Business in the Contemporary Legal Environment

Aspen College Series

Business in the Contemporary Legal Environment

Second Edition

Daniel V. Davidson

Professor of Business Law, Chair of Accounting, Finance & Business Law
College of Business and Economics
Radford University

Lynn M. Forsythe

Professor of Business Law
Craig School of Business
California State University, Fresno

Wolters Kluwer

ISBN 978-1-4548-7351-8

Library of Congress Cataloging-in-Publication Data

Names: Davidson, Daniel V., author. | Forsythe, Lynn M., author.
Title: Business in the contemporary legal environment / Daniel V. Davidson, Professor of Business Law, Chair of Accounting, Finance & Business Law College of Business and Economics Radford University; Lynn M. Forsythe, Professor of Business Law, Craig School of Business, California State University, Fresno.
Description: Second Edition. | New York : Wolters Kluwer, [2017]
Identifiers: LCCN 2016027773 | ISBN 9781454873518
Subjects: LCSH: Commercial law—United States. | LCGFT: Casebooks.
Classification: LCC KF889 .D38 2017 | DDC 346.7307—dc23
LC record available at https://lccn.loc.gov/2016027773

About Wolters Kluwer Legal & Regulatory US

Wolters Kluwer Legal & Regulatory US delivers expert content and solutions in the areas of law, corporate compliance, health compliance, reimbursement, and legal education. Its practical solutions help customers successfully navigate the demands of a changing environment to drive their daily activities, enhance decision quality and inspire confident outcomes.

Serving customers worldwide, its legal and regulator portfolio includes products under the Aspen Publishers, CCH Incorporated, Kluwer Law International, ftwilliam.com and MediRegs names. They are regarded as exceptional and trusted resources for general legal and practice-specific knowledge, compliance and risk management, dynamic workflow solutions, and expert commentary.

I want to dedicate this book to my wife, Dee Davidson, my best friend, the love of my life, and the best teacher I have ever known. I also want to dedicate it to our students who challenge us, delight us, and at times frustrate us. They are the reason we do this. Finally, a special thanks to my co-author, Lynn Forsythe. It is always a joy to work with her. She corrects all my mistakes and never rubs it in!
—Dan Davidson

I want to thank my family for their encouragement, support, and love, especially Jim and Mike Poptanich and Aileen and Robert Zollweg. I also dedicate this text to our students—past, present, and future. I enjoyed working with Dan Davidson again. His creative suggestions and collegial spirit make the process enjoyable. His positive attitude makes him a delightful writing partner.
—Lynn M. Forsythe

Summary of Contents

Contents

Chapter 2: Business Ethics 35

Chapter 3: The U.S. Legal System and Court Jurisdiction 67

Part II   Governmental Influences 167

Chapter 6: Constitutional Regulation of Business 169

Chapter 7: Administrative Regulation 201

Chapter 8: Protection of Intellectual Property 221

Part III   Contracts   251

Chapter 9: Contract Formation 253

Chapter 11: Contracts for the Sale of Goods 303

Part IV   Torts and Crimes 333

Chapter 12: Torts 335

Chapter 13: Crimes and Business 367

Part V — Agency and Business Organizations 397

Chapter 14: Agency 399

Chapter 15: Business Organizations 433

Chapter 16: Securities Regulation 465

Chapter 18: Consumer Protection 515

Chapter 19: Environmental Protection and Sustainability 541

Chapter 20: Labor and Fair Employment Practices 569

A BUSINESS-ORIENTED TEXT

Business in the Contemporary Legal Environment, Second Edition, serves as an introduction to the legal environment in which a business operates. Our goal is to explain various areas of the law in plain English, with an emphasis on the implications and applications of these areas in a business setting. We are not training aspiring lawyers. (Virtually every chapter in this text is a separate class in law school. For each topic that we cover in 20 or 30 pages a law student will study in depth for 14 or more weeks.) We are, however, offering useful information for aspiring—and practicing—business persons and professionals.

Business people need to be able to anticipate legal problems. Hopefully, this ability to foresee difficulties will permit them to avoid problems. However, sometimes the difficulties cannot be avoided. In these situations the business person needs to recognize the nature of the problem and know how to work with his or her attorney to resolve it. Legal issues, including lawsuits, are business problems that can and should be managed. A manager who understands many of the basics of the legal environment is better prepared to manage these situations.

Our goals in this text are:

- To provide a student-friendly introduction to those legal topics most relevant to business people;
- To demonstrate how these topics apply to a business;
- To show the interrelationship of many of the topics;
- To provide exercises and examples that help the student to identify and analyze legal issues that are frequently encountered in business; and
- To help the students develop critical thinking skills and habits.

We also want to provide help and support to the students and instructors using this text. Wolters Kluwer offers a wide variety of supplementary materials for students and instructors, including a comprehensive Instructor's Manual, Test Bank, PowerPoint slides, and other resources, available at the companion Web site that accompanies the text.

AN OUNCE OF PREVENTION

We have included a number of strategy boxes in every chapter. These boxes, which we call *An Ounce of Prevention*, discuss situations that frequently occur in a business environment and strategies for handling the situations in a manner that will help to avoid potential legal problems.

They may state a fact situation that has occurred with a recommendation for handling such situations in your own business. More often they simply suggest a practical method for dealing with potentially sticky legal problems.

EXHIBITS

There are numerous exhibits in the text. Tables, charts, and illustrations are used to assist students in organizing and understanding the material. These exhibits are not meant to replace the text. They provide a visual aid to comprehension and learning, but they do not replace reading and studying the text.

TOPICAL COVERAGE

Our goal is to provide a concise current introduction to the legal environment of business. We chose to break the text down into six parts:

Part I Foundations of the Law

In Part I we introduce students to the legal environment of business. Chapter 1 is an introduction to law and the legal process. Chapter 2 discusses business ethics, with an emphasis on the importance of ethics to a business and its decision making. Chapter 3 covers the U.S. legal systems, courts, and the concept of jurisdiction. Chapter 4 covers dispute resolution, both through litigation and various alternative dispute resolution (ADR) techniques. Chapter 5 looks at international considerations for business, a key concept in the global marketplace.

Part II Governmental Influences

In Part II the influence of governmental regulation is addressed. Every business, from the corner fruit stand up to and including the largest multinational enterprise, must be aware of and in compliance with a myriad of governmental regulations and requirements. Knowledge of this area is imperative for a business if it is to succeed.

Chapter 6 covers the constitutional bases for government regulation of businesses, as well as some of the limits on governmental regulatory power imposed by the Constitution. Chapter 7 addresses administrative regulation, the most pervasive regulatory area. Chapter 8 deals with intellectual property (IP). Many businesses rely on their IP in order to compete in the marketplace. It is essential to know the limits of IP protection and the best methods for protecting any IP the business owns.

Part III Contracts

Business as we know it could not exist without some form of contract law. In this section of the book we examine contract law as it affects businesses and consumers in the United States. We also briefly mention some areas of international trade that are affected by contract law. In Chapter 9 we discuss contract formation. We examine how a contract is made, and what will make that contract enforceable. We also examine the "negative elements" that may prevent a contract that appears to be valid and binding from being enforced. In Chapter 10 we discuss contract performance and remedies. What do the parties need to do in order to properly fulfill their contractual obligations? What remedies are available if one of the parties fails to carry out his or her duties? Finally, in Chapter 11 we look at a specialized area of contract law: The Law of Sales. This discussion focuses on the impact of Article 2 of the Uniform Commercial Code for the sale of goods in the United States, and also at the effect of the United Nations Convention on Contracts for the International Sale of Goods (CISG) on the international sales of goods.

Part IV Torts and Crimes

Businesses are also affected by civil wrongs, torts, and by criminal conduct. A business may be sued if any of its employees commit a tort. A business may also decide to sue another party if the other party commits a tort that harms the business. Crimes such as theft and shoplifting can harm a business; on the other hand, some business conduct is considered criminal. If convicted, the business may be fined and its officers may be imprisoned. Chapter 12 covers the law of torts, while Chapter 13 discusses crimes and business.

Part V Agency and Business Organizations

Many businesses are incorporated, while others assume a different organizational structure. Choosing the proper form for a business to take is a significant decision, and one that is frequently made without adequate thought. But regardless of the form chosen, most businesses will operate with or through agents. In Chapter 14 we examine agency law. The topics include an explanation of what an agent is and how his or her conduct can affect the principal. It also discusses employees and independent contractors. Chapter 15 addresses the various types of business organizations that exist in the United States, together with a discussion of the benefits and the disadvantages of each type of organization. Chapter 16 covers securities regulation. This includes an explanation of what a security is, the sale of various securities, including stocks, and the regulation of these sales. It also discusses other statutes affecting securities, including the Sarbanes-Oxley Act and the Dodd-Frank Act.

Part VI The Regulatory Environment

We conclude our coverage of the legal environment by examining the regulatory environment that every business must navigate. In Chapter 17 we cover strategic alliances and antitrust law. Strategic alliances provide many potential benefits, especially for smaller businesses that face competition from much larger enterprises. However, care must be taken to ensure that such alliances do not violate the federal antitrust laws. Chapter 18 deals with consumer protection. Any business that regularly extends credit to consumer customers must ensure that it complies with these laws and regulations. The material is also of immediate practical use to students, since the consumer protection statutes frequently affect most students. By learning their rights, students can help to protect their credit and their credit ratings. Chapter 19 discusses environmental protection and sustainability. This is a very complex area, but we have tried to simplify the coverage while still including the key issues and how they affect business. Chapter 20 deals with labor law and fair employment practices. Labor law protects the workers as a group, while fair employment laws protect the workers as individuals. The distinction is important, especially for entry-level managers. Since many students will enter the work force as entry-level managers, an understanding of these topics will give them a competitive advantage.

APPLICATIONS

Every chapter begins with a Classic Case, a case from the past that helped to set the precedents for some of the material covered in the chapter. We conclude each chapter with a Contemporary Case, a recent decision that shows a current application of one of the principles discussed in the chapter.

There are also three Short Answer Questions and two "You Decide" cases at the end of each chapter for student review, assignments, and discussions. These work well in class or in study group sessions.

In addition the Web site that accompanies the text contains materials for review and study. For example, it includes additional Classic and Contemporary Court Cases, exhibits, and Short Answer questions. There are also a number of links to "You Tube" videos that help to explain certain topics.

AACSB CURRICULAR STANDARDS

The AACSB curricular standards relevant to business law and the legal environment of business state that the business curriculum should include ethical and global issues; the influence of political, social, legal and regulatory, environmental, and technology issues; and the impact of demographic diversity on organizations. We believe *Business in the Contemporary Legal Environment* uniquely satisfies these standards in a readable yet rigorous format.

Global issues are treated in several areas, beginning with Chapter 1 and its introduction to different legal systems including those based on various religions. International law is discussed in Chapter 5. This discussion includes the role of sovereign immunity and the extraterritorial application of U.S. law. Chapter 8 includes a discussion of how a business can protect its intellectual property in other countries. The United Nations Convention on Contracts for the International Sale of Goods (CISG), discussed in Chapter 11, affects international trade between merchants in different countries.

Chapter 2, Business Ethics, addresses the ethical theories and how they can be applied in business. There is a helpful section addressing ethical decision making. The "Ounce of Prevention" boxes also offer some interesting tips and suggestions to avoid ethical problems.

We have created a text that we hope is engaging, intuitive, and oriented toward providing the legal skills students will need in the business world. The focus on applications through the use of "An Ounce of Prevention" boxes, exhibits, and end-of-chapter materials all contribute to a unique treatment of the legal environment of business. We cover issues ranging from employee privacy to employment law; from torts and crimes through contracts and securities. We examine governmental regulation of business and internal self-imposed regulation of business.

ACKNOWLEDGMENTS

Writing a textbook is a rewarding endeavor. However, it is also a significant undertaking. It would not have been possible without the help and support of a number of people along the way. We have enjoyed working together on this project. We each prepared half of the chapters and commented on the drafts prepared by our coauthor. We hope this team effort has been successful and that you enjoy using this book as much as we have enjoyed writing it.

We want to thank Louis McGuire whose initial contact led us to Wolters Kluwer Law and Business. This book would not have been possible without the support of David Herzig who recognized the need for a readable legal environment text with practical business applications. We are also indebted to our developmental editor, Betsy Kenny. Betsy's help and guidance improved the text as it evolved from the first draft to final product. We appreciate Paul Sobel and the team at The Froebe Group, LLC, who carefully supervised the final stages of production. We have enjoyed working with each—and all—of them.

A special thanks to our families. They have tolerated the late nights and short deadlines. They provided helpful suggestions and put up with us when we were out of sorts. Without their support and encouragement, we would not be able to accomplish our goal.

A sincere thank you to the reviewers of this text, whose suggestions, criticism, questions, and observations helped us write a text that contains the essential material and is user-friendly, readable, and enjoyable.

August 2016

Daniel V. Davidson
Lynn M. Forsythe

About the Authors

Dan Davidson is an alumnus of the Indiana University—Bloomington College of Business and the Indiana University—Bloomington School of Law.

Professor Davidson has been teaching business law and legal environment classes since 1974, with stops at five different campuses over his career. He is currently teaching and serving (for the second time) as Chair of the Department of Accounting, Finance & Business Law at Radford University in Radford, Virginia.

Professor Davidson has previously served as a part of the author team on four other textbooks, and he has authored or co-authored numerous journal articles. Some of his work can found on Google Scholar and/or Research Gate.

Professor Davidson has been the recipient of numerous teaching awards and several advising awards during his career.

Professor Davidson is married to Dee Davidson, a high school math teacher, and is the proud father of a son, Jaime, who works for Audience View and lives in Birmingham, AL, and a daughter, Tara, who is a high school English teacher in Lexington. Kentucky.

Lynn M. Forsythe received her B.A. from The Pennsylvania State University and her J.D. from the University of Pittsburgh School of Law. She passed the bar examinations in the states of California and Pennsylvania. She is professor of business law at the Craig School of Business at California State University, Fresno, where she serves as the course coordinator for Business and the Legal Environment.

Professor Forsythe has received numerous Craig School of Business awards, including those for research and service. She was a Craig Faculty Fellow for research and the Verna Mae and Wayne A. Brooks Professor of Business Law. She is a Coleman Fellow at the Lyles Center for Innovation and Entrepreneurship at California State University, Fresno.

Professor Forsythe is the author or co-author of numerous articles on business law and business law pedagogy. She served on the author team for four other textbooks. She has held the positions of editor-in-chief, staff editor, and reviewer for *The Journal of Legal Studies Education*. She is currently an advisory editor and reviewer. Her papers have been recognized by the Allied Academies, the Western Academy of Legal Studies in Business, and by inclusion in West's Entertainment, Publishing and the Arts Handbook of 2015. Some of her work can found on Google Scholar and/or Research Gate.

Professor Forsythe is active in the Academy of Legal Studies in Business and the Western Academy of Legal Studies in Business. Professor Forsythe is currently the Secretary of the Craig School of Business Chapter of Beta Gamma Sigma and a Life Member of Alpha Kappa Psi, professional business fraternity.

Business in the Contemporary Legal Environment

Part I

Foundations
of the Law

1

Business and Its Legal Environment

Learning Objectives

After completing this chapter you should be able to

- Explain why an understanding of law is important to businesspeople
- Contrast substantive law and procedural law
- Compare tort law, criminal law, and contract law
- Recognize the functions of the law
- Describe the sources of U.S. law
- Explain the role of precedents in U.S. law
- Compare law and equity

3

Classic Case

This U.S. Supreme Court case deals with an alleged criminal libel. It also addresses the old adage that ignorance of the law is no excuse. Barlow claimed on the export register that he was exporting refined sugar. If this was true, he was entitled to have the duties reduced, which was called a drawback. If this was not true, Barlow committed a criminal libel, an untrue statement treated as a crime, and Barlow would forfeit the sugar. He claimed that he could not be found guilty since he was unaware (ignorant) of the law: He thought that the sugar he was exporting was classified as refined sugar.

BARLOW v. UNITED STATES
32 U.S. 404, 1833 U.S. LEXIS 354 (1833)

FACTS Joseph Barlow allegedly made a false entry about sugar in the office of the duty collector, with the intent to defraud the government of its revenue. Barlow admits that he made the entry to obtain a reduction in export duties; but he denies that the entry was false. Barlow claims that the sugars are truly refined sugars as he listed them. Under the statute, goods will be forfeited to the federal government if a false entry is made. Barlow argued that the federal statute did not apply. He claimed that the sugar was refined sugar as he understood the term, and that under the statute he was entitled to the reduced duty for refined sugar.

ISSUE Is Barlow excused because he was ignorant of the law?

HOLDING No, ignorance of the law is no excuse. Barlow cannot avoid the forfeiture of the sugar.

REASONING Excerpts from the opinion of Justice Story:

... The ... question is whether the sugars were ... entered by a false ... [label.] They were

entered by the name of "refined sugars." They were, in fact, sugars known by the appellation of "bastar," or "bastard" sugards (sic), which are a species of sugars of a very inferior quality, of less value than the raw material; they are the ... refuse of clayed sugars, left in the process of refining, after taking away the loaf and lump sugar ... The question is, whether this species of sugar is, in the sense of the acts of Congress, "refined sugar." These acts allow a drawback "on sugar refined within the United States."

It has been contended ... that all sugars which have undergone the full process of refining, after they [are granulated] ..., are properly to be deemed refined sugars ... In a certain sense, they may certainly be ... deemed to be refined; that is, in the sense of being ... clarified and freed from their feculence. But the question is, whether this is the sense in which the words are used in the acts of Congress.

The acts of Congress on this subject, are regulations of commerce and revenue; and there is no attempt in any of them to define the distinguishing qualities of any of the commodities which are mentioned therein. Congress must be presumed to use the words in their known and habitual commercial sense; not ... in that of foreign countries, if it should differ from our own. ... [S]till, if among buyers and sellers generally in the course of trade and business, the appellation "refined sugars," is exclusively limited to ... lump and loaf sugar, and never includes bastard sugar, the acts of Congress ought to be construed in this restrictive sense. ... [W]e think that there is a decisive and unequivocal preponderance of evidence to establish that bastard sugar is not deemed ... "refined sugar." The appellation is exclusively limited to ... white refined loaf or lump sugars. This is established, not merely by the testimony of merchants and grocers, and persons in the custom house, but by the testimony of sugar refiners. ... [A delivery of bastard sugars would not satisfy a contract for the sale of refined sugars. This] puts an end to the question, whether the sugars in controversy were entered by a false denomination. . . .

There was no accident in the case; . . . [Barlow] knew what the article was when he entered it. The only mistake, if there has been any, is a mistake of law. The party in the present case has acted . . . with his eyes open. . . . He has not been misled; and his conduct . . . is not . . . free from . . . suspicion. . . . He has made every effort in his power to obtain the drawback by passing off as refined sugars what he well knew were not admitted to be such by the higher government officers.

. . . [This case] presents the broader question, whether a mistake of law will excuse a forfeiture. . . . We think it will not. . . . It is a common maxim, familiar to all minds, that ignorance of the law will not excuse any person, either civilly or criminally; and it results from . . . the extreme danger of allowing such excuses to be set up for illegal acts to the detriment of the public. There is scarcely any law which does not admit of some ingenious doubt; and there would be perpetual temptations to violations of the laws, if men were not put upon extreme vigilance to avoid them. There is . . . [no] reason to suppose that the legislature . . . had any intention to supersede the common principle. The safety of the revenue, so vital to the government, is essentially dependent upon upholding it. . . . [I]t is the opinion of the court that the judgment of the circuit court ought to be affirmed. . . .

BUSINESS AND THE LAW

Business

This book is about the legal environment of business. An organized society is established, to a significant extent, on duty. Each member of society having certain duties imposed upon him or her, while he or she voluntarily assumes other duties. A business is a part of the society in which it operates, and the business also must honor its duties as a member of the society.

U.S. society relies on business to satisfy many of its needs and desires. Most people in the United States are not self-sufficient. They purchase cell phones, food, tablet computers and utilities. They rent apartments and vehicles. They purchase services such as data plans and lawn care. Most of the things they acquire, they purchase or rent from businesses. U.S. citizens provide the labor and skills needed by business, so they are also the employees of businesses. Employees earn wages so that they, in turn, can purchase goods from businesses. Even nonprofit organizations operate like businesses and are subject to many of the same laws. Statutes and regulations define the obligations of each party to others. The emphasis throughout this book is to provide an understanding of that legal environment from the perspective of businesspeople.

An Ounce of Prevention

As you read the cases and examples in this text, think about each situation from a management perspective. Ask yourself how the dispute started. What, if anything, could the parties have done to avoid the problem? Ask yourself what you would do in similar circumstances. You may find that planning ahead and being proactive can help you avoid disputes and problems. At least, you will be able to better understand why the situation arose so that you can evaluate the problem from a businessperson's point of view.

Law

Before we begin our study, we must answer a basic question: What is *law*? Many definitions exist, ranging from the philosophical to the practical. Plato (427-347? B.C.), a Greek philosopher who studied and wrote in the area of philosophical idealism, said law was *social control*. Sir William Blackstone (A.D. 1723-1780), an English judge and legal commentator, said law is the set of rules specifying what is right and what is wrong. For our purposes, we shall define law as "rules that must be obeyed." People who disobey these rules are subject to sanctions such as paying a fine or going to jail. Our society has many kinds of rules, but not all rules can be considered "law." For example, rules in games or sports are not laws. What differentiates a law from other types of rules? A person who violates a mere rule does not face sanctions from the government. He or she may be subject to peer pressure, ridicule, or even shunning, but he or she does not face legal penalties. People who break *laws* can be held accountable for their actions through court-imposed sanctions, such as fines, imprisonment, or forfeitures. Laws are enforced by the government through the legal system. Mere rules are not enforced this way.

Many different types of legal rules exist. One type defines a specific way to create a legal document, for example, a contract or a will. A second type forbids certain kinds of conduct; criminal law is an excellent example of this kind of legal rule. (*Criminal law* is the body of law dealing with public wrongs called *crimes*.) A third type of legal rule compensates people who have been injured because someone else breached a duty by committing a tort. (*Tort law* is the body of law dealing with civil wrongs for which the victim is entitled to remedies.) For example, when an automobile manufacturer negligently fails to discover a defective brake system on one of its new cars, and the manufacturer's negligence is the direct cause of an injury to the driver and/or passengers, the manufacturer may have to pay monetary damages to the injured people. (*Negligence* is the failure to do something a reasonable and prudent person would do, or doing something that a reasonable and prudent person would not do.)

Rules that describe binding contracts, define crimes, and specify legal duties are generally rules about substantive law. (*Substantive law* is that part of law that creates and defines legal rights. It is distinct from *procedural law,* which is the law specifying the methods used to enforce legal rights or obtain compensation for the violation of these rights.) U.S. courts establish rules to take care of their everyday business. For example, all states have a rule concerning the maximum number of days a person has to answer a civil lawsuit; this is an example of a procedural law. The distinction between substantive law and procedural law is important.

Exhibit 1.1 compares some of the major areas of law discussed in this book. A *plaintiff* is the one who files a civil lawsuit. The *defendant* is the one who responds to the suit.

We will view the law as a body of rules that establish a certain level of social conduct, or of *duties*, that members of the society must honor. One way to view these duties is shown in Exhibit 1.2. The party or parties who are injured can seek enforcement against the wrongdoer. Enforcement consists of one of three legal remedies: (1) paying money as damages or as a fine; (2) providing equitable relief, such as being subject to an *injunction* (a court order that directs a person to do or not do something); or (3) going to jail or prison. This text will focus on what the law is and the purposes it serves.

Most of the U.S. legal system is based on voluntary compliance. People are assumed to know the law, as in the Classic Case of *Barlow v. United States.* In the United States, we also expect people to comply with the law. For example, drivers generally stop at stop signs and red lights. We expect other drivers to stop. When a driver stops at a red light and then drives through it, we are surprised because most

Exhibit 1.1

A Comparison of Tort Law, Criminal Law, and Contract Law

Question	Tort Law	Criminal Law	Contract Law
How is the obligation created?	Tort law imposes duties on all people to respect the rights of others	Criminal law imposes duties on all people to respect the social order; prohibits or requires certain conduct of all people	Individuals agree on a contract and voluntarily assume duties under the agreement
Who enforces the obligation?	Suit by injured plaintiff	Prosecution by a government entity	Suit by party to the contract alleging that a breach occurred
What is the burden of proof in court?	Preponderance of the evidence	Beyond a reasonable doubt	Preponderance of the evidence
What happens if the defendant loses?	Defendant can be required to pay for the injury caused	Defendant can be imprisoned, sentenced to probation, and/or fined	Defendant can be ordered to perform the contract or pay for the injury caused

Source: Courtesy of Lynn M. Forsythe, © Lynn M. Forsythe 2016.

Exhibit 1.2

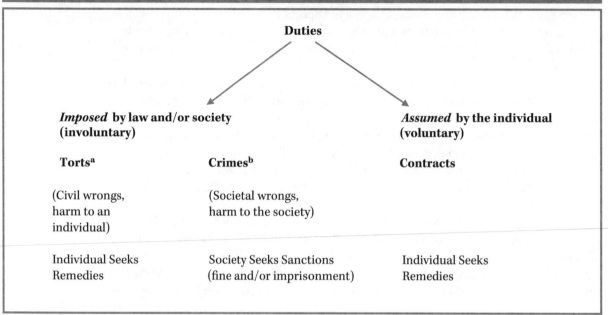

Duties in a Society

Duties

Imposed by law and/or society
(involuntary)

Assumed by the individual
(voluntary)

Torts[a]

Crimes[b]

Contracts

(Civil wrongs,
harm to an
individual)

(Societal wrongs,
harm to the society)

Individual Seeks
Remedies

Society Seeks Sanctions
(fine and/or imprisonment)

Individual Seeks
Remedies

[a] Some conduct may be both a tort and a crime. The victim of the conduct can seek civil remedies under tort law while the state can seek criminal sanctions under criminal law. Criminal sanctions can include restitution.
[b] Most crimes not only harm society, but also harm one or more individuals. The individuals who are harmed can seek civil remedies under tort law.

drivers obey the rules of the road. Similarly, U.S. tax law is based on voluntary compliance. This does not mean that an individual can choose whether to pay income tax. What it means is the taxpayer is supposed to fill out an accurate tax return and submit it to the government. (Some countries do not expect accurate tax returns. The tax form is merely the starting point for negotiations between the taxpayer and the government.)

Why Study the Law of Business?

Law is crucial to the way we conduct business in the United States. Businesspeople need to be aware of the legal implications of their actions. They need to know when they can sue and when they may be sued. They need to realize the potential for recovery if they file suit and the possible liability if they are sued. An understanding of the law allows businesspeople to know (or learn) the limits imposed on their actions by society. Some specific examples may illustrate its importance.

- **Contracts.** The law provides that valid contracts will be enforced. A business can establish a plan for the future, secure in the knowledge that its contracts with customers and suppliers will generally be performed. If they are not performed, the business can sue for its losses. A business will also be liable for its contracts with others if it does not perform, so it should live up to its contractual obligations. Some form of contract law is essential if a business is to operate in an efficient manner. Imagine a society where people could choose whether or not to perform their contracts. Would this be hard on businesses? Why?

- **Employment law.** The law provides rules and regulations regarding employment. These rules and regulations provide standards to ensure some protections for employees. For example, there are minimum wage laws, maximum hour laws, workplace safety rules, and equal employment opportunity rules. Businesses that do not comply may be subject to lawsuits and/or fines. Imagine a society where businesses are not obligated to provide safe workplaces. Would businesses be likely to invest funds to protect their workers? What would happen to the workforce? Would this be hard on workers? How would it affect business?

- **Intellectual property (IP) law.** IP law provides protection to a business that has acquired intellectual property. Patent law provides that a business can apply to the government for a patent for its invention. If the patent is granted, the business receives a government-sanctioned monopoly for the length of the patent. Once the patent is issued, the business can prevent others from using its invention in the United States without permission. Businesses can then license the invention to others who pay for the right to use the invention. Imagine a society where inventions cannot be protected by patents. Would businesses be less likely to invest their resources in research and development? Why? Would the society have fewer advances and less technology? How would this affect the economy?

- **Government regulations.** The social contract theory states that businesses exist because society allows them to exist. It also holds that society can change "the rules of the game" at any time, forcing businesses to adapt to the new rules or face sanctions. These sanctions may include losing the right to continue in existence. Many of the government regulations affecting business are an outgrowth of the social contract theory. For example, antitrust laws, consumer protection laws, environmental laws, and securities laws all originated to some extent from public pressure on government to address these issues. Imagine the United States without these laws. In some cases, you can examine history before the laws were enacted to see how society would be different.

Think about the role of law in business decision making. Law plays a significant part in the success or failure of many business enterprises.

You need to understand the legal implications of your actions as a businessperson and consumer. Otherwise, your actions may have unexpected legal consequences. If you can apply your legal knowledge to particular business situations, you may also save yourself great expense. It is helpful to understand the legal environment in which a business operates. If business executives "scan" their environment, they can often identify trends. Sometimes a business or industry may impact the direction of a change. When a business takes direct action it is called being proactive. (*Proactive* means to identify potential problem areas and actively participate in resolving them.) For example, industries may decide to self-regulate in an attempt to avoid government regulation. The video game industry created a rating system for games at least in part to avoid potential legislation. When a business is *reactive*, it waits to see what develops and *then* reacts. It does not initiate change. It makes change only when forced to do so. A business or industry may be proactive on some subjects and reactive on others. As you will learn, the law of business is a practical subject.

Another reason to study the law of business is because it will help you develop valuable decision-making skills. The legal style of analysis can be used in business decision making. This study will also alert you to particular situations in which you may need the assistance of a lawyer. Legal counsel can be helpful in preventing problems and in seeking remedies. For example, in the sale of commercial real estate the buyer or seller needs the assistance of a lawyer *before*, rather than after, an earnest money contract is signed.

We will focus on prevention, including (1) how to recognize potential legal problems; (2) how to avoid legal problems if possible; and (3) how to resolve them as quickly as possible if they do arise. *Preventive law* is law designed to prevent harm or wrongdoing before it occurs. Many statutes are intended to prevent certain conduct by providing for sanctions against people who violate the statutory provisions. *Remedial law* is designed to deal with problems that do arise.

An Ounce of Prevention

Potential legal problems can be disruptive for a business. When legal problems arise, you should go beyond a simple cost-benefit analysis. You should consider factors such as harm to your reputation, the time you will spend resolving the issue through litigation, alternative methods for resolving the conflict, and the importance of getting a "win" in your overall plans. Resorting to litigation should be viewed as a last resort rather than as a first step to resolving the problem.

Legal Language

The study of law requires learning legal terminology. This text defines many of the terms for you. Remember to read in context and to be aware of legal meanings. These three rules will help improve your mastery of this material:

1. Legal terms may appear to be synonymous with everyday words, but often they are not.

2.   Legal terms may have more than one legal meaning.
3.   Some legal terms have no relation to everyday language.

Role of the Attorney

Legal issues are critical to all businesses. Whether the business is facing litigation or practicing preventive law and attempting to avoid legal problems, attorneys can be important "partners" in a business. One of the primary purposes of this text is to assist you in working with your attorney and to enable you to more fully understand what he or she says. There may be situations when you are able to represent yourself in legal matters, such as negotiating a lease. When a person represents himself or herself in court, it is called appearing *pro persona*, or *pro per* for short. There are many situations in which it is unwise to represent yourself and you should hire a competent attorney.

An Ounce of Prevention

If you are considering representing yourself, you should consider how much is at stake. Is this a relatively minor issue or a complicated legal issue such as a patent dispute? You should also consider your skills. Can you conduct basic legal research? Do you have sufficient time to prepare an effective case? You may want to share the work with your attorney, with both of you doing some of the work. For example, you may be able to negotiate the basic terms of a commercial lease and then have the lease drafted by your attorney.

LEGAL SYSTEMS

When people refer to "the law" they are really referring to a legal *system*, which consists of some combination of law, order, and justice. Each legal system involves a variety of people, rules, and processes. Every culture and every society is built around its own system, including its own rules, expectations, and provisions for enforcement. Each legal system provides a structure for enforcing the rules in order to meet the expectations of that specific society.

Traits of a Legal System

Order   *Order* has different meanings in different contexts, and "an order" is significantly different from "order." The law usually considers *an order* as a legal command issued by a judge, while *order* is the absence of chaos. We are using *order* in this second sense. *Chaos* is confusion and total disorganization, producing a disorderly society. Chaos resulted when a large number of refugees flooded the European Union in 2015 and 2016. If the laws of a society were always followed and never broken, there would be perfect order. No crime would exist, and everyone would be safe. No society with perfect order has ever existed.

The words *law* and *order* are often linked together. It is natural to link them because, when the law is followed, there is order. However, perfect order does not exist because the law is not followed by everyone all the time. Society is always *somewhat* chaotic and disorganized. One of the reasons people do not always obey the law is that they may not be aware of what the law is in a particular situation. However, the U.S. legal system *presumes* that everyone is aware of the law and what it requires. If society did not presume that everyone knows the law, individuals accused of breaking the law would have an excellent defense: They could argue that they did not know they were breaking the law, and society would then have to prove the person's knowledge of the law before sanctions could be imposed. The presumption that everyone knows the law also creates an incentive for citizens to study the law. The U.S. educational system plays an important role in helping residents to learn the law.

Justice *Justice* is a difficult term to define. Different theories of justice exist, and individuals have varying beliefs about it. When we speak of *justice,* we normally mean *fairness*. Although perfect justice is fair, there is more to the concept of justice than merely being fair. Justice, as used in the Anglo-American legal system, refers to both the *process* followed and the *results* obtained in the process. Courts try to administer justice that conforms with the laws. From a social perspective, justice may be affected as much—or even more—by appearances than by results. So, judges, lawyers, and police officers are required to avoid the *appearance* of impropriety in their dealings. If the public perceives that the system is not just, they are less likely to accept the results the system provides. This perception can lead to the destruction of the order developed in society through enforcement of its laws. Protests over the killing of African Americans in 2013 and the ensuing "Black Lives Matter" movement are examples of what may occur when people perceive that the law is not being applied fairly. The protests disrupted the social order.[1]

The goal of any legal system should be attaining justice by continually searching for fairness and equity. Fairness is less abstract than justice and is easier to address on a practical level. Most people have a basic concept of "fairness" that can be applied to any given situation. For example, when you see a bully pick on a victim, you probably believe that this conduct is not fair. In this type of situation, the conduct is clearly unfair *and* unjust. In many situations, it is difficult to determine what a fair-and-just result would be. For example, suppose that a wealthy individual is accused of committing a crime. That wealthy individual hires the best attorneys he or she can find, and—in a very public trial—is found not guilty by the jury. Many people might question whether this result is *fair*. While there may be doubts about the fairness of the result, the process followed in the legal system assures—at least to some extent—that the result of the trial is *just*.

The Needs of a Legal System

The Need to Be Reasonable   A legal system needs to be reasonable. It should rely on reasonable conclusions based on facts. Laws prohibiting texting while driving are reasonable because we can prove that texting while driving is related to an increase in the number of accidents.

In addition to being reasonable, laws need to be applied in a reasonable manner. A law stating that Juana, a buyer on credit, will have property taken away from her if she does not make the payments on it is certainly reasonable. It would be an unreasonable law if Juana's children were taken away from her if she stopped making payments for the property. There is no reasonable connection between the conduct and the penalty.

The Need to Be Definite   The law needs to be definite, not vague. For example, a law stating that all contracts "for a lot of money" must be in writing would be unclear and confusing. By comparison the Statute of Frauds states that all contracts for the sale of goods costing $500 or more must be in writing: This rule is very clear. If one has a contract for $499.99 worth of goods, it need not be in writing; but if the contract is for $500 or more of goods it must be in writing.[2] There is a definite point at which a written contract is required.

Sometimes the law is unable to state precisely what a person must do. In such cases, the law applies the standard of *reasonable* behavior rather than setting precise boundaries. If Toni is driving her car and hits and hurts Miguel, a pedestrian, Miguel may sue Toni. In this situation, the law does not state that speed in excess of a particular amount is necessary in order to find the driver at fault. Is Toni at fault if the only information available is that the speed limit was 55 miles per hour and she was traveling at 50 miles per hour? Under these conditions, the law would ask the question: Was Toni's conduct reasonable under the circumstances? If so, she is not liable for damages. If Toni's conduct is not reasonable, she is liable to Miguel. In the final analysis, the law provides an answer and is definite.

The Need to Be Flexible   To say that the law needs to be both definite and flexible seems like a contradiction in terms. The law needs to be definite to establish a standard. In other respects, the law must be flexible so that it can be applied in many different situations. For example, if a drunk driver kills a family wage earner and the family files a wrongful death lawsuit, recovery would be based on the future earning capacity of the wage earner. (*Wrongful death* is unlawful death. It does not necessarily have to involve a crime.) Recovery would not be based on a table of damages. Another aspect of flexibility is the need to adapt to changes in society and technology. For example, old laws are now being applied to activities on social media, such as Facebook, Instagram, LinkedIn, SnapChat, Skype Qik, YikYak, and YouTube. If trees did not bend in the wind, they would break. The U.S. legal system is like those trees: It must bend without breaking. However, because of this flexibility, the U.S. legal system loses some of its predictability.

The Need to Be Practical   Because people depend on the law to guide their actions, the law needs to be practical and oriented to action rather than to thought. The law must deal with real issues created by real people. For example, most U.S. courts will only decide real disputes between the parties. They will not decide hypothetical cases. Courts will also avoid cases where the issue is *moot* (abstract; not properly submitted to the court for a resolution; not capable of resolution) or where there is no real case or controversy. (A *case or controversy* is a case brought before the court where the plaintiff and defendant are really opposed to one another on significant issues.) When the plaintiff and defendant really agree with each other and are trying to get a court decision confirming their position, there is no real case or controversy.

The Need to Be Published   If a society had the best set of laws imaginable, but no one knew about them, they would be virtually useless and the society would have chaos. Although ignorance of the law is generally no excuse, the U.S. system does try to provide notice of the rules and laws. In traffic law, for example, speed limits need to be posted so drivers know how fast they can legally drive. People cannot voluntarily comply with secret laws and rules. Posting also prevents arbitrary enforcement by police. So, all laws need to be published. Once a law has been published, we can presume that all people know it. Consequently, ignorance of the law is no excuse. For example, even if you did not see the posted speed limit, the police will still enforce it. Statutes are good examples of published laws.

The Need to Be Final   If a controversy exists and the parties use the legal system to resolve it, one thing is certain: At some point in time the matter will be resolved. It may not be resolved to the full satisfaction of the person who "won" the case, but it will be resolved. Parties who are unhappy with the results can appeal, but eventually the appeals end and the decision is final. Exhibit 1.3 outlines the needs of a legal system.

Compliance with the Law

Despite our assumption about voluntary compliance, people do not always comply with the law. When you observe people in your community repeatedly doing something, you might conclude that this behavior is lawful. This assumption may be unwise. For example, employers may repeatedly ask employees to violate the state labor code. During your study of business law, you should try to distinguish these three distinct questions:

1.   What is the law about this topic?
2.   How do people and businesses behave?
3.   What should the law be for this topic?

Answers to these questions will vary based on the state or region under analysis. The most variance will occur over what the law should be. Individuals will disagree based on their views and their ethical beliefs. Proactive businesspeople may suggest answers that will benefit their particular situation.

Exhibit 1.3

The Needs of the Legal System

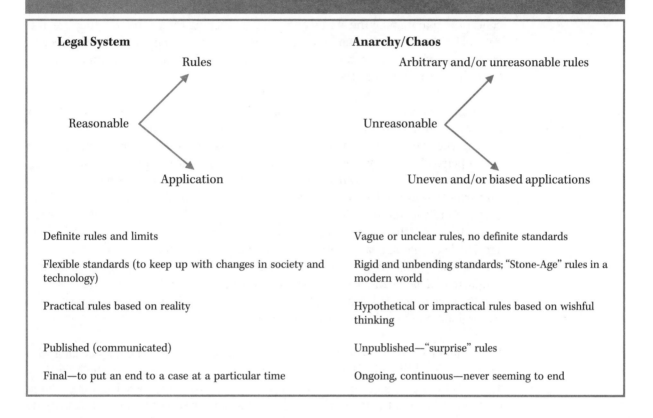

Legal System	Anarchy/Chaos
Definite rules and limits	Vague or unclear rules, no definite standards
Flexible standards (to keep up with changes in society and technology)	Rigid and unbending standards; "Stone-Age" rules in a modern world
Practical rules based on reality	Hypothetical or impractical rules based on wishful thinking
Published (communicated)	Unpublished—"surprise" rules
Final—to put an end to a case at a particular time	Ongoing, continuous—never seeming to end

The Purposes of a Legal System

Achieving Justice   Justice basically equates to fairness. Sometimes we achieve it and sometimes we do not. To some, the rule of *caveat emptor* (let the buyer beware) is a fair rule. The buyer who did not examine the goods will not receive damages in a lawsuit for defects that would have been revealed by an inspection.

Providing Police Power   Because justice is the ultimate purpose of a legal system, providing police power may be viewed as an intermediate purpose of a legal system. When you see the term *police power*, you may envision a uniformed police officer. That is just one part of what we call police power. Police power allows the government to create and enforce laws designed to protect the public's health, safety, and general welfare.[3] Laws and ordinances concerning police, fire, sanitation, and social welfare in state and local governments stem from police power.

Maintaining Peace and the Status Quo   One of the earliest purposes of the law was to "keep the King's peace." Most modern torts and crimes are based on a simple breaching of the King's peace. Today, laws that govern the relationships between private individuals, such as the laws governing assault, battery, false imprisonment, and trespass, are private forms of keeping the peace. Closely associated with keeping the peace is the concept of maintaining the status quo—that is, keeping things the way they are. It is natural for the law to maintain the status quo unless changing things benefits society. Under the proper circumstances, a court issues a preliminary injunction that maintains the status quo until the lawsuit is resolved.

Providing Answers   On a practical level, the law should provide answers. A party may appeal a court decision to a higher court if he or she does not like the answer. Assume Melanie sues Troy, a neighbor, because Troy is allegedly creating a private nuisance on his property. (*Nuisance* is the unreasonable or unlawful use of a person's own property when it interferes with another person's use and enjoyment of his or her property.) If Troy wins the case in the trial court, Melanie can appeal the decision to the next higher court. In most states, this higher court is called an *appellate court* (court that has the power to review the decisions of lower courts). If an appellate court rules in favor of Troy, Melanie may appeal to the state's highest court. In that court, Melanie may win or she may lose again. Regardless of the final outcome, once the appellate process is completed, Melanie and Troy are provided with an answer. The process is complete and the case is decided. This is called *res judicata*, which is the civil law equivalent of the prohibition of double jeopardy in criminal law.

Providing Protection   The law protects all kinds of interests. The laws dealing with the torts of assault and of battery are classic examples of protection of the individual. The law also protects persons when it protects their civil rights. The U.S. Constitution contains (1) the right to be protected from unreasonable searches and seizures; (2) the right against compulsory self-incrimination of a crime; (3) the right to be indicted by a grand jury before being tried for a federal capital or infamous crime;[4] (4) the right against *double jeopardy* (a rule of criminal law that states that a person cannot be tried in court more than once by the same government for the same criminal offense); (5) the right to a jury trial; and (6) the right to post bail. Most rights, even Constitutional rights, have limits and restrictions.

The law is also concerned with the protection of property. All property is characterized as either real or personal property. *Real property* is land and whatever is affixed to the land, such as a house. All other property is *personal property*. In general, if property is movable or tangible, it is personal property. Intangible property such as a patent or a copyright is also personal property. The U.S. legal system has a variety of laws that protect both types of property. Personal property can have another separate meaning. It can also mean property that is owned by individuals, as opposed to public property that is owned by the government or the community.

Enforcing Intent   The law of contracts is based on freedom of contract. When we enter into a contract we make our own "laws" of conduct. For example, suppose that you found some merchandise that you could resell at a very good price. You want to make the contract today so that you can "lock in" the price. You have a cash flow problem, and you cannot pay for the goods today. You are confident that you can quickly and easily resell the goods, so you enter into a contract promising to pay for the goods at the stated price, with payment due two weeks after delivery. Of course, if you cannot resell the goods as quickly as you anticipated, you will have a financial problem and you may breach the contract. If the supplier sues you, you would probably be found liable for breach of contract. This potential problem is really a question of your business judgment and not a question of law.

Providing Rehabilitation   Both criminal law and civil law are directed toward rehabilitation. Criminal law should, among other things, rehabilitate the criminal. Civil law is also involved in rehabilitation to some extent. Contract law provides rehabilitation

Exhibit 1.4

The Purposes of a Legal System

Purpose	Reason
Achieving justice	To provide "justice" so that the needs of the members of society are addressed.
Providing police power	To provide a social structure so that "wronged" individuals do not have to resort to self-help; to provide for the health and welfare of the members of society.
Maintaining peace and the status quo	To provide members of society with a feeling of personal security and a structure on which they can rely.
Providing answers	To achieve practical justice; lets the members of society know what is expected of them and what they may reasonably expect from others.
Providing protection	To define and establish social guidelines and protect the entire society if any of these guidelines are not followed and obeyed.
Enforcing intent	To provide some method for permitting private agreements and for ensuring that these agreements are honored or enforced.
Providing rehabilitation	To allow people who violate the guidelines of the society a second chance; recognizes that people make mistakes.
Facilitating commercial transactions	To support freedom of contract and private ownership of property. These concepts encourage and promote business transactions.

for a party harmed by a breach of the contract. Tort law provides for a form of rehabilitation by awarding damages to the victim of the tort. The federal bankruptcy law is directed toward the rehabilitation of honest debtors.

Facilitating Commercial Transactions   One of the major characteristics of the U.S. legal system is that it facilitates commercial transactions. Contract law allows for the use of credit to make sales. The use of checks, credit cards, debit cards, and bill-paying apps on cell phones reduces the need for people to carry large amounts of cash to make purchases. For example, very few automobiles would be sold in the United States if car dealers insisted on cash payment. The U.S. national economy still relies on the automobile industry. The prosperity of the energy, steel, and transportation industries are directly related to that of the automobile. A loss of sales could hurt the national economy, and not just the automobile industry. When U.S. automobile manufacturers suffered from the economic downturn in 2008-2009, the federal government offered bailout money to some of them.[5] Generally, the U.S. legal system fosters free and open competition and facilitates trade. Exhibit 1.4 outlines the purposes of a legal system.

Legal Systems in Other Countries

You should not assume that other countries have the same or similar legal systems. A U.S. citizen may find that behavior that is tolerated in the United States constitutes a crime in a foreign country or is punished more severely there. Zeng Chengjie, a real estate developer who has been called "China's Bernie Madoff," was executed by lethal injection by the Chinese government for fraud and illegal fundraising.[6] Many of the protections a citizen expects in the United States do not apply abroad. For example, U.S. citizen Amanda Knox was retried in Italy for the 2007 murder of her roommate.[7] In the United States, this trial would probably be barred by the rule against double jeopardy. Other countries have different historical and sociological backgrounds. Citizens' values and government rules may differ from those in the United States. For example, interest on loans (part of *Riba*) is prohibited under traditional Muslim law.[8] In Beijing, 60-70 Chinese workers angry over a pay dispute held their U.S. boss, Chip Starnes, hostage for five days. Apparently this is common practice in Chinese employment disputes, and police are reluctant to intervene.[9]

Court decision making also differs from nation to nation. Courts in common-law countries, such as the United States and Great Britain, rely on precedents as well as statutes in deciding cases. Courts look to prior cases for guidance in how previous courts interpreted the law in similar situations. This reliance on prior decisions is called *precedent*. In common-law countries, courts tend to follow precedents unless there is a compelling reason to change.

By contrast, civil-law countries such as France and Germany do not rely on precedents. In these nations the court applies statutes without reference to how earlier courts decided similar cases. Each case is treated as unique, and the court tries to apply the law in a logical and fair manner to the facts presented in that particular case.

Consequently, precedent is not significant in civil-law systems. It is interesting to note that in the European Union (E.U.), the role of precedents is increasing even though the E.U. is primarily a civil-law system. For example, decisions made by the E.U. Court of Justice become precedents in all the member countries.

In the former Union of Soviet Socialist Republics (USSR), private ownership of property was limited due to the government's socialist philosophy. The primary goal of its legal system was to preserve state ownership of all means of production. Consequently, the USSR's law mainly consisted of criminal law. The law of property, contracts, and business organizations did not play a role. Many of the former Soviet republics are now beginning to engage in *privatization* (the process of going from government ownership of business and other property to private individual ownership). A body of private law is being developed as these countries move toward a more traditional civil-law system. The new countries often rely on consultants, like attorneys from the United States, in developing their systems of commercial law.

The Role of Religion

There are a number of legal systems based on religious teachings. The Hindu legal system is one example. Their system is a personal and religious law system which states that Hindus should act in accordance with this law wherever they live. The Hindu system has been recorded in books called *smritis*. Most Hindu law applies to family matters. Anglo-Hindu law evolved in most Hindu countries while they were British colonies and judges applied a combination of English and Hindu laws. When India gained its independence from the United Kingdom, it replaced Anglo-Hindu law with a civil code primarily based on Hindu law.

Some Muslims believe in Islamic law or *Sharia*, which is based on the Koran and other religious writings. There are three basic types of Muslim legal systems. Some Muslim countries use classical *Sharia*. This is the approach in Iran and Saudi Arabia. Some Muslim countries have blended systems, including Afghanistan, Egypt, Indonesia, Malaysia, Morocco, Pakistan, and Sudan. Others have secular (nonreligious) legal systems, including Kazakhstan, Mali, Nigeria, and Turkey.[10] The following case is an example of how one country applies Islamic law. A 24-year-old Norwegian woman who was attending a business meeting in Dubai, United Arab Emirates (UAE), claimed that she was sexually assaulted by a co-worker. After the rape, she asked the hotel staff for help and asked them to call the police. The police came and arrested the victim for having sex outside of marriage. She was sentenced to 16 months in jail for the crime under the UAE's Islamic-influenced legal system. The alleged attacker received a 13-month sentence for sex outside of marriage and alcohol consumption.[11]

A number of other religions also have legal systems, including Catholicism and Judaism. These religions generally provide their own tribunals for resolving disputes.

SOURCES OF LAW

The U.S. legal system is based on the Constitution, treaties, statutes, ordinances, administrative regulations, common law, case law, and equity. Together they constitute the U.S. system. Although each of the elements is separate, the elements are interdependent. A change in one element will affect one or more other parts of the system. For example, in a civil rights suit a person may allege a violation of constitutional rights (Fourteenth Amendment), a statutory right (Civil Rights Act of 1964), an administrative regulation (Equal Employment Opportunity Commission guideline), past decisions of the court (precedents), and equity (if all else fails, the person should win because it is fair).

Constitutions

A *constitution* is the fundamental law of a nation. It may be written or unwritten. The U.S. Constitution is written. It allocates the powers of government and sets limits on those powers. The founders of the United States knew that all tyrants had two powers: the power of the purse and the power of the sword. The Constitution places the power of the purse exclusively with Congress and the power of the sword with the executive branch. The judiciary, the third branch of the U.S. government, has neither the power of the purse nor the power of the sword. However, it has the power to interpret the meaning of the U.S. Constitution and to decide the constitutionality of the laws passed by Congress. In the landmark case of *Marbury v. Madison,*[12] the U.S. Supreme Court created the doctrine of *judicial review* (the power of the courts to review and uphold or overturn the decisions of other departments or branches of government). The court held that the Supreme Court has the power to decide whether laws passed by Congress comply with the Constitution. If they do not, they are unconstitutional and are of no force or effect. We discuss the unique nature of the Constitution further in Chapters 3 and 6.

States also have constitutions, and they are the fundamental laws of those states. The U.S. Constitution is the supreme legal document in the United States and will take precedence over state constitutions if there are conflicts between them.

Treaties

Treaties are formal agreements between two or more nations. Treaties are often categorized by the number of nations involved. *Bilateral treaties* involve two nations, and *multilateral treaties* involve more than two nations. Treaties that are recognized by almost all nations, such as the Geneva Convention, are *universal treaties.* The United States enters into treaties for a variety of purposes, including providing protection, for example, through the North Atlantic Treaty Organization

(NATO), and promoting trade through the North American Free Trade Agreement (NAFTA). Treaties are the only elements of the U.S. legal system that do not stem from the Constitution. The power to make a treaty is a function of sovereignty and not one of a constitution. In most cases, treaties are negotiated by the president or his or her designee(s). The U.S. Constitution gives the Senate the power to approve treaties, and a two-thirds vote is required for approval.[13] The president sometimes involves senators in the negotiation process to ease the subsequent approval process.[14] The Senate has rejected relatively few treaties.[15] However, sometimes the president withdraws a treaty rather than have it defeated.[16] Other times the treaty "dies" in a Senate committee or is amended or changed by the Senate. In these situations, generally the United States and the other countries enter into further negotiations.[17] (The president can enter into executive agreements that are not subject to approval by the Senate.[18]) While the Constitution is the supreme law of the land for domestic issues, treaties are the supreme law of the land for international issues.

Statutes

Statutes are the acts of federal or state legislative bodies. They prohibit or command an action. It is preferable to use the word *statute* when you are referring to a legislative act to distinguish it from other types of laws, such as ordinances, regulations, common law, and case law. A good example of state statutory law is the Uniform Commercial Code (UCC). The UCC is a set of laws designed to aid business. All 50 states, the District of Columbia, and the U.S. Virgin Islands have adopted at least portions of the UCC. Unfortunately for businesspeople, some states adopted modified versions of the UCC. So, businesspeople still need to check the law in each specific state.

Ordinances

Ordinances are laws passed by municipal bodies. Cities, towns, and incorporated villages have the power to establish laws for the protection of the public's health, safety, and welfare. Counties generally do not have legislative power, but they usually have the power to enforce state laws within their boundaries.

Administrative Regulations

Administrative regulations are rules promulgated by government agencies, most of which are created by the legislative branch of government. Examples of agencies include the Federal Trade Commission (FTC) on the federal level and the public utility commission (PUC) on the state level. The rules and regulations of these entities have the full force and effect of law. Government agencies will be discussed in more detail in Chapter 7.

Common Law

The term *common law* has multiple meanings depending on the context. In its broadest sense it means the body of law that originated, developed, and was administered in England. In this context, common law is the Anglo-American set of legal rules and principles that make up the laws in most states. This meaning includes statutes in England at the time the colonists came to America, as long as the statutes were consistent with life in the colonies. In another sense, common law refers to principles or rules that developed from usages and customs dating from antiquity, and to the recognition by the courts of these usages and customs.[19] All U.S. states except for Louisiana have a common law system.[20] Louisiana, like most European nations, has a code-based legal system. These code-based legal systems, commonly called *civil law systems*, rely on statutory authority in deciding cases rather than following precedent. If there is no statutory authority to decide a case, the court cannot issue a ruling in a civil law system. Courts in a civil law system lack the authority or power to "make law" through judicial rulings that establish precedent. Courts in common law countries do "make law" by establishing and following precedent.

Case Law

Case law comes from reported court cases and is part of the common law. Quite often, judges must interpret statutes in order to apply them to actual cases and controversies. You will not fully understand a particular statute until you have read both the statute *and* the cases that have interpreted it. *Case law*, then, is the law articulated by judges.

The American Law Institute (ALI) is dedicated to clarifying the law, improving the administration of justice, and drafting the Restatements of the Law. *Restatements* are not actually part of the law; rather, they are treatises that summarize the law on a subject. When there are conflicting approaches, the Restatement recommends one of the alternatives. Restatements become part of the case law when a court relies on a particular section in reaching its opinion.

Stare decisis means the question has been decided. For example, if a particular legal point is well settled in a certain jurisdiction, a future case with substantially the same facts will be decided in accordance with the principle that has already been decided. This is one of the reasons that lawyers do a great deal of legal research. The doctrine of stare decisis is also called precedents. Even though a legal matter has been settled, it does not mean the legal system must remain static.

A precedent remains in effect until it is changed. The legal system evolves. Lawyers and petitioners in court may try to persuade the judge to modify precedents, and sometimes they are successful. When a court changes the precedents, it generally supports its decision with one of these three reasons:

1. The prior rule is out of date; it is not appropriate to present-day society.
2. The prior case is distinguishable because the facts are different in one or more significant details.
3. The judge or justice who made the prior ruling was incorrect or wrong.

Judges may be reluctant to state that the prior ruling was in error, especially if they participated in making that ruling. It is easier to state that someone else made an error. Judges *sometimes* do admit that the rule they created earlier is not the appropriate response to a particular legal problem.

When a court follows precedent, it is striving to make the law *definite*, satisfying one of the needs of a legal system. However, as times and situations change, courts need to be able to change the law. The law would not be *flexible*, another need of a legal system, if precedents could never be changed. Courts can have a difficult time balancing the need to be definite and the need to be flexible. *Brown v. Board of Education*[21] is an example of a court overturning precedents. In that 1954 case, the U.S. Supreme Court overturned precedents and decided that providing separate schools for African American and Caucasian children was unconstitutional. This overturned the precedent, established in *Plessy v. Ferguson*,[22] that "separate but equal" facilities were constitutional.

Dictum is language by a judge that is not necessary to the decision before the court. It is an observation or remark that is not essential to the case or its resolution. These remarks or asides are not part of the precedents. Dictum can provide valuable clues about how that judge might decide future cases.

An opportunity to "make law" occurs when jurisdictions are in conflict over a point of law. For example, many states are divided into judicial districts, and courts in each of these districts may issue written legal opinions. If two or more districts have published conflicting opinions on a particular point, the time is ripe for the creation of a new statewide rule that will resolve the matter. Until the statewide rule is created, however, each court creates precedents for itself and for any courts directly under it. When there are no prior court decisions on a point of law, the case is one of first impression. *First impression* occurs when an issue is presented to the court for an initial decision; the issue presents a novel question of law and is not governed by precedent.

Equity

Equity is a body of rules applied to legal controversies when no adequate remedy at law exists. Rules of equity were developed outside the common law courts in England by an officer of the King called the chancellor. The primary reasons for developing equity were the rigid and sometimes unfair decisions made by the courts of law and the limited types of remedies available in them.

Today, the rules of law and equity are joined into one legal system.[23] An injunction is an example of an equitable remedy. Before U.S. courts will issue an injunction, the person requesting it must prove that the remedy at law would be inadequate. For example, if your neighbors are burning rubber tires on their property and the wind carries the obnoxious odor directly across your property, their action will destroy

Exhibit 1.5

Distinctions between Actions in Law and in Equity[a]

Characteristic	In Law	In Equity[b]
Type of relief	Money to compensate plaintiff for his or her losses	Action, either in the form of ordering the defendant to do or not to do something, or in the form of a decree about the status of something[c, d]
Nature of proceeding	More restricted by precedents	More flexible and less restricted by precedents; supposed to create equity (justice)
Time limit for filing lawsuit	Applicable period fixed by the statute of limitations[e]	A reasonable period of time as determined by the judge on a case-by-case basis[f]
Decider of fact	Jury trial, if requested by a party	No jury trial, judge decides the facts[g]
Enforcing a decision	Plaintiff may begin an execution of the judgment[h]	Plaintiff may begin contempt proceedings if the defendant does not perform as directed; defendant may be placed in jail and/or fined[i]

[a] Actions at law and those in equity are no longer as distinct as they once were. As a result, many states allow "combined trials," with issues of law and issues of equity being tried together.
[b] Traditionally, a court of equity was called a court of chancery, and the judge was called a chancellor.
[c] Common equitable remedies include injunction, specific performance of a contract, rescission of a contract, and reformation (correcting or rewriting) of a contract.
[d] Courts would prefer to award monetary damages. Equitable relief is only granted when the plaintiff can convince the court that money would be inadequate.
[e] The statute of limitations period will depend on the state and the type of lawsuit. It will be a fixed period.
[f] If the plaintiff has waited too long to file suit under the circumstances, the judge will apply the doctrine of *laches*, and the suit will be dismissed.
[g] Some states permit the use of an advisory jury.
[h] In an execution, the clerk of the court issues a formal document and the sheriff seizes the defendant's money and/or other property. If property is seized, the sheriff will sell it and use the proceeds to pay the plaintiff.
[i] The court is authorized to place the defendant in jail until he or she complies (or agrees to comply) with the court decree.

the peaceful use and enjoyment of your land. You would not have an adequate remedy at law, since no amount of money would be sufficient to allow them to continue to burn rubber tires. You could request that the court issue an injunction to stop your neighbors from burning the tires. In a larger sense, equity may be viewed as a doctrine that results in the legal system's adherence to the principle of fairness. Exhibit 1.5 summarizes some of the differences between law and equity.

CLASSIFICATIONS OF LAW

Federal versus State Law

The U.S. legal system is divided into two branches: federal and state. Lawyers must learn not only the law of their states, but also federal law. In addition, lawyers should know the majority rule. The *majority rule* is the rule that most states have adopted. Often there is also a *minority rule*, which a smaller number of states follow. Rarely do the various states agree on all aspects of a law. Exhibit 1.6 outlines the sources of law in the United States.

Common versus Statutory Law

The legal system consists of both common and statutory laws. Judges in the United States and England generally have the power to "make law" by interpreting statutes or applying precedents, and those interpretations become "common" law. Judges also apply the statutory law. Statutory law refers to the statutes passed by the legislative bodies. Common law is "unwritten" law, developed over time by judicial action. It fills the gaps where other sources of law do not cover a particular topic.

Civil versus Criminal Law

The U.S. legal system also separates civil and criminal law. In this context, *civil law* is private law that permits one person to sue another. *Criminal law* is public law in which

Exhibit 1.6

The Sources of Law in the U.S. Legal System

Authority	Source	Definition
F, S	Constitution	Supreme law of the land; fundamental basis of domestic law
F	Treaties	Formal agreements between nations; fundamental basis of international law; not based on the Constitution
F, S	Statutes	Acts of the legislature; control of domestic conduct; subject to limits imposed by the Constitution
S	Ordinances	Laws passed by municipal bodies and designed to control purely local problems; subject to any limits imposed by statutes or by the Constitution
F, S	Administrative Regulations	Acts of administrative agencies; control of specific areas of conduct; subject to any limits imposed by statutes or by the Constitution
F, S	Case Law	Precedents; courts define and interpret areas of law
F, S	Equity	Special rules and relief when "the law" does not provide a proper and/or adequate remedy

Legend: F=federal; S=state

a government entity files charges against a person. For example, if Gisell becomes violent, attacks Brett, and inflicts bodily harm, the district attorney may prosecute Gisell for assault. The district attorney is the government representative in state court. If convicted, Gisell may go to jail or prison. In addition, Brett may sue Gisell in civil court for money damages. The additional suit would not constitute double jeopardy or its civil law equivalent, *res judicata*, since two different theories of action exist: criminal and civil. (*Res judicata* is a rule of civil law that prevents a person from being sued more than once by the same party for the same civil wrong.) Some courts permit criminal cases and civil cases to be heard as part of the same trial.

There are a number of significant differences between civil and criminal law. One of the most significant differences is the burden of proof. In a civil case, the plaintiff must prove his or her case by a preponderance of the evidence. (A *preponderance of the evidence* means that the evidence on this side is stronger than the evidence on the other side. In other words, the plaintiff must provide evidence of greater weight than the defendant in order to win.) In a criminal case, the judge or jury must start with the presumption that the defendant is innocent, and the government must convince the judge or jury that the defendant is guilty beyond a reasonable doubt. (A *reasonable doubt* means a belief that there is a real possibility that the defendant is not guilty.)

Substantive versus Procedural Law

Substantive law deals with rights and duties given or imposed by the legal system. *Procedural law* is devoted to how those rights and duties are enforced. For example, the law of contracts is substantive law. The law of pleadings is procedural law, it describes the steps used to enforce those rights or duties. (*Pleadings* are formal statements filed in court identifying the claims of the parties.) A controversy over the mental ability to form a valid contract is a substantive matter. Where one files the lawsuit, what must be alleged, how one notifies the defendant, and how long the defendant has to answer the allegations are all examples of procedural law. This book is devoted primarily to substantive law.

Public versus Private Law

Private law is the body of law that deals with the property and relationships of private persons. It includes the areas of *property law* (ownership and transfer of assets); *contract law* (rights and duties that arise from enforceable agreements); *tort law* (other private wrongs such as negligence, invasion of privacy, and defamation); and *business relationships* (agency, partnerships, corporations, and similar entities). *Public law* deals with the relations between private individuals and the government. It also deals with the structure and operation of the government itself. *Constitutional law* (law relating to the government and its activities under the Constitution), *criminal law* (law relating to offenses against the government), and *administrative law* (law relating to government agencies) are types of public law. Both private law and public law are very important to business decision making.

Contemporary Case

This Contemporary Case is part of an ongoing dispute among the petitioners and the District of Columbia about the constitutionality of Washington, D.C.'s attempts to restrict the possession of firearms and to require gun owners to register their guns. The first set of suits is called *Heller I* and the second is called *Heller II*. This is an appeal from the district court's summary judgment for the District in *Heller III*. In this case the federal court of appeals decided that some parts of the current statute were constitutional and other parts were not.

HELLER v. DISTRICT OF COLUMBIA

801 F.3d 264, 2015 U.S. App. LEXIS 16632 (D.C. App. 2015)

FACTS The District of Columbia wanted "to combat gun violence and promote public safety" by restricting gun ownership and requiring registration of guns. In *Heller I* the Supreme Court decided that the District's prohibition of handguns kept at home and used for self-defense was unconstitutional. The D.C. City Council then enacted the Firearms Registration Amendment Act of 2008 (FRA). The FRA required the registration of almost all firearms and imposed conditions on the registration. Individuals under the age of 18, or who had been convicted of certain drug or violent crimes within the past five years, or who had a severe mental health problem could not register firearms. The D.C. Council then enacted the Firearms Amendment Act of 2012, which repealed parts of the

FRA and reduced some of the burdens on gun registrants.

ISSUES Is the District of Columbia statute that requires the registration of long guns constitutional? Is it constitutional to require the photographing and fingerprinting of each gun registrant?

HOLDINGS Yes. It is constitutional to require owners to register their long guns. Yes. It is constitutional to require owners to register in person and be photographed and fingerprinted.

REASONING Excerpts from the opinion of Senior Circuit Judge Ginsburg:

... In *Heller II*, we adopted a two-step approach to determining the constitutionality of the District's gun registration laws: "We ask first whether a particular provision impinges upon a right protected by the Second Amendment; if it does, then we go on to determine whether the provision passes muster under the appropriate level of constitutional scrutiny." ... We determined that level was intermediate scrutiny. ... For a ... provision to survive intermediate scrutiny, the District has to show, first, that it "promotes a substantial governmental interest that would be achieved less effectively absent the regulation," and second, that "the means chosen are not substantially broader than necessary to achieve that interest." ... [T]he District must demonstrate that the harms to be prevented by the regulation "are real, not merely conjectural, and that the regulation will . . . alleviate these harms in a direct and material way." . . . [I]t is our . . . [job] to determine . . . whether the District "has drawn reasonable inferences based on substantial evidence." . . . If it has done so, and if the means chosen are not overbroad, then "summary judgment [for the District] . . . is appropriate regardless of whether the evidence is in conflict." . . .

In *Heller II* we held the basic registration requirement as applied to handguns did not impinge upon the Second Amendment and was therefore constitutional. . . . ("[T]he basic requirement to register a handgun is longstanding in American law. . . . [W]e presume the District's basic registration requirement . . . does not impinge upon the right protected by the Second Amendment. . . .")

Requiring the registration of handguns is legally different from requiring the registration of long guns only in that "basic registration of handguns is deeply enough rooted in our history to support the presumption that [it] is constitutional," . . . the registration requirement for long guns lacks that historical pedigree. . . . Because the burden of the basic registration requirement as applied to long guns is de minimis, it does not implicate the second amendment right. . . . It is therefore constitutional.

The additional registration requirements . . . cannot be said to be de minimis. . . . [The recent changes in the requirements somewhat reduced the burden.] Those requirements are . . . subject to intermediate scrutiny. We previously identified two substantial governmental interests served by the registration requirements . . . : (1) protecting police officers by enabling them to determine, in advance, whether guns may be present at a location to which they are called and (2) aiding in crime control. . . . On appeal, the District identifies more particularly its interest in "protecting police officers" and reiterates its interest in "promoting public safety" generally. Heller does not dispute that these are substantial governmental interests. Rather, he challenges the closeness of the fit

between the asserted interests and the various registration requirements. . . . The District responds that although the ". . . [Metropolitan Police Department (MPD)] does not routinely check registration records prior to responding to a call for service . . . such a check is a tool available for use in appropriate circumstances." . . . [T]he question remains whether that "tool" promotes the District's . . . interest in police protection. . . . District police "are trained to treat situations where there might be a crime in progress or domestic dispute or some other situation possibly involving violence as always having a potential to have a dangerous weapon present." . . . The testimony of the District's own witnesses . . . indicates that the records established via the registration requirements . . . have little to no effect upon the conduct or safety of police officers. . . .

[T]he District claims the various registration requirements advance its interest in public safety by "distinguishing criminals from law-abiding citizens, enabling police to arrest criminals immediately, facilitating enforcement against prohibited persons obtaining or continuing to possess firearms, reducing gun trafficking, and increasing the difficulty for criminals to acquire guns." . . . The District has presented substantial evidence from which it could conclude that fingerprinting and photographing each person registering a gun promotes public safety by facilitating identification of a gun's owner, both at the time of registration and upon any subsequent police check of the gun's registration. The requirement that registrants appear in person is necessary in order for a photograph and fingerprints to be taken. . . . The Report of the Committee on the Judiciary stated that "[t]he initial fingerprinting requirement is fundamental . . . to fulfill its public safety obligations in registering firearms—being able to screen the registrant to ensure that he or she is not disqualified from possessing a firearm." . . . [T]he District points to evidence suggesting background checks using fingerprints are more reliable than background checks conducted without fingerprints, which are more susceptible to fraud. . . . [T]he

District points to an investigation conducted by the U.S. Government Accountability Office [GAO], in which five "agents acting in an undercover capacity used . . . counterfeit driver's licenses in attempts to purchase firearms from gun stores and pawnshops that were licensed . . . to sell firearms." . . . Those attempts were [all] . . . successful. . . . The report concluded that federal background checks . . . "cannot ensure that the prospective purchaser is not a felon or other prohibited person whose receipt and possession of a firearm would be unlawful." . . . [A] disclosure measure such as the one . . . here survives intermediate scrutiny if the deterrent value of the measure will materially further an important governmental interest. . . . The GAO study indicates the fingerprinting requirement would . . . help to deter and detect fraud and . . . prevent disqualified individuals from registering firearms.

. . . Chief Lanier . . . asserted that "a certificate with a photo helps to quickly and safely communicate" the fact of registration to police officers, which, "in turn,

helps to keep both the officer and the registrant safe." . . . [W]e believe the District has adduced substantial evidence from which it reasonably could conclude that fingerprinting and photographing registrants will directly and materially advance public safety by preventing at least some ineligible individuals from obtaining weapons and . . . by facilitating identification of the owner of a registered firearm during any subsequent encounter with the police. . . . The additional requirement that registrants appear in person to be photographed and fingerprinted is . . . necessary to implement those requirements. . . .

[T]he district court's . . . order is AFFIRMED with respect to: the basic registration requirement as applied to long guns . . . ; the requirement that a registrant be fingerprinted and photographed and make a personal appearance to register a firearm . . . ; the requirement that an individual pay certain fees associated with the registration of a firearm . . . ; and the requirement that registrants complete a firearms safety and training course. . . .

Short Answer Questions

1. Benjamin Franklin wrote, "Laws too gentle are seldom obeyed; too severe, seldom executed."[24] Do you agree? Why or why not?

2. In addition to statutes criminalizing texting while driving, what other laws are commonly violated in the United States? In your opinion, why is there a low level of voluntary compliance with these laws? What issues does this low level of compliance cause?

3. A U.S. law enacted in 1996 prevents lawyers from soliciting victims of air disasters for the first 45 days after a crash. Clients are permitted to contact lawyers, however. After the crash of Asiana Flight 214 on July 6, 2013, the National Transportation Safety Board reminded attorneys of the rules in a mass email. The message said, "We are closely monitoring the activities of attorneys following this accident, and will immediately notify state bar ethics officials and other appropriate authorities if impermissible activity is suspected." What do you think is the purpose of this law? Is it effective in advancing that purpose? Is it necessary? Why or why not?[25]

You Decide...

1. On January 28 and 29, 2016, the Martells' house in San Francisco was demolished. Ronald Martell and his wife purchased the house in October 2015, for $2,149,000. It was on a hill with sweeping views of the Pacific Ocean. The Martells were considering some remodeling projects and had not yet moved into the house. The buyers' inspection during the sale did not reveal any problems. Within a week in January the house slipped 14 inches from the curb and dropped 12 inches. William Strawn, a spokesperson for San Francisco's Department of Building Inspection, said the city ordered an immediate teardown of the house because of the "imminent public safety hazard." The City was afraid that it would slide down the hill and damage other homes. The cause of the unstable soil conditions is under investigation. The soil seems to be full of water. It is not known if the water is from recent rains and/or other sources. The City ordered five other owners of nearby homes to hire engineers to inspect their homes and show the City that they are safe.

Assume that Ronald Martell and his wife contact you. They want to know who is responsible for the expenses of demolishing and then rebuilding their house. What advice would you give them? Why?

(*See* Jean Elle and Riya Bhattacharjee, "Sliding House, Sold for $2M, Demolished in San Francisco," NBC Bay Area, January 28, 2016, http://www.nbc bayarea.com/news/local/Sliding-House-Torn-Down-in-San-Francisco-366929101.html (accessed 2/6/16); Janie Har and Jeff Chiu, "Crews Demolishing San Francisco House Sliding Off Hill," Associated Press, January 29, 2016, http://hosted.ap.org/dynamic/stories/U/US_SLIDING_HOUSE_DEMOLISHED? SITE=OKSHA&SECTION=HOME (accessed 2/6/ 16); and Anton Nilsson, "Heartbroken San Francisco Homeowner Watches as His 'Dangerous' $2 million House Is Demolished to Stop It Sliding Down a Hill—Just Four Months After He Bought It," DailyMail. com, January 29, 2016, Updated: January 30, 2016, http://www.dailymail.co.uk/news/article-3422864/ San-Francisco-homeowner-watches-three-story-hill side-house-bought-2-million-October-demolished. html (accessed 2/6/16).)

2. Two Oregon ranchers, members of the Hammond family, were sentenced to five years in prison for burning on federal lands. Their sentence triggered an occupation at the Malheur Federal Wildlife Refuge in eastern Oregon beginning January 2, 2016. The protesters claimed that the lands should be returned to local ranchers and local governments. Interestingly, prior to the occupation the U.S. Fish and Wildlife Service had created a collaborative plan for managing the Malheur. The plan was based on input from environmentalists, ranchers, conservationists, and county commissioners.

LaVoy Finicum, an Arizona rancher, was a frequent spokesperson for the occupiers. He willfully violated rules and destroyed property on the refuge. Finicum was a friend of Cliven Bundy and had traveled to the Oregon refuge with Cliven's sons, Ammon and Ryan. Much of the Bundys' complaints stem from Cliven Bundy's standoff with federal officials in 2014. "'When the BLM [Bureau of Land Management] tried to round up

Bundy's cattle for trespassing on federal land, some of Bundy's crew took up sniper positions and threatened to shoot it out, so the BLM temporarily backed off to avoid bloodshed.'"[26] Bundy has still not paid the $1 million he owes the federal government for grazing fees.

Finicum was shot and killed by authorities on January 26, 2016 when authorities stopped a vehicle on local roads. When Finicum got out of the vehicle he allegedly reached for his loaded gun and was shot by authorities.

Following the shooting of Finicum, a number of protesters were arrested on various federal counts. Ten of the occupiers were charged with threatening federal officers. Some of the employees who lived on the refuge had to abandon their homes and the occupiers reportedly went through their belongings. One of the occupiers, Jon Ritzheimer, is accused "of having threatened a woman in the Safeway supermarket in Burns [Oregon] who was wearing a shirt with a Bureau of Land Management emblem on it, threatening to follow her home in her car and burn down her house."[27] Federal Magistrate Judge Stacie F. Beckerman in Portland, Oregon ordered the defendants "held as a risk of flight and a risk to the safety of the community."[28] The citizens of Harney County were on edge during the occupation. The Hammonds have tried to distance themselves from the occupation.

Assume this case has been filed in *your* federal court. How would *you* decide this case involving the occupiers? Be certain that you explain and justify your answer. What interests of a legal system were the authorities trying to enforce? What interests were the occupiers trying to advance? Why?

(See Patrik Jonsson, "Ransacked Oregon Refuge Shows Disdain Toward America's Rangers: What's the Fix?" *The Christian Science Monitor*, January 30, 2016; Patrik Jonsson, "Armed Oregon Occupation: Is It Really About White Poverty in the West?" *The Christian Science Monitor*, January 9, 2016; Dave Seminara, Julie Turkewitz, and Kirk Johnson, "Jailed Oregon Protest Leader Urges Followers: 'Please Go Home'," *The New York Times*, January 28, 2016, A1; and Julie Turkewitz and Jack Healy, "Protester Who Was Killed Was Group's Defiant Voice," *The New York Times*, January 28, 2016, A16.)

Notes

1. Steve Inskeep, Host, Nishat Kurwa, Guest, *Morning Edition*, December 4, 2014, "'Black Lives Matter' Slogan Becomes a Bigger Movement," NPR Youth Radio, http://www.npr.org/2014/12/04/368408247/black-lives-matter-slogan-becomes-a-bigger-movement (accessed 4/22/16) and Alisa Robinson, "Black Lives Matter: The Evolution of a Movement," Occupy.com, March 16, 2015, http://www.occupy.com/article/black-lives-matter-evolution-movement (accessed 4/22/16).

2. This section of the UCC was substantially revised in 2003. When states adopt the 2003 revisions, the amount will be increased to $5,000. Currently, no state has adopted the revisions. Uniform Law Commission Web site, "UCC

Article 2, Sales and Article 2A, Leases (2003)," http://www.uniformlaws.org/Act.aspx?title=UCC%20Article%202,Sales%20and%20Article%202A,%20Leases%20%282003%29 (accessed 2/5/16).

3. *Drysdale v. Prudden*, 195 N.C. 722, 143 S.E. 530, 536 (1928).

4. The grand jury requirement is included in the Fifth Amendment and applies to federal criminal cases. This is not a requirement at the state level under the U.S. Constitution, although it may be required under the state's constitution or statutes.

5. Kimberly Amadeo, "Auto Industry Bailout (GM, Ford, Chrysler)," *about news*, Updated February 08, 2016, http://useconomy.about.com/od/criticalssues/a/auto_bailout.htm (accessed 2/19/16); "Auto Bailout Saved 1.5 Million U.S. Jobs–Study," *Reuters*, December 9, 2013, http://www.reuters.com/article/autos-bailout-study-idUSL1N0JO0XU20131209 (accessed 2/19/16); and Jonathan Weisman, "U.S. Declares Bank and Auto Bailouts Over, and Profitable," *The New York Times*, December 19, 2014, http://www.nytimes.com/2014/12/20/business/us-signals-end-of-bailouts-of-automakers-and-wall-street.html?_r=0 (accessed February 19, 2016).

6. The businessman allegedly defrauded more than 57,000 investors out of approximately RMB 2.8 billion (US $460 million). Zeng's family claims that they were not notified by the Chinese government prior to his execution. Tara Clarke, "Why China's Bernie Madoff Should Give Pause to Americans Doing Business in China," *Money Morning*, July 19, 2013, http://moneymorning.com/2013/07/19/why-chinas-bernie-madoff-should-give-pause-to-americans-doing-business-in-china/(accessed April 22, 2016).

7. Associated Press, "Italian Court Sets Date for Amanda Knox Retrial," *MSN News*, http://news.msn.com/crime-justice/italian-court-sets-date-for-amanda-knox-retrial?ocid=ansnews11 (accessed July 10, 2013).

8. See Kerrie Sadiq and Ann Black, "Embracing Sharia-Compliant Products through Regulatory Amendment to Achieve Parity of Treatment," 34 Sydney L. Rev. 189 (March 2012).

9. Starnes claimed that it was all a misunderstanding about layoffs and severance packages. Some workers had a different story, claiming that they were owed back pay. They also thought that the factory was going to be closed and everyone was going to be laid off. David McKenzie and Connie Young, "U.S. Businessman Held Hostage by His Workers in China, He Says," *CNN*, June 25, 2013, http://www.cnn.com/2013/06/25/world/asia/china-us-businessman-hostage (accessed July 21, 2013) and "American Businessman Being 'Held Hostage' in China,"

Fox 19, posted June 25, 2013 and updated July 2, 2013, http://www.fox19.com/story/22682685/american-businessman-being-held-hostage-in-china (accessed July 21, 2013), source CNN.

10. Presentation by Babak Shakoory, "Islamic Commercial Law," Fresno, CA, April 16, 2012.

11. Brian Murphy, "Marte Deborah Dalelv, Alleged Norwegian Rape Victim, Sentenced to 16 Months Jail in Dubai for Sex Outside of Marriage," *Huff Post World*, July 19, 2013, http://www.huffingtonpost.com/2013/07/19/marte-deborah-dalelv-sentenced-norwegian-rape-dubai_n_3624867.html?icid=maing-grid7 | hp-desktop | dl14 | sec1_lnk3%26pLid%3D346961 (accessed July 21, 2013). After a public outcry and high level discussions between Norway and UAE, Sheikh Mohammed bin Rashid Al Maktoum pardoned Dalelv. She was permitted to leave UAE. Nicola Goulding, Jennifer Z. Deaton, and Laura Smith-Spark, "Dubai Pardons Norwegian Who Reported Her Rape," *CNN*, July 23, 2013, http://www.kcra.com/news/national/Dubai-pardons-Norwegian-who-reported-her-rape/-/11797450/21094226/-/u1lrnuz/-/index.html (accessed October 5, 2013).

12. 1 Cranch 137, 2 L. Ed. 60 (1803).

13. U.S. Constitution, Article II, Section 2. The case of *Missouri v. Holland*, 252 U.S. 416 (1920), established that statutes passed in accordance with a valid treaty cannot be declared unconstitutional.

14. United States Senate Web page, "Treaties," http://www.senate.gov/artandhistory/history/common/briefing/Treaties.htm (accessed February 5, 2016).

15. *Ibid.*

16. *Ibid.*

17. *Ibid.*

18. *Ibid.*

19. "Common law," *Ballentine's Law Dictionary*, 2010 LexisNexis [#174], a division of Reed Elsevier, plc.; Bryan A. Garner, *Black's Law Dictionary*, 7th ed. (St. Paul: West Publishing Co., 1999), 270.

20. Bryan A. Garner, *Black's Law Dictionary*, 7th ed. (St. Paul: West Publishing Co., 1999), 270.

21. 347 U.S. 483 (1954).

22. 163 U.S. 537 (1896).

23. Although it is one legal system, some states, like Delaware, still have separate courts of equity.

24. Benjamin Franklin, *Poor Richard Improved: Being an Almanack and Ephemeris . . . for the Year of our Lord 1756 by Richard Saunders*, printed and sold by B. Franklin & D.

Hall, Philadelphia (1756), and at Brainy Quote, http://www.brainyquote.com/search_results.html?q=Laws+too+gentle+are+seldom+obeyed (accessed 2/5/16).

25. USA Today, "Courts Will Treat Asiana Passengers Differently," *USA Today*, July 14, 2013, http://www.usatoday.com/story/news/nation/2013/07/14/courts-asiana-airlines/2515869/(accessed July 15, 2013).

26. Ray Ring and Marshall Swearingen, "Defuse the West," *High Country News*, October 27, 2014, quoted in Patrik Jonsson,

"Ransacked Oregon Refuge Shows Disdain Toward America's Rangers: What's the Fix?" *The Christian Science Monitor*, January 30, 2016.

27. Dave Seminara, Julie Turkewitz, and Kirk Johnson, "Jailed Oregon Protest Leader Urges Followers: 'Please Go Home'," *The New York Times*, January 28, 2016, A1.

28. *Ibid.*

2

Business Ethics

Learning Objectives

After completing this chapter you should be able to

- Explain why ethics are important to business
- Describe the main ethical theories
- Distinguish consequential and nonconsequential theories
- Recognize the ethical perspective of an author or speaker
- Select an ethical theory and analyze a dilemma from the perspective of that theory
- Identify the stakeholders in a business decision

Classic Case

In Chapter 1 the focus was on the law. In this chapter the focus is on business ethics. As you read the cases in this chapter consider the ethics of the participants. For example, in this Classic Case consider the ethics of Jacobson and the city of Cambridge officials. In this decision the U.S. Supreme Court analyzed whether the smallpox vaccine requirement was constitutional under the police power of the state. The court considered whether one person had the right to refuse a mandatory vaccination when the program was intended to help the common good.

JACOBSON v. MASSACHUSETTS

197 U.S. 11, 1905 U.S. LEXIS 1232 (1905)

FACTS Jacobson lived in the city of Cambridge. Cambridge had a smallpox outbreak that seemed to be getting worse. The Cambridge Board of Health passed a regulation that required all adults to get the smallpox vaccination. The city provided the vaccinations for free. Jacobson refused to have the vaccination. He appeared to be healthy at this time. He experienced a negative reaction to a vaccination as a child.

ISSUE Must adults within Cambridge comply with the Board of Health's regulation to have a smallpox vaccination?

HOLDING Yes, The vaccination requirement is constitutional.

REASONING Excerpts from the opinion of Mr. Justice Harlan:

... The authority of the State to enact this statute is ... commonly called the police power—a power which the State did not surrender ... under the Constitution. ... [This court] has distinctly recognized the authority of a State to enact quarantine laws and "health laws of every description." ... According to settled principles, the police power of a State must be held to embrace ... such reasonable regulations ... as will protect the public health and the public safety. ... It is equally true that the State may invest local bodies ... with authority ... to safeguard the public health and the public safety. The mode or manner in which those results are to be accomplished is within the discretion of the State, subject ... to the condition that no rule prescribed by a State, nor any regulation adopted by a local governmental agency ... shall ... [violate] the Constitution of the United States or infringe any right granted or secured by that instrument. ...

The defendant insists that his liberty is invaded when the State subjects him to fine or imprisonment for neglecting or refusing to submit to vaccination; that a compulsory vaccination law is unreasonable, arbitrary and oppressive, and, ... hostile to the inherent right of every freeman to care for his own body and health in such way as to him seems best ... But the liberty secured by the Constitution of the United States ... does not import an absolute right in each person to be, at all times and in all circumstances, wholly freed from restraint. There are ... restraints to which every person is necessarily subject for the common good. ... Society based on the rule that each one is a law unto himself would soon be confronted with disorder and anarchy. Real liberty for all could not exist under the operation of a principle which recognizes the right of each individual person [to make his own decisions] ... regardless of the injury that may be done to others. ... "[P]ersons and property are subjected to all kinds of restraints and burdens, in order to secure the general comfort, health, and prosperity of the State." ... "[A]ll rights are subject to such reasonable conditions as may be deemed by the governing authority ... essential to the safety, health, peace, good order and morals of the community. Even liberty itself, the greatest of all rights, is not unrestricted license to act according to one's own will. It is only freedom from restraint under conditions essential to the equal enjoyment of the same right by others. It is then liberty regulated by law." . . .

[T]he legislature of Massachusetts required the inhabitants of a city or town to be vaccinated only when, in the opinion of the Board of Health, that was necessary for the public health. . . . [I]t was appropriate for the legislature to refer that question . . . to a Board of Health, composed of persons residing in the locality affected and appointed . . . because of their fitness to determine such questions. To invest such a body with authority over such matters was not an unusual nor an unreasonable or arbitrary requirement. . . . [A] community has the right to protect itself against an epidemic of disease which threatens the safety of its members. . . . [W]hen the regulation in question was adopted, smallpox . . . was prevalent . . . in the city of Cambridge and the disease was increasing. . . . [T]he court would usurp the functions of another branch of government if it adjudged . . . that the mode adopted . . . to protect the people . . . was arbitrary and not justified by the necessities of the case. . . . There is, of course, a sphere within which the individual may assert the supremacy of his own will and rightfully dispute the authority of any human government . . . to interfere with the exercise of that will. But it is equally true that in every well-ordered society charged with the duty of conserving the safety of its members the rights of the individual in respect of his liberty may at times . . . be subjected to such restraint . . . as the safety of the general public may demand. . . .

[If there were two ways to protect the public from a disease, it is not the court's function to determine which one should be used.] That was for the legislative department to determine in . . . light of all the information it had or could obtain. . . . The state legislature proceeded upon the theory which recognized vaccination as . . . an effective if not the best known way in which to meet and suppress the evils of a smallpox epidemic. . . .

"It must be conceded that some laymen . . . and some physicians of great skill and repute, do not believe that vaccination is a preventive of smallpox. The common belief . . . is that it has a decided tendency to prevent the spread of this fearful disease and to render it less dangerous to those who contract it. While not accepted by all, it is accepted by the mass of the people, as well as by most members of the medical profession. . . ." A common belief, like common knowledge, does not require evidence to establish its existence, but may be acted upon without proof by the legislature and the courts. . . . "The fact that the belief is not universal is not controlling, for there is scarcely any belief that is accepted by everyone. The possibility that the belief may be wrong, and that science may yet show it to be wrong, is not conclusive. . . ."

We are not prepared to hold that a minority, residing or remaining in any city or town where smallpox is prevalent, and enjoying the general protection afforded by an organized local government, may . . . defy the will of its constituted authorities, acting in good faith for all, under the legislative sanction of the State. . . . While this court should guard with firmness every right appertaining to life, liberty or property as secured to the individual by the Supreme Law of the Land, . . . it should not invade the domain of local authority except when it is plainly necessary to do so in order to enforce that law. . . .

The judgment of the court below must be affirmed.

It is so ordered.

INTRODUCTION

A number of people view "business ethics" as a contradiction in terms. Recent corporate scandals and the resulting loss of trust by the public demonstrate that ethics is important in business. Even a *perceived* lack of ethics in a firm or in an industry can have devastating effects on the firm, the industry, or even the entire U.S. economy. These scandals often lead to additional government regulation. Remember the impact of these events, including economic harm they cause while studying this chapter.

Business ethics involves the ethics of individuals *and* the ethics of the organization to which they belong. For example, a chief financial officer (CFO) has ethics and the corporation has ethics. Or a senator will have certain ethics and the Congress as a whole has ethics. The individual's ethics may be the same or similar to those of the organization. Sometimes there is a mismatch between the two. If a company frequently asks the CFO to do acts that he or she feels are not ethical, the views of the two do not match well. In this text we will discuss the perspectives of both the individual and those of the organization.

Ethics and Law

Ethics and law are interrelated. For some individuals ethics and law are synonymous. For example, when these individuals face an ethical dilemma they ask whether the behavior that they are considering is legal. In their minds if it is legal, it is ethical. If it is not legal, it is not ethical. However, for many people, these questions are not identical. To illustrate the two positions, assume Justin oversleeps and leaves for work late. Justin is considering driving over the speed limit. If he believes that ethics and law are synonymous, he would believe that exceeding the speed limit is unethical *and* illegal. If he believes that they are separate questions, he would recognize that exceeding the limit is illegal. He may believe that speeding in order to arrive at work on time is ethical. He may believe that speeding is not an ethical question at all. In this chapter we will focus on ethics.

Some laws are based on the ethical beliefs of some members of society. Murder is a crime because most people believe that it is wrong to kill other human beings. The prohibition movement to prohibit alcohol consumption in the United States occurred because some people felt that consuming alcohol was unethical. The constitutional amendment and the related laws that enforced it were not successful. Eventually the laws were repealed. One of the reasons for repeal was that many residents of the United States felt that the consumption of alcohol was not intrinsically unethical. Throughout the book it is important to pay attention to the interrelationships between ethics and law.

Ethics and Morality

It is fairly standard for people to equate ethics with morality, and to use the words *ethics* and *morals* interchangeably. In so doing, they find it easier to discuss the topic of ethics. However, such usage is not altogether accurate. *Ethics* refers to a guiding philosophy—the principles of conduct governing an individual or a group.[1] By contrast, *morals* relate to principles of right and wrong behavior as sanctioned by or operative on one's conscience.[2] From the perspective of an individual, ethics and morals frequently have the same meaning. However, from the perspective of a group—including a society—it is more appropriate to speak of ethics. When we speak of ethics, we will be talking about societal values, the accepted standard of conduct within a given society. In contrast, when we speak of morals, we will be talking about individual values, the accepted conduct of an individual by that individual.

Exhibit 2.1 gives a few examples of how ethics and morals may be compared.

An individual with higher morals than society's values is one whose actions exceed those that are generally accepted. For example, while society may frown on jaywalking, it does not consider such conduct unethical. The person with higher morals might consider jaywalking to be wrong and immoral. A person with lower morals than society's values is one whose actions, or at least whose accepted values, fall below those of society at large. Such a person may see nothing wrong with cheating or stealing.

Different societies may have different ethics, but the morals of any given individual should remain relatively constant no matter which society that person should happen to be in at any point in time. Ethical conduct is conduct that is deemed right—or at least accepted as not wrong—within a societal setting. Moral conduct is conduct that

Exhibit 2.1

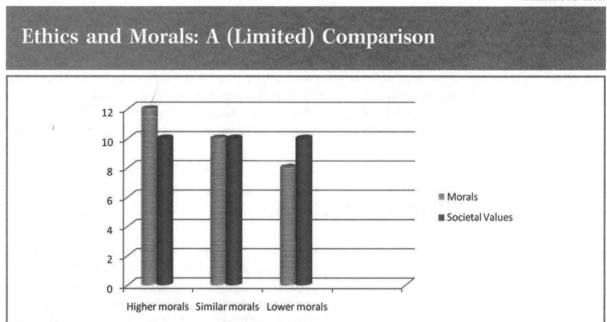

Ethics and Morals: A (Limited) Comparison

Source: Courtesy of Daniel V. Davidson. © 2016.

the individual considers right—or at least does not consider wrong—without regard to the attitude of the society.

To further complicate this already complex issue, societies also have standards that go beyond ethics. The ethical standards of a society reflect what is considered "right" and "wrong" within that society in a general manner. Some wrong behavior may be merely a matter of rude conduct, frowned on within the society. However, it is not of sufficient seriousness or severity to merit more than a social dislike of the conduct. For example, conducting a loud cell phone conversation in a public place is likely to be considered rude, but it is not likely to merit an official sanction. Other "wrong" conduct may be considered to be much more serious; this conduct may be so inappropriate that society fines or even incarcerates the person who acts in this "wrongful" manner. To help ensure that people within a society act in a socially acceptable manner, the society enacts laws and regulations, usually with penalties attached for violations of the laws or regulations. These laws enacted by society provide an ethical floor—a minimum standard of behavior that is expected from each member of that society.

Although it is a broad generalization, conduct that violates a law or a regulation of a society is generally deemed unethical by that society. This is not to say that all unethical conduct is also illegal; rather, it says that all illegal conduct is generally viewed as unethical. Of course there are situations where some members of a society will act in a manner that violates a law or a regulation to force the society to reconsider its official position and change the law. One such example involves Dr. Martin Luther King Jr., who encouraged civil disobedience in the 1950s. Much of his conduct was illegal at the time. People who view ethics and legality as the same would also view his conduct as unethical. The civil rights movement ultimately changed the laws regarding equal rights and racial discrimination and changed the social values in the United States. In retrospect, many believe that Dr. King acted in a *moral* manner by helping to change laws that they believe were unethical. There is a potential problem when an individual's personal morals call for conduct prohibited by society's ethics. For example, suppose Sydnie feels that stealing is moral as long as the victim of the theft is wealthy. Sydnie will encounter problems if she acts on the basis of this moral value by stealing from a wealthy person. If Sydnie decides to steal from the wealthy, she may be acting morally (adhering to her personal values), but she will be considered to have acted unethically by society (violating the society's values). U.S. society has decided that theft is both an illegal and an unethical act. Sydnie will find that her morals conflict with society's ethics.

ETHICAL THEORIES

It is important to begin with an introduction to some of the more widely used ethical theories and principles. This section introduces several of these ethical theories and compares them to one another. Each theory has proponents who argue for its use. Each also has critics who point out the weaknesses of the theory. As we study these ethical theories, remember that we do not have consensus on what is the "best" ethical theory. Each individual and each organization must choose the theory that best suits his, her, or its beliefs, morals, and values. Even people who are applying the same theory may come to a different conclusion as to what they should do. Some people combine theories or look at an ethical problem from the perspective of several different theories.

Although a business may be recognized as a legal person, the business is not a "particular person." It is really a collective of people. Generally, one individual is not a significant influence in providing moral or ethical guidance for the firm. The group to which a business belongs is generally too diverse to have a single system or code of morals.

Similarly, "business" is not a single profession, like medicine or law, which could adopt a single code of ethical conduct. Thus, for most people, the study of business ethics comes down to an analysis of the system or code of morals of a particular person, the specific businessperson whose conduct is being evaluated. Unfortunately, the ethical standard often applied in this situation is the ethical standard of the observer and not that of the person being observed. To properly treat the ethical issues of a businessperson, some kind of analytic framework must be established and some basic understanding of the ethical parameters of business needs to be developed.

An Ounce of Prevention

When you hear or read about someone saying "that is not right" or "that is not ethical," try to identify his or her ethical perspective. This practice will improve your ability to recognize the different theories. People generally want or expect others to share their ethical beliefs. For example, when a manager says that his or her employees need to be more ethical, the manager really wants the employees to share his or her ethical views. In other words, the manager wants the employees to act and be motivated by the same values as the manager. The observer (the manager) is frequently using his or her values in evaluating the conduct of those he or she is observing (the employees).

In your role as a business owner or manager, you should try to remember that other people in your organization may have different ethical beliefs than you do. If you remember this, you are less likely to be shocked when they act in a manner different from your expectations.

Cultural Relativism

Cultural relativism holds that what is good or bad depends on what is approved by the majority of a given society. Morality is a product of the culture. For example, the death penalty is a socially acceptable punishment in some societies, but not in others. Two societies may hold ethical views that are opposed to one another, and there is no clear way to resolve the differences. No culture is superior to any other culture. Other societies are different, but they are not "wrong." Cultural relativists view themselves as being tolerant of the differences. Critics of cultural relativism say that there are universal or hypernorms: Many diverse societies prohibit the same things, such as lying, stealing, adultery, and killing human beings. Critics also say that if a society does not prohibit something, such as killing other human beings, it is acceptable to judge that society and to point out that the society is defective.

Consequential and Nonconsequential Principles

Many ethical theories are based on either consequential (teleological) principles or on nonconsequential (deontological) principles. Consequential principles judge the ethics of a particular action by the *consequences* of that action. Consequential ethics determine the "rightness" or the "wrongness" of any action by comparing the amount of good to the amount of evil that a given action will produce. A person using consequential ethics needs to evaluate each of his or her possible choices, measuring the good (and the evil) that seems likely to result from the alternatives. The "right" action is that action that will produce the ratio of the greatest amount of good to evil. The major theories of ethical behavior under the consequential principles include ethical egoism and utilitarianism. These theories will be examined in more detail later in this section.

Nonconsequential principles tend to focus on the concept of *duty* rather than on the results of the action. Nonconsequential ethical theories are rule-based. Under the nonconsequential approach, a person acts ethically if that person is faithful to his or her duty, regardless of the consequences that follow from being faithful to that duty. The nonconsequential ethical theories are likely to reflect the values of the society. Remember that society imposes duties (in the form of rules and regulations) to maximize the values it wants, and by meeting that duty, the individual is furthering the interests of that society. The *categorical imperative* advanced by Immanuel Kant and the *veil of ignorance* advocated by John Rawls are two of the best-known theories in support of nonconsequential principles of ethics. Both of these theories will be discussed in detail later in this chapter.

Ethical Egoism

Ethical egoism is a prescriptive theory that says the proper goal of all people is their own self-interest.[3] In other words, you should do those things that maximize your own self-interest. (Do not confuse an *egoist*, a person who follows the ethical theory of egoism, with an *egotist*, a person who has an exaggerated sense of self-importance.) In ethical egoism, each person is expected to act in a manner that will maximize his or her long-term self-interests. In so doing, society will benefit because when each individual acts in a manner that produces his or her greatest good, the sum of all of these individual acts will produce the greatest total good for the society. Under this theory, an action is morally right if it maximizes the actor's self-interest. It does not need to do anything else.

One common misconception about egoism is that all egoists are hedonistic pleasure-seekers who emphasize instant gratification. This interpretation treats one's pleasure as being equal to one's best interests.[4] Most egoists take a broader view of what is in "one's best interests." Consequently, many egoists may decide to act in an apparently "selfless" manner because doing so will further their long-term self-interest. These egoists may be willing to make a personal sacrifice today to receive some benefit in the future. Doing so is perfectly consistent with the doctrine of egoism. An egoist may cooperate with others so that others will cooperate with him or her in the future. So an egoist may decide that it is in his or her interest to live up to a promise so that others will accept his or her promises in the future or so that others will not sue him or her for breach of contract. One problem with ethical egoism is whether a person can accurately choose what is in his or her best interest. The actor may not recognize the good or bad consequences of an act.

In the same manner that an individual may follow ethical egoism, so may an organization. From an organizational perspective, egoism involves those actions that best promote the long-term interests of the organization. A corporation using egoism may establish a minority hiring program or a college internship program. These programs may advance the long-term interests of the corporation by (1) improving its public image, (2) reducing social tensions, or (3) avoiding legal problems that might otherwise arise. These programs may help provide skilled employees in the future. The short-term expenses incurred in such programs can be offset by future benefits so that the programs may appear to be generous and public-spirited when in reality they are undertaken for self-interested reasons.

Utilitarianism

The second major consequential approach is utilitarianism. To a utilitarian, the proper course of conduct in any given setting is the course that will produce the greatest good (or the least harm) for the greatest number.[5] Rather than focusing on the interests of the individual (as an egoist would), the utilitarian focuses on the interests of the group. The ethical course of conduct is the one that best serves the interests of the social group as a whole, regardless of the impact on any individuals or any subgroups of the social system. Classical utilitarians equated good as pleasure and bad as pain. Under this hedonistic approach, the amount of good created would be the amount of pleasure minus the amount of pain.[6] Many utilitarians today use a broader definition of good. Most utilitarians do not care if the "good" is felt immediately or if it is felt later. One weakness of the theory, though, is determining at what point in time the "goodness" should be measured. There are two primary types of utilitarianism, act-utilitarianism and rule-utilitarianism.

Act Utilitarianism   Act utilitarianism is concerned with individual actions and the effect of those actions on the social group. An act utilitarian expects each person to act in a manner that will produce the greatest net benefit for the group. An act utilitarian makes each ethical decision by examining the options and selecting the option that will maximize the goodness. (Act utilitarianism has been called "direct utilitarianism.")[7] To an act utilitarian, telling a "little white lie" may be the most ethical course of conduct in a given situation if telling the lie produces more total good than would be obtained by telling the truth, by avoiding the answer, or by any other alternative. One area of weakness is determining how you define and measure benefit and goodness. (Hedonists would define it as pleasure.) Another weakness of the theory is the difficulty in deciding how large the group is. An act utilitarian needs to decide if the "group" is a town, a state, or the world. In practice some act utilitarians use a rule-utilitarian process to make decisions.[8]

Rule Utilitarianism   A rule utilitarian also wants to maximize goodness. He or she takes a different approach. A rule utilitarian would (1) make a list of every possible combination of moral rules (the lists can be very short or very complex, with different circumstances and contingencies); (2) select the set of rules that would maximize the utility if everyone followed them all the time; and (3) decide moral questions by asking himself or herself, "Is the action I am contemplating permitted by the rules? If so, I may do it."[9] (This has been called indirect utilitarianism.)[10] The best rule is the rule that causes the best consequences. The best rules may not be simple because they may have a long list of exceptions. For example, the formulation for promise-keeping might be "always keep your promises, except . . ." followed by a long list of exceptions.[11] "The rule utilitarian measures the consequences of the act repeated over and over again through time . . . as a rule whenever similar circumstances arise."[12] One criticism of rule utilitarianism is that when it is extended, it becomes the same as act utilitarianism.[13]

Kant and the Categorical Imperative

The nonconsequential ethical theories are best exemplified by the categorical imperative developed by Immanuel Kant, an eighteenth-century German philosopher. Kant thought that certain universal moral standards existed without regard to the circumstances of the moment or the values of any particular society.[14] Under Kant's theory, when people follow these universal moral principles, they are acting morally and ethically. When people do not follow these universal principles, they are acting unethically. Individual variations and consequences are irrelevant. The universal moral principles impose a duty on each person, and the performance of that duty is what determines the "rightness" or the "wrongness" of any action.

Kant also believed that there were perfect duties and imperfect duties. Perfect duties are those things a person must always do or refrain from doing, such as the duty of a merchant to never cheat a customer. Imperfect duties involve things a person should do, but not necessarily things a person must do. For example, a person should contribute to charities, but a person is not required to contribute to all charities. A person does not have to contribute to any particular charity every time that charity solicits contributions.

Based on his theories, Kant developed his *categorical imperative*. The categorical imperative says that each person should act in such a manner that his or her actions could become the universal law. In a perfectly ethical and moral world, each person is expected to act as every person ought to act. The rules to be followed are unconditional, and adherence to these rules is imperative. If each person carries out his or her duty by following these "universal rules," society will be properly served by each individual.

Kant's approach is also applicable to organizations. An organization is judged in the same manner as an individual. The organization is expected to obey the categorical imperative, just as an individual is expected to obey it. The organization is to act according to its duty, with its actions being judged against the "universal law" standard: Would such conduct be proper if all organizations were to act in the same manner? The organization is expected to act in a manner that discharges its duty to every aspect of society, which would include recognition of the rights of others and the duty owed to others.

Feminism

Feminism, or the feminist philosophy, is also sometimes called the ethics of caring. Advocates of this theory argue that men and women have different attitudes about how social life should be organized and how ethical conflicts should be resolved. The theory is based on the concept that everyone is interdependent. It gives a high priority to (1) empathy, (2) healthy and harmonious relationships, (3) caring for one another, and (4) avoiding harm. This ethical theory indicates that particular attention should be paid to the effect of decisions on individuals, especially those individuals in a close relationship with the decision maker.[15] This philosophy focuses on character traits such as sympathy, compassion, loyalty, and friendship. Important factors are social cooperation and the realization that in many situations the parties are not of equal power or ability. The social context of the decision is important. The structure of the society must be protected, and the rights and interests of the less capable people should be protected as well. This philosophy continues to develop. During its evolution, some aspects are more important to some philosophers than others. For example, some argue that this approach is a human strength and both men and women should be trained to use it. This approach with its focus on relationships may be difficult to use in business.

The relationships among these ethical theories are summarized in Exhibit 2.2.

Rawls and the Veil of Ignorance

John Rawls based much of his work on Kant as he developed his own theory about what constitutes a just society. Rawls described his theory, called *Rawlsianism*, by using the "Bargaining Game," a theoretical community of men and women who join together to bargain for a completely new set of moral rules (laws) that they must all obey in the future. The players start from the "Original Position." Once the rules are selected, the players must adhere to the rules, even if the rules are not in their self-interest in a particular situation. The players choosing the rules do not know their own positions in society, talents, or abilities. Rawls calls this the *veil of*

Exhibit 2.2

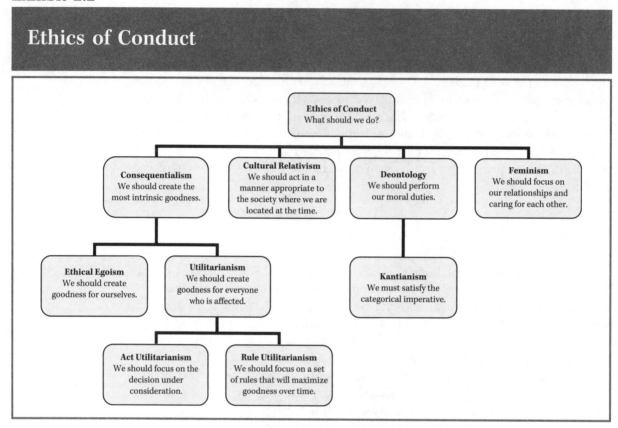

Ethics of Conduct

Ethics of Conduct
What should we do?

Consequentialism
We should create the
most intrinsic goodness.

Cultural Relativism
We should act in a
manner appropriate to
the society where we are
located at the time.

Deontology
We should perform
our moral duties.

Feminism
We should focus on
our relationships and
caring for each other.

Ethical Egoism
We should create
goodness for ourselves.

Utilitarianism
We should create
goodness for everyone
who is affected.

Kantianism
We must satisfy the
categorical imperative.

Act Utilitarianism
We should focus on the
decision under
consideration.

Rule Utilitarianism
We should focus on a set
of rules that will maximize
goodness over time.

ignorance.[16] Rawls felt that a society developed behind this veil of ignorance would be a just society. Since the people making the rules were wholly ignorant of their unique combination of race, religion, color, gender, wealth, age, and/or education, they would enact rules they would be willing to live under regardless of which combination of factors they might, theoretically, possess; they would have to live under the rules they created once they emerged from their veil of ignorance. For example, if the people were deciding if the society would provide health care for everyone, they would have to ignore whether they could afford to pay for health care for themselves. Rawls has been interpreted as saying, "In effect, the parties choose principles for the design of society as if their places in it were to be determined by their worst enemies."[17]

True justice can be obtained by the society, with each member willing to live under the rules developed behind the veil. A proper constitution will be adopted; an appropriate method for legislation based on the constitution will be created; and a proper method for dispute resolution will be developed.[18] The rules will be applied by judges and administrators and generally followed by the citizens. Rawls is often considered a political philosopher. Rawls's articles and presentations helped to revive the social contract theory, which will be discussed later in this chapter.

These theories and their relationship to business are summarized in Exhibit 2.3.

Exhibit 2.3

A Comparison of Ethical Theories

Ethical Theory	Positive Aspects in a Business Context	Negative Aspects in a Business Context
Ethical Egoism[19] (Consequential theory—An act is ethical when it promotes the best long-term interests of the firm.)	1. Provides a basis for formulating and testing policies. 2. Provides flexibility in ethical decision making for a business. 3. Allows a business to tailor codes of conduct to suit the complexity of its particular business dealings.	1. May ignore blatant wrongs. 2. Incompatible with the nature and role of business. 3. Cannot resolve conflicts of egoistic interests. 4. Introduces inconsistency into ethical decision making.
Utilitarianism[20] (Consequential theory—The most ethical decision is the one that produces the greatest good, or the least harm, for the greatest number of people.)	1. Provides a basis for formulating and testing policies. 2. Provides an objective manner for resolving conflicts of self-interest. 3. Recognizes the constituent groups of a business. 4. Provides the latitude in ethical decision making that business seems to need.	1. Ignores conduct that appears to be wrong in and of itself. 2. May be in conflict with the principles of justice. 3. Difficult to formulate satisfactory rules. 4. May result in harm if the organization does not accurately predict the consequences of an act.
Feminism[21] (The ethics of caring—Recognizes the importance of personal relationships in decision making.)	1. Provides a basis for formulating and testing policies. 2. Provides an objective manner for resolving conflicts of self-interest. 3. Recognizes the constituent groups of a business. 4. Provides flexibility in ethical decision making for business.	1. Places undue emphasis on those closest to the decision maker. 2. May be more concerned with the community than with the business. 3. Difficult to formulate satisfactory rules.
Kant and the Categorical Imperative[22] (Nonconsequential theory—Only when we act from a sense of duty do actions have ethical value.)	1. Takes the guesswork out of ethical decisions. 2. Introduces a needed humanistic dimension into business ethics decisions. 3. Concept of duty implies the ethical obligation to act from a respect for rights and the recognition of responsibilities.	1. Provides no clear way to resolve conflicts among duties. 2. Provides no compelling reason that certain rules should be absolute.
Rawls and the Veil of Ignorance[23] (Nonconsequential theory— Rational agents, unaware of their personal characteristics or places in society, choose the principles they wish to have govern the society.)	1. Takes the "guesswork" out of ethical decisions.* 2. Introduces a needed humanistic dimension into business ethics decisions. 3. Implies the ethical obligation to act from a respect for rights and the recognition of responsibilities.	1. Uses the better-off members of society to assume the welfare of the worst-off. 2. Provides no compelling reason for following universal principles that are agreed to by members of the society.

Source: Courtesy of Daniel V. Davidson. © 2016.
* There is no "guesswork" because the rules that are to be followed have been established.

An Ounce of Prevention

There are a number of competing theories. It is important to consider your decisions from the viewpoints of more than one theory. You may not agree with the other theories, but there are those in society who do. They will evaluate your decision and behavior from the perspective of their chosen theory. When it is a significant decision, such as shutting down a plant, you will want to know what they think about your decision. This will also help you defend your decision to the public if it is prudent to do so.

A SYNTHESIS FOR ETHICAL DECISION MAKING

Each of these ethical theories provides a possible framework for evaluating the ethics of a business and the ethics of the people who operate the business. Remember, there is no one universally accepted theory or approach to ethics in general, nor is there an accepted or universal approach to business ethics. Each firm can select a theory of ethics to follow in developing its own ethical approach to conducting its business. Before choosing a theory, the businessperson should also take into account several other factors. These factors should include, but not be limited to, the short-term versus the long-term impact of any decisions, the constituent groups that will be affected by the decision being made (constituent groups are discussed later in the chapter), and the way in which the ethical decision fits within the legal environment.

One problem that many people face in making ethical decisions is recognizing that an ethical issue is present. Before you can use your ethical "tools" to make a decision, you need to recognize that you are facing an ethical issue. When a business or economic issue is addressed, it is normally obvious, and the decision is made on business and/or economic bases. However, the issue may also contain ethical issues. For example, while most people agree that slavery is wrong and that having slaves is unethical, slavery was allowed in the United States for decades and was often justified as being the natural order of things. In fact, slavery was economically beneficial for the slaveholders, and its existence was rationalized on economic grounds. In a similar manner, unequal pay for women has been rationalized to justify the economic benefits to the employer rather than being addressed as an ethical issue. Once an ethical issue is identified, it is logical to apply your ethical tools and to make a decision that includes consideration of the ethical and business/economic issues.

Perhaps a business would be best advised to seek a synthesis of different ethical theories as it develops its approach to ethical issues. After all, other people will judge the business, and they may view its decisions from a different ethical perspective. This approach would provide a structure for evaluating actions and options regardless of the ethical theory that most closely reflects the values of the business. One such synthesis is suggested by the work of Vincent Ruggiero.[24] Ruggiero suggests that there are three common concerns in ethical decision making: obligations, ideals, and effects. From this foundation we can develop a framework for ethical decision making. In making a decision, the following three factors should be considered:

1. The obligations that arise from organizational relationships
2. The ideals involved in any decisions that are made
3. The effects or consequences of alternative actions

Any actions that honor obligations while simultaneously advancing ideals and have the effect of benefiting people can be presumed to be moral actions. Any actions that fall short in any respect become suspect.[25] This is not to say that these latter actions are necessarily unethical. However, since these actions have a negative impact on one or more of the areas of concern, the actions should be very carefully evaluated, and alternatives should be examined to see if a better choice has been overlooked.

With this in mind, the business should follow a two-step process to ensure that it is making ethical decisions. The first step is to identify the important considerations involved (obligations, ideals, and effects). The second step is to decide where the emphasis should lie among these considerations. This approach allows the firm to apply its ethical principles to an ethical problem while also taking into account the relative positions of each of the constituent groups of the business.

Informal Approaches

An individual, including a businessperson, may want to adopt a less formal approach to his or her ethical decision making. There are a number of informal approaches that can be used. Among the more popular—and effective—of these are the following:

1. The "Golden Rule" Test—The decision maker should "do unto others as he or she would have others do unto him or her." This is a generally accepted principle in Judeo-Christian religions.
2. The "Front Page" Test—Would the decision maker be comfortable seeing this decision or course of action as the lead story on the front page of local and national newspapers?
3. The "Other Side of the Fence" Test—How would the decision maker feel if he or she was standing on the "other side of the fence" observing this decision being made by someone else?
4. The "What Would Your Mother Think" Test—Is this a decision that would make the decision maker's mother proud when she learns that her child made it?

While none of these possess the elegance of more formal ethical theories, each provides an evaluation method that forces the decision maker to consider the impact of the decision from an outsider's perspective and may help the person reach a decision in which he or she can take pride and/or in which he or she can avoid embarrassment.

An Ounce of Prevention

Although many business ethicists use the more formal methods, you can use these informal techniques to provide a quick assessment of a decision. For example, the Front Page Test gives you an idea of whether you would be embarrassed or proud of your decision. It also gives you an idea of how the decision would be perceived by others. Would you need to explain or defend the position? Would it be defensible to most people? The Other Side of the Fence technique can be more personal. For example, if you are considering conduct that might be sexual harassment or demeaning, you could ask, "how would I feel if this conduct was directed at my wife, my mother, or my daughter?"

THE EVOLUTION OF BUSINESS AS AN ETHICAL ENTITY

Business as an Amoral Institution

Historically, many people viewed business as an amoral institution. Since any given business was inanimate, and since only animate objects could be expected to possess morality, it stood to reason that a business was not expected to possess morality. Because it could not be expected to be moral, it also could not be immoral. Morality and immorality were reserved for animate beings, and inanimate objects were *amoral*. This did not present much of a problem when most businesses were relatively small and local in nature. The owners and operators of businesses were known in the community, and even though the business was viewed as amoral, the owner or operator was held to community standards. Most businesses were operated in an ethical manner in order to keep the local customers satisfied. However, as businesses grew larger and more complex, they lost this local flavor. Businesses no longer operated in a restricted geographic market and no longer had to adhere to community standards. Eventually, society began to demand some minimal ethical standards from businesses. Included among these standards were the expectations of fair play and honesty and the expectation that a business would seek profits for its investors. If a business did not meet these demands voluntarily, society could seek intervention and help from the legislature. Sometimes the legislature would respond by setting minimum standards for business behavior. If the business obeyed these laws, it met the duty of fair play; if the managers did not blatantly lie to the customers, the business met the duty of honesty; if the firm generated profits for its investors, it met its duty towards them. Sometimes courts were asked to enforce these standards. The 1919 Michigan Supreme Court's opinion in *Dodge v. Ford Motor Company*[26] is an example. Ford Motor Company was an extremely successful enterprise at the time, and it was paying substantial dividends reflecting that success. Stockholders were receiving ordinary dividends of 5 percent *per month* and special dividends that had averaged more than *400 percent* per annum over the previous five years. Then Henry Ford and the board of directors announced a change. While Ford would continue to pay regular dividends of 5 percent per month, there would be no more special dividends. Instead, the board announced its intention to reduce the price of new cars *and* to make substantial investments in socially beneficial programs for the employees and the community. Two of the stockholders, the Dodge brothers, filed suit to prevent the conduct proposed by Ford. The Michigan Supreme Court ruled that the board of directors of a corporation may *not* place the interests of the public ahead of the interests of the stockholders and may *not* divert corporate funds to non-corporate purposes. The board was instructed to continue to maximize profits and to leave any charitable or public benefit contributions to individuals who chose to make such contributions from their personal funds.

The *Dodge v. Ford Motor Company* case was viewed as a landmark opinion, providing guidance for boards of directors in closely held corporations. While this opinion deals directly with the conflict between the desire of the Ford board to provide for the workers and society and the challenge by shareholders who want dividends, the basic thrust of the opinion is that the board has a legal duty to the shareholders to maximize the return on their investments. It is not supposed to look out for others.

Notice what the court said a corporation is expected to do. Would such conduct by a corporation be considered ethical today? If not, what has changed? Investors still want a return on their investments, and they expect to receive dividends from the corporations in which they invest. Businesses are still expected to earn a profit and to return at least a portion of that profit to the shareholders.

Game Theory

As society and the courts began to recognize the existence of corporate duties, the concept of business as an amoral institution became untenable. If a business had duties, it also had some ethical responsibilities. These responsibilities tended to be based on adherence to the rules and obeying those rules. If a business obeyed the rules and stayed within the law, it was deemed to be acting in an ethical manner. This approach to business ethics led to the development of *game theory* as a means of judging the ethical stance of the business.[27] Game theory equates the operation of a business with playing a game, and the rules of the game determine the ethics of the business. If a manager of a firm lied to his or her customers, the manager—and consequently, the business—had acted unethically. If the manager bluffed his or her customers, the manager—and the firm—may have acted in an ethical manner, presuming that bluffing is an acceptable part of the game. Bluffing is an accepted part of several games, including poker. Of course, one person's bluffing may well be another person's lying, but such problems were left for others to solve.

There is a basic flaw in the game theory of business ethics. Game theories and game rules are fair and equitable only if all of the participants in the game are aware that a game is being played. If any of the participants do not realize a game is being played, they will not be aware of the rules and they will be at a disadvantage. To take advantage of people under such circumstances would not be ethical.

Under game theory, a number of rules were developed and followed. For example, *caveat emptor* (let the buyer beware) was a "rule" of the business game for a substantial period in U.S. history. Similarly, *laissez faire* economic regulation was a rule of business in the United States. Business and its customers were aware of these rules and played the business game accordingly. Eventually, business began to industrialize and to gain an increasing ability to produce for larger markets. The game was no longer quite as fair. As the game became more one-sided in favor of business, the other "players" (the customers) began to seek new rules for the game. When business did not voluntarily change the rules, the customers asked the government to intervene. This led to government regulation of business and eventually an entirely new playing field on which the game of business was to be conducted. This new playing field is the one on which business must operate today.

Social Contract Theory

Many business executives today argue that U.S. business is too regulated by the government. These people want to be unfettered, set free from the "excessive" regulations imposed by the government and allowed to compete freely with foreign producers. Although this attitude can possibly be justified from a simplistic economic position, it fails to take into account two factors: the spillover costs society must pay when a business fails to act in a responsible and ethical manner and the "social contract" between business and society. When businesses became too large for local control, the society sought legislative intervention to force compliance with social demands. This is the basis of the social contract theory. Business must comply with the demands of society if it wants to continue to exist and to operate within that society. The social contract defines the permissible scope of business conduct and goes beyond the purely economic issues. If society wants more from business than profits, business must accept this mandate in order to survive in society. To do otherwise is to breach the social contract.

Social contract theory assumes that a business can exist only because society allows it to exist. Today, society expects (and demands) more from business than mere profits. Business must respond to a number of issues including consumer safety, environmental concerns, and quality of life. If these added demands cause costs to rise, so be it. If business will not meet these demands voluntarily, these demands will be enforced by regulation—or by society changing the form of business or the rules of doing business. The Dodd-Frank Wall Street Reform and Consumer Protection Act is an example of society changing the rules. Not only has the game theory of business been rejected by society, but the rules by which business is allowed to exist have also been changed by social contract theory.

Under social contract theory, the United States has responded to recent business problems from Ponzi schemes to sales of defective mortgages. In dealing with social contract theory and in evaluating the ethical stance of any given business, it is important to recognize that each business has a number of constituent groups and that each group of constituents will have different wants, needs, and desires. (Constituent groups are sometimes called *stakeholders*.) How the constituent groups are viewed, and how they are counted, is a matter of interpretation. For simplicity's sake, we have listed the constituents as belonging to one of four distinct groups. More members or more groups could easily be used, if so desired.[28] The business manager must base decisions affecting the business, at least in part, on the impact these decisions will have on the various constituents. Some decisions will affect all of the constituent groups, although not equally. Others will only affect some of the groups. Some decisions will have a positive impact on some groups and a negative impact on others. Deciding how each group will be affected, and how much weight to give to each group, is essential in reaching ethical decisions. Exhibit 2.4 shows some of the constituent groups a business must consider.

Corporate Social Responsibility

Social contract theory has influenced the development of corporate social responsibility (CSR). Although it is called *corporate* social responsibility, many individuals feel that it applies to all businesses and not just those organized in the corporate form. CSR is the concept that businesses can and should act ethically and that they are responsible for their conduct. "While CSR does not have a universal

Exhibit 2.4

Constituents of a Business

Owners and Creditors[a]

↑ ↓

Employees   →   ***The Business*** →   The Community
(including managers) ←   ←

↑ ↓

Customers

Note: The arrows indicate that duties and obligations are owed in both directions, *from* the business to its constituents and *to* the business from its constituents. A business exists within a set of symbiotic relationships with its various constituents.

[a] This group is sometimes referred to as "stakeholders"—"A person or group that has an investment, share, or interest in something, as a business or industry" (Dictionary.com). The term stakeholder includes both owners and creditors of the business. There are numerous other definitions of "stakeholder," some of which are much broader and more inclusive than the definition used here. R. Edward Freeman, in his book *Strategic Management: A Stakeholder Approach* (Marshfield, Mass.: Pitman, 1984), includes environmentalists, the media, government, and competitors, among others, as stakeholders. With a narrow definition, as used in this exhibit, there are fewer constituents. With a broader definition, more constituents are involved. This would make the exhibit more complex, and it makes it more difficult to address constituent issues and concerns.

definition, many see it as the private sector's way of integrating the economic, social, and environmental imperatives of their activities."[29] As CSR evolves, it has developed a number of different theories about how a responsible business should make decisions and what a responsible business should do. Some of these developments are discussed below.

Critics complain that there is no consensus on which CSR theory to use. They also complain that CSR is only used to improve the corporate image; in other words, it is a public relations effort. CSR is also criticized for distracting businesses from their economic responsibility to be profitable. There is an active debate about whether social responsibility helps or hinders a firm's profitability. There is some evidence that a company's reputation for being socially responsible helps it to attract and retain workers.

Maximize Profits Approach   The maximize profits approach is the traditional view of CSR. Under this theory, a business's duty is to maximize profits for its owners. For corporations, the owners would be the stockholders. The effect of a business's decisions on others is not important by itself. This approach is illustrated by the court's decision in *Dodge v. Ford Motor Company*.

Moral Minimum Approach   The moral minimum approach to CSR states that a business's duty is to make a profit and avoid causing harm to others. If it does cause harm to others, it has a duty to correct that harm or compensate those who are injured. Under this view, if a business pollutes a river, it has a duty to clean up the river or compensate those who are injured by the pollution. A business does not have an obligation to correct a problem when it did not contribute to the problem. Laws of the community may help establish what the moral minimum is.

Stakeholder Interest Approach   Another view of CSR is that a business owes duties to other groups in addition to its owners (shareholders). The business should consider the impact of its decisions on various stakeholders. Businesses owe duties to the constituent groups, and the constituent groups are likely to owe duties to the businesses. Thus, there is a reciprocal set of duties and expectations as illustrated in Exhibit 2.4.

Consider the following example of how these duties can affect a business in its decision making. A firm has developed a new production method that will lower costs, increase profits, and make safer products. Adopting this new method will benefit two constituent groups, owners/creditors and customers. However, this new method will require relocating the plant, and it may produce a number of pollutants. Relocating the plant will cause harm to current employees who may be unable or unwilling to relocate and to the current community, which will suffer economic harm from reduced employment. The possible increase in pollutants will harm the community at the site of the new plant, although this harm will be offset to some extent by the increase in employment and the economic "ripple effect" a new plant will cause. Somehow a balancing of these competing interests must be undertaken in reaching a decision that reflects the best short-term and long-term interests of the firm. As this example also illustrates, one problem with the stakeholder approach is that of how to select which group's interests deserve the greater weight in any particular decision. The interests of the stakeholders often will conflict.

Corporate Citizenship Approach   According to the corporate citizenship theory of CSR, businesses should be good citizens in the community by advancing society's goals. The business has a duty to "do good." The business should actively try to solve social problems, even social problems that it did not cause. This view is based on the concept that business controls much of the wealth and power; consequently, it has a responsibility to use the wealth and power in ways that benefit society. Under this view, a business would be evaluated based on (1) its contribution to social causes and (2) its business operations, especially how it deals with issues such as human rights, employment discrimination, and the environment. Businesses have finite resources, and there will always be social problems, so one difficulty with this approach is deciding how the business should choose which causes to support. Should it limit itself to causes that are related to its business operations? Should it choose causes that are important to its stockholders or key personnel? How much should it contribute? If a business spends too much on social problems, investors may be reluctant to invest in the business due to reduced profits and dividends.

Currently, most people seem to subscribe to either the stakeholder interest approach or the corporate citizenship approach.

Problems with Business Ethics

Any business that seeks to act in an ethical manner faces a basic problem. There are no fixed guidelines to follow, no formal code of ethics to set the standards under which the business should operate. Numerous professional organizations have their own codes of ethics or conduct. For example, the legal profession has the Code of Professional Responsibility; the medical profession has its Hippocratic Oath; the accounting profession has a code of ethics and also has generally accepted auditing standards (GAAS) and generally accepted accounting principles (GAAP); the real estate industry has a code of conduct; and various other groups or organizations have similar codes. However, "business" as a separate entity has no code of ethical conduct. The closest thing business has to an ethical guideline is the law. If a business is acting within the law, it is acting legally and is arguably meeting its minimum social requirements. However, this forces business into a reactive posture, always responding to legislative demands. It would seem that a proactive position in which business establishes its own path would be preferable.

Given this overriding problem, what can be done to provide a solution? At the present time, probably nothing can be done in the global, or even national, sense. But it may be possible for each industry to develop a code of ethics for that particular industry, in much the same manner that the real estate industry has developed a code for its members. If such an industry-wide approach does not prove feasible, each individual firm can develop its own personal code of ethics. Although such a micro-approach may not be ideal, it at least encourages business to embark on the journey toward formalizing its ethical posture.

The Human Factor

As was mentioned earlier, in the past business was frequently viewed as an amoral institution. Workers were expected to leave their personal values at the front gate when they reported to work. At the same time, workers were expected to be loyal agents of the firm. Generally, this was interpreted to mean that if a course of conduct was beneficial to the employer, the employee was to follow that course. If a course of conduct was not beneficial to the employer, the employee was not to follow it. The attitudes and opinions of the employees were ignored.

The "loyal agent" attitude was described—and then rebutted—by Alex C. Micholos in his article "The Loyal Agent's Argument."[30] The loyal agent's argument presumes that the principal follows the ethical theory of egoism, and that the loyal agent must also act egoistically for the principal. The argument runs as follows:

1. As a loyal agent of the principal, I ought to serve his interests as he would serve them himself if he possessed my expertise.
2. The principal will serve his interests in a thoroughly egoistic manner.
3. Therefore, as a loyal agent of this principal, I must operate in a thoroughly egoistic manner on his behalf.

To operate in a thoroughly egoistic manner, a person acts in the way that best advances his or her interests, presuming that everyone else is doing the same thing.

The gist of the loyal agent's argument is that a truly loyal agent will put the principal first in any decisions involving conflicting interests. The traditional loyal agent argument supposes that a loyal agent is expected to act without regard to ethical considerations as long as the conduct puts the principal first. There is a major flaw in this traditional loyal agent's argument. Too many people feel that a loyal agent, if acting in a truly egoistic manner, has license—if not a duty—to act immorally and unethically if doing so will advance the interests of the principal. Micholos argued that the truly loyal agent must exercise due care and skill in the performance of the agency duties and must act in a socially acceptable manner while furthering the interests of the principal. To do otherwise will have a long-term detrimental impact on the principal and will therefore be disloyal.

A businessperson tends to follow his or her personal moral and ethical values and to apply these values in judging the ethics of others. While the loyal agent's argument stresses that a truly loyal agent will put the interests of the principal ahead of the interests of the agent, that same agent will prefer to work for a principal whose interests and values are aligned with the interests and the values of the agent. If the demands and requirements of a job consistently conflict with the morals and the ethics of an employee, that employee will, or should, try to locate more acceptable employment before changing his or her ethical perspective. Be aware, however, that there are some who think that the employee becomes desensitized and begins to adopt the values of the employer. Those agents start doing things the way the company has always done them.

The Legal Aspect

The U.S. legal system contains numerous ethical components. For example, a person is presumed to be innocent until proven guilty in criminal law. Each person is entitled to due process of the law and to equal protection under the law. Protections exist against compulsory self-incrimination and cruel and unusual punishment. The Constitution provides for free speech, free exercise of religion, and the right to counsel, among other rights and guarantees.

Business law also attempts to reflect the ethical standards of the society and to promote ethical conduct in the realm of business. The law of sales imposes a duty on each party to a sales contract to act in good faith. Bankruptcy is designed to give an honest debtor a fresh start. Agency law imposes the duties of loyalty and good faith on the agent.

The laws that regulate business have developed, to a significant extent, under social contract theory. Governmental regulations of business were enacted initially, in many cases, in response to a public demand for protection from the abuses and excesses of big business. Antitrust laws were intended to control business and to protect the ideal of a free and competitive economy and the Federal Trade Commission was established to stop unfair and deceptive trade practices.

The government stepped in to deal with problems, ranging from protecting the environment to helping homeowners fight mortgage foreclosures. Similar steps were followed in other areas, such as labor and fair employment. When the steps business took toward solving a problem were less than the public demanded, the legislature was asked to intervene on behalf of the public. In virtually every circumstance, though, the legislature's treatment of the problems was relatively rigid and potentially expensive for business. The business community could have and should have developed solutions with a great deal less rigidity and a great deal less expense, had they been willing to meet the challenge directly. Instead, by waiting for the government response, business had a much stricter regulatory environment in which to operate. More recently, there has been an adverse reaction in the legislature over bonuses paid to executives of companies that were bailed out with government funds during the economic crisis of 2008. A new financial regulation bill was signed into law in response to the financial meltdown.[31]

In each of these areas, the application of social contract theory is apparent. Society perceived problems and demanded that corrective steps be taken to alleviate the problems. Business had an opportunity to take corrective steps in a manner devised by business but failed—or refused—to do so. When no satisfactory solutions were proposed by business, the government stepped in to resolve the problem in a rigid, statutory manner. By failing to respond in a proactive manner, which would have permitted a custom-tailored, micro-focused solution by each affected business or industry, the business community was presented with a reactive, macro-oriented solution that must, by definition, extend across industry lines and that is intended to control all aspects of the business community with one broad regulation.

MULTINATIONAL ETHICS

Businesses involved in international transactions have additional problems. How should they deal with constituents in multiple countries? For example, assume that a U.S. business opens two factories in foreign countries. It plans to produce and sell its products abroad and import them into the United States. Whose ethics should the business apply? How should it treat its employees in these other countries? When a firm operates within only one society, the ethical stance of the firm is *more* likely to be consistent with the ethical values of that society. If the firm does not conform to socially acceptable standards, the social contract theory is used to change the permissible scope of the firm's conduct.

What happens when a truly loyal and ethical agent of the firm is reassigned to a foreign post within the company? This reassignment may have serious ethical implications. The social contract between the new location and its businesses may well be different from the social contract between the firm and its home country, calling for a reassessment of what is acceptable—or even desirable—behavior. For instance, a firm may open a new plant in a nation with very lax environmental protection statutes. This same firm, in its home country, has been an environmentally concerned business that has taken many pro-environment steps to reduce its pollution. If the firm tries to be as environmentally active in its new location, it will be at a competitive disadvantage. If the company seeks to be economically competitive, it will be acting in a manner contrary to its stated policy of environmental concern and protection. What should the firm do?

Although there is no perfect solution, any firm that is considering expansion into another country needs to make every effort to learn about the cultural differences that exist between the two nations and to take steps to reduce any culture shock or conflict prior to the expansion. The firm may consider hiring citizens of the other nation, or it may consider requiring an educational program to prepare its employees for the move. The employees should be taught as much as possible about the new country, and they should also be urged to watch and learn. The firm and its employees should be aware that they are visitors, guests in another nation, and they should act as they would if they were personal guests at the home of a new friend. Above all else, the firm and its employees should avoid being judgmental. New countries and new cultures may seem strange and exotic, or they may merely seem different, but the new country will provide the social values that drive the social contract under which the firm will now be conducting business. Assimilation and acceptance are essential!

A RECOMMENDATION FOR BUSINESS

U.S. businesses need to develop a model or a framework of ethical behavior. It is likely that no single model can be developed that will apply equally to every industry, but it is possible to suggest a general outline for business. This general outline can then be tailored by each industry to the needs and the demands of that particular industry. For example, business should probably lean toward the consequential ethical theories rather than the nonconsequential theories. Consequential theories are more readily understood and more easily accepted by the public than nonconsequential approaches. Additionally, consequential theories are more flexible and more responsive to social and technological changes.

Regardless of the overriding theory, business should adopt a "synthesis" approach for resolving ethical issues. The firm should first identify the important considerations involved (obligations, ideals, effects) and should then decide where the emphasis should lie among them. The business should consider its impact on its constituents (owners, creditors, employees, customers, community, etc.). This approach works well with any ethical principle, takes into account the people to whom the firm must answer, and provides a framework for decision making that is comparable to other types of business decisions regularly made by managers.

Business should also consider its public relations image in deciding how to proceed within the consequential area. A utilitarian approach that is concerned with the greatest good for the greatest number is more acceptable to society than an egoistic approach. Society already tends to view business as being too egoistic. Also, many people seem incapable of distinguishing between *egoistic* and *egotistic*. (*Egoists* measure their conduct on the basis of self-interest, choosing the course of conduct that will provide the greatest benefit to themselves. *Egotists* are self-centered, characterized by excessive references to themselves.)

Next, business should avoid rigid rules that force specific actions or reactions, especially with the rapid changes that occur with modern technology. This does not mean business should not have rules and standards, but rather that the rules and standards should be flexible enough to change as society and the business environment change. Business should also emphasize that a truly loyal agent will act within the law while keeping the best interests of the principal in mind.

Whenever possible, businesses and industries should try self-regulation. Business should also learn to work with the government in establishing statutory regulations. By taking a proactive role in regulation, business can not only help to protect its own best interests, but also can show its concern for society and its various constituents.

The development of a comprehensive business ethic will not be easy, nor will it be greeted with open arms by all businesses or business leaders. The alternative, however, is increasing regulation, public distrust, and a general malaise in the business community. Proactive steps can be taken to benefit *both* business and society.

Contemporary Case

Notice in this Contemporary Case that the doctors are seeking a declaration. Not all courts have authority to provide declaratory relief. The doctors are attempting to clarify their roles in helping their terminally ill patients end their lives. After this decision the New Mexico Supreme Court granted a writ of certiorari, and will review this case.

MORRIS v. BRANDENBURG

356 P.3d 564, 2015 N.M. App. LEXIS 87
(Ct. of Appeals, 2015)

FACTS Dr. Katherine Morris is a surgical oncologist at the University of New Mexico (UNM) and Dr. Aroop Mangalik is a UNM physician. Aja Riggs is a patient who has been diagnosed with uterine cancer.

ISSUE Is it constitutional to apply the New Mexico statute to criminalize a physician's act of prescribing a lethal dose of a medicine at the request of a mentally competent, terminally ill patient?

HOLDING Yes. It is constitutional to apply the statute to physicians. Providing aid in dying is not a fundamental liberty interest under the New Mexico Constitution.

REASONING Excerpts from the opinion of Judge

Timothy L. Garcia:

... A New Mexico statute makes "assisting suicide" a fourth degree felony and defines the proscribed conduct as "deliberately aiding another in the taking of his own life." ... Uncertain about the legality of aid in dying in New Mexico, Drs. Morris and Mangalik filed suit seeking a declaration that they cannot be prosecuted under Section 30-2-4. They alleged that the statute does not apply to aid in dying, and if it does, such application offends provisions of our state constitution, including Article II, Section 4's

guarantee of inherent rights and Article II, Section 18's Due Process Clause. ...

Quality of life for terminally ill patients varies depending on the specific illness, its manifestations in the patient, and the patient's physical and psychological reserves. ... The dying process is often extremely difficult for patients with terminal illnesses. ... In some instances, a patient's suffering is such that doctors induce unconsciousness ... and then withhold hydration and nutrition until death arrives. ... [This palliative] sedation is an accepted medical practice and is allowed in New Mexico. ... The same is true for withdrawal of life-sustaining treatment measures. ... But these legal options for ending life arise only after the patient potentially endures a period of degeneration. ...

Dr. David Pollack ... testified at trial that patients choose to ingest the lethal dose of medication "to alleviate symptoms, to spare others from the burden of watching them dwindle away or be a shell of their former sel[ves] or to feel like they are in control, [to] have some autonomy and some control over the way that they die." ... The trial testimony identified the existence and substance of a standard of care for determining terminality and eligibility for aid in dying in other states ... [A] number of patients who have been prescribed aid-in-dying medication never ingest it. ... [T]he availability of the medication nonetheless provides patients the comfort of knowing that there is a peaceful alternative to being forced to endure unbearable suffering. ...

[The New Mexico statute states,] "[A]ssisting suicide consists of deliberately aiding another in the taking of his own life. Whoever commits assisting suicide is guilty of a fourth degree felony." ... "Our principal goal in interpreting statutes is to give effect to the Legislature's intent." ... To do so, we first look to the language used and the plain meaning of that language. ... "We refrain from further interpretation where the language is clear and unambiguous." ... In defining the proscribed conduct—"[a]ssisting suicide"—as "deliberately aiding another in the taking of his own life[,]" the statute necessarily also defines "suicide" as "the taking of [one's] own life." ... This statutory definition of "suicide" binds us. ... [A] patient's choice to "achieve a peaceful death" is still "the taking of [one's] own life" under the statute's plain terms. ... "[A]iding" ... means "providing the means to commit suicide[.]" ... Dr. Morris [stated] ... that a prescription for aid in dying is typically for the barbiturate Seconal ... calculated to have lethal effect. This conduct ... provides a patient the means to take his or her own life and is prohibited by the text of Section 30-2-4. ... [W]here the language is plain, the court's task of statutory interpretation ends. ... Since enacting Section 30-2-4 in 1963, the Legislature has twice considered "assisted suicide" in the healthcare context. In both ... the Legislature expressly refused to "authorize ... assisted suicide ... "..."

Plaintiffs argue that Section 30-2-4's criminalization of aid in dying violates two provisions of the New Mexico Constitution: the Due Process Clause of Article II, Section 18 ... and the inherent-rights guarantee of Article II, Section 4 ... [O]ur analysis of rights afforded by the New Mexico Constitution is not "inextricably tied" to federal constitutional analysis. ... Plaintiffs identify the fundamental rights implicated in aid in dying as (1) the "right to autonomous medical decision making" and (2) the right to "a dignified, peaceful death." ... We understand Plaintiffs' assertion to be that this narrowly defined interest is only fundamental where: (1) a mentally competent patient is capable of giving consent, (2) the patient is diagnosed as terminally ill, (3) the patient requests a prescription for medication that may be ingested to bring about an immediate end to his/her life, and (4) a willing physician applying the proper standard of care determines that it would be appropriate to provide and prescribe the terminal dose of medication for the patient to ingest and end the patient's life. ... There is also no dispute

that a physician may lawfully act ... to support a patient's desire to shorten the dying process by removing life-sustaining nutrition, hydration, or mechanical life support, and by administering palliative sedation (high doses of consciousness-lowering medications). ...

The Due Process Clause of the New Mexico Constitution provides that "[n]o person shall be deprived of life, liberty or property without due process of law[.]" ... The federal Due Process Clause similarly provides that no state "shall ... deprive any person of life, liberty, or property, without due process of law[.]" ... In *Glucksberg*,[32] the United States Supreme Court confirmed that the substantive component of the Due Process Clause under the Fourteenth Amendment protects certain aspects of personal autonomy as fundamental rights. ... The Court stated that the government may not interfere with certain liberty interests unless the government meets its burden under a strict scrutiny standard—proving that the infringing statute is narrowly tailored to serve a compelling governmental interest. ... In *Glucksberg*, four physicians, three terminally ill patients, and one nonprofit organization filed suit against the State of Washington, seeking a declaration that the state's ban on assisting suicide was unconstitutional. ... [T]he plaintiffs asserted a liberty interest to allow a mentally competent, terminally ill adult the right to choose physician-assisted suicide as a method to end life. ... The United States Supreme Court unanimously determined that "the asserted 'right'" to physician-assisted suicide is not a liberty interest entitled to any type of protection under the Due Process Clause of the Fourteenth Amendment. ...

Constitutions, including our New Mexico Constitution, are sacred because they were written to apply in perpetuity. ... The constitutional question here—whether aid in dying is a constitutional right, fundamental or otherwise—has only been directly answered by one case, *Glucksberg*. ... [N]o court, federal or state, has held that the concept of death, including a method of a more dignified premature death with the assistance of another person, is rooted within the protections of bodily integrity under the constitution. . . .

[I]t is our view that we should continue to be very careful when considering new constitutional interests and remain reluctant to deviate from United States Supreme Court determinations of what are, and what are not, fundamental constitutional rights. . . . [T]he substantive fundamental rights that are recognized to exist under the Due Process Clause of the Fourteenth Amendment have always originated from classic personal interactions or embedded principles in our democratic society. . . . In addition, the modern concerns associated with aid in dying . . . are medical circumstances that have only garnered growing consideration in modern society due to the longevity, pain management, and life-sustaining advancements that have been made more recently by the medical profession. . . .

Aid in dying . . . is a relatively recent human phenomena and deserves appropriate public evaluation and consideration. However, . . . it must also be carefully weighed against longstanding societal principles such as preventing a person from taking the life of another; preventing suicide; preventing assisted suicide; promoting the integrity, healing, and life preserving principles of the medical profession; protecting vulnerable groups from unwanted pressure to considering aid in dying as the best alternative to other medical options; and promoting human life where aid in dying is not the appropriate medical option despite a patient's request for its use. . . . The recent advances in life-prolonging medical care and the public acceptance of aid in dying in some states has not diminished the other longstanding societal principles and concerns regarding intentional killing, the dying process, the preservation of life, and the basic life saving principles embedded in the medical profession. . . . Yet, even where statutory approval has been achieved, improper application of the statutory protections that

allow aid in dying will still expose an offending physician or other responsible parties to criminal liability if they fail to comply with the statutes' narrow parameters. . . . Presently, aid in dying is best described as a legal and societal work in progress. . . . [W]e conclude that there is no fundamental right to aid in dying under Article II, Section 18 of the New Mexico Constitution. . . .

Article II, Section 4 specifically identifies three broad categories of individual interests that are entitled to constitutional protection in New Mexico—life, liberty, and happiness. However, Article II, Section 4 has been sparsely interpreted. . . . The Oxford English Dictionary defines "life" as "[t]he condition or attribute of living or being alive; animate existence. Opposed to *death*." . . . We decline to recognize Article II, Section 4 as protecting a fundamental interest in hastening another person's death because such an interest is diametrically "[o]pposed" to the express interest in protecting life. . . .

[A]id in dying challenges the longstanding and historic interest in the protection of life until its natural end as well as the equally longstanding prohibition against assisting another in hastening that process. . . . This treasured right to life is not only considered sacred under the common law but is also recognized as an inalienable right, even for those condemned to death. . . .

[D]eath and the process of dying are not rights expressly enumerated within Article II, Section 4 and can only qualify as inferences that might exist within the categories of liberty or happiness. . . .

Plaintiffs' narrowly defined asserted right to aid in dying would provide constitutional immunity from criminal prosecution to only physicians and no one else. . . . The selective discrimination embodied within Plaintiffs' concept of aid in dying is constitutionally unsound for recognition as a fundamental right embodied within Article II, Section 4 and does not protect all New Mexicans who have equal interests in dying with autonomy and dignity. . . .

We reverse the district court's ruling that aid in dying is a fundamental liberty interest under the New Mexico Constitution. Accordingly, we reverse the district court's order permanently enjoining the State from enforcing Section 30-2-4. . . .

It is so ordered.

Short Answer Questions

1. Assume that you have been hired as the ethics officer of a relatively new venture. You and the rest of the officers are considering developing a code of ethics for the company. What are the advantages and disadvantages of a code of ethics? Should this code be based on a consequential or a nonconsequential ethical theory, or should it be a combination of these? Why?

2. You are writing an essay for economics. Your roommate recommends a Web site that prepares and sells essays. You are considering using the site. Select an established ethical theory and analyze your dilemma from that position. Discuss the purchase and submission of such an essay from one of the informal approaches to ethical decision making. How might the result from an informal approach differ from the result from a more formal approach? What would explain the difference?

3. Nicotine is one of the addictive substances in regular cigarettes. Most e-cigarettes vaporize nicotine for the "smoker." Is it ethical for you to create a product that is addictive? Why or why not? Is it ethical to add substances that are addictive to your products? Why or why not?[33]

You Decide...

1. On September 18, 2015 the Environmental Protection Agency (EPA) ordered the Volkswagen Group (VW) to recall almost 500,000 U.S. diesel cars fitted with software that defeated emissions tests. According to Christopher Grundler, director of the EPA's Office of Transportation and Air Quality, "VW manufactured and installed software in the electronic control module of these vehicles that sensed when the vehicle was being tested for compliance with EPA emissions standards" and "Put simply, these cars contain software that turns off or significantly reduces the effectiveness of emissions controls when driving normally, and turns them on when the car is undergoing an emissions test."[34] The EPA claims the software allowed cars to pass emissions tests even though they produced up to 40 times more pollution than allowed. VW had received $51 million in U.S. green subsidies for its "clean diesel" cars based on the false data.

VW eventually acknowledged that at least 11 million of its diesel vehicles worldwide were built with devices that would cause inaccurate pollution test results. Apparently the false data was first discovered in 2013, when the International Council for

Clean Transportation (ICCT) paid researchers at West Virginia University to test diesel car emissions. The researchers tested a 2012 Volkswagen Jetta and a 2013 VW Passat and were surprised to find much higher levels of nitrogen oxide emissions than the legal limit. In May 2014, ICCT informed the EPA about the results. "By December 2014, VW issued a voluntary recall of all its US diesel cars from model years 2009-2014."[35] The U.S. government investigation may spread to other car manufacturers.

There have been investigations and recalls in a number of other countries. VW U.S. sales for November 2015 dropped by 25%. Its sales elsewhere also dropped significantly. VW suspended production at its Dresden, Germany plant for 2016. Many workers will be laid off to compensate for the costs associated with the false diesel emissions tests. VW imposed a spending cap of $12.8 billion on property, plant and equipment for 2016. "VW may face fines up to $18 billion."[36] Analysts have said that it could cost VW as much as $40 billion "to cover vehicle refits, regulatory fines and lawsuits."[37]

Assume that you are an officer of Volkswagen (VW) Group of America. What would you have done originally? Would you have permitted VW to install the software? Why? What would you have done after the U.S. government discovered the software? Be certain that you explain and justify your answer.

Michael Horn, president and CEO of Volkswagen (VW) Group of America, admitted that he knew about the emission rigging as early as Spring 2014.[38] Analyze the ethical perspectives of Horn, VW, consumers, and the EPA.

(See Collin Furtado, "Recap 2015: 10 Stories to Know In & Out of Volkswagen Emission Scam," Diligent Media Corporation Ltd., *DNA* (Daily News & Analysis), December 30, 2015 and Jana Kasperkevic, "Head of VW in US Will Tell Congress He Knew of Emissions Rigging in Early 2014," *The Guardian*, October 7, 2015.)

2. When the 2015 football season began, FanDuel and DraftKings saturated television stations with commercials enticing viewers to imagine that they could pick the right collection of players and win big. In many states U.S. residents can now gamble online in "fantasy sports," where fans pick a roster of players to create an imaginary team. Many of them place bets online. "The New York-based FanDuel and the Boston-based DraftKings provide websites that host these wagers, which range in entry fees from $1 to $250—with about 10 percent of the fees going to the companies."[39] If the fan's team "wins," he or she will make money on the bet. The companies contend that the contests are based on skill, and are not games of chance.

Many of the companies' employees were fantasy sports players before becoming employees, and continue to play on other sites. "Many of these employees set the prices of players and the algorithms for scoring. In short, they make the market."[40] In 2015 DraftKings' employee, Ethan Haskell, mistakenly released data early before the start of the third week of National Football League (N.F.L.) games that showed which particular players were most used in all lineups on one of the site's contests. "Getting it early . . . is of great advantage in making tactical decisions, especially when an entrant's opponents do not have the information at all."[41] DraftKings claims that Haskell did not make inappropriate use of the information. However, he reportedly won $350,000 at a rival site, FanDuel, that same week. "The episode has raised questions about who at daily fantasy companies has access to valuable data, such as which players a majority of the money is being bet on; how it is protected; and whether the industry can—or wants—to police itself."[42] "A spokesman for DraftKings acknowledged that employees of both companies had won big jackpots playing at other daily fantasy sites. . . . [T]he two companies temporarily barred their employees from playing games or taking part in tournaments at any other site; they already had prohibited their employees from playing on their own company sites."[43]

The federal Unlawful Internet Gaming Enforcement Act of 2006 excluded fantasy sports from its ban on online gambling under the theory that it is more skill than chance.[44] There was a significant amount of lobbying before the law was enacted. "Fantasy sports gambling is illegal in just five states: Montana, Washington, Louisiana, Iowa, and Arizona."[45] Other states may also take action to prohibit it.

"Eilers Research, which studies the industry, estimates that daily games will generate around $2.6 billion in entry fees this year and grow 41 percent annually, reaching $14.4 billion in 2020."[46] DraftKings and FanDuel have become cherished sponsors of sport teams. "Jerry Jones of the Dallas Cowboys and Robert K. Kraft of the New England Patriots have stakes in DraftKings."[47] "DraftKings has tapped hundreds of millions of dollars from Fox Sports, and FanDuel has raised similar amounts from investors like Comcast, NBC and KKR."[48] There is also a legitimate concern that teams might be corrupted by criminals to throw a game or bettors becoming gambling addicts.

What should DraftKings and FanDuel do and why? Analyze the ethics of the fantasy sports companies, their employees, and other bettors. Be certain that you explain and justify your answer.

Daniel Wallach, a sports and gambling lawyer, said "The single greatest threat to the daily fantasy sports industry is the misuse of insider information." ... "It could imperil this nascent industry unless real, immediate and meaningful safeguards are put in place. If the industry is unwilling to undertake these reforms voluntarily, it will be imposed on them involuntarily as part of a regulatory framework."[49] In your opinion does the industry need to be subject to more regulation? Why? Will self-regulation work? Why?

(See Frank Cerabino, "Fantasy Sports Gambling Wants to Save Fla. Action," *Palm Beach Post* (Florida), October 14, 2015, p. 1B; Joe Drape and Jacqueline Williams, "Scandal in Unchecked World of Fantasy Sports," *The New York Times*, October 6, 2015, p. A1; and *The Monitor's* Editorial Board, "The Outrageous Fortune of Fantasy Sports," *The Christian Science Monitor*, October 7, 2015.)

Notes

1. *Merriam Webster's Collegiate Dictionary*, 10th ed. (Springfield, MA: Merriam-Webster, 1993), 398.

2. *Ibid.*, 756.

3. William H. Shaw & Vincent Berry, *Moral Issues in Business*, 4th ed. (Belmont, CA: Wadsworth Publishing, 1989), 51. By contrast, psychological egoism is a descriptive theory. It describes what people do.

4. Some of the early writers in this area were hedonistic egoists. This interpretation of "best interest" is not prevalent today.

5. Shaw and Berry, 55.

6. Brad Hooker, "Rule Consequentialism," *Stanford Encyclopedia of Philosophy* (SEP), http://plato.stanford.edu/entries/consequentialism-rule/(accessed March 3, 2016).

7. Gary E. Varner, "Act v. Rule Utilitarianism," from online lecture on utilitarianism, Texas A&M University, http://philosophy.tamu.edu/gary/bioethics/ethicaltheory/actrule.html (accessed March 3, 2016).

8. Hooker, "Rule Consequentialism."

9. Varner, "Act v. Rule Utilitarianism."

10. *Ibid.*

11. Thomas Mautner, editor, *The Penguin Dictionary of Philosophy*, http://www.utilitarianism.com/ruleutil.htm (accessed March 3, 2016).

12. Philip A. Pecorino, "Utilitarianism," http://www.qcc.cuny.edu/socialsciences/ppecorino/introtext/Chapter%208%20Ethics/Utilitarianism.htm (accessed March 3, 2016).

13. Mautner, *Penguin Dictionary of Philosophy*.

14. Shaw & Berry, 63.

15. Rogene A. Buchholz & Sandra B. Rosenthal, *Business Ethics, the Pragmatic Path Beyond Principles to Process* (Upper Saddle River, NJ: Prentice-Hall, Inc., 1998), 68-69.

16. John Rawls, *A Theory of Justice* (Cambridge, MA: Harvard University Press, Belknap Press, 1971).

17. Chandran Kukathas & Philip Pettit, *Rawls: A Theory of Justice and Its Critics* (Palo Alto, CA: Stanford University Press, 1990), 39.

18. *Ibid.*, 195-201.

19. Shaw & Berry, 52-55.

20. *Ibid.*, 58-60.

21. Buchholz & Rosenthal, 68-69.

22. Shaw & Berry, 66-67.

23. Rawls, *Theory of Justice,* 195-210.

24. Vincent Ryan Ruggiero, *The Moral Imperative* (Port Washington, NY: Alfred Knopf Publishers, 1973).

25. Shaw & Berry, 77.

26. 170 N.W. 668 (Mich. 1919).

27. Albert Z. Carr, "Is Business Bluffing Ethical?" HARV. BUS. REV., (January-February, 1968), 143-153.

28. R. Edward Freeman, in his book *Strategic Management: A Stakeholder Approach* (Marshfield, Mass.: Pitman, 1984), includes environmentalists, the media, government, and competitors, among others, as stakeholders.

29. Government of Canada, Innovation, Science and Economic Development Canada, "Corporate Social Responsibility," *Industry Canada,* ic.gc.ca., http://www.ic.gc.ca/eic/site/csr-rse.nsf/eng/Home/(accessed March 3, 2016).

30. Tom L. Beauchamp & Norman E. Bowie, *Ethical Theories and Business,* 2nd ed. (Englewood Cliffs, N.J.: Prentice-Hall, Inc., 1983), 247.

31. See, e.g., Board of Governors of the Federal Reserve System, "Troubled Asset Relief Program (TARP) Information," http://www.federalreserve.gov/bankinforeg/tarpinfo.htm (accessed March 4, 2016); Investopedia, "Troubled Asset Relief Program—TARP," http://www.investopedia.com/terms/t/troubled-asset-relief-program-tarp.asp (accessed March 4, 2016); and U.S. Department of the Treasury, "TARP Programs," https://www.treasury.gov/initiatives/financial-stability/TARP-Programs/Pages/default.aspx (accessed March 4, 2016).

32. *Washington v. Glucksberg,* 521 U.S. 702, 117 S. Ct. 2258 (1997).

33. Bart Jansen, "E-Cig Ban Means No Vaping for Nicotine Fix on Flights," *USA Today,* March 2, 2016, http://www.usatoday.com/story/news/2016/03/02/dot-bans-e-cigs-airliners/81206904/ (accessed 3/4/16) and National Institute on Drug Abuse, "Drug Facts: Electronic Cigarettes (e-Cigarettes), Revised August 2015, https://www.drugabuse.gov/publications/drugfacts/electronic-cigarettes-e-cigarettes (accessed March 4, 2016).

34. Jana Kasperkevic, "Head of VW in US Will Tell Congress He Knew of Emissions Rigging in Early 2014," *The Guardian,* October 7, 2015.

35. Collin Furtado, "Recap 2015: 10 Stories to Know In & Out of Volkswagen Emission Scam," Diligent Media Corporation Ltd., *DNA* (Daily News & Analysis), December 30, 2015.

36. *Ibid.*

37. *Ibid.*

38. Jana Kasperkevic, "Head of VW in US Will Tell Congress He Knew of Emissions Rigging in Early 2014," *The Guardian,* October 7, 2015.

39. Frank Cerabino, "Fantasy Sports Gambling Wants to Save Fla. Action," *Palm Beach Post* (Florida), October 14, 2015, p. 1B.

40. Joe Drape and Jacqueline Williams, "Scandal in Unchecked World of Fantasy Sports," *The New York Times,* October 6, 2015, p. A1.

41. *Ibid.*

42. *Ibid.*

43. *Ibid.*

44. Frank Cerabino, "Fantasy Sports Gambling Wants to Save Fla. Action," *Palm Beach Post* (Florida), October 14, 2015, p. 1B.

45. *Ibid.* On November 10, 2015, New York Attorney General Eric Schneiderman ordered DraftKings and FanDuel to stop permitting New York gamblers to bet on their sites. Carl Campanile and Bruce Golding, "Bettor Knock It Off! NY Bans Fantasy Sites," *The New York Post,* November 11, 2015, 3.

46. Joe Drape and Jacqueline Williams, "Scandal in Unchecked World of Fantasy Sports."

47. *Ibid.*

48. *Ibid.*

49. *Ibid.*

3

The U.S. Legal System and Court Jurisdiction

Learning Objectives

After completing this chapter you should be able to

- Describe the power of the executive, judicial, and legislative branches of government
- Explain the major provisions in the U.S. Constitution
- Discuss the Bill of Rights
- Define subject matter jurisdiction
- Distinguish the type of cases that can be heard in federal court and state court
- Explain how courts obtain jurisdiction over defendants
- Compare subject matter jurisdiction to venue

The U.S. Supreme Court in this Classic Case considered whether the State of Washington had jurisdiction (or authority) over the International Shoe Company. Washington wanted the company to pay its state unemployment compensation tax. International Shoe had salespeople who lived in Washington and sold its shoes in that state. The company itself did not have facilities within the state.

INTERNATIONAL SHOE CO. v. STATE OF WASHINGTON

326 U.S. 310, 66 S. Ct. 154 (1945)

FACTS International Shoe manufactured and sold shoes. It was a Delaware corporation with its principal place of business in St. Louis, Missouri. It had places of business in several states, but not in Washington. Its merchandise was distributed through several branches located outside Washington. It had no office in Washington, made no contracts, and maintained no inventory there. During the years in question, International Shoe employed 11 to 13 salesmen under direct supervision and control of sales managers in St. Louis. These salesmen lived in Washington, their principal activities were confined to that state, and they were compensated by commissions based upon the amount of their sales. The commissions for each year totaled more than $31,000. The company supplied its salesmen with a line of samples that they displayed to prospective purchasers. Occasionally they rented rooms to display samples. The cost of the rent was reimbursed by the company. The authority of the salesmen was limited to exhibiting their samples and soliciting orders at prices fixed by the company. The salesmen sent the orders to the company's principal office to be accepted or rejected. When the orders were accepted, the merchandise was shipped and invoiced from outside Washington. No salesman had authority to enter into contracts or to collect payment. Notice of the tax assessment was served on a salesman in the State of Washington, and a copy was mailed by registered mail to International Shoe at its address in St. Louis, Missouri.

ISSUES Can the State of Washington require International Shoe to appear in its courts without violating the Due Process Clause of the Fourteenth Amendment? Can the state require International Shoe to pay the state unemployment compensation tax without violating the Due Process Clause?

HOLDINGS Yes, to both questions. The State of Washington's suit and assessment of the unemployment contribution do not violate the Fourteenth Amendment.

REASONING Excerpts from the opinion of Chief Justice Stone:

The statutes in question set up a comprehensive scheme of unemployment compensation, the costs of which are defrayed by contributions . . . by employers to a state unemployment compensation fund. The contributions are a specified percentage of the wages payable annually by each employer for his employees' services in the state. . . .

26 U. S. C. § 1606 (a) provides that "No person required under a State law to make payments to an unemployment fund shall be relieved from compliance . . . on the ground that he is engaged in interstate . . . commerce, or that the State law does not distinguish between employees engaged in interstate . . . commerce and those engaged in intrastate commerce." It is no longer debatable that Congress . . . may authorize the states, in specified ways, to regulate interstate commerce or impose burdens upon it. . . .

Since the corporate personality is a fiction, . . . it is clear that unlike an individual, its "presence" . . . can be manifested only by activities carried on in its behalf by those who are authorized to act for it. . . . [T]he terms "present" or "presence" are used merely to symbolize those activities of the corporation's agent within the state which courts will deem to be sufficient to satisfy the demands of due process. . . . Those demands may be met by such contacts of the corporation with the state . . . as make it reasonable . . . to require the corporation to defend the particular suit which is brought there. An "estimate of the inconveniences" which would result to the corporation from a trial away from its "home" or principal place of business is relevant in this connection. . . . "Presence" in the state in this sense has never been doubted when the activities of the corporation . . . have not only been continuous and systematic, but also give rise to the liabilities sued on, even though no consent to be sued or authorization to an agent to accept service of process has been given. . . . Conversely it has been generally recognized that the casual presence of the corporate agent or even his conduct of single or isolated . . . activities in a state . . . are not enough to subject it to suit on causes of action unconnected with the activities there. . . . To require the corporation in such circumstances to defend the suit away from its home or other jurisdiction where it carries on more substantial activities has been thought . . . too great and unreasonable a burden on the corporation to comport with due process. . . .

It is evident that the criteria by which we mark the boundary line between those activities which justify [subjecting] . . . a corporation to suit, and those which do not, cannot be simply mechanical or quantitative. . . . Whether due process is satisfied must depend . . . upon the quality and nature of the activity in relation to the fair and orderly administration of the laws. . . . [The Due Process Clause] does not contemplate that a state may make binding a judgment *in personam* against an individual or corporate defendant with which the state has no contacts, ties, or relations. . . .

But to the extent that a corporation exercises the privilege of conducting activities within a state, it enjoys the benefits and protection of the laws of that state. The exercise of that privilege may give rise to obligations. . . . [S]o far as those obligations arise out of or are connected with the activities within the state, a procedure which requires the corporation to respond to a suit brought to enforce them can, in most instances, hardly be said to be undue. . . .

[T]he activities carried on in behalf of appellant in the State of Washington were neither irregular nor casual. They were systematic and continuous throughout the years in question. They resulted in a large volume of interstate business, in the course of which appellant received the benefits and protection of the laws of the state. . . . The obligation which is . . . sued upon arose out of those very activities. It is evident that these operations establish sufficient contacts or ties with the state of the forum to make it reasonable and just, according to our traditional conception of fair play and substantial justice, to permit the state to enforce the obligations which appellant has incurred there. . . . [W]e cannot say that the maintenance of the present suit in the State of Washington involves an unreasonable or undue procedure. . . .

[Washington] . . . imposes a tax on the privilege of employing appellant's salesmen within the state measured by a percentage of the wages. . . . The right to employ labor has been deemed an appropriate subject of taxation in this country . . . [and] . . . a tax imposed upon the employer for unemployment benefits is within the constitutional power of the states. . . .

Affirmed.

THE FEDERAL CONSTITUTION

The Constitution of the United States is a unique document for two reasons: It is the oldest written national constitution, and it was the first to include a government based on the concept of a separation of powers. (A link to the Constitution is available on the Web site for this text.) The authors of the Constitution were reacting to the tyranny of British rule. The document was intended to prevent many of the problems the founders felt were present in Great Britain. The U.S. Constitution established a governmental structure that has three separate "divisions" and a series of checks and balances in which the power of one branch is offset, at least to some extent, by that of the others.

History taught the founders that all tyrants had at least two powers—the power of the purse and the power of the sword. Consequently, they separated these powers by placing the power of the purse (fiscal and monetary control) in the legislative branch of government and the power of the sword (control over armed forces) in the executive branch. The judicial branch does not have the formal, written power that exists in the other branches of government. It does possess what may be the most important power, at least from a constitutional perspective. The judicial branch has the power to decide where and how the other two branches may properly exercise their powers. This power was "created" by the court itself in the landmark case, *Marbury v. Madison*,[1] and is called the power of judicial review. We shall discuss judicial review in greater detail later in this chapter.

Allocation of Power

Legislative Power   Article I of the Constitution creates a Congress consisting of two houses: the Senate and the House of Representatives. Congress has the power to levy and collect taxes, pay debts, and pass all laws with respect to certain enumerated powers, such as providing for the common defense and general welfare, regulating commerce, borrowing and coining money, establishing post offices and building highways, promoting science and the arts, and creating courts inferior to the U.S. Supreme Court.

Executive Power   Article II creates the executive branch of government by establishing the offices of president and vice president. The president is the commander-in-chief of the armed forces of the United States. In addition, the president has the power to make treaties and to nominate ambassadors, judges, and other officers of the United States. The Senate must ratify all treaties, or the treaties will not be effective. The Senate must also confirm all presidential appointments or the appointee cannot take office. The vice president is the president of the Senate and also serves for the president when the president is unable to serve.

Administrative Agencies, an Additional Executive Power   Administrative agencies also wield power under the executive branch of government, even though they are not discussed in the U.S. Constitution. These agencies are sometimes called a fourth branch of government. They are generally created by Congress through the passage of a statute, often at the request of the executive branch. The statute that creates the agency is called the *enabling statute*, and it specifies the power and authority of the agency. Most federal agencies have the power, within their authority, to make rules and regulations that are similar to statutes. They also decide controversies involving these rules and regulations. (These controversies are resolved in administrative hearings; they are not cases in the literal sense of the word.) The exact authority and the organization of the agencies vary greatly. Administrative agencies exist on the federal, state, and local levels. See Chapter 7 for a more detailed discussion of administrative agencies.

Judicial Power   Federal judicial power is placed in one Supreme Court and in such other inferior courts as Congress may create. The U.S. president nominates all Article III federal judges. When the judges are confirmed by a majority of the Senate, they are permitted to serve in office for the rest of their lives, as long as their behavior is "good."

The actual wording of Article III limits rather than expands judicial power. Under Section 2 of Article III, generally the federal courts may only hear and decide *cases or controversies* (claims brought before the court in regular proceedings to protect or enforce rights, or to prevent or punish wrongs). Legally, cases or controversies can be defined as matters that are appropriate for judicial determination. For a matter to be appropriate for judicial determination,

> [t]he controversy must be definite and concrete, touching the legal relations of parties having adverse legal interests. It must be a real and substantial controversy admitting of specific relief through a decree of a conclusive character, as distinguished from an opinion advising what the law would be upon a hypothetical state of facts.[2]

Constitutional law has evolved through precedents so that, today, the following are *not* considered to be a case or a controversy:

- **Advisory opinions.** Opinions rendered by a court at the request of the government or of an interested party that indicate how the court would rule on a matter should such litigation develop.[3]
- **Moot cases.** Cases in which a determination is sought on a matter that, when decided, cannot have any practical effect on the controversy; a question is moot when it presents no actual controversy or when the issues have ceased to exist.[4]
- **Lack of standing.** Standing means that the party has a sufficient interest in the outcome of a controversy to assert his or her rights.[5]
- **Political questions.** Questions that the court refuses to decide, due to their purely political character or because their determination would encroach on powers of the other branches.[6]

The doctrine of the separation of powers requires that *federal* courts deal only with judicial matters. An *advisory opinion* is one in which the executive branch or an interested party refers a question to the judicial branch for a nonbinding opinion. However, that is not the purpose of the federal judicial system. Accordingly, whenever a member of the executive branch requires an advisory opinion, the question is referred to the justice department within the executive branch for an opinion from the attorney general. Under the U.S. federal system of government, the attorney general is the appropriate person to issue an advisory opinion. Contrary to the federal rule, some state courts are empowered to give advisory opinions. The International Court of Justice and the courts of a number of other nations also will issue advisory opinions.

The federal courts only hear cases that are appropriate for a judicial solution. *Moot cases* are those cases in which the matter has already been resolved or those cases in which any attempt at a resolution would have no practical effect. Sometimes the "resolution" occurs through the passage of time or a change in circumstances. In the case of *DeFunis v. Odegaard,*[7] the Supreme Court stated that the question of whether a student should be admitted to a law school was a moot case because while the case was moving through the court process the student had been admitted to the law school and was completing his degree. The law school informed the Supreme Court that regardless of the outcome of the suit, the law school would award DeFunis a degree if he passed his final quarter of coursework. Accordingly, the court chose not to write an opinion on the merits of the suit.

Only persons who can demonstrate that they have actually been harmed or injured have *standing* to sue. Courts will generally define standing as having a direct and immediate personal injury. For example, if you saw Taylor punch Kristen in the nose, you would not have standing to sue Taylor for *assault* (a threat to touch someone in an undesired manner) or *battery* (the unauthorized touching of another person without either legal justification or that person's consent); only Kristen would have standing to sue Taylor because she was the one who was injured. However, statutes may grant standing to sue in situations where it would not otherwise exist. For example, the Endangered Species Act (ESA) contains a citizen-suit provision which provides that in general, "any person may commence a civil suit" to enforce the ESA.[8]

Even though many political questions involve real controversies, the doctrine of U.S. courts is that courts will not hear them. While a political question may be considered a very real controversy, it is not considered to be a *judicial question* (a question that is proper for a court to decide). This rule is based on the concept of *judicial restraint*, a judicial policy of refusing to hear and decide certain types of cases. For example, if Darlene contends that a state is not based on a democratic form of government, she cannot argue that issue in a U.S. federal court because it is a political question. Similarly, if Luis thinks that a U.S. foreign policy is incorrect, he cannot debate that point in court because foreign policy is a political question. What constitutes a political question is not always clear. For instance, is *legislative apportionment*—the ratio of legislative representation to constituents—a political question? Historically, the courts have said no.

The Constitution contains four limits on judicial power, but does not mention the one concept that has *expanded* judicial power. The specific power of judicial review is not mentioned in the Constitution. The court itself created this doctrine in the land-mark 1803 case of *Marbury v. Madison*.[9] This power is based on an interpretation of the Constitution, which states that U.S. courts may examine the actions of the legislative and executive branches to ascertain whether those actions conform to the Constitution. If they do not, the courts have the power to declare those actions unconstitutional and unenforceable. Under this doctrine, the Supreme Court can declare an act of Congress invalid if the congressional act does not conform to the Constitution. Similarly, the court can declare conduct by the president, or any other member of the executive branch, invalid if the conduct conflicts with the Constitution. This concept of judicial power does not exist in Great Britain, where the parliament is supreme. The U.S. judicial branch, which has neither the power of the purse nor the power of the sword, has significant power because it can determine what action by the other branches is legal.

Since 1803, the power of U.S. courts to judicially review all actions of the legislative and executive branches has gone unchallenged. It has become the cornerstone of the doctrine of the separation of powers. This power of the Supreme Court to invalidate legislation also extends to all state legislation because of the Supremacy Clause in the federal Constitution.

Role of Judges and Juries   The role of a judge varies with the type of court over which the judge presides. In a trial court the judge has several different responsibilities. If it is a jury trial the judge:

1. Presides over the trial
2. Determines the admissibility of any evidence either side wants to present
3. Rules on any motions or objections raised by either side
4. Instructs the jury about the applicable law in the case and the standards that must be met in order to decide for the plaintiff or the defendant in a civil suit, *or* to decide for the government or the defendant in a criminal case
5. Awards remedies to the successful plaintiff in a civil suit or imposes a sentence on a criminal defendant who is found guilty of the crime with which he or she has been charged

In a jury trial the jury decides which evidence is more believable and whether a party has produced sufficient credible evidence to win. We called this role the "decider of fact." If there is no jury, the judge serves as the "decider of fact" in its place. The judge is the "decider of law."

A judge or justice serving on an appellate court has a significantly different role. He or she is expected to review the record of the trial court or a lower court of appeals to ensure that the law was applied correctly. Generally new evidence is not presented in appellate courts. The appellate courts are looking for errors of law—mistakes in how the law was applied or interpreted by the lower court. When there are errors, the appellate court justices must decide whether to reverse the lower court's opinion, remand the case for a new trial, or recommend other appropriate remedies.

Despite the role, the robes, and the titles, judges are people, too. As a result, the personalities of individual judges and justices may very well affect their rulings in any given case. The impact of the U.S. Supreme Court justices is particularly strong. As of this writing, the current justices on the Supreme Court are Chief Justice John G. Roberts, Jr., and Justices Samuel Anthony Alito, Jr., Stephen G. Breyer, Ruth Bader Ginsburg, Elena Kagan, Anthony M. Kennedy, Sonia Sotomayor, and Clarence Thomas.[10] There is currently one vacancy due to the death of Antonin Scalia. When there is a vacancy, the remaining justices continue to do the work of the court. The personal and jurisprudential views of the judges impact the rulings in particular cases and the precedents being set for a jurisdiction. For example, there are numerous articles about how Justice Ruth Bader Ginsburg's work experiences and views affect her decisions.[11] The same is true of other judges and justices. Justice Clarence Thomas made some pointed observations from the bench during a case involving cross burning that reportedly changed the tone of the proceedings.[12]

Judges who favor judicial restraint believe that the judge's role is to make sure that a law is legal and constitutional. These judges believe that if there is something wrong with the legal system, judges should not correct it. Corrections should be left to the legislature. For example, in addressing asbestos litigation, Justice Souter wrote, "[T]his litigation defies customary judicial administration and calls for national legislation."[13] Judges who are activists believe that their role is to encourage social change: These judges often believe it is not necessary to wait for the legislature to address the issue. This is often called "making law." Those who believe that judges should not be activists often complain when they feel that judges are "making law."[14]

Original Constitution

The original Constitution, signed on September 17, 1787, contained a number of rights pertaining to individuals. We will discuss some of the most significant rights. Among these rights is the right of habeas corpus. *Habeas corpus* is the name given to a variety of writs issued to bring a party before a court or judge (a *writ* is a writing issued by a court in the form of a letter ordering some designated activity). In Latin, *habeas corpus* means "You have the body."[15] This right may be used by all persons who have been deprived of their liberty. There are special forms of the writ; however, when the words "writ of habeas corpus" are used alone, the writ is addressed to the person who detains an individual. The writ commands the recipient to produce the individual in a court and to comply with any order by the court issuing the writ. This is probably the most common form of the writ.

Another right established by the Constitution is that Congress may pass no bills of attainder. A *bill of attainder* is a "legislative trial," whereby a person is judged a felon or worse by act of the legislature and not by a court of law.

Congress also may not enact ex post facto laws. An *ex post facto* law is a law passed after an occurrence or act that retroactively changes the legal consequences of such act. Assume that Iron Fortress Defense, Inc. legally purchased some equipment in January. In March Congress enacted a statute making the purchase of such equipment illegal. Iron Fortress Defense could not be prosecuted for making the purchase since it did so before the statute was enacted. Of course, Congress *can* declare similar transactions illegal in the future. The constitutional prohibition on ex post facto laws applies only to criminal law. This prohibition includes laws that make an act a crime, make a crime into a more serious crime, change the punishment for a crime, or alter the legal rules of evidence for proving a crime.[16] The constitutional basis for regulating businesses is discussed in greater detail in Chapter 6.

Selected Amendments to the Constitution

Four years after the U.S. Constitution was signed, the first ten amendments were passed. These amendments, known as the Bill of Rights, were designed to ensure that certain individual rights were protected. In all, twenty-seven amendments to the Constitution have been passed. The amendments to the Constitution reflect the citizens' concerns about particular topics and reflect changes in the society. The Constitution itself serves as the supreme law of the land for U.S. society. All of the amendments are important because they affect the rights of the citizens and/or limit the power of the government. Not all of the amendments have a significant impact on the legal environment of a business. We will briefly discuss the amendments that are most likely to impact business in this section.

First Amendment   The First Amendment provides that "Congress shall make no law respecting an establishment of religion, or prohibiting the free exercise thereof. . . ." The First Amendment provides the basis for the separation of church and state. This amendment also provides for freedom of speech, freedom to assemble, and freedom of the press. For example, California passed a statute that prohibited the sale or rental of "violent video games" to minors. Members of the software and video game industries challenged the statute on the grounds that it interfered with their free speech. The U.S. Supreme Court decided that the statute violated the businesses' rights under the First Amendment.[17]

An Ounce of Prevention

The Constitution may seem like a lofty document. You need to be aware of its provisions because it can have a practical effect on your business. Constitutional rights have limits. You cannot falsely yell fire in a crowded store because you could start a stampede. Likewise, you cannot defame your employees or your competitors. Before you attempt to restrict your employees' behavior and speech, you should remember that they may have constitutional rights in these areas. For instance, employee postings on their blogs or social media may be protected speech. Employee tattoos may be protected as a form of expression. Religious headwear and beards may be protected under freedom of religion.

Fifth Amendment   This amendment protects individuals from self-incrimination and double jeopardy. These protections are important in criminal matters. This amendment also provides that a person cannot be deprived of life, liberty, or property without due process of law. This provision applies to individuals and corporations. Sometimes courts expand their definition of "life, liberty, or property" and at other times they narrow their definition.

There are two types of due process—procedural due process and substantive due process. Procedural due process deals with the government's procedures when it deprives a person of life, liberty, or property. Procedural due process gives a person a right to a proper notice and hearing. The specifics of what will satisfy due process depend on the type of case. Generally, the more serious the case the more rights the person has. For example, if Avi is charged with murder, she will be entitled to a jury trial. If Matthew is charged with speeding, he will not be entitled to a jury trial in traffic court.

Substantive due process refers to the basic fairness of the laws that may deprive an individual of life, liberty, or property. Privacy rights are often protected under substantive due process. If the government passes a law that limits a person's liberty or limits how the person uses his or her property, the government has to have a proper purpose. This will be discussed in more detail in Chapter 6.

Fourteenth Amendment   The Supreme Court has decided that under the Fourteenth Amendment most of the guarantees in the Bill of Rights also apply to actions by state and local governments. Under this amendment the states cannot deprive individuals of life, liberty, or property without due process. In many states, a driver's license is considered to be a property right, so the state cannot terminate a person's driver's license without giving the driver an opportunity to be heard. A business license would also be considered a property right. In one case, Jeff Quon worked for the City of Ontario Police Department (OPD). He was a sergeant and member of the Special Weapons and Tactics (SWAT) Team. The city provided Quon and a number of other officers with alphanumeric pagers. The bills from the service provider indicated high usage, and for a while the city asked the officers to pay for their overages. Then the city decided to audit the usage for some of the officers who were exceeding the number of characters allowed under the basic service. The city asked the service provider to transcribe the officers' messages. The city then read the messages and determined which ones were personal and which ones were work related. Quon "sent or received 456 messages during work hours in the month of August 2002, of which no more than 57 were work related." Some of the messages were sexually explicit. Quon argued that the city violated the ban on "unreasonable searches and seizures" under the Fourth Amendment and made applicable to the states under the Fourteenth Amendment. The Supreme Court found that the search was reasonable because it was "motivated by a legitimate work-related purpose, and because it was not excessive in scope."[18]

An Ounce of Prevention

People in the United States generally believe that procedural due process is a key component of fairness. If you make business decisions affecting others—including customers, employees, investors, and suppliers—without due process, you will often be perceived as being unfair. People negatively impacted by your decision may be motivated to sue you. You should consider giving others "due process" when your decision may affect them. In these contexts, due process will include adequate advance notice of any changes and an opportunity to express their opinions. You may learn creative options from their suggestions. In addition, you will be perceived as being fair. People appreciate being heard on issues that are important to them. If they are heard and feel valued, they are less likely to sue you.

THE COURTS AND JURISDICTION

Jurisdiction is the power of a court to affect legal relationships. We will examine four aspects of jurisdiction:

1. *Subject matter jurisdiction*, which is the power of a court to hear certain kinds of legal questions
2. Jurisdiction over the persons or property
3. Concurrent versus exclusive jurisdiction
4. Venue

Subject Matter Jurisdiction

Subject matter jurisdiction refers to the power of the court to hear and decide particular types of cases. Article III of the Constitution defines the Supreme Court's subject matter jurisdiction as including all cases in law and equity arising under the Constitution, the statutes of the United States, and treaties. The subject matter jurisdiction granted to the Supreme Court is extensive. A state juvenile court, on the other hand, is limited solely to hearing matters concerning children that arise within that state and under its laws. If an adult were brought before a juvenile court, the court would lack subject matter jurisdiction. Likewise, a federal bankruptcy court may not decide a criminal matter because its jurisdiction is limited to bankruptcy matters. Subject matter jurisdiction determines which court is the "right" court to hear a particular type of case or controversy.

Jurisdiction over the Persons or Property

In addition to the appropriate subject matter jurisdiction, a court must also have jurisdiction over the persons or property whose rights, duties, or obligations the court will decide. The defendant may not want to have the case decided where the plaintiff filed the suit. Jurisdiction may be a particular problem for businesses that enter contracts with people outside their state or sell their products in many states and countries. Such a business may be subject to suits in many different states or countries, each of which may be able to assert jurisdiction over the business. A purchaser of the company's product may prefer to litigate any disputes in his or her "home court" rather than the home court of the business. For example, some people believe that Apple had such a "home court" advantage in one of its U.S. patent infringement suits with Samsung because the dispute was litigated close to Apple's corporate headquarters.[19]

Three techniques exist for obtaining jurisdiction over persons or property—*in personam, in rem,* and *quasi in rem.*

In Personam Jurisdiction   *In personam* jurisdiction refers to the court's authority over the defendant. It is also called personal jurisdiction. Questions do not arise about the court's jurisdiction over the plaintiff. The plaintiff chooses to file the suit in a particular court and so implicitly consents to the court's jurisdiction. It is inconsistent to allow the plaintiff to file the suit and then complain that the same court lacks jurisdiction over him or her.

The defendant does not choose the court. Often, if the defendant were given a choice, he or she would choose not to have any trial. If a trial must take place, he or she might well prefer to have it held somewhere else. The question, then, is how to get *in personam jurisdiction* of the defendant. When can the court legally compel the defendant to attend or face a *default judgment* if he or she refuses to attend the trial? (A default judgment is a civil judgment against a defendant who does not appear in court. It is only valid when the court has jurisdiction over the court case and the defendant.)

The defendant may simply consent to the court's jurisdiction. Consent can occur by responding to a lawsuit that has been filed. It can occur either by express consent or by failure to raise the issue of jurisdiction and, instead, responding to the legal questions. Consent can also be given prior to the lawsuit. This is commonly accomplished by a contract clause or by appointment of an agent to accept *service of process.* (Service of process is the delivery of a legal notice to inform the defendant of the nature of the legal dispute.) A corporation is considered to have given consent when it registers with a state as a *foreign corporation* (a corporation that had its articles of incorporation approved in another state) and asks permission to conduct business in a state. Courts have concluded that a corporation that engages in business as a foreign corporation without the required registration has given implied consent.

A court will also have *in personam* jurisdiction over a defendant who is physically present in the state when he or she is served with process. This would include a person who is on a trip to the state or even merely passing through the state on his or her way to another destination. Courts will generally decide that there is no jurisdiction over a defendant who is tricked into entering the state by the plaintiff. A corporation is physically present in a state in which it is *doing business*. (Doing business is also used as the basis of implied consent by some states.) The courts have decided numerous cases about what constitutes doing business and have devised various tests for recognizing doing business. Two of these tests are (1) whether the corporation's activities were single, isolated transactions or continuous and substantial activities or (2) whether the corporation's agents were only soliciting offers in the state or were engaged in additional activities.

In the Classic Case of *International Shoe Co. v. State of Washington*, [20] the U.S. Supreme Court concluded that before a defendant is required to appear in a state court, the defendant must have certain *minimum contacts* with the state. Otherwise, the suit would offend traditional concepts of fair play and substantial justice. This decision created a constitutional test for *in personam* jurisdiction. The defendant in this case was a corporation, but the ruling applies to other business entities and individuals as well.

In personam jurisdiction also exists in the defendant's state of domicile. Domicile is a complicated legal doctrine (and most of its complexity is outside the scope of this text). Human beings have one and only one domicile. A person may choose his or her domicile or the law may assign it. *Domicile* is usually the place where a person is physically present and he or she considers as home; it is his or her permanent home. When the person leaves for a while he or she intends to return to this place. Domicile does *not* require that a person live in a state for a certain minimum period of time. Consequently, domicile contrasts with residency statutes that require, for example, a person to live in a state for a set period of time before voting in the state or being eligible for in-state tuition at its colleges and universities.

Suppose that both the plaintiff and the defendant are domiciliaries of Alaska; Alaska has jurisdiction over them. If the plaintiff is a domiciliary of Oregon and the defendant is a domiciliary of Alaska, Alaska would once again have in personam jurisdiction. The defendant's domicile would create jurisdiction in the Alaskan court. On the other hand, if the plaintiff is a domiciliary of Alaska but the defendant is a domiciliary of Oregon, Alaska may not have proper jurisdiction over the defendant. If the plaintiff wants to sue the defendant in a state court, the plaintiff might need to go to Oregon and sue the defendant there, since a defendant's domicile is almost always an appropriate forum. (*Forum* is the court that is or will be conducting the trial.) Potential jurisdiction in a federal court is discussed later in this chapter.

Corporations are domiciled in the state in which they are incorporated. They are also considered to be domiciled in the state where they have their corporate headquarters, if this is a different state. A corporation may be sued where it is domiciled. A corporation is also subject to in personam jurisdiction in all states in which the corporation does business because it is physically present in these states.

Most states have laws called *long-arm statutes.* The purpose of these statutes is to permit the state to exercise in personam jurisdiction when ordinarily this would not be possible. A common long-arm statute permits a state to exercise authority over a person who drives on its roads. This type of long-arm statute is also called a *nonresident motorist statute.* (Note that despite the use of the term "nonresident" in many statutes, the legislatures probably mean "domicile.") Suppose that Cara, a domiciliary of Nebraska, drives a car on the roads of Kansas and injures Colin, a domiciliary of Kansas. In this situation, the courts of Kansas would have *in personam* jurisdiction over Cara, because Kansas feels that it would be unfair to force Colin to go to Nebraska to sue. Some states have enacted much broader long-arm statutes. For example, Illinois enacted a statute that listed certain acts that would confer jurisdiction, if done in the state. California, Iowa, Kansas, Pennsylvania,[21] and Texas,[22] on the other hand, enacted long-arm statutes that provide for in personam jurisdiction whenever it complies with the state and federal constitutions.[23] As with other matters under the control of the states, there is great variation among long-arm statutes.

E-commerce creates new problems in applying in personam jurisdiction. U.S. courts rely on the precedent established by *International Shoe* and apply it to Internet cases. One of the leading Internet cases is *Zippo Manufacturing Co. v. Zippo Dot Com, Inc.,*[24] which involved a dispute over the ownership of an Internet domain name. The court in *Zippo* talks about specific personal jurisdiction. Specific *in personam* jurisdiction permits courts to exercise jurisdiction related to the defendant's contacts with the forum. General *in personam* jurisdiction permits jurisdiction of the defendant for any dispute without showing that the claim arises from the contacts with the forum. The district court stated the criteria as follows:

> A three-pronged test has emerged for determining whether the exercise of specific personal jurisdiction over a non-resident defendant is appropriate: (1) the defendant must have sufficient "minimum contacts" with the forum state, (2) the claim asserted against the defendant must arise out of those contacts, and (3) the exercise of jurisdiction must be reasonable.[25]

From these criteria, the court decided that if a person enters into contracts with residents of another jurisdiction, and those contracts involve the knowing and repeated transmission of computer files over the Internet, personal jurisdiction over the person in that other jurisdiction would be proper. However, if a person simply posts information on an Internet Web site, there are not sufficient contacts with any "foreign" jurisdictions to permit the exercise of personal jurisdiction over the person posting the information. Such passive Web sites do no more than make information available. Between these two extremes lies the troublesome area. In this area a person might be involved with an interactive Web site that allows for the exchange of information between the user and the host computer. In these situations, personal jurisdiction will depend on the level of interaction and also on whether the exchange of information is commercial in nature.[26]

There are still a number of questions to be answered in this dynamic area. The ultimate resolution of some of these issues is likely to have a major impact on the growth and development of e-commerce.

In Rem Jurisdiction   If a state cannot obtain *in personam* jurisdiction on any of these grounds, *in rem* jurisdiction may be used. *In rem* jurisdiction exists when the court has authority over property or status of the defendant that is located within the control of the court. *In rem* jurisdiction allows the state to exercise its authority over something such as land, a marriage, or a partnership within its boundaries. The court's judgment will affect everyone's rights in that "thing." It does not impose a personal obligation on the defendant. For example, if an individual or a corporation has real property in one

Exhibit 3.1

Methods to Obtain Jurisdiction over the Defendant

Type of Jurisdiction	Type of Judgment	Differences Between Individual and Corporate Defendants	
		Individual	*Corporation*[a]
In personam			
Authority over a specific person or corporation within the control of the state. Authority may derive from consent, domicile, physical presence, or long-arm statutes.	Affects the person.	**Consent** Defendant consents to personal jurisdiction; consent can occur before or after a suit has begun.	**Consent** A corporation consents when it registers as a foreign corporation with the state.[d]
		Domicile Defendant has a residence—usually a home—at which he or she is/has been physically present and intends to remain for the time being; individuals have only one domicile.[b]	**Domicile** A corporation is incorporated (has filed its articles of incorporation with the state) and/or has its corporate headquarters in the state.
		Physical Presence Defendant is served by hand while he or she is within the geographic boundaries of the state.[c]	**Physical Presence** A corporation is recognized as "doing business" in the state.
		Long-Arm Statutes State has a statute that specifies that certain people are subject to its jurisdiction, such as anyone operating a motor vehicle, doing business, transacting business, or engaging in business within the state.	

Exhibit 3.1 Continued

Type of Jurisdiction	Type of Judgment	Differences Between Individual and Corporate Defendants
In rem		
Authority over property or status within the control of the state. Settles ownership interests in property or status for all persons.	Affects the property or status.	The rules for individuals and corporations are basically the same.
Quasi in rem		
Authority obtained through property under the control of the state. Settles issues of ownership, possession, or use of property; or settles personal disputes unrelated to the property.	Affects the rights of specific people to property.[e]	The rules for individuals and corporations are basically the same.

[a] This column applies to corporations. Other business entities have different rules. For example, a limited liability company is domiciled in the states where any of its members are domiciled.

[b] Some people are not capable of selecting domiciles for themselves; they have domiciles determined for them by legal rules (for example, minors).

[c] Most states will refuse to exercise jurisdiction if the defendant is brought into the state by force or enticed into the state by fraud.

[d] If the corporation fails to register, the court may imply consent from the act of doing business in the state. Generally, implied consent is limited to cases arising from the actual doing of business in the state.

[e] The maximum recovery for a successful plaintiff is the value of the property.

state but is domiciled in another, the state where the property is located can exercise *in rem* jurisdiction in a dispute over ownership of the property.

Quasi in Rem Jurisdiction   In this type of jurisdiction, the court determines the rights of particular persons to specific property. (It is distinct from *in rem* jurisdiction because a court with *in rem* jurisdiction will determine the rights of all persons in the thing. It differs from *in personam* jurisdiction because there is no authority over the person of the defendant.) *Quasi in rem* jurisdiction is authority obtained through property under the control of the court. The court obtains control of the property through one of two methods. In one, the property is within the jurisdiction of the court, and the plaintiff wishes to resolve issues of ownership, possession, or use of the property—for example, to foreclose a mortgage. In the second method, the dispute does not concern the property, but is personal to the plaintiff, such as a breach of contract or the commission of a tort. Jurisdiction will exist if the plaintiff can locate the defendant's property within the state and bring it before the court by *attachment* (seizure of the defendant's property) or *garnishment* (procedure to obtain possession of the defendant's property when it is in the custody of another person). The state will have limits on when attachment or garnishment is allowed.

Exhibit 3.2

A Comparison of Federal and State Court Jurisdiction

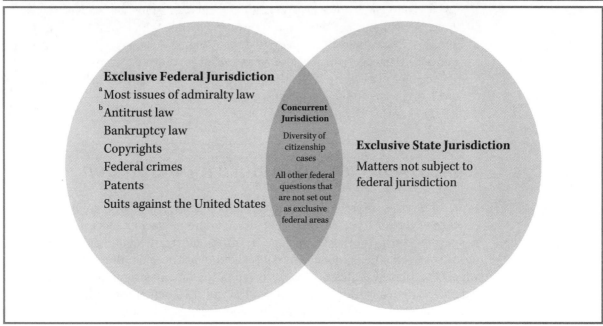

Exclusive Federal Jurisdiction
[a]Most issues of admiralty law
[b]Antitrust law
Bankruptcy law
Copyrights
Federal crimes
Patents
Suits against the United States

Concurrent Jurisdiction
Diversity of citizenship cases
All other federal questions that are not set out as exclusive federal areas

Exclusive State Jurisdiction
Matters not subject to federal jurisdiction

[a] States have concurrent jurisdiction over some aspects of admiralty law under federal statutes.
[b] Many states have state antitrust laws.

When the plaintiff's suit is successful, the recovery is limited to the value of the property. Exhibit 3.1 summarizes the techniques for obtaining jurisdiction over the defendant.

Service of Process   Regardless of the type of jurisdiction, the plaintiff must have the defendant properly served with process to inform him or her of the lawsuit. One type of service is *actual notice*, where the defendant is personally served by an officer of the court or is mailed service by registered mail. If actual notice cannot be arranged after reasonable attempts to do so, notice may be served publicly by a posting on the property or in a newspaper. This is called *constructive service or notice*. Constructive notice may also include service at the office of the state's secretary of state. For example, when an out-of-state corporation registers in Virginia, the state may specify that process may be served on Virginia's secretary of state.

An Ounce of Prevention

The person who serves process is considered an officer of the court because he or she is performing an important judicial function. In most states you do not have to be a court employee to be a process server. In many states any adult can serve process on the defendant. Some states even permit the plaintiff to serve the process. Even where it is permitted, you should not serve the defendant yourself. This could possibly lead to an exchange of heated words or even the commission of a battery. It is better to pay someone else, such as a sheriff, to hand the legal papers to the defendant.

Concurrent versus Exclusive Jurisdiction

In certain cases, more than one court may exercise jurisdiction. This is called *concurrent jurisdiction.* On the other hand, some subjects can be heard only by a specific court to the exclusion of other courts, which is called *exclusive jurisdiction.* Examples of exclusive jurisdiction in the federal courts are suits in which the United States is a party or suits that involve bankruptcy, copyrights, federal crimes, and patents. Most federal statutes set out whether jurisdiction under the statute is exclusive to the federal courts or concurrent with federal and state courts. Employment discrimination is an example of concurrent jurisdiction. An employee who sues based on unlawful discrimination can sue in either federal or state court. Generally, the employee can combine his or her federal claims and state claims. Exhibit 3.2 illustrates the jurisdictional domains of federal and state courts.

Venue

Once a court establishes that it has proper jurisdiction over the subject matter and the defendant, it must then ascertain whether it is the proper venue. *Venue* literally means "neighborhood." In a legal sense, however, it means the proper geographical area or district where a suit can be brought. In federal courts, the question of venue is which federal judicial district is the appropriate one. In state courts, it is usually a question of which county is appropriate. If both the plaintiff and the defendant are domiciled in the same state, *in personam* jurisdiction exists in that state's courts. But which of the state courts is best situated to hear the case? For example, venue could be proper in the area where an incident, such as an automobile accident, occurred. The court may consider the domicile of the defendant in determining the proper venue. More than one court may have proper venue. The laws of each state spell out in great detail the appropriate courts that would have venue.

An Ounce of Prevention

Concurrent jurisdiction in multiple courts is common. For instance, you may be able to have your dispute heard in California state court, Ohio state court, or federal court. When there is concurrent jurisdiction, you and your attorney must decide where to file the suit. This is commonly called forum shopping. In making your decision, you should consider a number of factors. One factor is whether you are more likely to be successful in one court compared to other courts. If you are requesting a jury trial, the probable makeup of the jury is also important. The parties, attorneys, and witnesses will also be required to travel to the court, so the relative cost and convenience of traveling to the forum is also a factor. Your attorney will only be licensed to try cases in certain courts. If the case is tried somewhere else, you will have to hire additional lawyers, or your attorney will have to obtain the court's permission to appear before it. You may be eligible to receive different remedies depending on the courts.

Choice of Laws

Choice of laws is the selection of which jurisdiction's laws should be applied to a particular incident, that is, what laws should govern the subject before the court. Although it is also called "conflict of laws," choice of laws is the more descriptive title. The forum court will use choice of laws rules to determine the *substantive laws* (the laws that create, define, and regulate rights) that should be applied to the dispute; however, the forum will use its own procedural laws. (*Procedural laws* are the methods of enforcing rights or obtaining redress for the violation of rights). Choice of law rules can be very complex. Since state laws can vary greatly, the forum's choice of which law to apply can often determine the outcome of the dispute.

An Ounce of Prevention

Choice of law rules can be confusing. It is often difficult for you and your attorney to predict what a court will do. When drafting contracts, a helpful strategy is for you to specify what state or national law should be applied. For example, you can state "In case of disputes, this contract is governed by the laws of New York." Courts will generally apply the law designated by the parties if the state chosen has some degree of contact with the agreement. Similarly, you can generally choose in your contract the court that will be the forum. If you sign a contract that says any lawsuits will be decided in Ohio, you have agreed to grant Ohio jurisdiction over you.

Federal Jurisdiction

Two specific grounds exist for federal jurisdiction: (1) federal question; and (2) diversity of citizenship *plus* amount in controversy. Most federal questions do not require a particular amount to be in controversy.

Federal Question Jurisdiction   Federal question jurisdiction comes directly from Article III of the Constitution. *Federal questions* are questions that pertain to the federal Constitution, statutes of the United States, regulations of federal administrative agencies, and treaties signed by the United States. For example, if Rachelle's Flowers, Inc. wants to file for bankruptcy protection, that will raise a federal question under the federal bankruptcy code. If Wolters Kluwer brings an action asserting that another publishing company has infringed its copyright, Wolters Kluwer raises a federal question because copyright is both a federal constitutional and statutory question. States do not have the right to issue copyrights, and state courts do not have subject matter jurisdiction to decide copyright cases.

Generally, state courts are presumed to have concurrent jurisdiction over civil cases under federal statutes unless Congress clearly intended for the federal courts to have exclusive jurisdiction.[27] Litigation can occur over whether the jurisdiction is concurrent or exclusive when the statute is not clear. For example, in 2012 the U.S. Supreme Court resolved the issue of whether individual private suits filed under the Telephone Consumer Protection Act (TCPA) could be tried only in state courts or whether federal courts had concurrent jurisdiction. It decided that jurisdiction under the act was concurrent.[28] Some other examples of concurrent jurisdiction between the federal courts and state courts are in the areas of civil rights[29] and trademark cases.[30] There is also concurrent jurisdiction over some areas of admiralty law.[31] Federal courts have exclusive jurisdiction over antitrust under federal statutes,[32] bankruptcy,[33] copyright,[34] federal crimes,[35] and patents.[36] Even where there is exclusive jurisdiction in the federal courts, state courts can try related cases. For example, a state court can hear a suit for breach of contract when the contract involves the sale of a copyright or patent.

Diversity of Citizenship Jurisdiction   Federal question jurisdiction is not necessary when diversity of citizenship is present. *Diversity of citizenship* exists when the plaintiff is a citizen of one state and the defendant is a citizen of another; it also exists when one party is a foreign country and the other is a citizen of a state. The primary reason underlying diversity jurisdiction is that if a citizen of Hawaii must file suit in Iowa in order to obtain jurisdiction over a citizen of Iowa, it is possible that the court of Iowa might favor its own citizen. If the plaintiff is worried about such potential favoritism, the plaintiff can file suit in federal court.

When federal jurisdiction is based on diversity of citizenship, a further requirement exists: a *minimum amount* in question. Federal law requires that the amount in question must exceed $75,000 in diversity cases.[37] The purpose behind the amount is to prevent federal courts from dealing with trifles and to reduce the caseload in federal courts. Many cases are highly complex, and the dollar amount is often unknown when the lawsuit is filed. Accordingly, the courts look to the amount the plaintiff, acting in good faith, claims to be in dispute. This is called the *plaintiff viewpoint rule.* In contrast, cases in which the federal courts have exclusive jurisdiction generally do not require a minimum amount in controversy.

Another aspect of diversity jurisdiction is called complete diversity. *Complete diversity* requires that no plaintiff be a citizen of the same state as any of the defendants. This rule poses complex problems when there are multiple plaintiffs and/or defendants. Complete diversity also prohibits having an alien plaintiff and an alien defendant in the same suit, even when the aliens are from different countries. (An *alien* is a person or corporation that is a citizen of another country.)

Exhibit 3.3 depicts the two grounds for federal jurisdiction.

The Federal Court System

Congress has, from time to time, created courts of *limited* jurisdiction. The court of military appeals, the court of international trade, and the tax court are examples of courts with limited jurisdiction. Congress has created *federal district courts* (general trial courts in the federal court system) in every state. Each state has at least one; some states have many. Rhode Island, for example, has one district court, and Texas has four. Most federal judges are nominated by the president, confirmed by a majority of the Senate, and entitled to serve for life.[38]

All of the district courts are grouped into 13 circuits. Each circuit has a court of appeals, which hears appeals from the trial courts. Courts of appeals do not retry the case; instead, they review the record to determine whether the trial court made errors of law. Generally, a panel of three judges from the circuit hears appeals. Decisions of the court of appeals establish precedents for all district courts in the circuit. For the most part, the decisions of these *circuit courts of appeals* are final. In a very few cases, the parties can appeal to the U.S. Supreme Court.

The 13 federal judicial circuits and their seats are: First: Boston, Massachusetts; Second: New York, New York; Third: Philadelphia, Pennsylvania; Fourth: Richmond, Virginia; Fifth: New Orleans, Louisiana; Sixth: Cincinnati, Ohio; Seventh: Chicago, Illinois; Eighth: St. Louis, Missouri; Ninth: San Francisco, California; Tenth: Denver, Colorado; Eleventh: Atlanta, Georgia; Twelfth: District of Columbia, Washington, D.C.; Thirteenth: Federal Circuit, Washington, D.C. For details on the 13 federal judicial circuits, see Exhibit 3.4.

Exhibit 3.3

The Two Grounds for Federal Jurisdiction

For Federal Jurisdiction the Case Must Involve	
Either	*Or*
Federal Question The controlling law involves a federal statute, rule, or regulation; an issue of U.S. constitutional law; or a treaty. The case involves an ambassador or other high-ranking public figure as a party. The United States is a party to the action. The case is between two or more states.	**Diversity of Citizenship** Parties on one side of the controversy are citizens of a state different from the parties on the other side. *and* **A Minimum Amount in Controversy (Excluding Costs and Interest)** The plaintiff must sue for more than $75,000.

Exhibit 3.5 describes how the federal courts are related to each other. There are three basic levels, the U.S. district courts (the trial courts in the federal system), the U.S. court of appeals, and the U.S. Supreme Court. Federal agencies are not courts; however, they often perform court-like functions, also called *quasi-judicial* functions. They are shown in Exhibit 3.5 to illustrate the appeal "path" from the agency to the court system.

The Supreme Court

The Supreme Court sits at the top of the U.S. judicial system. It is the only court created by the Constitution. The Constitution does not specify the number of judges, called justices, on the Supreme Court. The Supreme Court is led by the chief justice, and it has eight associate justices by statute.[39] The justices are nominated by the president and confirmed by a majority of the Senate, and they are entitled to serve for life during good behavior.

As previously mentioned, certain cases may be appealed to the Supreme Court. However, the court may affirm a case routinely without permitting oral arguments or formally considering the case. The court is more likely to hear a case under one of the following conditions:

- Whenever the highest state court declares a federal law invalid
- Whenever the highest state court validates a state law that is challenged based on a federal law
- Whenever a federal court declares a federal statute unconstitutional and the government was a party to the suit

Exhibit 3.4

The Thirteen Federal Judicial Circuits

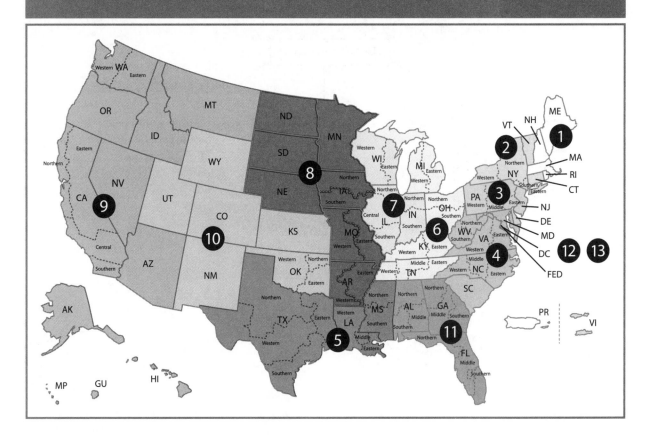

- ■ Whenever a federal appellate court declares a state statute invalid on the grounds that it violates federal law
- ■ Whenever a federal three-judge court decides a civil case involving an equitable remedy

Certiorari   Even when there is no right of appeal the Supreme Court can hear cases under certiorari. *Certiorari* means "to be more fully informed." When the Supreme Court decides to grant *certiorari*, it issues a writ that orders the lower court to certify a record of the proceedings and send it to the Supreme Court. A minimum of four justices must agree to hear the case on *certiorari*. Other than that requirement there are no hard-and-fast rules. However, there are certain situations in which the Supreme Court is more likely to grant *certiorari*:

Exhibit 3.5

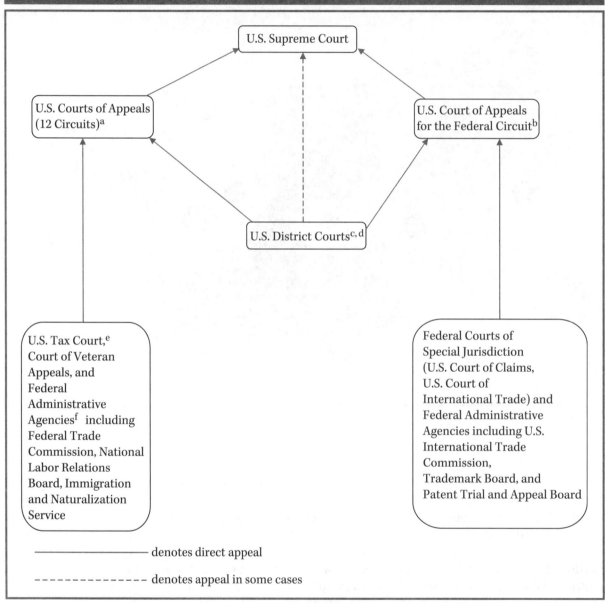

The Federal Judicial System

a Includes District of Columbia Circuit.

b Takes appeals from some specialized courts.

c Bankruptcy courts exist as units of the district courts.

d Appeals from some federal agencies go to the U.S. district courts.

e In some cases, there is Supreme Court review.

f Administrative agencies perform court-like functions; however, they are not courts.

- Whenever two or more circuit courts of appeals disagree with respect to the same legal issue;
- Whenever the highest state court has made a decision that conflicts with prior decisions of the U.S. Supreme Court;
- Whenever the highest state court has decided a question that has not yet been determined by the U.S. Supreme Court;
- Whenever a circuit court of appeals has decided a state law question that appears to be in conflict with established state law; and
- Whenever a circuit court of appeals has decided a federal question that has not yet been decided by the U.S. Supreme Court.

Original Jurisdiction   The Supreme Court also has original jurisdiction in a number of cases or controversies. When the Supreme Court exercises its *original jurisdiction* it serves as a trial court. Article III, Section 2 of the Constitution declares that the Supreme Court shall have original jurisdiction "In all cases affecting ambassadors, other public ministers and consuls, and those in which a state shall be a party."

State Courts

Like the federal system, most states have three basic levels: trial courts, courts of appeals, and a supreme court. The names of the courts vary from state to state. States also have *inferior trial courts*. These may include municipal courts, juvenile courts, domestic relations courts, traffic courts, small claims courts, probate courts, and justice courts presided over by justices of the peace. (Historically, justices of the peace were not required to be lawyers. Many states have changed their rules and now require new justices of the peace to be lawyers.) For the most part, inferior trial courts are not *courts of record*—that is, they make no record or transcript of the trial. In cases of appeals from their decisions, there is a *trial de novo*, a new trial, in a regular trial court.

The more significant cases involving matters of state law originate in *courts of general jurisdiction* (courts having unlimited or almost unlimited trial jurisdiction in civil and criminal cases). In some jurisdictions, two courts exist at this level. One court is charged with resolving all questions of law and the other with resolving all matters of equity. An example of a question of law is a suit seeking money damages. Most business law cases fall into this category. Equity suits, on the other hand, are those in which the plaintiff is seeking a special remedy, such as an *injunction* (a writ issued by the court of equity ordering a person to do or not do a specified act), because monetary damages will not make the plaintiff "whole."

Each state has at least one court of appeals. The highest court of appeals is usually called the supreme court. There are exceptions. In New York State, for example, the supreme court is a general jurisdiction trial court and the Court of Appeals is the highest court in the state. Sometimes intermediate courts of appeals also exist, as in the federal system. These appellate courts review the trial court record to determine whether the lower court made any errors of law. Appellate courts do not usually review

Exhibit 3.6

The Typical State Judicial System[a]

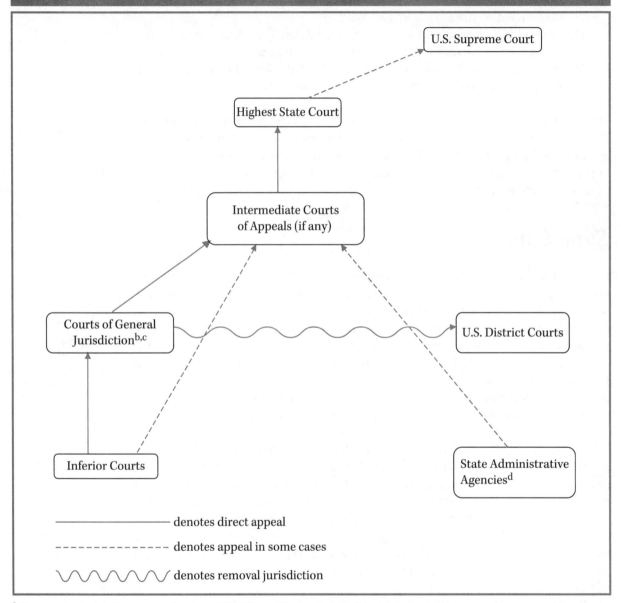

[a] There is great variation among the states. The titles of the courts vary from state to state.
[b] The state trial courts may be divided into divisions; for example, the civil division, the criminal division, family court.
[c] Removal jurisdiction generally is exercised when the defendant asks that the case filed in one court be moved to the other court.
[d] Administrative agencies perform some court-like functions; however, they are not courts.

decisions of facts made by the lower court. Some appellate courts hold trials *de novo*, which are exceptions to this general rule.

An example of a case history is *Bennis v. Michigan.*[40] It was originally decided by the Wayne County Circuit Court, then appealed (in this order) to the Michigan Court of Appeals, the Michigan Supreme Court, and then the U.S. Supreme Court.

Exhibit 3.6 describes a typical state system and its interrelationship with the federal system. State agencies, like federal agencies, are not courts; a person can appeal an unfavorable agency decision to the intermediate court of appeal in most states.

If you are interested in detail about how to locate the law and the meaning of legal citations, refer to the Web site for this text.

Contemporary Case

In the following Contemporary Case, the federal trial court decided whether the court had *in personam* jurisdiction. The court also attempted to reach a decision that would be efficient both for the parties and for the judicial system.

SKIDMORE v. LED ZEPPELIN
106 F. Supp. 3d 581, 2015 U.S. Dist. LEXIS 59113 (E. Dist. PA 2015)

FACTS Michael Skidmore is the trustee for the Randy Craig Wolfe Trust. He argues that Led Zeppelin's 1971 song "Stairway to Heaven" infringed the copyright of Randy Craig Wolfe's guitar composition "Taurus." On behalf of the trust he sues the living members of the band Led Zeppelin (James Patrick "Jimmy" Page, Robert Plant, and John Paul Jones) and music industry companies associated with Led Zeppelin. The companies include "(1) Super Hype Publishing, Inc., a publishing company owned and managed by Page that publishes the musical compositions of Led Zeppelin and Page; (2) Warner/Chappell Music, Inc., a global music publishing company that publishes and administers Super Hype's catalog of songs, including Led Zeppelin's music; (3) Atlantic Recording Corporation, the record company that manufactured,

sold, and distributed *Led Zeppelin IV*, the album containing the allegedly infringing song."

ISSUES Does the court lack personal jurisdiction over the individual defendants? Should the case be transferred to the Central District of California?

HOLDINGS Yes, the Eastern District of Pennsylvania lacks personal jurisdiction over the individual defendants. Yes, the case should be transferred to the Central District of California in the interest of judicial efficiency.

REASONING Excerpts from the opinion of Juan R. Sánchez:

Venue in a copyright action is governed by 28 U.S.C. § 1400(a), which provides that an action under the federal copyright laws "may be instituted in the district in which the defendant or his agent resides or may be found." A defendant in a copyright action "may be found" wherever the defendant is subject to personal jurisdiction. . . . "[A] District Court typically exercises personal jurisdiction according to the law of the state where it sits." . . . Pennsylvania's long-arm statute permits the exercise of personal jurisdiction "to the fullest extent allowed under the Constitution of the United States." . . . In order for the Court to have jurisdiction over the Defendants . . . they must have "certain minimum contacts with . . . [Pennsylvania] such that the maintenance of the suit does not offend traditional notions of fair play and substantial justice." . . . Once the defense of lack of personal jurisdiction is raised, "the plaintiff bears the burden of showing that personal jurisdiction exists." . . .

There are two categories of personal jurisdiction: (1) general or "all-purpose" jurisdiction, which a court may exercise to hear "any and all claims" against a defendant when the defendant's affiliations with the forum state are "so 'continuous and systematic' as to render [it] essentially at home in the forum State," . . . and (2) specific jurisdiction, which "depends on an affiliatio[n] between the forum and the underlying controversy" and is "confined to adjudication of issues deriving from, or connected with, the very controversy that establishes jurisdiction." . . .

For general jurisdiction to exist, "the contacts between the defendant and the forum need not be specifically related to the underlying cause of action." . . . For an individual, "the paradigm forum for the exercise of general jurisdiction is the individual's domicile," . . . and for a corporation, the paradigm fora are its "place of incorporation and principal place of business." . . . The Supreme Court has made clear that only in an "exceptional case" would an individual be "essentially at home" in a forum other that of its domicile. . . .

Plaintiff asserts the Court has general jurisdiction over the individual Defendants because they make millions of dollars on sales of their music and related goods and services in this District, including through CD sales, digital downloads, radio and television play, advertising, marketing, concert performances, other performances, licensing, merchandising, book sales, T-shirt sales, and poster sales. . . . In opposition, the individual Defendants have submitted declarations stating they (1) are citizens . . . of the United Kingdom, (2) reside in London, (3) have never resided in Pennsylvania or been issued a Pennsylvania driver's license, (4) have never owned any real or personal property located in Pennsylvania, (5) have never owned any bank or brokerage accounts in Pennsylvania, (6) have no employees in Pennsylvania, (7) are not currently . . . parties to any contract with a Pennsylvania resident or company, (8) have not been in Pennsylvania for the purpose of promoting the exploitation, sale or distribution of Led Zeppelin's music since at least 1980, and (9) have not performed as part of Led Zeppelin in Pennsylvania since 1985. . . .

The Court finds the individual Defendants are not subject to either general or specific jurisdiction in this District. First, none of the individual Defendants are domiciled in this District. . . . Next, in determining general jurisdiction, "[o]nly contacts occurring within a reasonable period of time prior to the filing of this action are relevant to this Court's general jurisdiction inquiry." . . . Copyright infringement claims are subject to a three-year statute of limitations . . . and Plaintiff filed this case on May 31, 2014. Because this case only involves acts of infringement arising after May 31, 2011, Plaintiff's reliance on contacts that are seventeen or more years old to establish general jurisdiction is unreasonable. . . .

Further, the sales of Defendants' music and products . . . in this District are not a regular or systematic contact by the Defendants; Plaintiff has not alleged any facts suggesting the individual Defendants exercised control over where these products are sold or marketed. "Due process requires that a defendant be haled into court in a forum State based on his own affiliation with the State," . . . and the corporate Defendants' alleged contacts with the District cannot be imputed to the individual Defendants. . . . These individual Defendants are not "essentially at home" in this District and subjecting them to general jurisdiction here would not comport with notions of fair play or substantial justice.

There are also insufficient contacts to justify the Court's exercise of specific jurisdiction over the individual Defendants. Other than Page's radio interview, the only acts alleged to have been performed by the individual Defendants in this District are concerts that occurred at least seventeen years ago. Given the three-year statute of limitations for copyright claims, these performances are not contacts upon which the Court may base its exercise of specific jurisdiction. Page's single radio interview . . . does not demonstrate he has purposefully directed infringing activities at this forum and is much too small and remote to comport with the requirements of due process. . . .

[J]urisdiction and venue in this District are improper as to the individual Defendants. These Defendants . . . have consented to personal jurisdiction and venue in the Central District of California. When venue is improper, the Court may dismiss the case or, in the interest of justice, transfer it to a district court in which the case could have been brought. . . . "[D]ismissal is a disfavored remedy because of the strains it imposes on judicial and party resources." . . . [A] court can transfer the case to a forum in which it could have been brought even if it lacks personal jurisdiction over the defendant. . . . [B]ecause this case cannot proceed against the individual Defendants in this District, but can proceed against all Defendants in the Central District of California, the Court finds that transfer is in the interest of justice. The Court will . . . transfer the claims asserted against the individual Defendants to the Central District of California.

. . . When venue is proper for some defendants but not for other defendants and dismissal is not appropriate, a district court can either transfer the entire case to a district where venue is proper for all defendants or sever the claims against the defendants for whom venue is improper and transfer only that portion of the case. . . . Severance and transfer of only the claims against the individual Defendants would impose unnecessary costs on the parties and the judicial system. All of Plaintiff's claims arise out of the same series of events, and a second, largely identical action filed against the individual Defendants would waste judicial resources and inconvenience witnesses. In addition, all Defendants consent to suit in the Central District of California; the Trust—the owner of the copyright that was allegedly infringed—is a creature of California law (and Defendants intend to challenge the creation of the Trust and Skidmore's standing as trustee); there are no Pennsylvania witnesses; there are a number of potential California witnesses regarding Wolfe's alleged ownership of the copyright to "Taurus" and the formation of the Trust; and California law governs the validity of songwriting and recording contracts Wolfe supposedly entered into before writing "Taurus," which bears on the ownership of the copyright. . . . Thus, the Court will transfer the entire action to the district in which all Defendants consent to jurisdiction and venue and in which the court is better-suited to rule on the state law issues. . . .

Accordingly, Defendants' motions to transfer will be granted. . . .

Short Answer Questions

1. Is it important who sits as a justice on the U.S. Supreme Court? Why or why not? Do you believe there should be some minimum requirements for a person to be appointed to the U.S. Supreme Court? Why? If so, what should they be? Some commentators have suggested a

mandatory retirement age for justices. Would you favor such a proposal? Why?

2. Native Americans generally have sovereignty on tribal lands. In one recent case, a 13-year-old American Indian boy and his parents filed a civil suit against the manager of a Dollar General Store for sexually molesting him. The manager was not a member of the tribe but the store was on Choctaw land. Dollar General had agreed to the jurisdiction of tribal courts over its lease. It is not clear whether it agreed to jurisdiction of the tribal courts in other matters. There is no evidence of consent by the manager to the court's jurisdiction. When do you think civil litigants that are not Native Americans should be subject to the jurisdiction of tribal courts? Why?[41]

3. Assume that you attend college in New York. During spring break, you and your best friend drive to Florida in your car. While in Florida, you have an automobile accident with Casey. Casey is a college student. His permanent home is in Tennessee. If you file a lawsuit for money to repair your car, what state court(s) could you use? Could you use a federal court? Why or why not?

You Decide...

1. Syed Farook and Tashfeen Malik were apparently radicalized and became supporters of the terrorist group ISIS. On December 2, 2015 they shot and killed 14 people at a holiday party for Farook's coworkers in San Bernardino, CA. The couple later died in a gun battle with police. Government agents conducted a number of searches during the subsequent investigation to determine the history of their radicalization and whether they had other conspirators involved in their activities. Farook tried to destroy his cell phone but his attempts were not successful.[42] The agents seized the iPhone but the government was not able to unlock the device. Apple, Inc. CEO Tim Cook stated that Apple would not cooperate with the government's attempts to obtain data from the device.

The U.S. government asked the court to issue an order directing Apple to help federal agents execute a search warrant. The government needed technical help to disable the security on an Apple device that the government lawfully seized pursuant to a warrant. Under the warrant the government has the right to look at the data on the device. The government law enforcement agents initially tried to bypass the lock but they were not been successful. Assume that the government's petition has been filed in your court.

How would *you* decide this case? Be certain that you explain and justify your answer. What do you think the law should be? Why?

(See Editorial, "Rotten Apple; The Tech Giant Is Wrong Not to Co-Operate with American Law Enforcement," *The Times* (London), February 18, 2016, 31; Patrick Seitz, "Apple Will Fight Feds on iPhone Backdoor," *Investor's Business Daily*, February 18, 2016, A01; and In re Order Requiring Apple, Inc. To Assist in the Execution of a Search Warrant Issued by this Court, 2015 U.S. Dist. LEXIS 138755 (E.D. New York 2015).)

Postscript: Technicians for San Bernardino County were able to reset Syed Farook's iCloud passwords. However, all information on the phone is not necessarily on the iCloud.[43] Eventually the federal government dropped its suit against Apple and paid over $1 million to have a third party unlock the phone.[44]

2. John Sanderson and George Taylor (plaintiffs) filed suit against Douglas Burdick and other defendants in a California court for a number of intentional torts such as defamation and infliction of emotional distress. The torts were based on Burdick's postings on the public part of his personal Facebook page. Burdick made the postings and later removed them while he was in Illinois. Burdick claims he has been a resident of Illinois since 1971 and has never lived in California. He also contends that he does not have assets, a place of business, or employees in California. Burdick apparently knew that Sanderson and Taylor were in California. The lawsuit is part of an ongoing dispute between the plaintiffs and the defendants, including Nerium Entities.

Nerium Entities are involved in advertising, marketing, and sale of a skin care product called NeriumAD. NeriumAD is marketed through multi-level marketing where salespersons are compensated for their own sales and sales generated by salespeople they recruit. Burdick is a "highly compensated representative of Nerium International and is the company's Corporate Consultant."[45] Sanderson and Taylor are entrepreneurs, physician-scientists, and bloggers. They have a noncommercial Internet blog Web site known as BareFacedTruth.com, which discusses the science behind skin care and other topics. Sanderson and Taylor began to question the science and safety of NeriumAD and its marketing organization. The defendants, including Burdick, "engaged in a campaign of harassment and defamation against Plaintiffs to destroy their reputations using false and misleading information."[46]

Burdick posted on his Facebook page as Corporate Consultant for Nerium that "more scandalous information would be revealed regarding the 'Blogging Scorpions.'"[47] The Facebook posting stated "BOY DOES THIS 'BLOGGING SCORPION' HAVE A LOT TO HIDE! More to come shortly about the Truth and Facts about this 'Blogging Scorpion[]', things like: [(1)] Why he lost his medical license (yes we have the documents directly from the Medical Board of California) [(2)] Why he personally uses multiple social security numbers [(3)] How many times has he been charged with domestic violence [(4)] Why he makes medical claims about his product that is not FDA approved (yes we have the video of him making these medical claims publically [sic]) [(5)] And much much more! Stay tuned as we reveal the 'REAL' truth behind this 'Blogging Scorpion.'"[48]

Burdick's contacts with California are not sufficient for general personal jurisdiction. Based on this information, is there sufficient minimum contact to support specific personal jurisdiction?

How would *you* decide this case? Be certain that you explain and justify your answer.

(See Burdick v. Superior Court, 233 Cal. App. 4th 8, 183 Cal. Rptr. 3d 1, 2015 Cal. App. LEXIS 32 (4th Cal. App Dist., 2015).

Notes

1. 5 U.S. 137 (1803).
2. Citations deleted. *Aetna Life Ins. Co. v. Haworth*, 300 U.S. 227, 240-241 (1937).
3. *Black's Law Dictionary*, 6th ed. (St. Paul: West, 1990), 54.
4. *Id.*, at 1008.
5. *Id.*, at 1045.
6. *Id.*, at 1158.
7. 416 U.S. 312 (1974).
8. Endangered Species Act of 1973 (ESA) (16 USCS 1540(g)) and *Bennett v. Spear*, 117 S.Ct. 1154 (1997).
9. 5 U.S. 137 (1803).
10. Official Supreme Court Web site, "Biographies of Current Justices of the Supreme Court," http://www. supremecourt. gov/about/biographies.aspx (accessed February 20, 2016).
11. Sheila M. Smith, "Comment: Justice Ruth Bader Ginsburg and Sexual Harassment Law: Will the Second Female

Supreme Court Justice Become the Court's Women's Right Champion?" 63 U. Cɪɴ. L. Rᴇᴠ. 1893, Summer 1995.

12. Lawrence Hammack, "Supreme Court Takes Closer Look at Virginia Ban on Cross Burning," *Roanoke Times*, December 12, 2002.

13. *Ortiz v. Fibreboard Corporation*, 1999 U.S. Lexis 4373 (1999).

14. There is a lot of commentary about the proper role of judges. Dean John Henry Wigmore . . . noted in 1917 that common law judges were constantly making law, and "our own Supreme Courts have long been drawing copiously and consciously from this unbounded field of public policy." Carol Nackenoff, "Symposium: 2015 Maryland Constitutional Law Schmoozeprivacy, Police Power, and the Growth of Public Power in the Early Twentieth Century: A Not So Unlikely Coexistence," 75 Md. L. Rev. 312 (2015) at 322 and 323. *See also* Richard Lavoie, "Issues Facing the Judiciary: Activist or Automaton: The Institutional Need to Reach a Middle Ground in American Jurisprudence," 68 Alb. L. Rev. 611 (2005).

15. *Black's Law Dictionary*, 7th ed. (St. Paul: West, 1999), 601.

16. *Ibid.*

17. *Brown v. Entertainment Merchants Association*, 131 S. Ct. 2729, 2011 U.S. LEXIS 4802 (S. Ct., 2011).

18. *City of Ontario, California v. Quon*, 130 S. Ct. 2619, 2010 U.S. LEXIS 4972 (S. Ct., 2010). Quote at 2632.

19. Choe Sang-Hun, "Mixed Emotions over Deft Imitator," *The International Herald Tribune*, September 3, 2012; Kim Tae-Jong, "Wharton Director Says Apple Claims Unreasonable," *Korea Times*, September 7, 2012.

20. 326 U.S. 310 (1945).

21. See *Skidmore v. Led Zeppelin*, 106 F. Supp. 3d 581, 2015 U.S. Dist. LEXIS 59113 (E.D. Pa 2015).

22. Tex. Civ. Prac. & Rem. Code Ann. § 17.042 (1997).

23. James Buchwalter, Laura Hunter Dietz, Sonja Larsen, Jeffrey J. Shampo, Thomas J. Czelusta, and Jane E. Lehman, Process VI. Methods of Service, C. Jurisdiction Acquired by Substituted or Constructive Service; Tests of Jurisdiction, 2. Over Nonresidents of State, b. Long-Arm Statutes, 62B Am Jur 2d Process § 160 Minimum-contacts formula; statutes coextensive with due process.

24. 952 F. Supp. 1119 (W.D. Pa. 1997).

25. *Id.*, at 1122-1123.

26. *Id.*, at 1124. The sliding scale in Zippo has created a number of inconsistencies. It has been argued that the sliding scale is not an effective notice system and consequently violates due process. "Without consistency in common law how can an internet user 'structure [his or her] primary conduct with some minimum assurance as to where that conduct will and will not render [him or her] liable to a suit[?]'" Citations deleted. Emily Ekland, "Comment: Scaling Back Zippo: The Downside to the Zippo Sliding Scale and Proposed Alternatives to Its Uses," 5 Alb. Gov't L. Rev. 380, 381-382 (2012).

27. John Bourdeau, Laura Hunter Dietz, Kerry Diggin, Romualdo P. Eclavea, Tracy Bateman Farrell, Alan J. Jacobs, Rachel M. Kane, Fern Kletter, Sonja Larsen, Lucas Martin, Jeffrey J. Shampo, Eric C. Surette, Barbara Van Arsdale, Mary Ellen West, Eleanor L. Grossman, Mary Babb Morris, and Jaqualin Friend Peterson, Federal Courts, XIV. District Courts, D. Jurisdiction, 5. Federal-Question Jurisdiction, c. Concurrent or Exclusive Jurisdiction, 32A Am Jur 2d Federal Courts § 912, § 912 Presumption of concurrent jurisdiction.

28. *Mims v. Arrow Financial Services, LLC,* 132 S. Ct. 740, 2012 U.S. LEXIS 906 (S. Ct., 2012).

29. John Bourdeau, et al., *supra* note 27.

30. Mary Babb Morris, Trademarks and Tradenames, VII. Infringement and Unfair Competition, H. Practice and Procedure, 1. In General, 74 Am Jur 2d Trademarks and Tradenames § 142, § 142 Jurisdiction.

31. John Bourdeau, et al., *supra* note 27.

32. U.S. Courts Web site, "Understanding Federal and State Courts," http://www.uscourts.gov/EducationalResources/ FederalCourtBasics/CourtStructure/UnderstandingFederal AndStateCourts.aspx (accessed September 16, 2012). States have authority to enact and enforce their own antitrust legislation when the antitrust behavior has significant local consequences. The contract, conspiracy, or monopoly may actually occur outside the state. When a combination affects interstate *and* intrastate commerce, federal control over the interstate part does not prevent state control over the intrastate aspects. See John Bourdeau, J.D., William H. Danne, Jr. J.D., Eleanor L. Grossman, J.D., Alan J. Jacobs, J.D., John R. Kennel, J.D., Sonja Larsen, J.D., Anne E. Melley, J.D., LL.M., and Mary Babb Morris, J.D., Jeffrey J. Shampo, J.D., Eric C. Surette, J. D., Barbara J. Van Arsdale, J.D., Monopolies, Restraints of Trade, and Unfair Trade Practices, VII. State Antitrust Laws: Introduction, D. State Antitrust Statutes, 1. In General, e. Extraterritorial Application; Effect of Federal Law, Am Jur 2d Monopolies, Restraints of Trade, Unfair Trade Prac. § 793 Effect on interstate commerce.

33. *Ibid.*

34. *Ibid.*

35. *Ibid.*

36. State courts do not have jurisdiction over any cases brought under federal patent law. Jane E. Lehman, Anne E. Melley, and Elizabeth A. Brainard, Patents, XXVIII. Patent Validity and Infringement Litigation, A. Jurisdiction, 60 Am Jur 2d Patents § 816, § 816 State courts.

37. 28 U.S.C. § 1332(a).

38. This applies to federal judges serving on the Supreme Court, the federal court of appeals, federal district courts, U.S. Court of Claims, and the U. S. Court of International Claims. These judges are called Article III judges. Article III judges serve "during good behavior." They cannot have their salaries reduced. Federal Judicial Center Web site, "How the

Federal Courts Are Organized, Federal Judges and How They Get Appointed," http://www.fjc.gov/federal/courts.nsf/auto frame!openform&nav=menu1&page=/federal/courts.nsf/page/183 (accessed February 20, 2016) and Federal Judicial Center, The U.S. Legal System: A Short Description, available at http://www2.fjc.gov/sites/default/files/2015/US-Legal-System-A-Short-Description-2014-08-04.pdf (accessed February 20, 2016).

39. The number of associate justices is established in 28 U.S.C. § 1. Supreme Court of the United States Web site, "A Brief Overview of the Supreme Court," http://www.supreme court.gov/about/briefoverview.aspx (accessed February 20, 2016).

40. 134 L. Ed. 2d 68 (1996).

41. See Garrett Epps, "Who Can Tribal Courts Try?," *The Atlantic*, December 7, 2015, http://www.theatlantic.com/politics/archive/2015/12/who-can-tribal-courts-try/419037/ (accessed February 26, 2016) and Adam Liptak, "Justices Weigh Power of Indian Tribal Courts in Civil Suits," *The New York Times*, December 7, 2015, http://www.nytimes.com/2015/12/08/us/politics/justices-weigh-power-of-indian-tribal-courts-in-civil-suits.html?_r=0 (accessed

February 26, 2016). The U.S. Supreme Court heard oral arguments in the case, *Dollar General Corp. v. Mississippi Band of Choctaw Indians*, No. 13-1496, on December 7, 2015. The oral argument before the court is available at The Supreme Court of the United States Web page, Oral Argument—Audio, http://www.supremecourt.gov/oral_arguments/audio/2015/13-1496 (accessed March 1, 2016).

42. Editorial, "Rotten Apple; The Tech Giant Is Wrong Not to Co-Operate with American Law Enforcement," *The Times* (London), February 18, 2016.

43. Jack Date, "San Bernardino Shooter's iCloud Password Reset with FBI Consent, Agency Says," *ABC News*, February 21, 2016, http://abcnews.go.com/US/fbi-san-bernardino-shooters-icloud-password-reset-consent/story?id=3709 3031 (accessed February 22, 2016).

44. Del Wilber, "TECHNOLOGY; FBI won't reveal more on hacking," *Los Angeles Times*, April 28, 2016, Pg. C 3.

45. 233 Cal. App. 4th 8, at 14.

46. *Id.*, at 15.

47. *Id.*, at 15.

48. *Id.*, at 16.

4

Dispute Resolution

Learning Objectives

After completing this chapter you should be able to

- Describe the stages in a typical civil lawsuit
- Explain the different types of fee arrangements clients can have with lawyers
- Compare the types of discovery
- Understand the role of small claims courts
- Recognize the advantages and disadvantages of using alternative dispute resolution
- Distinguish the different types of alternative dispute resolution

Classic Case

Historically courts were opposed to arbitration. This opposition was evident in the approaches courts took to contract clauses that said that the parties would arbitrate any disputes. In this Classic Case the U.S. Supreme Court resolved some inconsistent interpretations of the Federal Arbitration Act (FAA). It determined that the Dobsons were required to submit their claim to arbitration and they were not permitted to litigate their dispute. Notice that the Dobsons did not sign the contract. They purchased the home from the Gwins who had purchased the service.

ALLIED-BRUCE TERMINIX COMPANIES, INC. v. DOBSON
513 U.S. 265 (1995)

FACTS In 1987, Steven Gwin bought a lifetime "Termite Protection Plan" (Plan) for his house in Birmingham, Alabama, from the local office of Allied-Bruce Terminix Companies, a franchise of Terminix International Company. In the Plan, Allied-Bruce promised "to protect" Gwin's house "against the attack of subterranean termites," to reinspect periodically, to provide any "further treatment found necessary," and to repair up to $100,000 in damages caused by new termite infestations. The written contract provided that "any controversy or claim . . . arising out of or relating to the interpretation, performance, or breach of any provision of this agreement shall be settled exclusively by arbitration."

In the spring of 1991, Mr. and Mrs. Gwin wished to sell their house to Mr. and Mrs. Dobson. The Gwins had Allied-Bruce reinspect the house. The Gwins were told that the house was free of termites. Soon after the Dobsons bought the house and the Plan was transferred to them, they discovered that the house was swarming with termites. Allied-Bruce attempted to treat and repair the house, but the Dobsons thought that Allied-Bruce's efforts were inadequate. They sued the Gwins, Allied-Bruce, and Terminix. Allied-Bruce and Terminix immediately asked the court for a stay so that they could proceed with arbitration. The court denied the request to stay due to a state statute that made written, predispute arbitration agreements invalid and "unenforceable."

ISSUE Was the arbitration clause enforceable against the Dobsons?

HOLDING Yes, the clause could be enforced against the Dobsons.

REASONING Excerpts from the opinion of Justice Breyer:

. . . Several state courts and federal district courts, like the Supreme Court of Alabama, have interpreted the [Federal Arbitration] Act's language as requiring the parties to a contract to have "contemplated" an interstate commerce connection. . . . Several federal appellate courts . . . have interpreted the same language differently. . . . We granted certiorari to resolve this conflict. . . .

[T]he basic purpose of the Federal Arbitration Act is to overcome courts' refusals to enforce agreements to arbitrate. . . . The origins of those refusals lie in "ancient times," when the English courts fought "for extension of jurisdiction—all of them being opposed to anything that would . . . deprive . . . them of jurisdiction." . . . American courts initially followed English practice. . . . [W]hen Congress passed the Arbitration Act in 1925, it was "motivated . . . by a . . . desire" to change this anti-arbitration rule. . . . It intended courts to "enforce [arbitration] agreements into which parties had entered," . . . and to "place such agreements upon the same footing as other contracts." . . .

Did Congress intend the Act also to apply in state courts? Did the Federal Arbitration Act pre-empt conflicting state anti-arbitration law, or could state courts apply their arbitration rules in cases before them, thereby reaching results different from those reached in similar federal diversity cases? . . .

We must decide in this case whether that Act used language about interstate commerce that nonetheless limits the Act's application, . . . carving out an important statutory niche in which a State remains free to apply its anti-arbitration law or policy. We conclude that it does not. . . .

[Section] 2 [of the Federal Arbitration Act] gives States a method for protecting consumers against unfair pressure to agree to a contract with an unwanted arbitration provision. States may regulate contracts, including arbitration clauses, under general contract law principles and they may invalidate an arbitration clause "upon such grounds as exist at law or in equity for the revocation of any contract." . . . What States may not do is decide that a contract is fair enough to enforce all of its basic terms (price, service, credit), but not fair enough to enforce its arbitration clause. The Act makes any such State policy unlawful, for that kind of policy would place arbitration clauses on an unequal "footing" . . . contrary to the Act's language and Congress' intent. . . . For these reasons, we . . . [interpret] the Act's language as insisting that the "transaction" in fact "involve" interstate commerce, even if the parties did not contemplate an interstate commerce connection. . . . Consequently, the judgment of the Supreme Court of Alabama is reversed and the case is remanded for further proceedings not inconsistent with this opinion.

It is so ordered.

LITIGATION

Most people are not familiar with litigation. The thought of being involved in a lawsuit may make them anxious. This chapter explores the stages of a typical lawsuit so that you can be an active participant with your attorney if a legal dispute does arise and you are involved in litigation.

Costs of Litigation

Before an individual or business entity pursues litigation, he or she should consider the costs of the litigation. There are likely to be direct and obvious costs and indirect, often hidden, costs. The kinds and amounts of fees will vary depending on the type of litigation. To make an informed decision about whether to start or defend a suit, the parties should consider the probable outcomes of litigation. The parties should also consider the likelihood that alternative dispute resolution (ADR) will be effective and its costs. (*Alternative dispute resolution* consists of methods of resolving disputes other than traditional litigation.) Even though some forms of ADR are becoming more formal, time-consuming, and expensive, ADR may still reduce overall costs.

There are a number of factors that a person should consider before deciding to initiate a lawsuit or agree to settle a dispute. Some of the more important factors include the following:

- The difficulty in predicting the outcome of litigation
- The amount of money a party might potentially win (or lose)
- The ability and willingness of the other party to pay any judgment
- The amount that the lawyers would charge
- The timing of the legal bills
- The amount of court costs, including filing fees
- The additional fees that might be incurred, including the fees for expert witnesses (for example, accountants, economists, and doctors), fees for preparing exhibits, fees for medical tests and exams, fees for *depositions* (the formal process of asking a potential witness questions under oath outside the courtroom), and the cost for jury consultants
- The availability of insurance to pay some of the costs of litigation, such as automobile policies that may pay the costs of defending the insured or special legal insurance
- The amount of time that the parties, their families, friends, and employees would spend in preparing for the litigation
- The manner in which this lawsuit and/or additional publicity would affect the reputations of the parties
- The effect on the continuing relationship between parties to the suit
- The stress and emotional toll that the lawsuit will take on those involved
- The loss of time and effort; for example, employees may be preparing for litigation instead of focusing on normal work tasks. The distraction from personal and professional goals; for example, employees may be distracted from the goals of the enterprise

Litigation is also expensive for the court system. As a result, courts have rules to reduce the costs. For example, a court may permit a *class action lawsuit*, which is a lawsuit involving a group of plaintiffs or defendants who are in substantially the same situation. One lawsuit can be more efficient than having many individual lawsuits, each of which is likely to involve the same basic facts and issues of law. Of course, combining the plaintiffs or defendants into a class is not always appropriate. Courts will rule on whether the group is a proper class. When the court agrees that the group should be a class, it *certifies* the class. In *Wal-Mart Stores, Inc. v. Dukes,* the U.S. Supreme Court decided that the women suing for employment discrimination did not constitute a class. They could proceed with individual claims, but they could not be a class.[1] When a class is certified, the court will decide the best techniques for notifying potential class members. Common techniques include sending notices by e-mail or mail and publicizing the case through the media. The federal Class Action Fairness Act (CAFA) makes it easier to bring class action suits in district court under diversity jurisdiction. The CAFA requirements are that "(1) the total amount in controversy is greater than $5 million, (2) the putative class contains at least 100 members, and (3) there is minimal diversity."[2] In *minimal diversity*, one plaintiff and one defendant must have diverse citizenship.

Many courts have established procedures to make complex litigation run more efficiently and smoothly. For example, if there are 300 cases against four insurance companies, with each of the plaintiffs seeking recovery under the insurance policies for injuries allegedly suffered due to exposure to toxic mold, the court may designate an individual judge or panel of judges to handle the suits. In consultation with the attorneys, the judge(s) may impose additional rules to aid in managing the cases. The judge may require such things as electronic filing of complaints and motions. In civil practice, the *complaint* is the plaintiff's first pleading. It informs the defendant that he or she is being sued.

The Problem

We will use this hypothetical situation to illustrate many of the concepts in this chapter.

Nic Grant, a college sophomore, was taking his girlfriend, Nancy Griffin, to dinner at Cassie's Bar and Grille in Butler, Pennsylvania. (Cassie's Bar and Grille is owned by Cassaundra Hill and is incorporated in Pennsylvania.) Nic and Nancy enjoyed their dinner, including the clam chowder and seafood bisque. Unfortunately, later that night both Nic and Nancy became violently ill, and they were hospitalized. The doctors believe this probably was caused by food poisoning from their dinner at Cassie's.

Nic spent five days in the hospital. As a result, he did not show up for work and consequently lost his job. He was also unable to take his final examinations or to complete his research projects for several of his classes. Nic was forced to withdraw from college for the semester. Nancy spent three days in the hospital. Nic's roommate, who is taking a course in legal environment, advised Nic that he and Nancy probably have a claim against Cassie's and recommended that they consult a lawyer to learn about their potential rights.

Before Trial

Client's Interview with a Lawyer   Nic recognized that he needed legal assistance and consulted with the local bar association. The local bar association referred Nic to an attorney, Ms. Lyn Carroll. Nic called Ms. Carroll and scheduled an initial interview. At this initial interview, Nic told Ms. Carroll as much about the evening as he could remember. Nic mentioned that he had not notified Cassie's Bar and Grille. Ms. Carroll agreed to assist Nic in obtaining compensation and offered to help Nancy as well. Ms. Carroll recognized that it might be a potential conflict of interest for her to represent both Nic and Nancy. (In order for Ms. Carroll to comply with the ethics rules for attorneys, she would need to send each prospective client a letter disclosing the possible conflict of interest and seeking their consent to having her represent both of them despite this potential conflict.)

When meeting with Ms. Carroll, Nic asked a number of questions including what her payment terms are, and whether there are any opportunities to negotiate or arbitrate a settlement rather than going to trial. Nic wanted to know if Ms. Carroll was willing to work toward a negotiated settlement and whether this would affect the amount of attorney's fees that he would pay. Following this initial meeting, Nic and Nancy agreed to meet with Ms. Carroll a few days later to discuss, read, and sign the client-attorney contract. As indicated in the contract, payment was to be based on a contingency fee. (A *contingency fee* is a fee to be paid to an attorney based on some contingency or event. The most common provisions are that the fee is due only if the case is settled or won.) Other bases for attorney's fees are not dependent on results: for example, flat rate and hourly rate fees. Whatever the fee arrangement, it is specified in the contract between the client and the attorney. The contract with Ms. Carroll and examples of many of the court documents are available on the Web site for this text.

Since Cassie's Bar and Grille has insurance, an attorney hired by the insurance company is likely to be its "lead counsel" in this case. However, that attorney will focus more on protecting the interests of the insurance company than the interests of Cassie's Bar and Grille. If Cassie's Bar and Grille loses the case, the insurance company will pay for the damages covered by the insurance policy, and Cassie's Bar and Grille will have to pay for any other damages. Consequently, in many situations the defendant would hire its own attorney. The firm's attorney would normally work with the insurer's attorney, and the two of them would agree on the strategy to use. We will assume in this case that Cassie's Bar and Grille has no potential liability over the policy limits and will not need its own attorney. We will refer to Cassie's Bar and Grille and Cassaundra Hill as the defendants. The insurance company is not really a defendant. It is providing insurance for Cassie's Bar and Grille's liability.

In this case, the insurance company has selected Mr. Jefferson Jones of the Pittsburgh law firm of Jones, Murphy, Sabbatino, and Schwartz, which specializes in defending these types of suits. The insurer has worked with Mr. Jones numerous times in past cases. Cassaundra scheduled an appointment to meet with Mr. Jones to discuss the case.

Even though the incident occurred in Butler County, the defendants can hire an attorney from Pittsburgh, located in Allegheny County. Attorneys are licensed at the state level and not the county level. Once licensed, the attorney can practice law anywhere within the state's jurisdiction. Rules of court and court procedures may vary somewhat from county to county. The attorney will need to know (or learn) the rules in Butler County and the Pennsylvania Rules of Civil Procedure. Each state and the federal court system has its own rules of procedure for both civil and criminal trials.

People are not required to hire an attorney. The plaintiffs, the defendants, or both sides could choose to represent themselves in court. This is called appearing *Pro se* (appearing in one's own behalf). This may be very unwise, depending on the circumstances. A nonlawyer often mislabels concepts, misses key points, and is not familiar with procedures.[3]

An Ounce of Prevention

It is often difficult to select and hire an attorney. You should select your attorney as carefully as you select a doctor. Your attorney should be a person with whom you are comfortable. He or she should also be someone that you trust. The attorney should have some experience or expertise in the matter that is in dispute, and he or she should probably have courtroom experience if you anticipate going to trial. For example, you may be inclined to hire your business attorney to represent you in court because you have confidence in him or her. The attorney may not have much experience in court. In fact, many types of attorneys rarely appear in court and so they are not familiar with rules of procedure and rules of evidence. There are a number of places to get information about attorneys, including the state bar association. You should consult these sources, talk with friends and colleagues who have hired attorneys in the past, and arrange to have a conference with the attorney or attorneys who seem most likely to meet your needs.

Investigation of the Facts   In the interviews with her clients and in subsequent telephone conversations, Ms. Carroll gathered information concerning the incident. She obtained medical releases from both clients in order to review the hospital and medical records of each of them. Nic and Nancy also gave her copies of their hospital bills.

Ms. Carroll wrote to the university for proof that Nic and Nancy withdrew from classes after June 6, 2016. She also wrote to Nic's former employer for information about Nic's wages, normal work week, and proof that he was fired on June 10, 2016. She finished her preliminary investigation when she had all the information. It is important that Ms. Carroll determine that there is basis for a suit. Attorneys and clients who file frivolous lawsuits may be subject to penalties. Then Ms. Carroll wrote a letter to Cassaundra Hill.

Negotiation of a Settlement   When Cassaundra received the letter, she contacted Cassie's Bar and Grille's insurance company to inform them about the claim. The insurance carrier immediately assigned an adjuster to the case. The adjuster contacted Ms. Carroll to ascertain the nature of the injuries. On the basis of this information, the adjuster attempted to negotiate a settlement by offering $17,027 to Nic and $5,680 to Nancy. Since the offers covered only out-of-pocket expenses and did not include any amount for lost wages or for pain and suffering, both Nic and Nancy rejected the offers. When no other offers were made by the insurer, Ms. Carroll filed suit on November 15, 2016. (Note that Nic Grant is claiming at least $16,000 and Nancy Griffin is claiming at least $8,000 in pain and suffering in addition to any other losses either of them may be able to prove.) In many situations, the negotiations would be more extensive. Ms. Carroll might have a conference with the insurance adjuster, Cassie's Bar and Grille's attorney, or the insurance company's attorney in an effort to resolve the conflict and reach a settlement without resorting to a civil suit.

There is some advantage to waiting to initiate suit. Plaintiffs will want an accurate idea of their losses. In this case, waiting might also be an advantage to Cassie's Bar and Grille, since Nic may locate another job. In general, a plaintiff must be sure to initiate his or her suit by filing the complaint before the statute of limitations expires. The suit should be started before the memories of the parties and witnesses begin to fade. Before filing suit, the attorney should discuss alternatives to litigation with her clients.

Filing the Suit   The complaint should be definite, and it should contain sufficient information for the defendant to understand the nature of the litigation so that he or she can prepare a defense. In this case the plaintiffs' original complaint was filed in the *Court of Common Pleas* (title used in some states for trial courts of general jurisdiction). After it was filed, the prothonotary's office delivered a copy to the sheriff. Depending on the state the office may be called the prothonotary's office, the clerk of courts's office, or it may have another label. The sheriff then serves copies of the complaint on all the defendants named in the complaint. Depending on the type of suit and the state, any responsible adult who is not a party to the suit may be able to serve the complaint. In some states, the complaint is accompanied by a *summons* (a writ commencing an action and notifying the person named that he or she must appear in court to answer a complaint). The complaint was delivered by mail to Cassaundra at the principal office of the corporation.

Sometimes the defendant does not answer the complaint or does not appear on the date of trial. In these cases, the court will generally enter a *default judgment*, a judgment in default of the defendant's appearance. In these cases, the court is only "listening" to the plaintiff's side, so the court generally awards the plaintiff what he or she is requesting. Default judgments are valid in civil cases if the court has proper jurisdiction, including jurisdiction over the defendant, and the defendant has been properly served with the complaint. (See Chapter 3 for a discussion of jurisdiction.) If the plaintiff does not appear on the trial date, generally the case is dismissed.

Usually, the defendant will file an *answer* to the complaint. The answer will deny some or all of the allegations made by the plaintiff in the complaint. Any allegations that are denied become the issues to be resolved at trial. Any allegations acknowledged as true and accurate become facts that are stipulated and do not need to be addressed further. In our hypothetical case, Cassie's Bar and Grille filed an answer to the complaint. In the answer, Cassie's denied that it was the source of any food poisoning and claimed that it should not be held liable for any injuries incurred by the plaintiffs. At this point in the proceedings, the plaintiffs have sued the defendants in a court of law and the defendants have filed an answer. Before trial, both attorneys may simplify the legal issues, amend their complaints and answers, and

Exhibit 4.1

Discovery

Technique	Description	Purpose[a]
Deposition	Oral questions asked of a witness who is under oath	Used to preserve testimony or to impeach a witness at trial
Interrogatories	Written questions sent to a party who responds under oath	Used to preserve testimony or to impeach a witness at trial
Subpoena Duces Tecum	Order for the production of documents and things	Used to discover information which can be presented during the trial
Physical or Mental Examination	Request that a person submit to an exam by a doctor selected by the opposition	Used when physical or mental condition is an issue in the case
Request for Admission	Request that opposing party admit that a statement is true	Used to reduce the number of items that must be proven at trial

[a] One purpose of all discovery techniques is to obtain information.

attempt to limit the number of expert witnesses. The purpose is to reduce costs and the length of trial.

Discovery   At this point, the discovery process begins. *Discovery* is a general term that applies to specific methods used to find information and to narrow the issues to be decided during the trial. Discovery can shorten the trial and encourage the parties to settle. If one side realizes that he or she is likely to lose the suit, he or she may decide to settle the case. The scope of discovery is very broad. Normally, one can discover all information that is relevant even if it cannot be introduced as evidence during the trial. The standard used is whether the discovery request is reasonably calculated to lead to admissible evidence. Exhibit 4.1 depicts the five common discovery devices.

Electronic Discovery (E-Discovery)   Most businesses create and maintain a large quantity of records in their usual course of business, including e-mails, e-mail attachments, and text messages. When the records are electronic, they are called *electronically stored information (ESI)*. It is now estimated that 92 percent of information created is stored electronically.[4] The importance of ESI is obvious. The law about discovery of ESI is still developing. The federal government and many state governments are revising their rules of procedure to specifically deal with ESI. If a business has reason to expect litigation will occur, it has an obligation to maintain its records, including its ESI. If the business fails to maintain records, the court can sanction it.

An Ounce of Prevention

When you realize that you are about to be sued, you may be tempted to destroy all potential evidence. In some cases, the evidence you think is damaging may actually be the evidence that will help you win the suit. In addition it may be illegal to destroy evidence, and you may be charged with obstruction of justice. Some of your records may be privileged. The constitutional right to protect yourself from self-incrimination protects you from having to disclose information that may lead to a criminal prosecution against you. The incrimination must be for an actual crime. The right does not protect you if the information is merely embarrassing or there is potential civil liability. This constitutional right does not apply to corporations.[5]

Depositions   Traditionally, a *deposition* is a witness's sworn testimony taken outside of court and then reduced to writing by a court reporter. The process begins with the witness swearing that the testimony will be truthful. If it is not, the witness can be held in contempt, as President Clinton was in Paula Jones's case.[6] The attorneys then ask questions which the witness answers. Increasingly, attorneys also videotape the deposition. This is permitted in many jurisdictions, including federal courts[7] and California courts.[8] If the deposition is used later at trial, the jury will watch the video instead of listening to someone read the deposition. This is more interesting, and the jurors are more likely to pay close attention to the questions and answers. Depositions are used to preserve testimony from someone who, for good cause, may not be able to attend the trial. They are also used to impeach the witness when the witness appears at trial and gives evidence that conflicts with what he or she said during the deposition. (To *impeach* means to use some evidence to question the truthfulness of a witness.) A deposition may be obtained from any party or witness.

Interrogatories   *Interrogatories* are written questions from one party to the other. Like depositions, interrogatories produce a written record of answers to questions. Because both the questions and the answers are written, the answers are not as spontaneous as in a deposition. The answer is made under oath, but the respondent has time to contemplate and carefully phrase the written answers. Often, a person's attorney will review a draft of his or her answers before the answers are returned. Interrogatories are limited to parties. You cannot send interrogatories to other witnesses.

Production of Documents and Things   In many lawsuits, oral testimony alone will be insufficient to win the case. In Nic and Nancy's case, Ms. Carroll will introduce the records of the two doctors and the hospital. Ms. Carroll may also request that Cassie's

Bar and Grille produce records it possesses about the source of the ingredients, food-handling practices, and employee training. The legal form used to obtain these documents is called a subpoena duces tecum. (A *subpoena duces tecum* is an order to appear with records.)

Physical or Mental Examination   Whenever the physical or mental condition of a party to the suit is in question, the court may order that party to submit to an examination by a physician. Here, both the present physical condition of the plaintiffs and their condition prior to the food poisoning will potentially be an issue, so a medical examination may be necessary.

Request for Admission   One party can serve the opponent with a written request for an *admission*. The recipient must admit or deny the request under oath. If he or she is unable to either admit or deny the request, the party should explain why. The party can also qualify his or her answer. The recipient has a duty to answer in good faith. If the recipient fails to answer in a stated period of time (usually 30 days), the matter is considered to be admitted. For example, Ms. Carroll may request an admission that Cassaundra Hill trains her own employees in food safety.

The Result of Discovery   As a result of the discovery process, the attorneys for Cassie's Bar and Grille and Cassaundra Hill informed their clients that it appears the food poisoning was probably caused by the negligence of Cassaundra's staff. Mr. Jones recommended a settlement offer of $19,027 to Nic and $6,680 to Nancy and Cassaundra agreed. (A settlement offer is really an offer to negotiate.) Ms. Carroll informed her clients of the offer and recommended that it be rejected. Nic and Nancy rejected the offer. Since the defendants made no additional offers, the case went to trial.

Pretrial Conference   Many courts now use pretrial conferences to encourage the parties to settle the dispute themselves. However, not all judicial systems and judges favor these conferences. Often the pretrial conferences result in a settlement. Even if there is no settlement, the conference generally clarifies the legal and factual issues involved in the case. Depending on the situation, participation in settlement conferences may be mandatory or voluntary.

Businesspeople need to be aware that *many* courts require the parties to participate in pretrial conferences. Some jurisdictions base the requirement on the amount of damages. In Butler County during pretrial conferences, the attorneys meet with the judge. The court requests that the parties be available either outside the room or by telephone. Then, if a settlement offer is made, the attorney can quickly inform his or her client and obtain a prompt response. This procedure is common in many courts. Depending on the jurisdiction and the judge's preferences, the judge *may* take a very active role in attempting to fashion a compromise that would be acceptable to both parties. Some judges may be harsh with parties who do not accept reasonable settlement offers or who do not participate in pretrial conferences in good faith. In some jurisdictions, nonbinding arbitration may be required in addition to or instead of a settlement conference.

Motions to Dismiss and Demurrers   There are a number of techniques to remove issues and/or end lawsuits that are groundless. Procedures vary depending on the technique used and the jurisdiction. Some jurisdictions only use one of them. The purpose is to avoid the expense of unnecessary trials and parts of trials.

A plaintiff *or* defendant can make a motion to dismiss after the opposition has filed a pleading. Pleadings include the plaintiff's complaint, the defendant's answer, or the defendant's counterclaim. When a court considers a motion to dismiss, it *normally* accepts as true the material facts alleged in the opposition's pleading. The pleading is interpreted in the light most favorable to the opposition. (Consequently, the pleading is interpreted against the party making the motion.) If the pleading states a claim upon which relief can be granted, the motion to dismiss will be denied.

A demurrer claims that the other party's pleading is not sufficient. Common grounds for demurrers include failure to state facts sufficient to constitute a legal cause of action (general demurrer), lack of jurisdiction (special demurrer), lack of capacity to sue (special demurrer), and uncertainty or ambiguity (special demurrer). For purposes of the demurrer, the court must accept as true all the facts that were in the pleading. The standard for deciding the demurrer is, assuming that the facts are true, would they entitle the plaintiff to relief in court?

Motion for a Summary Judgment   A motion for a summary judgment also terminates issues and/or lawsuits that are groundless. It is a motion asking the judge to declare that side the "winner" because there are no material issues of fact. It goes beyond what is stated in the pleadings and attacks the basic merits of the opponent's case. This motion permits the examination of evidentiary material, such as admissions, affidavits, and depositions. The standard courts use is whether there is any genuine or triable issue. If there is no genuine or triable issue, the moving party is entitled to a summary judgment. The court can grant a summary judgment on some issues or claims and not on others. Summary judgment is procedurally distinct from motions on the pleadings, which only permit the court to review the pleadings and do *not* permit review of evidence.

On Nic and Nancy's behalf, Ms. Carroll made a motion for a summary judgment claiming that no material facts appear to be in dispute; rather, the case is merely a matter of applying the law.

The Trial

The judge denied Nic and Nancy's pretrial motions and the legal process continued. The actual trial proceeding is governed by technical rules of trial practice. A good plaintiff or defendant takes an active role in assisting the lawyer. However, it is best to leave trial work to attorneys.

An Ounce of Prevention

Court can be intimidating if you are a witness or a party. To prepare you should review your notes about the event, your depositions, and interrogatories. You should carefully consider your hairstyle and clothes. Your appearance and behavior should indicate that you take the lawsuit seriously. Your clothes should be conservative and not obviously expensive. You should remember that you are always "on stage," even when you are not in the witness box. The judge and jury (and any media present) will observe you while you testify, while you sit hearing other evidence, and even while you are in the hallway during breaks. Be especially careful in what you say and do when the judge or members of the jury may be nearby.

Jury Selection　A legal case can be resolved by a trial before a judge, without a jury. Then the judge decides questions of fact and questions of law. Such a trial is often less expensive and less time-consuming. Nic and Nancy agree with their attorney that a jury will generally favor the plaintiffs and their arguments, and they elect to have a jury trial. A request for a jury trial must be made in a timely manner. This was noted on the plaintiffs' original complaint.

Members of the jury are referred to as *petit jurors* (ordinary jurors on the panel for the trial of a civil or criminal action). Most states select potential jurors from the voter registration list or the list of licensed drivers or both. Traditionally, civil juries consisted of twelve jurors. Some jurisdictions have reduced this number. Generally, six to twelve jurors are used. In federal court, a civil jury also consists of six to twelve members.[9]

Alternate jurors may also be selected. Alternate jurors sit with the regular jurors and hear the evidence. If a regular juror becomes ill or has to leave the jury for some reason during the evidence phase, an alternate joins the jury and it continues to function. Without alternate jurors, the parties would have to select a new jury and begin the trial again. An alternate juror can substitute for a regular juror even during deliberations in some jurisdictions: The jury will then start its deliberations from the beginning.

Voir Dire　The prospective jurors may be required to complete a juror information form. The attorneys use this information to question potential jurors during the *voir dire* examination (examination of potential jurors to determine their competence to serve on the jury). Jurors need to be questioned in the proper manner to obtain helpful, accurate answers, without offending them. The information provided by the prospective jurors is used by the judge and counsel as the basis for challenging jurors as biased and ineligible to serve. The attorneys and/or the judge can ask the questions. For example, an attorney may request that the judge ask any potentially embarrassing questions so that the attorney can try to maintain good rapport with the potential jurors. In some jurisdictions, the judge may control voir dire by asking all the questions of the potential jurors. At the opposite extreme—New York, for example—voir dire is conducted by the attorneys without the judge; the judge is called in only if problems arise. The procedure depends on the rules of court and the judge's preferences. In civil disputes in Butler County, the judge usually conducts voir dire of all the prospective jurors at one time. In Nic and Nancy's case, for example, if a potential juror happened to work for Cassie's Bar and Grille, Ms. Carroll would challenge that person and request that the judge excuse the person. On the other hand, if one of the prospective jurors was a member of Nic's fraternity, Mr. Jones would challenge the student.

Challenges Based on Cause   Two methods exist for dismissing prospective jurors. First, a potential juror can be removed *for cause.* When a juror is removed for cause, generally an attorney first suggests to the judge that the juror will probably be biased. Challenges for cause can occur if (1) the juror has a financial stake in the case or similar litigation, (2) if members of the juror's family have such an interest, or (3) there is reason to believe the juror will be partial to one party. The judge then decides whether he or she agrees; if so, the potential juror is dismissed. The judge can also make this decision on his or her own initiative. (When a judge raises an issue on his or her own, we say that the judge does it *sua sponte*, which means voluntarily, without prompting or suggestion, of his or her own will or motion.) There is no limit on the number of potential jurors who can be removed for cause.

Peremptory Challenges   A second technique is to remove a prospective juror by the use of a *peremptory challenge.* Unlike removal for cause, each side is allotted a limited number of peremptory challenges. The judge decides the number of peremptory challenges prior to beginning the jury selection process. In federal court, for example, each side receives three peremptory challenges.[10] With peremptory challenges, the attorney does not need to discuss his or her reasons for wanting to remove the juror.

Peremptory challenges are often based on the attorney's intuition and/or past experiences. When an attorney doesn't feel comfortable with a prospective juror, he or she can use a peremptory challenge to remove that person from the jury. The attorney should be careful with peremptory challenges for two reasons: First, he or she has a limited number of them and later prospective jurors may be less favorable than ones removed by peremptory challenge earlier; second, courts have decided that such challenges cannot be used to exclude potential jurors on the basis of gender,[11] religion, race, or color. (The precedents began with *Batson v. Kentucky*,[12] a criminal case. The limitation is now used in criminal and civil cases.)

Selection Process   The decision about whether to exclude a person from the petit jury may be reached after that individual juror is questioned. In the alternative, it may be made after an entire set of jurors is sitting in the jury box. For example, the judge may then ask each attorney if the attorney has any objections to the jury sitting in the box. A judge may discuss excusing jurors at both points. The techniques used for jury selection will depend on the rules of court and the judge's preferences. Once a jury is selected, the jury is instructed to make its decision based only on the evidence presented in open court. Jurors are not to do their own research or read about the case from outside sources such as newspapers, television, and social media.

Jury Consultants   Parties can hire jury consultants to assist them in selecting sympathetic jurors. These jury consultants come from varying backgrounds, including marketing, psychology, and sociology. They investigate the backgrounds of potential jurors and collect statistics about the reactions of certain socioeconomic groups to trials generally and to issues that are expected to arise in the particular trial on which they are consulting.

Jury consultants sometimes arrange a *shadow jury* consisting of "jurors" with demographic backgrounds similar to the impaneled jurors. The shadow jury sits in the public area of the courtroom and its members report their impressions of the evidence. This can be particularly helpful in highly technical cases, where litigants are concerned that the jurors may be confused by the details. This technique provides attorneys with continuous feedback on how their presentation is perceived.

Another technique is the *mock jury* where the lawyers practice their case before a group of mock jurors with demographic backgrounds similar to those of the actual jurors.

Removal of Judges   California has a unique procedure that allows each party one peremptory challenge against the judge assigned to the case. This peremptory challenge must be filed before any proceedings begin in front of the judge being challenged.[13]

Most jurisdictions do not permit peremptory challenges to a judge; however, they have other procedures to disqualify a judge. A judge is not permitted to preside over any action in which he or she has any bias, has a financial interest, is related to any of the parties or attorneys, or there are any facts that would impair the judge's impartiality. For example, if the plaintiffs have appealed the judge's *gag order* (order by judge to be silent about a pending case) to the state supreme court, the judge may be biased. The judge may raise this issue *sua sponte* or it can be raised by one of the parties.[14]

Opening Statements   After the jury is chosen, each side has an opportunity to tell the jury what it intends to prove during the trial. This serves as an introduction to the party's case and helps the jury integrate the evidence that follows. The attorney for the plaintiff makes an opening statement, followed by the attorney for the defendant.

Direct Examination   After a witness has been sworn in, the attorneys question the witness. Witnesses who lie can be held in contempt. The plaintiffs' attorney questions his or her witnesses first. The rules of evidence include rules concerning what an attorney can ask and how he or she may ask it. Trial attorneys are reluctant to ask questions when they do not know how a witness will respond. This is the reason for pretrial preparation of witnesses. Failure to adequately prepare can be disastrous.

Cross-examination   After Ms. Carroll questions each of her witnesses, Mr. Jones has an opportunity to question them. The best way to clarify matters brought up in direct examination is the skillful use of cross-examination by counsel. After the cross-examination, the attorney who called the witness (Ms. Carroll) *may* examine the witness again on redirect, and the opposing counsel (Mr. Jones) *may* examine the witness on recross. The process of examination and cross-examination continues until Ms. Carroll has no other witnesses to call. Next, Mr. Jones directly examines his witnesses one at a time, and Ms. Carroll cross-examines each one until the defense has no further witnesses to call. At this point, both sides "rest" their cases.

Demeanor Evidence   Some cases are decided primarily on the oral evidence presented at trial with little supporting evidence. Sometimes cases are called "swearing matches" or "he said/she said" because the witnesses' testimonies conflict. The decider of fact, usually the jury, decides who is more believable. The decider of fact uses demeanor evidence to help it evaluate who to believe. (*Demeanor evidence* includes the witnesses or the parties' behavior, speech, mannerism, and dress.)

Expert Witnesses   An *expert witness* is a witness who possesses special knowledge. For example, the parties in our case may call medical experts and specialists in safe food handling. Expert witnesses are permitted to testify concerning their opinions. They are allowed to state their own conclusions and to discuss hypothetical situations described by the attorneys. In this way, expert witnesses are distinguished from regular witnesses, who are not permitted to give their opinions, draw conclusions, or respond to hypothetical questions. Courts may accommodate special witnesses, such as experts, by allowing them to testify when it is convenient for the witness's schedule.

Motion for a Directed Verdict   A motion for a directed verdict is addressed to the judge. It is usually requested at the close of the opponent's case. The standard used by the judge is whether the plaintiff has made a *prima facie* case (a case that is obvious on its face)[15] on which the plaintiff is entitled to recover. If the plaintiff has not presented a prima facie case, the defendant is entitled to a directed verdict. In most jurisdictions, the judge cannot weigh the evidence—the judge must (1) look solely at the evidence produced by the plaintiff, (2) accept any reasonable inference from that evidence, and (3) disregard all challenges to the credibility of that evidence. (A minority of jurisdictions permit the weighing of evidence.) If the defendant's motion is granted, it means that the court has determined that the defendant must win as a matter of law.

If the motion is not granted, the trial will continue. After the presentation of the defendant's evidence, the plaintiff may request a directed verdict on the defendant's cross-complaint and/or the defendant can again request a directed verdict. If either party's motion for a directed verdict is granted, it means that the court has determined that that party must win as a matter of law.

Closing Arguments   After both sides rest, each has an opportunity to persuade the jury by reviewing the testimony, restating the significant facts, and then drawing conclusions from those facts. Each attorney takes the same body of evidence and attempts to reach a successful result by emphasizing the evidence favorable to his or her client and minimizing unfavorable evidence. This stage is called *closing arguments* or *summation.*

The Verdict   At the conclusion of closing arguments, the judge instructs the jury about the law and charges them to answer certain questions. As part of the charge, he or she instructs them in the applicable areas of law and defines any legal concepts. This is called the *charge to the jury* or *jury instructions.* Many states have published standardized jury instructions so that the judge does not have to write new jury instructions each time.

The jury may be directed to reach a general verdict and/or a special verdict. In a *general verdict*, the judge asks who should win the lawsuit and how much he or she should receive. In a *special verdict*, the judge asks specific questions about the relevant factual issues in the case.

After the jury leaves the courtroom, they *deliberate* on the evidence in private and attempt to reach a verdict. In many jurisdictions, the jury may request that parts of the evidence be read back to them during the deliberation process. Many jurisdictions do not require a unanimous jury decision in civil cases; some even authorize a decision by a majority vote of the jurors. In Pennsylvania, the verdict is valid if at least five-sixths of the jurors agree to it.[16] In federal court, a civil jury must reach a unanimous decision unless the parties agree to accept a smaller vote.[17] After the petit jurors reach a verdict, it is announced in open court. The *verdict* is the stated opinion of the jury. If the judge concurs in the verdict, he or she enters a judgment.

In our case, the jury deliberated and held for the plaintiffs, Nic Grant and Nancy Griffin, for $21,026 and $5,498, respectively. The court then entered a judgment in those amounts for the two plaintiffs. The judgment is the court's official decision.

Judgment   In most cases, the judge will agree with the jury's verdict. When the judge disagrees with the jury verdict, the judge may enter a *judgment notwithstanding the verdict.* Traditionally, this was called a judgment *non obstante veredicto* or judgment n.o.v. When a judge declares a judgment n.o.v., the judge substitutes his or her own decision for that of the jury. Either a plaintiff or a defendant may be awarded a judgment n.o.v. A judgment n.o.v. is appropriate only if the jury's verdict is incorrect as a matter of law; that is, there is no substantial evidence to support the jury verdict. Most courts use the same standard as that used for a directed verdict. The court (1) disregards all conflicts in the evidence, (2) does not consider whether the witnesses are credible, and (3) gives face value to the evidence in favor of the party who received the verdict. The party who won the original verdict will likely appeal the judgment n.o.v.

Posttrial Proceedings

Execution and Attachment   Sometimes the defendant may "voluntarily" pay the judgment after losing the case. If not, the successful plaintiff will have to conduct the collection process himself or herself. First, the plaintiff has to locate the defendant's assets. Then the plaintiff uses a writ to obtain the court's permission to attach them. The plaintiff then takes the writ to the court where the assets are located, completes a form requesting execution, pays a fee, and asks a sheriff, marshal, or constable to collect the assets. State laws on execution and attachment vary.

Motion for a New Trial   A losing party may file a *motion for a new trial* with the judge. It will be filed with the same judge who originally heard the case, unless that judge is disabled or disqualified. (The party making the motion is requesting the court to order a new trial.) Common grounds for a motion for a new trial include: the judge committed a prejudicial error in conducting the trial; there were irregularities in the jury's behavior; or the evidence was insufficient to support the verdict. In extremely rare cases, a new trial may be granted based on newly discovered evidence. To obtain a new trial on this basis, the moving party must show that (1) the newly discovered evidence pertains to facts in existence at the time of trial, (2) the evidence is material, and (3) the moving party using reasonable diligence could not have obtained the information prior to trial. The last requirement prevents a party who was negligent in failing to locate the evidence from obtaining a new trial.

Additur or Remittitur   A party who believes that the damage award is too large or too small can also request a new trial. When the motion for a new trial is based on the amount of damages, a judge may grant a new trial unless a plaintiff agrees to accept a reduction in damages. This is called *remittitur*. Some states also permit granting a new trial unless a defendant agrees to accept an increase in the amount of the award. This is called *additur*. When the judge orders additur or remittitur, the parties can decide to accept it, request a new trial on damages, or appeal.

Appeal   After losing the decision, the attorney for Cassie's Bar and Grille might file a notice of appeal to hear the case before a higher court. The rules of court specify the time limit for filing a notice of appeal. Appeals are limited to questions of law. In other words, the appellate court will generally not reverse a lower court unless the lower court made an error of law. In this hypothetical case, the decision is in accordance with the law; consequently, Cassie's Bar and Grille does not appeal. Cassie's Bar and Grille now owes the plaintiffs $21,026 and $5,498, respectively.

If a case is appealed, the appellate court can *affirm* the decision, which indicates approval, or *reverse* the decision, which indicates an error of law. Appellate courts can affirm some parts of the decision and reverse others. Sometimes the appellate court reverses and *remands* the case because the lower court made a mistake of law, and the case is returned to it for correction. Exhibit 4.2 depicts the stages of a trial.

Exhibit 4.2

Common Steps of a Trial

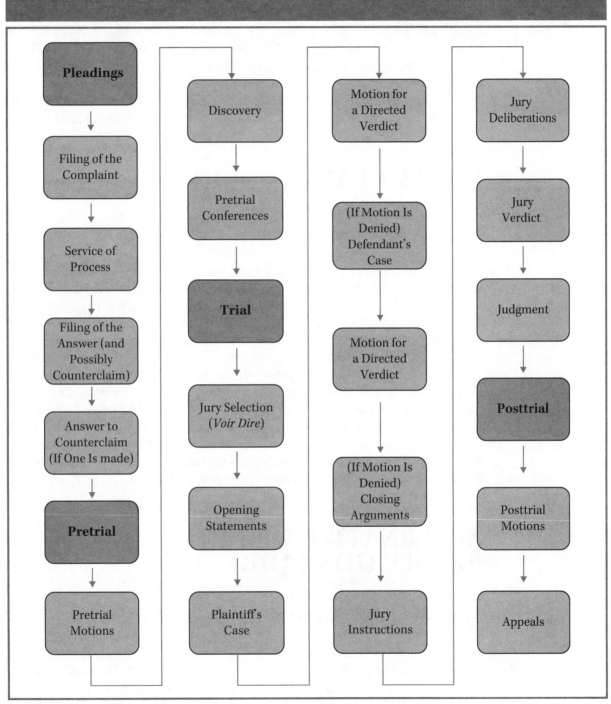

A Comment on Finality

One of the benefits of the law is finality. When a cause of action has been litigated and reduced to a judgment and all appeals have been exhausted, the matter comes to an end. In this case, the doctrine of *res judicata* applies. *Res judicata* means that when a court issues a final judgment, the subject matter of that lawsuit is finally decided between the parties to the suit. This doctrine prevents further suits from being brought by the same parties on the same issues. In other words, the matter comes to rest. Remember that *res judicata* does not prevent timely appeals nor does it prevent criminal proceedings based on the same behavior. (Note: *Res judicata* is the civil law equivalent of the prohibition against double jeopardy used in criminal law.)

SMALL CLAIMS COURT

One technique to reduce legal expenses is for a party to file the legal dispute in small claims court. Although this is still litigation, it significantly reduces the costs. This option permits a party to effectively represent himself or herself. Generally, the opponent can also appear without a lawyer. Small claims courts do not use legalese and standard rules of evidence. The procedures in small claims courts vary from state to state. Small claims courts can usually process a case more quickly. The jurisdictional amounts differ—the upper limit may range from $2,500 (Kentucky and Rhode Island) to $25,000 (Tennessee).[18] In most states, Nic and Nancy's claims would exceed the jurisdictional limits of small claims court.

Some small claims courts publish booklets to assist parties in small claims actions. There may also be government employees who provide free or low-cost legal services to parties involved in litigation in small claims court. Participants need to be organized and bring their witnesses and any physical evidence with them to the hearing. Participants should prepare a brief, coherent presentation of the case. It is also helpful to observe a few small claims cases in advance of the hearing date. The court can award a default judgment if the defendant does not appear for the trial.

ALTERNATIVE DISPUTE RESOLUTION (ADR)

The Need for Alternatives to a Civil Suit

Regular lawsuits are often expensive and time-consuming. A business that is plagued by frequent lawsuits will suffer financially. As a result, many businesses seek an alternative form of dispute resolution, such as arbitration. Even the federal government is participating in arbitration. For example, the United States arbitrated the amount owed to the amateur filmmaker Abraham Zapruder for seizing his film of the assassination of President John F. Kennedy.[19]

Litigation can be a lengthy process. First there is the delay before a suit is filed. Then additional time passes while the parties prepare for court. Although the length of time to trial varies from court to court, it can be a significant period of time. For example, the median length of time from filing the dispute to disposition of the case in federal district courts is 24.9 months.[20] Even if a plaintiff has a strong case, there is no guarantee that the plaintiff will prevail at trial, and it may be several years before the matter is finally resolved.

For a business, the time spent in preparing for the trial and then having employees attend the pretrial and trial proceedings represents a significant expense even if the business wins the case. Many businesses prefer to settle the case—the earlier the better—by paying the plaintiff and saving all the time and effort that a trial requires. If an alternative is available, these businesses are likely to use it.

Alternatives to litigation do exist, and these alternative forms of dispute resolution are becoming increasingly popular. ADR provides a number of benefits:

- The burden on the court system is reduced.
- An injured party with a legitimate claim is likely to be compensated more quickly. When one considers the time value of money, this can be a significant factor.
- Defendants may be less likely to settle groundless claims merely for the sake of expediency and/or because the settlement is less expensive than the expenses of a trial.
- ADR is less adversarial, allowing the parties to reach a more amicable resolution. This permits the parties to continue to do business together or to coexist in harmony in the future.
- ADR can be conducted with more privacy. Court cases are generally open to the public and trials may be reported in the media.

As a result of these and other benefits, the use of ADR is becoming more common, especially in the resolution of disputes involving a business. Increasingly, courts are requiring parties to attempt alternative methods of dispute resolution before allowing access to the courts. Because these processes are usually faster and less expensive, they tend to create less tension in the relationship of the parties. This is particularly important in disputes between family members, such as child-custody cases, and in business situations in which the parties may wish to continue to do business together. For example, difficulties arose when Whoopi Goldberg's firm was filming *T. Rex.* The parties agreed to use arbitration whenever problems occurred so that they could continue to produce the film.[21] Continuity of relationship is not an issue in Nic and Nancy's suit against Cassie's Bar and Grille, since the parties do not have an on-going relationship. ADR can be used with more than two parties. However, for the sake of simplicity we will talk about two-party disputes.

ADR has its limits, and it is not appropriate for resolving every form of legal dispute. ADR cannot be used in criminal matters, for example, and it does not establish legal precedent. ADR may not result in a fair resolution if there is significant power imbalance. Power imbalance may occur when one of the parties has a significant advantage over the other. Power imbalances include (1) emotional strength, (2) negotiating skills, (3) superior knowledge such as financial, legal, or technical knowledge, and (4) leverage such as the leverage a boss has over an employee. The impartial third party may be able to help "correct" some of the power imbalance depending on the intermediary's skill. In addition, some matters should be debated in a public forum, which is not provided by ADR. In both negotiation and mediation, a person can stipulate that he or she will not sign an agreement until it is approved by his or her lawyer or other advisor. Exhibit 4.3 summarizes the types of alternative dispute resolution that will be discussed below.

Exhibit 4.3

Types of Alternative Dispute Resolution

Type of Alternative Dispute Resolution	Description	Example
Negotiation	The parties talk to each other and resolve their dispute.	Nicole and Pam are roommates. They each have annoying habits. They sit down and talk to each other and reach a compromise.
Mediation	The parties use an impartial third party (mediator) to help them communicate with each other and resolve their dispute.	Glenda and Robert are neighbors. They are not getting along very well. They agree to meet with a volunteer neighborhood mediator. The mediator helps them resolve their differences.
Arbitration	The parties present their evidence to an impartial third party (arbitrator) who makes a decision called an award. Before the arbitration begins, the parties decide if the arbitration will be binding or advisory.	Rosie works for an office supply store. When she started work, she agreed that she would submit any employment disputes to binding arbitration. The store also agreed to submit its disputes with Rosie to binding arbitration. Rosie feels that her boss is discriminating against her because she is a woman. Rosie and the store submit the dispute to binding arbitration.
Minitrial	The parties present their evidence before an impartial third party. The parties then try to negotiate a solution. The neutral party may make an advisory award before or after the parties negotiate.	Two competing car manufacturers have a dispute about their competitor's advertising practices. They participate in a minitrial. After hearing the evidence, the manufacturers agree to change the content of their television commercials.
Rent-a-judge Trial	The parties present their evidence to a retired judge who serves as the arbitrator and makes an award.	Cassie's and one of its suppliers are having a dispute about the timing of shipments. They agree to submit their dispute to a rent-a-judge so that it can be resolved quickly and the shipments can continue.

An Ounce of Prevention

When a business relationship begins, most people tend to be optimistic. Typically, you are inclined to believe that everything is going to go well and that you and the other party will both profit from the arrangement. This is the time to add a contract clause requiring ADR to settle any future disputes. It is easier to agree to ADR when you are on friendly terms rather than after the dispute arises and you are having a hard time cooperating. You can select one or more types of ADR in your contract. You can also include where the ADR will occur, how you are going to locate a mediator or arbitrator, and who is going to pay the costs and expenses. Inclusion of this clause is a proactive step that may well save you time and money if a dispute arises.

Negotiation

The simplest form of ADR may be *negotiation*. It involves the discussion and resolution of a controversy by the parties involved. Negotiation is so common that most people do not even consider it as a form of ADR. Instead, they think of it as merely a method for settling disputes or controversies. That is the essence of ADR, however—settling a dispute or a controversy without using courts.

If the parties to the dispute are willing and able to negotiate an acceptable solution, negotiation is an excellent method of dispute resolution. If the parties are able to resolve the matter themselves, with or without consulting their attorneys, they can probably save time and money. Since negotiation is handled by the parties, all interested parties must be willing to negotiate before it can be effective. For example, Nic and Nancy could try to negotiate a settlement with Cassie's Bar and Grille's insurance company rather than take the case to trial. In so doing, they may wish to have Ms. Carroll assist them in the negotiation. The insurance adjuster or the attorney for the insurer may serve as the representative for the company.

Mediation

Mediation is similar to negotiation, although there is a significant difference. Mediation involves the use of an impartial third party, a *mediator*, who attempts to help the parties reach a mutually acceptable resolution to their dispute. Usually, just one mediator is used. The mediator does not act as a decision maker. Rather, he or she facilitates communication between the parties. The mediator listens to the parties and assists them in resolving their differences, or in resolving as many aspects of their dispute as possible. There are no formal procedures. The parties may choose to have a lawyer, a family member, or some other advisor present during the mediation. Generally, the mediator should not have any financial or personal interest in the outcome of the dispute. A prospective mediator should promptly disclose to the parties any circumstance likely to cause bias or the appearance of bias.

The advantages of mediation are that it is less expensive than litigation, it is quicker, and generally the results are perceived as more satisfactory. The American Arbitration Association (AAA) claims that its mediations are very effective, with 85 percent of commercial matters and 95 percent of personal injury matters resulting in written settlement agreements.[22] Participants are generally more satisfied because they agreed to the result. Nic, Nancy, and Cassaundra could use mediation to attempt to resolve their dispute. The insurance company also needs to be represented if they are going to pay for Nic and Nancy's losses. The parties may use a commercial service to locate an appropriate unbiased mediator. Generally, the mediator does not impose a solution on the parties. Some mediators, however, take a more forceful role in attempting to reach an agreement; others believe a more passive role is appropriate. Mediation sessions are private; usually only the parties, their representatives, and the mediator will be present. Other people generally may attend only with the permission of the parties and the mediator.

More than one mediation technique can be used in an attempt to resolve the disagreement. One mediation technique is *caucusing*. In this technique, the mediator meets with each party separately. Another mediation technique is *shuttle mediation*, where the mediator physically separates the parties during the mediation session and then runs messages between them. If mediation is not successful, the parties can use another ADR technique or submit their dispute to the court. Consequently, an important principle of mediation is confidentiality of the proceedings; otherwise, the parties will not discuss the issues freely. The parties must be confident that what they say or admit in mediation will not be used against them in court. The parties should agree to maintain the confidentiality of the mediation and not to rely on or introduce into evidence at any arbitration, judicial, or other proceeding (1) the views expressed by a party; (2) suggestions made by a party; (3) admissions made by a party; (4) proposals made by the mediator; (5) views expressed by the mediator; and/or (6) the fact that a party was or was not willing to accept a proposal. The mediator should not be required to testify or divulge records in any adversarial proceeding. No stenographic record is prepared of the mediation process.

Certification of Mediators There is a disagreement about whether mediators should undergo some certification process and become certified. The proponents of mediator certification believe that standards would encourage the confidence of the courts and the disputing parties. They also believe that certification would ease the backlog in civil courts. The opponents to certification feel that it would limit the diversity of mediators at a time when diversity is in demand. Lawyers, judges, psychotherapists, and ministers have entered the field of mediation. In addition, opponents argue that the profession is still developing and it is too early for certification: There are no adequate standards for certification. Certification at this time would be unfair and misleading to the public. In addition, there have been relatively few complaints against mediators.

Skills   Knowledge of the law, while important in some cases, is only one possible competency for a good mediator. Other necessary skills for mediators include the following:

- Patience, persistence, concentration, and focus toward the goal
- The ability to distinguish between stated positions of the parties and their real interests
- The ability to remain positive and constructive, even with difficult parties
- The ability to maintain confidentiality
- The ability to remain unbiased in the search for the truth of the situation and the solutions that work best for all concerned under the circumstances
- The ability to secure a resolution that is substantively, procedurally, and psychologically satisfactory for the participants[23]

Compensation   Many mediators are volunteers who serve as mediators through various community organizations. Others are professional mediators who rely on mediation to provide much of their income. The parties should discuss the compensation issue and how the expenses will be shared before agreeing to submit their dispute to mediation. There is no hard-and-fast rule regarding the compensation of mediators. Compensation among mediators can vary widely. For example, in the Boston area, mediators' fees range from approximately $100 to $800 per hour.[24] For a dispute such as Nic and Nancy's dispute with Cassie's Bar and Grille, mediation could take a few hours or even a full day. If the mediation is not making progress, at some point the participants may decide to stop mediating.

Arbitration

Arbitration is the process of submitting a dispute to the judgment of a person or group of persons called *arbitrators* for resolution. The final decision of the arbitrator or panel of arbitrators is called an *award*. It is usually binding on the parties. In nonbinding or advisory arbitration, the parties can consider the decision but do not have to follow it. (Television "judges" are arbitrators and not practicing judges, although some of them may have been judges in the past.)

Arbitration begins with an agreement between the parties to arbitrate, usually in the initial agreement. The parties *can* agree to arbitrate after an actual dispute arises, if they are willing to do so. The terms in an arbitration agreement can vary widely. An agreement to arbitrate is basically a contract or a portion of a contract. Like all contracts, to be valid it must be based on *mutual assent*, meaning the parties must agree to be bound by exactly the same terms. If a party agrees to an arbitration clause because of *fraud* (when one party enters into a contract relying on a false statement of material fact) or *duress* (when one party enters into a contract due to a wrongful threat of force), the agreement will not be valid. AAA recommends a standard contract clause such as the one below. The language in brackets can be added when appropriate.

> Any controversy or claim arising out of or relating to this contract, or the breach thereof, shall be settled by arbitration administered by the American Arbitration Association in accordance with its Commercial [or other] Arbitration Rules [including the Optional Rules for Emergency Measures of Protection], and judgment on the award rendered by the arbitrator(s) may be entered in any court having jurisdiction thereof.[25]

Generally, a party *cannot* appeal the decision in binding arbitration. There are exceptions. One ground for appeal is lack of mutual assent in the agreement to arbitrate. Some courts will also consider an appeal if the arbitrator refused to admit evidence which would have been admissible in court.

The arbitrator may be selected by the parties, selected by an arbitration organization, or selected by the parties from a list of panel members provided by an arbitration organization. Arbitrators charge about $400 to $700 a day.[26] Fees vary depending on the region and the type of case. Despite the expense, one finance company reported a 66 percent reduction in legal expenses by using arbitration.[27] If Nic, Nancy, and Cassie's Bar and Grille choose this option, their arbitration would probably take a day.

If both parties comply willingly with the arbitration award, no further action is required. If one side does not, court action to "confirm" the decision is necessary.

Organizations   There are a number of organizations that actively support arbitration and provide both the forum in which an arbitration occurs and the arbitrator. Some of these organizations operate exclusively within the United States, and others operate internationally. Within the United States, arbitration is supported by the Judicial Arbitration and Mediation Services, Inc. (JAMS), which employs only former judges as arbitrators; the Federal Mediation and Conciliation Service; and the AAA. Internationally, the AAA (which operates both domestically and internationally); the International Chamber of Commerce, headquartered in Paris; and the London Court of Arbitration (which is not a court, despite the title of the organization) support arbitration.

The AAA administers approximately 150,000 cases per year.[28] Its services include arbitration, mediation, minitrial, *fact-finding* (a process in which an arbitrator investigates a dispute and issues findings of fact and a nonbinding report), education, and training. When the AAA is involved in the arbitration process, it can refer a list of potential arbitrators, serve as an intermediary between the parties and the arbitrator in negotiating the arbitrator's compensation, and collect a deposit for arbitrator compensation. The AAA handles the administrative details so that the parties do not deal directly with the arbitrator. This helps ensure that the parties will not discuss the case privately with the arbitrator prior to the hearing.

An Ounce of Prevention

Because of its advantages, businesses often include arbitration clauses in their contracts with consumers. When you purchase a consumer good, you should be aware that an arbitration clause may be included in the lengthy terms of the contract. Whether the court will enforce the arbitration clause depends on the specifics of the agreement and the negotiation. Your business may be on the other side of the transaction when it sells goods or services. If your business wants to have its arbitration clause enforced, it should make sure that the agreement is fair to both sides. For example, the agreement will be uneven if the consumer cannot sue but the business can still use the courts to sue the consumer. When the arbitration agreement is uneven, the courts will be more likely to disregard it.

International Arbitration   At the international level, arbitration is most likely to be regulated by the 1958 U.N. Convention on Recognition and Enforcement of Foreign Arbitral Awards, an international treaty dealing with arbitration. This convention has 156 parties.[29] In this hemisphere, the Inter-American Convention on International Commercial Arbitration also facilitates international arbitration.[30] The International Chamber of Commerce also supports and encourages arbitration; and many firms involved in international business seek to resolve their disputes through its arbitration provisions. The Federal Arbitration Act and the international treaties are designed to increase the acceptance and use of arbitration as an alternative method for resolving disputes.

Minitrial

In ADR, the term *minitrial* describes a process in which the parties' attorneys present an abbreviated form of their best case. The parties are permitted to use expert witnesses to support their case. Usually a *neutral*, (an unbiased person), chairs the case. Senior executives from the firms involved also attend the presentation. After the presentation, the senior executives meet in an attempt to resolve the dispute. Prior to the presentation, the parties usually specify what will happen if the senior executives are unable to settle the case. For example, if the senior executives are unable to settle the case, the neutral may be empowered to (1) mediate, (2) provide a nonbinding advisory opinion informing the parties of the probable outcome of litigation, and/or (3) provide the parties with a detailed analysis of the strengths and weaknesses of their cases. (Note that in litigation, judges use the term *minitrial* to refer to an abbreviated judicial proceeding on a few issues, for example, a minitrial on damages.)

Rent-a-Judge Trial

A rent-a-judge trial is another alternative method of dispute resolution. When the parties elect to use this method, they pay a fee to a "judge" to hear and decide the dispute. Judges in these cases are typically retired judges, who are experienced in presiding over trials and who bring the reputation and prestige of their former positions to their current role. Rent-a-judge cases occasionally involve a "jury" of hired experts, particularly in technical cases.

The major advantage of the rent-a-judge option is that it is much faster than regular civil litigation. In addition, the proceedings are relatively private and do not become part of the public record. Many time-consuming trial procedures are eliminated, providing additional savings of time and money.[31] These trials are significantly less formal and are generally conducted in conference rooms.

It is common for the parties in a civil case to wait four to five years before they can get their case to trial. These same parties can get their case to trial with a rent-a-judge in a matter of weeks. As a result, rent-a-judge trials are becoming more popular. A number of companies now exist to assist clients in locating rent-a-judges. One company, Judicate, even has its own private courthouse in Los Angeles. In some jurisdictions, the clerk of court's office maintains a list of retired judges who are willing to serve as rent-a-judges. Depending on the jurisdiction, the decisions of rent-a-judges may be appealed to the public court of appeals.[32] Nic and Nancy might agree to use a retired judge from Butler County to serve as a rent-a-judge. If they are experiencing financial hardship, the speed of using a rent-a-judge and the opportunity for a quick payment would be attractive.

Online ADR

One of the changes in ADR is the trend toward using the Internet to conduct ADR. One advantage is that the parties do not need to spend time and money to travel to another location. This advantage is particularly strong if the parties are in different countries. If they are using asynchronous methods, such as e-mail and discussion boards, they do not even need to schedule a particular time for a "chat." One disadvantage is the lack of nonverbal communication. It is difficult to recognize if a person is joking or not being serious. A number of associations and businesses support online ADR, including CyberSettle.com, OnlineMediators.com, and Online Ombuds Office for disputes relating to online activity.

Disadvantages of ADR

ADR has a number of advantages for the individuals involved. It also helps reduce court congestion. However, it has a number of disadvantages for society and the general public as well. ADR may not be particularly helpful if:

- Society would benefit from an authoritative precedent.
- The matter involves significant questions of government policy, and ADR would not help to develop that policy.
- It is especially important to maintain established policies and increase consistency among cases.
- The matter significantly affects persons or organizations who are not parties to the ADR.
- It is important to have a full public record of the proceeding, and ADR will not provide such a record.

Contemporary Case

The U.S. Supreme Court was asked to interpret the Federal Arbitration Act in this Contemporary Case. California had judicial and legislative rules that said most consumers had the right to arbitrate their disputes as a class. The court calls this the *Discover Bank* rule based on the California precedent establishing the rule. The DIRECTV contract said that consumers waived the right to class action arbitration. The contract also said that it would apply the "law of your state." Note how the court addresses whether the "law of your state" included a law that was no longer valid because of a U.S. Supreme Court decision.

DIRECTV, INC. v. IMBURGIA

136 S. Ct. 463, 2015 U.S. LEXIS 7999 (2015)

FACTS DIRECTV, Inc. entered into a service agreement with its customers, including Amy Imburgia and Kathy Greiner. Section 9 of the agreement provides that "any Claim either of us asserts will be resolved only by binding arbitration." It also states "Neither you nor we shall be entitled to join or consolidate claims in arbitration." The agreement adds that if the "law of your state" makes the waiver of class arbitration unenforceable, then the entire arbitration provision "is unenforceable." Section 10 of the contract states the arbitration provision "shall be governed by the Federal

Arbitration Act." Imburgia and Greiner brought this lawsuit in state court alleging that the company's early termination fees violate California law. DIRECTV requested that the court enforce the arbitration clause.

ISSUE Is DIRECTV entitled to have the arbitration agreement enforced?

HOLDING Yes, the arbitration provision is enforceable against the customers.

REASONING Excerpts from the opinion of Justice Breyer:

The Federal Arbitration Act states that a "written provision" in a contract providing for "settle[ment] by arbitration" of "a controversy . . . arising out of" that "contract . . . shall be valid, irrevocable, and enforceable, save upon such grounds as exist at law or in equity for the revocation of any contract."

. . . At one point, the law of California would have made the contract's class-arbitration waiver unenforceable. In 2005, the California Supreme Court held in *Discover Bank v. Superior Court* . . . that a "waiver" of class arbitration in a "consumer contract of adhesion" that "predictably involve[s] small amounts of damages" . . . is "unconscionable under

California law and should not be enforced." . . . But in 2011, this Court held that California's *Discover Bank* rule "'stands as an obstacle to the . . . execution of the . . . objectives of Congress'" embodied in the Federal Arbitration Act. . . . The Federal Arbitration Act therefore pre-empts and invalidates that rule. . . .

The California Court of Appeal . . . held [in this case] . . . that, despite . . . [federal decisions], "the law of California would find the class action waiver unenforceable." . . . The court noted that *Discover Bank* had held agreements to dispense with class-arbitration procedures unenforceable under circumstances such as these. . . . [T]he Court of Appeal referred to two sections of California's Consumers Legal Remedies Act. . . . Section 1751 renders invalid any waiver of the right under § 1781(a) to bring a class action for violations of that Act. . . . As far as those sections apply to class-arbitration waivers, they embody the *Discover Bank* rule. . . . [We shall refer to the decisions and the statutes together as the *Discover Bank* rule.]

[W]e recognize that California courts are the ultimate authority on . . . [California] law. . . . We recognize . . . that when DIRECTV drafted the contract, the parties likely believed that the words "law of your state" included California law that then made class-arbitration waivers unenforceable. . . . [T]his Court subsequently held in *Concepcion*[33] that the *Discover Bank* rule was invalid. . . .

[W]e do not believe that the relevant contract language is ambiguous. The contract says that "[i]f . . . the law of your state would find this agreement to dispense with class arbitration procedures unenforceable, then this entire Section 9 [the arbitration section] is unenforceable." . . . Absent any indication in the contract that this language is meant to refer to *invalid* state law, it presumably takes its ordinary meaning: *valid* state law. . . . California case law itself clarifies any doubt about how to interpret the language. The California Supreme Court has held that under "general contract principles," references to California law incorporate

the California Legislature's power to change the law retroactively. . . . And judicial construction of a statute ordinarily applies retroactively. . . . [N]othing in the Court of Appeal's reasoning suggests that a California court would reach the same interpretation of "law of your state" in any context other than arbitration. The Court of Appeal did not explain why parties might generally intend the words "law of your state" to encompass "*invalid* law of your state." . . . [W]e can find nothing . . . suggesting that California would generally interpret words such as "law of your state" to include state laws held invalid because they conflict with, say, federal labor statutes, federal pension statutes, . . . or the like. . . . [I]ts conclusion appears to reflect the subject matter at issue here (arbitration), rather than a general principle that would apply to contracts using similar language but involving state statutes invalidated by other federal law. . . . [T]he Court of Appeal reasoned that invalid state arbitration law . . . maintained legal force despite this Court's holding in *Concepcion*. . . . And at the end of its opinion it reiterated that "[t]he class action waiver is unenforceable under California law, so the entire arbitration agreement is unenforceable." . . . But those statements do not describe California law. . . . The view that state law retains independent force even after it has been authoritatively invalidated by this Court is one courts are unlikely to accept as a general matter and to apply in other contexts. . . . [T]here is no other principle invoked by the Court of Appeal that suggests that California courts would reach the same interpretation of the words "law of your state" in other contexts. The court said that the phrase "law of your state" constitutes "'a specific *exception*'" to the agreement's "'*general* adoption of the [Federal Arbitration Act].'" . . .

The court added that it would interpret "'ambiguous language against the interest of the party that drafted it,'" namely DIRECTV. . . . [T]he reach of the canon construing contract language against the drafter must have limits, no matter who the drafter was. . . .

[W]e reach a conclusion that . . . falls well within the confines of . . . present well-established law. California's interpretation of the phrase "law of your state" does not place arbitration contracts "on equal footing with all other contracts" . . . For that reason, it does not give "due regard . . . to the federal policy favoring arbitration." . . . [T]he Court of Appeal's interpretation is pre-empted by the Federal Arbitration Act. . . . Hence, the California Court of Appeal must "enforc[e]" the arbitration agreement. . . .

The judgment of the California Court of Appeal is reversed, and the case is remanded for further proceedings not inconsistent with this opinion.

Short Answer Questions

1. Is there any conflict of interest if Ms. Carroll represents both Nic Grant and Nancy Griffin in the hypothetical case against Cassie's Bar and Grille? Why or why not? Is there any conflict of interest if Mr. Jones represents both defendants? Why?

2. If you were the CEO of Cassie's Bar and Grille, what would you consider in trying to decide whether to settle or litigate the dispute? What factors would be most important in making your decision?

3. Typical consumer contracts, such as banking services, cable services, and financial services, include clauses that customers must arbitrate their claims with the company. The clauses often also state that customers cannot form a group and have class arbitration and/or a class action lawsuit. The federal Consumer Financial Protection Bureau (CFPB) is considering rules that would prevent these clauses in contracts for financial products overseen by the CFPB. CFPB Director Richard Cordray said, "Companies are using the arbitration clause as a free pass to sidestep the courts and avoid accountability for wrongdoing." Assume that you work at the CFPB. Would you argue for restrictions in this area? Why?[34]

You Decide...

1. I.B., an Arizona resident and a minor, asked to use his mother's credit card to purchase items in a game called "Ninja Saga" on Facebook. He gave her $20 in cash and he charged $20 on her credit card. I.B. did not realize that Facebook kept the number on file and he ended up spending a few hundred dollars. He thought his remaining expenditures were with virtual money and not real money. I.B.'s mother asked Facebook for a refund. Facebook refused. They finally returned the funds after this suit was filed. He charged over $1,000. J.W.'s parents told Facebook that the charges were not authorized. Facebook refunded only a small portion of the $1,000. Facebook was aware that I.B. and J.W. were minors at the time of the purchases.

Facebook states that purchases made through its Web site are final. Facebook's refund policies for individuals between 13 and 17 are the same as its policies for adults. Facebook's Statement of Rights and Responsibilities must be accepted by all users joining Facebook or making any purchases through Facebook. It states that "[t]he laws of the State of California will govern this Statement, as well as any claim that might arise between you and us, without regard to conflict of law provisions."

I.B. and J.W. (and their parents) want to represent a nationwide class of Facebook users, who were minors according to Facebook's own records and made purchases on Facebook. They want an injunction to force Facebook to comply with California law. Under California law contracts of minors are generally voidable and can be disaffirmed by the minors. For a class action suit in federal court, Federal Rule of Civil Procedure 23 requires that the party "prove that there are in fact sufficiently numerous parties, common questions of law or fact, typicality of claims or defenses, and adequacy of representation." Assume that the motion to create a nationwide class of minors has been filed in your court.

How would *you* decide this case? Be certain that you explain and justify your answer. What benefits might a class receive that a single plaintiff might not enjoy?

(See I.B. v. FACEBOOK, INC., 82 F. Supp. 3d 1115, 2015 U.S. Dist. LEXIS 29357 (N. Dist. CA, San Jose Div., 2015).)

2. Lawyers representing Bill Cosby, the actor, filed a lawsuit contending that the release of his deposition from 2005 was not lawful. The released deposition was from a case involving Andrea Costand that was settled in 2005. Costand's lawyer had asked the judge to release the entire deposition arguing that Cosby and his team had violated their confidentiality agreement; consequently, the agreement should not be binding. Cosby's lawyers argued that Cosby has been damaged by news reports indicating that he had drugged women with powerful sedatives so that he could have sex with them. Over 50 women have accused Cosby of sexual assault. Many of them have pursued criminal charges and civil cases against him. In 2015 a court reporting service released the deposition because it believed a judge's order made the deposition public. Cosby's counsel argued that the documents were to remain sealed under the terms of the Costand settlement. Assume that Cosby's lawsuit has been filed in your court.

How would *you* decide this case? Be certain that you explain and justify your answer.

What additional information would you like to have? Why?

(See Graham Bowley and Sydney Ember, "Bill Cosby, in Deposition, Said Drugs and Fame Helped Him Seduce Women," *The New York Times*, July 18, 2015, http://www.nytimes.com/2015/07/19/arts/bill-cosby-deposition-reveals-calculated-pursuit-of-young-women-using-fame-drugs-and-deceit.html?_r=0 (accessed 3/20/16); Adam Carlson, "Bill Cosby Admits and Defends His Extramarital Affairs, Giving Women Drugs, in Newly Released Court Documents," *People*, July 19, 2015, http://www.people.com/article/bill-cosby-admits-affairs-drugs-deposition-released (accessed 3/20/16); and Kinsey Lowe, "Bill Cosby Lawyers: Release of Deposition Used to Smear Him Violates Settlement – Report," *Deadline*, July 21, 2015, http://deadline.com/2015/07/bill-cosby-release-of-deposition-violates-settlement-1201483189/ (accessed 3/20/16).)

Notes

1. *Wal-Mart Stores, Inc. v. Dukes*, 131 S. Ct. 2541, 2011 U.S. LEXIS 4567 (2011).

2. Class Action Fairness Act (CAFA) also makes it easier for the defendant to have the case removed to federal district

court. John Bourdeau, Laura Hunter Dietz, Kerry Diggin, Romualdo P. Eclavea, Tracy Bateman Farrell, Alan J. Jacobs, Rachel M. Kane, Fern Kletter, Sonja Larsen, Lucas Martin, Jeffrey J. Shampo, Eric C. Surette, Barbara Van Arsdale, Mary Ellen West, Eleanor L. Grossman, Mary Babb Morris, and Jaqualin Friend Peterson, Federal Courts, XIV. District Courts, J. Class Actions, 2. Jurisdiction and Venue, a. Jurisdiction, 32B Am Jur 2d Federal Courts § 1565, § 1565. Diversity jurisdiction under Class Action Fairness Act of 2005.

3. It is generally unwise for a lawyer to represent himself or herself even though he or she may know the rules, since the lawyer is emotionally involved in the case.

4. Citations omitted. Burke T. Ward, Janice C. Sipior, Jamie P. Hopkins, Carolyn Purwin, Kent McBride, and Linda Volonino, "Electronic Discovery: Rules For a Digital Age," 18 B.U. J. Sci. & Tech L. 150, 154 (Winter, 2012).

5. John R. Kennel, Depositions and Discovery, Part One: Depositions and Discovery in Civil Actions, II. Scope of Discovery, B. Particular Matters Discoverable, 23 Am Jur 2d Depositions and Discovery § 37, § 37 Corporate defendants.

6. David A. Lieb, "Clinton Ordered to Pay $90,000 in Penalty Fees in Jones Contempt Case," *Fresno Bee*, July 30, 1999.

7. Federal Rules of Civil Procedure § 30[b][2].

8. California Civil Procedure § 2025[p].

9. Federal Rules of Civil Procedure § 48.

10. See 28 U.S.C. § 1870.

11. See *J.E.B. v. T.B.*, 114 S. Ct. 1419 (1994).

12. 476 U.S. 79 (1986).

13. California Code of Civil Procedure § 170.6.

14. See 28 U.S.C. § 455 and California Code of Civil Procedure § 170.

15. A prima facie case can still be rebutted by evidence to the contrary.

16. See 42 Pa. C.S.A. § 5104.

17. Federal Rules of Civil Procedure § 48.

18. Sara Hill, "50-State Chart of Small Claims Court Dollar Limits," Nolo Web site, http://www.nolo.com/legal-encyclopedia/small-claims-suits-how-much-30031.html (accessed March 19, 2016). This chart provides additional information, for example, some types of plaintiffs and certain types of cases may have different limits.

19. Eric Lichtblau, "Zapruder Film Costs U.S. $16 Million," *Fresno Bee*, August 4, 1999.

20. United States Courts Web site, "Table C-5—U.S. District Courts—Civil Judicial Business (September 30, 2015)," http://www.uscourts.gov/statistics/table/c-5/judicial-business/2015/09/30 (accessed March 19, 2016).

21. *Whoop, Inc. v. Dyno Productions, Inc.*, 75 Cal. Rptr. 2d 90 (Cal. App. 2d Dist., 1998).

22. American Arbitration Association, *A Guide to Mediation and Arbitration for Business People* (September, 2007).

23. Teresa V. Carey, "Credentialing for Mediators—To Be or Not To Be?," U.S.F. L. Rev. 30 (Spring 1996), 641.

24. Boston Law Collaborative, LLC Web site, "About Mediation and Other Methods of Dispute Resolution," http://www.bostonlawcollaborative.com/blc/faqs/about-mediation-and-other-methods-of-dispute-resolution.html (accessed March 19, 2016).

25. American Arbitration Association, *Drafting Dispute Resolution Clauses—A Practical Guide* (September 1, 2007). Reprinted by permission of AAA.

26. "When You Need A Lawyer," *Consumer Reports*, February 1996, 39.

27. Curtis D. Brown, Esq., "New Law Lets Creditors Cut Court Costs," *Credit World*, July/August 1996, 30-31.

28. American Arbitration Association Web site, "Statement of Ethical Principles for the American Arbitration Association," http://www.adr.org/aaa/ShowPDF?doc=ADRSTG_009820 (accessed March 19, 2016).

29. United Nations Treaty Collection, Chapter XXII, Commercial Arbitration, Convention on the Recognition and Enforcement of Foreign Arbitral Awards, https://treaties.un.org/Pages/ViewDetails.aspx?src=TREATY&mtdsg_no=XXII-1&chapter=22&lang=en (accessed March 19, 2016).

30. Department of International Law, Organization of American States, "Inter-American Convention on International Commercial Arbitration," http://www.oas.org/juridico/english/sigs/b-35.html (accessed March 19, 2016).

31. Deborah Shannon, "Rent-A-Judge," *American Way Magazine*, February 1991, 33-36.

32. *Id.*, at 34.

33. *AT&T Mobility, LLC v. Concepcion*, 131 S. Ct. 1740, 2011 U.S. LEXIS 3367 (2011).

34. Kevin McCoy, "CFPB May Let You Sue Your Bank Instead of Going to Arbitration," USA TODAY, October 7, 2015, http://www.usatoday.com/story/money/2015/10/07/cfpb-considering-rules-banning-forced-arbitration/73455738/ (accessed March 20, 2016).

5

International Considerations for Contemporary Businesses

Learning Objectives

After completing this chapter you should be able to

- Recognize some of the ways in which a business can "go global"
- Describe how some U.S. law has international implications and applications
- Discuss the General Agreement on Tariffs and Trade (GATT) and the World Trade Organization (WTO) and their effect on international trade
- Explain free trade agreements and free trade zones and how they encourage international trade
- Identify the various methods of dispute resolution used in international business

Classic Case

This is a very early case addressing the issue of extraterritorial application of the Sherman Act of 1890, the nation's first antitrust law. Notice how the Court framed its argument around the fact that the acts in question all occurred in another nation and so were beyond the jurisdiction of the Court. The Court pays virtually no attention to the conduct's impact on the U.S. domestic market. Compare this opinion with the Contemporary Case at the end of the chapter to see how attitudes have changed in this area.

AMERICAN BANANA CO. v. UNITED FRUIT CO.
213 U.S. 347 (1909)

FACTS The [American Banana Co.] is an Alabama corporation, organized in 1904. [United Fruit Co.] is a New Jersey corporation, organized in 1899. Long before [American Banana] was formed, [United Fruit] ... made contracts with others, including a majority of [its] most important [competitors, to purchase the property and business of its previous competitors. These contracts also included a provision against these former competitors reentering the banana market. United Fruit made contracts with others] regulating the quantity to be purchased and the price to be paid [for their produce. It also] acquired a controlling interest in the stock [of other firms. All of this was done with the intent to prevent competition and to control and monopolize the banana trade. United Fruit also owned the company that sold all of the bananas of the combining parties at a fixed price. As a result, it was able to] monopolize[, to] restrain trade [in the banana market,] and [to] maintain[] unreasonable prices.

[In 1903,] one McConnell ... started a banana plantation in Panama, [which was at that time] part of the United States of Columbia. [McConnell also] began to build a railway, [which would be his only method for exporting his bananas. His actions were legal under] the laws of the United States of Columbia. He was notified by [United Fruit] that he must either combine [with it] or stop. [He chose to do neither.] Two months later ... the governor of Panama recommended ... that Costa Rica be allowed to administer the territory through which the railroad was to run ... [Shortly] afterwards, in September, the government of Costa Rica ... interfered with McConnell[, preventing him from proceeding in his venture. Both acts were believed to be instigated by United Fruit.]

In November, 1903, Panama revolted and became an independent republic. ... In June, 1904, [American Banana] bought out McConnell and went on with the work [he had started]. ... But in July, Costa Rican soldiers and officials, instigated by [United Fruit], seized a part of the plantation and a cargo of supplies ... and stopped the construction and operation of the plantation and railway. [Later,] in August, [an individual named] Astua ... [obtained] a judgment from a Costa Rican court declaring [that he owned the plantation]. Agents of [United Fruit] then bought the lands from Astua. [American Banana] has tried to induce the government of Costa Rica to withdraw its soldiers and also has tried to persuade the United States to interfere, [but both efforts failed due to United Fruit's intervention].

ISSUES Did the alleged conduct of United Fruit, if proven, constitute a violation of the Sherman Act? Does the Sherman Act have extraterritorial application in this situation?

HOLDINGS No to each question. The conduct in question took place in Panama, which is not subject to the provisions of the Sherman Act. All of the alleged wrongdoing took place outside the borders of the United States and involved the actions of other sovereign states. The doctrines of sovereign immunity and comity prevent the extraterritorial application of the Sherman Act.

REASONING Excerpts from the opinion of Justice Holmes:

It is obvious that, however stated, the plaintiff's case depends on several rather startling propositions. In the first place the acts causing the damage were done, so far as appears, outside the jurisdiction of the United States and within that of other states. It is surprising to hear it argued that they were governed by the act of Congress.

No doubt in regions subject to no sovereign, like the high seas, or to no law that civilized countries would recognize as adequate, such countries may treat some relations between their citizens as governed by their own law, and keep to some extent the old notion of personal sovereignty alive. . . . They go further, at times, and declare that they will punish any one, subject or not, who shall do certain things, if they can catch him, as in the case of pirates on the high seas. In cases immediately affecting national interests they may go further still and may make, and, if they get the chance, execute similar threats as to acts done within another recognized jurisdiction. . . . But the general and almost universal rule is that the character of an act as lawful or unlawful must be determined wholly by the law of the country where the act is done. . . . For another jurisdiction, if it should happen to lay hold of the actor, to treat him according to its own notions rather than those of the place where he did the acts, not only would be unjust, but would be an interference with the authority of another sovereign, contrary to the comity of nations, which the other state concerned justly might resent. . . .

The foregoing considerations would lead in case of doubt to a construction of any statute as intended to be confined in its operation and effect to the territorial limits over which the lawmaker has general and legitimate power. "All legislation is *prima facie* territorial." . . . Words having universal scope, such as "Every contract in restraint of trade," "Every person who shall monopolize," etc., will be taken as a matter of course to mean only every one subject to such legislation, not all that the legislator subsequently may be able to catch. In the case of the present statute the improbability of the United States attempting to make acts done in Panama or Costa Rica criminal is obvious, yet the law begins by making criminal the acts for which it gives a right to sue. We think it entirely plain that what the defendant did in Panama or Costa Rica is not within the scope of the statute so far as the present suit is concerned. Other objections of a serious nature are urged but need not be discussed. . . .

Further reasons might be given why this complaint should not be upheld, but we have said enough to dispose of it and to indicate our general point of view.

Judgment affirmed.

INTRODUCTION

National economies and economic policies are tied to and affected by the economies and the policies of other nations to a significant extent. The Great Recession that hit the U.S. economy several years ago had an impact on stock prices around the world. The devastation in Japan following the March 2011 earthquake and tsunami had a ripple effect on markets around the globe. The debt crises in Europe and the efforts to prop up the economies of Greece, Italy, and other nations while stabilizing the Euro also led to downturns in numerous economies both inside and outside the European Union. The 2014 vote in Scotland on whether to leave the United Kingdom had the potential to seriously affect a number of economies. It also had a potential impact on U.S. national defense policies. Many domestic issues in other nations have a "ripple effect" on the economies of other nations.

This interlacing of national economies at the macro level also has an effect at the micro level. Businesses today operate in this "global village," and the successful businessperson needs to be aware of the implications and the impact of international factors and events while planning for the future of his or her enterprise.

For example, suppose that LynnDan Novelties, Inc., a company based in Pittsburgh, decides to expand its business from national to international. LynnDan already sells a variety of items to its traditional buyers in the United States, but decides that it can also sell a similar variety of items to businesses in Mexico and Ireland. If LynnDan is correct, its profits will increase substantially, which may lead to further expansions into other countries.

While prospects look good for LynnDan, this planned expansion might also present some serious problems for the firm. By entering into contracts with customers in three different countries, LynnDan is making contracts that could possibly be governed by three entirely different sets of laws. Most of LynnDan's sales in the United States would be governed by Article 2 of the Uniform Commercial Code (UCC). The sale to the Mexican customer would possibly be governed by Mexican law, which has a strong European influence and is based on the Napoleonic Code, and by the North American Free Trade Agreement (NAFTA), a treaty to which both Mexico and the United States are signatories. The sale to the Irish customer would possibly be governed by Irish law, which has a strong English common law influence, and by the rules of the European Union (EU), of which Ireland is a member. What is the seller to do?

Historically, experienced international traders would specify in their contracts which law would govern the transaction; thus, LynnDan could have negotiated the contracts so that the UCC was controlling in all three transactions. Or, the parties could have agreed to have any disputes settled by arbitration. International sales contracts often call for any disputes to be arbitrated, rather than tried, so the parties could avoid using unfamiliar court systems and unfamiliar laws.

In 1988, the United Nations Convention on Contracts for the International Sale of Goods (CISG) went into effect. The CISG provides a law of sales contracts specifically for contracts between businesses in countries that have approved the convention. In the United States, the CISG replaces the UCC in any sales transactions between a U.S. firm and a business from another CISG country, unless the parties opt out of CISG coverage and specify that the UCC will be the controlling law. Fortunately, the CISG is much like Article 2 (the law of sales) of the UCC, and provisions of the CISG are often similar to the UCC's provisions, so it should not be too "foreign" to American managers. (Article 2 of the UCC, Sales; Article 2 of the UCC, Sales; and the CISG are discussed in detail in Chapter 11.)

As of September 24, 2014, 83 countries had ratified the CISG, including the United States and other important trading partners, such as China, France, Germany, and several republics of the former Soviet Union.[1] (The complete list of member nations is

Exhibit 5.1

Total U.S. International Trade in Goods and Services[a]

Year	U.S. Import of Goods	U.S. Import of Services	Total U.S. Imports	U.S. Export of Goods	U.S. Export of Services	Total U.S. Exports
1992	536, 528	119,556	656,094	439,631	177,251	618,882
1999	1,035,592	192,893	1,228,485	698,524	271,343	969, 867
2007	1,986,347	372,575	2,358,922	1,165,151	488,396	1,653,548
2014	2,374,101	477,428	2,851,529	1,632,639	710,565	2,343,205

[a] Amounts are stated in millions of dollars.

shown at the Web site for Chapter 5.) Over the next several years, the CISG is likely to become the law in even more countries. This should reduce the concerns faced by companies like LynnDan Novelties in the example above.

Such concerns are not far-fetched, nor are they unusual. In 1992 the United States exported $618.9 billion in goods and services and imported $656.1 billion. By 1999 those figures had grown, with exports of $969.9 billion and imports of $1.23 trillion. In 2007 the numbers were up again, with exports of $1.65 trillion and imports of $2.36 trillion. The most recent data show exports of $2.43 trillion and imports of $2.85 trillion in 2014.[2] (See Exhibit 5.1 for more information.) Many American companies such as McDonald's, General Motors, and Digital Equipment find most of their revenues or profits coming from overseas operations. Foreign investment in the United States doubled between 1985 and 1990. Marshall McLuhan was right.[3] We are so economically interdependent on one another that we do live in a global village. To succeed in the business world of the twenty-first century, every businessperson must be familiar with the basic rules of international business.

Going Global

As communications and transportation have improved, buyers and sellers in different markets have been able to find one another more easily, making it easier for them to do business together. Technology has opened the global marketplace to businesses of all sizes, allowing them to sell their goods, services, and technology. Future advances in technology will make interactions between buyers and sellers in different markets even easier, increasing the potential for international trade and the likelihood—or even the need—for a business to "go global."

A business has many options once it decides to go global. For example, as it develops its international customer base, the business may decide to change the way it organizes itself or the methods it uses for selling its goods or services in foreign markets. There are a number of options available, from the direct sale to customers to the opening of an operation center in the foreign market. Each company will have to decide which method or methods work best for it in each foreign market. Each company will also need to consider when it may need to change its method as its operation in other nations evolves. Some potential methods are set out in Exhibit 5.2.

An Ounce of Prevention

When considering expansion into one or more foreign markets, be certain to consider long-term prospects as well as short-term implications. If the long-term prospects are not clear, it is often best to choose the easiest and least expensive method to enter the market; for example, either direct selling to the customer or hiring a sales agent in the other country. If the long-term prospects seem positive, a distributorship arrangement may be a better alternative. If the business already has a positive image and a widely recognized brand, franchising is an attractive option. Joint ventures or direct investment for expansion purposes tend to be much more expensive and should involve careful analysis of the payback period and the stability of the government in the other nation.

Exhibit 5.2

Methods of Entry into a Foreign Market

Method	Potential Benefits	Potential Drawbacks
Direct sales by the seller to the consumer	• Ease • Simple retail or e-tail transactions	• Limited exposure to the target market • Export licenses and fees
Sales agents in other nations	• Increased exposure of product • Active and incentivized sales personnel	• Supervision of a foreign agent • Possible legal implications under the laws of other nations • Export licenses and fees
Distributorship arrangements	• Essentially becoming a wholesaler to foreign retailers • Can select a firm with an established market and reputation	• Increased cost to consumers may affect sales • Loss of control over marketing • Export licenses and fees

Exhibit 5.2 Continued

Method	Potential Benefits	Potential Drawbacks
Franchising	• Keeps brand name and recognition in control of the franchisor • Protects intellectual property rights (trademark, patent, etc.) • Popular expansion method for U.S. businesses	• Possible legal restrictions on franchising in other nations • Supervision of franchisee • Language differences and interpretation of the franchise expectations • Cultural differences
Joint venture	• "Partnering" with a business in the other nation—sharing of risks • The joint venturer is a native, who understands the culture and can help to avoid problems with red tape	• Sharing of profits may mean less return to the domestic joint venturer • Loss of autonomy
Direct investment—construction of facilities in the other nation	• Avoids many problems with export licenses and fees • Become a citizen of the foreign nation • Possible incentives from the host country to encourage the investment	• Potential for nationalization of the facility • Supervision of the foreign location • Possible legal implications under the laws of other nations • Tax implications

INTERNATIONAL IMPLICATIONS AND APPLICATIONS OF U.S. LAWS

There is an old adage that businesspeople need to remember: "When in Rome, do as the Romans do." American businesses are used to doing business in the United States under U.S. law. Many, if not most, businesses have a lawyer or a law firm on retainer, ready to help them deal with any legal issues that may arise in the course of doing business. But the legal issues they are used to dealing with are normally issues involving U.S. law. When the firm expands its operation into a foreign nation, management should know that they will have to follow the laws of that nation. Since they are unlikely to be familiar with those laws, the business should probably seek legal counsel there, as well. But the firm may also have to follow some of the laws of the United States even though it is doing business in another country. There are some circumstances in which the laws of the United States will have *extraterritorial* application, subjecting the firm to possible liability in an American court for its conduct in another nation. There may also be issues involving the exporting and/or importing of goods. It quickly becomes obvious that "going global" is more than just expanding the market.

Extraterritoriality

A U.S. firm operating in another nation may find that its conduct is potentially subject to U.S. laws involving antitrust, employment, the Sarbanes-Oxley Act, and the Foreign

Corrupt Practices Act. Other U.S. statutes may also have extraterritorial application, but these are the legal areas most likely to affect an American firm involved in international trade.

Antitrust Laws

U.S. antitrust laws are designed to provide a somewhat level playing field for businesses in the United States by protecting and encouraging competition. Various anticompetitive activities are prohibited by these statutes. For example, the Sherman Antitrust Act states in its first section that "every contract, combination . . . or conspiracy in restraint of trade or commerce among the several States, or with foreign nations, is declared to be illegal." Section 2 prohibits monopolizing or attempting to monopolize any line of trade or commerce. (Antitrust laws are discussed in some detail in Chapter 16.) Both sections of the Sherman Act have been frequently litigated in the United States, and most businesses have a good idea of what conduct is permitted under the statute. But do the prohibitions set out in the antitrust laws apply to conduct outside the United States as well?

Despite the Court's opinion set out in our Classic Case for this chapter, a number of subsequent cases have ruled that the antitrust laws do have extraterritorial application, at least in some circumstances. (One such case is the Contemporary Case for this chapter.) Unfortunately, the courts have not been in full agreement in determining when these statutes should apply to international transactions. There has been no consensus on how far the jurisdiction should extend. Some courts use the "direct and substantial effect" test; they examine the effect on U.S. foreign commerce as a prerequisite for proper jurisdiction. Other courts have used a test that looks at whether a conspiracy exists that adversely affects U.S. commerce.

Most courts prefer to evaluate and balance the relevant considerations in each case. The courts determine whether the contacts and interests of the United States are sufficient to support the exercise of extraterritorial jurisdiction. The standards for determining whether U.S. antitrust laws should apply to conduct outside the borders of the United States can be found in *Timberlane Lumber Co. v. Bank of America.*[4]

Timberlane purchased some forest land in Honduras and began planning a modern log-processing plant, with the goal of importing lumber from Honduras into the United States. Several Honduran lumber companies, all financed by Bank of America, allegedly conspired against Timberlane in an effort to drive Timberlane out of business in Honduras. Timberlane filed suit against Bank of American, seeking treble damages for its alleged violation of the Sherman Act. The Ninth Circuit Court of Appeals set out a three-part test for determining if or when the U.S. antitrust laws could be applied to conduct occurring outside the U.S. borders. This test requires a showing that

1. the alleged act has some impact on American foreign commerce;
2. the impact is large enough to have a recognizable effect on the plaintiff; and
3. the interests of the United States are sufficiently strong to justify the assertion of extraterritorial jurisdiction.

Timberlane ultimately lost its case when the court found that the conduct being challenged was intended to impact Honduran commerce, not commerce in America. But the three-part test used to reach the decision remains.

In an effort to resolve the issue, Congress passed the Foreign Trade Antitrust Improvements Act[5] in 1982. This amendment to the Sherman Antitrust Act says that the courts need to examine the site of the injury in determining whether the antitrust laws apply. The act is aimed at protecting the U.S. market from antitrust problems caused here in the U.S. and attempts to exclude pure export activities from antitrust coverage. Some of the language in this statute is based on the three-part test set out by the appellate court in the *Timberlane* case.

Employment Laws

The courts have also concluded that some U.S. employment laws apply beyond U.S. borders. Congress amended Title VII of the Civil Rights Act of 1964, extending protection against illegal employment discrimination to Americans working for American companies, even when the employee is working in another nation. The amendment extends the protections of Title VII across national boundaries, at least for U.S. workers employed by U.S. firms, regardless of the location to which the worker is assigned. This means that U.S. citizens subjected to discriminations that would be illegal in the United States, but possibly legal in the host nation, can successfully enforce their rights against their American employers in a U.S. court, even if the discrimination was legal in the country where it occurred. The same protections do not apply for employees of the American business who are not U.S. citizens.

An Ounce of Prevention

It is a common practice for U.S. firms that establish locations in foreign countries to hire citizens of that country as part of its workforce. It is also a common practice to have a number of U.S. citizens on site as supervisors and managers, especially in the earliest period of the expansion. Be certain that managers, both domestic and on site, are familiar with which U.S. employment laws apply, and to whom they apply. It is also beneficial to be familiar with the culture of the other nation and to avoid sending managers or supervisors who are likely to offend or antagonize the foreign workers due to the managers's personality or lack of sensitivity.

Imports and Exports

International trade normally involves the importing or exporting of goods. While some firms may choose to move facilities to other countries, producing their goods inside the targeted nation, others operate more traditionally. They export goods from their home nation into other countries. They may also be importing other goods or materials that are to be used in the production process in their own nation. This process seems simple and straightforward, but there are a significant number of issues that must be resolved in moving goods from one nation to another. These issues often begin with moving the goods out of their nation of origin.

Any exporting of goods from the United States requires a license. This is often as simple as stamping a general license statement on the export documents. Other goods, especially in the area of technology, require the firm to obtain a validated export license from the U.S. Department of Commerce. The Department of Commerce maintains a commodity control list that gives the licensing status of thousands of export items. Firms that plan to export goods need to ensure that they have proper licensing and clearances for all the goods they plan to export.[6] Companies that export goods in violation of U.S. export-licensing policy face criminal sanctions and may lose their exporting privileges. U.S. exports are regulated for three purposes: (1) to protect the nation in time of short supply; (2) to protect national security; and (3) to further U.S. foreign policy interests.

Goods must not only be cleared for exportation, they also must be cleared for importation into the destination country. Before goods can be imported into a country, the goods must pass through customs. Passing through customs normally requires the payment of a tariff or an import duty at the port of entry. This tariff or duty is generally based on the type and the value of the goods. While the average tariff worldwide is approximately 5 percent,[7] local and national taxes and fees and custom fees often increase the total. Also, while the *average* duty is about 5 percent, there are significant differences—both higher and lower—in some countries. The imposition of these fees will increase the cost of the goods to customers in the importing nation, which is likely to have a negative effect on the importer's competitive position in that nation.

All customs issues in the United States are initially handled by the U.S. Customs Service. If a business disagrees with an administrative decision handed down by the Customs Service, it can appeal that decision. The U.S. Customs Court, a specialized court, has exclusive jurisdiction over civil actions involving appeals regarding decisions of the U.S. Customs Service.

Intellectual Property

Historically, patent, copyright, and trademark protection extended only within the boundaries of each country. An inventor who wanted to protect an invention in additional countries would have to obtain a patent in each country. To complicate matters, some countries did not recognize exclusive patent rights for some kinds of products, such as pharmaceuticals. These countries felt it was more important to deliver life-saving drugs to their people than to protect the profits of the pharmaceutical companies. Although no worldwide intellectual property rights exist, a real trend has grown toward international protection of copyrights, patents, and trademarks. In 1988, for example, the United States became the eightieth member of the Berne Convention for the Protection of Literary and Artistic Works. Today there are 168 signatories to the convention.[8] A copyright holder who publishes a book in the United States will now receive the same protection in other member countries that local authors do.

The area of patent law is also moving toward international protection. The European Patent Convention (EPC) allows only one filing and one patent examination to obtain protection in 31 countries.[9] (The EPC is not a part of the European Union [E.U.] but each E.U. member is also in the EPC.) Similarly, the Patent Cooperation Treaty with 148 signatory nations also allows only one patent application and examination to serve as a basis for patent filings in all member nations.[10]

Trademark law has also moved toward some international recognition, though not as quickly as the other areas of intellectual property protection. The Madrid Agreement (also known as the Madrid Protocol) allows one application to potentially provide protection in all member countries. The Protocol is a filing agreement, allowing any person who has registered his or her mark to seek protection in any of the other member states. The filing results in the issuance of an International Registration. However, it is up to each individual state to determine whether any protections will be granted. If or when a nation grants protection, the mark is protected in that country as if it had been registered in that country. The Madrid Protocol is also administered by the WIPO. There are currently 96 contracting parties, including the United States.[11]

U.S. businesses have faced serious problems in recent years with counterfeit goods. Levi Strauss, Apple Computer, and other companies have reported significant losses of revenues due to imports that counterfeit company trademarks or patents. The International Chamber of Commerce (ICC) estimated that counterfeit goods were worth $650 billion in 2008, and expected that figure to exceed $1.7 trillion by 2015.[12] It also estimates that 2.5 million jobs have been lost due to counterfeit goods.[13] The International Standards Organization (ISO) is considering the development of standards to increase consumer confidence, make supply chains more secure, and to help public authorities in creating and implementing preventive, deterrent, and punitive policies to address the counterfeiting problem.[14] The U.S. Customs and Border Protection and Homeland Security's Immigration and Customs Protection reported more than 23,000 seizures of fake products worth approximately $1.2 billion in fiscal year 2014.[15] Additionally, the U.S. Department of Justice reported that as much as $2.6 billion in federal, state, and local taxes are lost each year in the United States due to the sale of pirated music, movies, video games, and software. This also results in more than 370,000 jobs being lost in the United States due to such piracy.[16]

Counterfeiting and pirating has a significant economic impact in the United States, and such conduct is becoming even easier. In response to this problem, the United States has toughened its enforcement of the laws designed to deter counterfeiters. Section 337 of the Tariff Act of 1930 was amended in 1988 to allow any owner of a registered U.S. intellectual property right, who believes that an import infringes on that right, to apply to the U.S. International Trade Commission (ITC) for an order banning the goods. The ITC can also issue a cease and desist order. Violations of the cease and desist order carry a potential fine of up to $100,000 per day or twice the domestic value of the goods.

In addition, Congress amended the Trade Act of 1974 by adding a section called Special 301, requiring the U.S. trade representative to identify countries that do not protect U.S. intellectual property rights. Once identified, the United States will negotiate improvements with those countries. If no improvements result, the United States must retaliate against those countries. Special 301 has been effective in getting many countries to improve their intellectual property laws.

The Foreign Corrupt Practices Act

Many businesses that are new to the international marketplace have some trouble understanding the different values of people from other cultures or the way business may be conducted in foreign nations. The differences may be relatively minor, or they may be substantial. One area that has been particularly troublesome involves payments to officials in other countries.

In an effort to address this problem and to provide guidelines for U.S. firms doing business in other nations, Congress passed the Foreign Corrupt Practices Act[17] (FCPA) in 1977. This act, an amendment to the Securities Exchange Act of 1934, covers foreign corrupt practices and provides accounting standards that firms must follow in reporting payments made to foreign officials. Significant amendments to the FCPA were made in 1988.

The FCPA applies only to firms that have their principal offices in the United States. The act prohibits giving money or anything else of value to foreign officials with the intent to corrupt. This is a very broad standard, but basically the act is intended to prevent the transfer of money or other items of value to any person who is in a position to exercise discretionary authority in order to have that person exercise his or her authority in a manner that gives an advantage to the donor of the "gift."

Interestingly, the act does not prohibit accommodation payments, also called "grease payments," to foreign officials, although these, too, may look like bribes. A grease payment is a payment to a person in order to have him or her perform a task or render a service that is part of the person's normal job. The "grease" is intended to get the person to do the job more quickly or more efficiently than he or she might have otherwise. By contrast, a payment that is made with the intent to corrupt is one that is designed to have the donee do something he or she might not have been obligated to do or to make a favorable choice among options.

Whistle-Blowers

The Dodd-Frank Wall Street Reform and Consumer Protection Act of 2010[18] includes a provision for "bounties" to whistle-blowers who assist the Securities and Exchange Commission (SEC) in uncovering illegal conduct. If the SEC imposes sanctions against a company that reach or exceed $1 million, any whistle-blower that provided original information that was not known to the SEC is eligible for a bounty of no less than 10 percent nor more than 30 percent of the money collected by the SEC. This provision only excludes some auditing firms or law enforcement officials, which at least implies that foreign nationals would be eligible for payment. It appears that the Dodd-Frank Act is intended to have extraterritorial application, including reports of violations of the FCPA. However, a 2014 opinion from the Second Circuit Court of Appeals[19] denied a claim by a Taiwanese employee who was allegedly fired due to his whistle-blowing against Siemens officials who, he alleged, had acted in violation of the FCPA. He claimed that the retaliatory dismissal was a violation of Dodd-Frank. The court held that the anti-retaliation provisions of Dodd-Frank do not apply extraterritorially. The issue is hardly settled, but this opinion raises questions about the applicability of Dodd-Frank beyond the borders of the United States.

INTERNATIONAL PRACTICES AND DOCTRINES

Nationalization

Any business that plans to expand its operation into another country needs to be aware of the risk of nationalization. Nationalization occurs when the government takes ownership from the business and vests it in the government. Nationalization can occur in either of two ways: expropriation or confiscation. With an expropriation, the government's conduct is generally considered to be legal and in compliance with international law. The business is given "just compensation," and the expropriation occurs for a proper public purpose. When a business is confiscated, on the other hand, the business is taken for any purpose, and there generally is no compensation given to the business. (In some cases there may be some compensation, but it is an inadequate amount.) While a confiscation does not comply with international law, it may be legal under the laws of the confiscating government. The act of state doctrine, discussed below, generally shields the conduct of the confiscating government from outside interference.

Congress passed the Foreign Assistance Act in 1961 to provide more structure to U.S. aid to foreign nations. The act established the United States Agency for International Development to oversee and administer nonmilitary aid to foreign nations. An amendment to the act requires the president of the United States to suspend all forms of assistance to countries that expropriate the property of U.S. citizens; nor will any assistance be given to any nation that "engages in a consistent pattern of gross violations of internationally recognized human rights, including torture or cruel, inhuman, or degrading treatment or punishment, prolonged detention without charges, causing the disappearance of persons by the abduction and clandestine detention of those persons, or other flagrant denial of the right to life, liberty, and the security of person, unless such assistance will directly benefit the needy people in such country."[20] While this act and its amendments provide some leverage to the U.S. government to negotiate with a foreign nation that has expropriated property of one or more U.S. citizens, it provides no direct relief to the citizens whose property was taken.

If a business plans to invest in other nations and wants more protection, it can obtain insurance against the risk of loss. The Overseas Private Investment Corporation (OPIC) furnishes low-cost insurance against nationalization, confiscation, lack of convertibility of foreign earnings, and general loss due to insurrection, revolution, or war. It also provides funding to eligible ventures through medium-term or long-term loans. OPIC will provide financing only to projects that are financially sound, promise to benefit the host nation socially and economically, and are not expected to cost any U.S. jobs or to have a negative impact on the U.S. economy. "OPIC achieves its mission by providing investors with financing, guarantees, political risk insurance, and support for private equity investment funds."[21]

Act of State Doctrine

One reason for seeking insurance protection for overseas investments is the act of state doctrine. The doctrine states that every sovereign state is bound to respect the independence of every other sovereign state and that the courts of one country will not sit in judgment on the acts of another government performed within its own borders. The concept of the act of state doctrine is embedded in the notion of sovereign immunity. Certainly, each sovereign state recognizes all other states' sovereignty. But the act of state doctrine is not a specific rule of international law. International law does not require that nations follow this rule, and in the United States the Constitution does not require it. Judicial decisions of the United States, however, have recognized the doctrine. The doctrine is based on the theory that a nation is not qualified to question the actions of other nations taken on their own soil. In fact, denouncing the public decisions of other nations can have a decidedly adverse effect on the conduct of a nation's foreign policy

Sovereign Immunity

In the traditions of international law, all nations are equal and sovereign. Thus, a nation is immune from suit for its actions, either by individuals or by other countries. To be sued, a nation must agree to give up its sovereign immunity. For example, the United States passed the Federal Tort Claims Act to allow individuals to sue the U.S. government for most negligent acts. On an international level, the doctrine of sovereign immunity causes businesses some trouble, especially because many governments operate businesses such as airlines, banks, auto companies, and even computer firms. The United States has taken actions to limit the effect of sovereign immunity in its courts. In 1976, Congress enacted the Foreign Sovereign Immunities Act, which declared that U.S. courts would not recognize sovereign immunity when the sovereign was engaged in commercial, rather than political, activities. So, for example, a state-owned bank could be subject to suit over its failure to pay a letter of credit. The United States has also negotiated many bilateral investment treaties containing provisions for other governments to waive the right to claim sovereign immunity.

The Foreign Sovereign Immunities Act was amended in 1996 with the passage of the Antiterrorism and Effective Death Penalty Act,[22] which permits American citizens to sue those foreign states that are officially classified as terrorist states for terrorist conduct that results in the death or injury of an American citizen. The act also provides for punitive damages to be assessed against the terrorist state if it is found guilty of the prohibited conduct.

THE GENERAL AGREEMENT ON TARIFFS AND TRADE AND THE WORLD TRADE ORGANIZATION

As mentioned earlier, tariffs and import duties can hamper the ability of a foreign firm to gain access to some markets. Even if access is not denied, the imposition of these fees puts the importing firm at a competitive disadvantage due to the increased cost that must be covered in the sale of the goods. Trade barriers such as tariffs and taxes have a negative effect on international trade, which can cause harm to the economies of both the exporting nation and the importing nation. It also reduces the availability of goods to the consumers in the importing nation. Many economists believe that the Great Depression was made much worse by the imposition of increased tariffs in a futile effort to protect domestic industries.

Following World War II, the western Allies envisioned an international economic organization that would provide leadership and coordination for international trade in the same manner as the United Nations was to provide leadership in the political environment. A charter was drafted for an International Trade Organization (ITO) in 1948, but the charter was effectively shelved because it was not adopted by a sufficient number of nations.

Prior to the proposed ITO charter, U.S. negotiators proposed a general agreement on tariffs and trades as a stepping-stone to prepare the way for ITO ratification. The western Allies accepted this U.S. proposal in 1947, creating the first General Agreement on Tariffs and Trade (GATT). When the ITO failed to generate sufficient support, GATT became the accepted framework for regulating international trade.

The GATT promoted free trade by seeking to reduce tariffs and quotas between nations. It promoted fair trade by defining such trade practices as unfair government subsidies of exports and dumping (selling goods below fair value in a foreign market). It also provided panels to resolve trade disputes. The GATT worked through "rounds" of discussions, during which countries agreed to reduce tariffs for all GATT members. The Uruguay Round, which began in September 1988 in Punta del Este, Uruguay, had a very broad negotiating agenda covering virtually every outstanding trade policy issue, including such non-goods-related issues as trade-related intellectual property rights, investment protection, services, and agricultural subsidies.

The breadth and complexity of the Uruguay Round, which ran until 1994, frustrated many of the participants and kept it from achieving a number of its objectives. However, it had one crowning achievement: the transformation of GATT into the World Trade Organization (WTO). In 1994 there were 128 GATT Members.[23] These 128 nations became the initial members of the World Trade Organization (WTO).

The WTO is an international economic organization that is intended to provide leadership and coordination for international trade. Thus, 47 years after the ITO was defeated, a world trade organization was created. The GATT did eventually provide an interim stepping-stone to an international organization, albeit for a much longer period than originally expected. The basic structure of the WTO is set out in Exhibit 5.3.

The World Trade Organization was officially established January 1, 1995. The WTO is not merely an extension of GATT; it has a completely different character and a completely different mission. GATT was a multinational agreement, not an organization, and was intended to regulate trade in merchandise (goods). There was no institutional foundation for GATT. By contrast, the WTO is an *organization* headquartered in Geneva, Switzerland, with a formal structure, a permanent staff, and a sizeable operating budget. The WTO has expanded coverage to not only include goods, but also to cover some trade in services and to provide protection for intellectual property. As of April 26, 2015, there were 161 member countries in the WTO, with nearly two dozen more nations listed as "observers." [24] Observer nations (except for the Holy See) must begin negotiation for admission (accession) within five years of becoming observers.[25] In addition, there are 48 nations recognized by the United Nations as Least Developed Countries (LDCs) and treated as such by the WTO. Thirty-four of these nations have joined the WTO, and another eight have applied and are negotiating for membership.[26]

The highest authority within the WTO is the Ministerial Conference, which is comprised of representatives from each member nation. The Ministerial Conference must meet at least once every two years and has the authority to make decisions on any matter under any of the multilateral trade agreements recognized by the WTO. While the Ministerial Conference is the highest authority, the day-to-day operations of the WTO are conducted by the General Council. The General Council serves as both the dispute settlement body of the WTO and the trade policy review body. It also reports to the Ministerial Conference. The General Council delegates a great deal of its responsibility to three other Councils: the Council for Trade in Goods, the Council for Trade in Services, and the Council for Trade-Related Aspects of Intellectual Property Rights. Obviously, the WTO has a much wider responsibility than did GATT, covering areas other than international trade in goods.

Dispute resolution under the WTO is considerably quicker than under GATT and promises to be much more effective. When controversies arise under the WTO, the dispute is submitted to a panel of trade experts. This panel will then have the authority to rule for one or the other of the complainants. When the panel rules for one of the nations, that nation will be given permission to retaliate against the other nation unless

Exhibit 5.3

The Structure of the World Trade Organization (WTO)[27]

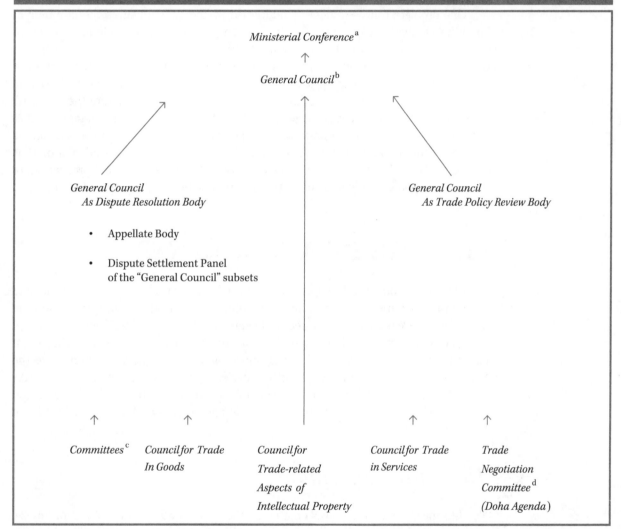

[a] The Ministerial Conference is the top decision-making body of the WTO. It meets at least once every two years. Decisions are normally made by consensus, although voting is permitted.

[b] The General Council is generally made up of ambassadors and heads of delegations. It meets several times a year. It is also meets as the Dispute Resolution Body and as the Trade Policy Review Body.

[c] At the third level are various branches. The Goods Council, Services Council, and Intellectual Property Council each report to the General Council. Various specialized committees and groups meet to discuss individual agreements and specific areas such as the environment.

[d] The Trade Negotiation Committee, set up by the Doha Agenda, addresses the issues to be covered in each round and establishes negotiating bodies to handle individual negotiating subjects. (All information taken from "What is the WTO?" found at http://www.wto.org/english/thewto_e/whatis_e/whatis_e.htm and "Doha Development Agenda," found at http://www.wto.org/english/tratop_e/dda_e/tnc_e.htm).

or until the losing nation changes the trade practice that was the subject of the dispute. In addition, the other member nations are expected to exert pressure on the losing nation to encourage a change in practice in order to ensure compliance. Since the member nations encompass a significant majority of world trade, such pressure and unofficial sanctions should prove to be very effective.

One problem that is frequently addressed by the WTO involves the dumping of goods into foreign markets. *Dumping* involves the selling of goods in foreign markets at a price below that charged in the domestic market. Very commonly, a firm that is dumping goods in a foreign market has a protected market at home, so the firm is not concerned about retaliatory pricing in its home market. The firm can then sell its products in other countries at an unfair price, often to the detriment of the domestic firms in that other country. As a result, many nations have anti-dumping duties that are used to raise the cost of importing the goods, thus offsetting the cost advantage enjoyed by the company that dumped goods. The WTO has been involved in numerous cases involving allegations of dumping. In many of these cases, the nation accused of dumping its goods challenges the anti-dumping reaction of the importing nation.

FREE TRADE AGREEMENTS

A number of nations saw the success of GATT in lowering trade barriers and decided to go even further in their quest to increase international trade. Countries in common geographical areas have formed free trade agreements. These agreements are created by treaties, a more formal arrangement than the GATT agreements, and they often cover much more than trade. The two most significant regional groupings are the European Union (E.U.) and the North American Free Trade Agreement (NAFTA). NAFTA includes all three nations in North America: the United States, Canada, and Mexico. There are numerous other free trade agreements in Asia, Africa, and Latin America.

The European Union

The European Union (E.U.) was created by the Treaty of Rome in 1957. As of July 24, 2015 the member states are Austria, Belgium, Bulgaria, Croatia, the Republic of Cyprus, Czech Republic, Denmark, Estonia, Finland, France, Germany, Greece, Hungary, Ireland, Italy, Latvia, Lithuania, Luxembourg, Malta, the Netherlands, Poland, Portugal, Romania, Slovakia, Slovenia, Spain, Sweden, and the United Kingdom.[28] In the Treaty of Nice, the E.U. proposed expansion of its membership, subject to approval by all of the current members. The proposal was approved on October 21, 2002.[29] Macedonia, Iceland, Montenegro, Serbia, and Turkey have also applied for membership, but their applications have yet to be approved.

The purpose of the E.U. is to establish a common customs tariff for outside nations importing goods into the community and to eliminate tariffs among E.U. members.

In furtherance of this purpose, the E.U. has its own legislative, executive, and judicial branches. The Treaty of Rome also covers the free movement of workers, goods, and capital within the community. The E.U. is governed by the Council of Ministers, the European Commission, the European Parliament, and the Court of Justice. Exhibit 5.4 depicts the governing structure of the European Union.

The Treaty of Rome established four main objectives for the freedom of movement within the E.U.: the movement of goods, people, services, and capital. Since the treaty, the E.U. has developed a large body of law designed to achieve these four objectives.

In 1986, the E.U. adopted the Single European Act, mandating the creation of a unified market by the end of 1992. In 1991, the heads of state of the EU member countries signed the Maastricht Treaty on European Political and Monetary Union, which strengthened the E.U. institutions and called for the establishment of a common currency, the European Currency Unit (ECU), by the close of the decade. The result was the "Eurozone," officially known as the *Euro Area*, a group of seventeen member states that adopted the Euro as their official legal currency. The European Central Bank, governed by a president and a board that comprises the heads of each national bank, is responsible for setting monetary policy for all of the members of the Euro Area.

Just as some U.S. law has extraterritorial application, some E.U. laws are applied beyond the borders of the union. It now appears that conduct anywhere in the world can be subject to E.U. competition rules (these competition rules are called antitrust rules in the United States) if the conduct is intended to affect and does affect the E.U. market. The European Court of Justice has ruled that Article 85, one of the major competition regulations of the EU, has *extraterritorial application* if the conduct in question is intended to affect parties or businesses located within the European Union.[30] This should serve as a warning to companies that engage in activities lawful in their home country but that also affect the European market.

The North American Free Trade Agreement

One powerful alternative to the E.U. is the free-trade agreement formed in North America, the North American Free Trade Agreement (NAFTA). The first piece of NAFTA went into effect in 1989, with the ratification of the Canada-U.S. Free Trade Agreement. One major purpose of the Canada-U.S. Free Trade Agreement was the elimination of tariffs on sales of goods between the two countries. The agreement called for the elimination of all tariffs between the nations by 1998. (As a practical matter, most such tariffs were already gone.) Goods qualify for tariff-free treatment if they are 50 percent North American in content. Also like the E.U., the Canada-U.S. Free Trade Agreement made it easier for Canadian and U.S. citizens to work in each other's countries and for investments to flow across the border. Unlike the E.U., however, the North American Free Trade Agreement did not set up a host of new institutions or require the two countries to give up much of their sovereignty. The only new institutions created by the agreement were binational panels of experts to be convened as needed to resolve trade disputes between the two countries. These expert panels replace the court systems for both countries in eligible cases.

Exhibit 5.4

The European Union

[a] The *Council of Ministers* issues directives, impelling each member state to ensure that its law is in compliance with E.U. policy. It also issues regulations, which are superior to national laws and may require amendments to national laws in order to ensure compliance with the E.U. regulations.

[b] The *European Commission* enforces E.U. law, primarily by the imposition of substantial fines for noncompliance. It also creates detailed regulations in the areas of competition and agricultural law (this authority is delegated to the Commission by the Council of Ministers).

[c] The *Assembly* consults with the Council of Ministers on legislation and proposes amendments to legislation. It can force the Council to resign with a vote of "no confidence."

[d] The *Court of Justice* is comparable to the U.S. Supreme Court. Its opinions become the domestic law for all member nations of the E.U.

In 1993, Mexico joined its Canadian and U.S. counterparts in the North American Free Trade Agreement. NAFTA creates a free trade area encompassing all of North America, a market large enough to compete successfully with Asian and European free trade groups. There are still some concerns about NAFTA, but there is no concerted effort by any of the governments involved to rescind the agreement. Free trade with Mexico presents different concerns than it did with Canada. U.S. environmental and labor groups object to Mexico's reputation for having a lax legal environment, and Canadians worry about more jobs moving south.

The Trans-Pacific Partnership (TPP), negotiated and adopted in 2015, will supplement NAFTA and address some of its perceived weaknesses. The TPP is not a free-trade zone, but it is a trade pact among twelve nations that has many of the attributes of a free-trade zone. The member nations are Australia, Brunei, Chile, Canada, Japan, Malaysia, Mexico, New Zealand, Peru, Singapore, Vietnam, and the United States.[31] Many questions remain about how or when it will be implemented, but its potential benefits seem significant for each of the member nations.

Other Free Trade Agreements

There are a number of other free trades agreements around the world, although none of the others possesses the economic strength of either the European Union or NAFTA. For example, there are at least four free trade agreements in Latin America. The Central American Common Market comprises Costa Rica, El Salvador, Guatemala, Honduras, Nicaragua, and Panama. The MERCOSUR Common Market comprises Argentina, Brazil, Paraguay, and Uruguay. The Andean Common Market is made up of Bolivia, Ecuador, Colombia, and Venezuela. And the Caribbean Community includes Barbados, Belize, Dominica, Jamaica, Trinidad and Tobago, Grenada, St. Kitts-Nevis-Anguilla, St. Lucia, and St. Vincent.

There are at least three African free trade agreements as well. These include the Economic Community of West African States, the Economic and Customs Union of Central Africa, and the East African Community. There is also a treaty, the Treaty Establishing the African Economic Community, which has 51 signatories. This treaty is intended to create an African equivalent to the European Union.

Each of these free trade agreements has the potential to influence international trade within its member states, and to help—or hinder—the economic growth and development of the member nations.

INTERNATIONAL STATUTES AND STANDARDS

There are a number of international statutes, treaties, conventions, commissions, agreements, and standards that directly impact international business. Among the most important of these are the following:

- The United Nations Convention on Contracts for the International Sale of Goods (CISG), which is briefly discussed in Chapter 11
- The United Nations Commission for International Trade Law (UNCITRAL)
- The International Organization for Standardization (ISO)

UNCITRAL and the ISO will be briefly discussed here.

The United Nations Commission for International Trade Law

UNCITRAL is perhaps the most important organization involved in addressing issues of private international trade. The U.N. General Assembly established UNCITRAL in 1966. This commission attempts to provide coordination of private international law to encourage and enhance international trade. UNCITRAL is actively involved in the development and enactment of U.N. Conventions (a U.N. Convention is a treaty that originates within the U.N.) dealing with international trade, such as the CISG and the Convention on the Recognition and Enforcement of Foreign Arbitral Awards. It is also actively involved in creating model laws and legal guides that are designed to serve as templates for the legislative bodies of any nations that are addressing international trade issues.

The International Organization for Standardization

The ISO is an international body dedicated to developing uniform standards in a number of different areas, thus enhancing international trade. There are 162 nations that belong to the ISO. Of these, 119 nations are "member bodies," 38 are "correspondent members," and 5 are "subscriber members." The member bodies are full members, and they influence the development of ISO standards; correspondent members observe the development of standards by attending meetings as observers; subscriber members keep up to date on the standards, but they do not adopt the standards.[32] According to the ISO:

> Standards are documented agreements containing technical specifications or other precise criteria to be used consistently as rules, guidelines, or definitions of characteristics, to ensure that materials, products, processes and services are fit for their purposes.[33]

As an example, the ISO developed the standards used for credit cards, phone cards, and "smart" cards, specifying the optimal thickness for these cards, among other things. Such standards allow the cards to be used worldwide.

The ISO has developed the Agreement on Technical Barriers to Trade (TBT), also known as the "Standards Code," in an effort to reduce any impediments to trade due to differences between national regulations and standards. This agreement "invites" the signatory nations to help ensure that the standardizing bodies within each nation accept and comply with a "code of good practice for the preparation, adoption and application of standards" as embodied in the agreement.[34] The ISO works closely with the WTO in an effort to enhance the development of international trade. In fact, the TBT is also known as the WTO Agreement on Technical Barriers to Trade.

The ISO has also developed two sets of quality standards for businesses. The first, ISO 9000, deals with quality management; the second, ISO 14000, deals with environmental management. Firms may voluntarily choose to seek ISO certification for their products under either of these plans; the requirements can be quite rigorous. Neither ISO 9000 nor ISO 14000 is a *product* standard. Rather, both are *management system* standards. The *quality* standards of ISO 9000 address those features of a product or service that are required by customers of the firm and then address the production process that is followed by the firm as it seeks to ensure that these features are present. Similarly, ISO 14000 addresses what the firm does in its efforts to minimize any harmful effects on the environment caused by its activities.[35]

INTERNATIONAL DISPUTE RESOLUTION

The best method of resolving an international business dispute is by providing a means for handling that contingency at the time the international transaction is created. Three principal options for settling a dispute are available: the International Court of Justice, national courts, and arbitration.

The International Court of Justice

The International Court of Justice (ICJ) has limited value in solving international business disputes. The ICJ is an agency of the United Nations, and its procedures were established in the United Nations Charter. A private person has no standing before the ICJ. Only nations may appear before the court. A private person who has a grievance against a state not his or her own must first secure the agreement of his or her own state to present the claim. If his or her state asserts the claim, the issue then becomes whether the other state will allow the matter to be submitted to the ICJ for resolution. Each state must agree to be bound by the court's decision; if they do not, there is no jurisdiction in the ICJ to hear the claim. Exhibit 5.5 lists the authorities the ICJ uses in reaching its decisions.

The International Court of Justice will use I, II, III, and IV as they apply. It will only use V if the parties agree to its use.

National Courts

A private person can usually resort to settlement of a dispute with a foreign nation by seeking redress through the courts of that state. Private persons can sometimes obtain adequate relief in their native state's judicial system. For example, a favorable judgment from a court in one nation may then be filed in the court of another nation. If the other

Exhibit 5.5

Authorities Used by the International Court of Justice

I	International Conventions—Treaties and other formal agreements between nations
II	International Custom—General practices accepted as law
III	General Legal Principles—Those general principles recognized and followed by "civilized nations"
IV	Judicial Decisions and Teachings of Experts—Applied after an examination of I, II, and III
V	Ex Aequo at Bono—That which is just and fair

nation's court recognizes the legitimacy of the judgment in the first nation, it will permit execution on the assets of the defendant based on the original judicial decision. United States courts are likely to enforce a judgment obtained in another country following a full and fair trial, before an impartial court, with an opportunity for the defendant to be heard. If the U.S. court thinks that the court and/or the case in the other nation was biased, that the court was corrupt, or that the defendant was not given an adequate chance to defend against the claims of the plaintiff, a U.S. court would probably not accept the judgment. Instead, the plaintiff would need to retry the entire claim in a U.S. court.

The recognition of foreign judgments is not a matter of international law, but rather a matter of comity. As the U.S. Supreme Court stated in the landmark case of *Hilton v. Guyot*,[36] comity is "the recognition which one nation allows within its territory to the . . . acts of another nation, having due regard both to international duty and convenience, and to the rights of its own citizens, or other persons. . . ." Comity is a matter of respect, goodwill, and courtesy that one nation gives to another, at least partly with the hope that the other nation will return the favor.

Arbitration

For variety of reasons, a particular international dispute may not be appropriate for resolution in the ICJ or national courts. In that case, international arbitration might be the best course of action. Many international commercial contracts include provisions for using arbitration. As of October 2015, 156 countries—including the United States—have signed the 1958 United Nations Convention on the Recognition and Enforcement of Foreign Arbitral Awards.[37] The countries that have signed this convention have agreed to use their court systems to recognize and enforce arbitration decisions. The fact that so many nations have ratified this U.N. convention provides persuasive evidence that arbitration is becoming the preferred method for resolving disputes in international business. In a controversy involving an alleged violation of the Sherman Act, the U.S. Supreme Court allowed the matter to be resolved by arbitration in Japan rather than hearing the case itself.[38]

In 2007, President Hugo Chávez nationalized a number of Exxon Mobil Oil's holdings within Venezuela. Exxon Mobil objected, and eventually the controversy ended up before the International Court of Arbitration (ICA), based in Paris. The ICA eventually found for Exxon Mobil and awarded it $908 million as compensation.[39] A subsequent action before the World Bank's International Centre for Settlement of Investment Disputes (ICSID) declared that Venezuela owed Exxon Mobil $1.6 billion, to be reduced by any amount Exxon Mobil recovered under the original ICA case.[40] As a signatory member of the U.N. Convention on the Recognition and Enforcement of Foreign Arbitral Awards, Venezuela is expected to honor the award.[41]

An Ounce of Prevention

Consider including a clause in any international contract that calls for the mandatory use of alternate dispute resolution (ADR). Whether calling for arbitration through the International Chamber of Commerce or some other arbitration agency, or specifying mediation, such a clause allows the firm to avoid the potential problems of dealing with a lawsuit in another nation. The savings in time and money make such a provision in the contract well worth considering. (It is even possible, if not yet probable, that mediation could be conducted through online dispute resolution [ODR].)

Online Dispute Resolution

A new form of alternative dispute resolution (ADR) has recently developed. This new form takes advantage of technology to provide a method for resolving disputes online, without requiring either of the parties to travel or to be overly inconvenienced. Online dispute resolution (ODR) is now available in a number of circumstances. NAFTA has a provision for online dispute resolution, especially in a controversy between a consumer and a business, to encourage consumers to assert their rights even though the business from which they purchased the goods is in another nation. A significant number of e-commerce businesses—businesses that may well have customers in a number of countries—have provided for ODR as a part of their sales contracts.

ODR is likely to involve mediation as the preferred method for resolving disputes. Each party submits its position to the online mediator, who then suggests settlement options to each party. However, the potential for growth is tremendous. All that is required to use this method is access to the Internet and a willingness to use the system. ODR can be synchronous or asynchronous; it can be extremely simple or relatively complex. While it is now normally used only for mediation, it can also be used for arbitration. This method of dispute resolution is relatively new, but it is likely to become extremely common and widespread in a relatively short time.

Contemporary Case

In this case the court is determining the scope of the Foreign Trade Antitrust Improvement Act (FTAIA) and when U.S. antitrust laws can apply to extraterritorial conduct that affects commerce within the United States. Note how the court analyzes the standards set out in the statute to reach its conclusion.

UNITED STATES v. LSL BIOTECHNOLOGIES

379 F.3d 672, 680 (9th Cir. 2004)

FACTS   This dispute grows out of a joint business venture—always a fertile ground for litigation. . . .

In the early 1980s, LSL Biotechnologies, Inc., an American corporation that develops and markets seeds, entered into a relationship with Hazera . . . in the hope [that they could] develo[p] a genetically-altered tomato seed that would produce tomatoes with a longer shelf-life. [The short shelf-life of a "normal" tomato restricts a seller to a small geographic market. A tomato with a longer shelf life would expand this market, allowing consumers to purchase "vine-ripened" tomatoes rather than tomatoes that were picked before ripening and then shipped. (Vine-ripened tomatoes have a better flavor and texture. U.S. consumers in more northern

locations can not get vine-ripened tomatoes for most of the year.)]

[The joint venture] eventually bred a ripening-inhibitor ("RIN") gene into tomato seeds to be grown in open fields. The RIN gene caused tomatoes to remain fresh longer after being picked. LSL obtained a patent for tomatoes and seeds containing the RIN gene; Hazera obtained no rights to the patent. The RIN gene tomatoes proved to be exceptionally successful when grown in Mexican climates, but failed to [produce as well] in cooler American climates. As a result, Mexican growers now dominate the fresh winter-tomato market. . . .

In 1987, Hazera sued LSL in an Israeli court. This . . . litigation led to mediation in Israel that produced the renegotiation of rather addendum to the [original contract between the two parties]. The addendum included a Restrictive Clause, which is the device the United States now claims violates the Sherman Act. The Restrictive Clause [prohibited Hazera from engaging in the development, marketing, or any other activities involving tomatoes having long shelf-life qualities. Hazera was also prohibited from any activities that would involve using LSL's proprietary rights.]

. . .

[The parties continued to work together until their contract] expired on January 1, 1996, and the Restrictive Clause became effective. [The United States filed its antitrust complaint on September 15, 2000,] alleg[ing] that the Restrictive Clause was "so overbroad as to scope and unlimited as to time as to constitute a naked restraint of trade in violation of Section 1 of the Sherman Act." [The clause was] also alleged [to be] illegal because "it has harmed and will continue to harm American consumers by unreasonably reducing competition to develop better seeds for fresh-market, long shelf-life tomatoes for sale in the United States."

The government [argued] that, "but for the [Restrictive Clause], Hazera would likely have become a significant competitor for [LSL] ..." [and LSL had eliminated one of the few firms capable of developing a seed for long shelf-life tomatoes that could be grown successfully in the United States.

At the time the suit was filed LSL controlled over 70 percent of the "fresh market tomato seeds," and Hazera had not developed a long shelf-life tomato seed.]

The district court first concluded that the Complaint failed to state a cause of action regarding conduct in the United States and dismissed that aspect of the action without prejudice. [The government appealed.]

ISSUE   Did the court have subject matter jurisdiction in this case under the provisions of the Foreign Trade Antitrust Improvement Act (FTAIA)?

HOLDINGS   No. The FTAIA provides the standard for establishing when subject matter jurisdiction exists over a foreign restraint of trade and that standard was not met here. The government failed to demonstrate that the implementation of the Restrictive Clause had a direct effect on U.S. business.

REASONING   Excerpts from the opinion of the Circuit Judge Tallman:

The Sherman Act prohibits "[e]very contract, combination in the form of trust or otherwise, or conspiracy, in restraint of trade or commerce among the several States, or with foreign nations" ... Federal courts have struggled for decades to determine when United States courts have jurisdiction over allegations of foreign restraints of trade. ... Prior to the passage of the FTAIA, courts applied varying tests to determine when foreign conduct fell within the purview of the Sherman Act. The most widely used standard was the "effects test," which was developed by Judge Learned Hand in *United States v. Aluminum Co. of Am.* ...

Application of the effects test ... has proved difficult and the precise extraterritorial reach of the Sherman Act remains less than crystal clear. In an effort to address this uncertainty, Congress enacted the FTAIA in 1982. The FTAIA "was intended to exempt from the Sherman Act export transactions that did not injure the United States economy." ... According to the House Report, another significant purpose of the FTAIA was to fix the problem that arose because "courts differ in their expression of the proper test for determining whether United States antitrust jurisdiction over international transactions exists." ... The FTAIA tackled this issue by "clarifying the Sherman Act ... to make explicit [its] application only to conduct having a 'direct, substantial and reasonably foreseeable effect' on domestic commerce." ...

It is manifest that our role is to apply the laws that Congress passes and the executive branch enforces unless those laws violate the Constitution. There is no suggestion that the FTAIA is unconstitutional. Thus, we must adhere to the FTAIA in determining whether a district court has subject matter jurisdiction over an alleged foreign restraint of trade. The government contends that the FTAIA merely codified the existing common law regarding when the Sherman Act applies to foreign conduct and that we should continue to employ the Alcoa effects test. We reject this contention.

Our task when interpreting legislation is to give meaning to the words used by Congress; we strive to avoid constructions that render words meaningless. . . . The FTAIA states that the Sherman Act shall not apply to foreign conduct unless it has a "direct, substantial, and reasonably foreseeable effect" on domestic commerce. . . . The Supreme Court reads the Alcoa test as conferring jurisdiction so long as the conduct creates "some substantial effect in the United States." . . . Unlike the FTAIA, the Alcoa test does not require the effect to be "direct." Adopting the government's argument and applying the Alcoa test would render meaningless the word "direct" in the FTAIA. We are not willing to rewrite a statute under the pretense of interpreting it.

Moreover, applying Alcoa instead of the FTAIA would contravene the FTAIA's purpose. The FTAIA created its jurisdictional test because the "enactment of a single, objective test—the 'direct, substantial, and reasonably foreseeable effect' test—will serve as a simple and straightforward clarification of existing American law." . . . It would be a serious departure from the goal of achieving clarity for us to conclude that Congress meant only "some substantial effect" . . . when it said "direct, substantial, and reasonably foreseeable effect." Clarity is not achieved by employing three modifiers ("direct," "substantial," and "reasonably foreseeable") as the standard for the required effect of the challenged conduct and then telling businesses that only one modifier ("substantial") is relevant to Sherman Act liability. . . .

The FTAIA provides the standard for establishing when subject matter jurisdiction exists over a foreign restraint of trade. This standard was not met here because the government cannot demonstrate that the district court clearly erred by determining that the alleged effects of the Restrictive Clause are not direct.

Because we conclude that the district court lacked subject matter jurisdiction over the entire Complaint, we do not consider the district court's Rule 12(b)(6) dismissal of the domestic aspect of the Complaint.

Affirmed.

Short Answer Questions

1. Assume that a mid-sized regional firm develops a product with very wide appeal. The management of the firm has even received some inquiries about its product from firms in several foreign nations. What sorts of things should this firm consider as it examines different ways for it to "go global"? What would you recommend as an immediate approach and what might you recommend for consideration later if there is significant demand in those other nations?

2. Many people believe that the Dodd-Frank whistle-blower provisions are meant to be applied extraterritorially. However, a 2014 opinion from the 2d Circuit Court of Appeals indicates that it does not apply beyond the borders of the United States. What reasons can you give for why the Dodd-Frank whistle-blowing protections should apply extraterritorially? What reasons can you give for why the 2d Circuit was correct? Which reasons do you find more persuasive?

3. The Trans-Pacific Partnership (TPP) is not a free-trade zone, but it shares some attributes with free trade zones. It should also provide a

more level "playing field" in a number of areas among the twelve signatories, including that of environmental protections. How would you compare the TPP with more traditional free-trade zones such as the European Union or NAFTA? What differences do you see between the TPP and traditional free trade zones?

You Decide...

1. The "Eight-Hour Law" provides, in effect, that every contract to which the United States is a party shall contain a provision that no laborer or mechanic doing any part of the work under the contract shall be required or permitted to work more than eight hours in any one day unless he or she is compensated at the rate of one and one-half times the basic rate of pay for all work in excess of eight hours per day.

In 1941, Foley Bros. entered into a contract to build certain public works on behalf of the United States in the East and Near East, particularly in Iraq and Iran. Foley Bros. agreed in the contract to "obey and abide by all applicable laws, regulations, ordinances, and other rules of the United States of America." The provisions of the Eight-Hour Law were not specifically included in the contract. Filardo, an American citizen, was hired to work on the construction projects as a cook at $60 per week. This contract of employment contained no provision concerning hours of work or overtime. Over the two-year course of his employment Filardo frequently worked more than eight hours per day, but he never received any overtime pay. When his request for accumulated overtime pay was refused, he sued Foley Bros. in the Supreme Court of New York. This court held that the Eight-Hour Law applied in this situation and a jury verdict in favor of Filardo was entered. Foley Bros. appealed, and the Appellate Division reversed on the ground that the law did not apply in this situation. The U.S. Supreme Court granted certiorari to decide whether the Eight-Hour Law applies to a contract between the United States and a private contractor for construction work in a foreign country. Should the Eight-Hour Law apply to a U.S. citizen working for a U.S. corporation in a foreign country apply? Would your answer be different if it was a citizen of the host nation working for a U.S. corporation in his or her home country? (See *Foley Bros., Inc. v. Filardo,* 336 U.S. 281 (1949).)

2. National Australia Bank (NAB) is an Australian Bank. Its Ordinary Shares (called common stock in the United States) are traded on the Australian Stock Exchange Limited and several other exchanges. All of its Ordinary Shares are traded in markets outside the United States. NAB's American Depository Receipts (ADRs) are traded on the New York Stock Exchange.

NAB bought HomeSide Lending, Inc., a mortgage servicing company headquartered in Florida, in 1998. HomeSide's business involved receiving fees for servicing mortgages. The value of servicing mortgages depends, to a significant degree, on the likelihood of the mortgages being repaid before their due date. Early pay-offs reduce the expected return. HomeSide calculated the present value of its mortgage-servicing rights by using valuation models designed to take the likelihood of early pay-offs into account. It recorded the net present value of its assets, and these figures appeared in NAB's financial statements. From 1998 until 2001, NAB's annual reports and other public documents touted the success of HomeSide's business. But in 2001, NAB twice reduced the value of HomeSide's assets, by $450 million in July and then by $1.75 billion in September. As a result, the prices of NAB's Ordinary Shares and ADRs slumped. NAB claimed that the September reduction was the result of a failure to anticipate the lowering of prevailing interest rates, other mistaken assumptions in the financial models, and the loss of goodwill.

Robert Morrison and other plaintiffs, all Australians who purchased NAB Ordinary Shares in 2000 and 2001, alleged that HomeSide executives fraudulently manipulated the financial models, making HomeSide appear more valuable than it really was. They also alleged that NAB and its executives were aware of this deception by July 2000, but did nothing about it. They sued NAB, HomeSide, and a number of the executives of each, alleging violations of §§ 10(b) and 20(a) of the Securities and Exchange Act of 1934 and SEC Rule 10b(5).

Should the provisions of § 10(b) of the Securities Exchange Act of 1934 be applied extraterritorially in order to provide a cause of action to foreign plaintiffs suing foreign and American defendants for misconduct in connection with securities traded on foreign exchanges?

(See *Morrison v. National Australia Bank*, 130 S. Ct. 2869 (2010).)

Notes

1. CISG Table of Contracting States, found at http://www.cisg.law.pace.edu/cisg/countries/cntries.html (accessed October 6, 2015).
2. "U.S. Trade in Goods and Services, 1992-Present," U.S. Department of Commerce, Bureau of Economic Analysis, report released July 7, 2015, found at http://www.bea.gov/newsreleases/international/trade/2015/trad0515.htm (accessed October 6, 2015).
3. Marshall McLuhan was a Canadian scholar who is credited with coining the phrase that the world is a "global village" due to the growth of electronic technology.
4. 549 F.3d 597 (9th Cir. 1976).
5. 15 U.S.C. § 6a.
6. While the Department of Commerce maintains the list, a number of different federal agencies or departments have control over the requirements for exporting different types of goods. It is the responsibility of the exporter to determine which agency or department must "sign off" on the proposed exporting and to show that it has performed its due diligence prior to applying for the license.
7. Tariff and Import Fees, Export. Gov., found at http://export.gov/logistics/eg_main_018130.asp.
8. "WIPO-Administered Treaties, Contracting Parties: Berne Convention, (Total Contracting Parties: 168)," found at http://www.wipo.int/treaties/en/ShowResults.jsp?treaty_id=15 (last visited October 7, 2015).
9. "The European Patent Convention (EPC)," Ius mentis, found at http://www.iusmentis.com/patents/epc/.
10. "The PCT now has 148 Contracting States," World Intellectual Property Organization, found at http://www.wipo.int/pct/en/pct_contracting_states.html (accessed October 7, 2015).
11. "Madrid–The International Trademark System," World Intellectual Property Organization, found at http://www.wipo.int/madrid/en/ (accessed October 7, 2015).
12. Steve Hargreaves, "Counterfeit goods becoming more dangerous," CNNMoney (New York, September 27, 2012), found at http://money.cnn.com/2012/09/27/news/economy/counterfeit-goods/ (accessed October 12, 2015).
13. Elizabeth Gasiorowski Denis, "Crackdown on counterfeiting," (January 8, 2014) International Standards Organization web site, found at http://www.iso.org/iso/news.htm?refid=Ref1809 (accessed October 12, 2015).
14. *Ibid.*
15. "CBP, ICE HSI Report $1.2 Billion in Counterfeit Seizures in 2014," U.S. Customs and Border Protection Web site (April 12, 2015), found at http://www.cbp.gov/newsroom/national-media-release/2015-04-02-000000/cbp-ice-hsi-report-12-billion-counterfeit-seizures (accessed October 12, 2015).
16. Jason Ryan, "Cyber Monday: Buyer Beware Counterfeit Goods," ABC News, The Blotter (November 28, 2011), found at http://abcnews.go.com/Blotter/cyber-monday-buyer-beware-counterfeit-goods/story?id=15041470 (accessed April 20, 2016).
17. 15 U.S.C. § 78dd-1 et seq.
18. Pub. L. 111-203.
19. *Liu Meng-Lin v. Siemens AG*, 763 F.3d 175 (2d Cir. 2014**).**
20. "Legislation on Foreign Relations," Government Printing Office (June 2001).
21. OPIC Web site, found at https://www.opic.gov/ (accessed October 14, 2015).
22. 28 U.S.C. §§ 1602-1611.

23. "The 128 nations that had signed GATT by 1994," found at https://www.wto.org/english/thewto_e/gattmem_e.htm (accessed October 6, 2015).

24. "Understanding the WTO: The Organization," World Trade Organization, found at http://www.wto.org/english/thewto_e/whatis_e/tif_e/org2_e.htm (accessed January 9, 2012). https://www.wto.org/english/thewto_e/whatis_e/tif_e/org6_e.htm (accessed October 6, 2015).

25. *Ibid.*

26. *Ibid.*

27. WTO organization chart, found at https://www.wto.org/english/thewto_e/whatis_e/tif_e/org2_e.htm (accessed October 20, 2015).

28. Countries in the E.U. and EEA, found at https://www.google.com/webhp?sourceid=chrome-instant&ion=1&espv=2&ie=UTF-8#q=members+of+the+european+union (accessed October 14, 2015).

29. "EU glows after Ireland 'yes' vote," MSNBCNews.com, October 21, 2001, http://www.civitas.org.uk/eufacts/FSTREAT/TR5.htm.

30. *Re Wood Pulp Cartel et al. v. Commission*, 4 C.M.L.R. 901 (1988).

31. "The Trans-Pacific Partnership," Office of the United States Trade Representative web site, found at https://ustr.gov/tpp/ (accessed October 14, 2015).

32. "ISO Members," the ISO Web site, found at http://www.iso.org/iso/about/iso_members.htm. (Last visited October 14, 2015).

33. "What are standards," ISO Web site (accessed July 17, 2002), http://www.iso.ch/iso/en/aboutiso/introduction/index.html/.

34. "The Agreement on Technical Barriers to Trade (TBT)," ISO web site (accessed July 22, 2002), http://www.iso.ch/iso/en/comms-markets/iso/.

35. "The basics," ISO web site, http://www.iso.ch/iso/en/iso9000-14000/tour/plain.html/.

36. 159 U.S. 113 (1895).

37. "Status: Convention on the International Recognition and Enforcement of Foreign Arbitral Awards," found at http://www.uncitral.org/uncitral/en/uncitral_texts/arbitration/NYConvention_status.html (accessed October 14, 2015).

38. *Mitsubishi Motors Corp. v. Soler Chrysler-Plymouth, Inc.*, 473 U.S. 614 (1985).

39. The International Court of Arbitration is the dispute resolution arm of the International Chamber of Commerce (ICC). More information can be found at http://www.iccwbo.org/court/.

40. Vyas, Kejal, and Daniel Gilbert, "Exxon Mobil Awarded $1.6 Billion in Venezuela Case," *The Wall Street Journal*, October 9, 2014, found at http://www.wsj.com/articles/exxon-mobil-awarded-1-4-billion-in-venezuela-case-1412879396 (accessed October 14, 2015).

41. Exxon has at least one other arbitration on this same issue pending before the World Bank's International Center for Settlement of Investment Disputes. It is scheduled for a hearing in early 2012.

Part II

Governmental Influences

6

Constitutional Regulation of Business

Learning Objectives

After completing this chapter you should be able to

- Explain the limits of the Commerce Clause
- Discuss the coverage of the Equal Protection Clause
- Describe the different tests applied in an equal protection case
- Distinguish *substantive due process* from *procedural due process*
- Identify when a taking has occurred under the Takings Clause
- Recognize the difference between commercial speech and private speech

Classic Case

This case established that the U.S. Supreme Court had the power of judicial review. Judicial review is the right to overturn actions by the other branches of the government if those actions conflict with the U.S. Constitution. The Constitution did not expressly state that the U.S. Supreme Court had the power to issue a writ of mandamus in such situations, a power Congress tried to grant in the Judiciary Act of 1789.

MARBURY v. MADISON

5 U.S. 137 (Cranch, 1803)

FACTS William Marbury was one of several people who had been nominated by President John Adams for a position as a justice of the peace in the District of Columbia. The nomination was submitted to the Senate, which consented to the appointment. Upon receiving confirmation by the Senate, the president signed the commission, duly appointing Marbury as a justice of the peace. The acting secretary of state at the time, Mr. Levi Lincoln, affixed the seal of the United States. President Adams's term of office ended before the commission was delivered to Marbury. The new secretary of state, James Madison, refused to deliver the commission.

The Judiciary Act of 1789 gave the Supreme Court original jurisdiction to issue writs of mandamus to any courts appointed or to any persons holding office under the authority of the United States. Marbury sought a writ of mandamus from the U.S. Supreme Court. (Marbury was asking the court to order Madison to deliver the commission.)

ISSUES Does Marbury have a right to the commission? Does the law afford him a remedy if he, in fact, has a right to the commission? Is mandamus issuing from the Supreme Court the appropriate remedy?

HOLDINGS Yes, he was entitled to the commission. The proper procedures were followed and all necessary steps were completed. Yes, the law does afford a remedy in this case, but perhaps only if it is done in the court's role as an appellate court.

REASONING Excerpts from the opinion of Chief Justice Marshall:

... The first [question] is ... has the applicant a right to the commission he demands? ... The appointment being the sole act of the president, it must be completely evidenced, when it is shown that he has done every thing to be performed by him. ... The last act to be done by the president is the signature of the commission. He has then acted on the advice and consent of the senate to his own nomination. The time for deliberation has then passed. He has decided. ... This appointment is evidenced by an open, unequivocal act; and being the last act required from the person making it, necessarily excludes the idea of its being, so far as it respects the appointment, an inchoate and incomplete transaction. ... Mr. Marbury, then, since his commission was signed by the president and sealed by the secretary of state, was appointed; and as the law creating the office gave the officer a right to hold for five years independent of the executive, the appointment was not revocable. ... To withhold the commission, therefore, is an act ... violative of a vested legal right.

This brings us to the second inquiry. ... If he has a right and that right has been violated, do the laws of the country afford him a remedy? The very essence of civil liberty certainly consists in the right of every individual to claim the protection of the laws, whenever he receives an injury. ... The government of the United States has been emphatically termed a government of laws, and not of men. It will certainly cease to deserve this high appellation, if the laws furnish no remedy for the violation of a vested legal right. . . .

It remains to be inquired whether . . . [h]e is entitled to the remedy for which he applies. This depends on, 1. The nature of the writ applied for, And 2. The Power of this court. . . .

This writ, if awarded, would be directed to an officer of government, and its mandate to him would be . . . "to do a particular thing therein specified, which appertains to his office and duty, and which the court has previously determined or at least supposes to be consonant with right and justice." . . . These circumstances certainly concur in this case. . . . It is not by the office of the person to whom the writ is directed, but the nature of the thing to be done, that the propriety or impropriety of issuing a mandamus is to be determined. . . .

This . . . is a clear case of mandamus . . . [I]t only remains to be inquired, [w]hether it can issue from this court. The act to establish judicial courts of the United States, authorizes the supreme court "to issue writs of mandamus, in cases warranted by the principles and usages of law. . . ." The constitution vests the whole judicial power of the United States in one supreme court, and such inferior courts as congress shall, from time to time, ordain and establish. . . . In the distribution of this power it is declared that "the supreme court shall have original jurisdiction in all cases . . . [involving] ambassadors, other public ministers and consuls, and those in which a state shall be a party. In all other cases, the supreme court shall have appellate jurisdiction." . . .

The authority, therefore, given to the supreme court, by the act establishing the judicial courts of the United States, to issue writs of mandamus to public officers, appears not to be warranted by the constitution; and it becomes necessary to inquire whether a jurisdiction, so conferred, can be exercised.

The question, whether an act, repugnant to the constitution, can become the law of the land, is a question deeply interesting to the United States; but, happily, not of an intricacy proportioned to its interest. It seems only necessary to recognise certain principles, supposed to have been long and well established, to decide it. . . .

It is emphatically the province and duty of the judicial department to say what the law is. Those who apply the rule to particular cases, must of necessity expound and interpret that rule. If two laws conflict with each other, the courts must decide on the operation of each. So if a law be in opposition to the constitution . . . the court must determine which of these conflicting rules governs the case. This is of the very essence of judicial duty.

If then the courts are to regard the constitution; and the constitution is superior to any ordinary act of the legislature; the constitution, and not such ordinary act, must govern the case to which they both apply. . . . Thus, the particular phraseology of the constitution of the United States confirms and strengthens the principle, supposed to be essential to all written constitutions, that a law repugnant to the constitution is void, and that courts, as well as other departments, are bound by that instrument. The rule must be discharged.

[The Judiciary Act of 1789 was declared to be unconstitutional. With the denial of the writ Marbury did not get his commission.]

AN HISTORIC PERSPECTIVE

The government provides significant regulation of business in the United States today. Federal regulations address important issues such as environmental pollution, employee safety, wage and hour issues, and labor relations. The federal government also mandates that publicly traded corporations accurately disclose material events, financial successes and failures, and, in some cases, the compensation packages of top executives. In addition, there are state regulations that cover such areas as consumer protection, the selling of securities, interest rates on loans, and highway weight limits. Local regulations cover issues such as zoning for commercial property and building codes. These represent only a few of the regulations that a business faces.

The regulation of business—overregulation in the minds of some—is a somewhat divisive issue within society. On one side of the issue are people like members of the Tea Party who favor less taxation, less regulation, and an emphasis on free enterprise. On the other side are people like participants in the "Occupy" movement who favor increasing taxation on the wealthy and stricter government regulation, especially at the federal level, to curtail what they see as unbridled corporate greed. It is likely that the political influence of one side or the other will affect the scope of government regulation of business in the future.

The United States has not always had such pervasive government regulation of business. As is often mentioned in American history texts, the United States was built on a *laissez faire* economy that reflected the belief that business operated best when uninhibited by the government. Business owners ran business and politicians ran government, and the two groups left each other alone. Buyers often were ignored, with *caveat emptor* ("let the buyer beware") being the rule of the land. Workers remained virtually unprotected. If they did not like their jobs, they could quit. If they did not go to work, they were fired. If they joined a union, they also were fired—and they quite often faced criminal conspiracy charges as well.

The nineteenth century was a great time to be an American entrepreneur, especially a wealthy one. However, public sentiment and the application of social contract theory brought a change in how the government viewed its interactions with business. Many people resented the abuses and mistreatments workers suffered. And, given the lack of land remaining for westward migration, people increasingly clamored for reform. Present-day governmental regulation emerged from these tumultuous times.

Business's "social contract" requires that it pay heed to the various social and economic issues mentioned above. Somewhere between the extremes of overregulation and underregulation, a happy medium must exist that can maximize the well-being of business, society, and government. The regulations businesses face are burdensome, and compliance can be expensive. But the lack of regulation has proved to be harmful to various elements of society. Since we seem unable to find that "happy medium," we need a method of maintaining the regulation of business while ensuring that businesses are not abused by overregulation. Since the law in many instances views firms as legal, or *juristic*, persons, businesses also can assert various constitutional rights and curb what they view as excessive governmental regulation.[1] Just as the Constitution stands as the guardian of individual rights, it also represents a significant weapon for businesses to use when they challenge the laws and regulations that affect them.

In the remainder of this chapter we will discuss the constitutional bases for government regulation of business, and we will also examine the protections afforded to business by the Constitution.

THE COMMERCE CLAUSE

The Articles of Confederation did not provide the federal government the authority to regulate interstate commerce, which left the states free to enact legislation that could impede trade among the states. Such state legislation, if enacted, would jeopardize the continuing existence of the nation, creating conflicts and commercial controversies among the various states. To avoid such an occurrence, the founders included the Commerce Clause in the Constitution to ensure that channels of commerce would remain open and to facilitate the transportation of goods. In so doing, they intended to foster economic integration among the states.

Article 1, Section 8, Clause 3 of the U.S. Constitution gives Congress the power "to regulate Commerce with foreign Nations, and among the several States, and with the Indian Tribes." This clause grants the exclusive power to regulate interstate commerce to the federal government. This power is exercised through the Congress and its power to enact statutes. From its language it is *not* an express limitation on the power of the states to also regulate commerce or the economy through each state's police power. However, the language of the clause implies that while the states can regulate intrastate commerce, their regulations may not unduly interfere with interstate commerce. The federal government has the sole authority to regulate interstate commerce, and interstate commerce includes commerce between the United States and foreign states (nations). It should also be remembered that at the time the Constitution was adopted, Native American tribes were recognized as separate and sovereign nations, albeit without fixed borders—unlike most other nations.

Interestingly, the Commerce Clause itself does not define commerce. That task fell to the Supreme Court and its power of judicial review. In 1824, the Supreme Court had its first occasion to interpret the Commerce Clause. Chief Justice Marshall's opinion in *Gibbons v. Ogden*[2] defined commerce as "the commercial intercourse between nations, in all its branches ... regulated by prescribing rules for carrying on that intercourse." Marshall also noted that the federal government can regulate commerce that *affects* other states, even if that commerce is local in nature. Basically, the Supreme Court broadly claimed that commerce included all aspects of business operations—even if many of these operations transpired wholly within one state.[3]

As a result of this interpretation, for nearly three-quarters of a century federal power to regulate commerce was broad. The Interstate Commerce Act of 1887 permitted the Interstate Commerce Commission (ICC) to regulate local railroad rates and local railroad safety because such issues directly affected interstate rates and safety.[4] The federal government also could regulate local grain and live-stock exchanges because they, too, involved transactions that affected the rest of the nation.

Not all the court opinions of the period favored regulation by the federal government, however. In 1869, the Court upheld a Michigan state law that banned the sale of illuminating oils that could ignite at lower temperatures. The state passed the statute to protect its inhabitants from the danger posed by oil fires. The majority in this case, *United States v. Dewitt*,[5] held that the ban was a valid use of a state's police power under the Tenth Amendment and that the Commerce Clause did not prohibit the use of this state power. In the 1873 Supreme Court decision *In re State Freight Tax*,[6] the court stated that the Commerce Clause's phrase *among* meant *between*. As a result, this opinion held that the federal government could regulate only interstate (that is, between two or more states; between a point in one state and a point in another state) commerce. In its 1888 *Kidd v. Pearson*[7] decision, the court ruled that commerce meant transportation. As a result of these opinions, federal regulation of business suddenly became restricted to actual interstate transportation and did not reach business deals that affected interstate business but that were conducted entirely in one state. Also, states were allowed some leeway to protect their citizens via their police power. Such transactions, defined as *intrastate* (that is, begun, carried on, and completed wholly within the boundaries of a single state), therefore remained beyond the scope of federal regulation.

This new, restricted definition of interstate commerce was a factor in the passage of the Sherman Act in 1890 (see Chapter 17 for a detailed treatment of this act). Indeed, this new definition of the federal authority to regulate business led the court to narrower interpretations and, consequently, the court's invalidation of many subsequent federal enactments. This period reflected back to the laissez-faire business philosophy of previous decades and lasted until around 1937.

A shift in the Court's restrictive view of the exercise of federal power occurred with the decision in *NLRB v. Jones & Laughlin Steel Corp.*,[8] which overturned 50 years of narrow interpretation. In the opinion Chief Justice Hughes wrote:

> When industries organize themselves on a national scale, making their relation to interstate commerce the dominant factor in their activities, how can it be maintained that their industrial relations constitute a forbidden field into which Congress may not enter when it is necessary to protect interstate commerce from the paralyzing consequences of industrial war?

Thus, the court had come full circle. As Justice Jackson noted in *United States v. Women's Sportswear Manufacturers Association*,[9] a 1949 case involving a Sherman Act challenge to a local price-fixing arrangement, "If it is interstate commerce that feels the pinch, it does not matter how local the operation which applies the squeeze." In upholding the right of the federal government to regulate the conduct in dispute, Justice Jackson provided us with both a picturesque definition of interstate commerce and the one most courts presently would accept as controlling.

This expansive definition of the reach of the federal government under the Commerce Clause also provided the federal government with a vehicle for removing discrimination and bigotry, as the *Heart of Atlanta Motel, Inc. v. U.S.*[10] decision demonstrates. The Heart of Atlanta Motel had a policy of refusing service to African Americans. The federal government challenged this policy as a violation of Title II of the Civil Rights Act of 1964, which prohibits racial, religious, or national origin discrimination by those who offer public accommodations. The government claimed that the motel was involved in interstate commerce and that federal intervention was justifiable. The motel argued that it was a purely intrastate business and so exempt from federal regulation under Title II. The Supreme Court held that because it provided services to interstate travelers, the motel was involved in interstate commerce. In reaching its decision, the court focused on the following facts: (1) The motel was readily accessible from two interstate highways; (2) it advertised in national magazines and placed billboards on federal highways; and (3) approximately 75 percent of its guests came from outside the state of Georgia. In the court's view, allowing such discrimination would discourage travel by the black community. Since the motel was set up to serve interstate travelers and it drew much of its business from interstate travelers, it was involved in interstate commerce. The court concluded that Title II gave the federal government authority to prohibit Heart of Atlanta Motel's discriminatory practice of renting rooms only to white people.

Exclusive Federal Power

From the earliest cases, the courts viewed three areas of commerce as lying exclusively within the regulatory power of the federal government: commerce with foreign nations, commercial activities involving Native American tribes, and commerce between the states (interstate commerce). Courts generally have recognized that Congress enjoys *plenary* (exclusive) power over foreign commerce or trade. For instance, the state of Washington does not have the authority to sign a treaty regulating tuna-fishing rights with Japan or Canada; only Congress has such power.[11]

Similarly, owing to the unique status that Native Americans have occupied in U.S. history, only Congress has the power to regulate such commerce. Congress's plenary power in this area stems from the quasi-sovereign status that historically has been accorded to Native American tribes. As such, Native American tribes have virtually complete control over their own reservations and land; the states have little say over reservation affairs. Federal law generally preempts even state or local regulation of off-reservation activities. This part of the Commerce Clause is referred to as the Indian Commerce Clause. Any federal law that is based upon the Indian Commerce Clause is restricted to commerce that occurs on Indian reservations.

The phrase "among the several states" has spawned a great deal of litigation concerning when federal power over interstate commerce is, in fact, exclusive. Precedents over the years have established three such areas as exclusively within the federal government's power: (1) Congress's power to regulate the use of the channels of interstate commerce; (2) Congress's power to regulate the instrumentalities of interstate commerce (including persons and things); and (3) Congress's power to regulate activities that have a substantial relation to interstate commerce. This means that Congress can regulate interstate carriers, roads, and television and radio stations since these would be *channels* or *instrumentalities* of interstate commerce. Congress also has the power to exclude from such interstate channels or instrumentalities the goods, persons, or services designated by Congress as harmful to interstate commerce. Consequently, Congress can stop the interstate shipment of stolen vehicles, diseased animals, spoiled meat, fungi-ridden fruit, or defective products. Businesses so affected can do little to challenge this exercise of federal power. Besides the channels or instrumentalities of interstate commerce, Congress has the exclusive power to regulate all commerce or activity that affects more than one state. Note that even intrastate commerce may be subject to such federal control *if* the intrastate activity has a "substantial effect" on interstate commerce or if Congress rationally could conclude that the activity in question affects interstate commerce.

As the *Heart of Atlanta Motel* case indicates, it takes very little commercial activity to trigger the application of this federal power over commerce. To illustrate, in *Burbank v. Lockheed Air Terminal, Inc.,*[12] the Supreme Court struck down a local ordinance that prohibited jet airplane takeoffs during specified hours (11:00 P.M. to 7:00 A.M. local time). The court invalidated this ordinance because of the need for national uniformity in airplane flight patterns (having this airport "off limit" for several hours could create clogs in air traffic) and because federal law, in the form of agencies concerned with aeronautical and environmental matters, preempted such local or state initiatives.

But keep in mind that this federal power is not boundless. For example, in *U.S. v. Lopez,*[13] the Supreme Court invalidated a federal law as exceeding congressional authority under the Commerce Clause. This was the first time the court had struck down a law allegedly based on the Commerce Clause in more than fifty years. The basis of the case was that Lopez, a high school student, was caught carrying a concealed handgun on school property. He was charged with violating a federal criminal statute, the Gun-Free School Zones Act of 1990. The act forbids "any individual knowingly to possess a firearm at a place that [he] knows . . . is a school zone."[14] The court held that the act exceeds Congress's authority under the Commerce Clause. Why? The possession of a gun in a local school zone is not an economic activity that might, through repetition elsewhere, have a substantial effect on interstate commerce. The advocates of the law argued that possession of firearms in a school zone could lead to violent crime, which, in turn, would hurt the national economy by (1) increasing the costs associated with violent crime; (2) reducing people's willingness to travel to areas they deem unsafe; and (3) threatening the learning environment, which would lead to poorly educated citizens. The court, however, concluded that this argument demonstrated too tenuous a nexus to interstate commerce for the court to uphold the law. The *Lopez* decision seemingly ended the Supreme Court's deference to congressional legislation based on the Commerce Clause. Five years later, the court's opinion in *United States v. Morrison*[15] struck down part of another federal law—the Violence Against Women Act—on the same grounds as in *Lopez*. The court held that the effects of violence against women were primarily noneconomic and that this subject had traditionally been regulated by the states. *Lopez* and *Morrison* indicate that Congress is no longer able to regulate noneconomic activity that merely *might* have an effect on interstate commerce simply by asserting that the activity may affect interstate commerce and so falls within the scope of the Commerce Clause.

Concurrent State Power

The Commerce Clause does not prohibit any state regulation of commerce. The states enjoy concurrent power with the federal government as to the regulation of commerce within the state. Just as the federal government wishes to promote the welfare of its citizens, so does each state. This means that state regulation of economic matters is permissible for activities within its borders. In addition, some state regulations that may impact interstate commerce are also permitted, so long as the regulation in question satisfies a so-called balancing test. The balancing test employed by the courts compares the burdens on interstate commerce caused by the regulation on the one hand and the importance of the state interest that underlies the regulation on the other. If a state regulation hampers interstate commerce in any way, the court is likely to strike it down under its dormant commerce clause authority. The Dormant Commerce Clause[16]—an implied power under the Commerce Clause—arises when Congress is silent on the issue but the state law at issue discriminates against out-of-state commercial interests. Such discrimination gives in-state commercial interests an unfair—and illegal—competitive advantage.

Some state regulations are valid. Courts generally uphold a state's initiatives aimed at promoting or protecting its citizens. Matters such as local health and safety measures are upheld as long as they do not merely protect local economic interests. For example, state regulation of milk products that involves testing or certification of the milk will survive a legal challenge based on the Commerce Clause unless the state is found to discriminate in favor of in-state producers to the detriment of out-of-state producers and/or the costs of compliance is prohibitive to out-of-state producers. When the alleged benefits of the law impose an unreasonable or undue burden on interstate commerce, the regulation will be struck down. In the absence of discrimination against out-of-state firms or the imposition of an undue burden, the states have concurrent power to regulate commerce.

The state's concurrent power to regulate commerce ceases if the state regulation conflicts with federal law. The Supremacy Clause of Article VI of the Constitution invalidates such state legislation. If Congress expressly prohibits state regulation in a given area or if federal law impliedly preempts the regulatory area, federal law supersedes the state's power to regulate as well.

State powers of taxation can pose special problems under the Commerce Clause because the states' legitimate interest in increasing their revenues by taxing business entities may burden interstate commerce. As will be discussed later, such discriminatory taxes, in addition to violating the Commerce Clause, may also pose due process and equal protection problems. Although Congress can authorize or prohibit state taxation that affects interstate commerce under the Commerce Clause, in the absence of such federal legislation the states can tax corporations and other business entities.

State tax laws that discriminate against out-of-state businesses usually violate the Commerce Clause. Nondiscriminatory taxation schemes—schemes that impose the same type of tax on local business and interstate entities require courts to employ a "balancing" test in which they weigh the state's need for additional revenue against the burden imposed on interstate commerce by such taxes. Entities of interstate commerce do not remain immune from paying state taxes. Such businesses need only pay their fair share. Taxation that amounts to undue burdens, unfair discrimination, or multiple taxation generally does not survive challenges brought under the Commerce Clause (and perhaps not under the Due Process Clause, either).

Most of the precedents in this area involve state legislative schemes that tax goods shipped in interstate commerce; taxes imposed on firms doing business in a given state; and highway, airport, sales, and use taxes. At present a few states are trying to impose sales taxes on Internet sales made to citizens of the state, even if the e-merchant is located in another state and has no or minimal contacts with the taxing state except for the shipment of goods to its customers who reside there.

The Marketplace Fairness Act of 2013[17] would grant states the authority to compel on-line retailers (e-tailers) to collect sales taxes on sales to citizens of the state, without regard to the location of the e-tailer. The bill passed the Senate but not the House of Representatives. A revised version, the Marketplace Fairness Act of 2015,[18] would compel remote vendors to collect and remit sales taxes to the 45 states that impose a sales tax, provided the vendor has gross out of state sales of one million dollars or more. To date the bill has not passed Congress. While these Acts have yet to become law, on-line and catalog businesses should recognize their potential exposure to use taxes.

Exclusive State Power

The state's plenary power to regulate commerce covers purely local activities that only very remotely affect other states. Given the interdependent nature of our economy and the Supreme Court precedents we have discussed, the instances in which a state has exclusive power over commerce remain comparatively rare.

Exhibit 6.1 provides a useful framework for understanding a court's analysis of a challenge based on the Commerce Clause.

Exhibit 6.1

An Analysis of the Commerce Clause

Exclusive Federal Authority	Concurrent Authority— Both State and Federal	Exclusive State Authority
1. Commerce with foreign nations. 2. Commerce involving the Indian tribes. 3. Commerce involving the channels and instrumentalities of interstate commerce. 4. Commerce that is interstate in nature or that has a "substantial effect" on interstate commerce even though primarily intra- state in nature. 5. Commerce where Congress has prohibited state regulation or where federal law implicitly preempts the regulatory area.	1. State regulations that have an impact on interstate commerce, if the regulation passes the "balancing test" in which the burden on interstate commerce is weighed against the state's interest in the regulation. 2. State regulations falling within the state's police power (providing for the general welfare of its citizens). Such regulations will be allowed unless the state regulation: (a) imposes an undue or unreasonable burden on interstate commerce, *or* (b) discriminates in favor of in-state firms and against out-of-state firms, *or* (c) conflicts with federal law.	1. Purely local activities with little or no effect on interstate commerce. 2. Intrastate activities that have only a remote and minimal effect on interstate commerce.

THE EQUAL PROTECTION CLAUSE

Another constitutional provision that acts as a curb on the government's power to regulate business is the Equal Protection Clause. The Fourteenth Amendment states: "[n]or shall any State . . . deny to any person within its jurisdiction the equal protection of the laws." Supreme Court precedents have determined that in most situations the Fifth Amendment's Due Process Clause provides that the *federal* government must guarantee equal protection to all persons as well. Basically, this guarantee means that when the government classifies people, it must treat similarly situated people similarly. It is interesting that the founders did not include such a provision within the seven articles of the Constitution itself. Many of the Constitutional Convention delegates reasoned that the federal government did not have the enumerated authority to treat similarly situated groups differently and that various state constitutional protections would be sufficient.[19] However, history proved otherwise, and the Equal Protection Clause continues to help remedy the negative effects of slavery and other forms of invidious discrimination in the United States. In recent years, courts have used the Equal Protection Clause to protect a broad range of individual rights. This provision also limits the types of regulations government can impose on businesses.

Before discussing the Equal Protection Clause, it is important to remember that discrimination itself is not illegal. It is true that the word *discrimination* has assumed a negative connotation, implying prejudicial treatment, often based on race or gender. However, *to discriminate* literally means "to distinguish or differentiate." When a person chooses to go to Fred's Fish Shack for dinner rather than Betty's Beef and Burgers, that person has made a discriminating choice. Fred's Fish Shack is a seafood restaurant, while Betty's Beef and Burgers is a steak house. If the diner would prefer fish on that evening, Fred's would be the more logical choice, and the person would make a discriminating choice to go to the seafood restaurant in order to have a fish dinner. Such discrimination would not be a violation of the Equal Protection Clause, even if the steak house was owned by a minority group member.

The Equal Protection Clause protects individuals and other entities only from *invidious discrimination* (discrimination stemming from bigotry or prejudice) when that bigotry causes harm to a member of a protected class or group. Many, perhaps most, governmental statutes and regulations classify (or discriminate) among groups. This kind of discrimination—mere differentiation—does not necessarily violate the Equal Protection Clause. For example, when the government requires someone to have a license to practice medicine, the government is differentiating (discriminating) among people. It is allowing people who qualify for a medical license to practice medicine, but prohibiting the practice of medicine by anyone not possessing such a license. Such differentiation does not constitute a violation of the Equal Protection Clause. However, if the government *also* prohibited members of certain distinct groups or classes, such as women or members of a particular religion from obtaining a license to practice medicine, such a differentiation—discrimination—would be a *per se* violation of the Equal Protection Clause. Illegal discrimination results when the differentiation stems from prejudice, bigotry, or stereotyping on racial, ethnic, gender, or similar bases.

It should also be noted that the Equal Protection Clause prohibits only discrimination that derives from state action. The clause does not apply to actions taken by private individuals. Individual citizens are allowed to discriminate for any reason, including reasons that would be illegal if state action was involved. Suppose, for example, that Sean, a U.S. citizen of Irish descent, refused to interact in any manner with people he believed were of British ancestry. Sean harbors resentment against England and all things English because of perceived injustices done to the Irish by the British. There is nothing illegal in Sean's actions, so long as it remains merely personal. However, if Sean operates a business and he refuses to consider hiring any applicant who is of British ancestry, Sean may encounter legal problems. If an applicant complains that he or she was discriminated against on the basis of national origin, a government agency, the Equal Employment Opportunity Commission (EEOC), becomes involved. At that point, given the federal laws prohibiting discrimination on the basis of ancestry, Sean's conduct violated the prohibition and the EEOC's involvement elevates Sean's action from merely personal to conduct involving state action. At this point, the Equal Protection Clause becomes applicable. Similarly, a person who litigates, alleging an illegal discrimination has affected him or her, the involvement of the court constitutes "state action" (the courts are a part of the government) and may make the Equal Protection Clause applicable.

Since at least 1950 the Equal Protection Clause has become a powerful tool in the civil rights movement, leading to numerous legal challenges and to the enactment of a number of federal statutes and agency regulations. As a result of this increased reliance on the clause, the Supreme Court has developed various tests for determining the legality of these regulations when they are challenged under the Equal Protection Clause. Under each of these three possible tests, courts will review the legislative classification at issue with regard to the fit that exists between the means the legislative body has used to accomplish a desired end or objective, and the impact the legislation has on the people affected by the regulation.

The Rational Basis Test

Any government standards that distinguish among similarly situated people (discriminatory standards) are likely to be challenged as unconstitutional. The government must, at a minimum, be able to show that the distinction is based on a rational basis (the *rational basis test*) for the standards to be upheld. If a regulation is challenged as violating the Equal Protection Clause, the government must show that the regulation is rationally related to a legitimate state interest. The prior example involving the practice of medicine would fall under the rational basis test. The state has a legitimate interest in protecting its citizens who need health care by ensuring that only those people who have satisfied the state's criteria for practicing medicine are allowed to do so within that state's borders. Courts generally do not second-guess the intent of the legislature in these situations, presuming instead that the regulation is valid unless no conceivable justification exists for the law. Since such regulations fall within the police power of the state, the courts will normally allow governmental entities wide latitude when enacting social and economic regulations; courts rarely invalidate such measures.

The rational basis test is the lowest level of scrutiny a court will place on governmental action. The only way a law will be struck down under this standard is if its provisions violate another constitutional provision or are irrational. An example of a law struck down under the rational basis test can be found in the case of *City of Cleburne v. Cleburne Living Center.*[20] In this case, a city ordinance required group homes for the mentally disabled to obtain permits because of neighbors' concerns, potential harassment of residents by high school students, and zoning issues. The court held that the law violated the Equal Protection Clause because it was not rationally related to a legitimate aim of government. The law did not cover similar institutions such as hospitals or nursing homes, and the law was arguably based on prejudices in the community against the mentally disabled. Such prejudices cannot be the foundation of a law when scrutinized under the Equal Protection Clause. This state law was too discriminatory—even under the rational basis test.

The Strict Scrutiny Test: A "Compelling State Interest"

If a regulatory measure involves invidious discrimination—that is, intentional discrimination against certain racial or ethnic groups—or certain fundamental rights, courts initially will apply the *strict scrutiny test*. When this test is applied, the courts presume that the regulation in question is *invalid*. The courts will only uphold the measure if it is founded on a rational basis and it is necessary to satisfy a compelling state interest. In these instances, the regulating body must show (1) that the regulation is necessary in order to attain a compelling state interest; (2) that no alternative, less burdensome way exists to accomplish the state objective or goal; and (3) that the regulation is tailored as narrowly as possible while still attaining the goal. The strict scrutiny test is the highest level of scrutiny the courts will use, and the state will rarely be successful in meeting this test.

Over the years, the Supreme Court has held that laws that impinge on so-called suspect classifications burden the rights of members of these groups, and it has held that the regulation must meet the compelling state interest standard. Race, color, creed, religion, and national origin are all suspect classifications. Any statutory or regulatory acts that seemingly discriminate against such persons will be subjected to strict scrutiny in court. One reason the court has protected these groups from the application of such laws is that they represent discrete, insular minorities, many of which have historically been victims of discrimination.

In order to justify the singling out of such *disenfranchised groups* (that is, groups restricted from enjoying certain constitutional or statutory rights owing to systemic prejudice or bigotry), the entity enacting the legislation must satisfy the compelling state interest test and the strict scrutiny approach that a court must apply to the law. For example, *Yick Wo v. Hopkins* [21] involved a denial of a permit to operate a laundry business in San Francisco. All but one of the non-Chinese permit seekers was granted a permit, but each Chinese-American applicant was denied a license. The court found that this violated the Fourteenth Amendment. Yick Wo was a member of a discrete, insular minority who had suffered historical disenfranchisement. His immutable physical characteristics—the shape of his eyes and his skin color, for example—also made him more easily identified and singled out by the government. The city council could not show that its denial of Yick Wo's permit represented the only means of accomplishing the state interest (avoidance of fire hazards) involved here; hence, the city council had failed to show that its treatment of Yick Wo satisfied the compelling state interest test.

Citing *Yick Wo v. Hopkins* and upholding its ruling, the Supreme Court's opinion in *Romer v. Evans* [22] held unconstitutional a referendum-based amendment to the Colorado state constitution that prohibited all legislative, executive, or judicial action at any level of state or local government designed to protect homosexual persons from discrimination. The court found the amendment to be a status-based enactment that could not be tied to a legitimate state interest. The court—using only the rational basis test—concluded that the amendment instead "classifie[d] homosexuals not to further a proper legislative end but to make them unequal to everyone else. This Colorado cannot do. A state [under the Equal Protection Clause] cannot so deem a class of persons a stranger to its laws."

Note that if the facts had been different in the *Yick Wo v. Hopkins* case and that if all the Chinese-Americans had obtained their permits and the lone unsuccessful applicant had been white, he also could, presumably, sue under the Fourteenth Amendment for "reverse discrimination." The Supreme Court since 1989 has said that "benign" racial classifications used by the government for affirmative action purposes (for example, a city's deciding to award a certain percentage of city contracts to minority-owned businesses because of the city's desire to correct societal discrimination) will be judged under the strict scrutiny/compelling state interest test as well. *Adarand Constructors, Inc. v. Pena,* [23] which involved a challenge to a federal program that granted preferential treatment to minority subcontractors, reinforces this 1989 decision.

In *Adarand*, the Supreme Court held that reviewing courts must subject all racial classifications imposed by any federal, state, or local governmental entity, to the strict scrutiny standard. This case makes it clear that racial classifications, like those set up by a state, must serve a compelling governmental interest and must be narrowly tailored to further that interest. Under this standard, only affirmative action plans that respond to specific, provable past discrimination and that are narrowly tailored to eliminate such bias would be legal. Although the court acknowledged that, practically speaking, it will be hard for the government to meet this test, the court did not view its decision as dealing a fatal blow to the vast network of federal affirmative action programs that currently exist.

Recently, the court has ruled on a few major affirmative action cases in the arena of higher education—cases that might have a future impact on business. The challenged affirmative action programs do not cite historical discrimination as their impetus. Instead, they are based on the idea that diversity is a valuable component of the educational experience. The court has upheld such programs if diversity is merely one aspect of the admissions decision (as opposed to part of an admissions quota) and only in the higher education context. On the other hand, public elementary schools are not allowed to justify admission preferences based on this "diversity for the sake of diversity" rationale.

Any governmental action that penalizes or unduly burdens *fundamental rights* (that is, rights expressly or impliedly guaranteed in the Constitution) is also judged by the compelling state interest test. Accordingly, the Supreme Court has struck down laws that prohibited a drugstore's selling birth control devices and a doctor's discussing birth control issues with his or her patients. The court believed these laws implicate the right of privacy, which the court interprets as encompassing the marital relationship and procreation. The 2015 Supreme Court decision in *Obergefell v. Hodges*[24] legalizing same-sex marriage was based, in part, on the Equal Protection Clause and in part on the Due Process Clause. (Due process is discussed later in this chapter.) The Court had previously held that marriage is a fundamental liberty that is important to both society and the individuals involved. Since a fundamental right was involved, the strict scrutiny test applied. The Court held that treating a couple differently based on the gender of the two people was a denial of equal protection and a denial of due process.

The arguments advanced by the states that prohibited same-sex marriage did not satisfy the "compelling state interest" test, so the prohibitions were stuck down.

An Ounce of Prevention

Companies that are running "help wanted" ads need to be very careful in the ad's wording. If a company lists any requirements for eligibility that have a negative impact on a suspect classification, the company can be sued for disparate impact,[25] a violation of the Equal Protection Clause. For example, a minimum height requirement may prevent a disproportionate number of women or Asian or Hispanic males from being considered. The company would need to show that the requirement was a bona fide occupational qualification (BFOQ) in order to avoid liability for illegal discrimination. The ad should also include a statement that the firm is an equal employment opportunity (EEO) enterprise.

The Heightened Scrutiny Test: A Substantially Important State Interest

In the 1970s, the Supreme Court flirted with the idea of placing gender-based laws under the strict scrutiny analysis, particularly if the challenged legislative enactment unduly burdened women. At that time, many commentators argued that, first, women represent a discrete, insular minority owing to their belated receipt of the right to vote and the existence of Married Women's Property Acts that denied women the capacity to own property and to enter into contracts. Second, women represent a group of individuals who manifest immutable physical characteristics; in other words, women's secondary sex characteristics ordinarily distinguish women from men and vice versa.

While the court never accepted these arguments—apparently it believed the discrimination caused by gender-based laws failed to rise to the invidious level found in most strict scrutiny cases—the Court carved out an intermediate tier of analysis for challenges to gender-based laws. At this intermediate level, a "heightened scrutiny" test, regulations require more justification than a mere rational basis, but less than a strict scrutiny. Any statutory schemes or regulations falling within this category must be "substantially related to an important state interest." If the enacting body cannot meet this test, courts will invalidate the legislation. Thus, older laws that prohibited women from entering certain occupations (becoming a barber rather than a hair stylist) would now be decided under this heightened scrutiny test. Similarly, if Yick Wo had been a woman and the city council's ordinance had said no woman can obtain a permit, the city council would need to show that its prohibition against women advanced a substantially important state interest. Otherwise, the ordinance would violate the Equal Protection Clause. Note that men are protected from burdensome laws as well. In *Craig v.*

Exhibit 6.2

An Analysis of the Equal Protection Clause[a]

Test	Rational Basis Test	Heightened Scrutiny Test	Strict Scrutiny Test
Applies to	Government action that distinguishes among similarly situated persons. The rational basis test must be satisfied in every case raising an equal protection argument if such distinctions are present.	Government action based on gender.	Government action that either (1) intentionally discriminates against certain racial or ethnic groups, e.g., suspect classifications, like race, color, creed, religion, and national origin or (2) affects certain fundamental rights.
Government's Burden	Government must convince the court that the regulation is rationally related to a legitimate state interest.	Government must convince the court that the regulation is rationally related to a legitimate government interest *and* is substantially related to an important state interest.	Government must convince the court that the regulation is rationally related to a legitimate government interest *and* (1) the regulation is necessary to attain a compelling state interest, (2) the state interest cannot be achieved in an alternative, less-burdensome way, and (3) the regulation is tailored as narrowly as possible while still attaining the state objective.
Government Will Lose if	Provisions violate another section of the Constitution *or* the regulations are not rationally related to a legitimate government concern.	Provisions violate another section of the Constitution *or* the regulations are not rationally related to a legitimate government concern *and* are substantially related to an important state interest.	Courts presume that the regulation is invalid: The government must convince the court otherwise. The government rarely wins.

[a] The Equal Protection Clause of the Fourteenth Amendment is limited to action by the state.

Boren,[26] the Supreme Court invalidated an Oklahoma law that allowed females to drink beer at age 18 but prohibited males from drinking beer until age 21.

The Supreme Court has held that the exclusion of women by the Virginia Military Institute (VMI) violated the Equal Protection Clause. VMI argued that accommodating women would require drastic alterations to its "adversarial" method of training. It further argued that such changes to its method would destroy VMI's program and its mission to produce citizen-soldiers. The court found that this argument fell well short of justifying the classification as "substantially related to an important state interest." The court concluded that because neither VMI nor the state of Virginia put forward an "exceedingly persuasive justification" for categorically excluding all women from VMI's programs, the school's policies were unconstitutional.[27]

THE DUE PROCESS CLAUSE

The Fifth Amendment to the Constitution provides that no person shall "be deprived of life, liberty, or property without due process of law." The Fourteenth Amendment expands this protection by stating "No State shall make or enforce any law which shall abridge the privileges or immunities of citizens of the United States; nor shall any State deprive any person of life, liberty, or property, without due process of law." This limitation on the power of the States is in addition to the guarantee of equal protection, also found in the Fourteenth Amendment.

Many people associate the Due Process Clause with the protection of individual rights, perhaps specifically with the protection of people accused of committing crimes. Obviously, the Due Process Clause provides some protection for criminal defendants. Such a person cannot be deprived of his or her life (capital punishment) without affording that defendant a full and fair "due process" trial. In the same vein, the government cannot deprive a person of his or her liberty, which includes the right to be free from involuntary constraints such as involuntary commitment to a mental institution, without affording a full and fair due process trial or hearing. The third protected area of the Due Process Clause is the area of property. No person can be deprived of his or her property without due process of law. Property, as interpreted by the courts, is not limited to real estate. Property includes anything that is capable of being owned: *real property* (land and anything permanently attached to land; real estate), and personal property, whether *tangible* (goods) or *intangible* (money, negotiable instruments, stocks, bonds, patents, copyrights, etc.). The court has also extended its definition of property to include certain entitlements to benefits provided under the applicable state or federal law. This means that a state or the federal government cannot deprive a person of property rights such as public employment, public education, continuing welfare benefits, or continuing public utility services without providing a procedure that ensures due process of law.

Due process has two facets, s*ubstantive due process* and *procedural due process*. If either element is lacking, the regulatory scheme will be struck down as unconstitutional. Substantive due process addresses the content of a given statute or regulation: Is the statute or regulation sufficiently clear, and does it properly address the issue the government is seeking to regulate, or is it overly broad and vague? Substantive due process protects people from arbitrary or unreasonable laws or regulations. It prohibits the enforcement of overly broad or vague statutes or regulations. Procedural due process, by contrast, is concerned with the procedures followed when a person is put in a position from which he or she may be deprived of life, liberty, or property. Procedural due process addresses such areas as having a fair and impartial person deciding the controversy, providing a fair proceeding, and maintaining the appearance of fairness as well as ensuring as fair a process as is possible.

Substantive Due Process

The *substantive* dimension of due process focuses on the content, the scope, and the purpose of a law or a regulation. It is not concerned with whether there were fundamentally fair procedures, but with the law itself. It is important to remember that each member of society has certain imposed duties he or she must satisfy. These duties are the "cost" of living in a given society. To ensure that people satisfy their duties, it is important for the government to ensure that the imposed duties are clearly communicated and bear a rational relationship to societal norms. If the government imposes arbitrary, capricious, or irrational expectations on its citizens, the government has violated substantive due process. Under substantive due process principles, a regulation is invalid if it fails to advance a legitimate governmental interest or if it constitutes an unreasonable means of advancing a legitimate governmental interest.

Courts generally defer to legislators' judgments regarding social and economic matters and thus presume such laws are valid *unless* the challenger can demonstrate to the courts that the laws are arbitrary and/or irrational. Judicial deference normally leads to the courts' upholding such laws. However, if the challenger can persuade the court that the law is arbitrary and/or irrational, the law will be held to be unconstitutional because it violated the concepts of substantive due process. For example, in 1879 Connecticut passed a law making it illegal to provide counseling or other medical treatment to married persons for the purpose of preventing conception. Estelle Griswold, the executive director of the Connecticut Planned Parenthood Association, was charged with violation of the statute, found guilty, and fined. She appealed, and the case ended up in the U.S. Supreme Court. The court opinion in the case, *Griswold v. Connecticut*,[28] found that the statute in question violated substantive due process, asserting that Connecticut had no legitimate interest in prohibiting such conduct and that, in fact, the law in question invaded the right to privacy that is implied in the Constitution. The court's analysis and decision applied what amounted to a strict scrutiny test, requiring the state to show a compelling state interest in order for the statute to be upheld. The *Griswold* opinion was one of the cases discussed in the *Obergefell* opinion (cited above), which addressed the issue of same-sex marriage. The Court in *Obergefell* pointed out that there is no difference in the *reasons* for marriage between a same-sex couple and an opposite-sex couple (the autonomy of the individual and the keystone of social order, among others), so prohibiting a same-sex marriage is a denial of due process.

There seems to be a complementary relationship between substantive due process and guarantees of equal protection under the law. Both constitutional guarantees require a rational fit between the objectives of the law and the impact on the group of people affected by it. When all persons are subject to a law that deprives them of a life, liberty, or property interest, due process probably applies. When a law classifies certain people for certain purposes, the equal protection doctrine probably is the appropriate vehicle for challenging the law.

An Ounce of Prevention

When an employer considers instituting a dress code, setting limits on hair length, having a policy regarding facial hair, or similar rules, he or she should be certain that the policy is job-related. Such a requirement may infringe on an employee's religious beliefs or constitute a disparate impact on the basis of race or gender. If the policy is overly broad, it may violate substantive due process, and it may also be viewed as a denial of equal protection. The employer should be prepared to justify any such policy and to make exceptions if there are legitimate reasons why some employees cannot abide by the policy.

Procedural Due Process

Before the government can deprive a person of life, liberty, or property, he or she usually must be afforded some kind of hearing. Such hearings generally require notice to the aggrieved party, an opportunity for that person to present his or her side of the story, and the presence of an impartial decision maker. The procedure may involve a trial, an administrative hearing, or some other dispute resolution method. The proceeding does not necessarily require the use of counsel, and if counsel is used by one side, the government does not have to provide an attorney to the other side to "level the playing field." (Note that in criminal law the defendant must be provided with counsel if he or she cannot afford an attorney to ensure procedural due process for the defendant.) The timing of the hearing—whether it must occur before or after the deprivation of a protected interest—and the extent of the procedural safeguards afforded to the affected individual vary.

Courts generally balance the individual interests involved with the governmental interest in fiscal and administrative efficiency. Prior Supreme Court precedents have held that a hearing must precede, for example, the termination of welfare benefits, the government's seizure and forfeiture of real estate allegedly used in connection with the commission of crimes, termination of public employment, and prejudgment garnishment of wages. Evidentiary hearings *prior* to the termination of benefits need not occur in situations involving disability benefits, some terminations of parental rights, and some drivers' license suspensions (for example, failure to take a breathalyzer test); but post-suspension hearings may be required in such circumstances.

For example, assume a state passes a law saying women can cut only women's hair and men can cut only men's hair. Patrick McCann, who runs a unisex barber shop, flouts the law and continues to cut women's hair. In response, the state licensing board notifies him that it plans to revoke his license (state action has occurred). The licensing board then holds a hearing in which McCann has an opportunity to present his side of the dispute, and convenes a panel (probably made up of other licensed barbers) that has no apparent biases against McCann. If the panel decides to revoke his license and McCann challenges the board's finding on the basis of a denial of procedural due process, he will likely be unsuccessful. The hearing described here would seem to satisfy the requirements of procedural due process. However, if the board unilaterally revoked his license without a hearing, did not allow him to present his side of the dispute in any hearing that was held, or convened a panel including one or more members who were biased against McCann, he would be able to assert that he had been denied due process, and a judicial review would probably follow. Note, also, that while McCann may lose an appeal based on procedural due process, he would seem to have an excellent case for a denial of substantive due process.

An Ounce of Prevention

Employers should provide employees with a handbook or with some other written statement of employee rights, especially covering disciplinary proceedings against employees. The policy set out should ensure that employees are provided with notice of any disciplinary actions and provide for a fair and impartial hearing before the employment is terminated. Doing so can help to prevent an action for wrongful discharge by an employee who loses his or her job. However, it is imperative that an employer who institutes such a policy strictly adheres to the policy since it can become a part of the employment contract.

THE TAKINGS CLAUSE

Besides guaranteeing procedural and substantive due process, the Fifth Amendment provides an additional protection of a person's property rights. The Fifth Amendment concludes with the Takings Clause, "nor shall private property be taken for public use, without just compensation." This Fifth Amendment restraint on the power of the federal government also applies to the states through the Fourteenth Amendment's Due Process Clause. Under the Takings Clause, the government cannot take privately owned property without ensuring that the property owner is afforded due process, and if the property is being taken for a public use, the owner must be paid "just compensation" for the property or property *right* that is taken.

In litigation, the disagreement often centers on whether a *taking* has occurred, in which case the Constitution obligates the government to pay just compensation, or whether the governmental action amounts only to *regulation* under the exercise of its police power, in which case no compensation is owed. While the court has set out no clear formula for judging when a taking has occurred, any actual appropriation of property will suffice. For example, if the state condemns privately owned property for the purpose of constructing a parking garage on a state college campus, a taking has occurred. Assuming that the condemnation occurred following proper procedures—and probably a public hearing of some sort—the condemnation does not raise any due process issues. The taking is for a public purpose, support of the state college, and the state will have to pay just compensation to the owner of the property. This is an example of the state's exercise of its power of *eminent domain*, the power of the government to take private property for public use. Eminent domain can also be used to acquire property for highway construction, the building of a school or a hospital, and numerous other reasons. The courts are likely to uphold the taking so long as a public purpose is asserted by the governmental body that is instituting the taking and the property owner is given just compensation.

Some takings involve a less-than-complete appropriation of property, but such takings may entitle the owner to just compensation. For instance, the court has held that federal dam construction resulting in the repeated flooding of private property and low, direct flights over private property located next to federal or municipal airports constitute takings *if* the activities in question destroy the property's present use or unreasonably impair the value of the property and the owners' reasonable expectations regarding it.

In *Lucas v. South Carolina Coastal Council*,[29] the court ruled that a taking had occurred although the owner of the land retained title to it. Lucas purchased two parcels of land on a barrier island off the South Carolina coast, intending to build single-family homes on each of the lots. After he purchased the land, the South Carolina legislature enacted a statute prohibiting new construction on sections of the island, preventing Lucas from building the houses and substantially impairing the value of the land. He sued, claiming that this constituted a taking for which he was entitled to compensation. The U.S. Supreme Court agreed with Lucas, deciding that the legislation made the land essentially worthless and concluding that "[W]hen the owner of real property has been called upon to sacrifice all economically beneficial uses in the name of the common good . . . he has suffered a taking." The *Lucas* opinion implies that any land use regulation that fails to substantially advance legitimate state interests or that denies an owner the economically viable use of his or her land is a taking subject to the Fifth Amendment. In the absence of such factors, zoning ordinances—the most common type of land use regulations—ordinarily are constitutional under the Takings Clause even if the regulations restrict the use of the property and cause a reduction in its value, so long as the ordinances substantially advance legitimate state interests and do not extinguish fundamental attributes of ownership.

During the attempted taking, the government must afford the affected property owner procedural due process. However, the just compensation paid by the governmental regulator need reflect only the fair market value of the property; the price paid need not compensate the owner for the sentimental value of the property, the owner's unique need for the property, or the gain the regulating body realizes by virtue of the taking.

The court has recently expanded the constitutional definition of taking property for "public use." Historically, condemnation proceedings transfer property from private owners to the government. The government then generally builds roads, bridges, railroads, government buildings, etc. The case of *Kelo v. City of New London, Connecticut*[30] seemingly expanded the right of eminent domain, causing a significant public outcry. The City of New London used its power of eminent domain to transfer property from private owners to private developers in order to develop a waterfront area for economic development. New London argued that this private-to-private transfer was a public use even without a governmental building project because of the increase in tax dollars and jobs that would flow into the city when the developers created an urban center on the condemned land. The property owners argued that this private development was not a public use as required by the Constitution. The court disagreed and ruled for the city. The majority opinion decided that the city, and not the developers, was the primary beneficiary of the condemnation and that this was part of the "broader and more natural interpretation of public use."

It should also be noted that such condemnations and takings for economic purposes had previously been upheld. In Washington, D.C., and in Detroit, Michigan, property had been taken from private owners and sold to developers to improve the economic base of the community. However, in these cases the properties taken were "blighted" urban eyesores that were essentially valueless, and the improvements were part of an overall urban renewal project. The property taken in New London was not blighted; it was primarily single-family homes and small businesses, and the neighborhood was well maintained. Nevertheless, in response to the precedent set in *Kelo*, many states amended their takings statutes to prevent condemnation and transfer for economic purposes. In 2006, President Bush issued an executive order that required the federal government to use its takings power only "for the purpose of benefiting the general public and not merely for the purpose of advancing the economic interest of private parties to be given ownership or use of the property taken."

THE FIRST AMENDMENT AND COMMERCIAL SPEECH

The First Amendment specifies that "Congress shall make no law ... abridging the freedom of speech. ..." This is a restriction on the power of the federal government, ensuring that certain fundamental rights cannot be restricted by the government. Freedom of speech is one of these fundamental rights, a right granted to all persons. Since a business is considered a legal (or *juristic*) person, businesses are also entitled to the protections of the First Amendment. While freedom of speech is a fundamental right, it is not an absolute right. The government can—and does— regulate speech and/or expression, whether oral, written, expressive, or symbolic. For example, there are restrictions on speech if the speech is defamatory, obscene, or constitutes "fighting words." Commercial speech can be limited if it is unfair or deceptive. In deciding whether to limit speech, the government engages in another balancing test in which it compares such factors as the importance of these rights in a democratic society, the nature of the restriction imposed by the law, the type and importance of the governmental interest the law purports to serve, and the narrowness of the means used to effect that interest.

Commercial speech is obviously different from individual or private speech. In private speech, a person is stating his or her opinions or beliefs. Such opinions and beliefs are viewed as almost sacrosanct and deserve the highest possible level of protection. Unless private speech falls into a clearly prohibited area, such as slander or obscenity, the speaker's right to utter these opinions or beliefs will be protected. Commercial speech is different. Speech that advertises a product or a service for profit or for a business purpose is uttered for a purpose different from that of private speech. Commercial speech is not given the same degree of protection as private speech.

The term *commercial speech* is of recent origin in the United States: It first appeared in a 1971 court opinion. It was 1976 before the court recognized that commercial speech was entitled to protection similar to that given to individual speech.[31] Today, commercial speech is evaluated under the test set out in *Central Hudson Gas & Elec. Corp v. Public Serv. Comm'n of N.Y.*[32] Assuming the speech does no more than propose a commercial transaction, the courts will apply a four-part balancing test:

- The speech in question cannot be illegal or misleading;
- the law regulating the speech must be based on a legitimate governmental interest, such as the health and safety of citizens;
- the law must directly advance this interest; and
- the law must be narrowly tailored, using the least restrictive means available to effectively meet the governmental interest.

In contrast, laws that burden or restrict individual speech are disfavored by the courts. Before they will be upheld, such laws must pass the "strict scrutiny/compelling state interest" test, and they must be narrowly drawn, adopting the "least restrictive alternative" available in order to attain a compelling state interest. Courts can strike down substantially overbroad and vague laws, as well as those that proscribe protected activity and thus "chill" others into refraining from the exercise of constitutionally protected expression. The government can also limit or restrict lawful speech to some extent by specifying the time, place, and/or manner in which such speech can occur. For example, demonstrators may be required to obtain permits prior to their demonstrations, and such demonstrations can be restricted to a particular venue. Free speech zones have become commonplace on college campuses.

The regulation of commercial speech is viewed differently by the courts, at least in part because the courts expect that advertisers will still advertise. By contrast, individual speech, especially political speech, is less resilient. When such speech is restricted, the effect may be to "chill" others, preventing them from speaking on the topic that led to the restriction. But what happens when commercial speakers enter into the arena of political speech?

In January 2010, the court issued a landmark opinion concerning a corporation's rights to political speech in *Citizens United v. Federal Election Commission*.[33] In this case, the court dealt with the controversy surrounding business involvement in political campaigns. Businesses have traditionally been allowed to engage in political speech. For example, businesses often donate money to political causes and committees. The Bipartisan Campaign Reform Act (BCRA) is a federal law that, among other things, banned direct campaign contributions from businesses to candidates for political office and more general contributions within a certain pre-election period. In *Citizens United*, a nonprofit group desired to run a documentary critical of Hillary Clinton, but refrained because of the BCRA. Instead, the organization sued, arguing that the campaign finance law infringed upon its freedom of political speech under the First Amendment. The court's majority opinion reasoned that political speech forms the heart of any democracy and that businesses are an important part of America's democracy. Therefore, many of the BCRA restrictions on corporate political speech were found to violate the First Amendment and were struck down. After the *Citizens United* decision, corporations and labor unions possess the same political speech rights as individuals. Corporations are now allowed to conduct "electioneering campaigns" that support or denounce individual candidates prior to an election; they are still banned from directly contributing to a politician's campaign.

Exhibit 6.3

An Analysis of Free Speech and Its Limitations

Type of Speech	Private Speech	Commercial Speech
Prohibitions	Defamation (both slander and libel) and perjury are prohibited. There are also less restrictive prohibitions for: Illegal speech Speech urging illegal conduct Fighting words Obscenity	Illegal speech, speech urging illegal conduct False or misleading speech Unfair or deceptive speech
Restrictions	Private speech can: be restricted to a particular area (free speech zones), and require a license or permit (demonstrations, parades).	Commercial speech can be restricted more significantly than private speech. Placement of advertising can be regulated, as can content to some extent. The restrictions include a ban on making direct contributions to a particular political candidate.
Standards Required to Uphold Restrictions	Freedom of speech is a fundamental right. Any restrictions must pass the strict scrutiny/compelling state interest test. Restrictions must be narrowly drawn, e.g., the least restrictive measure possible to protect the governmental interest.	Commercial speech is not as protected as private speech. Commercial speech is entitled to protection as a fundamental right of the speaker, but the courts *seem* to apply what amounts to a "substantial state interest/intermediate scrutiny test" to restrictions on commercial speech.

As an interesting side note, the Occupy Movement was allowed to conduct a parade in the wake of the Rose Parade in Pasadena, California, on January 2, 2012. This was considered protected political speech. Although the Occupy parade was not a part of the Rose Parade, its parade was immediately after the Rose Parade and along the same route.

Contemporary Case

This opinion from 2013 laid the foundation for the *Obergefell* decision reached in 2015 concerning same-sex marriage. It addresses issues of proper jurisdiction, state sovereignty, and the guarantees of due process (from the Fifth Amendment) and equal protection (from the Fourteenth Amendment).

UNITED STATES v. WINDSOR
133 S.Ct. 2675 (2013)

FACTS Edith Windsor and Thea Spyer, New York City residents, met in 1963 and began a long-term relationship. When they became concerned about Thea's health in 2007, they traveled to Ontario, Canada and were married. They returned to New York after the marriage, where they continued to live together until Thea's death in 2009. The State of New York recognized their marriage as valid, and accepted them as a legally wed couple.

Thea left her entire estate to her spouse, Edith, who sought the federal estate tax marital deduction. However, the Internal Revenue Service denied that she was entitled to this deduction under the provisions of the Defense of Marriage Act (DOMA). Section 3 of DOMA, enacted in 1996, amended the Dictionary Act[34] in title 1, § 7 of the United States Code for both "marriage" and "spouse." Under DOMA, marriage means "only a legal union between one man and one woman as husband and wife," and spouse refers "only to a person of the opposite sex who is a husband or a wife."

Windsor paid the estate tax ($363,053) and then asked the IRS for a refund. After the IRS declined her request, she filed suit, alleging that DOMA violated the principles of equal protection and due process. The District Court ruled against the United Sates and ordered it to pay the refund to Windsor. The appellate court upheld the judgment and the U.S. Supreme Court granted certiorari.

ISSUES Did the Court have jurisdiction to hear this case? Does DOMA improperly deny equal protection and/or due process to a subcategory of people?

HOLDINGS Yes to both issues. The Court did have proper jurisdiction despite the decision by the Justice Department to no longer defend § 3's constitutionality, and DOMA did deny both equal protection and due process to a subcategory of people without a showing of any substantial state interest.

REASONING Excerpts from the opinion of Justice Kennedy:

... It seems fair to conclude that, until recent years, many citizens had not even considered the possibility that two persons of the same sex might aspire to occupy the same status and dignity as that of a man and woman in lawful marriage. For marriage between a man and a woman no doubt had been thought of by most people as essential to the very definition of that term and to its role and function throughout the history of civilization. ... For others, however, came the beginnings of a new perspective, a new insight.

Accordingly some States concluded that same-sex marriage ought to be given recognition and validity in the law for those same-sex couples who wish to define themselves by their commitment to each other. The limitation of lawful marriage to heterosexual couples ... came to be seen in New York and certain other States as an unjust exclusion. ... And so New York recognized same-sex marriages performed elsewhere; and then it later amended its own marriage laws to permit same-sex marriage. New York, in common with ... 11 other States and the District of Columbia, decided that same-sex couples should have the right to marry and so live with pride in themselves and their union and in a status of equality with all other married persons. ...

Against this background of lawful same-sex marriage in some States, the design, purpose, and effect of DOMA should be considered as the beginning point in deciding whether it is valid under the Constitution. By history and tradition the definition and regulation of marriage ... has been treated as being within the authority and realm of the separate States. Yet it is further established that Congress, in enacting discrete statutes, can make determinations that bear on marital rights and privileges. Just this Term the Court upheld the authority of the Congress to pre-empt state laws, allowing a former spouse to retain life insurance proceeds under a federal program that gave her priority ... over the wife by a second marriage who survived the husband. ... Congress has the power both to ensure efficiency in the administration of its programs and to choose what larger goals and policies to pursue.

Other precedents involving congressional statutes which affect marriages and family status further illustrate this point. In addressing the interaction of state domestic relations and federal immigration law Congress determined that marriages "entered into for the purpose of procuring an alien's admission [to the United States] as an immigrant" will not qualify the noncitizen for that status, even if the noncitizen's marriage is valid and proper for state-law purposes. ... And in establishing income-based criteria for Social Security benefits, Congress decided that although state law would determine in general who qualifies as an applicant's spouse, common-law marriages also should be recognized, regardless of any particular State's view on these relationships. ...

Though these discrete examples establish the constitutionality of limited federal laws that regulate the meaning of marriage in order to further federal policy, DOMA has a far greater reach; for it enacts a directive applicable to over 1,000 federal statutes and the whole realm of federal regulations. And its operation is directed to a class of persons that the laws of New York, and of 11 other States, have sought to protect. ... In order to assess the validity of that intervention it is necessary to discuss the extent of the state power and authority over marriage as a matter of history and tradition. State laws defining and regulating marriage, of course, must respect the constitutional rights of persons ... but, subject to those guarantees, "regulation of domestic relations" is "an area that has long been regarded as a virtually exclusive province of the States." ...

The significance of state responsibilities for the definition and regulation of marriage dates to the Nation's beginning; for "when the Constitution was adopted the common understanding was that the domestic relations of husband and wife and parent and child were matters reserved to the States." ...

Against this background DOMA rejects the long-established precept that the incidents, benefits, and obligations of marriage are uniform for all married couples within each State, though they may vary, subject to constitutional guarantees, from one State to the next. Despite these considerations, it is unnecessary to decide whether this federal intrusion on state power is a violation of the Constitution because it disrupts the federal balance. The State's power in defining the marital relation is of central relevance in this case quite apart from principles of federalism. Here the State's decision to give this class of persons the right to marry conferred upon them a dignity and status of immense import. When the State used its historic and essential authority to define the marital relation in this way, its role and its power in making the decision enhanced the recognition, dignity, and protection of the class in their own community. DOMA, because of its reach and extent, departs from this history and tradition of reliance on state law to define marriage. "'[D]iscriminations of an unusual character especially suggest careful consideration to determine whether they are obnoxious to the constitutional provision.'"

The Federal Government uses this state-defined class for the opposite purpose—to impose restrictions and disabilities. That result requires this Court now to address whether the resulting injury and indignity is a deprivation of an essential part of the liberty protected by the Fifth Amendment. What the State of New York treats as alike the federal law deems unlike by a law designed to injure the same class the State seeks to protect.

In acting first to recognize and then to allow same-sex marriages, New York was responding "to the initiative of those who [sought] a voice in shaping the destiny of their own times." . . . These actions were without doubt a proper exercise of its sovereign authority within our federal system, all in the way that the Framers of the Constitution intended. The dynamics of state government in the federal system are to allow the formation of consensus respecting the way the members of a discrete community treat each other in their daily contact and constant interaction with each other.

The States' interest in defining and regulating the marital relation, subject to constitutional guarantees, stems from the understanding that marriage is more than a routine classification for purposes of certain statutory benefits. . . . For same-sex couples who wished to be married, the State acted to give their lawful conduct a lawful status. This status is a far-reaching legal acknowledgment of the intimate relationship between two people, a relationship deemed by the State worthy of dignity in the community equal with all other marriages. It reflects both the community's considered perspective on the

historical roots of the institution of marriage and its evolving understanding of the meaning of equality.

DOMA seeks to injure the very class New York seeks to protect. By doing so it violates basic due process and equal protection principles applicable to the Federal Government. . . . The Constitution's guarantee of equality "must at the very least mean that a bare congressional desire to harm a politically unpopular group cannot" justify disparate treatment of that group. . . . In determining whether a law is motived by an improper animus or purpose, "'[d]iscriminations of an unusual character'" especially require careful consideration. . . . DOMA cannot survive under these principles. . . . DOMA's unusual deviation from the usual tradition of recognizing and accepting state definitions of marriage here operates to deprive same-sex couples of the benefits and responsibilities that come with the federal recognition of their marriages. This is strong evidence of a law having the purpose and effect of disapproval of that class. The avowed purpose and practical effect of the law here in question are to impose a disadvantage, a separate status, and so a stigma upon all who enter into same-sex marriages made lawful by the unquestioned authority of the States.

The history of DOMA's enactment and its own text demonstrate that interference with the equal dignity of same-sex marriages . . . was more than an incidental effect of the federal statute. It was its essence. The House Report announced its conclusion that "it is both appropriate and necessary for Congress to do what it can to defend the institution of traditional heterosexual marriage. . . . [The bill] is appropriately entitled the 'Defense of Marriage Act.' The effort to redefine 'marriage' to extend to homosexual couples is a truly radical proposal that would fundamentally alter the institution of marriage." . . . The House concluded that DOMA expresses "both moral disapproval of homosexuality, and a moral conviction that heterosexuality better comports with traditional (especially Judeo-Christian) morality." The stated purpose of the law was to promote an "interest in protecting the traditional moral teachings reflected in heterosexual-only marriage laws." Were there any doubt of this far-reaching purpose, the title of the Act confirms it: The Defense of Marriage. . . .

The Act's demonstrated purpose is to ensure that if any State decides to recognize same-sex marriages, those unions will be treated as second-class marriages for purposes of federal law. This raises a most serious question under the Constitution's Fifth Amendment.

DOMA's operation in practice confirms this purpose. When New York adopted a law to permit same-sex marriage, it sought to eliminate inequality; but DOMA frustrates that objective through a system-wide enactment with no identified connection to any particular area of federal law. DOMA writes inequality into the entire United States Code. The particular case at hand concerns the estate tax, but DOMA is more than a simple determination of what should or should not be allowed as an estate tax refund. Among the over 1,000 statutes and numerous federal regulations that DOMA controls are laws pertaining to Social Security, housing, taxes, criminal sanctions, copyright, and veterans' benefits. . . .

The power the Constitution grants it also restrains. And though Congress has great authority to design laws to fit its own conception of sound national policy, it cannot deny the liberty protected by the Due Process Clause of the Fifth Amendment.

What has been explained to this point should more than suffice to establish that the principal purpose and the necessary effect of this law are to demean those persons who are in a lawful same-sex marriage. This requires the Court to hold, as it now does, that DOMA is unconstitutional as a deprivation of the liberty of the person protected by the Fifth Amendment of the Constitution.

The judgment of the Court of Appeals for the Second Circuit is affirmed.

Short Answer Questions

1. Suppose that a business institutes a policy that it will only hire applicants for any of its jobs if the applicant has at least a high school diploma or equivalent. Is such a policy permissible under the Equal Protection Clause?

    Suppose, instead, that a business has a policy of only hiring college graduates with a particular major and a stated minimum GPA. Is this different from the requirement that a successful applicant possesses at least a high school diploma or equivalent, from an equal protection perspective? Explain.

2. A public school district in a southern state has a dress code that has been in effect since 2002. This dress code prohibits wearing any clothing that has symbols that are likely to offend others, including any symbols that connote racism or that mock disabilities. One of the symbols included in the ban is the Confederate battle flag, which the school district deemed to be deeply divisive and offensive to African-American students.

    Following the church shootings in South Carolina in June 2015, the school district amended its "dress code," expanding the ban that already existed on articles of clothing to include decals on automobiles and the display of "disruptive" flags in the school parking lot. A number of students protested this extension, asserting that it is an illegal interference with their First Amendment right to freedom of speech. If this case is taken to court, how should the controversy be resolved?

3. Suppose that a city enacts a zoning ordinance that prohibits certain adult entertainment enterprises, primarily bookstores and theaters, from operating in certain parts of the city.

Specifically, the ordinance prohibits the operation of such establishments within one block of a school, a church, or a bar. Would such an ordinance survive a lawsuit seeking to overturn it? What standard would the court use in deciding this case? Would a rational basis be sufficient grounds to uphold the ordinance, or would a higher standard be applied?

You Decide...

1. Jennifer Gratz and Patrick Hemacher each applied for admission to the University of Michigan's College of Literature, Science, and the Arts (LSA). Gratz applied for admission in the fall of 1995; Hemacher applied for admission in the fall of 1997. Both Gratz and Hemacher were residents of the state of Michigan, both were Caucasian, and both were denied admission. Gratz was informed by the Admissions Office that she was "well qualified" but that she was "less competitive than the students who ha[d] been admitted on first review." She subsequently enrolled at the University of Michigan at Dearborn, from which she graduated in 1999.

Hemacher was notified that although his "academic credentials [were] in the qualified range, they [were] not at the level needed for first review admission." Hemacher subsequently enrolled at Michigan State University.

Gratz and Hemacher filed a class action lawsuit against the university alleging "violations and threatened violations of the rights of the plaintiffs and the class they represent to equal protection of the laws under the Fourteenth Amendment ... , and for racial discrimination in violation of [federal law]." They were seeking compensatory and punitive damages for past violations. They asked for a finding that respondents violated petitioners' "rights to nondiscriminatory treatment." They also requested an injunction prohibiting respondents from

"continuing to discriminate on the basis of race in violation of the Fourteenth Amendment" and an order requiring the LSA to offer Hemacher admission as a transfer student.

The university denied that it had acted inappropriately. The U.S. District Court upheld the university's admission policies, and the Supreme Court granted certiorari.

Did the university's admissions guidelines violate the Equal Protection Clause of the Fourteenth Amendment and Title VI of the Civil Rights Act of 1964?

(See *Gratz v. Bollinger*, 539 U.S. 244 (2003).)

2. Abercrombie & Fitch is a clothing store chain with locations throughout the United States. It has a "Look Policy" that is meant to emphasize its image as a purveyor of a "hip east coast" style. The "Look Policy" prohibits, among other things, facial hair or extreme hairstyles or hair colors. Employees should wear clothing that is clean and classic, but it should not be provocative. Earrings should be no larger than a dime and should not dangle, and men may not wear earrings. No scarves or caps may be worn, nor any black clothing. The Look Policy was also a part of the interview process, with the interviewer scoring the applicant on his or her appearance as a part of the evaluation of the candidate.

Samantha Elauf, a practicing Muslim, applied for a job as a salesperson with an Abercrombie & Fitch store in Oklahoma. In keeping with her religious beliefs, she wore a headscarf, a hijab, every day, including the day she interviewed for the position with Abercrombie & Fitch. Ms. Elauf did not mention the hijab or her reason for wearing it during the interview, nor did the interviewer mention it or question her about it. Ms. Elauf also did not ask for an accommodation from the store if she was hired.

Following the interview, the interviewer contacted the District Manager to discuss the situation.

The District Manager told the interviewer to lower Ms. Elauf's score in the "appearance" section of the interview. As a result, Ms. Elauf did not get hired. She filed a complaint with the EEOC, alleging that she was the victim of discrimination due to her religion. The EEOC filed suit against Abercrombie & Fitch on behalf of Ms. Elauf.

Did the Abercrombie & Fitch "Look Policy" violate Ms. Elauf's fundamental rights? Should the court uphold the store's dress code?

(See *Equal Employment Opportunity Commission v. Abercrombie & Fitch Stores, Inc.*, 135 S. Ct. 2028, 2015 U.S. LEXIS 3718 (2015).)

Notes

1. See, for example, *Citizens United v. Federal Election Commission*, 558 U.S. 310 (2010) in which the Supreme Court upheld the right of a non-profit corporation to exercise its freedom of speech in the form of political expenditures.
2. 9 Wheat (22 U.S.) 1 (1824).
3. This same interpretation was still followed more than a century later. See *Wickard v. Filburn*, 317 U.S. 111 (1942), in which a farmer was penalized for harvesting more wheat than he was authorized to harvest. Despite Filburn's assertion that the wheat was grown for his personal use, the court held that Filburn was subject to regulation because the "excess" wheat he harvested *might* have a substantial economic effect on interstate commerce.
4. 24 Stat. 379 (1887).
5. 76 U.S. 41 (1869).
6. 82 U.S. 232 (1872).
7. 128 U.S. 1 (1888).
8. 301 U.S. 1 (1937).
9. 336 U.S. 460 (1949).
10. 379 U.S. 241 (1964).
11. The Supreme Court has held that the Commerce Clause grants Congress—and not the executive branch—exclusive power to regulate commerce with foreign nations (i.e., commerce between United States citizens and citizens of foreign nations).
12. 411 U.S. 624 (1973).
13. 514 U.S. 549 (1995).
14. 104 Stat. 4789, § 1702 (1990).
15. 529 U.S. 598 (2000).
16. The "Dormant Commerce Clause" is not found in the Constitution. This phrase refers to the court's rulings over the years that have established limits on the power or the right of the states individually to enact legislation that imposes barriers on interstate commerce. The court has ruled that Congressional inaction in a particular area does not permit state regulation in the area until such time as Congress does act.
17. S. 743 (114th) (2013).
18. S. 698 (114th) (2015).
19. See the Web site for this chapter for links and additional information on this topic.
20. 473 U.S. 432 (1985).
21. 118 U.S. 356, 6 S. Ct. 1064, 30 L. Ed. 220 (1886).
22. 517 U.S. 620 (1996).
23. 515 U.S. 200 (1995).
24. 135 S. Ct. 2028, 2015 U.S. LEXIS 3718 (2015).
25. Disparate impact occurs when an employer's practices have a statistically significant effect on distinct classes or groups of people. Disparate impact does not require any showing of intent to discriminate.
26. 429 U.S. 190 (1976).
27. *U.S. v. Virginia*, 518 U.S. 515 (1996).
28. 381 U.S. 479 (1965).
29. 505 U.S. 1003 (1992).
30. 545 U.S. 69 (2005).
31. *Virginia Board of Pharmacy v. Virginia Citizens Consumer Council*, 425 U.S. 728 (1976). Virginia made it illegal for pharmacists to advertise their prescription drug prices.

The Virginia Citizens Consumer Council (VCCC) challenged this statute, and the Court ruled that commercial speech is entitled to First Amendment protections, and that prohibiting the advertisement of prices does not advance a legitimate government interest.

32. 447 U.S. 557 (1980).

33. 558 U.S. 08-205 (2010).

34. 1 U.S. Code § 7. Chapter 1 of the Dictionary Act provides rules of interpretation for federal statutes. DOMA amended § 7 to define "marriage" and "spouse" in a manner that would prohibit the use of either term for a same-sex couple under any federal law or provision.

7

Administrative Regulation

Learning Objectives

After completing this chapter you should be able to

- Explain the administrative procedure process
- Describe the administrative rule-making process
- Discuss the investigative authority of an agency
- Explain what is involved in an administrative hearing
- Recognize the limitations of judicial review of agency actions

This is a landmark Supreme Court opinion in which the Court addressed the issue of whether Congress could delegate authority to the executive branch to carry out the objectives of its statutory enactments. Such delegation of authority to the executive branch is necessary if administrative agencies are to function.

J. W. HAMPTON. JR., & CO. v. UNITED STATES
276 U.S. 395, 48 S.Ct. 348 (1928)

FACTS J.W. Hampton, Jr. & Co. (Hampton), a freight customs broker, imported barium oxide into New York. The customs collector assessed a tariff on the barium oxide of six cents per pound, two cents more per pound than the tariff specified in the Tariff Act of September 21, 1922. The tariff rate was raised by a proclamation of the President of the United States, Calvin Coolidge. The President's authority to decree increases or decreases in the tariff rates set out in the statute was found in § 315 of Title 3 of the Tariff Act of September 21, 1922, the so-called "flexible tariff provision."

In the statute, Congress delegated the authority to adjust tariff rates to the President, upon the recommendation of the Tariff Commission, which was to investigate any perceived inequities in tariffs.

Such adjustments were to be made in order to "regulate the foreign commerce of the United States" in order to equalize the cost of production between U.S. products and foreign imports of the same or competing items. The President was not authorized to transfer any article from the dutiable list to the free (non-dutiable) list, or from the free list to the dutiable list.

In this case the President was informed that the prior duty of four cents per pound on barium oxide did not equalize the cost of production between imported barium oxide and barium oxide produced in the

United States, and so he issued a proclamation increasing the duty to six cents per pound to equalize the cost of production.

Hampton objected, arguing that Congress's delegation of such authority to the President was unconstitutional since only Congress is authorized to exercise legislative power. Hampton also argued that taxes, duties, imposts, and excises could only be used to generate revenue, and not for the purpose of protecting American industries.

The Customs Court upheld the increase in the tariff, as did the U.S. Court of Customs Appeals. The Attorney General certified that the case should be reviewed by the U.S. Supreme Court, and a writ of certiorari was granted in June 1927.

ISSUES Was this delegation of authority to the president an unconstitutional delegation of legislative authority to the executive branch? Was the increase in the tariff an unconstitutional imposition of duties for a purpose other than raising revenues?

HOLDINGS No to each issue. The authority granted to the president in this case was not a legislative authority, it was a carefully defined executive authority. The power to impose taxes, duties, imposts, and excises is not specifically limited to the raising of revenues.

REASONING Excerpts from the opinion of Chief Justice Taft:

First. It seems clear what Congress intended by § 315 ... [was] to secure by law the imposition of customs duties on articles of imported merchandise which should equal the difference between the cost of producing in a foreign country the articles in question and ... [selling them] in the United States, and the cost of producing and selling like or similar articles in the United States, so that the duties not only secure revenue, but at the same time enable domestic producers to compete on terms of equality with foreign producers in the markets of the United States. It may be that it is difficult to fix with exactness this difference, but the difference which is sought in the statute is perfectly clear and perfectly intelligible. Because of the difficulty in practically determining what that difference is, Congress seems to have doubted that the information in its possession was such as to enable it to make the adjustment accurately, and also to have apprehended that, with changing conditions, the difference might vary in such a way that some readjustments would be necessary to give effect to the principle on which the statute proceeds. To avoid such difficulties, Congress adopted . . . the method of describing with clearness what its policy and plan was, and then authorizing a member of the executive branch to carry out its policy and plan and to find the changing difference from time to time and to make the adjustments necessary to conform the duties to the standard underlying that policy and plan. As it was a matter of great importance, it concluded to give by statute to the President . . . the function of determining the difference as it might vary. He was provided with a body of investigators who were to assist him in obtaining needed data and ascertaining the facts justifying readjustments. . . .

The Tariff Commission does not itself fix duties, but, before the President reaches a conclusion on the subject of investigation, the Tariff Commission must make an investigation, and in doing so must give notice to all parties interested and an opportunity to adduce evidence and to be heard. . . .

Congress may feel itself unable conveniently to determine exactly when its exercise of the legislative power should become effective . . . and it may leave the determination of such time to the decision of an executive. . . .

It is conceded by counsel that Congress may use executive officers in the application and enforcement of a policy declared . . . by Congress, and authorize such officers, in the application of the congressional declaration, to enforce it by regulation equivalent to law. But it is said that this never has been permitted to be done where Congress has exercised the power to levy taxes and fix customs duties. The authorities make no such distinction . . . If Congress shall lay down by legislative act an intelligible principle to which the person or body authorized to fix such rates is directed to conform, such legislative action is not a forbidden delegation of legislative power. If it is thought wise to vary the customs duties according to changing conditions of production at home and abroad, it may authorize the Chief Executive to carry out this purpose, with the advisory assistance of a Tariff Commission appointed under congressional authority . . .

It was contended that this section delegated to the President both legislative and treatymaking powers, and was unconstitutional. After an examination of all the authorities, the Court said that, while Congress could not delegate legislative power to the President, this Act did not in any real sense invest the President with the power of legislation, because nothing involving the expediency or just operation of such legislation was left to the determination of the President; that the legislative power was exercised when Congress declared that the suspension should take effect upon a named contingency. What the President was required to do was merely in execution of the Act of Congress. It was not the making of law. He was the mere agent of the lawmaking department to ascertain and declare the event upon which its expressed will was to take effect.

Second. The second objection to § 315 is that the declared plan of Congress . . . [is] one directed to a tariff system of protection that will avoid damaging competition to the country's industries by the importation of goods from other countries at too low a rate to equalize foreign and domestic competition in the markets of the United States. It is contended that the only power of Congress in the levying of customs duties is to create revenue, and that it is unconstitutional to frame the customs duties with any other view than that of revenue raising. It undoubtedly is true that . . . there has been much discussion between parties as to the wisdom of the policy of protection ... [and] as to its constitutionality, but no historian ... would contend that Congress, since the first revenue Act in 1789, has not assumed that it was within its power in making provision for the collection of revenue to put taxes upon importations and to vary the subjects of such taxes or rates in an effort to encourage the growth of the industries of the nation by protecting home production against foreign competition ...

So long as the motive of Congress and the effect of its legislative action are to secure revenue for the benefit of the general government, the existence of other motives in the selection of the subjects of taxes cannot invalidate congressional action ...

And so here, the fact that Congress declares that one of its motives in fixing the rates of duty is so to fix them that they shall encourage the industries of this country in the competition with producers in other countries in the sale of goods in this country cannot invalidate a revenue Act so framed. Section 315 and its provisions are within the power of Congress. The judgment of the Court of Customs Appeals is affirmed.

INTRODUCTION

When the topic of government regulation of business is discussed, many people immediately envision statutory enactments by Congress. Some may think of the Sherman Antitrust Act or the Clayton Act, while others will think about Sarbanes-Oxley or the Foreign Corrupt Practices Act. The Dodd-Frank Act or the Civil Rights Act of 1964 may come to mind for others. Each of these laws is, in fact, an integral part of government regulation of business. And each was passed by Congress to address a particular broad issue that a significant number of people believed needed to be addressed. Such enactments are an important part of social contract theory. But while statutory enactments are a key element of government regulation and of social contract theory, they are not the most common, and they may not be the most important.

Administrative regulation is the most common and the most pervasive form of governmental regulation at both the federal and the state levels. The discussion in this chapter focuses on federal administrative regulation. Each state has similar administrative agencies and administrative regulations, and must follow similar rules.

The use of administrative regulation began in earnest in the late 1800s with the creation of government agencies, such as the Interstate Commerce Commission (ICC). Since then Congress added agencies like the Federal Trade Commission (FTC) in 1914, the Securities and Exchange Commission (SEC) in 1934, and then a multitude of "alphabet agencies" over the remainder of the twentieth century. Each of these agencies was created by statute and charged with providing regulations and guidance in dealing with the specific area provided for in the statute. Congress delegates regulatory authority to administrative agencies and expects those agencies to hire experts in the field to exercise that delegated authority. The relevant skill of the agency's experts allows it to recognize particular issues or areas that may be unique to that field, and for which most members of Congress lack experience or expertise.

One interesting aspect of administrative regulation is that administrative agencies tend to wield more (relative) power than does any one branch of the federal government or any of the state governments. (While some people refer to agencies as the "fourth branch" of government, they are actually within the executive branch and not an independent branch of the government.) Americans tend to take great pride in our separation of powers, as provided for in the U.S. Constitution. The legislative branch (Congress) enacts laws and controls the purse (the budget); the executive branch (the president) enforces the laws and controls the military (the sword); and the judicial branch (the courts) interpret and apply the law. This *separation of powers* provides a system of checks and balances that has worked well for more than 200 years. Administrative agencies, on the other hand, have a *combination* of powers. An agency enacts rules and regulations, a quasi-legislative role; it enforces those rules and regulations, an executive role; and it holds hearings in which it interprets and applies the regulations, a quasi-judicial role. Each of these powers will be discussed in subsequent sections as we examine the role of administrative agencies and administrative regulation in the United States today.

ADMINISTRATIVE AGENCIES

As previously mentioned, administrative agencies are frequently created by Congress through a legislative enactment called an enabling statute. The enabling statute grants the agencies their rule-making authority to allow them to effectively oversee and regulate the specific area covered by the statute. For example, the Federal Communication Commission (FCC) has broad regulatory authority over interstate and international communications by radio, television, wire, satellite, and cable. Similarly, the FTC has broad regulatory authority to protect consumers by preventing unfair and deceptive trade practices. Each of these, and many other agencies, is deemed to be an independent agency. An independent agency is an agency over which the president has limited power to remove the head of the agency. The president is closely involved in appointing the head of the agency, however.[1]

There are also executive agencies, such as the Environmental Protection Agency (EPA), that are headed by a member of the president's cabinet. These executive agencies are created by executive order of the president rather than by an act of Congress and are thus somewhat beyond the control of the legislative branch.

Regardless of the classification, agencies are created to provide expertise in a particular field or area that may be lacking in the Congress (for independent agencies) or the executive branch (for executive agencies). The agencies are then delegated the authority (1) to oversee this particular area; (2) to propose necessary regulations to accomplish the objectives of the enabling legislation or the executive order; and (3) to otherwise help to ensure that activities within the particular area are in compliance with public policy. To carry out its obligations, each agency has rule-making authority, investigative authority, and adjudicatory authority. Each of these areas of authority is discussed in the following sections.

STATUTORY PROVISIONS AND LIMITATIONS ON ADMINISTRATIVE AGENCIES

Before discussing what regulatory agencies do or how they do it, it is helpful to examine the parameters within which these agencies operate. When an administrative agency is created, it has certain authority delegated to it. But this delegation is not carte blanche to do whatever the agency desires. Its authority is limited by both constitutional and statutory restrictions. When an agency oversteps its bounds, its conduct is subject to challenge in court, and the court may strike down any actions that exceed the agency's delegated authority.

Every regulation that an agency enacts must comply with the constitutional requirements of providing due process and equal protection. Regulation must be enacted in a manner that provides for procedural due process, including a need to announce proposed rules in advance and to allow for a period of public comment and feedback. The final regulation must also be published so that the public is aware of the regulation and its effective date prior to its implementation. This procedure is discussed in more detail in the next section of the chapter.

Even if the agency follows all of the procedural steps and properly proposes and then enacts a regulation, the regulation must assure substantive due process in order to withstand a challenge. The regulation cannot be overly broad, restricting conduct or activities that are beyond the scope of the agency's authority. Nor can the regulation be vague or ambiguous, leaving the public in doubt as to what is or is not prohibited by the regulation. For example, suppose that the Drug Enforcement Administration (DEA)[2] decided that most of the illegal drugs that entered the United States were being brought into the country through the southern border of the United States. In an effort to stop or reduce such smuggling of controlled substances, the DEA enacted a regulation prohibiting the entry into the United States of any persons or carriers from south of the border. All motor vehicles would be turned away, all ships would be refused entry to any U.S. ports, and all aircraft would be diverted away from any U.S. airports. While such a regulation might very well stop, or significantly reduce, the illegal importation of drugs from south of the border, the regulation would be overly broad, and thus it would violate substantive due process. Thousands of people who were not involved in the drug trade would be inconvenienced or denied entry—or reentry—to the United States due to this regulation. Obviously, the diverted aircraft would land elsewhere, the diverted ships would enter other ports, and the motor vehicles would not enter the United States, but at what cost? The drug smugglers would simply find a way to avoid entering the United States from the south. Perhaps they would fly to Canada and try to enter from the north, or fly to Europe to attempt their smuggling from the east.

The Equal Protection Clause requires that similarly situated people are to be treated similarly. An administrative regulation will frequently call for the application of some discriminating factor such as licensing or the imposition of a residency requirement in determining who is entitled to benefits or is subject to a particular regulation. There is nothing wrong with requiring or applying such a factor, provided that the application is done in a manner that does not discriminate on an improper basis. Recall, for example, the *Yick Wo*[3] case from Chapter 6, in which a requirement for attaining a license seemed to be based on public safety concerns, but was in fact based on racial discrimination against people of Chinese ancestry. The courts are likely to examine very closely any regulations that seemingly have a disparate impact and are likely to apply the strict scrutiny test in evaluating such regulations.

There are also some statutory restrictions that affect agency conduct. The two most important of these are the Administrative Procedures Act[4] (APA) and the Freedom of Information Act[5] (FOIA). The APA specifies the procedures that an agency must follow in enacting and in enforcing regulations, adding to regulatory action an additional procedural component to the procedural due process requirements of the Constitution. The FOIA requires agencies to publish or disclose their rules, regulations, procedures, policies, and reports. Any citizen can file an FOIA request if he or she believes that an agency has failed to comply with the disclosure requirements, and the agency must provide the requested information unless it falls within one of the areas exempted in the statute. There are nine exemption areas under the FOIA.[6] These exemptions are set out in Exhibit 7.1.

The FOIA applies to Census Bureau data, but it does not apply to records held by Congress, federal courts, state and local governments, private businesses, schools, private organizations, or private individuals.[8] Every state also has an FOIA, although the scope of these statutes is likely to differ somewhat from the federal law.

Exhibit 7.1

Exemptions to the Freedom of Information Act

Exemption (b)(1)	Classified matters of national defense or foreign policy
Exemption (b)(2)	Internal personnel rules and practices
Exemption (b)(3)	Information specifically exempted by other statutes
Exemption (b)(4)	Trade secrets, commercial or financial information
Exemption (b)(5)	Privileged interagency or intra-agency memoranda or letters
Exemption (b)(6)	Personal information affecting an individual's privacy
Exemption (b)(7)	Investigatory records compiled for law enforcement purposes
Exemption (b)(8)	Records of financial institutions
Exemption (b)(9)	Geographical and geophysical information concerning wells[7]

RULE-MAKING AND REGULATORY AUTHORITY

Administrative agencies are charged with overseeing and monitoring specialized areas. In order to do so, the agencies must make rules and regulations. The federal APA, as the controlling law for how federal administrative agencies must conduct themselves, has "rules" for rule making that administrative agencies must follow. (Many states have their own APA.) Under the APA, a rule or a regulation is defined as

> the whole or a part of an agency statement of general or particular applicability and future effect designed to implement, interpret, or prescribe law or policy or describing the organization, procedure, or practice requirements of an agency.[9]

The APA also defines rule-making as the "agency process for formulating, amending, or repealing a rule."[10] Adding some detail to this definition, rule-making involves

> agency action which regulates the future conduct of either groups of persons or a single person; it is essentially legislative in nature, not only because it operates in the future but because it is primarily concerned with policy considerations.[11]

The agency's focus changes once a rule that it proposed goes into effect. The agency now becomes responsible for enforcing the rule and for adjudicating any perceived or alleged violations of the regulation. Exhibit 7.2 shows a typical rule-making process.

An Ounce of Prevention

Because administrative regulations have such significant impact on businesses, it is important for any business to continue to be informed about regulations and proposed regulations that directly or indirectly affect the business and/or its industry. It is beneficial to regularly check the Federal Register to see if any new regulations have been proposed that may have a direct impact on the business. However, the number of regulations that are proposed in any given period may make this an ungainly task. Another option—and possibly a better one—is to join (or establish) a listserv of firms and organizations that face comparable regulations and regularly deal with the same agencies. The listserv group can then share information about proposed regulations, comment periods, and concerns that members have with any regulations or proposals. The most recent versions of LISTSERV include a Web interface to make communication easier and more intuitive. The Web interface is richly populated with on-screen information, tutorials, and wizards to help you use the program quickly and effectively.[12] A business can also join trade groups which actively track regulations.

Exhibit 7.2

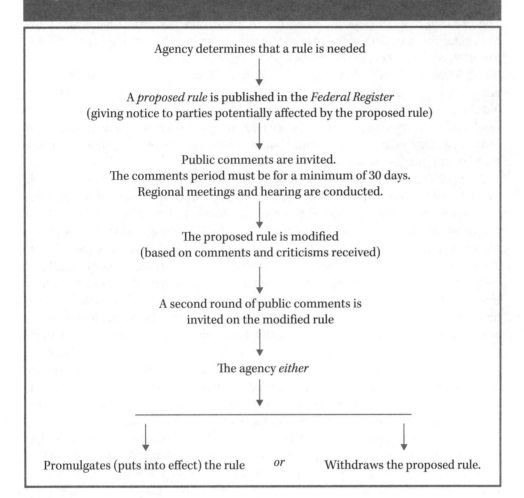

Rule-making Procedures for an Administrative Agency

Agency determines that a rule is needed

↓

A *proposed rule* is published in the *Federal Register*
(giving notice to parties potentially affected by the proposed rule)

↓

Public comments are invited.
The comments period must be for a minimum of 30 days.
Regional meetings and hearing are conducted.

↓

The proposed rule is modified
(based on comments and criticisms received)

↓

A second round of public comments is
invited on the modified rule

↓

The agency *either*

↓

Promulgates (puts into effect) the rule   *or*   Withdraws the proposed rule.

INVESTIGATIVE AUTHORITY

To properly fulfill its oversight responsibilities an agency needs to be able to conduct investigations or have some other means of acquiring information. It is interesting to note that an agency must have specific authority to conduct investigations. This authority is normally found in the enabling statute that created the agency or in other statutes that are enacted to complement the enabling statute. In fact, the APA limits the right of an agency to investigate or to demand information. An investigation or a demand for information is valid only if the agency follows the procedures specified in the statute.

Courts often issue *subpoenas*[13] in order to compel a person to testify in a judicial proceeding. Courts also issue *subpoenas duce tecum*[14] to compel the production of documents to be used as evidence in a trial. An administrative agency can only issue subpoenas of either type if the authority to do so is authorized by statute. This restriction makes it more difficult for an agency to investigate, but provides a layer of protection for the members of the regulated areas. Remember that the agency legislates, executes, *and* adjudicates within its area of expertise. If agencies had the power to issues subpoenas at will, they could easily begin "witch hunts" against certain suspect groups or organizations that operate within those areas of expertise. The APA's limitation on subpoena power provides protection for the regulated group from overreaching by the regulating agencies. Congress can grant such subpoena power in the enabling statute or in complementary statutes, but such power is generally limited even when agencies are allowed to issue subpoenas.

Agencies may be accused of conducting a "witch hunt" even absent subpoena power. The Internal Revenue Service (IRS) is an agency under the jurisdiction of the Treasury Department. Its agents are allowed to issue summonses to investigate a variety of tax-related issues. The IRS was accused of conducting witch hunts against various Tea Party organizations seeking tax-exempt status between 2010 and 2013. A subsequent Senate investigation determined that "gross mismanagement at the highest levels of the I.R.S . . . confirms that the I.R.S. is prone to abuse."[15] Agencies are allowed to conduct inspections to ensure that the organization being inspected is in compliance with administrative regulations. This right to inspect is not an unlimited right. The Fourth Amendment's protection against unreasonable searches and seizures applies to administrative agencies as well as to law enforcement personnel, even in the area of administrative inspections. However, the requirement of showing probable cause that applies to law enforcement personnel does not apply as strictly to an administrative agency. If the agency can show that there is a governmental interest at stake requiring an inspection of an organization or a facility, the court is likely to find sufficient probable cause to issue a warrant for the search.

Administrative agencies do not have unlimited authority to conduct investigations. Even if the agency asserts that there is a governmental interest at stake and that an investigation is necessary, the agency must show that the investigation is for a legitimate purpose that will further that governmental interest. The investigation must seek only relevant information, and the demand for such information must be specific and it cannot be unreasonably burdensome on the investigated party. Agencies are not allowed to conduct "fishing expeditions" in the hope of finding evidence of wrongdoing. These restrictions apply even if the agency has acquired a search warrant.

For example, the Occupational Safety and Health Administration (OSHA) conducts a number of inspections every year. OSHA inspectors will frequently show up at a location requesting permission to conduct an inspection. The OSHA inspectors are supposed to request access only during regular business hours, and they are expected to provide proper identification and credentials before being granted access.[16] If the inspector is denied access, he or she can obtain a warrant from the court, compelling the manager of the facility to grant access for the inspection.

An Ounce of Prevention

Inspections by administrative agencies are inevitable for many, if not most, firms. Agencies are granted broad discretion in their enabling statutes, and the courts tend to apply a limited probable cause requirement when an agency requests a search warrant. As a result, a firm should consider allowing an agency to inspect its facilities when asked without requiring a warrant, unless the request takes place at an unreasonable time. Cooperation with the inspector may not garner any favorable points, but refusing the request for an inspection without a warrant may well generate suspicion and cause the inspectors to look a little more closely once they acquire the warrant and gain access for the inspection.

The National Environmental Policy Act (NEPA), signed into law in 1970, requires federal agencies to prepare and submit an environmental impact statement (EIS) for projects that are likely to have a significant impact on the environment. The EIS is a detailed report that includes the consideration of reasonable alternatives and an analysis of potential impacts on the environment, and it shows compliance with environmental laws and executive orders.[17] The EPA is charged with enforcing NEPA, in conjunction with the Council on Environmental Quality (CEQ). The EPA reviews and evaluates the EIS that is filed for "any major federal actions that will significantly affect" the environment.

The power granted to administrative agencies to investigate, to inspect, and to compel action is very broad. The areas and the organizations that are subject to the regulatory authority of agencies must keep abreast of proposed regulations and must be aware of the need to comply with the regulations. Keep in mind, however, that there are limitations and restrictions placed on the agencies, providing protection to the entities being regulated from abusive or overly broad efforts to regulate.

HEARINGS AND ADJUDICATORY AUTHORITY

When an agency determines that there is reason to believe one of its regulations is being violated or that one of the organizations subject to its oversight is guilty of some improper conduct, the agency will notify that organization. This notification will include a statement of the area or areas of concern and allow the organization the opportunity to address the issue and for an informal resolution of the perceived problem. This is often all that is required to settle the matter.

If no settlement is reached, the agency will issue a formal complaint against the other party. This complaint is a public document, and it must be announced to the public through a press release. Following this formal complaint the agency will conduct further investigation, and the parties will continue to negotiate, trying to reach a settlement. If the parties are still unable to resolve the matter, an administrative hearing will be scheduled so that the matter may be formally adjudicated within the administrative process.

Some agencies are allowed to issue cease and desist orders. A *cease and desist order* is delivered to an individual or an organization subject to administrative regulation to halt the practice in question or face sanctions. (*Cease* means to stop or to halt; *desist* means to refrain from doing something. Thus, a cease and desist order is an order to stop the action and to refrain from doing the action any longer.) The order will normally include a time period for the person receiving the order to request a hearing to determine whether its actions should be stopped or to show that it should not be subject to such an order. If no hearing is requested within the specified time frame, the order becomes final. If the recipient continues to act in the challenged manner after the order becomes final, it is likely to be fined. For example, the FTC is authorized to impose a fine of up to $16,000 per violation of a final cease and desist order, and each day constitutes a separate violation.[18] The EPA, the SEC, and the FTC are among the agencies authorized to issue cease and desist orders. Agencies that are not authorized to do so on their own may petition a court to issue a cease and desist order to stop prohibited conduct. For example, the Department of Housing and Urban Development (HUD) does not have the authority to issue such an order, but can ask a court to do so when it discovers conduct that violates its policies. If the recipient of a cease and desist order requests a hearing, the issuing agency will grant that request.

Administrative hearings are similar in many respects to a trial, although there are some significant differences. Such hearings are conducted by *administrative law judges* (ALJs) rather than by a traditional judge, there is no right to a jury, and the rules of evidence are less restrictive. There is also a limited right of appeal from an administrative hearing. At the federal level, an administrative law judge is an Article I judge, and is within the executive branch of the government. By contrast, federal judges are Article III judges and are part of the judicial branch. Article I judges are not subject to approval by the Senate, while Article III judges require approval by the Senate. Article I judges are not appointed for life during good behavior, and an Article III judge is appointed for life during good behavior. ALJs are protected, however, although not as protected as an Article III judge. An ALJ can only be discharged for good cause, and that good cause must be affirmed by the Merit System Protection Board. An ALJ has immunity for his or her judicial acts, and he or she is insulated from political pressure or influence while serving as the finder of fact in a hearing.

The ALJ conducts the hearing in a manner similar to a trial. Since there is no jury, the ALJ fills the roles of both the jury (the finder of fact) and the judge (interpreting and applying the regulations to the facts). The ALJ has to decide what evidence is admissible and what evidence should be excluded. After the presentation of all the evidence, the ALJ will issue a ruling on the merits of the hearing. The ALJ is expected to rule based on a preponderance of the evidence. (Recall that in a civil case the plaintiff has the burden of proof and must provide a preponderance of the evidence. In a criminal case, the state has the burden of proof and must provide evidence establishing its case beyond a reasonable doubt.) The APA addresses the burden of proof issue with this statement: "A sanction may not be imposed or rule or order issued except on consideration of the whole record or those parts thereof cited by a party and supported by and in accordance with the reliable, probative, and substantial evidence."[19]

JUDICIAL REVIEW OF ADMINISTRATIVE ACTIONS

A person subject to administrative regulation who loses the hearing may be able to seek judicial review of the administrative action. However, he or she needs to be aware that the courts tend to defer to the administrative agency in such circumstances, so judicial review is not a guaranteed right. There is also a requirement that the person must exhaust his or her administrative remedies before judicial review can even be considered. This means that any reviews or appeals that are available within the agency must first be pursued, before a person can ask the court to review the agency's decision.

In determining whether a person has exhausted his or her administrative remedies, the courts apply the "exhaustion of remedies rule." The exhaustion of remedies rule says that a person or organization cannot appeal a decision to the courts until the person has taken all the appeals permitted within the agency. If a person files in court prematurely, the agency will ask the court to dismiss the case because the person has not exhausted his or her remedies. The person can avoid the application of the exhaustion of remedies rule if he or she can convince the court of one of three things:

1. It would be useless to exhaust the remedies.
2. The appellant would suffer irreparable harm while taking his or her appeals within the agency.
3. The agency exceeded its authority.

If all internal remedies have been exhausted and the person still believes that he or she was denied due process, was the victim of errors by the ALJ, or otherwise did not receive a fair and impartial hearing, he or she can ask a federal court (if it is a federal agency) to review the matter. Even if all of the internal remedies have been exhausted, the person cannot seek judicial review unless he or she can establish "standing." The person seeking review must be a person who is—or will be—harmed by the agency's actions and/or ruling.

An Ounce of Prevention

Administrative hearings are adversarial proceedings. A business that is involved in an administrative hearing needs to pay close attention to, and abide by, the agency's procedures. The business also needs to be aware of any internal appeals processes and to any time limits that may apply to these appeals. The business must exhaust its administrative remedies before it can seek judicial review. Missing an appeal deadline or failing to properly exhaust these internal remedies will preclude any efforts to have the court revisit the issues.

Generally, even if judicial review is granted, it will be a limited review. The APA provides that courts are not supposed to second-guess agency decisions or actions that are within the discretion of the agency. Courts follow the substantial evidence rule in most judicial reviews of administrative findings. The _substantial evidence rule_ "is a principle that a reviewing court should uphold an administrative body's ruling if it is supported by evidence on which the administrative body could reasonably base its decision."[20] This means that if the court finds that there is substantial evidence—an undefined amount—that the agency could reasonably rely on in reaching its decision, the court must uphold the decision.

However, if the court decides that the agency decision was "arbitrary or capricious, an Abuse of Discretion, or is otherwise not in accordance with law,"[21] the court can overrule the agency's action. This may even include a _de novo_ (from the beginning) review by the court. A de novo review involves the court holding a trial as if the original hearing did not occur. The court will make its own finding of fact and then apply the law to the facts as found in the "new" trial.

TECHNOLOGICAL ADVANCES CREATE NEW CONCERNS

As technology opens new windows of opportunity for entrepreneurs and for business in general, it also presents new problems and new concerns. Many of these problems are likely to require administrative agency oversights, and some will require the creation of new agencies or the expansion of current agencies.

Two recent examples illustrate some current concerns. Drones, unmanned aircraft piloted by remote control, have been newsworthy for quite some time. The use of drones in military operations is well known and widely reported. However, the use of drones by civilians is relatively new, and it has become a concern. There have been reports of near-collisions with commercial aircraft, there are concerns about potential invasions of privacy, and other concerns are sure to surface as the availability of privately owned drones increase. There have also been reports of neighborhood altercations and the suspension of flights to fight wildfires.[22] In response to some concerns, and in anticipation of others, the Federal Aviation Administration (FAA) is preparing regulations for privately owned drones. Federal law requires that an aircraft can only be operated legally if it is registered with the FAA. Drones have been classified as aircraft since 2012, but the registration requirement has not been enforced. The FAA now intends to begin registering and regulating the use of even small drones (5.5 pounds to 55 pounds).[23]

Similarly, many people are concerned about GMOs (genetically modified organisms) in their food, believing that people should not consume such foods. On November 19, 2015 the Food and Drug Administration (FDA) approved an application from AquaBounty Technologies for approval of its genetically engineered (GE) salmon, called AquaAdvantage Salmon. (The FDA does not approve of the GMO classification, believing it to be too broad and somewhat misleading.) This was the first time the FDA has approved a genetically engineered animal, certifying that the fish is fit for human consumption.[24]

These two examples may well be the mere "tip of the iceberg," and they illustrate that the need for administrative oversight is not likely to decrease in the foreseeable future.

Contemporary Case

This case held that while a corporation may be a "legal" person, it does not enjoy the same right to privacy that an individual enjoys. Personal rights apply to humans, but not to juristic "persons," an important distinction.

FEDERAL COMMUNICATIONS COMMISSION v. AT&T, INC.
131 S.Ct. 1177, 2011 U.S. LEXIS 1899 (2011)

FACTS AT&T participated in an FCC-administered program (the E-Rate or Education Rate program) that was created to enhance access to advanced telecommunications and information services for schools and libraries. In 2004, AT&T voluntarily reported to the FCC that it may have overcharged the government for the services it provided as part of the program. As a result of this disclosure by AT&T,

the FCC's Enforcement Bureau began an investigation. During the investigation AT&T provided a number of documents to the Enforcement Bureau. The FCC and AT&T resolved the matter in December of 2004, with AT&T agreeing to repay the government $500,000 and to institute a plan to ensure future compliance with the program.

Several months later, CompTel, a trade association representing some of AT&T's competitors, submitted a Freedom of Information Act (FOIA) request to the Enforcement Bureau seeking all the pleadings and correspondence in the bureau's file on the AT&T investigation. AT&T opposed the request.

The bureau issued a letter ruling in response to the FOIA request in which it determined that some of the information provided by AT&T should be protected from disclosure as "trade secrets and commercial or financial information." Other information was withheld under FOIA Exemption 7(C), which exempts "records or information compiled for law enforcement purposes" that "could reasonably be expected to constitute an unwarranted invasion of personal privacy." The bureau concluded that "individuals identified in [AT&T's] submissions" have "privacy rights" that warrant protection under the exemption. But the bureau decided that the exemption did not apply to the corporation itself, reasoning that "businesses do not possess 'personal privacy' interests as required" by the exemption. The FCC agreed with the bureau's decision, and AT&T appealed. The Third Circuit Court of Appeals overturned the FCC's ruling, and the Supreme Court granted certiorari.

ISSUE Are corporations entitled to "personal privacy," allowing them an exemption from disclosing law enforcement records under the Freedom of Information Act?

HOLDING No. The "personal privacy" provision was intended only for individuals and does not extend to artificial persons such as corporations.

REASONING Excerpts from the opinion of Chief Justice Roberts:

Like the Court of Appeals below, AT&T relies on the argument that the word "personal" in Exemption 7(C) incorporates the statutory definition of the word "person." . . . The Administrative Procedure Act defines "person" to include "an individual, part-nership, corporation, association, or public or private organization other than an agency." . . . Because that definition applies here, the argument goes, "personal" must mean relating to those "person[s]": namely, corporations and other entities as well as individuals. This reading, we are told, is dictated by a "basic principle of grammar and usage." . . . for "[t]he grammatical imperativ[e]" that "a statute which defines a noun has thereby defined the

adjectival form of that noun." According to AT&T, "[b]y expressly defining the noun 'person' to include corporations, Congress necessarily defined the adjective form of that noun—'personal'—also to include corporations." . . .

We disagree. Adjectives typically reflect the meaning of corresponding nouns, but not always. Sometimes they acquire distinct meanings of their own. The noun "crab" refers variously to a crustacean and a type of apple, while the related adjective "crabbed" can refer to handwriting that is "difficult to read," Webster's Third New International Dictionary 527 (2002); "corny" can mean "using familiar and stereotyped formulas believed to appeal to the unsophisticated," . . . which has little to do with "corn," . . . ("the seeds of any of the cereal grasses used for food"); and while "crank" is "a part of an axis bent at right angles," "cranky" can mean "given to fretful fussiness." . . . What is significant is that, in ordinary usage, a noun and its adjective form may have meanings as disparate as any two unrelated words. The FCC's argument that "personal" does not, in fact, derive from the English word "person," but instead developed along its own etymological path . . . simply highlights the shortcomings of AT&T's proposed rule.

"Person" is a defined term in the statute; "personal" is not. When a statute does not define a term, we typically "give the phrase its ordinary meaning." . . . "Personal" ordinarily refers to individuals. We do not usually speak of personal characteristics, personal effects, personal correspondence, personal influence, or personal tragedy as referring to corporations or other artificial entities. This is not to say that corporations do not have correspondence, influence, or tragedies of their own, only that we do not use the word "personal" to describe them. . . .

Dictionaries . . . suggest that "personal" does not ordinarily relate to artificial "persons" such as corporations. . . . AT&T dismisses these definitions, correctly noting that "personal"—at its most basic level—simply means "[o]f or pertaining to a particular person." . . . The company acknowledges that "in non-legal usage, where a 'person' is a human being, it is entirely unsurprising that the word 'personal' is used to refer to human beings." . . . But in a watered-down version of the "grammatical imperative" argument, AT&T contends that "person"—in common legal usage—is understood to include a corporation. "Personal" in the same context therefore can and should have the same scope, especially here in light of the statutory definition. . . .

The construction of statutory language often turns on context, . . . which certainly may include the definitions of related words. But here the context to which AT&T points does not dissuade us from the ordinary meaning of "personal." We have no doubt that "person," in a legal setting, often refers to artificial entities. . . . But AT&T's effort to ascribe a corresponding legal meaning to "personal" again elides the difference between "person" and "personal." When it comes to the word "personal," there is little support for the notion that it denotes corporations, even in the legal context. AT&T notes that corporations are "protected by the doctrine of 'personal' jurisdiction," . . . but that phrase refers to jurisdiction in personam, as opposed to in rem, not the jurisdiction "of a person." The only other example AT&T cites is an 1896 case that referred to the "personal privilege" of a corporation. . . . These examples fall far short of establishing that "personal" here has a legal meaning apart from its ordinary one, even if "person" does. . . .

Regardless of whether "personal" can carry a special meaning in legal usage, "when interpreting a statute . . . we construe language . . . in light of the terms surrounding it." . . . Exemption 7(C) refers not just to the word "personal," but to the term "personal privacy." . . . AT&T's effort to attribute a special legal meaning to the word "personal" in this particular context is wholly unpersuasive. AT&T's argument treats the term "personal privacy" as simply the sum of its two words: the privacy of a person. Under that view, the defined meaning of the noun "person," or the asserted specialized legal meaning, takes on greater significance. But two words together may assume a more particular meaning than those words in isolation. We understand a golden cup to be a cup made of or resembling gold. A golden boy, on the other hand, is one who is charming, lucky, and talented. A golden opportunity is one not to be missed. "Personal" in the phrase "personal privacy" conveys more than just "of a person." It suggests a type of privacy evocative of human concerns—not the sort usually associated with an entity like, say, AT&T.

Despite its contention that "[c]ommon legal usage" of the word "person" supports its reading of the term "personal privacy," . . . AT&T does not cite a single instance in which this Court or any other (aside from the Court of Appeals below) has expressly referred to a corporation's "personal privacy." Nor does it identify any other statute that does so. . . . On the contrary, treatises in print around the time that Congress drafted the exemptions at hand reflect the understanding that the specific concept of "personal privacy," at least as a matter of common law, did not apply to corporations. . . .

We reject the argument that because "person" is defined for purposes of FOIA to include a corporation, the phrase "personal privacy" in Exemption 7(C) reaches corporations as well. The protection in FOIA against disclosure of law enforcement information on the ground that it would constitute an unwarranted invasion of personal privacy does not extend to corporations. We trust that AT&T will not take it personally.

The judgment of the Court of Appeals is reversed.

Short Answer Questions

1. Assume that an administrative agency decides to enact a new regulation. The proposed regulation is published in the *Federal Register* on the first day of the month with the notation that it will take effect on the 15th day of the month. When the proposed regulation was published in the *Federal Register* it was the first time that any of the firms in the affected industry were aware of any pending regulation. Several of these firms would like to challenge the implementation of the proposed regulation in this manner. What arguments might these firms raise in their challenge? What should the agency have done differently in its effort to enact the regulation?

2. A firm has been found to be in violation of an administrative regulation after a full administrative hearing conducted by an ALJ. The firm does not believe that it was treated fairly in the hearing and would like to have the court review the results of the hearing. What, if anything, must the firm do to obtain judicial review of the hearing? How likely is the firm to prevail in a judicial review if or when such a review is granted?

3. Near the end of a workweek, late on a Friday afternoon, the manager of a manufacturing facility is notified that an OSHA inspector has arrived and would like to enter the facility for an inspection. The inspector claims that he has heard that the facility has several significant safety issues, in violation of OSHA regulations. Does the manager have to allow the inspection when the OSHA representative requests it? If the manager would prefer not to allow the inspection at that time, what can she do to prevent the inspection without jeopardizing her position with the firm?

You Decide...

1. Section 5 of the Indian Reorganization Act authorizes the secretary of the interior at his or her discretion to acquire land for the purpose of providing that land to Native Americans. Such land can be within or outside the boundaries of a tribal reservation. The title to the land is to be held by the United States in trust for the Indian tribe and will be exempt from state and local taxation. The secretary of the interior has promulgated regulations and procedures to govern the acquisition of such land, and the Bureau of Indian Affairs (BIA) oversees this area. The regulations require that the BIA provide notice to the state and local governments having jurisdiction over any such land and gives them thirty days to provide comments. The affected tribe is then given an opportunity to respond to the governments' comments. Following this, the secretary makes a decision about the proposed acquisition.

A tribe in South Dakota purchased a 39-acre parcel of land used as a "travel plaza," with a gas station and a convenience store, from private owners in 1992. In 2004 the tribe asked the BIA to acquire the land in trust for the tribe. The request included a commitment to continue to use the land as a travel plaza. The local and state government were duly informed of the proposal and asked for comments. Both opposed the acquisition of the travel plaza in trust. Despite this opposition, the decision to approve the acquisition in trust was approved. Among the factors considered in this decision were (1) that placing the plaza in trust would provide for economic development for the tribe; (2) that it would ensure the survival of the tribe as a sovereign nation; and (3) that removal of the property from the tax rolls would have a minimal effect on the county and state governments.

The county then sued, asserting (among other issues) that the secretary had acted in an arbitrary and capricious manner under the APA and that the county's due process rights had been violated.

How would *you* decide this case? Be certain that you explain and justify your answer.

(See *County of Charles Mix v. United States Department of the Interior*, 2012 U.S. App. LEXIS 6946 (8th Cir., 2012).)

2. The International Association of Machinists and Aerospace Workers filed a petition with the National Labor Relations Board (NLRB) seeking certification as the representative of Mercedes-Benz service technicians employed at Contemporary Cars, Inc. The board's regional director held a hearing, determined the proposed bargaining unit was appropriate, and directed that an election occur. Contemporary Cars requested that the board review the regional director's decision regarding the bargaining unit. Despite only having two members, the board summarily denied the request. Members

of the bargaining unit voted in favor of representation by the union, and the regional director certified the union. Contemporary Cars refused to bargain with the union in order to preserve its right to challenge the validity of the bargaining-unit determination in a court of appeals, The union filed an unfair labor practice charge with the board. Contemporary Cars conceded the violation, and the two-member board issued an order finding Contemporary Cars in violation of the National Labor Relations Act.

Contemporary Cars then filed a petition for review of the NLRB's order with the U.S. Court of Appeals, seeking review of the bargaining-unit determination. During this period the U.S. Supreme Court issued a ruling that the National Labor Relations Act requires a minimum of three members to participate on the board in hearings. As a result of this ruling, the NLRB issued an order setting aside its previous two-member decision and to "take further action as appropriate." Subsequently, the original two members plus a third board member issued a new order, again affirming the regional director's bargaining-unit decision and finding Contemporary Cars in violation of the act. The NLRB filed a petition for enforcement of its order with this court.

How would *you* decide this case? Be certain that you explain and justify your answer.

(See *NLRB v. Contemporary Cars, Inc.*, 667 F.3d 1364; 2012 U.S. App. LEXIS 1503 (11th Cir. 2012).)

Notes

1. "Administrative Agencies," USLegal.com, http://system.uslegal.com/administrative-agencies/ (accessed November 16, 2012).
2. According to the DEA Web site, the mission of the Drug Enforcement Administration is "to enforce the controlled substances laws and regulations of the United States" and to bring to justice any persons violating these laws. http://www.justice.gov/dea/agency/mission.htm.
3. *Yick Wo. V. Hopkins*, 118 U.S. 356, 6 S. Ct. 1064, 30 L. Ed. 220 (1886).
4. 5 U.S.C. §§ 511-599
5. 5 U.S.C. § 552.
6. 5 U.S.C. § 552 (b).
7. FOIA exemptions, http://www.osec.doc.gov/omo/foia/exemptions.htm (accessed November 16, 2012).
8. Freedom of Information Act (FOIA) Office, United States Census Bureau, http://www.census.gov/foia/foiarequests/ (accessed November 16, 2012).
9. 5 U.S.C. § 551 (4).
10. 5 U.S.C. § 551 (5).

11. Robert Longley, Federal Regulations, "The Laws Behind the Acts of Congress," About.com Guide.

12. lsoft.com Manuals, "Section 3, Communicating with LIST-SERV," found at http://www.lsoft.com/manuals/15.5/html help/list%20owners%20-%20beginners/CommwithLS.5.1 .html (accessed December 1, 2015).

13. A subpoena (sub = under; poena = penalty) is a mandatory writ or process directed to and requiring one or more persons to appear to give testimony for the party named or face penalties. *Black's Law Dictionary*. A subpoena is used to compel a person to appear in order to provide testimony in a proceeding.

14. A process by which the court commands a witness who has in his or her possession or control some document or paper that is pertinent to the issues of a pending controversy or to produce it at trial.

15. Jackie Calmes, "Senate Report Cites I.R.S. Mismanagement in Targeting Tea Party Groups," N.Y. Times (Aug. 5, 2015), found at http://www.nytimes.com/2015/08/06/us/politics/ senate-report-cites-irs-mismanagement-in-targeting-of-tea-party-groups.html?r=0 (accessed December 1, 2015).

16. Walter D. James, "Agency Inspections: What Do You Do?", http://www.jamespllc.com/publication%5Cwaltjamespdf1 .pdf (accessed November 16, 2012).

17. NEPA Documentation, U.S. Department of Transportation, http://www.environment.fhwa.dot.gov/projdev/docueis.asp (accessed November 16, 2012).

18. Federal Trade Commission Act, 15 U.S.C. § 45 (l).

19. 5 U.S.C. § 556(d).

20. "Substantial Evidence Rule Law & Legal Definition," U.S. Legal. Com, http://definitions.uslegal.com/s/substantial-evidence-rule/ (accessed November 16, 2012).

21. "Administrative Law and Procedure," http://legal-dictionary .thefreedictionary.com/Administrative+Law+and+Procedure (accessed November 16, 2012).

22. Fred Barbash, "Drones impede air battle against California wild fires. 'If you fly we can't,' pleads California Firefighter," *Washington Post* (July 31, 2015), found at https://www .washingtonpost.com/news/morning-mix/wp/2015/07/31/ if-you-fly-we-cant-pleads-california-firefighter-as-drones-impede-spreading-wildfire-battle/ (accessed December 8, 2015).

23. Patrick Fowler, Troy Roberts, Snell & Wilmer "Almost Ready to Fly: New Federal Registration Requirements for Small UAS/Drones," *JDSupra Business Advisor* (November 30, 2015), found at http://www.swlaw.com/blog/product-liability-update/2015/11/25/almost-ready-to-fly-new-federal-registration-requirements-for-small-uasdrones/ (accessed December 7, 2015).

24. Bergerson & Campbell, P.C., "FDA Approves First Genetically Engineered Animal," *JDSupra Business Advisor* (November 24, 2015), found at http://www.jdsupra.com/ legalnews/fda-approves-first-genetically-31163/ (accessed December 7, 2015).

8

Protection of Intellectual Property

Learning Objectives

After completing this chapter you should be able to

- Recognize the importance of intellectual property to businesses
- Discuss the advantages and disadvantages of the different types of intellectual property
- Distinguish trademarks, service marks, and trade dress
- Identify how a business can protect its intellectual property from employees and those outside the enterprise

Classic Case

The Classic Case for this chapter is a Supreme Court decision concerning the rights of Coca-Cola in its trademark. The Koke Company argued that the trademark should be cancelled because it was a fraud, since the drink did not contain cocaine.

THE COCA-COLA COMPANY v. THE KOKE COMPANY OF AMERICA

254 U.S. 143, 41 S. Ct. 113, 1920 U.S. LEXIS 1177 (1920)

FACTS Coca-Cola filed suit seeking an injunction to restrain The Koke Company of America from using the word "Koke" to describe its product. Coca-Cola alleged that the words infringed Coca-Cola's trademark and constituted unfair competition. Coca-Cola asserted that Koke was a trademark infringement, clearly intended to capitalize on Coca-Cola's goodwill. The Koke Company argued that Coca-Cola's trademark should be declared void because it fraudulently represented the contents and/or effects of the product.

ISSUES Did Koke infringe on the trademark of Coca-Cola? Did Koke's action constitute unfair competition? Was the Coca-Cola trademark a fraudulent representation of the product?

HOLDINGS Yes, Koke infringed the Coca-Cola trademark. Yes, Koke was guilty of unfair competition. No, the Coca-Cola trademark was not a fraudulent representation of the product.

REASONING Excerpts from the opinion of Justice Holmes:

. . . Whatever may have been its original weakness, the mark for years has acquired a secondary significance and has indicated the plaintiff's product alone. It is found that defendant's mixture is made and sold in imitation of the plaintiff's and that the word Koke was chosen for the purpose of reaping the benefit of the advertising done by the plaintiff and of selling the imitation as . . . the plaintiff's goods. The only obstacle found by the Circuit Court of Appeals . . . was its opinion that the trademark . . . and the advertisements accompanying it made such fraudulent representations to the public that the plaintiff had lost its claim to any help from the Court. That is the question . . . that we shall discuss.

Of course a man is not to be protected in the use of a device the very purpose and effect of which is to swindle the public. . . . The defense relied on here should be scrutinized with a critical eye. . . . Before 1900 the beginning of the good will was more or less helped by the presence of cocaine, a drug that, like alcohol or caffeine or opium, may be described as a deadly poison or as a valuable item of the pharmacopoeia. . . . The amount seems to have been very small. . . . [A]fter the Food and Drug Act of June 30, 1906[,] . . . if not earlier, . . . it was eliminated from the plaintiff's compound. . . . It is argued that the continued use of the name imports a representation that has ceased to be true and that the representation is reinforced by a picture of coca leaves and cola nuts upon the label and by advertisements, . . . that the drink is an "ideal nerve tonic and stimulant," . . . and that . . . the very thing sought to be protected is used as a fraud.

The argument does not satisfy us. We are dealing here with a popular drink not with a medicine. . . . The name now characterizes a beverage to be had at almost any soda fountain. It means a single thing coming from a single source, and well known to the community. . . . [W]e see no reason to doubt that . . . it has acquired a secondary meaning in which perhaps the product is more emphasized than the producer but to which the producer is entitled. The coca leaves and . . . cola nut . . . may be used to justify the continuance of the name or they may affect the flavor as the plaintiff contends ... [B]efore this suit was brought the plaintiff had advertised to the public that it must not expect and would not find cocaine ... [Plaintiff] had eliminated everything tending to suggest cocaine effects except the name and the picture of the leaves and nuts, which probably conveyed little or nothing to most who saw it. ... [I]t would be going too far to deny the plaintiff relief ... because possibly here and there an ignorant person might call for the drink with the hope for ... cocaine intoxication. The plaintiff's position must be judged by the facts as they were when the suit was begun, not by the facts of a different condition and an earlier time. ...

Decree reversed.

Decree of District Court modified and affirmed.

INTRODUCTION

In this chapter, we will examine how the law protects intellectual property. Intellectual property is intangible property that is created or invented by human beings. Intellectual property law encompasses several substantive legal areas: patents, copyrights, trademarks, service marks, trade dress, and trade secrets. Computers and the Internet make it easy to discover and infringe on someone's intellectual property rights. Once the information is obtained, it can be readily shared on blogs and online publications, such as WikiLeaks.

Article I, Section 8 of the U.S. Constitution authorizes Congress "to promote the Progress of Science and the useful Arts, by securing for limited Times to Authors and Inventors the exclusive Right to their respective Writings and Discoveries." This constitutional grant of authority to Congress is the cornerstone on which U.S. intellectual property law is built. The "exclusive right" to authors is the basis of copyright law, and the "exclusive right" to inventors is the basis of patent law. These "exclusive rights" provide the holders of copyrights and/or patents with government-issued monopolies on their covered works. It is hoped that these monopolies will encourage creativity. The "limited times" mentioned in this section ensures that the monopoly will not last forever, but rather will expire after a reasonable time. Congress establishes what will be a reasonable time.

Although not specifically addressed in the U.S. Constitution, the United States recognizes other types of intellectual property. The symbol, mark, or device that identifies a business or an organization (trademark, service mark, certification mark, trade dress) is entitled to protection. Trade secrets are also protected provided the person who has the secret treats it with an appropriate level of confidentiality. Generally, the owner has the task of protecting his or her intellectual property and suing others who use that property without permission. The Classic Case is an example of the trademark owner filing suit to "police" its trademark.

The United States has four different intellectual property systems which will be discussed in this chapter. They are represented in Exhibit 8.1. The Type of System describes who will generally own the intellectual property unless there is a contract stating otherwise.

Exhibit 8.1

Types of Intellectual Property Systems in the United States			
Type of Intellectual Property	**Type of System**	**Federal or State Protection**	**Type of Protection**
Patents	First to file[a] with the Patent and Trademark Office has the rights.	Federal	Owner can sue to protect his or her rights.
Copyrights	First to reduce it to a tangible medium has the rights. The "artist" owns the exclusive rights and can prevent use by others.	Federal	Owner must register with the Copyright Office of the Library of Congress in order to recover monetary damages.
Trademarks, Service Marks, and Trade Dress	First to use the mark or trade dress in business.	Federal and state	Owner is not required to file with the Patent and Trademark Office but the owner will have better protection by filing.
Trade Secrets	Must be treated as confidential and must attempt to keep it secret.	State	Owner may seek an injunction and sue for damages for improper acquisition by others.

Source: Courtesy of Lynn M. Forsythe. © 2016.

[a] This system began in the United States in 2013 after the effective date of the America Invents Act. It is a first to file system similar to that used in most of the other countries. However, the U.S. law provides for an administrative derivation proceeding to determine if the first to file is really an inventor.

PATENTS

A *patent* is a federally authorized and issued *monopoly* (exclusive right) granted to the inventor. To obtain this legal monopoly, the inventor must file an application with the U.S. Patent and Trademark Office (PTO). The filing requires a full description of the item or design. If the patent is granted, the patent holder has the exclusive right to the item or the design for the life of the patent. The holder can use it, sell it, or license it for use by others. Once the patent protection ends, anyone can copy, make, use, or sell the product formerly protected by the patent. Currently, the exclusive right lasts for twenty years (for a utility or a plant patent) or fourteen years (for a design patent).

In 2011, Congress enacted the Leahy-Smith America Invents Act (AIA), which made some significant changes to U.S. patent law.[1] The AIA became effective with new patent applications filed on or after March 16, 2013. One of the most significant changes is from a "first to invent" system to a "first to file" system similar to that used by many other countries. This system rewards the inventor who files the patent application first. Under the AIA usually the inventor must file the application within one year of its public disclosure of the invention.[2] Public disclosure includes a number of activities including printed publications, presentations at conferences, foreign patent filings, and even YouTube videos. Generally, the inventor has a one year "grace period" between the public disclosure and the effective date of the patent application. However, someone else may file during that period. If more than one person independently creates the same invention, normally the patent will be awarded to the first one who files. There are also changes in what an inventor includes in his or her patent filings.

The Standards of Patentability

To be eligible for patent protection, the invention must be (1) new; (2) useful; and (3) not obvious to persons of ordinary skill in the trade or area. All three requirements must be satisfied before a utility patent will be issued. The patent application will be denied if:

- there is already something substantially similar to the invention in existence or available,
- there has been public use by others in this country prior to the application, *or*
- the inventor has either sold or publicly used the invention for more than one year prior to his or her application.

Before the PTO will issue a patent, the invention must be shown to be useful. The person requesting the utility patent needs to demonstrate that there is the potential for society to obtain significant current benefits from the invention.

Finally, the invention must involve a development that is not obvious to others in the field. If the invention would be obvious to a person of ordinary skill in the field, the public will not benefit by permitting the inventor to have a 20-year monopoly. There is an assumption here that if the invention is truly useful and it is obvious, someone would come forward with the idea in due time, and the protections afforded by a patent would not be beneficial to society.

Utility patents can be obtained for:

1. Any processes (earlier this was called *art*, now it is called *processes* which includes processes, art, or methods);
2. Machines;
3. Articles of manufacture;
4. Business methods (provided that the business method is shown to produce a useful, concrete, and tangible result);[3]
5. Compositions of matter, including certain non-naturally occurring plants, such as hybrids;[4] or
6. Any new and useful improvements thereof.

Ideas *per se* are not patentable. Neither are laws of nature (for example, "for every action there is an equal and opposite reaction"), mathematical formulas, scientific truths or principles, and mental processes.

Inventors who believe they have met these requirements begin the process of obtaining a patent by filing an application with the PTO. This application includes (1) a declaration that the applicant discovered the invention for which he or she seeks the patent; (2) any drawings necessary to explain the patent; (3) detailed descriptions, specifications, and disclosures (including all prior processes) of the subject matter the applicant claims as his or her invention; and (4) the required filing fees. The information provided in the specifications should (1) enable any person skilled in the process to make or use the invention after the expiration of the term of the patent and (2) inform the public of the limits of the monopoly claimed by the inventor.

The application will be assigned to a PTO examiner for review. The commissioner of Patents and Trademarks will issue a patent if the PTO examiner approves the application. Common grounds for rejection include the finding of a prior process or the existence of "double-patenting" (two patents for the same invention). Applicants who receive rejection notices can appeal to the PTO Patent Trial and Appeal Board and then either to the U.S. Court of Appeals for the Federal Circuit or the U.S. District Court for the District of Columbia.

An Ounce of Prevention

If you believe that you have discovered something new, useful, and nonobvious, you should consider filing for a patent. Remember, though, when you apply for a patent, you must make a full disclosure of how to make the item. This disclosure will allow others to copy the invention and possibly compete with you. Not all applications are approved. The PTO can deny a patent application. For example, in calendar year 2014 the PTO received 615,243 applications and it granted 326,033.[5] In addition, courts can invalidate a patent if they decide that the PTO incorrectly granted it. This poses a significant risk. If the PTO denies an application or the court invalidates the patent, the invention will be publicly disclosed, and you will have no protection for it. In addition, once it is disclosed it cannot be a trade secret. Consequently, it is important to be fairly confident that your invention is patentable before you file an application.

Protection from Infringement

A patent can be an extremely valuable asset. Possession of a valid plant or utility patent gives the patent holder exclusive rights to the invention and a twenty-year head start over his or her competitors. If another person uses the patented item without the patent holder's permission, the patent holder can file suit for infringement. A person can infringe a patent intentionally or accidentally. Patent infringement does not require proof of an intent to infringe. The issuance of a patent serves as constructive notice to the world of the patent's existence. This means that the person being sued for the infringement will try to prove that his or her invention is sufficiently different from the patented item or that the patent is invalid because one of the conditions is absent. If either can be shown, there is no infringement.

A defendant may also argue that the patent holder has abused the patent rights, for example, by using the patent to engage in anticompetitive behavior or to extend its monopoly beyond the scope of the patent rights. If the defendant can establish that the patent holder violated antitrust laws in the use of the patent, the defendant will be found not guilty of infringement. Generally it is not a misuse of the patent if the patent holder refuses to sell or license the patent to others,[6] or even to use the patent he or she has acquired.[7]

Remedies for Infringement

Remedies for patent infringement include damages and equitable relief in the form of injunctions. Courts award damages in an amount adequate to compensate the holder of the patent for the infringement, including lost profits attributable to the infringement. At a minimum, the patent owner is entitled to a reasonable royalty representative of the infringer's use of the invention. Courts have authority to treble the damages assessed.

Courts can also award an injunction under the usual, well-established principles of equity. Under these principles, a plaintiff must show "(1) that it has suffered an irreparable injury; (2) that remedies available at law, such as monetary damages, are inadequate to compensate for that injury; (3) that, considering the balance of hardships between the plaintiff and defendant, a remedy in equity is warranted; and (4) that the public interest would not be disserved [hurt] by a permanent injunction."[8] Courts are authorized to award attorney's fees to the prevailing party in exceptional cases. However, courts rarely award such fees.

International Dimensions

Patent laws vary significantly from country to country. For example, some countries do not patent drugs, computer programs, or business methods. Some countries do not perform a patent search to determine whether the invention is novel. These countries will accept the patent and allow the courts to determine later if the patent is valid. In addition, some countries do not provide for a one-year grace period after the first publication, disclosure, or commercialization of the invention.[9] In these countries, the inventor must apply *before* disclosing, publishing, or commercializing the invention. The recent disagreement between Apple and Samsung illustrates the complexity of international patent disputes. The dispute spans ten countries including, the United States.[10] A Japanese court rejected some of Apple's patent claims. However, there are still other patent claims pending in Japanese courts. A judge in South Korea entered a split decision and a court in England ruled against Apple.[11] In their complex relationship, Samsung is both a competitor and a major supplier for Apple. However, Apple has been reducing the orders it places with Samsung for components.[12]

Patents may have significant value beyond the patent holder's national borders. Consequently, there are a number of international treaties. The United States is a signatory nation to the Paris Convention for the Protection of Industrial Property, administered by the World Intellectual Property Organization (WIPO). The Paris Convention currently has 176 contracting countries.[13] The Paris Convention gives anyone who files a basic application in one signatory country the benefit of the same filing date in any other member country where he or she files a national application within one year. The inventor benefits from the earlier date, especially in first-to-file jurisdictions. The United States is also one of the 148 signatory nations to the Patent Cooperation Treaty (PCT).[14] The PCT is also administered by WIPO. Under the PCT a U.S. resident can file a PCT application with the PTO within one year after filing a U.S. national application with the PTO. The PTO will have it searched and examined to determine patentability. Eventually, the inventor will have to file national applications in each country where he or she wants patent protection. Under both treaties, when the inventor files in the individual countries, he or she pays the costs of filing and the costs of translating the application and description into other languages. Patent attorney David Pressman recommends that an inventor not apply for a patent in a foreign country unless (1) it is likely that there is a significant market for products using the invention in that country; (2) it is likely that there will be significant commercial production of the invention there; or (3) the inventor has located a licensee for the invention or someone else who is willing to pay for the foreign patent.[15]

An Ounce of Prevention

You can gain powerful information about technology by performing a patent search. Some businesses perform patent searches even though they do not intend to apply for a patent themselves. The patent search can reveal information about competing technologies. It also can help you avoid activities that infringe an existing patent. If you discover superior technology already exists, you may benefit by licensing the technology instead of conducting your own research. The patent holder is more likely to license the technology to you at competitive rates if you are not a direct competitor. The patent search may also help you with your creative processes. Searching the patents of your competitors may also provide valuable clues about the direction of their research and development.

Computers

Neither the original U.S. patent statute nor recent amendments included computers or computer program-related inventions. After a period of uncertainty, computer programs are now patentable in the United States, provided that they satisfy the three requirements of novelty, uniqueness, and nonobviousness. The European Union reached a similar position under its patent law in 2005.

COPYRIGHTS

Writers, composers, and other types of artists are protected by copyright law. We will refer to them as artists or authors. The Copyright Act protects an original work of authorship fixed in any "tangible medium of expression" from which the work can be perceived, reproduced, or otherwise communicated. A person cannot receive a copyright by thinking about or telling an original story. Nor can a person copyright a song that he or she hummed, or even sang, to himself or herself or to others. But if the person writes down the original story or records the original music, he or she is entitled to copyright protection. It is the "reduction to tangible form"—the writing or the recording—that makes the work copyrightable.

Works of authorship include, but are not limited to: (1) literary works, including computer programs; (2) musical works, including any accompanying music; (3) pantomimes and choreographic works; (4) pictorial, graphic, and sculptural works; (5) motion pictures and other audiovisual works; (6) sound recordings; (7) architectural works; and (8) vessel hull designs. Note that copyright laws protect only *expressions of ideas*, not the ideas themselves. To acquire protection, the artist must express his or her original artistic idea in some tangible medium, providing proof of his or her creation of the artistic work. In one case, Shepard Fairey created a poster of Barack Obama, commonly called the "Hope" poster. The Associated Press claimed that it owned the photograph on which the poster was based. Mannie Garcia, a freelance photographer, actually took the photograph in 2006. The Associated Press argued that it was a work for hire and that it owned the photo. The Fairey-Associated Press case was settled in January 2011. Both sides contend that their view of the law is correct. However, they have agreed to work together and share the image and the right to make merchandise bearing the image. The financial terms were not released. Fairey was then found guilty of misdemeanor contempt for his intentional destruction of trial evidence and creation of fake trial evidence during the early stages of the dispute.[16]

Copyright protection extends much longer than does patent protection. Generally, for works created after January 1, 1978, a copyright runs for the life of the author plus 70 years. If the author is anonymous, the work is created under a pseudonym, or it is a "work for hire," the copyright runs for the lesser of 95 years from its first publication or 120 years from its creation. Copyrights cannot be renewed. Different rules apply for works first published before January 1, 1978.[17]

Under current law, a new artistic work is automatically entitled to copyright protection as soon as it is fixed into tangible form. This means that a person does not need to (1) register with the Copyright Office of the Library of Congress; (2) affix the copyright symbol (©); or (3) take any other steps in order to be protected under copyright law. In order for an artist or author to acquire copyright protection today, his or her work must simply be original, it must be at least somewhat creative or artistic, *and* it must be fixed in a tangible medium of expression. However, for the copyright holder to file suit for damages against an infringer, the copyright must be registered with the Copyright Office. If the copyright is not registered, the holder can seek other remedies (e.g., an injunction) but cannot sue for damages.[18] A copyright cannot be based on a mere recitation of facts (the listings in a telephone directory, for example); consequently, many computer databases cannot be copyrighted. An idea may not be copyrighted, but the method of expressing an idea may be.[19]

The U.S. Copyright Office (1) registers copyrights; (2) issues certificates of registration; (3) keeps records of copyright registrations, licenses, and assignments; and (4) oversees deposits of copyrighted materials. Unlike the PTO's stringent and detailed oversight of patents and trademarks, the Copyright Office merely determines whether applications involve copyrightable subject matter and have fulfilled all the registration requirements. Consequently, the registration process is relatively simple and inexpensive. The artist or author can register the copyright online for a nominal fee.

Protection from Infringement

A copyright provides a bundle of rights that enables the copyright owner—usually the author or one to whom the author has transferred rights—to exploit a work for commercial purposes. These exclusive rights include: (1) reproducing the copyrighted work; (2) preparing derivative works (or adaptations) based on the copyrighted work; (3) distributing copies or audio recordings of the copyrighted work; (4) performing publicly literary, musical, dramatic, and choreographic works; pantomimes; and motion pictures or audiovisual works; and (5) displaying the works themselves or individual images of the works mentioned in (4), as well as pictorial, graphic, or sculptural works. Public performance includes performing songs at a political campaign event.

However, members of the public can use copyright-protected work in certain ways without obtaining the permission of the copyright holder. Under the fair use provisions of the Copyright Act[20] certain reproductions are permitted without obtaining permission from the copyright holder. In order to qualify as a "fair use," the use must be for purposes such as comment, criticism, news reporting, research, scholarship, and teaching. Section 107 of the Copyright Act sets out four factors that should be considered in deciding whether a challenged use qualifies as a fair use and is not an infringement:

1. The purpose and character of the use, including whether the use is for a commercial purpose or is for nonprofit educational purposes;
2. The nature of the copyrighted work;
3. The amount and substantiality of the portion used compared to the copyrighted work as a whole; and
4. The effect of the use upon the potential market for, or value of, the copyrighted work.[21]

Because the distinction between fair use and infringement is not clear, it is preferable to seek permission and to avoid using the copyrighted material if permission is not obtained. However, if a person believes that the use is necessary, and he or she is unable to obtain permission, he or she should carefully review the standards generally followed for determining whether the use will qualify as fair use. The standards are included in *Reproduction of Copyrighted Works by Educators and Librarians*,[22] provided by the U.S. Copyright Office. The user should also document his or her analysis of why the use was "fair."

The fair use doctrine also includes parody to some extent. A work created by one person in which he or she imitates another person's copyrighted work as a parody or a satire may be viewed as a fair use. While the owner of the copyrighted work may not appreciate the parody or satire, the courts tend to allow such use, even without permission from the copyright holder. The Supreme Court reached such a conclusion in a 1994 opinion, upholding the use by the rap group 2 Live Crew in which the group performed a parody of "Oh, Pretty Woman," a song written by Roy Orbison and William Dees in 1964. (Orbison and Dees had assigned their rights in the song to Acuff-Rose Music, Inc.) When 2 Live Crew asked for permission to use the song, Acuff-Rose refused.[23] Rather than being deterred, they used the song in their recording of "Pretty Woman." Acuff-Rose sued for infringement, but the court found for 2 Live Crew, noting that the parody was within the scope of fair use and was not an infringement.

Many U.S. copyright holders of recorded music assign their rights to control public performance of their music to either the American Society of Composers, Authors, and Publishers (ASCAP) or to Broadcast Music, Inc. (BMI) to ensure that they receive royalties when their songs are played in public. Both ASCAP and BMI collect royalties from various entities that play songs and then distribute these royalties to their signed artists on a predetermined schedule of payments. By assigning their rights to either of these organizations, the artist loses some control over the use of the covered recordings. In 2008 when Sarah Palin was running as the Republican vice-presidential candidate, she used "Barracuda" as her song at the convention. Ann and Nancy Wilson from the rock group *Heart* contended that the Republicans should have asked permission before using their song. A spokesman for John McCain, the presidential candidate, responded that the campaign had obtained the license to use the music. The song was licensed for public performance under a blanket fee paid by the convention venue to ASCAP.[24] (There are also *compulsory* licensing sections in the act that apply to cable television systems' secondary transmissions of primary broadcasts, satellite retransmissions, electronic video game arcades, and jukeboxes.)

Copyright infringement does not require intent on the part of the infringing party. A totally innocent reproduction of another's copyrighted work is still an infringement of the owner's copyright, unless there is permission or the fair use exception applies. George Harrison was found to have innocently and inadvertently infringed the copyright held by Bright Tunes Music for the song "He's So Fine," recorded by The Chiffons, when he recorded "My Sweet Lord."[25] Typically, the copyright owner will show that the defendant had access to the copyrighted work and that the defendant's work shows a striking similarity to the copyrighted work. If the court finds that the similarities are more likely than not to have been the result of copying the protected work, it will find that infringement has occurred.

Remedies for Infringement

Civil remedies for infringements include injunctions, the impoundment and destruction of infringing items, and damages. Monetary damages are available if the copyright was registered with the U.S. Copyright Office. Plaintiffs can request actual damages, including the infringer's profits attributable to the infringement, or statutory damages ranging from a minimum of $750 to $30,000 for all infringements involved in the action with respect to one work. The court will award what it thinks is just under the circumstances. A court may increase the damages to $150,000 for willful infringements. Similarly, the court may lower the damages to $200 if the infringer can prove it was unaware that its actions constituted an infringement. The court in its discretion may award court costs and/or attorney's fees.[26]

Criminal penalties can involve substantial fines and/or prison sentences depending on the type of copyright infringement.[27] In addition, the No Electronic Theft Act of 1997 provides for both civil and criminal penalties for copyright infringement involving the Internet. Under the act infringement is a crime only where it is done "willfully and for purposes of commercial advantage or private financial gain."[28]

International Dimensions

The United States became a member of the International Union for the Protection of Literary and Artistic Works (the Berne Convention) in March 1989. Under the Berne Convention, each member nation must automatically extend the protection of its laws to nationals of other signatory nations and to works originally published in a member nation's jurisdiction. The United States has taken a minimalist approach to compliance with the Berne Convention, not accepting every provision of the treaty. However, the United States has enacted into law many of the treaty's provisions. WIPO has updated the Berne Convention to reflect developments in information technology. These revisions have closed some loopholes that made the U.S. recording industry vulnerable to infringement in the international arena.

The Universal Copyright Convention (UCC), administered by the United Nations, is another international copyright treaty. The United States has been a member of the UCC since 1955.[29] The UCC imposes fewer substantive requirements on copyrights than does the Berne Convention. However, some Berne Convention members also joined the UCC as a means of establishing relationships concerning copyrights with UCC members who have not signed the Berne Convention.

Recent amendments to the General Agreement on Tariffs and Trade (GATT) expand the protections afforded to copyrighted works, including computer programs.

Computers

Web sites and computer programs may be copyrighted as long as the subject matter is appropriate. For example, they do not include "ideas, program logic, algorithms, systems, methods, concepts, or layouts."[30]

Keep in mind that while the computer program can be copyrighted, the idea behind the program cannot be protected by copyright law. Original works can receive a copyright, but ideas—even original ideas—cannot receive copyright protection. A program that provides a word-processing function can be copyrighted, but the idea of word processing cannot be copyrighted. Copyright law does not prevent other software developers from devising competing word-processing programs. The software program for the video game Halo® can be copyrighted, but the idea behind the game is "fair game" for others to "borrow" by creating a similar game with a different program to run it.

Similarly, the audiovisual display aspects of a video game may be copyrightable, whereas the idea—for example, a crazy character that "munches" everything—behind the game, or the game *per se,* ordinarily will be ineligible for copyright protection. The same may be true in general of flowcharts, components of machines, and printed circuit boards that do not have computer programs embedded in them: These normally are not copyrightable.

There are some important limitations and differences in the copyright protections for computer software. While it would probably be viewed as an infringement for a person to buy a book and then make a copy of it for his or her "archives," this copying is not an infringement with software. It is also not considered an infringement if a person makes a copy or an adaptation of a computer program when such a copy or adaptation is essential for proper utilization of that program on the buyer's computer. It is a violation for a person to make and sell a backup copy separately from the original authorized copy.

The fair use doctrine also applies to software. Software that is protected by copyright can be used in the classroom for instructional or demonstration purposes without acquiring permission from the copyright owner and without the need to pay royalties for the use. In addition, libraries can reproduce and distribute software in some circumstances without infringing the copyright.

TRADEMARKS, SERVICE MARKS, AND TRADE DRESS

Trademarks, service marks, and *trade dress* each involve a distinctive mark or design that identifies the provider of goods or services. As a business develops a reputation and establishes goodwill, customers who see the mark recognize the provider and rely on that provider's reputation as evidence of the quality customers expect from the business. As a result, these distinctive marks can be quite valuable to business.

From their inception, trademarks have served as a means by which people engaged in the trades and crafts identify their goods. Archaeologists have found centuries-old artifacts bearing such symbols. The medieval guilds used trademarks as a means of controlling quality and fostering customer goodwill. Early statutes were intended to prohibit "palming off," in which one producer passes off its goods as the goods of a competitor by copying the competitor's trademark.

Current trademark law continues this tradition of protecting against consumer confusion as to the origin of goods. It provides protection by creating a registration system. The U.S. Constitution does not protect trademarks. Federal regulation is based on the Commerce Clause, which grants the federal government authority to regulate interstate commerce. At the federal level, the 1946 Lanham Act[31] provides for the registration of trademarks with the PTO. When a trademark is issued, the owner of the trademark can use the ® symbol. Once a trademark is issued, the owner of the trademark must protect it and enforce it. Many businesses have established policies on the use of their trademarks. For example, Twitter has posted its policy online.[32]

State laws also protect trademarks. Over the years, an extensive body of state trademark law has developed, principally through the application of state laws governing unfair competition. Most states have their own registration provisions.[33]

Protection from Infringement

Each of these devices is entitled to protection, but the protections vary significantly. This is primarily due to how a business uses the devices and how the public perceives them.

Trademarks   The Lanham Act defines a trademark as "a word, symbol, or phrase, used to identify a particular manufacturer or seller's products and distinguish them from the products of another."[34] Trademarks are used to distinguish one manufacturer's goods from those of its competitors. A mark must be distinctive in order to be registered. In determining whether any given "word, symbol, or phrase" is distinctive and deserving of protection, the courts have established four separate classifications. The mark is either

1. arbitrary and fanciful,
2. suggestive,
3. descriptive, or
4. generic.

An *arbitrary and fanciful term* is distinctive by definition. "Exxon" and "Xerox" are arbitrary and fanciful words that had no meaning until they were created by the respective companies. The mark is identified with the product and what the product is. Exxon *is* a type of gasoline. Xerox *is* a type of copier. Creating a word, symbol, or phrase that did not exist prior to the introduction of the product with which it is identified satisfies the test for an "arbitrary and fanciful term" and is entitled to trademark protection.

A *suggestive term* is one that conjures an image or an idea of what the product is intended to do rather than what the product is. As a result such terms are also distinctive and entitled to trademark protection. For example, Coppertone, a sun-tanning product, suggests what the product does rather than what it is. Note that all these marks embody some degree of imagination. The word, symbol, or phrase acquires an association that suggests a particular product to the consumer that did not previously exist. A "copper tone" might ordinarily have implied a color before the sun-tanning product was introduced. Now many consumers associate the term "Copper-tone" with the product.

A descriptive mark is one that basically describes the business that the mark intends to portray. "Holiday Inn" is a descriptive mark, "describing" what the mark represents—an inn for people on holiday, or a hotel/motel. (Sometimes the description is less obvious, as in "Vision Center," a mark for a business that sells glasses and contact lenses. While not selling vision *per se,* the business is selling products that enhance one's vision.) Purely descriptive marks—adjectives such as *sweet* or *chicken;* geographic designations, like *California* or *New York* in reference to wines; and people's names, like *L.L. Bean,* used as marks—do not qualify as distinctive until they have acquired a "secondary meaning." When consumers no longer view the marks as purely descriptive terms but rather as indicative of the source of the goods or products, the marks have become distinctive.

Generic marks are not entitled to trademark protection. Generic marks describe the classification or category of the product rather than the product itself. If a computer company decided to incorporate as Computers, Inc., and to sell its product as "Computer," it would not be able to acquire a trademark on "Computer." Generic terms cannot qualify for trademark protection. In addition, some terms that were once trademarked have lost that protection because the term became generic. There are numerous examples of words that have passed into generic usage and have lost their trademark status. *Aspirin, calico, cellophane, escalator, linoleum, shredded wheat, thermos, yo-yo,* and *zipper* represent a few such former U.S. trademarks. Aspirin may no longer be a trademark in the United States, but may still be a trademark under the laws of other nations.

An Ounce of Prevention

Some products are more likely to become generic than others. The first entry into a market is more exposed to this risk. If you produce the first photocopier or individual music player and then other businesses enter the field, members of the public may start calling them all by your name. For example, people commonly call copy machines Xeroxes and MP3 players iPods, even though those labels may be inaccurate. Xerox copiers are made by Xerox and iPods are made by Apple. To avoid genericide, you should always use your trademark with the generic label, for example, Xerox copy machine. You should always capitalize your trademark, for example Xerox and not xerox. You should not use the trademark as a general noun; for example, don't call a photocopy a Xerox. You should not use the trademark as a verb, for example, "I am Xeroxing this" or "I am going to Google that." If you fail to monitor the use of your trademark, it can result in the loss of trademark protection. When you notice a potential problem with genericide, you should launch a campaign to remind people that the term is your trademark and that it should only be used properly.

Not every distinctive word, symbol, or phrase can be protected as a trademark. The Lanham Act prohibits the issuance of a trademark for a deceptive mark or for marks that are immoral, scandalous, or offensive.[35] Specifically, the act excludes trademark protection for marks that (1) disparage any person (living or dead), institution, belief, or national symbol; (2) use the name, portrait, or signature of a living person without that person's consent; (3) use the name, portrait, or signature of a deceased U.S. president during the lifetime of his or her spouse without the spouse's consent; and/or (4) so resemble an already registered mark as to be likely to cause confusion, mistake, or deception.

A trademark belongs to the first person or entity to use the mark in trade or commerce. In order to register the mark and gain statutory protection, the owner must demonstrate either prior use or a *bona fide* intent to use the mark in the future. An applicant submits his or her application with the proposed trademark to the PTO. The PTO examines the application for compliance with the statute and also to ensure that the mark is not confusingly or deceptively similar to previously registered marks. Once granted, registration ordinarily lasts for ten years and is renewable for ten-year periods so long as the mark remains in commercial use. The PTO requires periodic filings confirming that the mark is still in use.

The law protects the trademark owner from infringement when the infringer's use will likely cause an appreciable number of consumers to be confused about the source of the goods or services. The factors courts have used to determine the "likelihood of confusion" include, but are not limited to, the following: (1) similarities in the two marks' appearance, sound, connotation, meaning, and impression; (2) similarities in the customer base, sales outlets, or the character of the sale ("impulse" versus "nonimpulse" sales); (3) the strength of the mark; (4) evidence of actual confusion; and (5) the number and nature of similar marks on similar or related products and services. For example, independently, two men created radio programs and did announcing and voice work. One was using the name "Spider Harrison" and the other was using "Spyder Harrison." The similar names caused confusion in the market.[36]

Defenses to infringement include "fair use" or abandonment of the mark. The Lanham Act expressly provides that nonuse of the mark for two consecutive years constitutes *prima facie* evidence of an intent to abandon the mark. Generally, a person can also use his or her surname in a business—even if it is the same as another famous, trademarked name, like McDonald's, Campbell's, or Hilton—as long as such use does not create the likelihood of consumer confusion.

Service Marks, Trade Dress, and Certification Marks   Service marks, trade dress, and certification marks are given similar treatment and protection. Each of these can also be registered with the PTO and can acquire trademark protection.

A *service mark* is a word, symbol, or phrase used to identify the provider of that service. The only appreciable difference between a trademark and a service mark is that a trademark is used to identify a product and a service mark is used to identify a service. In each case, the mark is intended to call to the mind of potential customers a particular company. The value of a service mark lies in the goodwill and the reputation of the business using the mark.

Trade dress is the use of a specific design, including shape or color, to identify a business, its goods, or its services. Some examples include the *shape* of a product (e.g., the iconic Coca-Cola bottle) and the *color* of the product (e.g., the pink of Owens-Corning fiberglass insulation). However, a product's shape cannot be protected by trademark if that shape would provide a competitive advantage, such as making the product easier to stack. Courts have extended trade dress to include floor plans, color schemes, and even some restaurant menu designs.

Certification marks are used (1) to identify the specific geographic region from which a product comes (e.g., the Real California Cheese seal); (2) to certify that the goods or services meet certain standards in relation to quality, materials, or mode of manufacture (e.g., Good Housekeeping Seal of Approval or the Better Business Bureau logo); (3) to certify that the work or labor on the products or services was performed by a member of a union or other organization; or (4) to certify that the performer meets certain standards (e.g., ISO 9000 certified). (Note that a certification mark is not used by the owner of the mark, nor does it identify the provider of the goods or services. It merely certifies that the goods or services possess certain traits or characteristics often identified with quality.)

Remedies for Infringement

The Lanham Act sets out certain statutory remedies for trademark infringement, including the equitable remedies of an injunction or an accounting to recover the profits the defendant unfairly obtained from the infringing use. In addition, the plaintiff may recover actual damages. The court can treble these damages in its discretion if the circumstances justify it (for example, willfulness or bad faith on the infringer's part). If the defendant used a counterfeit mark, the court will usually award treble damages, attorneys' fees, and prejudgment interest.

International Dimensions

Trademark laws vary by country. Some countries, like the United States, require use of the mark. In other countries, registration is the basis of ownership and use can follow later. In some countries, the business must register its trademark in order to import its goods into the country.[37]

The Madrid Protocol, administered by WIPO, allows for simultaneous registration in more than one member country. The United States is a member country.[38] Under the Madrid Protocol, a U.S. business first registers with the PTO. This registration is called the basic application or the basic registration. The business selects the other countries in which it wants protection. This is referred to as countries in which it wants "extension of protection." These other countries then decide whether to accept the trademark, using their own criteria. If one country rejects the mark, it will not affect registration in the other countries. However, if the United States registration is declared invalid, it will affect the "extension."[39]

Canada and Mexico are logical markets for U.S. goods. However, they do not belong to the Madrid Protocol, so the owner will have to register in each of them separately.[40]

If the firm is going to do business in European Community (EC) countries, it might consider applying for a Community Trademark (CTM). After applying, if even one member country rejects the trademark, the business will not receive a CTM. It can then apply in individual member countries. If the business receives a CTM, it can enforce its trademark by filing one lawsuit instead of filing suits in each individual country where the infringement is occurring.[41]

The Paris Convention also applies to trademarks. Under the Paris Convention, a signatory nation grants "outside" trademark holders the same rights as it grants native trademark holders. Since the United States is a signatory country, once a U.S. trademark holder registers with the PTO, his or her registration date will be the effective date in all Paris Convention countries as long as he or she registers in those countries within six months of filing with the PTO.[42]

TRADE SECRETS

Protection of Trade Secrets

Patents and copyrights each offer significant protection to a successful applicant. However, not all applications are approved. Even if an application is approved, the information concerning the covered material becomes available to the public and increases the risk that a competitor may use that information to compete with the holder of the right. Some people would prefer to treat their intellectual property as a secret, avoiding the need to reveal how something is done. When a business makes this choice, the business is treating its method as a trade secret, and relying on its ability to keep the information confidential. The business is also relying to a much greater extent on state law to provide legal protection, although some federal protections also exist. In determining whether given information is a trade secret, courts generally consider:

1. The extent to which the information is known outside the owner's business;
2. The extent to which it is known by employees and others involved in the business;
3. The extent of measures taken by the owner to guard the secrecy of the information;
4. The value of the information to the owner and to its competitors;
5. The amount of effort or money expended by the owner in developing the information; and
6. The ease or difficulty with which others could properly acquire or duplicate the information.

To qualify as a trade secret, the know-how, manufacturing processes, customer lists, or other proprietary information must be used continuously in the business. In addition, the owner must show that it has taken steps to protect and to ensure that the information is handled in a confidential manner. This is likely to require a showing that: (1) steps were taken to ensure the physical security of the information; (2) disclosure of the information was limited to only those who actually need the information to complete their jobs; and (3) the firm gave notice to those who had access to the information that the firm expects them to keep it in confidence. At a practical level, the business may: (1) require employees to sign confidentiality agreements and covenants not to compete (where they are legal); (2) review papers that employees will present publicly; (3) conduct exit interviews with departing employees; and so on. One need only take reasonable precautions to guard and/or prevent access to the proprietary information. In 2010, "an Apple engineer misplaced a top secret prototype iPhone at a bar." This prototype was the basis for the iPhone 4. When the prototype was discovered, it was sold to Gizmodo.com, an electronics blog for consumers. Gizmodo examined the prototype and posted images and a discussion of the iPhone on its blog. Apple subsequently reported that the prototype had been stolen. Steve Jobs and Apple's general counsel then contacted the blogger who had the phone and the blogger returned it. After the phone was returned to Apple, "a special task force of armed police officers and investigators broke down the front door of the home of Gizmodo's editor and confiscated several personal items in connection with the misplaced phone."[43]

Liability for Misappropriation

Courts base liability for misappropriation of a trade secret on two principal theories: (1) breach of contractual or confidential relations and (2) acquisition of the information through improper means. Under the first line of reasoning, courts will prohibit persons in an agency relationship (including employment) and/or a fiduciary relationship from disclosing or using information acquired in the course of the relationship. Sometimes an employee expressly promises not to compete with the employer for a given period of time in a specified geographical area if the employee leaves this particular job. (Note, however, that some states will not enforce covenants not to compete between employees and their former employers.) In the absence of such an express agreement, courts generally will not imply such a restrictive covenant. But in some circumstances—for example, where a third party learns of confidential information from the employee—the law *will* imply a confidential relationship between the third party and the owner of the trade secret. In such circumstances, the third party's disclosure or use of the information will be actionable as misappropriation.

The law also imposes liability for acquiring the trade secret improperly. The law will not tolerate conduct that falls below generally accepted standards of commercial ethics. If a competitor of a firm induces that firm's key engineer to disclose proprietary information, the competitor will have acquired the information through improper means. Liability will also result from the acquisition of information through bribery, commercial espionage, fraud, theft, and trespass. However, information obtained through reverse engineering, independent discovery, or the owner's failure to take reasonable precautions is probably acquired lawfully.

An Ounce of Prevention

You may be interested in hiring a competitor's employee because of his or her technical expertise. If you do so, you need to avoid violations of your competitor's trade secrets. You should also state in the employment contract that the new employee will not violate the competitor's trade secrets. If the employee does so, he or she will be liable and not you. (Based on the agreement, you may be able to collect reimbursement from the employee if you have to pay for the violation.) Both you and your new employee may be sued civilly or charged with crimes for any potential violations. For example, American Potash tried to obtain a license from DuPont to use its chloride process, a trade secret. When the negotiation failed, American Potash decided to develop its own chloride process by hiring an employee with expertise in the area. It eventually hired Donald Hirsch, a DuPont chemical engineer. Hirsch had earned a doctorate degree and he had been involved in DuPont's extended effort to develop its own chloride process. When DuPont sued, it obtained a preliminary injunction against American Potash and Hirsch. The court said that there was an imminent threat that Hirsch would disclose DuPont's trade secrets in his new position at American Potash.[44]

Civil and Criminal Remedies

Remedies for misappropriation of a trade secret include injunctions and damage awards. Such damages may include the plaintiff's lost profits, the profits made by the defendant, or the royalty amount a reasonable person would have agreed to pay. State criminal laws may apply to misappropriations of trade secrets as well.

On the federal level, the Economic Espionage Act of 1996 (EEA) seeks to punish a broad range of activities that interfere with an owner's proprietary rights in commercial trade secrets. The EEA addresses (1) economic espionage, including activities on behalf of foreign instrumentalities; and (2) theft of trade secrets, resulting from certain domestic commercial endeavors. Prohibited activities include misappropriating, concealing, procuring by fraud or deception, possessing, altering or destroying, copying, downloading-uploading, or conveying trade secrets without permission. The sanctions that can be imposed for prohibited activities include fines, imprisonment, and criminal forfeiture. The penalties are more severe for individuals or organizations that are acting in concert with or on behalf of foreign instrumentalities. The criminal forfeiture provision permits the seizure and forfeiture of the property used to facilitate the misappropriation or impermissible possession of a trade secret.

Computers

To protect trade secrets involving hardware or software an employer should create confidentiality, nondisclosure, and noncompetition agreements with employees, where these agreements are legal. Employers also should limit physical access to areas where the development and/or storage of privately and exclusively owned software takes place. All software and documents containing trade secrets should have proprietary labels. To ensure the security of the information, the software should use encrypted code so that only those who have the key for unscrambling it can make the program intelligible. Employers should provide regular reminders to employees about their secrecy obligations and conduct exit interviews with departing employees where they remind the employee about his or her obligations regarding proprietary information.

If the owner of the trade secret will be licensing the software, it will need to take special care. Besides restricting disclosures by the licensee, the licensor/owner should limit the rights the licensee obtains in the software by virtue of the license. The licensor should specifically prohibit copying except for use or archival purposes. The licensor should (1) formulate special coding techniques to identify misappropriated software; (2) distribute the software in object code as opposed to source code; and (3) stipulate that the breach of any confidentiality provision will result in the immediate termination of the licensing agreement. Trade secrets may be lost through another party's independent discovery of the secret or any other legitimate means, such as reverse engineering or the public dissemination of the knowledge underlying the trade secret through either a failure to keep the information secret or weaknesses in the security methods the owner has used. Mass distribution of software copies to those with whom the software owner has a confidential relationship by itself generally does not eliminate trade secret protection.

Exhibit 8.2 on pages 242-243 compares the different types of intellectual property discussed in this chapter.

An Ounce of Prevention

You need to make strategic decisions about how to protect your intellectual property. Some types of assets can be protected in more than one way. You should consider the advantages and disadvantages of the various options. You need to make this decision early in the process. In the United States and internationally, you can lose protection if you act too slowly; for example, if you disclose the information in a patent application and then decide that it should have been kept as a trade secret.

Exhibit 8.2

Types of Intellectual Property

Type of Intellectual Property	What is protected?	What is not protected?	Does it have to be registered?[a]	Where is it registered?	How long does the protection last?
Patent	• Invention must be new, useful, and nonobvious • Invention that is a process, machine, article of manufacture, or composition of matter, or invention that is a new and useful improvement of one of these 4 categories	• Ideas • Laws of nature • Mathematical formulas • Scientific truths • Mental processes	• Yes	• U.S. Patent and Trademark Office	• 20 years for a utility or a plant patent, 14 years for a design patent • Patents are not renewable
Copyright	• Original works of art/authorship that have been fixed in a tangible medium • Includes: Architecture Computer software Movies Music Novels Paintings Photographs Poetry Songs	• Facts • Ideas • Inventions • Methods of operation • Systems (It may protect how these things are expressed.)	• No • You do have to register if you wish to file a U.S. lawsuit for monetary damages	• U.S. Copyright Office	• Life of author/creator plus 70 years • If the work is "created" by or for a business entity, the shorter of 95 years from first publication or 120 years from creation

Exhibit 8.2 Continued

Type of Intellectual Property	What is protected?	What is not protected?	Does it have to be registered?[a]	Where is it registered?	How long does the protection last?
• Trademark • Service Mark • Certification Mark	• Word, term, or mark used to identify a product, service, or group	• Purely descriptive terms • Generic terms • Marks that are deceptive • Immoral marks • Marks that use a person's name or likeness without permission • Official symbols of the U.S. or any state	• No	• U.S. Patent and Trademark Office	• Registered trademark is valid for 10 years • Trademarks are renewable for 10 year periods • There are no limits on the number of renewals as long as it remains in use
• Trade Dress	• Unique design, color, shape, sound, or other decorative aspect of a product that is used to identify a product or producer	• Trade dress that is functional, for example, a square package that stacks well on store shelves	• No	• U.S. Patent and Trademark Office	• Registered trade dress is valid for 10 years • Trade dress is renewable for 10 year periods • There are no limits on the number of renewals as long as it remains in use
• Trade Secret	• Method of doing business that has value because it is not known to the competition • The owner treats it as a secret	• Failure to keep the information secret • Independent discovery of the secret • Information that is public • Legal reverse engineering	• No	• N.A.	• Indefinite period
• Domain Name	• Internet address of a business	• Some names are no longer available	• Yes	• Register with the company hosting the domain name • It also may be possible to obtain a trademark or service mark in the domain name	• Registrant selects period from 1 to 10 years • Domain names are renewable • There are no limits on the number of renewals

Source: Courtesy of Lynn M. Forsythe. © 2016.

[a] If registration is not required, the owner may still benefit by registering. For example, by registering the owner may be permitted to sue in federal courts or obtain assistance of the U.S. Customs Office. State registration may also be required or recommended.

Contemporary Case

Apple began this U.S. litigation by filing a patent suit against Samsung on February 8, 2012. It involves five Apple patents and two Samsung patents used in smartphones. This excerpt is limited to one of the patent disputes in the case, Apple's '721 patent. Notice how the court analyzes the standard for what is patentable. This is the third appeal to the Federal Circuit in this ongoing dispute.

APPLE, INC. v. SAMSUNG ELECTRONICS CO., LTD.
2016 U.S. App. LEXIS 3432 (Fed. Cir., 2016)

FACTS Apple claimed that Samsung infringed its U.S. Patent No. 8,046,721 (the '721 patent). The district court awarded Apple $119,625,000 in damages and ongoing royalties for infringement of its '647 patent, the '721 patent, and the '172 patent. Apple's '721 patent covers the iPhone's "slide to unlock" feature. The feature allows a user to slide an image across the screen to unlock the phone. Both companies appealed.

ISSUE Is Apple's '721 patent valid?

HOLDING No. The patent is not valid because it is obvious based on the prior art.

REASONING Excerpts from the opinion of Chief Judge Dyk:

. . . Samsung argues . . . that the district court erred in not granting its motion for . . . [judgment as a matter of law (JMOL)] that the '721 [patent] . . . would have been obvious in light of the various prior art references. . . . Obviousness is a question of law based on underlying findings of fact. . . . Secondary considerations, such as commercial success, long felt but unsolved needs, and the failure of others, must be considered. . . .

Samsung contends that the district court should have granted its motion for JMOL that the '721 patent would have been obvious. We agree. . . . [O]ne problem with a portable device with a touchscreen is the accidental activation of features. When a user puts the portable device in a pocket, features may be activated by unintentional contact with the screen, and, for example, a phone call might be made. . . . The '721 patent claims a particular method of unlocking. The user touches one particular place on the screen where an image appears and, while continuously touching the screen, moves his finger to move the image to another part of the screen. . . .

Samsung presented two prior art references, the NeoNode N1 Quickstart Guide ("Neonode") from 2004 and a video and paper by Plaisant that were presented at a computer-human-interactivity conference in 1992. . . . Both NeoNode and Plaisant are prior art. . . . The Neonode reference describes an unlocking mechanism for a touchscreen phone where a user can, through movement of a finger continuously touching the screen of the device, unlock the phone. . . . Neonode discloses using a touch gesture on the screen to unlock a phone but does not have a moving image associated with the gesture. . . .

The Plaisant paper "compares six different touchscreen-based toggle switches to be used by novice or occasional users to control two state (on/off) devices in a touchscreen environment." . . . [In] the "slider toggle," "a sliding/dragging movement is required to change the position of the yellow pointer from one side of the toggle to the other. . . . Users can [ ] grab the pointer and slide it to the other side." ... The "lever toggle" has the same functionality with a different appearance. ...

Apple does not dispute that Plaisant, when combined with Neonode, discloses all of the claimed features of the '721 patent. Rather, Apple argues that the jury could have reasonably found that (1) Plaisant teaches away from using the "slider toggle" and (2) a skilled artisan would not have had the motivation to combine Neonode and Plaisant because Plaisant describes wall-mounted devices rather than portable mobile phones. ...

The fact that the Plaisant paper ... notes that users did not prefer the particular design of the slider toggles is not evidence of teaching away. The reference simply discloses that users were able to figure out the push-button-type toggles more intuitively than the slider toggle. ... This was so primarily because of the design of Plaisant's sliding toggle. The Plaisant paper notes that a simple alteration of the design could solve this problem. ... The reference also lists many benefits of sliding toggles, noting that "many other controls can be designed using sliding motions. Another advantage of the sliding movement is that it is less likely to be done inadvertently therefore making the toggle very secure." ... There was no criticism of sliding toggles that would lead one of skill in the art to be "discouraged from following the path." ... [T]he reference extolls the virtues of sliding toggles as a possible solution to particular problems in computer-human-interaction design. ... [A] reasonable jury could not have found that Plaisant teaches away from using sliding toggles. ... A reference qualifies as analogous prior art if it is "from the same field of endeavor, regardless of the problem addressed" or "if the reference is not within the field of the inventor's endeavor, ... the reference still is reasonably pertinent to the particular problem with which the inventor is involved." ... We conclude that no reasonable jury could find that the Plaisant reference is not analogous art in the same field of endeavor as

the '721 patent. The field of endeavor is determined "by reference to explanations of the invention's subject matter in the patent application, including the embodiments, function, and structure of the claimed invention." ...

Samsung presented expert testimony that a person of skill in the art "would be highly interested" in both Neonode and Plaisant ... because "they both deal with touch base[d] systems, they both deal with user interfaces. They both talk about changing state. ... [A] person looking at this would just think it natural to combine these two." ... [T]he patentee included as potentially relevant many prior art references relating generally to human-interface design, including the Plaisant reference. ... The specification clearly describes the field of the invention as being related to "transitioning" touch screen devices between interface states. ... The Plaisant paper describes exactly this same function. ... A skilled artisan would naturally turn to references like Plaisant to find solutions. ... A reasonable jury could not conclude otherwise.

... We have held that evidence of a long-existing need in the industry for the solution to a recognized and persistent problem may lend support to a conclusion that an invention was nonobvious. ... The idea behind this secondary consideration is that if a particular problem is identified by an industry but left unsolved, the failure to solve the problem (despite the incentive to do so) supports a conclusion of nonobviousness. ... [T]o demonstrate long felt need, the patentee must point to an "*articulated identified* problem and evidence of efforts to solve that problem" which were ... unsuccessful. ... No reasonable jury could find testimony by a single expert about his personal experience with one device as evidence of an industry-wide long-felt need. ...

Apple presented expert testimony that the attendees at an Apple event manifested approval when Steve Jobs first presented and unlocked the iPhone. We have held that "[a]ppreciation by contemporaries skilled in the field of the invention is a useful indicator of whether the invention would have been obvious to such persons at the time it was made." . . . [I]ndustry recognition of the achievement of the invention, such as awards, may suggest nonobviousness. . . . Evidence of approval by Apple fans—who may or may not have been skilled in the art—during the presentation of the iPhone is not legally sufficient. . . .

Apple also argues that internal Samsung documents show that a feature of the Samsung unlock mechanism was copied from the iPhone. These documents show that Samsung engineers recommended modifying Samsung software to "clarify the unlocking standard by sliding" to make it the "[s]ame as [the] iPhone." . . . What was copied was not the iPhone unlock mechanism in its entirety, but only using a fixed starting and ending point for the slide, a feature shown in the Plaisant prior art. We have found, "[i]n some cases, evidence that a competitor has copied a product embodying a patented invention can be an indication of nonobviousness." . . . Evidence of copying of a feature in a patent owner's commercial product is "not sufficient to demonstrate nonobviousness of the claimed invention." . . .

Apple points to the commercial success of the iPhone as evidence of nonobviousness. . . . [E]vidence that customers prefer to purchase a device "with" a slide-to-unlock capacity does not show a nexus when the evidence does not show what alternative device consumers were comparing that device to. For example, it is not clear whether the alternative device had any unlocking feature. A reasonable jury could therefore not find a nexus between the patented feature and the commercial success of the iPhone.

. . . Apple's evidence of secondary considerations is "insufficient as a matter of law to overcome our conclusion that the evidence *only* supports a legal conclusion that [the asserted claim] would have been obvious." . . . We reverse the judgment of infringement and no invalidity because the asserted claim of the '721 patent would have been obvious in light of Neonode and Plaisant. . . .

Short Answer Questions

1. You are very creative. You script and stage an original video, which you produce with some help from your friends. In order to make your video more interesting and professional, you add background music from some CDs that you have purchased. You post the finished video on YouTube®. Are there any potential legal problems with your video? If so, what are they?

2. Your friend Cara just returned from the tattoo parlor. She proudly showed you her new Elsa tattoo. Assume that Elsa from the movie *Frozen* is a copyright of Disney, Inc., and that Disney finds out about the tattoo. What rights does Disney have? Why?

3. Delaware North had been the concessionaire at Yosemite National Park since 1993. It lost its bid for a new 15-year contract. In 2002, Delaware North registered some Yosemite names as trademarks with the U.S. Patent and Trademark Office without informing the National Park Service. The trademarks claimed include The Ahwahnee Hotel, Curry Village, Wawona Hotel, Badger Pass Ski Area, Yosemite Lodge

at the Falls, and Yosemite National Park. Delaware North claims that there was a public record of the registration and the Park Service did not object to the trademarks. Delaware North did not reveal the trademarks to the Park Service until 2014. Since it lost the concessionaire contract, Delaware North wants to be compensated for the trademarks and other Yosemite assets. The federal government contends that Delaware North "has apparently embarked on a business model whereby it collects trademarks to the names of iconic property owned by the United States."[45] It has been reported that Delaware North wants $51 million for the return of the names of the Yosemite landmarks.[46] On March 1, 2016, many of the attractions at Yosemite had new signs. The signs were changed overnight. Delaware North said it is "shocked and disappointed" that the Park Service would change "the beloved names of places in Yosemite National Park."[47] March 1st is also the date that the new concessionaire took over. Can places on federal land and in federal parks be trademarked? Do you think that they should be able to be trademarked? Why?

You Decide...

1. The Washington Redskins are a professional football team. The "Redskins" trademark was first used by the team in 1933 while the team was located in Boston, Massachusetts. Pro-Football, Inc. (PFI) selected the name to distinguish the team from the Boston Braves, the professional baseball team. PFI admits that all six Redskins Marks refer to Native Americans. The name has been used continuously since 1933. The United States Patent and Trademark Office approved and registered the mark in 1967. Variations of the marks were registered between 1974 and 1990. The owner has repeatedly renewed the marks. PFI has made continuous efforts to associate its football team with Native Americans during the relevant time period. There were a number of newspaper articles in 1971 and 1972 describing the opposition to the name by some Native Americans. "[I]n 1972 Leon Cook, President of the National Congress of American Indians ("NCAI"), among others, met with Edward Bennett Williams, the president of PFI, to explain that the team name was a slur."[48] Following the meeting Williams wrote to NFL Commissioner Pete Rozelle to inform him that the American Indian leaders objected to the continued use of the name "Redskins." Williams did not change the team name, but he did modify the fight song and the cheerleaders' outfits so that they were less stereotypical. On August 11, 2006, Amanda Blackhorse and other defendants filed a petition to cancel the registrations of the Redskins Marks. The Trademark Trial and Appeal Board (TTAB) canceled the registration of the trademark. It did not cancel the mark itself.

Section 2(a) of the Lanham Act provides ... that a trademark shall be refused registration if it "consists of or comprises immoral, deceptive, or scandalous matter; or matter which *may disparage* or falsely suggest a connection with persons, living or dead, institutions, beliefs, or national symbols, or bring them into contempt, or disrepute. ..."[49] Section 2(a) does not require that the mark holder possess an intent to disparage. PFI challenges the constitutionality of Section 2(a) of the Lanham Act claiming that: "(1) Section 2(a) of the Lanham Act violates the First Amendment by restricting protected speech, imposing burdens on trademark holders, and conditioning access to federal benefits on restrictions of trademark owners' speech; (2) Section 2(a) of the

Lanham Act is unconstitutionally vague in violation of the Fifth Amendment because it does not provide notice as to which marks "may disparage," it authorizes arbitrary and discriminatory enforcement, and it is impermissibly vague as-applied to PFI; and (3) the TTAB Order violates the Due Process and Takings Clauses of the Fifth Amendment because it deprives PFI of its property without due process and constitutes an unconstitutional taking of PFI's property."[50]

Assume that this case was appealed to your court. How would *you* decide this case? Be certain that you explain and justify your answer.

(See *Pro-Football, Inc. v. Blackhorse*, 2015 U.S. Dist. LEXIS 90091 (E. Dist. VA, Alexandria Div., 2015). Many of the trademarks involved in this dispute are included in the judge's opinion.)

2. Center Point was a general commercial construction company. It hired Richard Burleigh as its operations manager and estimator. Center Point wanted to expand its business in steel fabrication. Center Point did not provide Burleigh any specialized training in steel fabrication. Instead it relied on his expertise and experience in the construction industry. It also relied on his contacts with general contractors in Northwest Arkansas. Center Point did not use proprietary software or formulas to bid on jobs. Company officials assumed Burleigh used his own experience in developing estimates and bidding on jobs. Center Point did tell him how it did things in its office, such as record keeping. Center Point obtained its customer list from Datafax, a subscription service. The service listed the jobs available for bid.

Burleigh left his employment with Center Point after about two and a half years and formed KB Structural with a friend. He began bidding jobs for this competitor of Center Point. Center Point filed suit, alleging that Burleigh had breached the terms of his non-complete clause and had breached his duty of loyalty to Center Point. Burleigh denied that Center Point gave him any training, proprietary formulas, trade secrets, or a secret customer list. Burleigh claimed that he did not learn anything at Center Point that would give him an unfair advantage in the bidding process against it. Did Center Point share any trade secrets with Burleigh that he cannot use for a competitor?

Assume that this case was appealed to your court. How would *you* decide this case? Be certain that you explain and justify your answer.

(See *Burleigh v. Center Point Contractors, Inc.*, 2015 Ark. App. LEXIS 704 (Ct. of App., Div. 3, 2015).)

Notes

1. Leahy-Smith America Invents Act, Pub. L. No. 112-29, 125 Stat. 284. The AIA became effective in 2013. The PTO is writing new regulations to conform to the statute. One of the significant changes is that the patent process is more transparent and accessible to members of the public, which now have multiple opportunities to argue against granting the patent before the PTO. See Robert A. Armitage, "Understanding the America Invents Act and Its Implications for Patenting," AIPLA Q.J. Vol. 40:1, Page 1 Winter 2012.

2. The rules are complex and vary depending on whether the public disclosure is by the inventor, someone associated with the inventor, or someone not related to the inventor. For a detailed discussion, see "United States Patent and Trademark Office, First Inventor to File (FITF) Comprehensive Training, Prior Art Under the AIA," http://www.uspto.gov/sites/default/files/aia_implementation/fitf_comprehensive_training_prior_art_under_aia.pdf (accessed May 8, 2016). If the disclosure is by someone not related to the inventor, then the inventor will have an issue with whether the invention is patentable.

3. Michael Cohen, "Patentability of Business Methods," *Ezine Articles*, submitted January 17, 2006, http://ezinearticles.com/?Patentability-of-Business-Methods&id=129647 (accessed February 27, 2016).

4. *J.E.M. Ag Supply, Inc. v. Pioneer High-Bred International, Inc.*, 534 U.S. 124 (2001).

5. U.S. Patent and Trademark Office, "U.S. Patent Statistics Chart Calendar Years 1963-2014," http://www.uspto.gov/web/offices/ac/ido/oeip/taf/us_stat.htm (accessed March 2, 2016).

6. John Bourdeau, William H. Danne, Jr., Eleanor L. Grossman, Alan J. Jacobs, John R. Kennel, Sonja Larsen, Anne E. Melley, Mary Babb Morris, Jeffrey J. Shampo, Eric C. Surette, and Barbara J. Van Arsdale, "Monopolies, Restraints of Trade, and Unfair Trade Practices I. Federal Antitrust Laws: Sherman and Wilson Acts K. Patent Misuse," Am Jur 2d Monopolies, Restraints of Trade, Unfair Trade Prac. § 121.

7. Id., Paul M. Coltoff, Eleanor L. Grossman, Jill Gustafson, Janice Holben, John Kimpflen, Jack K. Levin, Karl Oakes, and Kimberly C. Simmons, "Patents XXVI. Patent Validity and Infringement Litigation I. Defenses," 60 Am Jur 2d Patents § 791.

8. *eBay, Inc. v. MercExchange, L.L.C.,* 547 U.S. 388, 391, 2006 U.S. LEXIS 3872 (2006).

9. David Pressman, *Patent It Yourself,* 13th ed. (Anaheim, CA: Nolo Press, 2008). For an excellent discussion of international patent law, see Chapter 12, "Going Abroad."

10. Choe Sang-Hun, "Mixed Emotions Over Deft Imitator," *The International Herald Tribune,* September 3, 2012, Section: Finance, p. 16.

11. Harriet Alexander, Shane Richmond, and Harry Wilson, "Battle of the Giants; The Feuding Over Patents Between Hi-Tech Heavyweights Apple and Samsung May End in a US Court, Says Harriet Alexander, But It Will Define the Future of the Mobile Phone Across the Globe," *The Sunday Telegraph* (London), August 26, 2012, Section: Sport, p. 21.

12. Reuters, "Apple Cuts Orders from Samsung for iPhone Chips," *The New York Times,* September 8, 2012, and *The International Herald Tribune, supra* Note 10, "Samsung estimates that it provides about a quarter of all the components inside the iPhone and the iPad, including the much talked-about retina display and the processor and memory chips. Apple is also Samsung's single biggest customer. Neither can walk away from this relationship quickly, however nasty the court battle gets. . . ." Jennifer Hughes and Stuart Kirk, "Samsung: Not a World Leader Yet," *The Straits Times* (Singapore), August 23, 2012, Section: Opinion.

13. WIPO, "Treaties and Contracting Parties, Paris Convention," http://www.wipo.int/treaties/en/ShowResults.jsp?lang=en&treaty_id=2 (accessed February 27, 2016).

14. Information about the Patent Cooperation Treaty can be found at the following Web sites, among others: WIPO/PCT, "Patent Cooperation Treaty ("PCT")(1970)," http://www.wipo.int/pct/en/treaty/about.htm (accessed February 27, 2016), WIPO/PCT Web site, "PCT—The International Patent System," http://www.wipo.int/pct/en/ (accessed February 27, 2016), and United States Patent and Trademark Office, "International Patent Legal Administration (formerly PCT Legal)," http://www.uspto.gov/patents-getting-started/international-protection/international-patent-legal-administration-formerly (accessed February 27, 2016).

15. Pressman, *supra* Note 9.

16. Tristin Hopper, "Running Out of Hope; Creator of Iconic Obama Poster Facing Prison, Millions in Fines," *National Post* (f/k/a The Financial Post) (Canada), September 7, 2012, Section: News, p. A3; Compiled by Dave Itzkoff, "Judge Urges Resolution in Use of Obama Photo," *The New York Times,* May 29, 2010, Section: C, p. 2; and Randy Kennedy, "Shepard Fairey and the A.P. Settle Legal Dispute," *The New York Times,* January 13, 2011, Section: C, p. 2.

17. For detailed information on the length of copyrights, see the chart published by Peter B. Hirtle of Cornell Law School, entitled "Copyright Term and the Public Domain in the United States." The chart is updated annually and is available at http://copyright.cornell.edu/resources/publicdomain.cfm (accessed February 27, 2016).

18. See the sources on the Patent Cooperation Treaty, *supra* Note 14.

19. *Feist Publications, Inc. v. Rural Telephone Service Co., Inc.,* 499 U.S. 340 (1991).

20. 17 U.S.C. §§ 107-118.

21. U.S. Copyright Office, "Fair Use Index," http://www.copyright.gov/fls/fl102.html (accessed February 27, 2016).

22. U.S. Copyright Office, *Reproduction of Copyrighted Works by Educators and Librarians,* http://www.copyright.gov/circs/circ21.pdf (accessed February 27, 2016).

23. Note that the copyright holder is unlikely to grant permission for a parody based on his or her work.

24. Tom Leonard, "Song Protest Band Wants Barracuda Ban," *The Daily Telegraph* (London), September 9, 2008, Section: NEWS, International, 17.

25. See *Bright Tunes Music v. Harrisongs Music,* 420 F. Supp. 177 (S.D.N.Y. 1976).

26. 17 U.S.C. § 504.

27. 18 U.S.C. § 2319.

28. 17 U.S.C. § 506(a).

29. U.S. Copyright Office, International Copyright Web page, http://www.copyright.gov/fls/fl100.html (accessed February 27, 2016).

30. U.S. Copyright Office, *Copyright Registration for Computer Programs, Circular 61,* available at http://www.copyright.gov/circs/circ61.pdf (accessed February 27, 2016).

31. 15 U.S.C.A. § 1051 et seq.

32. Twitter Brand Portal, https://about.twitter.com/company/brand (accessed February 27, 2016).

33. Stephen Elias & Richard Stim, *Trademark, Legal Care for Your Business & Product Name,* 8th ed. (Anaheim, CA: Nolo Press, 2007), 35.

34. 15 U.S.C. § 1127.

35. To see a court's discussion of an offensive mark, refer to *Pro-Football, Inc. v. Blackhorse,* 2015 U.S. Dist. LEXIS 90091 (E. Dist. VA, Alexandria Div., 2015).

36. *Shottland v. Harrison,* 2012 U.S. Dist. LEXIS 94876 (S. D. FL, 2012).

37. Elias & Stim, *supra* Note 33, 274.

38. U.S. Patent and Trademark Office, "Madrid FAQs," http://www.uspto.gov/trademarks/law/madrid/madridfaqs.jsp#q3 (accessed February 27, 2016).

39. Elias & Stim, *supra* Note 33, 277-278.

40. *Id.,* 274.

41. *Id.,* 278.

42. *Id.,* 278-279.

43. Information and quotes from Tom C.W. Lin, "Executive Trade Secrets," 87 NOTRE DAME L. REV. 911, 915-915 (February, 2012).

44. See *E.I. duPont de Nemours & Co. [DuPont] v. American Potash & Chemical Corp.,* 200 A. 2d 428 (Del. Ch., 1964).

45. Oakland Tribune Editorial, "Park Service Right Not to Pay $51 Million Yosemite Ransom," *Contra Costa Times* (California), March 2, 2016.

46. *Ibid.*

47. *Ibid.*

48. See *Pro-Football, Inc. v. Blackhorse,* 2015 U.S. Dist. LEXIS 90091 (E. Dist. VA, Alexandria Div., 2015) at *8.

49. 15 U.S.C. § 1052(a).

50. See *Pro-Football, Inc. v. Blackhorse,* 2015 U.S. Dist. LEXIS 90091 (E. Dist. VA, Alexandria Div., 2015) at *2 and *3, *supra* Note 48.

Part III

Contracts

9

Contract Formation

Learning Objectives

After completing the chapter you should be able to

- Explain how and why the three positive elements of a contract are used to establish contract formation
- Discuss what constitutes consideration and why consideration is essential in the creation and enforcement of a contract
- Recognize the negative elements that may affect a contract and what effect each might have
- Describe when a writing is necessary to make a contract enforceable, and explain what satisfies the writing requirement
- Discuss what makes a contract valid, voidable

Classic Case

This case addresses the issue of consideration. Consideration is the element that elevates a promise to a legal obligation, turning the agreement into a contract. Note the careful language of the court in explaining why consideration is present in this situation.

HAMER v. SIDWAY
124 N.Y. 538, 27 N.E. 256 (N.Y. 1891)

FACTS On March 20, 1869, William E. Story and his nephew, William E. Story, 2d, agreed that if the nephew would refrain from drinking liquor, using tobacco, swearing, and playing cards or billiards for money until the nephew became 21 years of age, the uncle would pay his nephew $5,000. The nephew satisfied all of the terms of the agreement, and so informed his uncle in a letter on January 31, 1875. In a letter dated February 6, 1875, the uncle acknowledged that he placed the money in a bank for "Willie" (the nephew) and would prefer to hold it, with interest, for his nephew until the uncle deemed the nephew capable of taking care of it. Willie consented to this arrangement.

On March 1, 1877, William E. Story, 2d, with his uncle's knowledge and consent, "transferred and assigned all his right, title and interest" in the funds to his wife, Libbie H. Story. Libbie Story subsequently "sold, transferred and assigned" her rights to Louisa Hamer, the plaintiff and appellant in this case.

William E. Story died without releasing the funds to his nephew, and the executor of his estate, Franklin Sidway, refused to release the funds to Ms. Hamer, asserting that there was no contract between the uncle and nephew, and therefore no legal claim to the money.

Ms. Hamer filed suit against the executor, seeking recovery of the $5,000, plus interest. The trial court's judgment for Ms. Hamer was reversed on appeal. Hamer then appealed.

ISSUE Is forbearance from legal and permissible activities or conduct sufficient consideration to support a valid contract?

HOLDING Yes. Forbearance from legal and permissible activities or conduct, asked for and given in exchange for a commitment, is sufficient consideration to support a valid contract.

REASONING Excerpts from the opinion of the Court of Appeals:

... The defendant contends that the contract was without consideration to support it, and, therefore, invalid. He asserts that the promisee by refraining from the use of liquor and tobacco was not harmed but benefited; that that which he did was best for him to do independently of his uncle's promise, and insists that it follows that unless the promisor was benefited, the contract was without consideration. A contention, which if well founded, would ... leave open for controversy in many cases whether that which the promisee did or omitted to do was ... of such benefit to him as to leave no consideration to support the enforcement of the promisor's agreement. Such a rule could not be tolerated, and is without foundation in the law. The Exchequer Chamber, in 1875, defined consideration as follows: "A valuable consideration in the sense of the law may consist either in some right, interest, profit or benefit accruing to the one party, or some forbearance, detriment, loss or responsibility given, suffered or undertaken by the other." Courts "will not ask whether the thing which forms the consideration does in fact benefit the promisee or a third party, or is of any substantial value to anyone. It is enough that something is promised, done, forborne or suffered by the party to whom the promise is made as consideration for the promise made to him." (Anson's Prin. of Con. 63.)

"In general a waiver of any legal right at the request of another party is a sufficient consideration for a promise." (Parsons on Contracts, 444.)

"Any damage, or suspension, or forbearance of a right will be sufficient to sustain a promise." (Kent, vol. 2, 465, 12th ed.)

Pollock, in his work on contracts . . . says: "The second branch of this judicial description is really the most important one. Consideration means not so much that one party is profiting as that the other abandons some legal right in the present or limits his legal freedom of action in the future as an inducement for the promise of the first."

Now, applying this rule to the facts before us, the promisee used tobacco, occasionally drank liquor, and he had a legal right to do so. That right he abandoned for a period of years upon the strength of the promise of the testator that for such forbearance he would give him $5,000. We need not speculate on the effort which may have been required to give up the use of those stimulants. It is sufficient that he restricted his lawful freedom of action within certain prescribed limits upon the faith of his uncle's agreement, and now having fully performed the conditions imposed, it is of no moment whether such performance actually proved a benefit to the promisor, and the court will not inquire into it. . . . Few cases have been found which may be said to be precisely in point, but such as have been support the position we have taken . . .

The order appealed from should be reversed and the judgment of the Special Term affirmed, with costs payable out of the estate.

All concur.

INTRODUCTION TO CONTRACTS

Contract law is one of the cornerstones upon which business is built. Without contract law, or something very similar to it, business as we know it could not exist. Virtually every member of our society will enter into hundreds, if not thousands, of contracts every year. In most circumstances, people don't even realize that they have entered into a contract, nor do they concern themselves with the legal implications of that contract. In fact, many people are not aware of their contracts and have little, if any, knowledge of the rights and responsibilities that arise in a contractual setting.

In its simplest sense, a contract is an agreement between two people in which each person agrees to do something in exchange for some reciprocal conduct by the other person. Since the parties have made an agreement, each party has an obligation to perform his or her side of that agreement. But in a mere agreement, whether the obligation is only social—a date or meeting socially—or moral, as in a promise to make a gift, there are no legal rights established for the parties. When the agreement is supported by consideration, it becomes a contract, and contract law elevates that social obligation into a legal obligation. Contract law provides for judicial enforcement and possible sanctions if either of the two parties does not carry out his or her part of the agreement.

A BRIEF HISTORY OF CONTRACT LAW

Contract law existed under the common law of England, but it was considered much less important than real property law. England was, after all, an agrarian society when the common law developed, and land was the basis of survival. The earliest forms of contract law found in the English common law involved actions in debt or in covenant. When a fixed amount of money was owed for a thing or a benefit given, the person to whom it was owed could seek to recover through an action at debt.[1] An action at debt could also arise for a breach of promise, if that promise was in a writing under seal and called for the payment of a fixed sum of money. An action for a breach of other promises made in writing and under seal was an action in covenant.[2] These actions were not of much use in agreements entered into by a merchant and a customer since most of these were not written and were not under seal.

These early beginnings were supplemented by the development of the law merchant, an unofficial set of rules that the merchants developed sometime around the thirteenth century to resolve common mercantile problems: Merchants believed that the common law did not provide adequate protections. Merchant courts were common at trade fairs, presided over by merchants, since these merchants were familiar with the problems that customers and merchants regularly encountered.[3] Parliament eventually adopted the law merchant's provisions into the common law, allowing the King's courts to decide a broader range of contract disputes.

While the law merchant was a huge step forward, it became outdated over the years. Technological advances led to new issues and new problems that were not contemplated when the law merchant was developed. Eventually, new statutes were enacted in an attempt to reflect contemporary commercial reality in the resolution of contract cases. The Uniform Sales Act, the Uniform Negotiable Instrument Law, and other uniform acts were passed in the early 1900s, providing a "modern" standard under which contract issues would be resolved. By the 1950s these uniform acts were nearly as outdated as the law merchant had been fifty years earlier. (Note that each of these uniform laws was adopted by the states. Contract law in the United States is primarily a matter of state law.)

The U.S. solution was the adoption of the Uniform Commercial Code (UCC), an updated set of laws promulgated by the National Conference of Commissioners on Uniform State Law (NCCUSL).[4] (The NCCUSL is now referred to by the less cumbersome Uniform Law Commission, or ULC.) The UCC addressed a number of the more common commercial contracts in a uniform and contemporary manner. The UCC was first published in 1952, the result of a collaboration between the NCCUSL and the American Law Institute (ALI). It has been adopted, in whole or in part, by all fifty states, Washington D.C., Puerto Rico, Guam, and the U.S. Virgin Islands. It is regularly reviewed, and revisions are proposed as technology and business practices change, allowing the UCC to remain current and providing an extremely useful and beneficial framework for resolving many of the contract law issues that arise in our society.

Note that contemporary contract law in the United States is a combination of common law rules and the UCC, with (1) some areas governed by "traditional" common law rules; (2) some governed by special statutory treatments; and (3) still others governed by one or more articles of the UCC. We will be discussing contract law in broad general terms, primarily with an emphasis on the common law rules, but we will point out differences between specific types of contracts and the rules that govern them when appropriate.

THE ELEMENTS OF A CONTRACT

As mentioned earlier, a contract is simply a moral obligation that has potential legal ramifications if the obligation is not performed as agreed. For these potential legal ramifications to come into existence, the parties must make a contract. The courts recognize seven different elements that must exist before a contract is found. These elements are as follows:

1. An offer—A communication of an intent to make a contract is made by the offeror.
2. An acceptance—A communication by the offeree to the offeror that the offeree agrees with the proposed terms.
3. Consideration—The exchange of value establishing that the agreement is more than a moral obligation.
4. The legal capacity to make a contract—Each party is sufficiently mature and mentally sound to appreciate the significance of the agreement.
5. Reality of consent to the terms of the contract—Each party has freely and voluntarily entered into the agreement.
6. Legality of purpose—The exchanges of value do not violate the law or public policy.
7. Proper form—The contract complies with any requirements as to its form. (Some contracts must be evidenced by a writing before the courts will enforce them; others can be either oral or written.)

If one party denies that a contract exists in court, the other person must prove its existence by showing that all of the positive elements are present. Alternatively, one of the parties may admit that there is a contract but that he or she should not be held to its terms because of some negative element in the contract's formation.

Exhibit 9.1 lays out the positive and the negative elements of a contract.

Exhibit 9.1

The Elements of a Contract

Positive Elements[a]   (These elements must be proven to show that a contract was made.)

Offer+Acceptance=Agreement
Agreement+Consideration=Prima facie contract

Negative Elements[b]   (It is assumed that each party satisfies each one of these requirements. Their absence must be proven to "escape" the contract.)

- Lack of capacity or lack of reality of consent makes the contract *voidable* at the option of the disadvantaged party.
- Lack of legality makes the agreement, at least the illegal portions of the contract, *void*.
- Lack of proper form makes the contract *unenforceable* by the courts.

[a] The party asserting that a contract exists must be able to establish that each of the positive elements is present. The court does not assume the existence of any of the positive elements.
[b] A party seeking to escape a prima facie contract must establish that an element assumed to be present is absent. He or she must be able to show a *negative*: the absence of capacity, a lack of reality of consent, absence of a legal purpose, or *improper* form.

THE POSITIVE ELEMENTS

When a plaintiff sues for breach of contract, he or she is asserting that a contract was formed and that the defendant has breached that contract. The plaintiff will have the burden of proof to establish that a contract was, in fact, formed if the defendant denies that a contract was made. The plaintiff will have to show that an offer was made to the offeree, that offer was accepted by the offeree, and that the agreement is supported by consideration from each party. The court will not assume that any of these three elements is present. The plaintiff will have to present positive evidence of the existence of each. In so doing, the plaintiff has established the existence of a prima facie contract.

The Offer

A person who wants to initiate the formation of a contract must make an offer to the party or parties with whom he or she wants to deal. This party, the offeror, has the ability to control any and all of the terms of any prospective contract. However, the offeror does not create the contract. That ability rests with the person to whom the offer was made, the offeree.

The common law requires the existence of three things to establish that an offer has been made:

1. A communication to the offeree. This communication can be in any form or manner of communicating.
2. The communication must contain reasonably definite terms. The communicated terms must provide sufficient details to allow a court to determine the respective obligations of the parties if an agreement is reached.
3. The communication must show an objective intent to make a contract. A reasonable person viewing the communication would conclude that the offeror communicated with the offeree with the intention to enter into a binding legal arrangement. This means the communication was not made in anger or in jest, and the offeror should reasonably expect the offeree to respond.

If these three things exist, an offer has been made, and the focus shifts to the next step. When an offer is made, one of four things will happen next:

1. The offeree may accept the offer, creating an agreement. If the agreement is supported by consideration, a prima facie contract exists.
2. If the offeree rejects the offer, it is terminated. There is no longer a valid and viable offer because that offer no longer exists. Generally, the rejection must be communicated to the offeror before it is effective.
3. The offeror may decide that he or she no longer desires to make the contract. In this situation the offeror can revoke the offer. Revocation is possible under common law rules at any time prior to the offeree's acceptance of the offer, even if the offeror promised the offeree that he or she would have a certain amount of time to decide whether to accept the offer. The revocation must be communicated to the offeree before it is effective.
4. The offer will lapse if it is not accepted, rejected, or revoked before the time stated in the offer. If no time is stated, the offer will lapse after the passing of a reasonable time, taking into consideration the nature of the offer. There is no need to communicate to the offeree the fact that an offer has lapsed.

The Acceptance

When the offeror makes his or her offer, he or she sets the terms of the proposed contract. However, the offeree controls whether the contract comes into existence. If the offeree accepts, an agreement has been reached, and a contract now exists, assuming that there is an exchange of consideration to support the agreement. If the offeree rejects the offer, the offer is terminated and there is no longer a possibility of an agreement on the basis of that offer. (Note that either party may resurrect the terms included in the original offer by making a "new" offer that consists of the same terms. Still, technically, this is a new offer because the original offer was terminated by the rejection.)

The common law also requires a showing of three things in order to establish that an acceptance has occurred:

1. A communication of the acceptance to the offeror.
2. An objective intent to enter into the contract proposed by the offeror.
3. A "mirror image" acceptance. The acceptance must comply with each and every term of the offer. Any variations, deviations, or changes in any term of the offer are treated as a counteroffer rather than as an acceptance. A counteroffer is also treated as a rejection. So if an offeree makes a counteroffer, the original offer has been rejected, a new offer (the counteroffer) has been made, and the roles of the parties have reversed.

There is an interesting variation on the requirement that the acceptance must be communicated to the offeror. The "mailbox rule" treats an acceptance as communicated to the offeror when it is *sent*, even if the offeror never receives the acceptance. In order for the mailbox rule to apply, the offeree must send his or her acceptance in the manner specified by the offeror in the offer. If the offeror does not specify a manner, the offeree must use the same manner as the offeror used. This means that if the offeror sends a letter containing an offer, the offeree must communicate his or her acceptance by mailing a letter of acceptance back to the offeror. The law views the post office (or other designated carrier) as an implied agent of the offeror. Since the offeror *implied* that the carrier was his or her agent by using it to deliver the offer, delivery of the acceptance to this "agent" is treated as the legal equivalent of delivering the acceptance to the "principal." (Note: The carrier is not a true agent of the offeror. The "agency" is implied because the offeror failed to include more specific terms for the proper method for accepting the offer.)

In common law, the offeree can reject the offer by simply saying "no thanks" or something comparable. He or she also rejects an offer by making a counteroffer, proposing different terms from the terms included in the original offer.

The common law rules regarding offer and acceptance are very strict and rigid, seemingly making it difficult for a party to establish that a contract existed. By contrast, the treatment of offers and acceptances under the UCC is significantly more relaxed. Article 2 of the UCC allows the formation of a contract for the sale of goods to be "made in any manner sufficient to show agreement, including conduct by both parties which recognizes the existence of such a contract."[5] The UCC goes on to state that "an agreement sufficient to constitute a contract for sale may be found even though the moment of its making is undetermined"[6] and that a contract can exist even if one or more terms are left open despite any lack of definiteness "if the parties intended to make a contract and there is a reasonably certain basis for giving an appropriate remedy."[7]

The UCC permits acceptance in any reasonable manner and by any medium of communication unless the offer has specifically restricted the manner of acceptance by its explicit terms. It allows the offeree to add additional terms in his or her acceptance, and those terms become part of the contract—even though not included in the offer—unless the offeror objects to the additional terms or the additional terms materially alter the obligations of the parties.

By looking at these exceptions from common law rules, it is obvious that modern commercial reality is more concerned with encouraging contracts and providing remedies where necessary than in erecting barriers to the legal enforcement of agreements under the strict technical requirements of the common law rules.

An Ounce of Prevention

If you make an offer and want to avoid the risks involved with the mailbox rule, you can specify a deadline and that the acceptance has to be received by you. This can be especially important if you have a limited inventory and you have sent offers to multiple parties. By doing so, if one or two acceptances could deplete your available inventory, you can revoke any outstanding offers for which an acceptance has not been received once you reach your capacity to perform.

Consideration

The third positive element, consideration, is the bargain element of the contract. Consideration is the quid pro quo, the "something for something," that justifies enforcing the agreement of the parties. In other words, consideration is the exchange of value that justifies imposing legal remedies when an agreement is not fulfilled by either of the parties. Consideration involves the *assumption of a legal duty* that the party did not previously have or the *surrender of a legal right* that the party did have, bargained for, and given in exchange for the assumption of a new duty or the surrender of an existing right by the other party. (The issue in our Classic Case for this chapter was whether the surrendering of legal rights by the nephew was sufficient to support a contract with the uncle who requested the surrendering of those rights by his nephew.) The exchange of value must be simultaneous or prospective: It is not consideration if one of the parties has already assumed the duty or surrendered the right without first making an agreement to do so; nor is it consideration if one of the parties attempts to use a preexisting duty to support a new and unrelated agreement. Exhibit 9.2 illustrates when consideration is present.

As a general rule, the court will not question whether the consideration exchanged is adequate. Common law views consideration as the old adage views beauty: It is in the eye of the beholder. If Juanita offers to sell an asset that has been appraised for $4,000 to her friend Allie for a used car with a book value of $2,000, and Allie agrees to make the deal, Juanita and Allie have made a contract. The fact that Allie appears to be the

Exhibit 9.2

The Presence of Consideration

Classification	Example	Is This an Exchange of Consideration?
Assumption of a legal duty	Javier promises to pay Evelyn $500 for a painting Evelyn is trying to sell.	Yes. Evelyn is assuming a new duty—to deliver the painting to Javier, and he is assuming a new duty—to pay $500 to Evelyn.
Surrender of a legal right	Ron backs into Yolanda's car in the parking lot. Ron agrees to pay Yolanda for the damage to her car if she agrees not to sue him.	Yes. Ron is assuming a new duty—to pay Yolanda for the damages to her car. In exchange, Yolanda is surrendering a legal right—the right to sue Ron to collect for the damages to her car.
Preexisting obligation	Karen is a waitress in a restaurant. A celebrity makes a reservation to eat at the restaurant, and Karen's boss promises her a $50 bonus if she provides exceptional service to the celebrity.	No. Karen already has an obligation to provide service to all customers and the boss already has an obligation to pay Karen for her work. (One might argue that providing "exceptional service" is assuming a new duty, but the courts are unlikely to accept that argument.)
Past consideration	While Abhay was on vacation, his neighbor Axel mowed and watered his lawn, even though Abhay never asked Axel to do so. Upon Abhay's return, he is so pleased with the condition of his yard that he thanks Axel and promises to pay him $50 for the yard work.	No. While Abhay would be assuming a new duty—paying Axel for the work, Axel is not providing any consideration. He has already performed the service without any legal obligation or any expectation of being paid. Since there is no exchange of value, there is no contract.

winner in the exchange, gaining $2,000 in total asset value, is irrelevant. Juanita received the benefit she was seeking at a price she was willing to pay: Allie also agreed to surrender an asset she possessed in exchange for an asset that Juanita offered to her.

While courts are not inclined to quibble over whether party A got a "square deal" from party B in any given contract, a lack of adequacy of consideration may be raised by one of the parties as evidence of the presence of a negative element. For example, a person who received what appears to be an unreasonably low price for an asset that she was selling may be able to argue that the other party was guilty of fraud or misrepresentation in getting her to agree to the contract. A person who paid what appears to be an unreasonably high price for an asset may be able to argue that he was the victim of duress or undue influence and that he never would have agreed to such a deal absent the duress or the undue influence. Combining an allegation of the presence of a negative element with an apparently unfair and inadequately balanced exchange of consideration may allow the disadvantaged person to disaffirm (avoid) the contract. Be aware, however, that the basis for avoiding the contract is not the inadequacy of the consideration; rather, it is the presence of the negative element. The inadequate consideration is merely evidence of the presence of the negative element as the reason for the unfair agreement.

THE NEGATIVE ELEMENTS

Many contract cases do not hinge on the issue of whether a contract was formed (all three positive elements were present), but rather focus on the absence of one of the other elements of a contract. The court assumes that if a prima facie contract exists there is a valid contract. The existence of a prima facie contract carries an assumption that each party had capacity, that each party voluntarily consented to the terms of that agreement (reality of consent), that the purpose of the agreement is legal, and that the agreement is in the proper form for the court to recognize and enforce it. The party asserting that an essential element is missing must show that one of these elements assumed to be present is, in fact, missing. In other words, that party must show a negative. That party may argue a lack of capacity or a lack of reality of consent. He or she also may argue that the agreement is illegal, violating a statute or public policy, or that the agreement is not in the proper and required form.

Remember that the court will not make these inquiries. The court will not ask each party whether he or she had capacity at the time of the agreement. It is up to the party alleging a lack of capacity to raise that issue as an affirmative defense to the contract. The same is true for a party claiming that he or she did not really consent, or that the agreement did not have a legal purpose, or that the agreement was not in the proper legally required form to be enforceable by the court.

Since the law presumes each of these criteria is satisfied, the issue becomes whether such a presumed criterion was in fact present and satisfied. The party seeking to disaffirm the contract must establish a negative element, the absence of the presumed element. Each of these "negative elements" is examined below.

(Lack of) Capacity to Contract

A person who has attained the age of majority and is of sound mind is said to possess the legal capacity to contract. If a person has not yet attained the age of majority, he or she is a minor (also sometimes referred to as an infant), and minors lack capacity to contract as a matter of law and of public policy. Similarly, a person who is insane or lacks sufficient mental capacity to recognize the significance of entering into a contract lacks capacity. In some rare circumstances a person may lack the necessary mental clarity to enter into a contract due to intoxication. Such a person might be found to temporarily lack the capacity to contract during the period of intoxication. There are some limitations on capacity imposed by statute, but they are not common under contemporary contract law.

Minority   Historically, the law has protected children from overreaching by adults. Persons of "tender years" are viewed as being unable to protect themselves from the superior knowledge and experience of businesses and/or adults. As a result, a minor had an absolute right to disaffirm (avoid) his or her contracts. The right to disaffirm lasts up to and for a reasonable time after reaching the age of majority. The age of majority today is eighteen. If the minor notified the other party that he or she wished to disaffirm the contract and he or she returned the consideration received, the minor was entitled to recover the consideration given. This was true even if the consideration the minor received has been damaged or has declined in value. The right to avoid the contract belongs only to the minor. If the minor decides to honor the contract, the other party (assuming he or she has capacity) must perform his or her obligation or face a suit for breach of the contract.

If a minor misrepresents his or her age, the right to disaffirm still exists for the minor, but in this situation he or she may be held liable in tort for any damages caused by the misrepresentation. (While a minor can disaffirm a contract, he or she cannot disaffirm liability for torts.)

A minor who enters a contract during minority can ratify the contract after attaining majority. This is especially important if the minor has not executed all his or her obligations under the contract. Ratification can be expressed or implied. If the former minor indicates an intent to be bound by the contract after attaining majority status, he or she has ratified. If the former minor does not disaffirm within a reasonable time after attaining majority, the ratification is implied. Continuing to perform an executory contract after attaining majority is also likely to be viewed as an implied ratification.

An exception of sorts exists when a minor makes a contract for *necessaries*. While the minor retains the right to disaffirm the contract, he or she may be held liable in quasi-contract for the reasonable value of the goods or services provided if those goods or services are deemed to be necessaries for the minor. Note that this is not necessarily the contract price. Necessaries are those things that a person requires in order to maintain a reasonable lifestyle. Historically, necessaries were viewed as food, shelter, and clothing. Today a number of other things may also be considered necessaries: Medical care, tuition or other education expenses, and even transportation expenses might be treated as necessaries for a person. Even if something would normally be viewed as a necessary, the minor will not be held liable if the good or service is already being provided by the minor's parents or guardians.

This absolute right to disaffirm has been modified somewhat by statute, but the right of a minor to disaffirm his or her contracts remains *almost* absolute even with these statutory enactments. Legislation in some states requires a minor to honor contracts made for education loans, medical expenses, bank account contracts, insurance contracts, and contracts for transportation by common carriers. There is significant variation among the states. Any minor who would like to disaffirm a contract should check his or her state's statutes to see if the contract falls within one of the state's legislative exceptions to the traditional rules.

Insanity   The law also historically protected the "feebleminded," those persons who have a mental disease or defect that leaves them unable to appreciate and to accept the implications of entering into a contract. Mental retardation, senility, stroke, Alzheimer's disease, and alcohol or drug addiction, among others, may provide evidence of the person's mental incompetency. A person seeking to avoid a contract due to insanity must establish that he or she was insane at the time the contract was made. Generally the person must also return any consideration received in order to recover any consideration given and to disaffirm the agreement. The disaffirmance must also be done seasonably, within a reasonable time after regaining sanity. If a guardian is appointed to manage the person's affairs, he or she must disaffirm within a reasonable time after becoming the guardian of the insane person.

The rules regarding necessaries are applied in contracts involving insane persons in a manner very similar to the rules regarding necessaries for minors. Again, the insane person (or his or her guardian) will be held liable in quasi-contract for any necessaries provided even if the contract is avoided due to the insanity.

Intoxication   Intoxication may also be used to establish lack of capacity, but generally this is not successful in court. The person must establish that he or she was so intoxicated that he or she was unable to understand the nature, purpose, or effect of the transaction. A person who becomes voluntarily intoxicated is less likely to be able to successfully argue that he or she should be allowed to disaffirm any contracts made during the intoxication. The intoxication in these circumstances would tend to show poor judgment, and the law does not protect people from their own poor judgment. However, if the intoxication is involuntary and the person can show that he or she would not have entered the contract but for the intoxication, the court may well allow that person to disaffirm the contract. For example, assume that Percy, who was in an accident, is in the hospital on pain medication and Reginald, the person who caused the accident, visits Percy in the hospital and convinces Percy to sign a release in exchange for a nominal payment. Upon recovering somewhat from the injury and being weaned off of the medication, Percy realizes what he did and wants to disaffirm the contract, retracting the release. In this situation, a court may well allow the disaffirmance due to Percy's involuntary intoxication.

(Lack of) Reality of Consent

The concept of freedom of contract presupposes that the parties to a contract freely and voluntarily agreed to be bound to the agreement. The law assumes when a person consents to a contract, the consent is real. If a person is induced to make a contract due to a misrepresentation or fraudulent representation of material facts, it can be argued that he or she did not really consent. Similarly, if the agreement was obtained through duress or undue influence, the disadvantaged party did not really consent. In these situations, the lack of *real* consent—consent given freely and voluntarily after all the terms and details are communicated—makes the contract voidable.

Misrepresentation   Misrepresentation involves the misstatement or miscommunication of a material fact that induces the other person to enter into a contract.

A material fact is a fact of sufficient importance that the contract is not likely to be made without it. A misrepresentation can occur without any wrongful intent. A person who states a fact while honestly believing that the statement is true will have committed a misrepresentation if the fact is material and the statement is untrue. The victim of a misrepresentation must decide whether to avoid or maintain the contract. He or she can decide to disaffirm, returning the consideration received and recovering the consideration given, or decide to honor the contract. There are no other remedies for a misrepresentation.

Fraud   Fraud also involves the misstatement of a material fact, but with fraud the party who misstated the fact did so with the intent to deceive the other party. The defrauding party acted with *scienter* (guilty knowledge), having the intent to deceive the other party into entering into a contract. In order for fraud to be shown, the victim must establish that the other person (1) intentionally misstated a material fact; (2) with the intent to deceive; (3) in order to induce the victim to enter into a contract; and (4) the victim suffered harm as a result of the fraud. The victim has four alternatives from which to choose if he or she can prove fraud:

1. Honor the contract and do nothing, which means, foregoing any lawsuits or the seeking of any damages. (This is generally not a good alternative.)
2. Honor the contract and sue for damages under contract law and/or for the tort of deceit (also called the tort of fraud in some states).
3. Avoid the contract and do nothing else. (This is the same remedy that is available for a mere misrepresentation.)
4. Avoid the contract and sue for damages under contract law and/or for the tort of deceit or fraud.

(Note: Alternatives 1 and 3 are the same as the alternatives with misrepresentation. Alternatives 2 and 4 add the availability of a suit for damages because of the presence of *scienter* and the intent to deceive.)

Duress   Duress occurs when a person makes a wrongful threat against the victim as the means for coercing the victim into a contract that he or she would not otherwise have made. To constitute duress, there must be a wrongful threat against the victim, the threat must be sufficient to remove the victim's ability to refuse the "offer," and the victim must accept. Historically, the threat had to be to inflict imminent bodily harm that the victim reasonably believed would occur if he or she did not agree to the proposed terms. The threat also had to be of a type that would objectively cause a reasonable person to feel that he or she had no choice but to consent.

Contemporary courts are likely to find duress if the person (1) threatens to harm the victim or to harm a member of the victim's immediate family; (2) threatens to cause substantial damage to the victim's property; (3) threatens to cause harm to the victim's livelihood; and/or (4) threatens to have the victim unlawfully prosecuted for a crime. Under the law today, a threat that causes severe mental anguish may constitute duress. The wrongful threat is no longer restricted to the imposition of imminent bodily harm.

Courts also recognize that economic threats may be sufficient to constitute duress. Economic duress occurs when the victim is forced to agree to a wrongful and coercive demand for future or additional performance in order to receive goods or services to which he or she is already entitled under a current contract. For example, suppose Custom Computer Emporium has a contract with Microprocessors Unlimited under which Custom Computer Emporium is to receive component parts that it must have to fulfill its current orders. Microprocessors Unlimited is aware of Custom Computer's need and refuses to deliver any more parts unless Custom Computer also agrees to enter into an additional contract, perhaps even at a substantially higher price. Without the parts, Custom Computer will breach its contracts with its own customers, and the liability from these breached contracts will bankrupt the business. Given these alternatives, Custom Computer agrees to the additional contract with Microprocessors Unlimited at the higher price, even though it has no real desire to do so; Custom Computer would likely not have entered into such a contract absent the threat of non-delivery.

The victim of duress can avoid the contract and can sue for damages for any of the torts that the person making the threat has committed. If the duress can be established, it is quite likely that one or more torts can also be shown.

Undue Influence Undue influence occurs when a person takes advantage of a victim's weakened condition or takes advantage of a fiduciary relationship to persuade the victim to make a contract he or she would not otherwise make. For example, Elaine has cancer and after months of radiation and chemotherapy, Cody convinces her to enter into a contract that is not beneficial to Elaine and that under ordinary circumstances she would reject. She may be able to avoid this contract by establishing her weakened condition due to her cancer treatments, asserting that Cody took advantage of her condition to persuade her to enter the contract. Her case will be strengthened if Cody is a close friend or relative. A person asserting that such an undue influence occurred will normally need to show the following:

- That he or she was in a weakened condition;
- That the other person unfairly benefitted from the contract, possibly by grossly inadequate or inappropriate consideration; and
- That this other person was in a position from which he or she could dominate the will of the victim.

If this can be shown, the victim of such undue influence can avoid the contract. Generally, other remedies are not available.

Undue influence may also arise when a person enters into a contract with a fiduciary. A fiduciary is a person occupying a special position of trust with the victim. Due to the fiduciary nature of the relationship, the victim is not likely to question the motives of the other person or to be as cautious as he or she would be normally. The victim enters into a contract that he or she would not have made if he or she had been dealing with a person "at arm's length."[8] Fiduciaries include, at a minimum, one's spouse, other members of one's immediate family, business partners, attorney, doctor, and minister. Each of these persons may be in a position to exert control or "overmastering influence" in convincing the victim to enter into a contract that the victim might not have considered had he or she been dealing with a person other than the fiduciary.

Mistake   Mistake can also establish a lack of reality of consent, but only if the mistake is a mutual (bilateral) mistake about the existence or the absence of a fact that is material to the contract. If such a mistake is found, the court may permit rescission of the contract, returning each party to his or her pre-contract position. If only one party is mistaken, there is a unilateral mistake and the court is not likely to grant relief. A unilateral mistake is often a sign of poor judgment or inadequate investigation prior to entering the contract, and that is the fault only of the person who made the mistake. However, if the other party knew—or should have known—that the person was mistaken as to a material fact and went ahead with the agreement, the court may allow the mistaken party to disaffirm the contract.

In some situations the parties will agree to terms and put the contract in writing, only to discover later that there is an error in the writing, in other words the writing is not an accurate reflection of the agreement made by the parties. In these situations the court will allow reformation, the correcting of the error in the writing so that the writing reflects the true terms of the agreement.

(Lack of) a Legal Purpose

A contract must have a legal purpose. It is unrealistic to expect that the court would help to enforce an agreement that called for the commission of an illegal act, the commission of a tort, or an act that violates public policy. If an agreement entered into by the parties is, in fact, for an illegal purpose, that agreement is void. If the agreement is generally for a legal purpose, but one portion of the agreement is for an illegal purpose, the contract is valid except for the illegal portion, which will be severed, or removed, by the court. If the illegal portion of the agreement would effectively nullify the value of the overall agreement, the overall agreement is void and the court will not enforce any part of the agreement.

Agreements in Violation of a Statute   Obviously, a court will not enforce an agreement to commit arson in order to collect on an insurance policy or to beat someone who has defaulted on a debt. Each of these agreements would violate a statute and would have an illegal purpose. However, there are numerous less obvious examples of agreements that violate statutes. A price-fixing agreement or an agreement to divide a market to reduce competition and/or to increase profits would violate a statute. An agreement to perform a service when the person who is to perform does not have a mandatory license for performing the service is likewise illegal. An agreement that involves wagering is likely to be illegal unless the wagering is of a sort that the state specifically permits (for example, bingo games operated by a church or other nonprofit organization, legal casinos, or pari-mutuel betting). Agreements that call for the payment of a usurious interest rate are illegal. In each of these situations, the agreement violates the statute and is illegal. Most of these agreements will also be void due to the statutory violation in them. There are a few exceptions, such as the following: Some occupations require a person to have a license before he or she is allowed to practice the occupation. Suppose that a person who is required to have a license is not, in fact, licensed, but enters into an agreement to perform the service despite his or her lack of the license. In some states the agreement may be a contract, despite the lack of a required license, but only if the license requirement is seen as a revenue-generating requirement.

If the license is viewed as a method of protecting the public, the agreement is void. This is based on public policy: The state has determined that a person must possess the appropriate license in order to provide services in the field, and unlicensed persons are likely to pose a threat to the health and/or well-being of the customer or client. Doctors, for example, must be licensed to practice medicine in the state. But if the license requirement exists to generate revenue, the contract is valid, but the unlicensed party is likely to be fined for failure to obtain a license prior to performing the service. (Note that this is not the rule in every state.) In these situations the person who is required to have a license may generally acquire a license by completing an application and paying a fee. There are no educational or experiential requirements that must be satisfied to become licensed. For example, many communities require a "peddler's license" for individuals who are selling items door-to-door. Even the Girl Scouts may need to get a license or a permit to sell their Girl Scout Cookies.[9]

If a contract calls for the payment of interest at a usurious and illegal level, some states will enforce the agreement, but will lower the interest to be paid to the maximum legal interest for the state. Other states may allow the lender to recover the principal, but not the interest. Still other states treat the entire arrangement as illegal and void, relieving the debtor of any legal obligation to repay the principal or the interest.

Agreements in Violation of Public Policy   Public policy is "that principal of the law which holds that no subject can lawfully do that which has a tendency to be injurious to the public or against the public good."[10] From this definition, it is obvious that public policy is a broad and somewhat vague term. Public policy sets the parameters for acceptable behavior within society. Its limits are set by the Constitution, statutes, rules and regulations, ordinances, common law, precedent, and—last, but not least—the court's opinion of what the public wants and/or what is most beneficial to the public.

There are some contracts or contract clauses that are acceptable (and enforceable) in some circumstances and not in others. Often, the difference is a matter of degree, with the court striking down a clause because it appears to be overly broad or vague or because one of the parties appears to be overreaching.

A covenant not to compete (a noncompete contract or clause) will be upheld if it is reasonable in time and in geographic scope. However, it will be deemed illegal if it is overly broad in either time or geographic scope. An employer who insists that his or her employees sign a contract including a noncompete clause that prohibits an employee from leaving and going to work for a competitor for two years and within fifty miles of the employer's location might be able to enforce the agreement. But if the same employer tried to restrict the employee for five years rather than two, or for five hundred miles rather than fifty, the court would probably strike the clause down as overly broad and illegal since it would violate public policy. A number of states, including California, will not enforce an employee covenant not to compete for any period. Some people think this policy and the unrestricted movement of employees contributed to the success of many start-up businesses in Silicon Valley.

If a noncompete clause is part of a contract to sell a business, the courts are likely to give effect to broader terms than courts would in an employment contract. The person buying the business does not want to face competition from the seller since the seller will probably have some accumulated goodwill and name recognition, and his or her reentry into the local market could seriously damage the buyer's prospects. But even in this situation, if the clause is overly broad, the court will strike it down as illegal.

An Ounce of Prevention

If you want to include a noncompete clause in a contract you need to check the applicable state law. Does it permit covenants not to compete in this context? What are its rules about what is reasonable in area and length of time? If you do not comply with state law the noncompete clause may be deemed to be unconscionable and/or illegal. If you request a covenant that is too long or specify an area that is too large, some courts will "rewrite" the agreement to make it reasonable. Other states will "discard" the entire covenant.

(Lack of) Proper Form

As a general rule, oral contracts are valid and enforceable. While the lack of any written evidence of a contract may make it difficult to prove all of the terms, the court will enforce the contract if the evidence shows the parties agreed. (If one of the parties is particularly persuasive or appealing to the jury and the other is not as engaging, the more engaging party may persuade the jury that his or her version of the facts is the proper one, but that is a matter of evidence and the ability of the jury. The oral contract as agreed upon should be enforced by the court, but the absence of any written evidence puts the burden on the finder of fact to "find" what the parties agreed upon in their contract.) A contract supported by written evidence is less open to these interpretive issues. This means that a contract evidenced by a writing is easier to prove, but it is no better legally.

An Ounce of Prevention

When you go through the process of writing out your agreement it helps you clarify the terms. As you work to commit the agreement to writing, you may discover that you do not really have a meeting of the minds. You also may discover that you have omitted some critical details, such as which party is going to select and pay for shipping. You can avoid some future problems by resolving them at this stage. A written agreement provides better evidence of your agreement. It may help you avoid a lawsuit or to be successful in any litigation.

However, some contracts are deemed of sufficient importance that written evidence of the contract is required before the court will enforce the agreement. If the parties to a contract in one of these areas enter into an oral contract and each performs, with neither objecting, there is no problem. But if they enter such a contract orally and then there is an issue over performance, the court may well choose not to enforce the oral agreement. Note that this is an issue that must be raised by the party using the lack of any writing as a defense. The court will not ask the parties if there is any writing.

The Statute of Frauds requires that certain types of contracts must be evidenced by a writing in order to be enforceable. There are five traditional areas covered by the Statute of Frauds:

1. Contracts to answer for the debts of another person;
2. Contracts to answer for the debts of a decedent from one's personal funds;
3. Contracts for the sale of an interest in land;
4. Contracts that cannot be performed within one year from the date of the contract's formation; and
5. Contracts in contemplation of marriage.

If a contract involves any of these five areas, there must be written evidence that the parties have made a contract, and the party against whom the contract is being asserted must have signed some portion of the writing, before it will be enforceable in court.

There are also two Statute of Frauds provisions under the UCC's coverage of the sale or leasing of goods that require written evidence of a contract. Under Article 2, any contract for the sale of goods in an amount of $500 or more must be supported by a writing.[11] Under Article 2A, any contract for the leasing of goods in an amount of $1,000 or more must be supported by a writing to be enforceable.[12] There is also an exception to the requirement that the party against whom enforcement is sought must have signed the writing, but this exception only applies to merchants. Assume that two merchants enter into an oral agreement that falls within the Statute of Frauds. Later, one of the merchants realizes that the contract should be in writing, so he sends a written and signed confirmation of the oral agreement. If the other merchant receives the writing and does not object to its contents or to the existence of the agreement within ten days after receiving the writing, the second merchant is also bound to the terms of the written confirmation.[13]

In addition, no written evidence is needed under either Article 2 or Article 2A if:

- the goods are to be specially manufactured for the buyer and would not be suitable for sale to others in the ordinary course of the seller's business, or
- the party against whom enforcement is sought admits in his pleadings, testimony, or other communications in court that a contract was made, or
- if there has been partial performance of the contract by either party, but only to the extent of such performance.[14]

It is important to note that the contract itself does not need to be in writing to satisfy the requirements of the Statute of Frauds. The requirement is that there be *written evidence* of the *formation* of the contract. Consequently, the court can enforce the agreement if there is any note, memorandum, or other written evidence sufficient to show that the parties entered into a contract and that adequately describes the terms of that contract. Such written evidence will satisfy the writing requirement. Even electronic communications such as emails, faxes, or text messages can satisfy the writing requirement. The rule for deciding if something was a writing used to require "reduction to tangible form," something that could be held and read by a person. But under the provisions of the Uniform Electronics Transactions Act (UETA)[15] and the Electronic Signatures in Global and National Commerce Act (E-SIGN),[16] electronic communications that are capable of being stored and later called up for examination and perusal will satisfy the requirement that there must be written evidence to show the formation of a contract.

The Statute of Frauds is not the only statutory provision requiring that some contracts must be in writing. State law may require other types of contracts to be in writing to be enforceable. Insurance contracts generally must be in writing to be enforceable, although a short-term "binder" agreement, whether oral or written, is valid and enforceable until the official policy is issued. Some types of employment contracts may also need to be written before they will be enforceable under some state statutes.

It is always a good idea to have written evidence of a contract, and even to have a detailed written contract if possible. However, it is essential to remember that in most instances an oral contract is valid and binding, and proof of its contents and terms is an issue for the finder of fact.

Contemporary Case

This case addresses the application of the mailbox rule to a more modern method of communication than the postal service—the use of a fax machine to transmit an acceptance. It raises some questions about how the transmittal of an electronic communication can be verified in order to have the mailbox rule apply.

TRINITY HOMES, LLC v. FANG
63 Va. Cir. 409, 2003 Va. Cir. LEXIS 349 (2003)

FACTS Stewart, an agent for Trinity Homes, LLC, alleges that he placed the Agreement for the purchase and sale of real estate addressed to T.H. Nicholson III, the agent for Fang, in his facsimile machine, dialed the number for Nicholson, pushed the button to start the facsimile, and then went on an errand. The facsimile machine utilized by Stewart was not a modern version and did not provide any verification that a facsimile was being transmitted and/or that such facsimile was received. There are no phone records relative to the alleged transmission of the facsimile transmission by Stewart. Shortly after the time Stewart alleged he forwarded the facsimile to Nicholson, he received a phone call from Nicholson indicating that the Fangs did not wish to sell the property or enter into a contract with Trinity Homes, LLC for that purpose. Trinity Homes contends that the mailbox rule should apply and that Steward's facsimile transmission was an acceptance of the offer. Trinity Homes asserts that this acceptance was sent prior to the revocation of the offer by Nicholson, and that a contract resulted from the facsimile transmission.

ISSUES Should the "mailbox rule" apply in this case? What is the status of the facsimile acceptance allegedly sent by Stewart?

HOLDINGS Yes, the mailbox rule should apply. There was no showing that the facsimile transmission actually occurred, which means that there was no acceptance prior to the revocation of the offer.

REASONING Excerpts from the opinion of Judge Marc Jacobson:

Initially, it is necessary to consider whether facsimile (fax) transmissions are similar to or should be treated the same as the Mailbox Rule in regard to the acceptance of a contract. . . . The Mailbox Rule states that, once an offeree has dispatched his acceptance, it is too late for the offeror to revoke the offer. The Mailbox Rule has been accepted in most American jurisdictions and by the Restatement of Contracts. . . . The Restatement addresses the issue of the application of the Mailbox Rule to electronic communication in § 64, which states: "Acceptance given by telephone or other medium of substantially instantaneous two-way communication is governed by the principles applicable to acceptances where the parties are in the presence of each other." . . . This is, therefore, a two-prong test: (1) the communication must be "substantially instantaneous"; and (2) the communication must be two-way. . . .

To be substantially instantaneous, the transmission must occur within a few seconds, or, at most, within a minute or two. . . . For a communication to be two-way, one party must be able to "determine readily whether the other party is aware of the first party's communications, through immediate verbal response or, when the communication is face-to-face, through nonverbal cues." . . . Further, if a communication is not two-way, "the offeror will not know exactly when the offeree accepts and may attempt to revoke the offer after the offeree has already sent his instantaneous acceptance to the offeror. . . . In such a situation, the Mailbox Rule should continue to apply and the contract should be considered accepted upon dispatch of the offeree's acceptance." . . .

The Supreme Court of Oklahoma considered this issue in *Osprey, L.L.C. v. Kelly-Moore Paint Co.* . . . In *Osprey* . . . [t]he plaintiff denied receiving the fax, despite a fax record and telephone record confirming the transmission. Applying the Mailbox Rule, the court held that the faxed notice . . . was sufficient . . . because the notice was in writing and the delivery of the notice by fax transmission served the same purpose of the authorized methods of delivery. The court stated specifically: "the fax log and telephone records show that the notice was property transmitted to Osprey. Transmitting the fax *was like mailing an acceptance under the Mailbox Rule,* where an offer is accepted when it is deposited in the mail." . . .

This Court concludes that the Mailbox Rule is applicable in the instant cause and thus the issue is one of fact, whether or not the facsimile transmission of [the acceptance] was actually forwarded or transmitted by Stewart to Nicholson.

. . . Stewart's fax machine was apparently one of early vintage and provided no verification of the transmission . . . to Nicholson. Unlike the *Osprey* case, there was no fax log and/or telephone records to show that the fax was properly transmitted to Nicholson. Stewart cannot say with certainty if the fax actually went through other than to say that he placed the fax in the fax machine, turned it on, and then left before viewing and/or verifying its transmission. Further, Stewart did not recall looking at the fax machine by or through which [acceptance] allegedly was transmitted, when he returned later in the afternoon from his errand.

The burden is on [Trinity Homes, LLC] to prove by preponderance of the evidence that the fax transmission . . . was actually made and accomplished. The Court in considering the totality of the evidence and the totality of the circumstances, finds and concludes that the burden has not been met nor satisfied and finds for the [Fangs].

Short Answer Questions

1. What are the three positive elements involved in contract formation? Which party has the burden of proof if any of the positive elements are in controversy? Why does that party have the burden of proof?

2. What are the four negative elements that may be involved in a contract formation case? Which

party has the burden of proof if any of the negative elements are in controversy? Why does that party have the burden of proof?

3. Why are the rules for contract formation different under the Uniform Commercial Code's Articles 2 and 2A than they are under the common law of contracts?

You Decide . . .

1. Assume the basic facts from the Grimms' fairy tale "Jack and the Beanstalk":

Jack lived with his mother, a poor widow, in a small house and they had little in the way of assets. Their most valuable asset was a milking cow.

The cow had gotten old and was no longer giving as much milk, so his mother told Jack to take the cow to town and sell it. (It is likely she planned to use the money from the sale to purchase a new cow, but this is just speculation.) On the way to town Jack met a stranger who offered a trade: The stranger would give Jack some magic beans in exchange for the cow. Jack agreed to the trade, handed over the cow, took the allegedly magic beans in exchange, and rushed home to share his good fortune with his mother. Unfortunately for Jack, his mother was furious with him for making this trade.

Here we will depart from the Grimms' version. Jack's mother decided to hire a lawyer and seek legal recourse. She found a lawyer who was willing to discuss her case and explain her options. You are that lawyer!

What issues do you think the mother might be able to argue to avoid the contract with the stranger? Would this case be decided under common law principles, or would it be resolved under the provisions of Article 2 of the UCC? If the case were to go to court, what result would you expect? Explain your reasoning in answering these questions.

2. Bob Britton, a general contractor and the agent for Ashton Development, Inc. in all dealings with Rich & Whillock, Inc (R&W)., signed a contract for grading and excavating services to be provided by R&W at a price of $112,990. The contract also stated "any rock encountered will be considered an extra at current rental rates."

R&W encountered rock on the project site and meeting was held to discuss the problem. Everyone agreed the rock would have to be blasted. The $112,990 contract price expressly excluded blasting. Whillock and Rich estimated the extra cost to remove the rock would be at least $100,000, for a total contract price of approximately $213,000. They also emphasized that the estimate was not firm and the actual cost could go much higher due to the unpredictable nature of rock work.

Britton directed R&W to go ahead with the rock work and bill him for the extra costs. R&W proceeded accordingly, submitting invoices and receiving payments every other week. The invoices separately stated the charges for the regular contract work and the extra rock work and were supported by attached employee time sheets. When Whillock asked Britton if he had any questions about any of the billings, Britton had no questions and told Whillock to continue with the rock work because it had to be done.

When the work was nearly finished, and after receiving payments totaling $190,363.50, R&W submitted a final billing for an additional $72,286. Britton refused to pay, alleging that he was short on funds for the project and had no money left to pay the final billing. Up until he received that billing, Britton had no complaints about the work done or the invoices submitted by R&W and had never asked for any accounting of charges in addition to that already provided. Whillock told Britton he and Rich would "go broke" if not paid because they were a new company, the project was a big job for them, they had rented most of their equipment and they had numerous subcontractors waiting to be paid. Britton replied he would pay them $50,000 or nothing, and they could sue for the full amount if unsatisfied with the compromise.

Britton then presented Rich with an agreement for a final compromise payment of $50,000, with $25,000 to be paid "upon receipt of this signed agreement," to be followed by a second $25,000 payment "upon receipt of full and unconditional releases for all labor, material, equipment, supplies, etc., purchased, acquired or furnished for this contract" . . .

Rich repeated Whillock's earlier statements about the probable effects of nonpayment on their business. Britton replied: "I have a check for you, and just take it or leave it, this is all you get." Rich then signed the agreement and received a $25,000 check after telling Britton the agreement was "blackmail" and he was signing it only because he had to in order to survive. R&W received the second $25,000 and signed a standard release form.

R&W then sued for damages for $22,286, alleging breach of contract. It argued that the agreement with Britton was obtained due to economic duress. Britton claimed that the $50,000 payment constituted a legitimate accord and satisfaction and should be upheld.

How would *you* decide this case? Was this economic duress, or was it an accord and satisfaction? Explain and justify your reasoning.

(See *Rich & Willock, Inc. v. Ashton Development, Inc.,* 157 Cal. App. 3d 1154 (Cal. Ct. App. 1984).)

Notes

1. Arthur Taylor von Mehren, "Contract," *Encyclopaedia Britannica.* http://www.britannica.com/topic/contract-law (accessed December 11, 2015).
2. *Ibid.*
3. *Ibid.*
4. The Uniform Law Commission (ULC) was formerly called the NCCUSL. This organization has been in existence since 1892.
5. UCC § 2-204(1).
6. UCC § 2-204(2).
7. UCC § 2-204(3).
8. "Beyond the reach of personal influence or control." "Parties deal 'at arm's length' when each stands upon the strict letter of his rights and conducts business in a formal manner, without trusting the other's fairness or integrity, and without being subject to the other's control or overmastering influence." *Black's Law Dictionary,* 7th ed. (St. Paul: West Publishing Co., 1999).
9. "Savannah rule bans cookie sale at Girl Scouts' home," *Savannah Morning News* (March 2, 2012), http://savannahnow. com/news/2011-02-26/savannah-rule-bans-cookie-sales-girl-scouts-home# (accessed December 11, 2015).
10. Judicial and Statutory Definitions of Words and Phrases, vol. 6, p.5813 (West Publishing Co.).
11. UCC § 2-201(1). The proposed amendments to Article 2 would raise this amount to $5,000 for the sale of goods. To date, no state has adopted the amended Article 2.
12. UCC § 2A-201(1)(b).
13. UCC § 2-201(2).
14. UCC §§ 2-201(3) and 2-201(4).
15. Uniform Electronic Transactions Act (UETA) is a uniform act put forward by the Uniform Law Commission (ULC) and has been adopted in 47 states, the District of Columbia, and the U.S. Virgin Islands. Illinois, New York, Washington State, and Puerto Rico have not yet adopted it. http://www.uniformlaws.org/Act.aspx?title=Electronic%20Transactions%20Act (accessed May 3, 2016).
16. Public Law 106–229 (June 30, 2000).

10

Contracts: Performance and Remedies

Learning Objectives

After completing the chapter you should be able to

- Discuss performance of a contract
- Distinguish between perfect tender, substantial performance, and breach of contract
- Explain when performance of a contract is excused
- Recognize when a breach of contract occurs
- Discuss the various remedies available at law and in equity for a breach of contract

Hadley v. Baxendale is a venerable case in contract law, which addresses what types of damages are available when a contract is breached.

HADLEY v. BAXENDALE
9 Exch. 341, 156 Engl Rep. 145 (1854)

FACTS Hadley owned and operated a mill in Gloucester. The mill was forced to shut down when the crank shaft broke, and Hadley needed to ship the broken crank shaft to an engineering firm in Greenwich. The broken crank shaft was to be used as a pattern in manufacturing a replacement crank shaft. Hadley hired Baxendale to deliver the broken crank shaft, informing Baxendale's clerk that "a special entry, if required, should be made to hasten its delivery." The clerk promised that it would be delivered the next day. However, the delivery was delayed several days due to neglect on the part of Baxendale. As a result, the mill was shut down for several days more than it would have been had the crank shaft been delivered the next day, as was promised. Hadley then sued Baxendale for £300, the amount of profits allegedly lost due to the lengthy closure of the mill. The jury found for Hadley on the issue of the lost profits, awarding him £25, and Baxendale appealed.

ISSUE Is Hadley entitled to recover lost profits due to Baxendale's failure to deliver the crank shaft in a timely manner?

HOLDING No. Hadley is not entitled to recover lost profits because there was no proof that Baxendale was aware that the mill would sit idle until the new crank shaft was delivered.

REASONING Excerpts from the opinion of Alderson, B.:

We think that there ought to be a new trial in this case; but in so doing, we deem it to be expedient and necessary to state explicitly the rule which the Judge, at the next trial, ought . . . to direct the jury to be governed by when they estimate the damages. . . . Now we think the proper rule . . . is this: Where two parties have made a contract which one of them has broken, the damages which the other party ought to receive in respect to such a breach of contract should be such as may fairly and reasonably be considered either arising naturally . . . or such as may reasonably be supposed to have been in the contemplation of both parties, at the time they made the contract, as the probable result of the breach of it. If special circumstances under which the contract was actually made were communicated by the plaintiffs to the defendants, and thus known to both parties, the damages resulting from the breach of such a contract which they would reasonably contemplate would be the amount of injury which would ordinarily follow from a breach of contract under such special circumstances so known and communicated. But . . . if these special circumstances were wholly unknown to the party breaking the contract, he, at most, could only be supposed to have had in his contemplation the amount of injury which would arise generally . . . from such a breach of contract. . . . Now in the present case, . . . we find that the only circumstances here communicated by the plaintiffs to the defendants at the time the contract was made, were, that the article to be carried was the broken shaft of a mill, and that the plaintiffs were the millers of the mill. But how do these circumstances shew [sic] reasonably that the profits of the mill must be stopped by an unreasonable delay in the delivery of the broken shaft by the carrier to the third person? . . . It follows . . . that the loss of profits here cannot reasonably be considered such a consequence of the breach of contract as could have been fairly and reasonably contemplated by both parties when they made this contract. For such loss would neither have flowed naturally from the breach of this contract in the great multitude of such cases occurring under ordinary circumstances, nor were the special circumstances, which, perhaps, would have made it a reasonable and natural consequence of such a breach of contract, communicated to or known by the defendants. The Judge ought . . . to have told the jury that upon the facts . . . before them they ought not to take the loss of profits into consideration at all in estimating the damages. There must . . . be a new trial.

INTRODUCTION

Contract law allows a party injured by a breach of the contract to use the legal system to compel performance by the breaching party or to determine the proper remedy or remedies awarded to the victim of the breach. It is hoped that the remedies available will make him or her "whole." In most cases the remedy provided will be the awarding of damages, in the form of monetary compensation, to give the victim the "benefit of his or her bargain." This is the remedy sought in *Hadley v. Baxendale*. However, before one can seek any remedies or relief, one must show that the contract was, in fact, breached. To establish that a breach has occurred, the victim must show that the other party failed to perform the contract or that the performance was inadequate and/or was not excused. To understand this area we must first examine *performance* and how it is measured. Next we will look at a variety of events and occurrences that may *excuse* performance. Finally, we will turn to the area of remedies to be applied when a breach of contract has been established by the plaintiff.

PERFORMANCE OF THE CONTRACT

When a person enters into a contract, he or she reasonably expects to receive what was bargained for; the person also should expect to perform his or her reciprocal obligations in order to discharge the contract. If a party does not perform as promised and that failure to perform is not excused for some reason, obviously there is a breach of the contract. However, in some circumstances a party believes that he or she has performed as agreed, but the other party insists that the performance was inadequate or unacceptable. In this situation, how should the court decide which party is correct? The court will need to look at the performance, look at the terms of the contract, and make a decision based on what should reasonably be expected in the way of performance. In so doing, the court must decide whether the promisee (the person to whom the performance is owed) should reasonably expect a *perfect tender*[1] of performance or should be satisfied with *substantial performance* of the obligation. Exhibit 10.1 outlines the process for evaluating contract performance.

Exhibit 10.1

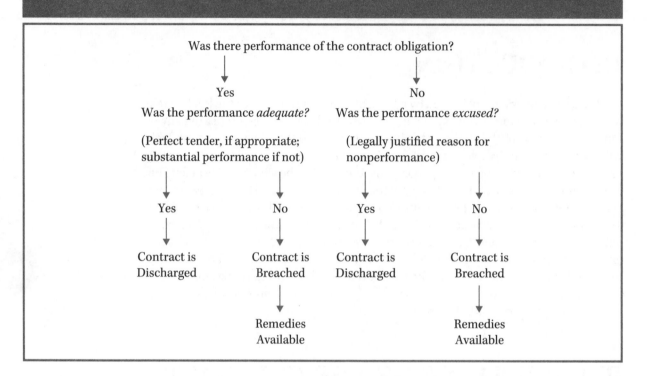

Evaluating Contract Performance

Was there performance of the contract obligation?

Yes — Was the performance *adequate?* (Perfect tender, if appropriate; substantial performance if not)

No — Was the performance *excused?* (Legally justified reason for nonperformance)

Yes → Contract is Discharged

No → Contract is Breached → Remedies Available

Yes → Contract is Discharged

No → Contract is Breached → Remedies Available

Perfect Tender

In common law it is reasonable for a promisee to expect perfect tender in most contracts. *Perfect tender* is performance that completely fulfills the promisor's commitments. For example, if Ronnie promises to pay Amanda $500 for a painting that Amanda has offered for sale, Ronnie would be expected to pay exactly $500 in order to complete his obligation, and Amanda would be expected to tender delivery of the painting to Ronnie. If Ronnie gave Amanda only $499.95, he would not have offered *complete performance* of his obligation. His *tender* (offer) of performance would not be *perfect*, even though a perfect tender should reasonably be expected by Amanda. Similarly, Amanda must tender delivery of the painting that Ronnie agreed to buy. She cannot decide to give Ronnie a different painting, even if she decides after their agreement that the painting Ronnie wanted is worth more than $500, but that the one she is willing to deliver for $500 is "just as good" as the one Ronnie agreed to buy.

Suppose that Rolando and Sofia enter into a contract for the sale of apples. Rolando agrees to sell 200 bushels of apples to Sofia at a price of $20 per bushel.

Under the perfect tender rule, Sofia should expect to receive 200 bushels of apples. The contract would not be performed completely if Rolando only sends 180 bushels, or even 199 bushels and 2 pecks of apples. Similarly, Rolando should expect to receive $4,000 from Sofia. Assume that each party does perform as agreed, but that when Sofia checks the apples she finds that there are some spoiled, bruised, or otherwise unacceptable apples in the delivery. In fact, when the "bad apples" are separated, Sofia discovers that two full bushels are bad and unacceptable. This means that she only received 198 bushels of apples that are fit for her intended use. Has Rolando provided perfect tender in this example? It is possible that he has provided perfect tender. He delivered 200 bushels of apples as per the contract, and the buyer of apples should reasonably expect that there will be some bruising or other problems with apples (apples are produce and a buyer should reasonably expect some bruising or spoilage when purchasing produce). The issue then becomes what percentage of spoilage is expected and accepted in the industry. If the industry expects up to 1 percent spoilage, then Rolando has provided perfect tender. While Sofia should expect to receive 200 bushels of apples, she should also expect that up to 1 percent of those apples would be bad.

Substantial Performance

Perfect tender constitutes complete performance, and when a party provides perfect tender, his or her obligations under the contract are discharged. When each party provides perfect tender, the contract itself is discharged, with no further obligations owed by either party. But there are times and circumstances in which perfect tender will not be a reasonable expectation. In these situations the court will examine whether the tender of performance, while short of perfection, is sufficient to satisfy the obligations under the contract. The court will look to see if substantial performance has occurred. If the court finds that substantial performance has occurred, the party who provided that substantial performance will be discharged from any further obligations under the contract.

For the court to find that substantial performance has occurred, the court must find that the party has (1) made a good faith effort to perform the contract and (2) performed at a level that is "good enough" to satisfy a reasonable and prudent person. To find substantial performance, the court must be satisfied that the party did not intentionally depart from the terms of the contract and that the party did not omit any essential points. It must also find that the party has honestly and faithfully performed the contract's material and substantial terms, with only technical or unimportant omissions.[2]

Suppose that Paul, a particularly persnickety[3] person, hired Hal to build a 30-foot-by-10-foot deck on the front of Paul's house. When the deck was completed, Paul used some extremely accurate scientific instruments to measure the deck and to determine whether the deck was level. Upon completing the measurements, Paul discovered that the deck was 3 degrees ($3°$) out of level. Paul then refused to pay Hal until Hal leveled the deck to Paul's satisfaction. If Hal sued Paul to recover the amount owed for the installation, it is likely that the court would rule in Hal's favor. Hal has seemingly provided substantial performance in this situation. Unless the contract specified that the deck had to be level within some tolerance that was less than 3 degrees out of level, Hal has performed in good faith and at a standard that appears to be good enough to satisfy a reasonable and prudent person; he should be paid for his efforts and granted a discharge under the contract.

An Ounce of Prevention

When a promisee needs or desires assurance of at least a minimum level of performance by the promisor, he or she can use language in the contract that will compel performance to at least that level. The contract may specify a "tolerance level" (a certain percentage or variance from the stated expectation) or even a requirement that the work be performed "to the satisfaction of the promisee." The promisor will have to meet the standards set out in the contract in order to obtain a discharge by performance unless the court deems such a clause unreasonable.

In some circumstances, a party will receive a discharge based on substantial performance, but some measure of damages will be imposed for his or her less-than-perfect tender. In other circumstances, the court may find that the substantial performance was all that the promisee could reasonably expect and that no damages should be assessed.

Obviously, substantial performance is more likely to apply to contracts that call for the construction of a building than for the sale of goods. When a person buys goods that are not "perfect," the goods can be returned or exchanged relatively easily. However, a construction project is not easily returned, and it would be unfair to allow the owner of the land to retain the finished construction project without paying something for the effort, assuming that the effort substantially complies with the original contract. The doctrine of substantial performance protects the contractor from a total loss in the event that his or her performance is less than perfect and prevents the unjust enrichment of the landowner when there is any deviation from the strict literal terms of the contract.

EXCUSED PERFORMANCE

Parties can enter into a contract, and those same parties can subsequently agree to "unmake" the contract. In so doing, they agree to end the contract without further performance and without any breach of the contract. In these circumstances, the parties have discharged their contractual obligations by agreement of the parties. There are also some situations in which the law itself provides an excuse for nonperformance of the contract, granting a discharge without a breach and without any liability, often due to circumstances beyond the control of the parties to the contract.

Discharge by Agreement of the Parties

There are several different methods of discharge by agreement of the parties. Some contracts include specific terms that allow either or both parties to agree to cancel the contract. In other situations the parties may decide, for any number of possible reasons, that their contract is no longer as beneficial as they initially expected, and they decide to terminate their contract without any performance and without a breach.

Release A release is "the relinquishment, concession, or giving up of a right, claim, or privilege by the person in whom it exists or to whom it accrues, to the person against whom it might have been demanded or enforced."[4] Or to put it in layman's terms, a release is the surrender of a right, and a release is often used as consideration for a "new" contract. When a release discharges a contract, one party gives up his or her right to receive the agreed consideration called for in the contract. To be effective a release (1) should be in writing; (2) should be supported by consideration; and (3) should provide for an immediate surrender of any right or claim against the party being released from his or her obligations. For example, Stephanie, a homeowner, may have a contract with Greg, a builder, to remodel her kitchen. For whatever reason, Greg informs Stephanie that he will not be able to complete the work in a timely manner, and offers to pay her some amount in exchange for being released from his obligations under the contract. If Stephanie agrees, she accepts the payment from Greg and releases him from any further obligations. Note that the parties have, in effect, made a contract (the exchange of money for the release) to cancel the remodeling contract.

Insurance claims commonly involve a release, as well. The insurance company agrees to settle a claim with an injured party in exchange for the injured party's signing of a release. The injured party receives a payment from the insurance company, and the insurance company receives a release in which the injured party agrees not to pursue any additional compensation or remedies from the insurer. In these cases the release is the consideration given by the injured party in his or her contract with the insurance company. This use of the term *release* does not discharge a contract; rather, the "release" supports and validates the new contract that fulfills a potential legal obligation. The injured party *releases* (surrenders) his or her right to sue in exchange for a monetary settlement of the claim without resort to litigation.

Rescission A rescission involves annulling a contract by mutual agreement and returning the parties to their *status quo ante* (their respective positions prior to the contract). In effect, the parties agree to "unmake" a contract, although legally speaking they have made a (second) contract that offsets and cancels the first contract. Suppose that Bob and Ted enter into a contract that calls for Bob to deliver some topsoil to Ted in exchange for Ted's payment of $350. Later, the parties decide to rescind this contract. In so doing they agree that Ted will surrender his right to receive the topsoil in exchange for Bob's relinquishment of the right to receive $350. Note that the consideration each is *giving* in the rescission agreement is the same consideration that each was to *receive* in the original contract. Bob was initially to receive money for delivering the topsoil, now Bob is giving up the right to the money in exchange for being released from the duty to deliver topsoil. Ted was initially obligated to pay money for a load of topsoil, now he is giving up the right to the topsoil in exchange for being released from the obligation to pay the money.

Novation   A novation is a new contract that replaces a prior (existing) contract, in which at least one of the parties to the prior contract is replaced by a new party. It is common for the new contract to provide for the same benefits as were expected in the prior contract, but the benefits will be delivered by at least one different person. The effect of the novation is that the party who is replaced is discharged from any obligations arising from the original contract. For example, assume that John and Betty enter into a contract in which John agrees to paint Betty's garage and Betty agrees to pay John $500 and to provide the paint for the job. Before John begins the job, he is offered a full-time position with a local business. John's brother, Roger, is willing to paint the garage, and to do so for the same terms. John then notifies Betty and asks her if she is willing to release him from his contract and to enter into a new contract with Roger. Betty knows both John and Roger, and she has no concerns about making the change. Betty agrees to the arrangement. A novation has occurred: John is discharged from his obligations, the original contract is terminated, and a new contract to replace the original one now exists between Betty (a party to the original contract) and Roger (a new party replacing John, a party on the original contract).

Accord and Satisfaction   An accord and satisfaction is somewhat different from the previous methods for discharging a contract by agreement of the parties. In an accord and satisfaction there is a prior contract or other obligation in existence that has not been performed or otherwise satisfied. The parties then agree to a new, substitute performance by one of the parties; the *accord* will replace the original obligation. When this substitute performance occurs there has been a *satisfaction*, which discharges both the original contract or obligation *and* the new obligation created in the accord. It should be noted that if an accord is reached, but there is no subsequent satisfaction, the party entitled to receive the substitute performance can sue the defaulting party. In most states the party can choose to sue based on either the accord or on the original contract.

An accord and satisfaction often involves an unliquidated amount allegedly owed by one of the parties. An *unliquidated amount* is an amount in controversy, an amount that was not agreed on at the time the contract was made. If a party who disagrees with the amount offers to settle for some specified amount and the other person agrees, an accord has been reached. When the agreed upon amount is paid, satisfaction has occurred and the contract is discharged. Suppose that Donna is on vacation and she loses a filling in a tooth. She contacts a local dentist to get the filling replaced, but does not discuss the cost for the procedure. Once the dentist has replaced the filling he informs Donna that the cost of the procedure will be $400. Donna is aghast! She thinks that $400 for replacing a filling is an outrageous amount and she refuses to pay. Unfortunately for Donna, she and the dentist have a contract. Fortunately for Donna, the amount of the contract is unliquidated; she never agreed to pay $400, or any other specific amount. If Donna offers to pay the dentist $250 and the dentist agrees to accept that amount as payment in full, an accord has been reached. If Donna then pays the $250, the accord was satisfied, and the payment will not only discharge her obligation under the accord, but will also discharge any obligations under the original contract for the unliquidated amount.

Now assume that Donna tells her brother Terry about her "adventure" with the dentist and the bill. Terry believes that he has just learned an invaluable lesson. When he receives his next credit card bill he notes that, ironically, the amount he owes is $400. He then writes a check for $250 to the credit card company, writes "payment in full" on the memo line, and mails the check. The company accepts and cashes the check and then bills Terry for the remaining $150 it claims he owes on his account. He denies owing anything, citing the rules for an accord and satisfaction. In this situation Terry will lose his argument. The amount owed on the credit card account was liquidated. It was an amount that was not in controversy, which means that his offer to pay less and to be released from any further obligation was not accompanied by any consideration and is not binding. There was no accord, and therefore there can be no satisfaction.

Conditions   The contract between the parties may contain conditions that affect the duty of one or both parties to perform. The failure to satisfy such conditions may discharge the contract, relieving both parties of any duty to perform. The presence of a condition in the contract limits or qualifies the obligation of the promisor in the contract. Contract law categorizes conditions based on the timing of the condition. It also examines whether a condition is expressed or implied.

There may also be external conditions that can affect the duty and/or ability to perform the contract. These conditions are not a part of the contract, but the fact that they exist may still have an impact on the parties to the contract and to the contract itself. We will only address those conditions the parties include in the contract in this discussion.

A *condition precedent* is a condition that must be satisfied before the promisor's duty to perform becomes legally binding. A condition precedent most commonly takes the form of *if* [occurrence of condition], *then* [performance obligation]. For example, Bill and Esther may enter into an agreement for the sale of Esther's home. The contract between them contains a condition precedent that may excuse Bill's duty to complete the purchase. Suppose the contract says, "If Bill can obtain a mortgage at or below the prime rate within 30 days of the agreement," then the parties will proceed to closing on the sale. If Bill is unable to obtain such a mortgage, he will be excused from his obligation to complete the purchase. Of course, Bill must make a good-faith effort to obtain the mortgage, and the contract must show that the condition is an essential element of the contract.

An Ounce of Prevention

If you are entering into a contract and you have any concerns about the ability of the other party to perform, you may want to include a condition precedent specifying that the other party must present some evidence of his or her progress toward performance before you are obligated to begin your own performance under the contract.

By contrast, a *condition subsequent* is a condition that must be satisfied before the final performance occurs. With a condition subsequent, the duty to perform is assumed to exist, but that duty will be cut off if the condition is not satisfied. Conditions subsequent frequently take the form of [performance obligation exists] *unless* [condition is not satisfied]. Using our contract between Bill and Esther, the purchase agreement may have a condition subsequent stating that Bill will be obligated to buy Esther's house unless Esther is unable to get a certificate that the house is free of termites and vermin. In this situation Bill is obligated to make the purchase, but his obligation will be cancelled if Esther is unable to obtain the required certificate.

A *concurrent condition* is one that requires the parties to exchange their performance obligations at the same time. Absent some understanding between the parties or specific language in the contract, most contracts are expected to be performed by a simultaneous exchange of consideration. A failure by one party to tender performance by the performance date will discharge the obligation of the other party.

An *express condition* is one that is specified in the agreement. An *implied*, or *constructive, condition* is one that is not spelled out by the parties in the agreement. Rather, it is "read into" the contract by the court to ensure justice and to avoid unjust enrichment.

Discharge by Operation of Law

The law can provide for the discharge of a contract, either by discharging the obligations entirely or by excusing nonperformance due to some external event or occurrence. In some of these situations, the contract is considered to be terminated at this point, with no provision for any adjustments or the return of any unearned consideration. In other situations there may need to be some adjustments to complete the discharge.

Bankruptcy   Bankruptcy law provides an honest debtor with a fresh start. One way to provide this fresh start to an honest debtor is to discharge some of his or her contractual obligations. A person who owes money to a creditor on a contract may be relieved of the duty to pay this debt if he or she files for bankruptcy. If the bankruptcy is successful, the creditor will be unable to recover the amount even if the creditor has fully performed his or her obligations under the contract. After bankruptcy the creditor will not be able to repossess any goods delivered or otherwise pursue any remedies against the debtor.

Statutes of Limitations   Statutes of limitations set some time period during which a person must file his or her claim. If this time period expires without a claim being filed, the right to pursue any remedies based on that claim lapses. A claim for damages due to a breach of contract must be filed within the time specified under the state's statute of limitations for a contract case or the party alleging the breach will lose his or her right to pursue remedies. At common law, the statute of limitations was typically six years from the date of the breach. Some states have a different statute of limitations for a written contract than for an oral contract. (Under the Uniform Commercial Code, UCC § 2-725, the suit must be filed within four years of the breach.)

Material Alteration of the Contract   Assume that two people enter into a written contract. Later, one of them makes material changes to the written contract without the permission of the other person and then tries to enforce this altered document as if it were the contract the parties originally made. If it is established that the alteration was done intentionally, and without the consent of the other person, the court may discharge the contract by operation of law.

Note that if the parties enter into a contract that is to be put in writing before it becomes effective, and the writing then contains any errors that materially alter the obligations of either party, the court may use *reformation* to correct the written contract. The court will allow the writing to be "re-formed" into compliance with the agreement on which the writing is based. This reformation is done to reflect the true agreement and is not based on any material alteration of the contract by one of the parties. Reformation may be available for an innocent mistake in reducing the agreement to writing, or when one of the parties intentionally makes a material alteration in an effort to gain an extra benefit without the consent of the other party.

Intervening Illegality   If there is a change in the law that makes performance of the contract illegal, the contract will be discharged. Any remaining obligations under the contract will be cancelled without any liability on the part of either of the parties. Any performance that had occurred prior to the change in the law will be upheld. For example, assume that Acme Fisheries has a contract to deliver one ton of redfish to Seafood, Inc. each month for a year, with Seafood paying for the deliveries within 30 days of receiving the fish. Six months into the contract the government imposes a moratorium on catching and eating redfish due to excessive mercury levels in the redfish population. Acme Fisheries will be excused from performance until such time as the moratorium is lifted. However, Seafood, Inc. will be obligated to pay for any deliveries made prior to the imposition of the moratorium for which payment has not yet been made.

Impossibility   Performance of the contract may be excused if such performance becomes impossible. This sounds perfectly reasonable and fair. If a person cannot possibly perform, how can that person be held responsible for failing to perform?

However, this is a somewhat tricky issue. The court will examine why performance is allegedly impossible before it applies this rule. There must be an unforeseen event or condition that should not reasonably have been contemplated by either party, and it must be an event or condition that is beyond the control of the parties. Suppose that Harry owns an apricot orchard and he and Sally enter into a contract that calls for Harry to sell 500 bushels of apricots to Sally this year. Unfortunately for Harry, a tornado touches down in his orchard and destroys his trees. As a result, Harry claims that his performance should be excused due to impossibility. Is he correct? That will depend on the terms of the contract. If Harry was to deliver 500 bushels of apricots from *his* orchard, his performance will probably be excused. But if the contract did not specify that the apricots had to come from Harry's orchard, the court may expect Harry to buy the apricots from another orchard and then deliver them to Sally. His performance would not be considered impossible—it would merely be inconvenient.

If a court finds that there is *objective* impossibility—circumstances are such that no one could perform the contract under the present conditions—the contract will be discharged. But if the court finds that it is only *subjective* impossibility—the circumstances are such that the obligor cannot perform, although another party could perform—the contract is not likely to be discharged. In fact, the nonperforming party is probably in breach of the contract. If a person enters a contract by promising to perform in a particular manner because he or she overestimates his or her ability, but then learns that he or she cannot actually deliver, the courts will view this as a subjective impossibility and will hold the nonperforming party liable for breach.

It is increasingly common in some industries for the parties to include a *force majeure* clause in their contracts. A *force majeure* (literally "a superior force") clause provides for excused performance due to *acts of God* (an act caused exclusively by forces of nature) or due to acts of a foreign enemy that interfere with and/or prevent performance. In our example involving Harry and Sally, a force majeure clause might have provided more protection for Harry than he would have under the concept of impossibility.

An Ounce of Prevention

If you are entering a contract in which substitute performance (or a substitute performer, if you should become unable to perform as agreed) would be unreasonable or unacceptable, you should consider including a force majeure clause. This clause would protect you from liability if your inability to perform were due to certain external and uncontrollable factors. You may also want to consider specifying some factors that would be included in the definition of force majeure beyond the normal "acts of God" that are traditionally relied on.

Commercial Frustration   Because of the difficulty of establishing impossibility, and also due to the seeming harshness of the rules relating to impossibility, a new concept has recently emerged. Some courts today will discharge a contractual obligation due to commercial frustration. Commercial frustration may be applicable when a change in conditions or circumstances has caused a "frustration" of the essential purpose of the contract. While less restrictive than impossibility, commercial frustration is still very difficult to establish. The change in conditions or circumstances must (1) be an occurrence that was unforeseen and unforeseeable to a reasonable person; (2) make performance impractical; and (3) both parties must have made the basic assumption that the condition or event would not occur. (UCC § 2-615 uses the phrase *commercial impracticability* rather than commercial frustration, but the concept is essentially the same.)

BREACH

When one (or more) of the parties to a contract fails to satisfactorily perform his or her obligations under the agreement, and the failure to perform is not excused either by agreement of the parties or by operation of law, a breach of contract has occurred. When a breach of contract occurs, the non-breaching party may elect to file suit seeking remedies. He or she may also attempt to hold the breaching party to the terms of the agreement, or may even decide to do nothing, waiving his or her rights to any available remedies. A breach also relieves the non-breaching party of any further obligations under the contract, at least until such time as the breaching party completes his or her obligations.

The breach may occur at the time that performance is due under the contract. This is often referred to as a complete or an actual breach of the contract and allows the other party to treat his or her duties under the contract as terminated: He or she still retains his or her right to seek remedies. The breach may also occur prior to the time that performance is due. This is referred to as an *anticipatory repudiation* or *anticipatory breach*. If one of the parties to the contract indicates in advance that he or she will not or cannot perform as agreed, that party has repudiated the contract. The other party then has the option of treating the contract as breached at the time of the repudiation, immediately seeking any available remedies. He or she may also choose to wait, giving the other person the opportunity to perform as agreed despite the earlier indication that performance would not be forthcoming.

The anticipatory repudiation must be clear and unequivocal. It is not enough for a party to be concerned that the other party may not perform as agreed. For example, if Jonathan and Thelma has a contract, and prior to the date for performance Thelma informs Jonathan and she may have trouble delivering the goods by the due date, Thelma has not repudiated the contract. She has notified Jonathan that she may be delayed in performing, but she gave no indication that she would not perform. But if Thelma notified Jonathan a month prior to the due date that she was unable to get the materials needed to perform, and therefore she would not be able to deliver the goods as agreed, Jonathan could treat this as an anticipatory repudiation.

The UCC provides a less strict method for finding an anticipatory repudiation in contracts for the sale of goods. Under UCC § 2-609, if either party to a contract for the sale of goods has reasonable grounds for believing that the other party will not perform as agreed, that party may request adequate assurances that performance will occur. He or she may also suspend his or her own performance while awaiting receipt of these "adequate assurances." If these assurances are not provided within 30 days of the request, UCC § 2-610 allows the party requesting the assurances to treat the contract as repudiated and seek any and all appropriate remedies.

An Ounce of Prevention

Many businesses regularly grant credit to their customers. This is especially true with commercial customers. For example, suppose that you made a sizeable sale to a customer and agreed to give that customer 90 days to pay for the goods. Shortly after the goods are delivered you learn that the customer is having financial problems. Rather than wait for the remainder of the 90-day period to see what happens, you might consider asking for "adequate assurances" that you will be paid on time. If the customer cannot provide such assurances, you can treat the contract as breached and begin the legal process to recover whatever you can. You are likely to minimize your losses with this technique, if the customer was in fact in financial difficulty. However, if the customer is able to provide the required assurances, you may have ensured that you will be paid, but you may also have offended the customer. He or she, in turn, may seek other sources for future purchases. Consider all the possible repercussions before deciding to seek "adequate assurances," especially from customers who may return in the future.

REMEDIES

The availability of *remedies* is what distinguishes contracts from mere social obligations. If one party to a contract breaches that contract, the other party is able to file a suit, seeking judicial relief in the form of remedies. As stated earlier in this chapter, when the parties enter into a contract, each expects to receive the "benefit of his or her bargain." In most contracts the parties do, in fact, perform as agreed, and the contract is discharged by performance. There are times, however, when one of the parties does not perform, or does not perform adequately, and his or her lack of performance is not excused. In these circumstances, the other party did not receive the benefit of the bargain. When this occurs, the non-breaching party is entitled to seek remedies.

There are two broad categories of remedies: remedies *at law*, and remedies *in equity*. Remedies at law take the form of damages, a monetary assessment of the harm suffered by the non-breaching party. The non-breaching party can only recover damages for such harm as should have been reasonably anticipated by the breaching party if he or she did not perform. (This was the issue in our Classic Case for this chapter.) Remedies in equity are specially tailored remedies for those situations in which money won't make the non-breaching party "whole." Equitable relief is only available in certain situations where a monetary settlement will not be equitable (fair) in that particular set of circumstances. Exhibit 10.2 shows the most common remedies.

Exhibit 10.2

Remedies

At Law	In Equity
Monetary award granted by the court due to a breach of contract	*Nonmonetary awards granted by the court in an effort to "do equity," to be fair to the non-breaching party when money won't "make it right"*
Compensatory Damages—Monetary award for actual, foreseeable harm caused by a breach of contract. Direct damages.	Rescission—A court order rescinding (cancelling) a contract.
Consequential Damages—Monetary award for indirect or secondary damages arising from a breach. Only available if the breaching party knew, or should have known, that the potential secondary losses were likely to occur if the contract were breached.	Restitution—A court order for the return of any consideration that has already been rendered or delivered following the discharge of a contract between the parties.
Punitive Damages—Monetary award granted by the court to punish a breaching party for particularly egregious conduct. Often based on willful, wanton, and malicious harm caused by the breach. Not commonly awarded in contract cases.	Specific Performance—A court order to perform the contract as agreed. Normally, only available for the sale of goods or land. If goods, the goods must be unique or not currently available from another source. For example, antiques and collectibles are likely to be considered unique. Winter coats would not normally be considered unique, even if being sold in mid-summer.
Nominal Damages—Monetary award granted by the court despite the fact that the non-breaching party had no measureable or appreciable loss.	Injunction—A court order to a party either to perform an act or to refrain from performing a particular act.
Liquidated Damages—Monetary award agreed upon by the parties in the original contract and upheld by the court if necessary. Liquidated damages are used in place of other damages when actual damages would be difficult to establish. May *not* be used as a penalty clause.	Reformation—A court ordered correction to an agreement, so that the writing conforms to the original agreement of the parties. Often used for a transcribing error in which the writing differs from the original agreement.
	Quasi-contract—A court order requiring a party that received a benefit to pay the reasonable value of the benefit received. Used to avoid unjust enrichment of one party when he or she received a benefit for which there was no contract or received a benefit from an avoided contract. Best viewed as a contract implied in law when no enforceable contract exists.

Remedies at Law—Damages

When one party breaches a contract, the other party is entitled to payment for his or her lost expectations. The injured party can then file suit seeking a monetary recovery for the losses suffered, known as *damages*. The breaching party will be held liable only for those losses that are a natural and proximate result of the breach and that the breaching party should have foreseen as a likely result of his or her failure to honor the terms of the contract. There are several types of damages that might be imposed following a breach, each of which is discussed below.

Compensatory Damages   *Compensatory damages* are the most common, and the easiest to prove, of the possible damage awards. Compensatory damages are *direct* damages, the amount of loss suffered as a direct consequence of the breach of the contract. The court assesses the amount of money that will place the injured party in the same economic position as he or she would have occupied if the contract had been performed: The court orders the breaching party to pay this amount. For example, suppose that Stan has recently started a lawn care business. He purchased a new lawn mower and an edger for his business from Lou's Lawn Equipment, Inc. Unfortunately, the mower was defective and needed to be repaired at a cost of $250. As a result of the defective mower, Stan lost several customers he had lined up for his lawn care business, a loss that he estimates at $50 per month for the six months he expected to be caring for their lawns. If Stan files suit against Lou's, he can reasonably expect to recover the $250 needed to repair the new mower. This is a loss that he can show is directly related to Lou's failure to provide him with a mower in proper working order. However, he probably will not be able to recover the $50 per lost customer. This is not a direct loss, and there is (currently) no evidence that Lou's knew or should have known that Stan intended to use his mower for a commercial purpose. The injured party can only recover for direct losses in the compensatory damages category.

Consequential Damages   *Consequential damages* are indirect damages, the amount of loss suffered by the non-breaching party as a secondary, or "spillover," effect of the breach. The breaching party will not be held liable for these secondary losses unless he or she knew or should reasonably have known that these damages were likely to occur if he or she did not perform the contract in an adequate manner. In our earlier example, if Stan informed Lou's at the time he was purchasing the mower that he was starting a lawn care business, it would be reasonable for Lou's to expect that the mower was being purchased for that business. In these circumstances Lou's might well be held liable for the $50 per lost customer that Stan was seeking. If Stan was more specific, informing Lou's at the time of the purchase that he was starting a lawn care business, that he already had some customers lined up, and that he needed the mower in order to begin work, the likelihood of recovering from Lou's for these consequential damages would increase significantly.

Remember the Classic Case at the beginning of the chapter. Hadley was seeking recovery of £300 for losses due to the closing of the mill while waiting for the replacement crankshaft. The court ruled that Baxendale had no reason to expect that the delay in shipping the crankshaft would result in a closure of the mill, and so it denied Hadley's claim for these damages.

Punitive Damages   Punitive damages are rarely imposed in a contract case. *Punitive damages* are not meant to compensate the victim of the breach. Rather, they are imposed by the court to punish the breaching party in order to deter such conduct in the future. Awarding punitive damages is sometimes a windfall for the plaintiff. Punitive damages may be imposed by a court if the breaching party is found to have acted willfully and intentionally in breaching the contract and the conduct of the breaching party caused additional losses or placed undue stress on the victim of the breach. There are also some statutory provisions for imposing punitive damages, such as the treble damages provisions of antitrust law. It should be noted that appellate courts are unlikely to uphold a punitive damages award that is grossly excessive and thus unfair to the breaching party.[5]

An Ounce of Prevention

The parties to a contract in which actual damages for breach may be difficult or impossible to calculate are advised to include a liquidated damages clause. Limiting damages to an amount that is agreed upon in advance, a reasonable estimate of what the damages are likely to be, and is mutually acceptable removes an area of uncertainty if things go wrong and reduces or even eliminates the need for a lawsuit to recover damages in the event of a breach.

Liquidated Damages   *Liquidated damages* are damages the parties have agreed to in advance of the contract's performance. Liquidated damages are contained in a written contract clause and call for a specified sum of money to be paid to the injured party in the event the contract is breached. Often the amount will be a specific sum per day (or possibly per week or per month) if the contract is not completed by the specified date. Courts are likely to uphold such a clause (1) if the amount is reasonable and not out of proportion to the injuries likely to be incurred upon a breach and (2) where damages would be difficult, if not impossible, to calculate upon breach.

It should be noted that a liquidated damages clause can be based on any time unit. For example, in Los Angeles recently there was a contract for renovations on the 405, a major freeway and traffic artery. To perform the job, the 405 was to be closed for three days, from July 15, 2011, through July 17, 2011. (The closing of the 405 for the work was referred to by the local media as "Carmageddon.") The job was to be completed and the road reopened by 5:00 A.M., Monday, July 18. The contract also specified that the contractor would be liable for damages of $6,000 for each side of the freeway that was not open every 10 minutes past the 5:00 A.M. deadline—a total of up to $72,000 per hour![6]

Suppose that Raul hires Better Builders, LLC to build a house on his vacant lot. The house is to be completed no later than June 30 of next year so that Raul can move in at the expiration of his current apartment lease. The total price of the construction contract is $150,000, and the contract includes a liquidated damages clause calling for the payment of $100 for each day after the June 30th deadline that the house is not completed. Would such a clause be upheld by the court, or is the amount unreasonable? If the house is not completed on time, Raul will need to find a new residence, since his apartment lease will expire at the end of next June; he may need to store furniture and other items until such time as he can move into the house; he may not be able to cook since he will no longer be in his apartment. There are other possible expenses he will incur while waiting for the house to be ready. The amount is probably reasonable. However, if the amount was set at $10 per day, it would appear to be unfair to Raul, and the court would likely reject it. Similarly, if it was set at $1,000 per day it would appear to be unfair to the builder, and again the court would likely reject it.

Nominal Damages   *Nominal damages* are damages in name only. There are times when a party breaches a contract, but the other party does not suffer any appreciable loss. In fact, there may be no actual measurable loss suffered. Still, a contract *was* breached, and contracts are supposed to be performed. If the victim of the breach files suit even though he or she suffered no actual (or appreciable) loss, the court, upon proof of the breach, will impose some small amount of damages ($25, for example) against the breaching party simply because there was a breach. *If* the court also imposes court costs and the attorney's fees of the other party, the breaching party may well end up paying several hundred dollars. While the plaintiff may only receive the $25 nominal damages, the defendant will have suffered a more significant cost, and the court will have "sent a message" regarding the sanctity of contracts.

Duty to Mitigate Damages   Even when the other party breaches a contract, the injured party is not assured that he or she will collect money for all of the damages incurred. The injured party has a duty to *mitigate* (minimize) the damages suffered before he or she will be allowed to recover. The duty to mitigate is based on the concept of fairness. While the victim of a breach of contract should be able to recover his or her damages attributable to the breach, the breach is not a carte blanche to run up the losses to increase his or her recovery. To ensure fairness, the victim of the breach is required to exercise due diligence in mitigating damages, but he or she is not required to incur any undue risk or inconvenience in attempting to keep the damages as low as is reasonable.

Suppose that Solar Today, Inc. entered into a contract with a local dealership to purchase ten new Hyundai Elantras for its sales force. The price quoted for the cars was $17,000 per car, a total of $170,000. For some reason, the dealer was unable to provide the cars as required in the contract, so the corporation decided to purchase ten cars from another dealer and to sue the original dealer for any losses incurred due to its breach. If the corporation decided to purchase ten Kia Optimas from another dealer at a cost of $19,200 per car, and then to sue for the $22,000 in added costs due to the breach, the court would be likely to agree with the damages claimed since the Kia would be considered a comparable vehicle to the Hyundai. (This assumes that the cars purchased were equipped similarly to the cars originally ordered.) However, if the corporation decided instead to purchase ten Nissan Maximas from another dealer, at a price of $32,400 per car, the court would be likely to deny any recovery due to base cost difference in the cars. The corporation would need to find cars that would logically be seen as comparable in cost as well as in equipment and options, and purchasing the Nissans at a cost nearly double that of the Hyundais would not be evidence of mitigating damages.[7]

Remedies in Equity

The Courts of Chancery in England developed equitable remedies for those situations in which the law did not provide an adequate remedy for the victim of a breach of contract. Equitable relief is only available in those circumstances in which the recovery of money will not satisfy the plaintiff or the concepts of justice and fairness. Keep in mind that equitable relief is the exception rather than the rule and that the collection of damages, the remedy *at law*, is by far the more common result of a breach of contract.

Rescission   *Rescission* is an equitable remedy relieving the parties from their obligations under the contract on the grounds of mutual mistake, fraud, impossibility, etc.[8] If the court grants the relief, the parties are returned to their original positions prior to the formation of the contract. Rescission nullifies the contract between the parties.

Restitution   *Restitution* is "[A]n equitable remedy under which a person is restored to his or her original position prior to loss or injury, or placed in the position he or she would have been, had the breach not occurred."[9] Restitution is commonly granted to prevent the unjust enrichment of one party. It will require the return of any consideration that has changed hands or the recovery of its reasonable value if it no longer exists or is no longer in the other party's possession.

Specific Performance   *Specific performance* is an equitable remedy in which the court requires "exact performance of a contract in the specific form in which it was made, or according to the precise terms agreed upon."[10] Specific performance can only be used if the subject matter of the contract is unique. This essentially restricts its use to contracts for the sale of unique items of tangible personal property[11] (e.g., an antique or a work of art) or the transfer of an interest in land. Land, by definition, is unique. This means that in any contract for the sale of an interest in land, specific performance is available as a remedy for breach. When the sale of tangible personal property (goods) is involved, the uniqueness of the goods—or the temporary unavailability of such goods—is necessary before specific performance is available as a remedy. If Franklin and Jefferson make a contract for the sale of five tons of coal for $50 per ton and then Franklin does not deliver, Jefferson cannot sue for specific performance. Coal is hardly unique, and Jefferson will be able to buy coal from another source. If he has to pay more than $50 per ton, he can sue Franklin for the difference. The monetary remedy is adequate to protect Jefferson.

Suppose that Jefferson and Franklin agreed that Franklin would buy Jefferson's rare antique porcelain eggs, but that Jefferson later decided that he didn't want to sell them. If Franklin files suit seeking specific performance, he is likely to win the case. The eggs are, from the facts stated, rare and thus unique. Franklin cannot acquire the eggs or their equivalent elsewhere. Franklin is entitled to the benefit of his bargain, and the court will order Jefferson to perform the contract according to the precise terms agreed upon, Jefferson will have to perform specifically as agreed. (If Jefferson still refuses to complete the contract, the court may hold him in contempt and incarcerate and/or fine him. In addition, the court will then act "on behalf" of Jefferson in completing the sale by delivering the porcelain eggs and holding any payment by Franklin on Jefferson's behalf.)

Injunction   An *injunction* is an equitable remedy in which the court prohibits a party from doing, or continuing, a specified action, or in which the court orders the person to undo some wrong or injury.[12] When an injunction is issued, the party against whom it applies is enjoined from some conduct, under penalty of a contempt citation and other appropriate sanctions. A temporary injunction may be issued pending a trial to determine the rights of the parties. In our earlier example involving the rare porcelain eggs, suppose that Jefferson had another buyer who was willing to pay more than Franklin had agreed to pay. Upon Franklin's request, the court would probably issue a temporary injunction against the sale pending its decision in the suit seeking specific performance. By contrast, a permanent injunction will normally be issued only after a court has resolved a matter and determined that the defendant's conduct (1) was unlawful; (2) was harmful to the plaintiff; and (3) must be prohibited on a permanent basis.

It should be noted that a court will not order specific performance of a contract that calls for the personal services of one of the parties, but it can—and often will—issue an injunction if a person breaches his or her contract calling for the performance of some personal services. Many students ask why the courts will not use specific performance in these circumstances. The answer is that, while the court may be able to compel the person to show up for work, there is no way the court can be assured that the person will provide his or her best efforts or will do anything except pass time until the time for performance has elapsed. But suppose that Sonya Singer, a cabaret performer, has signed a contract to perform at a local nightclub. The contract is for her exclusive work in the area and calls for her to perform three nights a week for the next three months at a rate of $750 per night. Shortly after signing the contract, Sonya's newest song becomes a hit and she has an offer to sing at a competing nightclub for $1,500 per night. She informs the first nightclub's owner that she is leaving for the other gig. He, in turn, seeks an injunction prohibiting her from performing anywhere else until such time as she satisfies her obligation to him under their original contract. If the court grants the injunction, Sonya has two choices: (1) honor the original contract for the remainder of the three months or (2) find some other source of income besides performing until such time as she completes her obligation to the owner of the first nightclub. While the court cannot force her to perform, it can prevent her from performing!

Reformation   *Reformation* is a court-ordered correction of a written contract to make the writing reflect the true intentions and agreement of the parties. Reformation is only available when the parties reach an agreement, and when the agreement is put in writing, there is an error that causes the writing to be an inaccurate statement of the agreement. The error may be caused by either a mutual or a unilateral mistake, a transcription error, or actual or constructive fraud on the part of one of the parties. Note that it may be difficult to prove that a written and signed contract does not accurately detail the agreement between the parties unless both parties acknowledge the inaccuracy, and if both parties are willing to do so, they should not need to go to court for the reformation. They should be able to correct it themselves.

Quasi-Contract   A *quasi-contract* is "[A]n obligation which law creates in [the] absence of agreement; it is invoked by courts where there is an unjust enrichment."[13] A quasi-contract is also called a contract implied-in-law, as opposed to a contract implied-in-fact. The court will create an obligation in quasi-contract in order to prevent one of the parties from obtaining benefits to which he or she is not entitled. The court will require the unjustly enriched party to pay the reasonable value of the benefits received, treating the parties as if a contract had been made. For example, a minor has the legal right to disaffirm his or her contracts, a rescission of the contract. However, the minor can be held liable in quasi-contract for the reasonable value of the benefits received to protect the other party and to prevent the minor from taking advantage of his or her minority to get something for nothing. It should be noted that a minor's duty of restitution in quasi-contract can vary widely from one state to another. The traditional common law view that a minor has no duty of restitution, except for any necessaries provided by the other party, is still followed in some states, while other states have taken a different view.

Contemporary Case

This case involves a plaintiff seeking equitable relief to prevent unjust enrichment of the defendant. The plaintiff is seeking recovery of monies advanced under its contract with the defendant, who later recovered funds in a lawsuit against a third party.

U.S. AIRWAYS, INC. v. McCUTCHEN

133 S. Ct. 1537, 185 L. Ed. 2d 654, 2013 U.S. LEXIS 3156 (2013)

FACTS McCutchen, an employee of U.S. Airways, was seriously injured in an automobile accident. At the time of the accident he was covered by U.S. Airways' health plan. The plan paid $66,866 in medical expenses incurred by McCutchen as a result of the accident.

McCutchen retained attorneys to sue the person who had caused the accident, agreeing to pay a 40% contingency fee for any recovery he received. (His medical expenses were expected to exceed $1 million.) The attorneys sued the other driver, but were only able to recover $10,000 from her due to her limited insurance coverage and lack of other assets. (Three other people had been killed or seriously injured in the accident.) The attorneys were also able to obtain $100,000 from McCutchen's insurance company, the maximum allowed under this policy. McCutchen thus received a total of $110,000, from which his attorneys received $44,000, leaving him with $66,000.

U.S. Airways then demanded reimbursement of the $66,866 it had advanced to McCutchen, relying on this statement from the insurance plan's description:

> **If [U.S. Airways] pays benefits for any claim you incur as the result of negligence, willful misconduct, or other actions of a third party ... [y]ou will be required to reimburse [U.S. Airways] for amounts paid for claims out of any monies recovered from [the] third party, including, but not limited to, your own insurance company as the result of judgment, settlement, or otherwise.**

McCutchen denied that U.S. Airways was entitled to any reimbursement, arguing that since he had only recovered a small portion of his actual damages, the right to reimbursement did not apply. He also argued that, if he was liable to U.S. Airways, the employee's claim should be reduced by the 40% contingency fee, its "fair share" of the cost of his recovery.

U.S. Airways then filed suit, seeking "appropriate equitable relief" to enforce the plan's reimbursement provisions. The District Court granted summary judgment to U.S. Airways on the ground that the plan "clearly and unambiguously provided for full reimbursement." The Third Circuit vacated the District Court's order, and the Supreme Court granted certiorari.

ISSUE Do equitable defenses override an insurance plan's reimbursement provisions provided for in the insurance contract?

HOLDING No. The terms of the contract prevail. However, since the plan did not address the costs of recovery, the common law's common fund rules apply.

REASONING Excerpts from the opinion of Justice Kagan:

... The question in this case concerns the role that equitable defenses alleging unjust enrichment can play in such a suit. ... [T]he Third Circuit held that "the principle of unjust enrichment" overrides U.S. Airways' reimbursement clause if and when they come into conflict. ... McCutchen offers a more refined version of that view, alleging that two specific equitable doctrines meant to "prevent unjust enrichment" defeat the reimbursement provision. ... First, he contends that in equity, an insurer in U.S. Airways' position could recoup no more than an insured's "double recovery"—the amount the insured has received from a third party to compensate for the same loss the insurance covered. That rule would limit U.S. Airways' reimbursement to the share of McCutchen's settlements paying for medical expenses; McCutchen would keep the rest (*e.g.,* damages for loss of future earnings or pain and suffering), even though the plan gives U.S. Airways first claim on the whole third-party recovery. Second, McCutchen claims that in equity the common-fund doctrine would have operated to reduce any award to U.S. Airways. Under that rule, "a litigant or a lawyer who recovers a common fund for the benefit of persons other than himself or his client is entitled to a reasonable attorney's fee from the fund as a whole." ... McCutchen urges that this doctrine, which is designed to prevent freeloading, enables him to pass on a share of his lawyer's fees to U.S. Airways, no matter what the plan provides ...

[The] logic [from precedents] dooms McCutchen's effort. U.S. Airways ... is seeking to enforce the modern-day equivalent of an "equitable lien by agreement." And that kind of lien—as its name announces—both arises from and serves to carry out a contract's provisions. . . . So enforcing the lien means holding the parties to their mutual promises. . . . Conversely, it means declining to apply rules—even if they would be "equitable" in a contract's absence—at odds with the parties' expressed commitments. McCutchen therefore cannot rely on theories of unjust enrichment to defeat U.S. Airways' appeal to the plan's clear terms. Those principles, as we said . . . are "beside the point" when parties demand what they bargained for in a valid agreement. . . . In those circumstances, hewing to the parties' exchange yields "appropriate" as well as "equitable" relief.

We have found nothing to the contrary in the historic practice of equity courts . . .

Yet McCutchen's arguments are not all for naught. If the equitable rules he describes cannot trump a reimbursement provision, they still might aid in properly construing it. And for U.S. Airways' plan, the common-fund doctrine (though not the double-recovery rule) serves that function. The plan is silent on the allocation of attorney's fees, and in those circumstances, the common-fund doctrine provides the appropriate default. In other words, if U.S. Airways wished to depart from the well-established common-fund rule, it had to draft its contract to say so—and here it did not.

Ordinary principles of contract interpretation point toward this conclusion. Courts construe . . . plans, as they do other contracts, by "looking to the terms of the plan" as well as to "other manifestations of the parties' intent. The words of a plan may speak clearly, but they may also leave gaps. And so a court must often "look outside the plan's written language" to decide what an agreement means. . . . In undertaking that task, a court properly takes account of background legal rules—the doctrines that typically or traditionally have governed a given situation when no agreement states otherwise . . .

This Court has "recognized consistently" that someone "who recovers a common fund for the benefit of persons other than himself" is due "a reasonable attorney's fee from the fund as whole." . . . We have understood that rule as "reflect[ing] the traditional practice in courts of equity." . . . And we have applied it in a wide range of circumstances as part of our inherent authority . . .

A party would not typically expect or intend a plan saying nothing about attorney's fees to abrogate so strong and uniform a background rule. And that means a court should be loath to read such a plan in that way.

The rationale for the common-fund rule reinforces that conclusion. Third-party recoveries do not often come free: To get one, an insured must incur lawyer's fees and expenses. Without cost sharing, the insurer free rides on its beneficiary's efforts—taking the fruits while contributing nothing to the labor. Odder still, in some cases—indeed, in this case—the beneficiary is made worse off by pursuing a third party . . .

Our holding today has two parts, one favoring U.S. Airways, the other McCutchen. First, in an action . . . based on an equitable lien by agreement, the terms of the . . . plan govern. Neither general principles of unjust enrichment nor specific doctrines reflecting those principles—such as the double-recovery or common-fund rules—can override the applicable contract. We therefore reject the Third Circuit's decision. But second, the common-fund rule informs interpretation of U.S. Airways' reimbursement provision. Because that term does not advert to the costs of recovery, it is properly read to retain the common-fund doctrine. We therefore also disagree with the District Court's decision. In light of these rulings, we vacate the judgment below and remand the case for further proceedings consistent with this opinion.

It is so ordered.

Short Answer Questions

1. Explain the different methods for evaluating performance in a contract. Why do *you* think there are different methods for evaluating the performance of a party?

2. What is meant by *excused performance*? What reasons, from either a legal or a public policy perspective, can be asserted to justify excusing performance by operation of law?

3. What are remedies? Why are there different types of remedies? When is it appropriate to seek remedies in equity?

You Decide...

1. An actress hired to portray a victim in a wrongful injury case used by a law firm in a tongue-in-cheek commercial has filed suit for breach of contract against the company that produced the commercial. She was paid $600 for "starring" in the commercial.

The "spoof" ad became a sensation, even being mentioned in the *New York Times*. The producer of the ad licensed it and the rights to the actress's likeness to a number of other law firms across the country. The production company did this without her knowledge or consent. Her image was also used on a number of billboards advertising law firms across the country, again without her knowledge or permission. According to her complaint, the production company earned at least $250,000 from her commercial without compensating her.

She is now asserting that she should be entitled to payment for each use of the commercial beyond the original use, for which she was compensated. She also alleges that she did not give permission for use of her image on billboards or in other ads for other law firms.

How would *you* decide this case? Was there a breach of contract? If so, is the amount being sued for appropriate in this situation? Be certain that you explain and justify your answer.

(See Barbara Ross, Ginger Adams Otis, "Actress from law firm ad files $1 million breach of contract lawsuit," *New York Daily News* (June 8, 2013), http://www.nydailynews.com/new-york/actress-files-1-million-breach-contract-lawsuit-article-1.1366762 (accessed December 9, 2015).)

2. Mr. Carney entered into a contract with Lake Ridge Academy that assured his son, Michael, would be admitted to the fourth grade class at the academy. The contract called for an initial deposit of $630, with the remainder of the tuition, $5,610, to be paid later. The contract also specified that Mr. Carney could cancel the agreement, surrendering his son's position at the academy without further liability for the unpaid tuition balance, provided that he did so no later than August 1 of that year. However, if he failed to give such notice by August 1, he would be liable for the full balance of the tuition, whether or not his son attended the academy. Mr. Carney decided not to send his son to Lake Ridge Academy, and wrote a letter to the academy giving notice of his decision. The letter was dated August 1, but it was not mailed until August 7, and Lake Ridge Academy did not receive the letter until August 14.

Lake Ridge asserted that Mr. Carney had not properly notified it of his intention to withdraw his son's application in time and demanded payment of the balance of the tuition. Mr. Carney refused to pay, and the academy sued. Mr. Carney argued that the $5,610 was a penalty clause, and thus illegal. The academy asserted that the amount represented liquidated damages and that the academy was entitled to the full amount.

How would *you* decide this case? Be certain that you explain and justify your answer.

(See *Lake Ridge Academy v. Carney*, 66 Ohio St. 3d 376, 613 N.E.2d 183, 1993 Ohio LEXIS (1993).)

Notes

1. *Tender* is an offer to do or perform an act that the party offering is bound to perform to the party to whom the offer is made. See http://www.lectlaw.com/def2/t076.htm (accessed June 4, 2016).
2. *Black's Law Dictionary,* 6th ed. (St. Paul: West Publishing Co., 1990), 1429.
3. According to *Merriam-Webster's Dictionary*, a *persnickety* person is fussy about small details, requires great precision. http://www.merriam-webster.com/dictionary/persnickety (accessed November 10, 2012).
4. *Black's Law Dictionary,* 1289.
5. See *BMW of North America v. Gore*, 517 U.S. 559 (1996), in which an award of $2 million in punitive damages due to BMW's "fraudulent failure" to disclose that it had repainted a $40,000 automobile prior to its sale.
6. Pearl Jam Forum, "Carmeggedon in Los Angeles," http://forums.pearljam.com/viewtopic.php?f=14&t=163409 &start=15 (accessed November 10, 2012).
7. The prices used in this example were representative of the prices in effect in southwest Virginia at the time of writing, and are not meant to endorse any brand or manufacturer, nor to imply anything about the quality of any of the cars used in the example.
8. *Black's Law Dictionary,* 1307.
9. *Id.,* 1313.
10. *Id.,* 1139.
11. The Uniform Commercial Code (UCC) defines tangible personal property as "goods." This topic is treated in more detail in Chapter 9.
12. *Black's Law Dictionary,* 784.
13. *Id.,* 1245.

11

Contracts for the Sale of Goods

Learning Objectives

After completing the chapter you should be able to

- Define both *goods* and *sales* as those terms are used in Article 2 of the Uniform Commercial Code (UCC)
- Discuss warranty law under Article 2
- Compare the rules for contract formation under Article 2 and the common law
- Explain what is meant by a *firm offer* and when the firm offer provisions apply
- Identify the major differences between a contract governed by Article 2 of the UCC and one governed by the provisions of the CISG

303

Classic Case

This case deals with conflicting terms in the formation of a sales contract. Specifically, the seller included an arbitration term in its acknowledgement forms, but the buyer did not want any disputes decided by arbitration. Note how the court treated the proposed arbitration clause in the acknowledgement form. In 1960 arbitration was frequently disfavored by the courts. Courts today are much more likely to uphold the arbitration clause in a similar case.

IN THE MATTER OF THE ARBITRATION BETWEEN DOUGHBOY INDUSTRIES INC. AND PANTASOTE COMPANY

17 A.D.2d 216, 233 N.Y.S.2d 488 (N.Y. App. 1st Dept. 1962)

FACTS Doughboy Industries and Pantasote had prior contracts before the contract at issue in this case. In these previous contracts Doughboy used its purchase-order form with its insulating conditions, and Pantasote used its acknowledgement form with its self-actuating conditions. Each ignored the other's printed forms, but proceeded with the contracts.

This case began on May 6, 1960 when Doughboy mailed two purchase orders for plastic film from its office in Wisconsin to Pantasote in New York. Each purchase order provided that 20,000 pounds of film were to be delivered on specified dates. Further quantities were ordered on a "hold basis," that is, subject to "increase, decrease, or cancellation" by the buyer. On May 13, 1960 Pantasote orally accepted both purchase orders without change except to suggest immediate shipment of the first part of the order. Doughboy agreed, and that day Pantasote shipped some 10,000 pounds of film in partial fulfillment of one purchase order. On May 16, 1960, Doughboy received Pantasote's first acknowledgment dated May 13, 1960, and on May 19, 1960 the second acknowledgment dated May 16, 1960. Although the

purchase orders called for written acceptances and return of attached acknowledgments by the seller no one paid any attention to these requirements. Neither party, orally or in writing, objected to the conditions printed on the other's commercial forms. Later, Doughboy sent change orders with respect to so much of the orders as had been, according to Doughboy, on a "hold basis."

The terms and conditions contained on Doughboy's purchase-order forms included the following language:

> Alteration of terms—None of the terms and conditions contained in this Purchase Order may be added to, modified, superseded or otherwise altered except by a written instrument signed by an authorized representative of Buyer and delivered by Buyer to Seller, and each shipment received by Buyer from Seller shall be deemed to be only upon the terms and conditions contained in this Purchase Order except as they may be added to, modified, superseded or otherwise altered, notwithstanding any terms and conditions that may be contained in any acknowledgment, invoice or other form of Seller and notwithstanding Buyer's act of accepting or paying for any shipment or similar act of Buyer.

This language plainly states that Doughboy wants any disputes settled under the terms it includes in its purchase order. But Pantasote was equally clear in its acknowledgement form, stating, among other items, that:

> IMPORTANT
>
> Buyer agrees he has full knowledge of conditions printed on the reverse side hereof; and that the same are part of the agreement between buyer and seller and shall be

binding if either the goods referred to herein are delivered to and accepted by buyer, or if buyer does not within ten days from date hereof deliver to seller written objection to said conditions or any part thereof.

On the reverse side the obligations of the buyer set forth above are carefully repeated. Among the conditions on the reverse side is the general arbitration clause.

ISSUE Should this case be submitted to arbitration, as specified in the acknowledgement form used by Pantasote?

HOLDING No. While it is true that Doughboy did not object to the additional terms within ten days, the arbitration clause constituted a material change in the obligations of the parties. Any proposed material change in obligations is invalid unless expressly agreed to by each party.

REASONING Excerpts from the opinion of Judge Breitel:

... This case involves only the application of the arbitration clause. Arguably, a different principle from that applied here might, under present law, govern other of the terms and conditions in either of the commercial forms. The reason is the special rule that the courts have laid down with respect to arbitration clauses, namely, that the agreement to arbitrate must be direct and the intention made clear, without implication, inveiglement, or subtlety ...

It should be evident ... that a contract for the sale of goods came into existence on May 13, 1960 when the seller made a partial shipment, especially when following upon its oral acceptance of the buyer's purchase order. ... The contract, at such time, was documented only by the buyer's purchase-order form. However, that is not dispositive. It is equally evident from the prior transactions between these parties, and general practices in trade, that more documents were to follow. Such documents may help make the contract, or modify it. ... Whether the subsequent

documents were necessary to complete the making of the contract ... or whether they served only to modify or validate the terms of an existing contract ... is not really too important once the commercial dealings have advanced as far as they had here. By that time, there is no question whether there was a contract, but only what was the contract.

Recognizing ... that the business men in this case acted with complete disdain for the "lawyer's content" of the very commercial forms they were sending and receiving, the question is what obligation ought the law to attach to the arbitration clause. And in determining that question the traditional theory is applicable, namely, that of constructive knowledge and acceptance of contractual terms, based on prior transactions and the duty to read contractual instruments to which one is a party ...

But, and this is critical, it is not only the seller's form which should be given effect, but also the buyer's form, for it too was used in the prior transactions, and as to it too, there was a duty to read. Of course, if the two commercial forms are given effect, they cancel one another ...

As pointed out earlier, an agreement to arbitrate must be clear and direct, and must not depend upon implication, inveiglement or subtlety. ... It follows then that the existence of an agreement to arbitrate should not depend solely upon the conflicting fine print of commercial forms which cross one another but never meet ...

Consequently, as a matter of law there was no agreement to arbitrate in this case, if one applies existing principles ...

On this exposition, the arbitration clause, whether viewed as a material alteration under subsection (2), or as a term nullified by a conflicting provision in the buyer's form, would fail to survive as a contract term. In the light of the New York cases, at least, there can be little question that an agreement to arbitrate is a material term, one not to be injected by implication, subtlety or inveiglement. And the conclusion is also the same if the limitation contained in the offer (the buyer's purchase order) is given effect, as required by paragraph (a) of subsection 2 of the new section.

Accordingly, the order denying petitioner-appellant buyer's motion to stay arbitration should be reversed, on the law, with costs to petitioner-appellant and the motion should be granted. . . .

INTRODUCTION

The common law of contracts, which was discussed in Chapters 9 and 10, developed in an era and in a society in which recourse to the courts was a relatively rare occurrence. While the basic tenets of the common law of contracts are still followed today, some elements of the common law have become outdated. As society has changed over time, there have been changes in the treatment of contract law. For example, the Statute of Frauds was enacted, adding the requirement for written evidence of the formation of certain types of contracts in order for those contracts to be enforceable in court. This requirement was implemented in an effort to prevent frauds and perjuries in specified types of contracts: (1) contracts for the sale of an interest in land; (2) contracts that could not be completed within one year of the contract's formation; (3) contracts in contemplation of marriage; (4) contracts to answer for the debts of another; and (5) contracts to answer for the debts of a decedent.

In our contemporary society the law of contracts has changed in its treatment of the sale of *goods*. This change was made, to a significant extent, due to the volume of such contracts that are regularly made. When students are asked, "How many contracts have you entered into this past year?" Most of them will reply with a very small number. Some, in fact, will state that they have not entered into any contracts in the past year. If a student is asked how he or she got his or her laptop computer, the standard response is that he or she purchased it. Similar answers follow when asked how they acquired their shoes, their pens or pencils, their notebooks, etc. Many students seem astounded when informed that each of these purchases was a contract! It then becomes obvious to the students that they have likely entered dozens, perhaps hundreds, of contracts in the past year. Each of these contracts was likely to be a contract for the sale of goods. This chapter addresses the differences between common law contracts and contracts for the sale of goods.

THE SALE OF GOODS

A contract for the sale of goods is the most common type of contract entered into by most people. Under Article 2 of the Uniform Commercial Code (UCC), goods "means all things (including specially manufactured goods) which are moveable at the time of identification to the contract for sale other than the money in which the price is to be paid, investment securities (UCC Article 8) and things in action."[1] This definition of goods also includes "the unborn young of animals and growing crops and other identified things attached to realty" that are to be severed from the realty.[2] Any time a person purchases an item of clothing, a gallon of gas, or a burger and fries in a fast-food restaurant he or she has purchased *goods*. If the item purchased is tangible personal property, meaning that it is moveable and is not land or anything permanently attached to land, the item is a good. If that item is sold in the United States under the provision of U.S. law, the sale is treated as a sale of goods and the contract is governed by the provisions of Article 2 of the Uniform Commercial Code (UCC). If that item is sold in an international contract and both parties to the contract are merchants, it is very likely that the contract will be governed by the terms of the United Nations Convention on the International Sale of Goods (CISG) unless the parties have agreed to "opt out" of the CISG's coverage in their contract. The legal implications for such transactions, and some of the significant differences between these contracts and the provisions under traditional common law, are discussed in the sections below.

ARTICLE 2 OF THE UNIFORM COMMERCIAL CODE

Article 2 of the UCC applies to contracts for the sale of goods. As stated above, goods are defined as tangible personal property. A *sale* is defined as the passing of title from a seller to a buyer for a price.[3] Many, if not most, of the contracts into which an individual enters will involve the sale of goods. The UCC, which was first published in 1952, is intended to reflect contemporary commercial customs and practices. In other words, the UCC strives to make current commercial law consistent with the conduct that is regularly followed in modern business practice.

Merchants or Nonmerchants

In common law the court normally views the parties as possessing equal bargaining power, with each party assumed to be able to protect his or her best interests. Common law principles do not distinguish between the parties as to their relative experiences, wealth, or position unless such an issue is raised by one of the parties. For example, if one party is able to establish that the other party used duress in the formation of the contract, the victim of that duress may be allowed to avoid the contract. (Duress was addressed as one of the negative elements in a contract in Chapter 9.) The UCC distinguishes between merchants and nonmerchants in a contract for the sale of goods, and the merchant is held to a higher standard of conduct. A *merchant* is a person who regularly deals in goods of the kind involved in the contract, *or* by his occupation holds himself out as a person possessing knowledge or skill particular to transactions involving such goods, *or* employs a person possessing such knowledge or skill as an agent, broker, or intermediary.[4] While every party to a sales contract is required by law to act in good faith and to cooperate with the other party, a merchant is also required to act in a *commercially reasonable* manner. This means that a merchant must not only act in good faith, but that he or she must also act in a manner that conforms to the normal fair dealings and practices of the trade while also acting in a manner that is consistent with normal business practices. A nonmerchant must act in good faith and must cooperate with the other party, but he or she is not required or expected to act in a commercially reasonable manner.

Warranties

Warranties can be included in a contract entered into under the provisions of common law. Any warranty so included is likely to be expressly agreed to by the parties, and no such warranties will exist unless they are agreed to in the contract itself. Article 2 of the UCC also allows the parties to expressly create warranties affecting their agreement. But Article 2 also provides for the inclusion of implied warranties; these warranties are implicitly included in the contract unless such warranties are expressly excluded in the contract. The implied warranties that may be present in a contract for the sale of goods are:

1. A warranty of title
2. A warranty against infringement
3. A warranty of merchantability
4. A warranty of fitness for a particular purpose

Exhibit 11.1 explains the implied warranties found in Article 2 of the UCC.

Exhibit 11.1

Implied Warranties in a Sales Contract

Warranty	Scope/Coverage	Exclusions/Limitations
Warranty of Title	The seller warrants that the title conveyed to the buyer shall be good, that the transfer of the goods is rightful, and that there are no hidden liens, claims, or encumbrances on the goods.	Warranty can be excluded or modified only by the use of specific language or by circumstances that give the buyer reason to know that the seller is not including the warranty of title.

Exhibit 11.1 Continued

Warranty	Scope/Coverage	Exclusions/Limitations
Warranty Against Infringements	A merchant seller warrants that the goods being sold will be delivered free of any rightful claims of any third person by way of infringement. (Intellectual property rights such as patents and copyrights are the primary areas for which infringements may occur.) A buyer who provides specifications to the seller for the construction or manufacture of goods warrants that the specifications do not infringe the rights of any third person.	Only a merchant seller gives this warranty to his or her buyers; only a buyer who provides specifications for the construction or manufacture of goods gives this warranty to the seller, and then only if the goods produced conform to the specifications provided by the buyer.
Warranty of Merchantability	A merchant seller warrants that the goods sold in the contract are merchantable. In order to be merchantable, the goods must be suitable for their ordinary use, be able to pass without objection in the trade, be adequately and properly labeled and packaged, and conform to any affirmations or promises contained on the label.	A seller can exclude the warranty of merchantability by the use of a written disclaimer that is conspicuous and contains the word *merchantability*. The warranty can also be excluded with language such as *as is* or *with all faults*.
Warranty of Fitness for a Particular Purpose	A seller, who has reason to know at the time of the contract that the buyer has in mind a particular purpose or use for the goods and knows that the buyer is relying on the seller's skill, judgment, or expertise in selecting goods suitable for that particular purpose, warrants that the goods are fit and appropriate for such use.	The seller must make clear to the buyer that there is no such warranty at the time of sale. A buyer will waive any claims under this warranty if the buyer restricts or limits the seller's selection or recommendation of the goods by imposing a restriction as to price, brand name, or similar limitations.

An Ounce of Prevention

You should be careful in labeling or advertising your product. Any claims made on the label or in advertisements might be treated as an express warranty, and you can be held liable for breach of that warranty if the product does not measure up. If the labeling or the advertisement creates a belief in the mind of the reasonable buyer concerning the character, quality, or nature of the goods, the courts may determine that the belief constitutes a warranty. If the goods do not comply with the belief created in the buyer's mind, you may be found to be in breach of the warranty.

Contract Formation

Common law takes a somewhat rigid view of contract formation. Under the common law rules, the parties must reach an agreement that shows a mirror image of terms: The offer and the acceptance must match exactly in every particular. Any deviation or variation is treated as either a counteroffer or as a negotiation toward a final agreement. The UCC, on the other hand, allows the parties to make a contract in any manner sufficient to show that a contract was made.[5] The acceptance of an offer can be made in any manner, and the parties are deemed to have an agreement if they *act* as if they have an agreement. The UCC even allows for the omission of some terms without affecting the existence of a contract.[6]

An Ounce of Prevention

Historically, writing was defined as "reduction to tangible form." In other words, it had to be capable of being held. . . . You should be aware that this is no longer true. Common electronic communications such as text messages, faxes, tweets, or e-mails are now writings under either the Uniform Electronic Transactions Act (UETA) or the E-SIGN Act. Consequently these communications may satisfy the Statute of Frauds. You should be careful when using any of these electronic communication methods since the communication may enable the other party to show that a contract was made and is evidenced by a writing.

The Statute of Frauds

The UCC also includes a Statute of Frauds provision. Any contract for the sale of goods that has a total price of $500 or more is unenforceable unless there is some written evidence that the parties have a contract. This written evidence must also be signed by the party against whom enforcement is sought.[7] There are several exceptions to this rule. There is no need for any writing if the goods are to be specially manufactured for the buyer and would not be suitable for use by anyone else. There is also no need for a writing if the party against whom enforcement is sought admits during any judicial proceeding that a contract was made. Nor is there a need for a writing to the extent that the contract has been performed. This means that if one of the parties has accepted some portion of the goods called for in the agreement but has not paid for them, the seller could collect for the goods already accepted, although he or she could not hold the buyer liable for the balance of the contract. Similarly, if the buyer has paid a portion of the total price, the seller will be liable for the delivery of the percentage of the total contractual obligation that equals the payment received.

There is another exception if both parties to the contract are merchants. If one merchant sends a written confirmation of his or her contract to the other merchant, and the second merchant knows or should know that the writing contains a confirmation, he or she must object in writing to the alleged confirmation within ten days of receiving it. A failure to object within ten days establishes the existence of a contract: It is binding on the second merchant even though he or she has not signed anything to evidence the contract. Assume that Roberto, a merchant seller of watches, and Fergie, a jewelry store owner, enter an oral agreement for the sale of an assortment of watches, with a total price of $12,000. Two days later, Roberto sends a written confirmation of the agreement to Fergie via e-mail. The e-mail accurately summarizes the terms the parties discussed. Fergie receives the e-mail on the 14th of the month but does not respond. If Fergie does not send a written objection to Roberto by the 24th, she will have "validated" the contract terms as written in Roberto's e-mail, and she can be held to the contract as if she had signed and returned the confirmation. (Recall that electronic communications such as e-mails and faxes are now deemed to be writings under the UETA and E-SIGN.)

Firm Offers

The common law of contracts allows an offeror to revoke an offer at any time prior to its acceptance by the offeree. This means that the offeror can withdraw the offer, ending the possibility of a contract being formed, so long as he or she does so before the offeree accepts. Suppose that on Thursday, Stan makes an offer to sell his concert tickets to Betty for $50 and tells her she has until next Monday to decide and let him know. On Saturday Ivan offers to give Stan $75 for the tickets. Stan accepts Ivan's offer and calls Betty to revoke the offer made to her. Even though Stan had told Betty that she had until next Monday to accept, Stan has the legal right to revoke the offer. Since Betty had not yet accepted the offer when it was revoked, she can no longer accept and create a contract. The same rule would apply even if Stan's original offer had been in writing.

The UCC takes a similar position in some circumstances, but there is an exception when the offeror is a merchant. If a merchant makes an offer in writing which includes a promise to hold the offer open for a stated time, the UCC treats this as a firm offer, and a firm offer cannot be revoked until the time stated has expired. The offeror cannot revoke his or her offer and must allow the offeree the time specified in writing to decide whether to accept or reject the offer. Furthermore, if no time is stated, the firm offer is irrevocable for a reasonable time, but the period may not exceed three months.

Performance of the Contract

The performance of a sales contract is relatively simple and straightforward—in theory. However, it may become much more complicated in practice. The seller is required to tender delivery of conforming goods as per the contract and to notify the buyer. The buyer is then required to accept and pay for the goods. As a result, the buyer has the goods that he or she agreed to purchase, and the seller has the money that he or she agreed to accept. Unfortunately, the reality of the situation can be more complicated. In practice, there are four steps involved in the performance. Two steps are legal obligations and two steps are intervening rights. Exhibit 11.2 diagrams the process.

Risk of Loss

Under Article 2, title to the goods and risk of loss are treated as separate and distinct topics. Title to the goods refers to ownership of the goods. Risk of loss refers to a financial or legal obligation in the event that, after the contract is entered but before performance is complete, the goods are lost, damaged, or destroyed prior to their delivery by the seller and acceptance by the buyer. If risk of loss lies with the seller and goods are lost, damaged, or destroyed before they are delivered to the buyer, the seller will have to send a second shipment or face liability for breach of contract. The seller in this situation failed to deliver the goods as agreed, and the risk of loss was still on the seller. If the buyer has risk of loss, he or she must pay for any goods that are lost, damaged, or destroyed after the risk shifted to the buyer.

Risk of loss lies with the seller until he or she completes his or her obligations under the contract. Once he or she completes these obligations, the risk shifts to the buyer. If the seller is a merchant and he or she is to deliver the goods to the buyer directly, risk of loss lies with the seller until the buyer takes possession of the goods. If the seller is a nonmerchant and he or she is to deliver the goods to the buyer directly, risk of loss passes to the buyer as soon as the seller tenders delivery and notifies the buyer that the goods are available. For example, if Boris, a merchant, sells a television to Natasha but agrees to retain possession until Natasha can return with her van to take possession, Boris retains risk of loss until Natasha returns. If a worker in Boris's warehouse knocks the television over and it breaks, Boris will have the risk of loss and will have to replace the broken television or pay damages due to his breach of contract.

However, if Natasha, a nonmerchant, had sold her old television to Sven, a friend from work, and told Sven that he could pick up the television any time after noon on

Exhibit 11.2

Performance of a Contract for the Sale of Goods

Step	Status	Application
Seller *tenders delivery* of conforming goods	Legal obligation	The seller must tender delivery—put and hold conforming goods at the buyer's disposition and notify the buyer. This may entail the use of standard shipping terms and/or the use of a carrier or warehouseman.
Buyer *inspects* goods	Legal right—may be waived by the buyer	The buyer can inspect the goods at any reasonable time and any reasonable place once the goods are identified to the contract. The buyer bears the cost of inspection unless a defect is discovered. Any defects that could be discovered in a reasonable inspection may not be asserted after the buyer has accepted the goods.
Seller *cures any defects* found in the inspection	Legal right—seller may choose not to do so	The seller must cure any defect discovered by the buyer in the course of his or her inspection within the original contractual time limits *unless* the seller reasonably and honestly believed that the goods as shipped were acceptable. Failure to do so is a breach of the contract.
Buyer *accepts and pays* for the goods	Legal obligation	If the buyer finds no defects in the goods upon inspection or chooses not to inspect, he or she must accept and pay for the goods. If the buyer finds any nonconformity, notifies the seller, and the seller seasonably cures the defect, the buyer must accept and pay for the goods. The buyer can pay in any reasonable manner unless the contract specifies a particular method of payment.

Tuesday and Sven agreed, Natasha has tendered delivery to Sven and the risk of loss has passed to him as of noon on Tuesday. If the television were somehow to be broken or damaged after that time—and without any negligence by Natasha—Sven would be liable for the contract price even though the television was broken or damaged.

Standard Delivery Terms

It is common for goods to be delivered by common carrier, especially in contracts between remote merchants. If the contract is a shipping contract, the seller completes his or her delivery when he or she makes appropriate arrangements for the transportation of the goods and turns possession of the goods over to the carrier. At that point, the seller has completed his or her performance and the risk of loss passes to the buyer. If the contract is a destination contract, the seller has agreed to retain risk of loss until the goods are tendered at their destination. The court will determine whether a contract between the seller and the carrier to transport the goods to the buyer creates a shipment contract or a destination contract, although a shipment contract is assumed.

An Ounce of Prevention

If you are involved in a contract in which the goods are to be delivered by a common carrier, be certain that you know whether you bear the risk of loss. If you do bear the risk of loss, consider carefully the likelihood that the goods will be damaged during transit and the cost of acquiring insurance to cover any possible losses. You will need to decide whether the amount at risk if there is a loss during shipment is sufficient to make purchasing insurance coverage a prudent use of your funds.

Because the use of a common carrier is such a common occurrence, the UCC has developed and defined certain standard shipping terms. One advantage to standard shipping terms is that they provide for the allocation of risk of loss. There are six standard shipping terms under the UCC, as set out in Exhibit 11.3.

Special Rules under Article 2

Standard Form Contracts   It is a common practice for many merchants to use standard form contracts when dealing with customers. If a merchant seller is dealing with a nonmerchant buyer, the use of a standard form contract does not provide many problems. The nonmerchant buyer is seldom in a position to negotiate any changes to

Exhibit 11.3

Standard Shipping Terms Under the UCC

Standard Shipping Term	Meaning	Application
FOB	*Free on Board*	The seller enters a contract with the carrier, and the goods are loaded on board the carrier. The seller has paid all fees and borne the risk of loss until the goods are at the FOB point. This can be either a shipment or a destination contract.
FAS	*Free Along Side*	FAS is normally followed by the name of a ship and a port. The seller is responsible for getting the goods alongside the named ship at the named port and retains risk of loss until the goods are so delivered. Historically, FAS was used in a shipment contract for the carriage of goods on navigable waterways.
CIF	*Cost, Insurance, Freight*	The seller quotes the buyer a price that includes the cost of the goods, the cost of insuring the goods, and the freight to the buyer's location. This is a shipment contract, and the buyer has risk of loss. The buyer also has the benefit of insurance on the goods.
C & F	*Cost and Freight*	The seller quotes a price that includes the cost of the goods and the cost of carriage. The buyer will be responsible for purchasing his or her own insurance, if so desired. This is a shipment contract.
Ex-Ship	*Off the Ship*	The contract will include the name of a ship and a port. The seller is responsible for getting the goods onto the dock at the named destination port and has risk of loss until the goods reach the named port's dock. This designation is used for water carriage.
No Arrival, No Sale	*Excuses further performance if the goods are shipped but never arrive*	In this contract, the parties have agreed that if the goods are properly shipped, but do not arrive, the contract is canceled. If the goods have deteriorated to such an extent that they no longer conform to the contract, the buyer may inspect and make an adjusted payment based on the condition of the goods. Either party may insure the goods during transit.

the contract, and in fact many such buyers seem blissfully unaware that they could, at least in theory, negotiate different terms. But when the contract is between merchants, a different scenario is involved. This was an issue in both the Classic Case and the Contemporary Case in this chapter. The merchant buyer will often send an order to the seller on a standard purchase order form prepared by and for the buyer. Obviously, such a form will include those terms and conditions most favorable to the buyer. If the seller is willing to accept this purchase order and enter into a contract, he or she will often send an acknowledgment form back to the prospective buyer confirming receipt of the purchase order and agreeing to enter into a contract. This acknowledgment form is often on a standard form prepared by and for the seller. Equally obviously, this form will include those terms and conditions most favorable to the seller. When this occurs, the forms do not agree with one another, which means that the terms are likely to conflict.

Under common law principles, there would not be a contract due to the failure to reach a mirror image agreement. But the UCC provides that the parties have a contract if they act as if they have a contract, without regard to the need for a mirror image agreement. It is apparent that the buyer wants to buy the goods and that the seller is willing to sell the goods, so there is a solid basis for finding a contract. The issue becomes one of determining what is included in the contract. The UCC provides for such a situation, allowing the parties to form a contract without the need for protracted negotiations to resolve the differences in the conflicting forms they have exchanged.

The offeree, the seller in our example, must accept in a reasonable time. However, the UCC allows the offeree to accept in any reasonable manner, and the acceptance is deemed to be valid, even if the acceptance includes additional terms or includes terms that disagree with the terms in the original offer. The only exceptions to this rule arise when:

- The offer specifically limits acceptance to the terms of the offer
- The additional terms would materially alter the obligations under the contract
- The offeror objects to the proposed additional terms within a reasonable time

Unless one of these exceptions exists, the court will find that the parties have a valid and enforceable contract despite the lack of an identical agreement.

On occasion the parties have to go to court due to an alleged breach of the contract, and the court then has to interpret the contract. In doing so, the court is most likely to rule that:

- All terms common to both the offer and the acceptance are included in the final contract
- Any term in one of the forms that contradicts any term in the other form cancels the terms out so that neither of the terms are part of the contract
- Any term included in the offer that is neither matched in nor contradicted in the acceptance becomes part of the contract

■ Any additional term included in the acceptance that is not objected to in a reasonable time also becomes part of the contract unless the additional term would materially alter the obligations of one of the parties, usually the offeror

For example, assume that Axis International sends a purchase order to Sure-Supply, offering to purchase $25,000 in equipment. In the offer, Axis specifies that the goods are to be delivered FOB Sure-Supply's warehouse; that any disagreements between the parties are to be settled by arbitration; that payment terms of 2-10, net 30 (the buyer can take a 2% discount if paying within ten days, the net amount is due in thirty days), are to be used. Sure-Supply responds to the purchase order with an acknowledgment form that provides for shipment FOB Sure-Supply's warehouse and that no discount for early payment will be provided. Sure-Supply also adds a clause that a 10 percent surcharge will attach to any late payment. Axis receives the acknowledgment form and does not object or notify Sure-Supply of any concerns or disagreements.

Given these facts, the contract provides for the sale of $25,000 of equipment, with shipment to be made via common carrier (implied by the standard shipping term) and shipped FOB Sure-Supply's warehouse. (This would normally mean a shipment contract, with risk of loss on Axis.) Since Sure-Supply did not object or cancel the arbitration clause, arbitration will be used to resolve any disputes. Since Sure-Supply objected to the 2 percent discount for payments within ten days of delivery, there will be no discount available. And since Axis did not object to the surcharge for late payments, Axis will be liable for a 10 percent surcharge if it makes payment more than thirty days after delivery. (Note that if the court decides that the 10 percent figure is unreasonable and constitutes a penalty, the surcharge will be disallowed.)

Open Terms The UCC allows the parties to omit some terms in their contracts without affecting the validity of the contract. By contrast, in common law the parties must have reasonably definite terms, and the omission of such terms would negate the existence of a contract. Under the provisions of Article 2, the parties can omit price, time of delivery, place of delivery, time and/or manner of payment, and even the quantity of goods involved, and still have a valid contract. Of course, the more terms omitted, the less likely the court is to find that a contract exists. Exhibit 11.4 outlines the treatment of open terms under the UCC.

The UCC also allows the parties to enter into a *requirement contract* or an *output contract*, although the quantity of goods involved in such a contract would not be considered "reasonably definite" under common law rules. A requirement contract specifies that the seller will deliver a sufficient quantity of goods to meet the buyer's requirements for those goods for the life of the contract. In an output contract, the buyer agrees to purchase the seller's output (production) or a specified percentage of that output for the life of the contract.

In each of these contracts the parties are required to operate in good faith and in a commercially reasonable manner. For example, a buyer would not be allowed to enter a three-year requirement contract with the seller and then to notify the seller shortly thereafter that the buyer had opened two new facilities and its requirements are now three times what was expected in the original contract. Nor could a seller enter into an

Exhibit 11.4

The Treatment of Open Terms in a Sales Contract

Open Term	Treatment	Code Section
Price	• The buyer or the seller sets the price in good faith if the contract so provides, or	§ 2-305(2)
	• The price is set by a third person if the contract so provides, or	§ 2-305(1)
	• The price is a reasonable price at the time and place of delivery.	
Delivery	• If no place for delivery is mentioned, delivery is at the seller's place of business, or the seller's home if the seller has no place of business.	§ 2-308(a)
	• If the goods to the contract are identified, and if both parties know the goods are at a place other than the seller's location, delivery is presumed to occur at the location of the goods.	§ 2-308(b)
	• If the time of delivery is not mentioned, delivery is to occur within a reasonable time considering the nature of the goods (calendar time) and the nature of the buyer's business (clock time).	§ 2-309
Payment	• Payment is expected at the time and place of delivery unless some other payment terms are specified.	§ 2-310
	• Payment may be made in any reasonable manner or in any manner current in the ordinary course of business.	§ 2-511(1)
	• If the seller insists on payment in cash, but did not specify cash payment in the contract, the buyer must be given a reasonable amount of time to procure cash for the payment.	§ 2-511(2)

output contract with the buyer for two years and then, several weeks later, notify the buyer that the seller had opened a new factory and had quintupled its production capacity.

Sale on Approval   In a sale on approval, the seller delivers goods to the buyer for a free trial period. The buyer will be purchasing the goods for personal use and consumption rather than for resale, and the seller is giving the buyer the opportunity to try the goods to see if they are satisfactory for the buyer's needs before the buyer commits to the contract. The seller retains title and risk of loss during the approval period, and if the buyer does not indicate that the goods meet his or her approval or act in a manner that would be seen as evidence of acceptance, the buyer can return the goods by the end of the approval period with no obligation to the seller.

Sale or Return   In a sale or return contract, the buyer purchases goods from the seller for the purpose of reselling the goods to the buyer's customers. The parties agree that the buyer can return any unsold goods after a specified period, receiving a credit to his or her account or a refund for the returned goods. Normally, the terms only provide for a credit to the account of the buyer. This arrangement encourages the buyer to carry more of the goods in inventory than the buyer might otherwise carry, since it can return the unsold goods for full credit or for a refund. The buyer has title and risk of loss during the specified period, and if he or she does not return any of the goods, he or she is liable for them, even if the goods were not returned due to theft or breakage.

Remedies for Breach of Contract

When a contract governed by common law is breached, the innocent party is entitled to recover damages. The same is true when a sales contract governed by Article 2 is breached, but there is a difference. At common law, the innocent party is entitled to compensatory damages and may also be allowed to recover for consequential damages. In some circumstances the nonbreaching party may be entitled to an equitable remedy because damages are not sufficient.

Under Article 2, the remedies available to the nonbreaching party are spelled out in the UCC itself. The available remedies are determined, to a significant degree, by when the breach occurred: Remedies are either preacceptance or postacceptance, depending on the timing of the breach. Preacceptance breaches are more common, and there are more preacceptance remedies available. Postacceptance breaches are rarer, and there are fewer available remedies when the breach is postacceptance.

Seller's Remedies   If the buyer breaches the contract prior to accepting the goods, the seller is entitled to any or all of six potential preacceptance remedies. The breach may be due to a failure to accept conforming goods, to a wrongful rejection of conforming goods, or an anticipatory repudiation of the contract. When the buyer breaches after accepting delivery of the goods, it is normally due to the buyer's refusal or inability to pay for the goods that have been accepted. In this situation, the seller is entitled to either or both of two available remedies. The remedies available to the seller are set out in Exhibit 11.5.

Buyer's Remedies   If the seller breaches the contract prior to the buyer's acceptance of the goods, the buyer is entitled to any or all of six potential preacceptance remedies. The breach may be due to a failure to make delivery, a tender of delivery of nonconforming goods, a failure or refusal to cure a defective delivery after notification of the nonconformity, or an anticipatory repudiation of the contract. If the seller's breach is not discovered until after the buyer has accepted delivery of the goods, the buyer is entitled to choose from a list of three available remedies. This breach will normally be

Exhibit 11.5

Seller's Remedies under Article 2	
Preacceptance Remedies	**Description**
Withhold delivery of the goods	The seller withholds delivery of goods still in his or her possession unless or until the buyer agrees to, or does, perform as agreed.
Stoppage in transit	The seller notifies the common carrier transporting the goods to stop the shipment. The seller must give adequate notice to the carrier to allow for the stoppage of the shipment and must indemnify the carrier for any losses or liability it suffers as a result of the stoppage.
Resell the goods	The seller can resell the goods. The resale may be of finished goods, any work in process, and any raw materials procured to fulfill the contract. The resale must be made in good faith and in a commercially reasonable manner, taking into consideration the nature of the goods and the existing market for such goods.
Sue the buyer for damages	The seller can sue the buyer for lost profits and/or any other damages that can be established due to the breach. This would include compensatory and consequential damages, as they are used under the common law.
Sue the buyer for the contract price	The seller can sue the buyer for the contract price. Should the buyer pay the contract price, the seller is then obligated to complete his or her portion of the contract by delivering conforming goods.
Cancel	The seller can notify the buyer that he or she is cancelling any remaining obligations under the contract. This cancellation terminates the seller's obligations under the contract but does not release the buyer from his or her obligations and responsibilities due to the breach.
Postacceptance Remedies	**Description**
Sue the buyer for the unpaid balance	The seller can file suit for the amount still owed under the contract, plus any expenses incurred in trying to collect.
Reclaim or recover the goods	The seller can reclaim the goods that were delivered and accepted, but for which payment has not been received. This is a very restricted right because the seller must initiate proceedings to recover or reclaim the goods within ten days of delivery or the right to reclaim or recover will lapse. (There is a waiver of the ten-day restriction if the buyer provided a written statement of his or her solvency within the three months preceding the delivery.)

due to the existence of a hidden defect not discovered until after the goods have been accepted or due to the seller's failure to provide a promised cure if the buyer would accept the goods. The remedies available to the buyer are set out in Exhibit 11.6.

Exhibit 11.6

Buyer's Remedies under Article 2

Preacceptance Remedies	Description
Sue the seller for damages	The buyer can sue the seller for lost profits and/or any other damages that can be established due to the breach. This would include compensatory and consequential damages, as they are used under the common law.
Cover	The buyer can purchase the goods from another seller, suing the original seller for any losses due to the efforts and expenses of covering. (Remember that the goods acquired as cover must be commercially reasonable substitutes for the goods originally called for in the contract.)
Resell the goods	The buyer can *resell* the goods, if the goods are nonconforming and (1) the seller asks the buyer to resell them on the seller's behalf; or (2) the goods are likely to spoil or appreciably decline in value unless they are promptly resold. The buyer is entitled to a reasonable fee or commission for his or her efforts to effect a resale and is entitled to hold the balance of any proceeds toward his or her claim for damages due to the breach. The resale must be made in good faith and in a commercially reasonable manner, taking into consideration the nature of the goods and the existing market for such goods.
Specific performance or replevin	If the goods covered by the contract are unique, the buyer can seek the equitable remedy of specific performance, having the court order the seller to deliver the goods as provided in the contract. If the goods are not unique, but are currently unavailable, or if cover was attempted and did not occur, the buyer can seek replevin. (Replevin has the same result as specific performance.)
Claim any goods identified to the contract	The buyer can claim any goods that are identified to the contract and that are still in the seller's possession. This is also a very restricted right because (1) the seller must be insolvent; (2) the buyer must have paid for the goods in advance; and (3) the buyer must initiate proceedings to claim the goods within ten days of the payment date.
Cancel	The buyer can notify the seller that he or she is canceling any remaining obligations under the contract. This cancellation terminates the buyer's obligations under the contract but does not release the seller from his or her obligations and responsibilities due to the breach.

Exhibit 11.6 Continued

Postacceptance Remedies	Description
Sue the seller for damages	The buyer can file suit for any compensatory and/or consequential damages incurred as a result of the breach.
Revoke acceptance	If the buyer discovers a hidden defect that substantially impairs the value of the contract or the seller fails to provide a cure after promising to do so, the buyer can revoke his or her acceptance, returning to his or her preacceptance position. The buyer can then seek any appropriate preacceptance remedies.
Recoupment	The buyer can recoup his or her losses by notifying the seller of the intent to use recoupment and then deduct any damages incurred from the balance due on the contract.

THE UNITED NATIONS CONVENTION ON CONTRACTS FOR THE INTERNATIONAL SALE OF GOODS (CISG)

The United Nations Convention on Contracts for the International Sale of Goods (CISG) was developed through the United Nations Commission on International Trade Law (UNCITRAL) to provide a widely accepted basis for governing and regulating the international sale of goods. Its treatment of sales contracts is similar in many respects to the provisions in the United States under Article 2 of the UCC. The CISG applies to any international contracts for the sale of goods under either of two sets of circumstances:

1. The contract is made between firms in different nations, and each of the nations has ratified the convention, or
2. The contract designates that it will be governed by the laws of a particular nation (a choice of law clause), and the designated nation has ratified the CISG.

Even if the contract should seemingly be governed by the CISG under either of these conditions, the parties can specifically opt out of the application of the CISG by including opt out language in their contract. The parties can also use a choice of laws clause to specifically opt in to the CISG's provisions if the contract would otherwise not be governed by its terms. In addition, the International Chamber of Commerce (ICC) views the CISG as part of the *lex mercatoria*, or law merchant, of international trade. As a result, if the ICC is arbitrating a dispute between firms in different nations and the dispute involves the sale of goods, the ICC will follow the provisions of the CISG unless the parties have opted out of its coverage in their contract.

Scope of the CISG

The CISG applies to contracts for the sale of goods between merchants in two different countries. It is not meant to apply to sales to consumers. International trade is seldom thought to apply to a business-to-consumer (B2C) transaction, and international trade law is primarily concerned with addressing business-to-business (B2B) transactions. The CISG does not require the showing of consideration in forming a contract. Evidence of an offer and an acceptance is sufficient to show a contract if such evidence would establish a contract under the national laws of the plaintiff. For example, if a United States merchant is suing a merchant from Mexico in a U.S. court, offer and acceptance alone would not show a contract. The national law of the plaintiff—the U.S. merchant—requires a showing of consideration as well as an offer and an acceptance to show that a contract was made. If the roles were reversed, with the Mexican merchant as the plaintiff in a Mexican court, there would be no need to show consideration. The offer and acceptance would establish a contract.[8]

Offers are treated in a manner similar to their treatment under the UCC, but acceptances are treated differently. Under the UCC (and under common law principles), an acceptance is not valid until *communicated* to the offeror. Remember, though, that the "communication" to the offeror can be effective upon dispatch, as in the mailbox rule. An offer can be also be revoked at any time prior to acceptance, unless an option was given or a firm offer was made by a merchant. Under the CISG, the acceptance is not valid until it is literally *received* by the offeror. However, the offer cannot be revoked after an acceptance has been *sent*, even though the acceptance is not valid until it is received. This means that a contract governed by the CISG may have a hiatus period, a period of inactivity, after the acceptance is sent but prior to its receipt, in which neither party can do anything except wait to see if the acceptance arrives in a timely manner. The CISG also contains a provision that is similar to the firm offer provision of Article 2. Under the CISG an offer is irrevocable under either of two situations:

1. Either the offer states that an acceptance must be made within a stated time, or
2. It is reasonable for the offeree to rely on the offer remaining open, and the offeree does, in fact, rely on the offer remaining open, to his or her detriment.

There are no Statute of Frauds provisions under the CISG. Any contract can be made orally, regardless of the size of the contract or the time required for performance of the obligations, unless the parties themselves have included a requirement in the contract that the agreement must be in writing before it is valid and enforceable.

Risk of Loss under the CISG

The CISG treats risk of loss in a manner similar to the treatment provided for in Article 2 of the UCC. The allocation of risk of loss is determined by the seller's delivery obligation under the contract. Generally, when the seller completes his or her delivery obligation, the risk of loss passes to the buyer. If a common carrier is to be used, the type of carriage contract will determine when risk of loss passes. There is an interesting provision in the CISG that is not specifically addressed under the UCC. If the parties enter into a sales contract while the goods are in transit, risk of loss passes to the buyer upon the formation of the contract. Assume that a seller in Germany shipped goods to the United States prior to finding a buyer, but planning to sell the goods either during shipment or after their arrival in the United States. While the goods are en route, the German seller enters into a contract with a U.S. buyer. As soon as the parties agree to the terms of the contract, the U.S. buyer assumes the risk of loss, and the German seller has completed his obligations under the contract (assuming that the goods conform).

The CISG also provides for the use of standard shipping terms, but there is a significant difference in the terms and their meanings from the standard shipping terms found in the UCC. The CISG uses the ICC shipping terms, also called Incoterms (International Commercial Terms). Incoterms are broken down into four categories:

1. E Terms
2. F Terms
3. C Terms
4. D Terms

There is only one E term, *EXW*, which means Ex-Works. The seller completes his or her duties when the goods are made available to the buyer at the seller's premises, and risk of loss passes to the buyer at that point in time.

The F terms include *FCA, FAS*, and *FOB*. FCA means Free Carrier, and requires the seller to turn the goods over to a carrier cleared for export, at a named location. This is similar to the UCC's *FOB* term. *FAS* means Free Along Side, and is virtually identical to the FAS term under the UCC. The Incoterm *FOB* means Free on Board, but here it is only used for seagoing or inland waterway transport. The seller is required to get the goods off of the dock and over the ship's rail to complete his or her obligations and pass risk of loss to the buyer.

There are four C terms, each of which implies that the seller must bear certain costs. The first C term is *CFR*, Cost and Freight (similar to C&F under the UCC). As an Incoterm, CFR requires the seller to clear the goods for export, pay all costs, and bear all risks until the goods pass over the ship's rail at the port of shipment. Note that CFR is again used for waterways and seagoing transport. A similar term is *CIF*, Cost Insurance Freight, which imposes the same obligations on the seller as does CFR, plus the seller must procure insurance on the goods. The standard requirement is to insure the goods for the contract price plus 10 percent, unless the contract specifies a different coverage. The third C term is *CPT*, Carriage Paid To (named location). The seller makes arrangements to have the goods transported to a named location, turns the goods over to the carrier, and pays the freight charge. The final C term is *CIP*, which means Cost and Insurance Paid to a particular location. This is the same as CPT, plus the obligation to procure insurance, again at contract price plus 10 percent.

There are five D terms, with the D referencing a named destination. The seller's duty varies with the different D terms. The first of these terms is *DAF*, which means Delivered at Frontier. The seller makes the goods available and cleared for export at the named destination, but is not responsible for getting the goods through customs. (Goods are cleared for export when a relevant government agency has determined that the goods may be legally exported.[9]) DAF is commonly used with overland transportation, whether by rail or by truck. The second term is *DES*, Delivery Ex-Ship, at a named port. The seller must get the goods to the named port and cleared for export. Again, the seller is not responsible for getting the goods through customs. *DEQ*, Delivery Ex Quay, is similar to DES, but now the seller is also required to get the goods off the ship and on the quay (dock) cleared for importation before the buyer assumes risk of loss. Both DES and DEQ are used for water transport. The final two D terms are *DDP* and *DDU*. DDP means Delivery, Duty Paid. The seller must get the goods to the destination with all fees paid, including import fees and expenses, and cleared for importation. For DDU, Delivery, Duty Unpaid, the seller gets the goods to the destination with all fees paid except for import fees and expenses.

Remedies under the CISG

Like Article 2 of the UCC, the CISG also specifies the remedies that are generally available to the parties in the event of a breach of contract. Note, however, that the CISG is not as concerned with balancing the rights of the buyer with the rights of the seller, as the UCC seems to be, nor does it distinguish between remedies for pre- and postacceptance breaches. The CISG remedies are set out in Exhibit 11.7. Note that suing for damages is not listed as an available remedy under the CISG. If either party would prefer to sue for damages, he or she must do so under the national laws that are applied to the contract.

Warranties under the CISG

The CISG does not specifically provide for warranties, but its language implies that warranty protections do exist in the contract. If warranties are found to exist, whether expressed in the contract or implied from the context of the contract and the language in the Convention, the buyer will be entitled to seek remedies for the breach of any such warranty.

Article 8 of the CISG says that any statements or conduct of either party are to be interpreted according to the intent of the party making the statement or carrying out the conduct. If such intent cannot be determined from the circumstances, the statements and/or the conduct are to be interpreted as a reasonable and prudent person would interpret them. If such statements or conduct would be interpreted as creating a warranty, a warranty has been created. Such warranties will be treated as expressed warranties since they are created by the statements or the conduct of the party against whom they are being asserted.

Exhibit 11.7

Remedies under the CISG

Seller's Remedies	Buyer's Remedies
The seller may require the buyer to pay the contract price and to take delivery or otherwise perform the contract. (Not available if the seller has chosen another remedy that is inconsistent with this one.)	The buyer may require the seller to perform, unless the buyer has chosen another remedy that is inconsistent with performance.
The seller can set another reasonable time during which the buyer can perform, provided the buyer is notified of the extension. (No other remedies can be sought during the extension period.)	The buyer can set an additional time for performance, provided that the seller is notified of this additional time. (No other remedies can be sought during this additional time.)
The seller can declare the contract avoided as to any unperformed portions of the contract.	The buyer can declare the contract avoided if the seller does not deliver the good within the time permitted under the contract or within the additional time allowed if the buyer sets an additional time.
The seller may supply any specifications as to form, measurements, or other features if the buyer has failed to do so.	The buyer can require the seller to deliver conforming substitute goods, or to cure any nonconformity if the seller delivered nonconforming goods. If the seller delivered nonconforming goods, the buyer can reduce the price to be paid to reflect the value of the goods delivered.
	If the seller tenders delivery prior to the agreed delivery date, the buyer can accept or refuse the tender; if the seller tenders delivery of a larger shipment than called for, the buyer can accept any or all of the amount over the contractual amount, paying for the goods at the contract rate.

Article 9 says that if the parties have established any practices between themselves in this or prior contracts, such practices become part of the contract. It also provides that if the parties implied that they will follow common trade usages and practices, such usages and practices become part of the contract. This seems to be perfectly logical, and there would seem to be no controversy involved in such an interpretation of the contract. However, if normal trade usage or practices includes the giving of implied warranties, such warranties become a part of the contract, even if the party giving the warranty never intended to do so.

Article 35 requires the seller to provide goods that are of the quality and quantity specified in the contract and that match any description of the goods in the contract. It also requires that the goods be packaged or contained appropriately and must be fit for their normal and intended usage. Such requirements mirror the UCC's standards for merchantability. Furthermore, if at the time the contract is made the seller is aware of a particular purpose for which the buyer is purchasing the goods, Article 35 requires that the goods be fit for that particular purpose. This is strikingly similar to the UCC's standards for fitness for a particular purpose. Even though the CISG does not use the term *warranty*, Article 35 provides protections similar to the UCC's implied warranties covering the quality of the goods sold.

Contemporary Case

This case, like the Classic Case for this chapter, involves a disagreement over an arbitration provision in a contract involving the sale of goods. Here the arbitration clause was included in proposed additional terms in the acceptance. Note the court's attitude toward arbitration clauses in general. Compare this attitude with that shown in the Classic Case.

ACEROS PREFABRICADOS, S.A. v. TRADEARBED, INC.

282 F.3d 92, 2002 U.S. App. LEXIS 2349 (2d Cir. 2002)

FACTS On December 17, 1999, Tradearbed (TA), an affiliate of the world's largest steel manufacturer, and Aceros, a major Central American contractor, began negotiations for Aceros's prospective purchase of steel. The letters included a list of the products Aceros desired and several purchase orders that included tonnage and proposed prices. On January 12, 2000, TA replied to Aceros with a letter that stated that TA "hereby confirms the orders for beams as follows," but the parties disagreed as to the translation of the next sentence. (Most of the letters were written in Spanish.) Aceros asserts that it reads: "We hereby confirm that the above-mentioned orders will be shipped in the next few days." In contrast, TA contends that the correct translation is:

"The confirmations of the above-mentioned orders will be shipped in the next few days."

Aceros argues that the January 12 letter constituted an acceptance of Aceros' prior offers, resulting in a binding contract between the parties as of that date. TA maintains that it accepted Aceros' offers only when it sent three confirmation orders (dated January 17, January 28, and March 9, 2000), that each confirmation constituted a separate acceptance, and that the parties therefore entered into three distinct contracts for the sale and purchase of steel.

Each of TA's "confirmation orders" included a cover sheet stating that the confirmation included the sale terms and conditions for the steel, and also contained a note on the last page. This note provided that the confirmation was "Subject to terms stated on General Conditions of Sale enclosed. Your failure to object to any term within 10 days of receipt of this contract shall be deemed an acceptance by you."

Aceros contends, and TA does not dispute, that the General Conditions of Sale were not included with any of the three confirmation orders. The General Conditions of Sale contain the following arbitration provision: "Any controversy arising under or in connection with the contract shall be submitted to arbitration in New York City in accordance with the rules then obtaining of the American Arbitration Association." Aceros did not sign or return the January 17 confirmation, and it is undisputed that Aceros never objected to any term in any of the confirmation orders. It is also undisputed that an Aceros agent accepted the January 28 confirmation order, by writing "[a]ceptado" on and signing each of the four pages of the confirmation order and then mailing it back to TA. Aceros neither signed nor returned the third confirmation order dated March 9.

Aceros decided that the contract had been breached, and filed suit against TA seeking damages for the alleged breach on December 11, 2000. On January 5, 2001, TA relying on the arbitration clause found in its General Conditions of Sale, filed a motion to stay the action pending arbitration. Aceros responded that the arbitration clause was not part of the parties' agreement as memorialized on January 12 because the General Conditions of Sale were (1) not accepted by Aceros; (2) not incorporated by reference into the confirmation orders; and (3) not enclosed with the confirmation orders as the orders themselves stated.

The District Court denied TA's motion, and TA filed an interlocutory appeal.

ISSUE Should this case be resolved in arbitration, as specified in the General Conditions of Sale?

HOLDING Yes. The arbitration clause was included in a proposed additional term when TA accepted the offer and Aceros did not object to any of these terms within ten days. They therefore became part of the contract.

REASONING Excerpts from the opinion of Miner, Circuit Judge:

... Aceros maintains that it could not have accepted the arbitration clause because the General Conditions of Sale (which include the arbitration clause) were not enclosed with the order confirmations nor mentioned by TA. That the General Conditions of Sale were not themselves included with the order

confirmations does not render the arbitration provisions invalid. Applying New York law, we have found that "[p]arties to a contract are plainly free to incorporate by reference, and bind themselves *inter sese*[1] to, terms that may be found in other agreements." ... Indeed, we have specifically found that parties were bound to arbitrate under arbitration clauses they never signed, where those clauses were contained in other documents that were incorporated by reference. ... Thus, TA's failure to include the General Conditions of Sale with the confirmation orders does not prevent those terms from being included in its contract with Aceros ...

For the reasons discussed below, we conclude that whether the January 12 letter formed a single contract or the confirmation orders formed three separate contracts, the parties are bound by the arbitration provisions. We therefore find it unnecessary to determine the precise moment of contract formation.

Under the New York Uniform Commercial Code ... an expression of acceptance or written confirmation that sets forth terms in addition to those initially agreed upon will not defeat formation of a binding contract. ... Instead, a contract will be found and the additional terms ... are then treated as "proposals" for addition to the contract. ... This analysis applies to both expressions of acceptance that form the contract ... and written confirmations of agreements already reached. ... An Official Comment to section 2-207 makes clear the applicability of that provision to these two situations: ...

> [A] proposed deal which in commercial understanding has in fact been closed is recognized as a contract. Therefore, any additional matter contained *either in the writing intended to close the deal or in a later confirmation* falls within subsection (2) and must be regarded as a proposal for an added term. ...

---

[1] A legal term meaning among or between themselves.

Therefore, were we to find that the contract between Aceros and TA was formed on January 12, as Aceros claims and as the district court held, then the three confirmation orders would constitute written confirmations stating terms additional to the January 12 agreement, and analysis would proceed under section 2-207(2).

Were we to agree instead with TA's argument that each of its order confirmations served as a separate acceptance of individual prior offers by Aceros to purchase steel, the confirmations would then constitute acceptances proposing additional terms and analysis would likewise proceed under section 2-207(2), albeit of three individual contracts. Both contract formation scenarios lead us to the same conclusion regarding the parties' obligation to arbitrate disputes.

We ... turn to an examination of whether the arbitration provisions are part of the parties' contract pursuant to section 2-207(2). It is undisputed that both TA and Aceros are merchants for the purposes of the UCC. ... Under the UCC, proposed additional terms become part of a contract between merchants unless one of three statutory exceptions is satisfied. ... Aceros invokes only the "material alteration" exception of section 2-207(2)(b), which prohibits inclusion in a contract of a proposed additional term that would "materially alter" the contract unless the other party agrees. ... Aceros agreed to arbitrate disputes in regard to goods shipped under the January 28 confirmation order when it wrote "[a]ceptado" on and signed every page of that confirmation order and mailed it back to TA. Aceros therefore bound itself to arbitrate disputes arising out of that order of goods. In contrast, neither the January 17 nor the March 9 confirmation order was expressly accepted by Aceros, and we must therefore determine whether the arbitration clause, as a proposed additional term in those two confirmation orders, is included in the parties' contract.

The district court stated that [a]s a matter of law, an arbitration provision materially alters ones' [sic] legal rights under a contract." ... The two authorities cited

by the district court ... restated the so-called New York rule that "parties to a commercial transaction will not be held to have chosen arbitration as the forum for the resolution of their disputes in the absence of an express, unequivocal agreement to that effect; absent such an explicit commitment neither party may be compelled to arbitrate." ... Thus, unlike nonarbitration agreements, which need only be proven by a preponderance of the evidence, New York law requires a higher degree of proof for arbitration agreements. ... While state law generally governs issues of contract interpretation in cases arising under the FAA[2] ... such disparate treatment of arbitration provisions is not permitted ...

In *Perry*, the Supreme Court held that under the FAA "[a] court may not, ... in assessing the rights of litigants to enforce an arbitration agreement, construe that agreement in a manner different from that in which it otherwise construes nonarbitration agreements under state law." ... Following the dictates of *Perry*, we considered the rule cited ... "preempted by the FAA because of its discriminatory treatment of arbitration provisions." ... Thus, contrary to the district court's holding, arbitration agreements do not, as a matter of law, constitute material alterations to a contract; rather, the question of their inclusion in a contract under section 2-207(2)(b) is answered by examining, on a case-by-case basis, their materiality under a preponderance of the evidence standard as we would examine any other agreement ...

"[T]he burden of proving the materiality of the alteration must fall on the party that opposes inclusion." ... This is so because the UCC presumes that between merchants additional terms will be included in a contract. ... Thus, "if neither party introduced any evidence, the [proposed additional term] would ... become part of the contract." ... Aceros was therefore required to establish that the arbitration provision constituted a material alteration to its contract with TA.

[2.] Federal Arbitration Act, 9 U.S.C. § 1 et seq. (Pub.L. 68–401, 43 Stat. 883, enacted February 12, 1925)

A material alteration is one that would "result in surprise or hardship if incorporated without express awareness by the other party." ... Surprise includes both a subjective element of what a party actually knew and an objective element of what a party should have known. ... We have stated that "[a] profession of surprise and raised eyebrows are not enough." ... Instead, "[t]o carry [its] burden ... [the nonassenting] party must establish that, under the circumstances, it cannot be presumed that a reasonable merchant would have consented to the additional term." ...

Aceros has failed to submit any evidence demonstrating either subjective or objective surprise at the inclusion of an arbitration clause in its contract with TA. ... In a footnote in its brief on appeal, Aceros "submits that surprise and hardship are self-evident where, as here, there was no reference to nor mention by [TA] to arbitration until after suit was filed." ... This claim ignores the fact that Aceros has the burden of *establishing* the elements of surprise or hardship, not merely stating that they are present. As with the statement in the affidavit, this assertion is conclusory and unsupported by any evidence in the record. ... Aceros has failed to establish surprise ... — [I]t has also failed to establish that it would suffer any hardship in being bound to arbitration.

Moreover, TA's vice-president submitted ... that "arbitration clauses, like the one here, are commonplace and the norm in the industry and have been for a very long time." ... Aceros did not rebut this assertion. Under New York law, an arbitration agreement does not result in surprise or hardship where arbitration is the custom and practice within the relevant industry. ... The logic of this rule is obvious: a merchant in a given industry will have, by definition, a difficult time establishing either subjective or objective "surprise" regarding a proposed contract term that is standard in that industry ...

Aceros did not submit any evidence of surprise or hardship and therefore has failed to demonstrate that the inclusion of an arbitration provision in its contract with TA constitutes a material alteration under section 2-207(2)(b). Moreover, TA submitted unrebutted evidence that arbitration is standard practice within the steel industry, thereby precluding Aceros from establishing surprise or hardship. Accordingly, we hold that the arbitration provisions proposed in TA's confirmation orders became part of the contract, and that Aceros and TA are therefore required to arbitrate their disputes ...

Short Answer Questions

1. The UCC imposes different standards on merchants than on nonmerchants. What test is used to decide if a person is a merchant under Article 2? Why do you think merchants should be held to a different and higher standard than nonmerchants?

2. The CISG does not apply to nonmerchants in most circumstances, while the UCC does apply to both merchants and nonmerchants. Why do you think this international law excludes nonmerchants? Why do you think the UCC's coverage includes nonmerchants?

3. The UCC provides for the inclusion of implied warranties in its contracts. These warranties only exist in certain situations. Assume that you are the purchaser in a sales

contract. When would you get the protection of each of the four implied warranties? Are implied warranties only given by merchant sellers?

You Decide...

1. Black Prince Distillery, Inc. distills and bottles whiskey. Home Liquors operates a number of retail liquor store outlets. Home Liquors purchased whiskey from Black Prince for nearly 25 years. During this entire period the whiskey sold to Home Liquors was transported by Royal Trucking. On May 10, Home Liquor called Black Prince and placed an order for whiskey. The order totaled $21,300. Black Prince prepared the order for shipment, called Royal Trucking and told the dispatcher that the order was ready for pick-up. As was their custom, Home Liquors telephoned a purchase order which was then confirmed by a writing executed by Home Liquors, and directed to Black Prince. The writing was entitled "Request for Release," and was signed by Home Liquors's agent. It read, in part, "please release the following to Royal Trucking Company," and set forth the quantity and type of goods being purchased. Black Prince would then prepare the shipping documents, which did not designate a destination for the goods. The shipping papers were signed and received by Royal's driver, who then took possession of the goods.

On May 11 the shipment was allegedly hijacked while in the possession of Royal Trucking and en route to one of the Home Liquors locations. Since the goods were never delivered to any of its locations, Home Liquors refused to remit payment. Black Prince decided to file suit for the contract price, alleging that Home Liquors had the risk of loss. Home Liquors denies this, asserting that since delivery was never properly tendered, risk of loss remained with Black Prince.

Assume this case was filed in your court. How would *you* decide this case? Be certain that you explain and justify your answer.

(See *Black Prince Distillery, Inc. v. Home Liquors,* 148 N.J. Super. 286, 372 A.2d 638 (1977).

2. Ron Fleming, a Texas resident, discovered a used 1964 Chevrolet Corvette convertible for sale in Memphis through an Internet advertisement. Fleming contacted Jim Murphy, who had prepared the Internet advertisement for Buggs Buggys and who provided him with the phone number of the seller. Fleming and Murphy agreed that Fleming would travel to Buggs Buggys, located in Memphis, to see the car and decide whether to purchase it for $38,000. Fleming and his stepson drove to the seller's location in Memphis, inspected the car, and took it on a short test drive. Fleming noted several problems with the car during the test drive, but declined the seller's offer to have the car inspected by a Memphis-area mechanic prior to purchase. Fleming tendered full payment for the car, and he and the seller signed a bill of sale that contained "as is" disclaimers of warranty. After Fleming arrived back home in Texas, he took the car to a mechanic for routine maintenance. The mechanic informed him that the car's frame was severely rusted, making it dangerous to drive. Fleming received the same opinion from a restoration specialist. Fleming claims to have ultimately spent nearly $35,000 restoring the vehicle. Fleming filed suit in Shelby County Circuit Court in Tennessee, asserting claims under the Tennessee Consumer Protection Act, for breach of the warranty of merchantability, negligent misrepresentation, and breach of contract. Fleming claimed actual damages which included over $25,500 in restoring the car to the condition represented by the seller.

Buggs Buggys denied any liability, asserting that the contract specifically stated that the sale of the car was made "as is," negating the warranty of merchantability. Buggs Buggys further argued that when Fleming declined the opportunity to have the car inspected by a Memphis-area mechanic prior to completing the purchase, he waived his right to inspect, which also waived his right to raise any alleged nonconformities that a reasonable inspection would have revealed.

Assume this case was filed in your court. How would *you* decide this case? Be certain that you explain and justify your answer.

(See *Fleming v. Murphy*, 2007 Tenn. App. LEXIS 451 (2007).)

Notes

1. UCC § 2-105(1).
2. *Ibid.*
3. UCC § 2-106(1).
4. UCC § 2-104(1).
5. *Ibid.*
6. UCC § 2-204(3).
7. UCC § 2-201(1). Note, however, that the proposed amendments to Article 2 would raise this amount to $5,000. At the time of writing, no state has ratified this proposed amendment.
8. Christopher Klein, *Mexican Contract Formalities and Interpretations: A Guide for the U.S. Legal Practitioner*, ISLP Law Journal (American University Washington College of Law) 35. Accessible at https://www.wcl.american.edu/journal/ilsp/v1/1/articles/klein.pdf (accessed June 4, 2016).
9. Answers.com, http://www.answers.com/Q/What_does_cleared_for_export_mean (accessed May 4, 2016).

Torts and Crimes

12

Torts

Learning Objectives

After completing this chapter you should be able to

- Explain the policies underlying tort law
- Describe the differences between intentional torts, negligence, and strict liability
- Recognize the defenses available for specific torts
- Compare the bases for product liability
- Discuss the theories for holding business entities liable for torts

Classic Case

Businesses can defame an individual, including an employee, or another business. The Classic Case for this chapter is an important Supreme Court decision limiting state defamation laws where the state laws may interfere with the constitutional protections of freedom of press and speech. Here the court created a new test that a public official must show "actual malice" when he or she is claiming defamation.

NEW YORK TIMES CO. v. SULLIVAN

376 U.S. 254, 1964 U.S. LEXIS 1655 (1964)

FACTS L. B. Sullivan was one of three elected Commissioners of the City of Montgomery, Alabama. He sued four individuals and the New York Times Company, claiming that he had been libeled by statements in a full-page advertisement that was printed in the *New York Times*. Some of the statements about the civil rights movement contained in the ad were not accurate descriptions of events that occurred in Montgomery. None of the statements in the ad named Sullivan, but he contended that the word "police" referred to him because he was the Montgomery Commissioner who supervised the Police Department. Sullivan contended that since arrests are ordinarily made by the police, the statement about arresting Dr. Martin Luther King, Jr. would be understood as referring to him.

The *Times* published the ad based on an order from a New York advertising agency. The agency attached a letter from A. Philip Randolph, Chairman of the Committee, which certified that the persons who "signed" the advertisement had given their permission. Some of these individuals testified that they had not authorized the use of their names and that they were not aware that their names were being used. The *Times*'s Advertising Acceptability Department knew Mr. Randolph and believed that he was a responsible person. It accepted the letter as sufficient proof of authorization following its established practice. No one at the *Times* tried to confirm the accuracy of the advertisement by checking it against *Times* news stories or by other methods.

The trial judge instructed the jury that the statements in the advertisement were libelous per se, and that legal injury was implied without proof of actual harm. Sullivan received a $500,000 judgment at the trial court. The *New York Times* appealed.

ISSUE Does Alabama's libel law violate freedom of speech and freedom of the press?

HOLDING Yes, Alabama's libel law is unconstitutional.

REASONING Excerpts from the opinion of Justice Brennan:

. . . [The] law applied by the Alabama courts is constitutionally deficient for failure to provide the safeguards for freedom of speech and of the press that are required by the First and Fourteenth Amendments in a libel action brought by a public official against critics of his official conduct. . . . [T]he evidence presented in this case is constitutionally insufficient to support the judgment for respondent. . . . The publication here was not a "commercial" advertisement. . . . It communicated information, expressed opinion, recited grievances, protested claimed abuses, and sought financial support on behalf of a movement whose existence and objectives are matters of the highest public interest and concern. . . . That the Times was paid for publishing the advertisement is as immaterial . . . as is the fact that newspapers and books are sold. . . . Any other conclusion would discourage newspapers from carrying "editorial advertisements" of this type, and so might shut off an important outlet for . . . information and ideas by persons who do not themselves have access to publishing facilities—who wish to exercise their freedom of speech even though they are not members of the press. . . .

The present advertisement . . . would seem clearly to qualify for the constitutional protection. . . . The constitutional protection does not turn upon "the truth, popularity, or social utility of the ideas and beliefs which are offered." . . . If neither factual error nor defamatory content suffices to remove the constitutional shield from criticism of official conduct, the combination of the two elements is no less inadequate. . . . It is true that the First Amendment was originally addressed only to action by the Federal Government. . . . But this distinction was eliminated with the adoption of the Fourteenth Amendment and the application to the States of the First Amendment's restrictions. . . . What a State may not constitutionally bring about by means of a criminal statute is likewise beyond the reach of its civil law of libel. . . . The fear of damage awards . . . may be markedly more inhibiting than the fear of prosecution under a criminal statute. . . .

Allowance of the defense of truth, with the burden of proving it on the defendant, does not mean that only false speech will be deterred. . . . The constitutional guarantees require . . . a federal rule that prohibits a public official from recovering damages for a defamatory falsehood relating to his official conduct unless he proves that the statement was made with "actual malice"—that is, with knowledge that it was false or with reckless disregard of whether it was false or not. . . . [T]he proof presented to show actual malice [in this case] lacks the convincing clarity which the constitutional standard demands. . . . [The proof] would not constitutionally sustain the judgment for respondent. . . . As to the Times, we . . . conclude that the facts do not support a finding of actual malice. . . . [T]here is evidence that the Times published the advertisement without checking its accuracy against the news stories in the Times' own files. The mere presence of the stories in the files does not . . . establish that the Times "knew" the advertisement was false. . . . [T]he record shows that they relied upon their knowledge of the good reputation of many of those whose names were listed as sponsors of the advertisement, and upon the letter from A. Philip Randolph. . . . [T]he persons handling the advertisement saw nothing in it that would render it unacceptable under the Times' policy. . . . We think the evidence against the Times supports at most a finding of negligence. . . .

We also think the evidence was constitutionally defective in another respect: it was incapable of supporting the jury's finding that the allegedly libelous statements were made "of and concerning" respondent. . . . There was no reference to respondent in the advertisement, either by name or official position. . . .

The judgment of the Supreme Court of Alabama is reversed and the case is remanded to that court for further proceedings not inconsistent with this opinion.

Reversed and remanded.

OBJECTIVES OF TORT LAW

A tort is a *civil* wrong. *Tort law* is concerned with a body of private wrongs, whereas *criminal law*, which we shall study in Chapter 13, is concerned with public wrongs. Tort law helps protect an individual's rights with respect to his or her person and property. It is a complicated body of law because it developed over hundreds of years. The discussion here is fairly general since most tort law is based on precedents in state courts and can vary significantly from state to state. There are a number of exceptions to many of the rules.

Torts provide a mechanism for persons who have been wronged to seek remedies in U.S. courts. In general, the remedy sought is monetary damages to compensate for the injury. People can avoid committing these wrongs by adhering to various "duties." For example, society recognizes a duty to refrain from physically injuring other persons or their property. Society also recognizes a duty to refrain from injuring the reputation of others.

Because tort law recognizes certain duties, it raises the policy question of exactly which rights society should protect by imposing duties. For example, should society recognize as a wrong only behavior *intended* to be a wrong? Should society also recognize as a wrong an unintended wrong due to someone's negligence? Should society also recognize as a wrong unintended consequences when the person is not negligent? These are the questions discussed in this chapter.

Society has developed the body of tort law to resolve social and economic policy questions. The law has to take into consideration a number of factors, including: (1) the social usefulness of the conduct of a person; (2) the interests asserted by the plaintiff; (3) the justification (if any) for the defendant's conduct; (4) the economic burden placed on the defendant if liability is imposed; and (5) the question of spreading the cost of liability from one to many persons. The law also has the unique problem of respecting past decisions while maintaining the flexibility to provide solutions to modern problems. For instance, tort law has to adjust to technological advances, such as defamation and invasion of privacy on social media.

THEORIES OF TORT LIABILITY

This chapter discusses intentional torts, negligence, and strict liability. Exhibit 12.1 depicts these three theories of tort liability. *Intentional torts* occur when the actor behaves in a willful or intentional manner; he or she either wants the act to occur or knows that the act would probably occur. A few examples involving the tort of battery will help.

Battery involves an intentional offensive contact, a "wrongful touching." The "act" involved is the contact. If you intentionally punch Christopher, you wanted the act to occur. Assume Denise is riding her horse and you intentionally frighten her horse. The horse bolts and jumps a fence, knocking Denise to the ground. You should have known that Denise would probably fall off the horse and contact the ground: In other words, you knew the act would probably occur. For battery, the actor intends or expects the contact to occur. He or she does not necessarily expect the injury. Assume Sara intentionally pushes Allen to the ground. Sara is not aware that Allen is a hemophiliac. When his blood does not clot due to the disease, Allen has to be hospitalized for a week. It is sufficient that Sara pushed him on purpose. It is not required that she intended to seriously injure him. Suppose that Wade said something offensive to you, and you said, "If you don't apologize, I'll punch you in the nose." If Wade did not apologize and you punched him in the nose, the law states that *you* are the party in the wrong. When you punched Wade, you committed the tort of *battery* on him. Provocation is not an issue here, since generally the law does not recognize the privilege of striking someone for making offensive remarks. (In this context, a *privilege* is a defense where the defendant claims that his or her conduct was authorized or sanctioned by the law.)

The law of *negligence* is based on a concept of fault in which morality and law are intermingled. How should society apportion the costs of accidents? Often, society has to make a moral statement when an injury occurs. Suppose a child darts out from behind a parked car an instant before Larry, an approaching driver, reaches that point. Larry immediately brakes in an effort to avoid hitting the child but is unable to stop in time to avoid the accident. In all likelihood, this accident would be considered unavoidable—it occurred without any negligence on Larry's part. The child, even though injured, would be denied any compensation from Larry for the accident.

On the other hand, if a child is walking across the street in a designated crosswalk and Donovan hits the child because Donovan is texting while driving or driving too fast, then society says that Donovan breached a duty to drive the car in a reasonable manner. Accordingly, Donovan will have to pay for damages suffered by the child.

Exhibit 12.1

The Three Theories of Tort Liability

Tort Liability		
Intentional Torts	*Negligence*	*Strict Liability in Tort*
The accused acts in a willful or intentional manner.	The conduct of the accused is compared to the conduct of a "reasonable and prudent" person.	The accused is generally involved in conduct that is deemed abnormally dangerous.
Involves a simple duty to avoid the act or conduct.	Involves a reasonable duty to avoid the act or conduct.	Involves a strict duty to be responsible for the harm caused.
There must be a showing of fault.	There must be a showing of fault.	There is no need to show fault.
The harm must be foreseeable.	The harm must be foreseeable.	The harm must be foreseeable.

The amount of injury is not a factor in determining liability: What is relevant is how the injury occurred.

Since most negligence cases will not fall at the ends of the spectrum, as the two previous examples did, the law has developed a test for determining whether negligence occurred in any given situation. The law applies the standard of the "reasonable and prudent person," comparing the conduct of this hypothetical individual to the conduct of the defendant. This topic is discussed in more detail later in this chapter.

Under *strict liability*, persons can be held liable to injured parties for conduct that was not intentional or negligent. That is, they can be held liable even if the damage arising from their conduct was not their fault. Some activities are classified as either ultrahazardous or abnormally dangerous, and if injury results from activities fitting either category, the actor will be held liable. For example, suppose you have a pet rattlesnake in a sealed glass cage and you place the cage in your backyard with signs on the fence that say: *Danger—Poisonous Snake, Beware.* If the snake somehow gets out and bites someone, you can be held liable for the resulting injuries despite your warnings or your best efforts to avoid injuring anyone. The law prevents you from trying to prove how careful you were. If your rattlesnake caused injury, you simply have to pay. It has been argued that horizontal fracking should be added to the list of abnormally dangerous activities.[1]

The Role of Duty

Residents in the United States have a duty to protect other persons from harm. The question the courts must examine is what degree of duty exists under any specific set of facts. With respect to intentional torts, we all have a simple duty to avoid liability-causing behavior. However, with respect to negligence, we all have a "reasonable" duty to avoid this type of behavior. Generally, the law states that this reasonable duty is a standard of ordinary skill and care, based on the facts of each individual case. The law tests a person's conduct by comparing it to a purely hypothetical person known as the *reasonable and prudent person*. Note that this hypothetical person is not perfect: He or she is merely reasonable and prudent.

The Role of Foreseeability

Both intentional torts and negligence are based on the concept of fault. Strict liability is not. All three theories of liability require *foreseeability*, the knowledge or notice that a specific act is likely to cause a certain type of result.

Foreseeability addresses the likelihood that something will happen in the future. It is easy to see that if you point a loaded gun at someone and pull the trigger, you can cause that person harm. But suppose you get in your car and drive down a dark street with your lights on. You are driving under the posted speed limit. A child darts out from behind a parked car, and you hit the child. Were you negligent, or was it merely an unavoidable accident? This is a more difficult question. Foreseeability is determined by what a "reasonable and prudent person" would expect. The foreseeability of a child darting into the street in front of your car would depend on such factors as the degree of darkness, the lateness of the hour, how densely populated the area was (for example, rural or urban, residential or business), other children observed in the area, signs regarding children at play, and so forth. These factors must be considered to determine whether the child's action is foreseeable and whether you were negligent.

INTENTIONAL TORTS

Assault

Assault is wrongful, intentional conduct that would cause a victim to have a reasonable apprehension of immediate harmful or offensive contact. Verbal threats alone are not an assault. Some movement toward the person must accompany the verbal threat. The threats of harm must be immediate: Threats of future harm are not sufficient to constitute an assault. The actor must have the actual or apparent ability to cause immediate harm to the victim. Pointing an unloaded pistol at a person, for example, is an assault if the victim has no way of knowing whether the pistol is loaded. The victim must feel apprehension: Actual fear is not required.

Battery

Some legal authorities have defined *battery* as a consummated assault. It is the wrongful, intentional, offensive, and nonconsensual touching of the victim. Common-law battery does not require an injury to the victim.[2] Touching an extension of the victim's body, such as a purse or backpack, also constitutes a battery. For example, assume that Ted is talking to Charese. She stands up briefly and begins to sit down. Ted removes the chair. It is battery when Charese hits the ground. The key element is that Ted intended the natural consequence of removing the chair: Charese falling to the ground. As far as the law is concerned, it is the same as pushing Charese to the ground. On the other hand, if the removal of the chair was done innocently, and the ultimate result of Charese falling to the ground was not intended, there is likely to be no tort of battery. The victim does not need to be aware of the battery at the time that it occurs. It can be battery if a person kisses a sleeping woman or a doctor performs surgery on an unconscious man without consent.

Conversion

Conversion occurs when a person intentionally exercises exclusive control over the personal property of another without the permission of the owner. In such a case, the converter is liable for damages. If a person lawfully obtains possession of property but then refuses to return it at the request of the owner, that person is also a converter. If the owner seeks the return of the property in court, the lawsuit is called *replevin* (an action to recover possession of goods taken unlawfully). Damages can also be obtained if the owner suffered harm during the conversion. Sometimes the owner does not desire the return of the property, for example, if it has been damaged. In this case, the owner asks for reimbursement for his or her loss.

Defamation

Defamation occurs when an actor intentionally makes an untrue statement concerning a victim, the statement is heard or read by someone else, and the statement injures the victim's reputation. As with other intentional torts, it is sufficient that the actor made the statement willfully. The defamatory remark must be *published*, which is defined as "read or heard by others." Consequently, a negative remark made directly to the victim that is not overheard by anyone else is not "published." The statement need not name the victim; however, the statement must be reasonably interpreted as referring to the victim. That was one of the issues in the Classic Case of *New York Times Co. v. Sullivan*. The statement must injure or reduce the victim's reputation among well-meaning individuals. If the actor curses at the victim, this will not injure the victim's reputation. It is interpreted more as an indication that the *actor* is extremely angry and may not be controlling his or her temper. Some courts apply the *libel-proof plaintiff doctrine* when the fact finder decides that the plaintiff's reputation for a specific trait is so poor that it could not be further damaged by the statement.[3] Suits against businesses are on the rise as disgruntled ex-employees are suing their ex-employers for defamation for remarks to former coworkers and/or potential new employers.

Two forms of defamation exist: *Slander* occurs when the statement is oral, and *libel* occurs when the statement is written or printed. Slander is spoken communication that causes a person to suffer a loss of reputation. The common law rule distinguished between *slander per se* and *slander per quod.* Slander per se occurs when an actor says that another person is seriously immoral, seriously criminal, has a social disease, or is unfit as a businessperson or professional. In these cases, there is no need to prove actual damages. Slander per quod is any other type of oral defamatory statement. A victim of slander per quod must show harm in order to recover any damages.

Libel is a written, printed, or other permanent communication that causes a person to suffer a loss of reputation. There are also two kinds of libel. *Libel per se* is libelous without having to consider the context of the remark. For example, if a newspaper printed a story that referred to a person as a "known assassin for hire," there is no need to show the context of the statement. On the other hand, *libel per quod* requires proof of the context. In other words, the statement is only negative in context. For example, Armour and Company ran a newspaper ad that consumers could purchase bacon in its new packages at a number of meat markets. The ad listed the names and addresses of several meat markets. Armour accidentally listed Max Braun's meat market. By itself, the statement does not seem negative. However, Braun operated a traditional kosher meat market which would not sell bacon. Braun sued for defamation because in context this was a very negative statement. The court ruled that Braun was entitled to sue for defamation.[4]

It is obvious that a book, a magazine, or a newspaper is written, so that defamatory remarks in any of these constitute a potential libel. Films and videos that contain defamatory remarks are also considered libelous. Since the medium containing the remark is relatively permanent, the remark can be "republished" any time the film or video is replayed. Consequently, these forms of communication are viewed as the equivalent of a writing rather than the equivalent of a spoken defamation. Electronic communications have created new areas where defamation can occur, such as blogs, e-mails, social network sites, and other Web sites.

Public Officials and Public Figures   The tort of defamation is an important exception to the First Amendment's guarantee of free speech. Consequently, U.S. courts have modified some of the common law rules. Our Classic Case for this chapter, *New York Times Co. v. Sullivan*,[5] is a landmark in U.S. jurisprudence. The U.S. Supreme Court held that when a public official sues for libel, the public official must also prove that the false statement was made with actual malice in addition to the other elements of libel. The court defined actual malice as knowledge that the statement was false or with reckless disregard of whether it was false or not. Some courts actually refer to it as *New York Times malice*.

Since the decision, the Court has applied the requirement to candidates for public office, incumbents, and "public figures." A *public figure* is a person who has a degree of prominence in society. There are two types of public figures. An "all purpose" public figure is someone who has achieved so much fame or notoriety that he or she becomes a public figure for all purposes and in all contexts. A "limited purpose" public figure is someone who voluntarily involves himself or herself in or is drawn into a particular public controversy: He or she then becomes a public figure for a limited range of issues. For the *New York Times* rule to apply, the alleged defamation must be relevant to the plaintiff's participation in that public controversy. The justifications for treating public figures differently from private individuals is: (1) public figures usually have greater access to the channels of communication and have a better opportunity to counteract false statements than private individuals; and (2) public figures have asked for the attention and comments, so they must accept the consequences of their choice, including the chance that false and injurious statements will be made about them.

Disparagement

Disparagement occurs when a business product is defamed. Generally it requires that (1) a person make a false statement about a business's products, services, reputation, honesty, or integrity; (2) the speaker publishes the remark to a third party; and (3) the speaker knows the remark is false, or the speaker makes the statement maliciously and with intent to injure the victim. It is sometimes called *product disparagement*. It is also called *trade libel*, if the statements are written, or *slander of title*, if the statements are oral. In this tort, the plaintiff is a business; often the defendant is another business. The Texas Beef Group's unsuccessful lawsuit against Oprah Winfrey for her statements about beef was based in part on product disparagement.[6]

False Imprisonment

False imprisonment is the unlawful detention of one person by another against the victim's will, and without just cause, for an appreciable amount of time. This tort protects a person from the wrongful loss of liberty and freedom of movement. For example, if after the end of a college class your professor locks the door and says that no one can leave the room, the professor has committed false imprisonment. Sometimes, merely standing in a doorway and refusing to let a person pass is also false imprisonment. As with other torts, there are defenses. For example, a privilege exists when a store employee has just cause to suspect a customer of shoplifting. If the employee detains the customer, the employee's acts will be privileged as long as the length of time and the manner of the detention are reasonable.

Fraud

Depending on the situation, fraud can be a crime, a tort, and/or a defense to a contract. In this chapter we will discuss the tort. *Fraud* is an extremely complex tort.[7] It involves the misrepresentation of a material fact made with the intent to deceive. If an innocent person reasonably relies on the misrepresentation and is harmed as a result, the injured person may successfully sue for fraud. There are five elements of fraud:

1. A material fact was involved: An opinion usually will not constitute fraud (fact).
2. The fact was misrepresented (a falsehood).
3. The falsehood was made with the intent to deceive (*scienter*).
4. The falsehood was one on which another person justifiably relied (reasonable reliance).
5. That person was injured as a result (damage).

For example, if an owner of a small business knowingly obtains a loan on the basis of a false financial statement, it is fraud. If a corporation solicits persons to buy stock for the purpose of building a new plant when in reality the corporation wants the money to pay off existing liabilities, it is fraud. The list is virtually endless.

Infliction of Emotional Distress

The law protects an individual from suffering *serious indignity* that causes emotional distress. This right of the individual is balanced against the interest of the state in not having frivolous and trivial claims tried in its courts. Most states recognize causes of action for both the intentional infliction and the negligent causing of emotional distress. The torts are often called *the intentional infliction of emotional distress* and *the negligent infliction of emotional distress*. In many states, the elements of intentional infliction of emotional distress are that (1) the defendant acted intentionally or recklessly; (2) the defendant's conduct was extreme and outrageous; (3) the defendant's actions caused emotional distress to the plaintiff; and (4) the plaintiff's emotional distress was severe. Some states require a physical injury in addition to emotional distress. For example, in one case a mortician training school was held liable for causing mental distress to twenty-three people who took their loved ones to funeral homes and instructed that the bodies *not* be embalmed. However, the training school "wrongfully" obtained the bodies and used them for instructional purposes in the embalming clinic.[8] There have been some cases in which former employees sued their former employers for intentionally inflicting emotional distress. While the threat of future harm cannot be treated as an assault (the threat must be imminent for an assault), it can constitute the intentional infliction of emotional distress depending on the reaction of the victim.

Intentional Interference with Contractual Relations

This tort occurs when a person (or business) intentionally interferes in a contract of another. It has various names, depending on the state, and may be called *unlawful interference with contractual relations*, *interference with a contractual relationship*, *inducement of breach of contract*, or *procurement of breach of contract*. It occurs when the defendant intentionally induces a party to breach his or her contract with the plaintiff, causing damage to the plaintiff. The defendant must be aware that a contract exists between the plaintiff and the other party. In some jurisdictions, a defendant may have a privilege to "interfere" in the contractual relationship. However, the interference is not privileged if the defendant is in competition with the plaintiff and wants the contract for himself or herself. Many of the cases based on privilege involve defendants who have legal or fiduciary duties to the other party to the contract.

Interference with Prospective Advantage

This tort is closely related to intentional interference with contractual relations. It is also called interference with a business relationship. It occurs when an actor interferes with another person or business's *potential* business relationships. Since the parties are still negotiating their arrangement, the relationship has less protection than an actual contract would have. The interference may occur as the plaintiff attempts to obtain employment or customers. Generally the plaintiff must show that:

1. The plaintiff reasonably expected to enter a business relationship with the other party;
2. The defendant was aware of the negotiation between them;
3. The defendant purposely and unjustifiably interfered with the potential relationship;
4. The defendant's actions caused the other party to terminate the negotiation with the plaintiff; and
5. The defendant's actions caused harm to the plaintiff.

Fair competition with the plaintiff is not a tort. In many situations, the defendant can use the privilege to compete as a valid defense to this tort.

Invasion of Privacy

U.S. courts recognize that some unwarranted or unreasonable invasions of privacy are grounds for a legal action. Originally, this tort began with someone's peering into a home without permission. *Privacy* refers to an individual's right to be left alone, his or her "zone of privacy." A person's privacy is invaded if that person becomes subject to unwarranted intrusions into his or her right to be left alone. These unwarranted intrusions have led to lawsuits and to the awarding of damages to the victim. Liability has been found for the public disclosure of private matters, such as playing a tape of a private citizen's telephone call without permission. The singer Adele is very private about her personal life. However, in 2016, a hacker obtained a number of very personal pictures, such as the ultrasound of her son and some of his baby pictures. The hacker posted them on a Facebook group for her fans. It is believed that the hacker obtained the pictures by breaking into the email account of Adele's partner.[9] Some colleges and employers have been asking applicants and employees to divulge the username and password to their Facebook[TM] and Twitter[TM] accounts. There is a trend to prohibit this practice. Twenty-three states now prohibit this practice by employers and 14 prohibit the practice by educational institutions.[10]

In most states, simple invasion of privacy has been expanded to include (1) appropriation of plaintiff's name, face, or likeness for commercial purposes; (2) presenting the plaintiff in a false light in the public eye; (3) intrusion on physical solitude; (4) public disclosure of private information; and (5) unauthorized use of the plaintiff's likeness or life story. For example, the use of a famous person's name, photograph, image, song, or voice in an advertisement without permission is an appropriation of the person's likeness. This version of invasion of privacy is often described as an invasion of the famous person's right of publicity, since he or she is deprived of the opportunity to sell his or her name or likeness to some other company. Publication is not required for most types of invasion of privacy. Unlike defamation, truth is not a defense. Under the First Amendment, the courts have created a privilege for the media when it is reporting on newsworthy events. The media will be protected even when the news report is inaccurate, unless the error was made deliberately or recklessly. The types of invasion of privacy are illustrated in Exhibit 12.2

Exhibit 12.2

The Tort of Invasion of Privacy

Type of Invasion of Privacy[a]	Definition	Example[b]
Appropriation of Name, Face, or Likeness	Defendant uses the plaintiff's name, face, or likeness for commercial benefit.	Without permission, a company uses the picture of a celebrity in its advertising and claims that he or she prefers its energy drink.
False Light	Defendant publicly attributes to plaintiff views or positions plaintiff does not hold.	Speaker falsely claims that Conrad is a member of a racist organization.
Intrusion on Physical Solitude	Defendant interferes with the plaintiff's seclusion.	Individual takes a picture of Bree while she is alone in her hotel room and posts it on the Internet.
Public Disclosure of Private Information	Defendant reveals private information that the plaintiff did not make public.	Manager informs coworkers that Ravi, an employee, is HIV positive.
Unauthorized Use of Likeness	Defendant publishes the plaintiff's likeness or life story.	Film company makes a movie about Toni's experiences as a kidnapping victim without obtaining Toni's consent.

[a] Some states may not recognize all types of invasion of privacy. The categories listed may be combined in some states.
[b] These actions would not constitute invasion of privacy if the person gave consent. Users who post pictures and private information on some social media, give consent under the user agreement.

Misappropriation of Trade Secrets

Misappropriation of trade secrets occurs when an actor unlawfully acquires and uses the trade secrets of another business enterprise. The victim must prove that a trade secret exists. A *trade secret* is some exclusive knowledge of commercial value that has been created by the labors of a specific person or group of people. The owner must have implemented reasonable steps to protect the trade secret. The actor must have acquired it by some unlawful or improper means, such as bribery, industrial espionage, or theft. Some states, like Texas, require that the actor acquire the secret as a result of a confidential relationship with the victim.[11] Texas also requires that the actor "use" the trade secret.[12] This tort is also called *theft of trade secrets*. Most states have adopted the Uniform Trade Secrets Act to codify their laws on trade secrets.[13]

An Ounce of Prevention

Trade secrets are valuable assets of many businesses. You need to protect your trade secrets from misappropriation by employees, competitors, and foreign countries. One of the most successful strategies is also one of the most obvious. If it is a trade secret, keep it secret! You should establish a policy for treating confidential information in a private and confidential manner. Restrict access to the information. Tell only employees and consultants who actually need to have the information. If an employee or consultant needs part of the information, share only the information that he or she needs to do the job. You should consider requiring employees and consultants to sign nondisclosure agreements stating that they will not disclose the trade secrets. You should also remind them periodically that they have trade secrets that they need to keep secret. When the relationship ends, you should remind the employee or consultant that they are still obligated to maintain the trade secret.

Racketeer Influenced and Corrupt Organizations Act (RICO) Violations

The Racketeer Influenced and Corrupt Organizations Act, commonly referred to by the acronym RICO,[14] is discussed in more detail in Chapter 13 since most of its provisions deal with criminal law. It is mentioned here because RICO also provides for civil suits by the victim. RICO is a federal statute directed at a pattern of racketeering activity. A *pattern* means two or more racketeering acts within a ten-year period. The RICO statute includes a long list of racketeering acts. Racketeering acts range from violent acts, such as murder, to less violent acts, such as mail fraud. Individuals and businesses that are injured by the RICO violation can sue those who violated it. The U.S. Justice Department can also file a civil RICO lawsuit. Successful plaintiffs in a civil action may recover treble damages, attorney's fees, and reasonable court costs. (*Treble damages* are three times the amount of actual damages.) A civil plaintiff can sue even though there has been no criminal conviction.

Trespass

The tort of *trespass* is used to protect property interests against nonconsensual infringements. There are two types of trespass—trespass to land and trespass to personal property. We will refer to the victim as the owner in this section, but another person who has the right to possession of the land or personal property also can bring a lawsuit for trespass.

A person who goes onto the real property of another without permission is a trespasser. The trespasser must *intentionally* go onto the land. A person who accidentally goes on the land of another may be negligent but is not trespassing. An example would be a driver who skids off the road and collides with a building: The driver did not intend to go onto the property. The actor does not need to realize that he or she is trespassing or that the land belongs to someone else. It is sufficient if the trespasser intends to go onto the land. For example, it would be trespass even if the person reasonably believes he or she owns the land or has permission of the owner. Trespass can also occur by intentionally causing an object to go onto the land of someone else. The trespasser will be liable for any actual damages that he or she causes. The trespasser will be liable for nominal damages if there is no actual damage.

Trespass to personal property is also called *trespass to chattels*. It occurs if the trespasser's action is intentional. The intent required is that the trespasser intended to deal with the property in the manner in which he or she did. It is irrelevant if the trespasser thought he or she had the right to do so. The trespass may dispossess the owner or "intermeddle" with the owner's possession of the personal property. An example of intermeddling would be if Alyse intentionally scratched Debbie's car. Debbie is not entitled to nominal damages for intermeddling; she can only collect actual damages. If Alyse's actions oust or evicts Debbie from her property, she may choose to sue for trespass or conversion.

Exhibit 12.3 summarizes the intentional torts discussed in this chapter.

Defenses to Intentional Torts

There is a great deal of variation from state to state in how the defenses are actually defined and what constitutes a defense. The following sections contain brief descriptions of some of the common defenses.

Consent   Even though a tort has been committed, the law may not compensate the injured party if that person consented to the tort. Consent is either expressed or implied. Most cases involve issues of implied consent. (Courts find *implied consent* when the overall conduct of the parties raises a presumption that there was an agreement.) The law will not infer consent unless it is reasonable under the circumstances. For example, football players obviously batter each other throughout the course of a game. Even though the tort of battery may have been committed, it is not actionable because the law views each player as having consented to the touching. However, if a player intentionally exceeds the implied consent, he or she may be liable for the tort. For example, a professional boxer consents to being punched during the bout. However, most courts would hold that a boxer does not consent to being bitten on the ear during a match, or to being punched by the other fighter after the bout is over. For example, Mike Tyson bit Evander Holyfield on both ears during a boxing match on June 28, 1997. Tyson was disqualified and Holyfield won the match.[15]

Exhibit 12.3

Intentional Torts

Specific Tort	Definition	Defenses
Assault	Conduct that would put a reasonable person in apprehension of an imminent offensive and nonconsensual touching (a battery)	Conditional privilege Consent Necessity/justification Self-defense
Battery	Intentional offensive and nonconsensual touching	Conditional privilege Consent Necessity/justification Self-defense
Conversion	Intentional exercise of exclusive control over the personal property of another without permission	Consent Necessity
Defamation: Slander (spoken) or Libel (written)	Statements *published* (commu-nicated) by the actor to another person about the victim that harm the victim's reputation	Absolute privilege (legal or congressional proceeding) Conditional privilege Truth
Disparagement	Defamation of a business's product, service, or reputation	Privilege
False Imprisonment	Detention of one person by another against his or her will and without just cause	Consent Privilege

Privilege Privilege is a defense that protects certain social interests. It may be recognized in a number of situations, including:

- If someone moves to strike you, you have the privilege of self-defense. Most states also recognize the privilege to defend family members.
- Retail businesspersons have a privilege to detain persons who they reasonably believe have committed theft from the business.
- Persons whose property is stolen have the privilege of going onto another person's property in order to retrieve it.
- Judges and legislators have the privilege of saying things that might be defamatory under other circumstances in order to stimulate debate and encourage independence of thought and action.

Exhibit 12.3 Continued

Specific Tort	Definition	Defenses
Fraud	Misrepresentation of a material fact made with the intent to deceive	
Infliction of Emotional Distress (can be done intentionally or negligently)	Action that causes a serious indignity or severe emotional distress	Consent Privilege for intentional infliction
Intentional Interference with Contractual Relations	Action that induces a party to break his or her contract	Privilege
Interference with Prospective Advantage	Interference with a potential contract or business relationship	Privilege
Invasion of Privacy	Unwarranted intrusions on the privacy of another	Consent Privilege
Misappropriation of Trade Secrets	The taking of secret business data or information for unauthorized use	Lack of secrecy
Racketeer Influenced and Corrupt Organizations Act (RICO)	Violation of federal statute by engaging in a pattern of racketeering activity	
Trespass Real property or personal property	Harm or infringement of the property of others	Privilege Consent Necessity

Necessity   Whenever a person enters another's land for self-protection, the law recognizes that as a necessity. Courts will not award the nominal damages ordinarily available for trespass. For example, if you are in a boat on a lake and a storm suddenly develops, you may enter a private cove, tie up to a private dock, and take shelter on the land in order to protect yourself. Due to the necessity, no trespass exists. However, the law permits the landowner to collect actual losses if, for example, you also use the food in his or her cabin. This example illustrates a *private necessity*, because the necessity applies only to you. There is also *public necessity*, where the act is for the public good. An example would be if you destroy a person's orchard to prevent a fast-moving fire from spreading to nearby homes.

Truth   Truth is one of the best defenses for the tort of defamation. A defendant will win if the defendant can prove that the statement was true. For example, if Tulio accuses Derek, an owner of a pawn shop, of being a crook and Derek sues for defamation, Tulio will win if Tulio can prove that Derek is a "fence" for stolen property.

NEGLIGENCE

Negligence occurs when a person fails to act as a reasonable and prudent person would act. *Negligence* exists when four conditions are met: (1) the defendant must have owed the plaintiff a duty; (2) the defendant must have breached the duty by acting in a particular manner or failing to act as required; (3) the breach of that duty must be the actual, as well as the legal, cause of the plaintiff's injury; and (4) the breach must cause a harm or injury that the law recognizes and for which money damages may be awarded by a court. In addition, the law requires that the type, but not necessarily the degree, of harm was or should have been foreseeable to the actor. *Foreseeability*, in negligence, addresses the likelihood that something will happen in the future. It is determined by what a "reasonable and prudent person" would expect in those or similar circumstances.

In addition to the general tort of negligence, the courts have developed a number of special types of negligence, including malpractice by accountants, doctors, and lawyers. Malpractice occurs when the professional does not perform as a reasonable member of his or her profession would. Courts have also developed torts dealing with the hiring of employees, including negligent hiring, negligent retention, and negligent supervision. These torts are discussed in Chapter 14.

Duty

The reasonable-and-prudent-person rule has been established in negligence law to determine the "degree" of duty each person owes to others. With respect to negligence, everyone has a duty to avoid behavior that does not measure up to the standards of the reasonable and prudent person. This standard is more difficult to define, explain, and apply than is the standard of simple duty applied to intentional torts. Generally, the law states that *reasonable duty* is a standard of ordinary skill and care, based on the facts of each individual case.

If, while you are quietly fishing on the shore of a lake, you see Lor 100 feet away fall out of his boat and begin to drown, do you have a legal duty to help him? The answer is *no*! You do not owe a duty to Lor because you did not create the hazard in the first place. On the other hand, suppose you were in the boat with Lor and you pushed him out of the boat as a joke, unaware that Lor could not swim. Now you will have a duty to help him. Since you have created the hazard, you have a duty to help Lor. Similarly, if Ali rents boats she is not likely to have a duty to ensure the safety of every person who rents a boat from her rental business. Assume Ali rents a boat to Shannon, the boat springs a leak because it is improperly maintained, and this causes Shannon to drown. Ali is likely to have breached her duty to rent safe boats and she could face liability for negligence due to her breach of duty.

To test for a duty in any particular situation, the law has constructed a person against whom the conduct of the defendant will be compared. As stated earlier, this purely hypothetical person is known as the *reasonable and prudent person*. It is important to remember that this "person" is not perfect: He or she is merely reasonable and prudent. Three areas help to define the reasonable and prudent person: knowledge, investigation, and judgment. There is also a statutory standard that is applied in certain situations.

Knowledge   As the amount of knowledge in the world increases, so does the amount of knowledge that the reasonable and prudent person is expected to possess. In this sense, the law presumes that everyone has complete knowledge of the law. If we have no knowledge of the law, how can we be expected to obey it?

Investigation   Investigation is closely related to knowledge. It is our obligation to find out. We assume that a reasonable person knows certain information. We also assume that the reasonable person will do research or tests to discover additional information. Before you drive a car, for example, the law presumes that you will check that the brakes are working properly. If you are a drug manufacturer, the law presumes that you will have investigated whether your drug will cause any harmful side effects. If you have failed to do adequate testing, you will have violated the standard of care of a reasonable and prudent person. Note that a harmful side effect does not necessarily mean that the manufacturer is negligent. Some drugs are still beneficial for the majority of the patients even though they have harmful side effects for some people. In this case, distribution of the drug with proper warnings attached is permitted. The adequacy of the warning was an issue in a lawsuit against a manufacturer of the oral polio vaccine when a father alleged that he contracted polio as a result of his daughter receiving the vaccine.[16]

Judgment   You have probably heard people say that one person has "good" judgment or another has "bad" judgment. The law measures both persons against the same standard. In a tort case, the defendant must have acted reasonably or else he or she will be found to have breached the duty of reasonable care. We have no universal rules. The outcome always depends on the facts of each case. A missing fact, discovered later, can change the outcome. Before beginning any activity, the law expects people to consider questions such as: What is the likelihood that this particular activity will harm someone else? If harm might occur, what is the likely extent of the harm? What must I do to avoid the risk to others?

Assume that Margaret just purchased a new rifle and wants to test it and adjust the scope for maximum accuracy for the deer season. Margaret finds an isolated field in the country and sets up a target at the base of a bald hill 300 yards away. No one else is present. After firing the first shot, however, she begins to attract a crowd. Assume that with each shot the crowd gets larger. At what point does she stop shooting to avoid injury to an innocent person? The decision to stop involves the exercise of reason. The exercise of reason is *judgment.*

Statutory Standard   In some cases, the law solves the problem of limits, like the ones just raised, by providing a standard in a statute, regulation, or ordinance. For example, most state traffic laws say that when it begins to get dark, all drivers are required to turn on their headlights. If Max is traveling down a road at night without his lights on, and he hits and injures a pedestrian, the law will conclude that Max breached a standard of reasonableness no matter what his excuse. Most of these statutes provide a criminal penalty, but that penalty is irrelevant in a tort case. In most states, breaching the statutory standard is *negligence per se* (inherent negligence; negligence without a need for further proof). However, the states are not in agreement as to whether this should be treated as a *conclusive presumption* where evidence to the contrary is not permitted. Some states, such as California,[17] instead treat negligence per se as a *rebuttable presumption.* The person is allowed to present evidence that, under the circumstances, violating the statutory standard was the most careful behavior.

Res Ipsa Loquitur

In general, the plaintiff has to prove that the defendant caused injury by not adhering to the reasonable-and-prudent person standard. *Res ipsa loquitur* relaxes that standard. *Res ipsa loquitur* means "the thing speaks for itself." To apply *res ipsa loquitur* in a case, the injury must meet the following three tests: (1) this occurrence would ordinarily not happen in the absence of someone's negligence; (2) the occurrence must be caused by a device within the exclusive control of the defendant(s); and (3) the plaintiff in no way contributed to his or her own injury. For example, if Nicole agrees to an operation to have her infected tonsils removed and after the surgery Nicole has a surgical instrument embedded in her throat, direct testimony is not necessary. It speaks for itself; someone in the surgery room was negligent. In some states, *res ipsa loquitur* creates a presumption of negligence. Its effect is to shift the burden of proof from the plaintiff to the defendant(s). In this hypothetical, the hospital personnel and the surgeons will each need to show that he or she exercised reasonable care. In other states, the burden of proof remains with the plaintiff. *Res ipsa loquitur* creates an inference of negligence. The jury then weighs the evidence, including the inference of negligence.

Causation

Causation is central to the law of negligence. It has two components: actual cause and "legal" cause, which is also called proximate cause.

Actual Cause   The court determines whether X, an act by one party, is the actual cause of Y, an injury to the other party. The court examines whether "but for" the occurrence of act X, would result Y have happened. This is called the *but-for test.* For example, a defendant in an automobile accident case may have failed to signal a turn properly. But if the accident would have happened even if he had signaled properly, the failure to signal is not the actual cause of the accident. It fails the but-for test.

Proximate Cause   *After* actual cause has been established, the focus shifts to *policy questions.* What the court decides here is whether the law should hold the defendant liable. At some point the law will say, "Enough." Beyond this point the defendant will not be held liable. To solve these policy questions, the law has developed a three-pronged test:

1. What is the likelihood that this particular conduct will injure other persons?
2. If injury should occur, what is the degree of seriousness of the injury?
3. What interest must the defendant sacrifice to avoid the risk of causing the injury?

For example, if the defendant is negligent with respect to Emilio, and Carla tries to rescue Emilio and suffers some injury as a result, the defendant may be held liable for Carla's injuries as well as Emilio's. It is foreseeable that people may try to rescue someone in peril. If Emilio is the one who is negligent and he puts himself in danger, he will probably be liable to Carla if she is injured trying to rescue him.

Harm

If the plaintiff is not injured, the defendant will not be held liable for damages. For example, Chad, speeding down a city street at 70 miles per hour, is clearly breaching the duty to drive in a safe and reasonable manner; but if no one is injured, no one can successfully sue for negligence. If harm is caused, it must be of a type for which the law allows damages to be awarded. For example, hurt feelings may be real, but the law does not generally award damages for hurt feelings.

Defenses to Negligence

Contributory Negligence   One defense in common law is *contributory negligence*, which bars recovery. (In the legal sense, *bar* means to prevent or to stop.) Suppose Justin wears a black raincoat at night and jaywalks on campus; he is hit by a car. If Justin sues and the driver can prove Justin actually contributed to the injury, Justin will lose in a state that applies contributory negligence.

Comparative Negligence   In a number of jurisdictions, the doctrine of contributory negligence has been replaced by the doctrine of *comparative negligence* through judicial precedents or legislative acts. Here, the fact finder (usually the jury) determines to what degree the plaintiff contributed to his or her own injury. Comparative negligence is generally perceived to be a more just method since it allocates fault; however, it may be difficult for the trier of fact to determine the relative faults. For example, assume Jason has $100,000 in damages, but he contributed 35 percent to his injury. Jason can recover the amount of his damages reduced by the amount that his conduct contributed to the incident. In this example he will be awarded $65,000. In a contributory negligence jurisdiction he would recover nothing.

Jurisdictions generally select from three variations of comparative negligence. *Pure* comparative negligence allows the plaintiff to recover no matter how negligent he or she was. (For example, the California Supreme Court adopted pure comparative negligence in *Li v. Yellow Cab Co.*[18]) However, some jurisdictions feel it would be unfair to allow the plaintiff to recover if he or she was the primary cause of the injury, for example, if the plaintiff was 95 percent responsible for causing the accident. Consequently, two other variations prevent recovery by the party who was mostly to blame. One version only permits recovery if the plaintiff contributed less than 50 percent of the negligence to his or her injury. This is commonly called the "less than" type of comparative negligence. This is probably the most common variety of comparative negligence. Another version allows recovery if the plaintiff contributed 50 percent or less to his or her injury, which is commonly called the "equal to or less than" version. The differences may appear minor, but they are significant to the parties of a lawsuit who may be denied recovery because the jury concluded that they were each 50 percent at fault.

Comparative negligence becomes even more difficult to apply when there are more than two parties. States have different ways of handling multiple party situations.[19] The effect of comparative negligence laws may be minimal in automobile accidents in "no fault" states. Medical groups, insurance groups, and others advocate for change in the tort liability system, particularly as it applies to their businesses. This is often called *tort reform* since they want to change or reform the tort system.

Assumption of the Risk   Common law developed a doctrine in which the defendant will win if the defendant can prove that the plaintiff voluntarily assumed a known risk. For example, have you ever examined cigarette packages? They bear various warnings, some of which are "Surgeon General's Warning: Smoking by pregnant women may result in fetal injury, premature birth, and low birth weight," or "Quitting smoking now greatly reduces serious risks to your health," or "Cigarette smoke contains carbon monoxide." Historically, a longtime cigarette smoker who contracted lung cancer and sued the cigarette manufacturer would lose because the manufacturer defended on the basis of the plaintiff's voluntary assumption of the risk. (Some courts are now reexamining tobacco company liability in light of new scientific evidence.)

Courts will generally apply assumption of the risk to sports when the risk of injury should be obvious, such as the risk to a skier who breaks her leg while skiing on a mountain slope or the risk of a variety of injuries for a person who participates in skydiving. Even when the activity is risky, generally courts will hold that the customer does not assume the risk of *all* possible types of injury. The business can still be liable if the customer is hurt in an unexpected manner. For example, a court held that a scuba outfitter was liable when the pilot returned to shore, leaving two customers in the ocean. The employees on the boat negligently failed to count all the customers before leaving the dive site.

The traditional view of assumption of the risk was that it prevented recovery. However, some states that have adopted comparative negligence now view assumption of the risk as a factor in determining the comparative negligence of the parties.[20]

An Ounce of Prevention

You can improve your chances in court by making sure that your customers are aware of the risks of the activity, whether the risks are being hit by a fly ball or spraining an ankle. In sports, you may prepare an explanatory video that covers the common risks. One of the advantages of the video is that it helps standardize the explanation so that all customers hear and see the key points. After the customers view the video, you can require them to sign a statement that they are aware of the risks and that they agree to assume them.

It hurts a business's reputation when customers are injured, even when the customer assumes the risk. Consequently you should try to minimize the risk of injury. Courts often state that although a business does not have a duty to remove all the risks involved in an activity, it has a duty not to increase the risks involved.

STRICT LIABILITY

With respect to intentional torts, everyone has a duty to avoid such behavior. With respect to negligence, we have a duty to use reasonable care. This section examines situations in which the law states that we have an absolute duty to make something safe, regardless of whether we are at fault or not. This is called strict liability.

Whenever a person undertakes an extremely hazardous activity and it is foreseeable that injury may result, that person can be held "strictly liable" if injury does result, whether or not the person was at fault. *Strict liability* is imposed without regard to fault. For example, if you use explosives on your property and a blast breaks your neighbor's windows, you will be held liable no matter how careful you were in handling the explosives. Generally, the areas in which we have strict liability are set out in the applicable statutes and/or court precedents.[21]

The doctrine seems to be expanding in scope. Some U.S. courts have shifted from ultrahazardous activity to dangerous activity. Today, the following activities are considered strict liability activities in most states: the keeping of wild animals, the use of explosives, and dangerous activities. Some states have added strict liability for the owner of a motor vehicle if injury occurs when the driver operates the vehicle with the owner's permission.[22] Some states are also adding strict liability for the owners of dogs or specific breeds of dogs. California imposes strict liability on parents for the willful misconduct of their minor children. There is a $25,000 limit on this type of parental liability.[23] Strict liability does not automatically arise. It is created by court decisions or legislation.

NUISANCE

There are two types of nuisances—a private nuisance and a public nuisance. A *private nuisance* is the unreasonable interference with the interest of a person in the use or enjoyment of his or her land. An example would be a dairy farm that causes a foul smell on the property of its neighbor, Kahn. Kahn could sue for a private nuisance. For Kahn to recover, it must be a situation in which the interference would be offensive, inconvenient, or annoying to normal people in the community. Kahn must not be either an overly sensitive person or a person who is using his land in an overly sensitive manner. In most states the court will balance the utility of the defendant's conduct with the severity of the harm the defendant is inflicting. In many situations, the defendant's conduct is intentional, but that is not a requirement for the tort of nuisance. Nuisance can be based on intentional acts, negligent acts, or strict liability. For example, there may be strict liability for storing explosives in a residential neighborhood. Nuisance should be distinguished from the tort of trespass. Trespass interferes with the owner's *exclusive* possession of the land, but nuisance interferes with the owner's *use and enjoyment* of the land.

A *public nuisance* causes an inconvenience or damage to the public at large (for example, if protestors block a highway). A private individual can only sue for a public nuisance if he or she suffers a different type of injury than that suffered by the rest of the public. The private individual does not need to own land to sue for his or her private harm. For example, if Oscar is operating a commercial fishery on a river that is polluted by the defendant's factory, Oscar can sue for this private harm.

PRODUCT LIABILITY

Product liability is a growing concern of businesses. Manufacturers and distributors of products may be held liable based on these legal theories: (1) fraud in the marketing of the product; (2) express or implied warranties (warranties will not be discussed in this chapter, since they are based on contract theories); (3) negligence; and (4) strict liability. People who are injured by a product may claim and attempt to prove more than one theory of liability since these theories are not mutually exclusive. Fraud in marketing will follow the general rules of fraud previously discussed in this chapter.

Negligence in product liability can include negligence in assembly, construction, design, instructions, labeling, and packaging. When an injured person uses the negligence theory for product liability, there must be a close causal connection between the negligence and the injury. The lawsuit will be subject to the usual defenses for negligence, including contributory negligence, comparative negligence, and assumption of the risk. To establish a negligent failure to warn claim, many states require the plaintiff to prove the following elements: (1) that the defendant designed the product; (2) that the defendant knew or had reason to know that the product was likely to be unreasonably dangerous; (3) that the defendant had no reason to believe that the users would realize the risk; (4) that the defendant failed to use ordinary care in warning the user of the risk of harm; and (5) that the failure to warn directly caused the injury. In addition, the product must malfunction or fail.[24]

Strict liability for products is clarified by § 402A of the *Restatement (Second) of Torts*,[25] a publication of the American Law Institute (ALI).[26] This section has been adopted by most states. It is used by courts as an authoritative reference, but the *Restatement* is not binding on them. It becomes precedence in court only after a judge has relied on a section and referred to it in his or her opinion.

Section 402A of the *Restatement (Second) of Torts* establishes the strict liability rule: A seller will be held liable for a product that contains a defect or is unreasonably dangerous to use. ("Unreasonably dangerous" seems vague to both laypersons and lawyers; there have been many court decisions attempting to define and clarify the term.) The defect must be in the product when it leaves the control of the defendant. As with other forms of strict liability, the plaintiff does not need to prove negligence or fraud in order to recover. Generally, the plaintiff must show (1) that strict liability applies to this situation; (2) that the product had a defect when it left the defendant's possession or was unreasonably dangerous; and (3) that the plaintiff was harmed. Since this is a tort cause of action, the seller cannot avoid liability by disclaiming it. Contributory or comparative negligence by the plaintiff cannot be used as a defense. The manufacturer may prove the following defenses depending on the situation—assumption of the risk, product misuse by the plaintiff, and *obviousness of hazard* (the risk in the product is evident, such as the risk of being cut when using a sharp knife).

An Ounce of Prevention

You may manufacture products and/or sell products manufactured by others. Consequently, you have potential product liability. Some products are extremely dangerous, and you may decide that the risk is too high and that you should avoid selling the product all together. Other products are potentially dangerous, but they have value and you may decide to sell them. You can reduce your liability by using care in your advertisements not to promise more than the product can deliver. The business should also label the product carefully and include the appropriate warnings. Since the Liebeck case (discussed below), McDonald's has improved its warnings.

You should try to follow the "better safe than sorry" maxim. If there is a chance that your customers will use the product in an unsafe manner, you should warn against such use. You should give the warning even if the danger seems obvious. This is especially true if the warning will not significantly increase costs. The tag attached to a hair-dryer cord warning against use around water is an inexpensive warning. Likewise a warning telling users not to use a curling iron to curl eyelashes is inexpensive. Both warnings reduce the risk to the businesses selling the products.

There is also a strict liability failure to warn theory. Missouri, for example, uses five elements for a strict liability failure to warn claim. They are: (1) the defendant sold the product in the course of its business; (2) the product was unreasonably dangerous at the time of sale when it is used as reasonably anticipated and without knowledge of its characteristics; (3) the defendant did not give an adequate warning of the danger; (4) the product was used in a reasonably anticipated manner; and (5) the plaintiff was harmed as a direct result of the product being sold without an adequate warning.[27] The courts often assume that if adequate warnings were given, the user would have followed them. This is a rebuttable presumption in some states, including Missouri.[28] Courts also consider whether adequate information is available absent a warning from the manufacturer.

The following case illustrates how a product liability lawsuit can develop from injury through settlement. On February 27, 1992, Stella Liebeck was sitting in the passenger seat of a parked car in Albuquerque, New Mexico. Liebeck, 79 years old, was trying to remove the lid from a Styrofoam cup of coffee to add cream and sugar when she spilled hot coffee. She suffered third-degree burns to her groin area. The car did not have cup holders and it had a sloped dashboard. When initially she could not open it, Liebeck put the cup between her legs to secure it.[29] She had bought the coffee four minutes earlier at a McDonald's drive-through window. McDonald's made and sold coffee at 180 to 190 degrees Fahrenheit. By comparison, coffee served at home is generally 135 to 140 degrees, and other businesses sell coffee at substantially lower temperatures than McDonald's. During the trial, the McDonald's quality assurance manager testified that a burn hazard exists with any food substance served at 140 degrees or higher.[30]

"Liebeck was hospitalized for more than a week. Despite a series of skin grafts, she was partially disabled for almost two years and permanently disfigured." After the accident, Liebeck wrote to McDonald's asking them to pay "any medical costs that were not covered by Medicare and the lost wages for her daughter who took care of Liebeck while she recovered." This would have been between $10,000 and $15,000. McDonald's offered her only $800. Liebeck hired an attorney and sued, seeking compensation for her losses and punitive damages based on the theory that McDonald's knew its coffee could cause serious burns and it acted with reckless indifference to the welfare of its customers. Liebeck offered to settle for $300,000, but McDonald's would not agree. A court-ordered mediator recommended that McDonald's settle for $225,000, but it refused to do so.

Prior to hearing the evidence, the jurors leaned toward McDonald's side and thought Liebeck's suit was frivolous. The evidence presented at the one-week trial changed the jurors' minds. "McDonald's admitted that it served its coffee very hot and that it did so because marketing studies 'showed that customers prefer their coffee very hot.'... [T]he evidence showed that: McDonald's coffee was dangerously hot and McDonald's knew it; McDonald's coffee was served hotter than coffee served elsewhere; most McDonald's customers were unaware that McDonald's coffee was both hotter than coffee served elsewhere and that, if spilled, it posed a serious risk to their safety; and McDonald's knew and did not care that its customers were not aware of the danger because hotter coffee meant greater sales." The jury deliberated for only four hours. "They found ... that Liebeck had suffered $200,000 in injuries and that both Liebeck and McDonald's were responsible." The jury decided that Liebeck was 20 percent responsible and McDonald's was 80 percent responsible for failing to protect and adequately warn its customer. After deducting the 20 percent, the jury awarded Liebeck $160,000 in compensatory damages. The jury decided that McDonald's conduct was reprehensible "in serving coffee that, based on more than 700 complaints, it knew could cause and had caused other incidents of severe burns." The jury awarded Liebeck $2.7 million in punitive damages, the amount it calculated was equal to two days of McDonald's coffee revenues. The trial judge later reduced the amount of punitive damages. It is not known how much Liebeck actually received because the parties then participated in another settlement conference. As a condition of the settlement McDonald's required that the amount not be disclosed. Inaccurate reporting of this case fueled the tort reform movement for some time.[31]

TORT LIABILITY OF BUSINESS ENTITIES

Before leaving this introduction to tort law, we should mention that businesses *can* be held liable for the torts of their employees. Liability is generally imposed through the doctrine of *respondeat superior*. *Respondeat superior* means that the superior should answer or pay for the torts of employees that occur in the course and scope of employment. *Respondeat superior* does not excuse the employee; the employee will be held liable in addition to his or her employer. *Respondeat superior* is discussed in more detail in Chapter 14.

An Ounce of Prevention

When a business commits a tort, most often an employee is the one who commits it. So, you should try to reduce the likelihood that an employee will commit a tort. You also need to strike a balance between micromanaging your employees and giving them freedom to do whatever they please. You should consider the types of jobs and the types of employees in determining what kind of supervision is appropriate. You can be liable for special forms of negligence, such as negligent hiring, negligent promotion, and negligent supervision. For example, one construction company hired day laborers to clean a construction site. One worker was assigned to collect partially empty canisters that had contained fuel for torches and welding equipment. He decided that they were too heavy, so he rolled and kicked them instead of picking them up. This resulted in an explosion in the building.

You may want to write a procedures manual to educate your employees. What seems obvious to you may not be obvious to all the employees. If you decide to write a manual, it is important that you and your employees follow it. Courts may determine that you are negligent if your employees fail to follow your manual.

Contemporary Case

In this Contemporary Case the court is applying the requirements for establishing defamation under New York state law. Note that there are several versions of defamation under New York law, including defamation by implication and defamation based on a mixture of opinion and fact. Regardless of the type of defamation, the plaintiff must show that the allegedly defamatory language is directed at him or her.

SORVILLO v. ST. FRANCIS PREPARATORY SCHOOL

607 Fed. Appx. 22, 2015 U.S. App. LEXIS 6424 (2nd Cir. 2015)

FACTS Elizabeth Sorvillo, a former employee of St. Francis Preparatory School, filed suit against the school, alleging defamation. Sorvillo's complaint is based on a letter sent by St. Francis's principal, Brother Leonard Conway (Brother Leonard) to alumni, parents, faculty members, administrators, trustees and others in the St. Francis community. Brother Leonard's letter stated that he had received several disturbing emails from members of the school's community stating that the content of numerous recent 'blog' postings on Sorvillo's internet site were defamatory and had crossed over the line of free speech. He then stated that he was investigating those postings with the assistance of legal counsel, and he added that speech is not "free" when its purpose is to bully, to convey hatred, or to spread malicious lies and unsubstantiated rumors.

The District Court dismissed Sorvillo's suit, and she appealed to the Circuit Court.

ISSUE Is Sorvillo entitled to a trial on her defamation claim?

HOLDING No. Sorvillo's complaint failed to state a claim since there were no allegations that she had made any of the postings on the blog.

REASONING Excerpts from the Summary Order of the Court:

... We review the district court's dismissal of Sorvillo's defamation claims de novo, accepting all factual allegations in the complaint as true and drawing all reasonable inferences in the plaintiff's favor. ... On appeal, Sorvillo advances two primary arguments. First, she argues that the district court erred by "erroneously characteriz[ing] [her] claim as one based on a defamatory implication." ... Second, she argues that under the correct legal standard, the district court had no basis on which to dismiss her complaint.

To establish libel under New York law, a plaintiff must prove five elements: "(1) a written defamatory factual statement [of and] concerning the plaintiff; (2) publication to a third party; (3) fault; (4) falsity of the defamatory statement; and (5) special damages or *per se* actionability." ..."Whether particular words are defamatory presents a legal question to be resolved by the court[s] in the first instance." ... It is "the responsibility of the jury to determine whether the plaintiff has actually been defamed ... [but] a threshold issue for resolution by the court is whether the statement alleged to have caused plaintiff an injury is reasonably susceptible to the defamatory meaning imputed to it." ...

While a plaintiff generally must plead that the defendant made specific false statements of fact in order to make out a prima facie case of defamation, there are several exceptions to this rule. One exception is defamation by implication. Under New York law, defamation by implication is "premised not on direct [false] statements but on false suggestions, impressions and implications arising from otherwise truthful statements." ... Defamation by implication occurs where "[a] combination of individual statements which in themselves may not be defamatory might lead the reader to draw an inference that is damaging to the plaintiff." ...

Another exception to this general rule is mixed opinion-fact defamation (also sometimes referred to as "mixed opinion defamation"). Under New York law, a plaintiff may maintain a mixed opinion-fact defamation claim where ... [the defendant] makes otherwise non-actionable statements of opinion, but where

> the statement of opinion implies that it is based upon facts which justify the opinion but are unknown to those reading or hearing it.... The actionable element of a "mixed opinion" is not the false opinion itself—it is the implication that the speaker knows certain facts, unknown to his audience, which support his opinion and are detrimental to the person about whom he is speaking ...

[The] Restatement (Second) of Torts § 566 ... says "A defamatory communication may consist of a statement in the form of an opinion, but a statement of this nature is actionable only if it implies the allegation of undisclosed defamatory facts as the basis for the opinion." That said, where "a statement of opinion ... is accompanied by a recitation of the facts on which it is based or ... does not imply the existence of undisclosed underlying facts," a mixed opinion-fact defamation claim is not actionable. ...

While we agree with Sorvillo that the district court mischaracterized her complaint as one alleging "defamation by implication," rather than "mixed opinion-fact defamation," we nevertheless affirm the district court's dismissal of the defamation claim because, even under the correct standard, Sorvillo's complaint failed to state a claim upon which relief may be granted. ... First, as the New York Court of Appeals has held, "a statement of opinion that is accompanied by a recitation of the facts on which it is based or one that does not imply the existence of undisclosed underlying facts," is not actionable. ... None of the three statements in the letter indicated

that Brother Leonard had any additional facts upon which his opinions were based. To the contrary, the first statement in the letter expressly shared with the reader the basis of Brother Leonard's opinion, namely that he "received several disturbing emails from members of [the St. Francis] community stating that the content of numerous recent 'blog' postings on [an] internet site [were] defamatory." Nothing in this statement indicated that he had any additional facts other than those that had been presented by the e-mails he received from individuals within his community. The second statement asserts that Brother Leonard was in the process of investigating the postings and evaluating all potential remedial actions with St. Francis's legal counsel. Far from implying that Brother Leonard had any knowledge about Sorvillo that he was not sharing with his readers, the letter explained that he was in the process of gathering additional information. Finally, the third statement—that "[s]peech is not 'free' when its purpose is to bully, to convey hatred, or to spread malicious lies and unsubstantiated rumors"—is pure opinion and does not concern or imply any facts about Sorvillo.

In addition, even a mixed opinion-fact defamation claim must be "of and concerning" the plaintiff. ... [Precedents establish that "[t]he 'of and concerning' requirement stands as a significant limitation on the universe of those who may seek a legal remedy for communications they think to be false and defamatory and to have injured them."] Here, as the district court correctly explained, the allegedly defamatory statements were made about the authors of the blog posts, and were not "of and concerning" Sorvillo in her capacity as the manager of the website ...

Because we conclude that Sorvillo's complaint failed to state a claim, we need not consider the defendants' argument that Brother Leonard's statements were protected by a qualified privilege. We have considered Sorvillo's remaining arguments and find them to be without merit. For the reasons given, we *AFFIRM* the judgment of the district court.

Short Answer Questions

1. Late one night Sonia, an employee at Better Burger Hut, was assigned to clean the eating area and empty the trash cans. She took the bags holding the trash to the dumpster outside. The dumpster was hidden in a cinderblock structure in the center of the parking lot. When it began to rain, Sonia hurried back into the restaurant and forgot to close the metal doors. She left them protruding into the parking lot. Later, when Tom tried to back out of his parking spot, the doors interfered with his line of vision. Tom ran into Zoe's car. Can Zoe successfully sue Sonia and Better Burger Hut in addition to Tom? Why? If so, what legal basis should Zoe use?

2. Blake Flovin, a high school wrestler, claims that he contracted *herpes gladiatorum* during a recent tournament. "Contracting the disease during matches from fellow wrestlers or the mats themselves is not uncommon." It is sometimes called "mat herpes." Wrestlers have "skin checks" before the matches and athletes with visible, active infections are not permitted to compete. However, wrestlers sometimes cover lesions with makeup or adhesive bandages in order to compete. It is also possible to spread the virus during the incubation period even if lesions are not present. The herpes virus can become dormant but it never goes away. Do high school and college wrestlers assume the risk of catching herpes? Why?[32]

3. E-Trade had a commercial created for the 2010 Super Bowl. It shows an E-Trade baby explaining to his cute baby girlfriend that he did not call because he was busy diversifying his portfolio on E-Trade. She asks him, "And that milkaholic Lindsay wasn't over?" Lindsay Lohan has filed a $100 million libel lawsuit against E-Trade. Should she succeed? Why or why not?[33]

You Decide...

1. In 2007 Terry Bollea, a.k.a. Hulk Hogan, had consensual sex with Heather Clem, the wife of Todd Clem. Clem was a friend of Bollea at the time. The sexual encounter was videotaped without Bollea's knowledge. Gawker Media obtained a copy of the video, made a one minute and 40 seconds excerpt, added a graphic description, and posted it online in October 2012.

Gawker, which claims to be an irreverent source of news, maintained that it has the right to free expression and freedom of the press in posting the video. Gawker Media and its chief owner "argue that Mr. Bollea is a flashy celebrity who in radio appearances and writings had often discussed details of his sex life, stoking public fascination that . . . made the topic fair game for journalists—a matter of 'public concern.'" The existence of the tape had been discussed in the media and by Bollea himself before Gawker posted the excerpt. Bollea sued for invasion of privacy. Bollea's attorneys claimed that at least seven million people viewed the video.

In a trial in 2016 the jury awarded Bollea $115 million in damages and $25 million in punitive damages. The judge ordered that the sex tape be sealed. Assume that Gawker Media's appeal has been filed in your court.

How would *you* decide this case? Be certain that you explain and justify your answer.

(See Erik Eckholm, "Hulk Hogan's Suit Over Sex Tape May Test Limits of Online Press Freedom," *The New York Times*, March 5, 2016, and Greg Toppo, "Jury Awards Hulk Hogan $25 Million in Punitive Damages for Posting Sex Tape," *USA TODAY*, March 21, 2016, http://www.usatoday.com/story/news/2016/03/21/jury-awards-hulk-hogan-25-million-punitive-damages-posting-sex-tape/82093604/ (accessed March 23, 2016).)

2. Raymond Gallie exited the 210 Freeway at a high rate of speed in his Ford Mustang. He was traveling between 70 and 86 miles per hour when he slammed into a line of vehicles stopped at an intersection. This caused a chain reaction. One of the vehicles traveling between 42 and 43 miles per hour hit the back of Jaklin Mikhal Romine's Nissan Frontier pickup truck. Romine was wearing her seatbelt. The force of the collision caused Romine's seat back to collapse backwards. Romine slid up the seat striking her head on the vehicle's back seat. Because of the position, the seatbelt was not able to stop her from sliding backwards. She is now a quadriplegic. She sued various persons and entities, including Ikeda Engineering Corporation (Ikeda), which helped design the seat, and Vintec Co. (Vintec), which manufactured it. The parties stipulated prior to trial that "[T]here is no manufacturing defect in the 2000 Nissan Frontier Driver's seat.... That means the seat met the plans and specifications applicable to that component part." The jury allocated 20 percent of the fault for plaintiff's harm to Ikeda and Vintec and 80 percent of the fault to Gallie. Assume that Romine's appeal has been filed in your court.

How would *you* decide this case? Be certain that you explain and justify your answer. What additional information would you like to know? Why would this information be important? Do you agree with the assignment of fault? Why?

(See *Romine v. Johnson Controls, Inc.*, 169 Cal. Rptr. 3d 208, 2014 Cal. App. LEXIS 244 (CA App., Dist. 2, Div. 5, 2014).)

Notes

1. Richard Rinaldi, "Fracturing the Keystone: Why Fracktng [sic] in Pennsylvania Should Be Considered an Abnormally Dangerous Activity," 24 WIDENER L.J. 385 (2015).
2. Jack K. Levin, "Assault and Battery," I. General Principles, 6 Am Jur 2d Assault and Battery § 5, Need for bodily injury. *American Jurisprudence*, Second Edition, © 2013 West Group.
3. *Church of Scientology Int'l. v. Time Warner, Inc.*, 932 F. Supp. 589 (S.D.N.Y. 1996), 593-594.
4. *Braun v. Armour & Co.*, 254 N.Y. 514, 1930 N.Y. LEXIS 1096 (Ct of App. N.Y. 1930).
5. 376 U.S. 254, 1964 U.S. LEXIS 1655 (1964).
6. "Oprah in Trouble," *The Economist*, June 19, 1997, http://www.economist.com/node/597502 (accessed March 22, 2016); Paul McMasters, *The First Amendment and the Media*, "Section IV of Libel Law/Punitive Damages/Tort Actions: A," http://www.mediainstitute.org/ONLINE/FAM99/LPT_A.html (accessed March 22, 2016); Sam Howe Verhovek, "Talk of the Town: Burgers v. Oprah," *The New York Times*, January 21, 1998, http://www.nytimes.com/1998/01/21/us/talk-of-the-town-burgers-v-oprah.html (accessed March 22, 2016).
7. In some states, the tort is called deceit, or there may be a tort of deceit that is closely related to the tort of fraud.
8. "Mortician Training Schools' Wrongful Acts Were Not Insured," *Death Care Business Advisor*, September 4, 1997, Vol. 2, No. 5.
9. Laura Lambert, "Adele's Horror as Hacker Puts Pregnancy Scan Photo Online," *Daily Mail* (London), March 21, 2016.
10. National Conference of State Legislatures (NCSL), "State Laws about Social Media Privacy," January 29, 2016, http://www.ncsl.org/research/telecommunications-and-information-technology/state-laws-prohibiting-access-to-social-media-usernames-and-passwords.aspx (accessed March 23, 2016). For a list of state legislation proposed in 2015 and 2016, see National Conference of State Legislatures (NCSL), "Access to Social Media Usernames and Passwords," March 18, 2016, http://www.ncsl.org/research/telecommunications-and-information-technology/employer-access-to-social-media-passwords-2013.aspx (accessed March 23, 2016).

11. *Texas Tanks, Inc. v. Owens-Corning Fiberglass Corp.,* 99 F.3d 734 (5th Cir. 1996).

12. *Ibid.*

13. The Uniform Trade Secrets Act, with the 1985 amendments, has been adopted in Alabama, Alaska, Arizona, Colorado, Delaware, District of Columbia, Florida, Georgia, Hawaii, Idaho, Iowa, Kansas, Kentucky, Maine, Maryland, Michigan, Minnesota, Mississippi, Missouri, Montana, Nebraska, Nevada, New Hampshire, New Jersey, New Mexico, North Dakota, Ohio, Oklahoma, Oregon, Pennsylvania, South Carolina, South Dakota, Tennessee, Texas, U.S. Virgin Islands, Utah, Vermont, Virginia, Washington, West Virginia, Wisconsin, and Wyoming. In 2016 the act was introduced in New York and Massachusetts. The following states have adopted the 1979 act, but not the 1985 amendments: Arkansas, California, Connecticut, Illinois, Indiana, Louisiana, Puerto Rico, and Rhode Island. (Although technically Puerto Rico and the U.S. Virgin Islands are not states, the Uniform Law Commission treats them as states and for purposes of uniform laws we will also.) Email from Katie Robinson, Legislative Program Director & Communications Officer, Uniform Law Commission, March 23, 2016.

14. See 18 U.S.C., §§ 1961 *et seq.*

15. Michael Tarm, "No Punches, Just Praise as Tyson, Holyfield Meet," *Associated Press,* October 16, 2009.

16. Michael Riccardi, "Drug Manufacturer Must Warn of Risks," *The Legal Intelligencer,* July 15, 1999, 4.

17. See Justia, California Civil Jury Instructions (CACI), 418. Presumption of Negligence per se, https://www.justia.com/trials-litigation/docs/caci/400/418.html (accessed March 22, 2016).

18. 119 Cal. Rptr. 858, 532 P.2d 1226 (1975).

19. The Uniform Law Commission (ULC) has adopted the Uniform Apportionment of Tort Responsibility Act (2003). The purpose of this act is to provide rules for apportioning fault among multiple wrongdoers. ULC Web site, "Apportionment of Tort Responsibility Act Summary," http://www.uniformlaws.org/ActSummary.aspx?title=Apportionment%20of%20Tort%20Responsibility%20Act (accessed March 22, 2016).

20. See *Rountree v. Boise Baseball, LLC,* 296 P.3d 373, 379-380, 2013 Ida. LEXIS 55 (2013) discussing its precedents in *Salinas v. Vierstra,* 107 Idaho 984, 989, 695 P.2d 369, 374 (1985). In Idaho, implied assumption of risk does not bar recovery. An express oral or written statement could still bar recovery.

21. *Rylands v. Fletcher,* L.R. 3 H.L. 330 (1868), is credited with creating the legal doctrine of strict liability. See, for example, Richard Rinaldi, "Fracturing the Keystone: Why Fracktng [sic] in Pennsylvania Should Be Considered an Abnormally Dangerous Activity," 24 WIDENER L.J. 385 (2015), *supra* Note 1.

22. For example, California Vehicle Code, § 17150.

23. California Civil Code, § 1714.1.

24. *Tenbarge v. Ames Taping Tool Systems, Inc.,* 1999 U.S. App. LEXIS 15028 (8th Cir. 1999).

25. American Law Institute (ALI) adopted significant revisions to § 402A and published them in *Restatement (Third) of Torts: Product Liability.*

26. The *Restatement (Second) of Torts* states the drafting committee's preferred version of the common law of torts.

27. *Tenbarge v. Ames Taping Tool Systems, Inc.,* 1999 U.S. App. LEXIS 15028 (8th Cir. 1999), *supra* Note 24.

28. *Ibid.*

29. Ginny Carroll & Steven Waldman, "Are Lawyers Burning America?," *Newsweek,* March 20, 1995, United States Edition, 32.

30. 'Lectric Law Library's Stacks, *The Actual Facts about the McDonalds' Coffee Case,* http://www.lectlaw.com/files/cur78.htm/ (accessed March 22, 2016).

31. Most of the facts and all the quotes are from Caroline Forell, "*McTorts: The Social and Legal Impact of McDonald's Role in Tort Suits,*" 24 LOY. CONSUMER L. REV. 105 (2011).

32. Julia Prodis Sulek and Natalie Jacewicz, "Wrestlers Face Possible Exposure to Herpes Virus; Infected High School Student Urges Delay of State Championship Meet," *Monterey County Herald* (California), March 3, 2016, A1.

33. "Lohan Sues Over E-Trade Babies Spot," *Monterey County Herald* (California), March 10, 2010; Anne Neville, "The Best and Worst Commercials from Super Bowl XLIV, from Betty White to Danica Patrick," *Buffalo News* (New York), February 7, 2010, Online Edition, Blogs, Pop Stand.

13

Crimes and Business

Learning Objectives

After completing this chapter you should be able to

- Discuss the objectives of criminal law
- Describe how criminal law differs from tort law
- Recognize some of the common crimes
- Compare the defenses of duress, insanity, intoxication, and justification
- Explain some of the ways that businesses can commit crimes and be victims of crimes

Classic Case

This case is a Supreme Court decision that illustrates how a business can violate a criminal statute. Businesses, like individuals, have some protection from police searches and seizures. The business here contended that the search of its premises was unconstitutional but the court disagreed.

NEW YORK v. BURGER

482 U.S. 691, 1987 U.S. LEXIS 2725 (1987)

FACTS Joseph Burger is the owner of a junkyard that dismantles automobiles and sells their parts. Five officers of the Auto Crimes Division of the New York City Police Department entered Burger's junkyard to conduct an inspection pursuant to New York Vehicle & Traffic Law § 415-a5.[1] The Division conducts five to ten inspections each day. The officers asked to see Burger's license and his record of the automobiles and parts in his possession. Burger replied that he did not have a license or a record. The officers then announced their intention to conduct a § 415-a5 inspection. The officers checked the vehicle identification numbers of several vehicles and determined that some were stolen. Burger was arrested and charged with possession of stolen property and operating as an unregistered vehicle dismantler.

ISSUES Is the warrantless search of an automobile junkyard unconstitutional, or does it fall within the exception for administrative inspections of highly regulated industries? Is an administrative inspection unconstitutional just because the ultimate purpose of the regulatory statute is the deterrence of criminal behavior and the inspection may disclose violations of the criminal code?

HOLDINGS No, the search is constitutional because an automobile junkyard is a highly regulated industry. No, the fact that the statute was intended to deter criminal behavior and the inspection may disclose crimes does not make it unconstitutional.

REASONING Excerpts from the opinion of Justice Blackmun:

... The Court ... has recognized that the Fourth Amendment's prohibition on unreasonable searches and seizures is applicable to commercial premises.... An expectation of privacy in commercial premises ... is ... less than a similar expectation in an individual's home.... [There is even less expectation in "closely regulated" industries.] Because the owner or operator of commercial premises in a "closely regulated" industry has a reduced expectation of privacy, the warrant and probable-cause requirements ... have lessened application.... This warrantless inspection[,] ... even in the context of a pervasively regulated business, will be deemed to be reasonable only so long as three criteria are met. First, there must be a "substantial" government interest that informs the regulatory scheme pursuant to which the inspection is made.... Second, the warrantless inspections must be "necessary to further [the] regulatory scheme." ... Finally, ... the regulatory statute must perform the two basic functions of a warrant: it must advise the owner of the commercial premises that the search is being made pursuant to the law and has a properly defined scope, and it must limit the discretion of the inspecting officers.... To perform this first function, the statute must be "sufficiently comprehensive and defined that the owner of commercial property cannot help but be aware that his property will be subject to periodic inspections undertaken for specific purposes." ...

Searches made pursuant to § 415-a5 ... clearly fall within this established exception to the warrant requirement for administrative inspections in "closely regulated" businesses.... First, the nature of the regulatory statute reveals that the operation of a junkyard ... is a "closely regulated" business in the State of New York.... The provisions regulating the activity of vehicle dismantling are extensive. An operator cannot engage in this industry without first obtaining a license, which means that he must meet the registration requirements and must pay a fee. . . . [T]he operator must maintain a police book recording the acquisition and disposition of motor vehicles and vehicle parts, and make such records and inventory available for inspection by the police or any agent of the Department of Motor Vehicles. The operator also must display his registration number prominently at his place of business, on business documentation, and on vehicles and parts that pass through his business. . . . [T]he person engaged in this activity is subject to criminal penalties, as well as to loss of license or civil fines, for failure to comply with these provisions. . . . That other States besides New York have imposed similarly extensive regulations on automobile junkyards further supports the "closely regulated" status of this industry. . . .

[A]n administrative scheme may have the same ultimate purpose as penal laws, even if its regulatory goals are narrower. . . . New York, like many States, faces a serious social problem in automobile theft and has a substantial interest in regulating the vehicle-dismantling industry because of this problem. The New York penal laws address automobile theft by punishing it or [punishing] the possession of stolen property, including possession by individuals in the business of buying and selling property. . . . [T]he State . . . has devised a regulatory manner of dealing with this problem. Section 415-a . . . serves the regulatory goals of seeking to ensure that vehicle dismantlers are legitimate businesspersons and that stolen vehicles and vehicle parts passing through automobile junkyards can be identified. . . .

The discovery of evidence of crimes in the course of an otherwise proper administrative inspection does not render that search illegal or the administrative scheme suspect. . . . Finally, we fail to see any constitutional significance in the fact that police officers, rather than "administrative" agents, are permitted to conduct the § 415-a5 inspection. . . . [M]any States do not have the resources to assign the enforcement of a particular administrative scheme to a specialized agency. So long as a regulatory scheme is properly administrative, it is not rendered illegal by the fact that the inspecting officer has the power to arrest individuals for violations other than those created by the scheme itself. . . .

Accordingly, the judgment of the New York Court of Appeals is reversed, and the case is remanded to that court for further proceedings not inconsistent with this opinion.

INTRODUCTION

Why should a business law textbook contain a chapter on criminal law? The reason is that businesses are constantly confronted with the *effects* of crimes such as computer crimes, embezzlement, and forgery. As can be seen in the Classic Case, a business can be subjected to police searches and business owners can commit crimes. To prevent a crime from happening, or to deal effectively with a crime once it has occurred, you need to know what constitutes a crime and the legal consequences of criminal conduct. You also need to be aware that technology is changing some aspects of criminal law. Social media can make it easier for criminals to locate victims, such as burglars who use postings to identify when no one will be home or kidnappers who befriend children and convince them to run away. In some cases it is also making things easier for law enforcement. For example, Cathy Bernstein was driving her Ford in Florida when she allegedly hit two vehicles. She left the scenes of both accidents. However, her vehicle was equipped with Ford Sync Emergency Assistance technology, which automatically called the emergency dispatcher. When the dispatcher contacted Bernstein, she denied being in an accident. The dispatcher was not convinced. Police were sent to Bernstein's home, where they located her damaged vehicle.[2]

Criminal law developed through a long history of precedents. However, most states have codified their criminal laws. As you should expect, the exact rules vary from state to state. Begin by referring to Exhibit 13.1, which summarizes the primary distinctions between civil law and criminal law. Try to distinguish between the two areas throughout this chapter. Remember that one action or series of actions may constitute *both* a civil wrong and a criminal wrong. Generally the civil suit will occur independently of the criminal suit. Some jurisdictions permit civil and criminal matters to be joined into one lawsuit. It will also be helpful to look at Exhibit 13.2, which examines the six steps in a typical criminal proceeding.

Exhibit 13.1

Distinctions Between Civil Law and Criminal Law

Question	Civil Law	Criminal Law
What type of action leads to the lawsuit or case?	Action against a private individual or business entity	Action against society
Who initiates the action?	Plaintiff	Government
Who is their attorney?	Private attorney	District Attorney (D.A.), State or Commonwealth's Attorney General, or the U.S. Attorney General
What is the burden of proof in the case?	Preponderance of the evidence	Beyond a reasonable doubt
Who generally has the burden of proof?	Plaintiff	Government
Is there a jury trial?	Yes, except in actions in equity	Yes, except in cases involving certain infractions and misdemeanors
What jury vote is necessary to win the case?	Jury vote depends on jurisdiction or agreement of the parties. Often a simple majority or two-thirds jury vote is sufficient.	Unanimous jury vote needed in federal court. Unanimous jury *may* be required in state court.
What type(s) of penalty or punishment is imposed?	Monetary damages or equitable remedies	Capital punishment, prison, fines, and/or probation

The Six Steps in a Typical Criminal Proceeding

1. Preliminary Hearing or a Grand Jury Hearing

A preliminary hearing is generally a public hearing where a magistrate considers the evidence against the accused and determines if there is probable cause to hold a criminal trial. The prosecutor presents sufficient evidence to have the case go to trial: he or she does not present all the government's evidence.
OR
A hearing before the grand jury. The grand jury hears the evidence in secret. Generally, the witnesses appear before the grand jury one at a time. The District Attorney may lead the questioning of the witnesses. The grand jury determines if a crime has been committed and, if so, which individuals were probably involved. If a grand jury issues an indictment against an individual, there will be a trial.

2. Arraignment

The suspect appears before the court and is informed of the criminal charges. The suspect is asked how he or she pleads. Generally, the amount of bail is set at this stage.

3. Discovery

Both sides gather facts and information to prepare for trial. Discovery can involve examining documents, records, and other pieces of physical evidence, as well as taking the depositions of witnesses or the parties themselves. Some discovery actually occurs at the preliminary hearing and arraignment. Discovery is generally more limited in criminal cases than in civil cases. One of the concerns is that if the defendant knows who will testify for the government, the defendant, defendant's relatives, and friends may intimidate the witnesses.

4. Pretrial Motions

If the parties want the court to make procedural decisions or other rulings, they do so by filing the appropriate motions with the court. Before a criminal trial, this may include a motion to suppress evidence defendant claims was obtained illegally by the police.

5. Trial

The court hears the evidence offered by both sides and decides issues of both fact and law. In a jury trial, the jury is the decider of facts.

6. Sentencing

If the defendant is found guilty beyond a reasonable doubt, the defendant will be sentenced to jail, probation, parole, and/or to pay a fine.

Crimes versus Torts

It is important to remember that one act can be the legal basis for both a criminal lawsuit and a civil lawsuit. In many situations, a *criminal act* (an act against the rules of society) will also involve an infringement on the legal rights of an individual. If one act is both a crime and a tort, it may be prosecuted by the criminal system and the injured individual may be able to seek remedies in the civil system. The two separate suits will not be barred by either the doctrine of *res judicata* or by the rule against double jeopardy. For example, the state of California prosecuted O.J. Simpson for the murder of Nicole Brown Simpson. Her relatives sued him for the tort of wrongful death.[3]

OBJECTIVES OF CRIMINAL LAW

The objectives of criminal law are the protection of persons and property, the deterrence of criminal behavior, the punishment of criminal activity, and the rehabilitation of the criminal.

Protection of Persons and Property

Someone once said that a lock was designed to keep an honest person honest. It is for the same reason that the government declares certain conduct to be illegal. The government believes that all persons and their property should be protected from harm. The primary difference between tort law and criminal law is that tort law may result in money damages being paid by the actor to the individual victims, whereas criminal law may result in loss of freedom by sending the actor to jail or prison. Private interests are served through the awarding of damages. The public interest, on the other hand, is served by deterring and punishing criminal activity. If all persons respected everyone else's person and property, there would be very little reason for criminal law. However, there is evidence that they do not. "There's an old saying . . . in fraud prevention circles called the 10-10-80 rule: 10 percent of people will never steal . . . , 10 percent of people will steal at any opportunity, and the other 80 percent of . . . [people] will go either way depending on how they rationalize a particular opportunity."[4]

Deterrence of Criminal Behavior

One method used to reduce criminal behavior is to present a sufficient deterrent to antisocial behavior. The presumption inherent in criminal law is that if we make the punishment sufficiently harsh, people and businesses who contemplate criminal behavior will avoid it because they fear punishment. If people fear the punishment, they will not commit the criminal act. If a sufficient number of people fear the punishment, there will be a reduction in that crime. The severity of the punishment is often an issue with corporate defendants. What constitutes a substantial penalty for an individual would be a minimal penalty for a corporation such as UBS Bank.[5] Criminologists have noted that severity alone is not a sufficient deterrent.

Individuals considering criminal behavior must also believe that they are likely to be identified and punished. The deterrent effect is reduced when criminals believe that they will not be identified, tried, or found guilty.

The U.S. Constitution states that there shall be no cruel and unusual punishment. If U.S. laws allowed the death penalty for even minor offenses, there would probably be fewer minor offenses. But is that just? Most people would argue that the loss of one's life for stealing a loaf of bread seems too high a price to pay for fewer loaves of bread being stolen. Similarly, many feel that caning a teenager for vandalism or castrating a rapist is too extreme. The problem is to decide how much punishment will deter criminal behavior without being deemed excessive and unconstitutional.

An Ounce of Prevention

You should consider where you are vulnerable as part of your risk management strategy. What types of crimes are likely to be perpetrated against you and by whom? You may be at risk from employees, forgers, shoplifters, thieves, and vandals. Once you have identified your exposure to risk, you should consider techniques to reduce that risk. You should consider installing burglar alarms, security cameras, and additional locks. In many situations when employees embezzle from their employers it is because the employer did not institute common checks and balances to protect itself. A small business may hire a new employee and then trust the employee to handle all the bank accounts, including the review of bank statements. In this case, there is no oversight of the employee. Oversight is recommended even if the employee is a trusted long-time employee. You may want to institute a criminal background check on new employees or otherwise attempt to screen out "unsavory" characters from your workplace. However, you need to use care not to violate federal and state employment laws, including laws that prohibit discrimination against ex-convicts who have served their punishment.

Punishment of Criminal Activity

Society cannot deter all criminal activity, so the U.S. legal system accepts that a certain level of criminal activity will exist. Accordingly, the system punishes criminal activity for punishment's sake. If a criminal takes something without paying for it, the criminal law makes that individual pay for it by depriving him or her of freedom for a period of time. Convicted criminals can be imprisoned, sentenced to probation, fined, or subjected to criminal forfeiture. (*Criminal forfeiture* is when the government confiscates property as a punishment for criminal activity.)

Rehabilitation of the Criminal

The criminal justice system does not *end* with punishment. The government has designed various programs to educate and train criminals in legitimate occupations during their incarceration. Theoretically, then, criminals should have no reason to return to a life of crime. Sometimes a sentence is suspended; that is, it is not put into effect. In such cases, the court supervises the individuals' activities to ensure that they have learned from their mistakes.

SERIOUSNESS OF THE OFFENSE

Criminal law classifies offenses into categories according to their level of seriousness. These categories are, from least to most serious, infractions, misdemeanors, felonies, and treason.

Infractions

Some states or local governments have a separate category for petty offenses called *infractions* or *violations*. Infractions are the violation of a rule or a local ordinance. They are generally punishable only by fines. Some examples include illegal gaming and breach of the peace. If a college fraternity party becomes noisy, the police may be called for breach of the peace.

Misdemeanors

Misdemeanors are minor offenses that are punishable by confinement of up to one year in a city or county jail, a small fine, or both. Public intoxication, speeding, texting while driving, and vandalism are likely to be classified as misdemeanors.

Felonies

Felonies are major offenses punishable by confinement from one year to life in a state or federal prison, a large fine, or both. Special capital felony statutes provide for punishment by death for designated felonies. Arson, burglary, grand theft, murder, and rape are normally classified as felonies.

Treason and Sedition

Treason is the only crime defined in the U.S. Constitution[6] and it is the most serious offense against the government. It is currently defined as "Whoever, owing allegiance to the United States, levies war against them or adheres to their enemies, giving them aid and comfort within the United States or elsewhere, is guilty of treason and shall suffer death, or shall be imprisoned not less than five years and fined . . . not less than $10,000; and shall be incapable of holding any office under the United States."[7] Treason is based on the concept that the person owed either a perpetual or temporary allegiance to the United States. Every citizen of the United States owes perpetual allegiance to it. Aliens who are domiciled in the United States owe temporary allegiance to it. If a citizen mutters words of discontent, the words by themselves will not constitute treason. The general view is that treason requires an overt act or a confession in court. The overt act does not have to be a crime by itself. The purpose of the overt act requirement is to show that the accused actually gave aid and comfort to the enemy. However, the overt act *can* be the oral or written communication of an idea, such as conveying military intelligence to the enemy or broadcasting radio shows of support and encouragement to the enemy.

Sedition is an agreement, communication, or some other activity intended to incite treason or some lesser commotion against the public authority. It includes advocacy intended and likely to incite or produce imminent lawless behavior. Sedition may be committed by taking some preliminary steps, as compared to treason, which requires an overt act. If the plan is for some minor disturbance, then, even if the plan is actually completed, it will be sedition instead of treason.

ELEMENTS OF A CRIME

Generally, an individual is presumed innocent until proven guilty. The government has the burden of proving that the suspect is guilty *beyond a reasonable doubt.* (Beyond a reasonable doubt is proof to a moral certainty; there is no other reasonable interpretation.) Technology can make it easier for the government to catch the suspect or prove its case. For instance, observers may take videos of the fight or the getaway vehicle with their cell phones.

The government must prove all the elements of the crime. There are two primary elements in every crime. The government must prove beyond a reasonable doubt that the defendant committed the prohibited criminal act *and* that the defendant possessed the necessary *mental state* at the time the act was committed. The wrongful act is called the *actus reus*, and the state of mind required for each crime is called the *mens rea.* If only one element is present, no crime exists. For example, if Nashira decides to embezzle from her employer and then takes no steps to implement her decision, she has not committed a crime. The intent was present, but no prohibited act occurred. Similarly, if Tony is smoking in a motel room and his cigarette ignites the draperies in his room and causes a motel fire, he has not committed the crime of arson. A prohibited act occurred, but there was no criminal intent. In the latter case, Tony may be liable for negligence, but he has not committed arson. Even *if* an actor has committed a prohibited act and possessed the necessary criminal intent, no criminal conviction will occur unless the government can convince the jury of both elements beyond a reasonable doubt. (Note that the jury does not find the defendant to be *innocent*. Rather the defendant is found *not guilty*; the jury decides that the government did not satisfy its burden of proof in the case.)

The Act

The law generally imposes criminal liability only when an individual acts in a manner that is prohibited by law. Ordinarily, the prohibited act must be voluntarily committed by the person before criminal liability will attach. This means that a person who is forced to act illegally against his or her will does not act voluntarily and may not be legally responsible for the act. However, the court *may* still impose liability if it decides that the threat used to force the conduct was not sufficient to remove the free will of the actor.

Some situations may *require* an individual to act or respond to the circumstances in a particular way. In these situations, a failure to act may be deemed a criminal "action" sufficient to justify prosecution by the government. This responsibility to act may be imposed by a statute as it was in the Classic Case or by judicial precedent.

The Mental State

To be held criminally responsible for an illegal act, the actor must intend to do the act. Each crime has a specified level of intent associated with the prohibited act. The terms commonly used today to describe intent are as follows:

1. **Purpose**—An actor acts with purpose if it is his or her conscious objective to perform the prohibited act.
2. **Knowledge**—An actor acts with knowledge if he or she is aware of what he or she is doing.
3. **Recklessness**—An actor acts with recklessness if he or she disregards a substantial and unjustifiable risk that criminal harm or injury may result from his or her action.
4. **Negligence**—An actor acts in a criminally negligent manner if he or she should have known that a substantial and unreasonable risk of harm would result from his or her action.
5. **Strict liability**—An actor will be held strictly liable if he or she acts in a manner that the law declares criminal, even if none of the above four elements is present. This intent is used primarily for crimes that have a light punishment—for example, violating food safety laws. This *mens rea* is also used in statutory rape cases simply because society has a vested interest in protecting its youth.

SELECTED CRIMES AND DEFENSES

We are unable to list all of the common crimes and defenses in this text. We will mention selected crimes that have applications for either detection or prevention in the marketplace. In many situations, the business is the victim of the crime and not its perpetrator. It is possible for a business to be the perpetrator of a crime, and there are a number of criminal statutes aimed primarily at business activities.

Murder/Manslaughter

Homicide is the killing of one human being by another. It is not necessarily a criminal act. It will *not* be a criminal act if the killing was lawful; for example, if there was a justification such as self-defense. *Murder,* however, is the willful, unlawful killing of a human being by another with *malice aforethought* (deliberate purpose or design). *Manslaughter* occurs when the killing is unlawful, but without malice. Manslaughter is usually divided into two categories—*voluntary* (upon a sudden heat of passion) or *involuntary* (in the commission of an unlawful act or in the commission of a lawful act without due caution). It is common for the state to charge a defendant with both murder and manslaughter and to let the *decider of fact* (the jury, if there is one; the judge, if there is no jury) determine which crime was actually committed. Corporations have been charged with manslaughter in a number of cases, including when a construction site accident killed seven of the corporation's workers[8] and when a defective product accidently killed the user.[9]

Arson

Arson is the intentional or willful burning of property by fire or explosion. Originally, this crime was limited to the burning of a house. In most states, the crime has been expanded to include the burning of all types of *real property* (land and items of property permanently attached to land) and many types of *personal property* (property other than land). Businesses may be the victim of arson in some cases. In other cases, a business person may commit arson by burning his or her business as part of a plan to defraud an insurer.

Burglary

Burglary is the breaking and entering of a structure with the intent to commit a felony inside the structure. Originally, this crime was restricted to the breaking and entering of a house at night, but like arson, it has been expanded to include other structures, such as stores and warehouses. Burglary is no longer limited to nighttime conduct, but can occur at any time of day or night. In some states the crime of burglary has been expanded to include burglary of a motor vehicle.

Embezzlement

Embezzlement is the taking of money or other property by an employee who has been entrusted with the money or property by his or her employer. Businesses should establish practices and procedures to reduce the likelihood of being victimized by embezzlement.

Forgery

Forgery is the making or altering of a negotiable instrument or credit card invoice in order to create or to shift legal liability for the instrument. It generally consists of signing another person's name to a check, promissory note, or credit card invoice or altering an amount on any of those documents. The government must generally prove that the accused acted with the intent to defraud. A business entity should use care in maintaining checks and signature stamps. It also should promptly reconcile bank statements to discover potential forgeries. A good internal control system can help deter forgery and embezzlement.

Credit Card and Check Legislation

Customers make extensive use of credit cards, debit cards, checks, and electronic payments. This creates a number of problems for businesses. For instance, criminals may steal an individual's credit card, debit card, or account number and use it to make substantial purchases. Credit card account numbers may be obtained by criminals in a number of ways. Computer hackers have stolen millions of credit card numbers from retailers such as Sears, Target, and T.J. Maxx. Phishing scams have obtained card information from thousands of individuals. Remote skimmers can be used to steal credit card information, even when the card is in the person's wallet. Physical skimmers can be attached to ATMs and gas pumps to capture the customer's information.[10] In addition, dishonest employees might obtain card information and then sell it to other criminals. Some states have enacted separate legislation making it a crime to misuse someone else's credit card or debit card information without permission. Other states treat this as a type of forgery. Criminals may steal the checks of an individual or business and forge the signature on the checks.

A different type of problem arises when the owner of a bank account writes checks when there are insufficient funds in the account. Most states have enacted statutes that make it a crime to write or transfer (make, draw, or deliver) a check when there are insufficient funds in the account. These are commonly called *bad check statutes*. Some states require the *mens rea* that the suspect intended to defraud the recipient of the check before there will be any criminal liability. Businesses are generally the recipients of the bad checks.

Identity Theft

Identity theft occurs when a thief steals personal information, such as the victim's name, address, Social Security number, and/or employment history, and then uses this information to access the victim's credit. The thief can obtain the personal information on the Internet, through public records, stealing mail from the victim's mailbox,[11] or going through the victim's trash. Thieves stole the identity of a Homeland Security Agent in Fresno, California. The officer left his pay stub and bank information in his vehicle. When thieves stole his car, they were also able to steal his identity.[12] *Hackers* (outsiders who gain unauthorized access to computers or computer networks) may gain access to personal information through an individual's personal computer, an employer's computer system, the records of a business with whom the individual dealt, or a credit card company's records. In one day in November 2008, an international ring of hackers hacked into a U.S. credit card processor and stole $9.4 million.[13] In some cases, the thief may actually work for a credit card company or credit card department of a retailer. In some state or federal prisons, cheap inmate labor is used for various enterprises. In one case, the state was using inmates to process credit card applications, and some of the inmates were stealing personal information from the applications.

Once the thief has obtained the information, he or she may apply for credit using the victim's name or may access the victim's accounts, such as bank accounts, retirement accounts, or Social Security accounts.

An Ounce of Prevention

You share some of the responsibility for protecting your identity. Identity theft can be very expensive and time consuming to correct. Remember to use high-quality passwords with a combination of symbols, letters, and numbers. Change your passwords periodically. Keep your anti-virus software up to date. Use current firewall software to prevent hackers from accessing your computer. You are especially vulnerable when you are using a high-speed Internet connection. Use a secure browser. Try to use Web sites with good privacy policies and a good history of protecting personal information. Don't open files or follow links from sources you do not know. Avoid storing personal information on laptop computers and other mobile devices. These devices can be hacked. In addition, if your device is stolen or you lose it, someone will have access to your information. When you dispose of electronic devices, delete all your personal information. You may not be aware that some devices may have information stored on them, such as some printers/scanners. You should also check your credit reports at least once a year.[14]

Criminal Fraud

Fraud is a broad term that covers many specific situations. The tort of fraud was discussed in Chapter 12. The English courts were very reluctant to criminalize fraudulent behavior. Over the years, legislation was passed in both England and the United States to change the historic view of "[we] are not to indict one for making a fool of another."[15] Today, most states have statutes that cover variations of what is generally called *criminal fraud*, *false pretense*, or *theft by deception*. Most states require proof of all of the following elements to convict a person of criminal fraud:

- The speaker (or writer) made a false statement of fact;
- The statement was material, that is, the statement would affect the listener's decision;
- The listener relied on the statement; and
- The speaker intended to mislead the listener.

Note that the fraudulent party can be either the buyer or the seller. For example, suppose that a savings and loan association creates the false impression that certain real estate assets are worth $100,000 by distributing false appraisals to induce a person to invest in those assets. In fact, the assets are worth substantially less than the false appraisals indicate. The savings and loan and its officers could be found guilty of criminal fraud if a person invests in those assets based on the false appraisals.

The federal mail fraud statute[16] applies to fraud conducted, at least in part, through the mail. The federal wire fraud statute[17] applies to frauds conducted in part using e-mail,[18] radio, telephone, or television.

One type of fraud that has received a lot of notoriety recently is the Ponzi scheme. Ponzi schemes are named after Charles Ponzi. However, he was not the first to operate such a scheme. In a Ponzi scheme, the money from later investors is used to repay early investors or to pay them dividends. The early investors generally receive "a high rate of return," attracting other investors to join the fund. Generally, there is no real revenue-producing activity or investment. Eventually, the scheme is uncovered when the "financier" cannot obtain sufficient new investments to pay the earlier investors. Bernard (Bernie) Madoff was sentenced to 150 years in prison for the Ponzi scheme he ran. The government claimed that he operated the scheme for at least twenty years and caused $13 billion in net losses to investors.[19] Similarly, R. Allen Stanford was convicted of thirteen counts in his $7 billion Ponzi scheme.[20]

Pyramid schemes are a variation on Ponzi schemes. In a pyramid scheme, an investor commits a certain amount of money (say $100) to join the program. Often the "investment" involves an exclusive territory for that investor to "harvest." He or she then gets other investors to buy in at the same price, subdividing his or her territory to these investors, with part of their investment going to the original investor and the balance going to the originator of the scheme. This continues down the pyramid, with each successive level of investors buying a smaller and smaller portion of the original territory. Some pyramids involve actual products to be sold, whereas others involve a product to be developed in the future. In either case, investors toward the bottom of the pyramid tend to lose the money they invested. Both Ponzi and pyramid schemes are crimes committed by the business or the businessperson.

Larceny

Larceny is the wrongful taking and carrying away of the personal property of another without the owner's consent and with the intent to permanently deprive the owner of the property. The most common forms of larceny are shoplifting and pickpocketing. Larceny does not require the use of force. Larceny is a serious problem for retail businesses. Merchandise is often lost through shoplifting. In addition, if customers feel unsafe due to pickpocketing or other crimes, they will avoid certain neighborhoods and shopping centers.

In common law, the theft of a trade secret was not considered larceny. However, many modern statutes have changed that by recognizing the misappropriation of trade secrets as a theft. Some of these are federal statutes, including the National Stolen Property Act,[21] the Economic Espionage Act,[22] the mail fraud statute,[23] and the wire fraud statute.[24] There are also state statutes that specifically deal with the misappropriation of trade secrets.

Robbery

Robbery is a form of aggravated theft. It is basically larceny *plus* the threat to use force or violence. To be classified as a robbery, the robber must use either violence or the threat of injury sufficient to place the victim in fear. The robber then takes something in the possession or in the immediate presence of the victim. If the same property had been carried away without the use of violence or a threat of injury, the act would be larceny.

Espionage

The Economic Espionage Act of 1996 (EEA)[25] makes the theft of trade secrets a federal crime. EEA covers both domestic economic espionage—for example, by competitors[26]—and the theft of trade secrets to benefit foreign powers.[27] It was the first federal statute to provide criminal penalties for the misappropriation of trade secrets. Misappropriation of trade secrets is also called economic spying or espionage.[28] The EEA makes espionage a federal crime punishable by 25 years in jail or a $25,000 fine for a person. It also provides for fines of up to $10 million for companies found guilty of such conduct.[29] Under the EEA, almost anything can be a trade secret as long as the owner takes reasonable steps to keep it a secret and it has economic value because it is a secret.

Computer Crime

Advances in computer technology have led to the development of new criminal activities. Companies like the Gap, Hitachi America, PeopleSoft, Playboy Enterprises, and Twentieth Century Fox each attract from 1 to 30 hacker attempts a day.[30]

With our increased dependence on technology, computer criminals can create extensive damage. "The going estimates for financial losses from computer crime reach as high as $10 billion a year. But the truth is that nobody really knows. Almost all attacks go undetected—as many as 95 percent says the FBI."[31] In addition to civil liability for improper use, many states now recognize the following activities as computer crimes:

1. **Unauthorized use of computers or computer-related equipment.** This may include the use of business computers for personal projects, including homework and personal e-mail. It also includes transferring software purchased by a business to a personal computer.
2. **Destruction of a computer or its records.** Computer viruses destroy or alter records, data, and programs. Annually there are numerous virus alerts—some are fakes and some are legitimate. Businesses expend significant resources to protect themselves from viruses and to correct the damage they cause. This includes a virus that "infects" the computers in a college computer lab and subsequently infects students' travel drives and home computers. In 2012 the FBI warned that more than 252,000 computers worldwide might be infected by the DNS Changer, a virus that interferes with a computer's ability to properly process domain names. The virus was planted by a fraud ring that intended to redirect computers to its own servers.[32]
3. **Alteration of legitimate records.** This would include altering a student's grade record in the registrar's office.
4. **Accessing computer records to transfer funds, stocks, or other property.** This would include entering a bank's computer system and transferring funds without authorization.

Congress enacted the federal Counterfeit Access Device and Computer Fraud and Abuse Act of 1984 to strengthen state attempts to deal with computer crime. The Act criminalized the *unauthorized*, knowing use or access of computers in the following ways:

1. To obtain classified military or foreign policy information with the intent to injure the United States or to benefit a foreign country. This would include accessing classified Pentagon files.
2. To collect financial or credit information, which is protected under federal privacy law. This would include accessing credit card accounts to obtain credit card numbers and credit limits.

3. To use, modify, destroy, or disclose computer data and to prevent authorized individuals from using the data. This would include intentionally transferring a virus to a computer.
4. To alter or modify data in financial computers that causes a loss of $1,000 or more. This would include the unlawful transfer of funds.
5. To modify data that impairs an individual's medical treatment.
6. To transfer computer data, including passwords, which could assist individuals in gaining unauthorized access that either affects interstate commerce or allows access to a government computer. This would include the use of a "sniffer" program, which can hide in a computer network, record passwords, and then transfer this information to others.

The first category listed above constitutes a felony, and the remaining five categories constitute misdemeanors.

One way criminals access cell phones, computers, and tablets of victims is by embedding viruses in applications that the owners purchase or download for free. Another technique is *war-drivers* (drive-by hackers) who hack into wireless computer networks from streets or parking lots to obtain information and/or plant sniffer programs. Often, the goal is to obtain credit card and debit card numbers to sell on the black market. A ring of hackers who hacked into the computers of Marshalls department stores and its subsidiary, T.J. Maxx, stole up to 45 million credit and debit card numbers. The attack cost the parent company more than $130 million to settle with banks and customers.[33]

An Ounce of Prevention

Computer crimes cause some unique problems for businesses. Criminals are constantly inventing new techniques to access computers, so you should keep up-to-date with the technology. You should make effective use of passwords, filters, encryption techniques, and virus scanners. If someone breaches your computer security you need to decide whether or not to report it. Businesses are reluctant to report the breach and often try to solve the issue on their own. This is one reason why we do not have accurate data about the frequency of breaches. If you do report the breach, the government can help locate the hackers. However, disclosure of the information can harm your reputation. For example, in 1994, Citibank discovered that Russian hackers made $10 million in illegal transfers. Initially, the bank called in a private security firm. When Citibank finally spoke to the FBI and the media, it lost some of its top customers. Competitors enticed customers away by advertising that the competitors' systems were more secure than those of Citibank.[34]

Corporate Liability for Crimes

Originally, courts held that a corporation could not be held responsible for crimes because the corporation was not authorized to commit crimes and so lacked the power to commit them. Some states define their crimes in terms of conduct by a human being. For example, homicide may be the killing of one person by another. There is a growing trend in many states to hold corporations criminally responsible when their officers and agents commit criminal actions in the execution of their duties. This trend is evidenced by court decisions, statutory law, and the Model Penal Code.[35] A specific example is the California Corporate Criminal Liability Act, which increased the criminal liability of corporate managers.[36] Corporate directors, officers, and employees are also *personally* liable for crimes they commit while acting for the corporation.

It can be difficult to convict a corporation of some crimes because the government has to prove the mental state necessary for the crime. Corporate liability is more common when the corporation is accused of violating a statute that does not require a specific mental intent, such as serving alcohol to a minor. In contrast, when the criminal act requires a specific mental state, such as battery with intent to kill, the courts generally refuse to hold the corporation liable unless the corporation itself participated in the acts or a high-ranking official participated in the acts with the intent to benefit the corporation.

In some states, corporate liability is limited to *white-collar crime*. Although this term does not have a precise meaning, it generally means crimes committed in a commercial context by professionals and managers. The officers and agents can be tried individually and convicted for their behavior. When liability is imposed against the corporation, punishment is usually in the form of a fine.

An Ounce of Prevention

A business entity is an artificial person. The entity itself cannot commit a prohibited act (the actus reus), but your officers and directors may commit such an act to advance your interests. You can be held liable as a perpetrator of the crime when the prohibited acts are done on your behalf. Generally, the penalty imposed on the business is a fine. Courts tend to levy substantial fines against businesses because courts want to make an impression on them and to send a message to other businesses that this behavior is not acceptable. There are some crimes, such as violations of the antitrust laws, which can also result in the imprisonment of corporate officials as well as the imposition of fines against the business and/or its officers. These statutes also provide for civil penalties.

Any criminal trial against you will probably tarnish your reputation. Consequently, it is in your interest to establish policies and procedures designed to prevent criminal conduct by officers. Your company policies should include methods for reporting suspicious behavior to corporate officials and protections for people who "blow the whistle."

Knowledge of the law, information about best practices in the particular industry, and internal safeguards are all helpful. Proper supervision of employees and agents will also reduce criminal activity. Where potential criminal sanctions are involved, prevention is, indeed, the best medicine.

Racketeer Influenced and Corrupt Organizations Act (RICO)

The Racketeer Influenced and Corrupt Organizations Act (RICO)[37] was included as part of the Organized Crime Control Act. Congress intended to remedy a serious problem: the infiltration of criminals into legitimate businesses as both a "cover" for their criminal activity and as a means of "laundering" profits derived from their crimes. For example, Mark has a profit from his sales of illegal drugs. He approaches Maddy about investing in her restaurant. He becomes a "partner" in the legitimate business. Mark now receives his profits by check. He can report them on his tax returns without arousing suspicion. Sometimes the drug dealer will also use the restaurant as a distribution site for his drugs. RICO makes it a federal crime to obtain or maintain an interest in, use income from, or conduct or participate in the affairs of an enterprise through a pattern of racketeering activity.

Under RICO persons employed by or associated with any enterprise are prohibited from engaging in a pattern of racketeering activity. A *pattern* constitutes committing at least two racketeering acts in a ten-year period. These racketeering acts are called *predicate acts* under RICO. Racketeering activity has been broadly defined and includes most criminal actions, such as bribery, antitrust violations, securities violations, fraud, acts of violence, and providing illegal goods or services. Racketeering acts also include acts relating to the Currency and Foreign Transactions Reporting Act, which is discussed later. RICO charges are added to other criminal charges when there is a pattern of corrupt behavior, such as bribery. Defendants may raise issues of double jeopardy when they are tried for both the predicate acts and the RICO violation. Courts generally determine that the prohibition against double jeopardy is not violated because the predicate acts and the RICO offenses are separate and distinct crimes.[38]

Criminal prosecutors and plaintiffs' attorneys soon recognized the opportunity to use RICO against commercial enterprises. Plaintiffs' attorneys are involved because the statute permits individuals who are injured by a violation of RICO to file a civil action. Successful plaintiffs in a civil action may recover treble damages, attorney's fees, and reasonable court costs. For example, beneficiaries of group health insurance policies used RICO to sue the insurance company.[39] This is an example of the overlap between criminal and civil law systems. A prior conviction in a criminal suit is not required in order to file a civil RICO suit. Some critics argue that RICO is leading to unfounded lawsuits and out-of-court settlements by intimidated firms. The government can also file civil RICO actions where the burden of proof will be lower. High civil penalties can provide a lucrative law enforcement technique.

Individuals convicted of criminal RICO violations can be fined up to $25,000 per violation, imprisoned for up to 20 years, or both. RICO also provides for the forfeiture of any property, including business interests, obtained through RICO violations. The property will be forfeited even if the property or business itself is legitimate. The defendant's assets can be temporarily seized before the trial begins to prevent further crimes. Some states have enacted their own RICO laws.

Since the federal RICO law can be applied to legitimate business activities, it presents a potential concern for all business organizations, public and private.

Currency Crimes

The Currency and Foreign Transactions Reporting Act is a federal statute passed to prevent money-laundering. Under the Act financial institutions have to electronically file Currency Transaction Reports (CTRs). A *currency transaction report* is a report the institution must file if a customer brings $10,000 or more in cash to the business during one day.[40]

The Uniform Law Commission (ULC) has written the Uniform Money Services Act (2000) for adoption by state legislatures. It enhances enforcement of existing money laundering laws and provides a framework for regulating nondepository providers of financial services. *Nondepository providers* offer services such as check cashing and currency exchange. While these businesses provide some financial services tradition-ally related to banking, they do not hold client's deposits or provide other banking services.[41]

Defenses

The four classic defenses to criminal liability are duress, insanity, intoxication, and justification. Each is briefly discussed below.

Duress   *Duress* exists when the accused is *coerced* into criminal conduct by threat or use of force that any person of reasonable firmness could not resist. Not all govern-ments permit this defense. Those governments that do recognize the defense varies with respect to the crimes to which it is applicable. Generally, the three essential elements of the defense are

1. An immediate threat of death or serious bodily harm,
2. a well-grounded fear that the threat will be implemented, *and*
3. no reasonable opportunity to escape the threatened harm.

Exhibit 13.3

Intoxication as a Defense

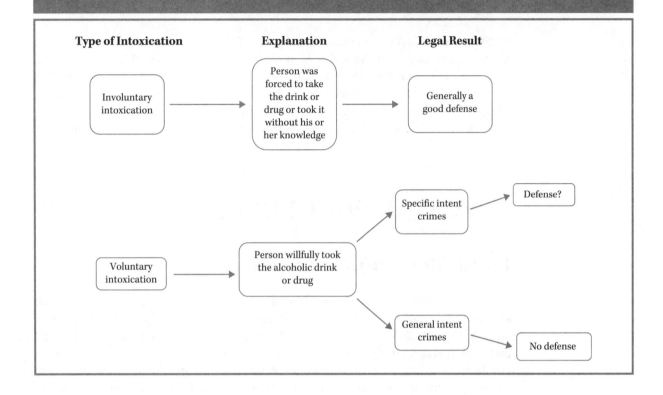

Type of Intoxication	Explanation	Legal Result
Involuntary intoxication	Person was forced to take the drink or drug or took it without his or her knowledge	Generally a good defense
Voluntary intoxication	Person willfully took the alcoholic drink or drug	Specific intent crimes → Defense? General intent crimes → No defense

Insanity   *Insanity* exists when, as a result of a mental disease or defect, the accused either (1) did not know that what he or she was doing was wrong or (2) could not prevent himself or herself from doing what he or she knew to be wrong. The exact definition varies from state to state. Some states do not permit the defense. Most states permit some version of the defense. Generally the defendant has the burden of proof; however, in some states the government has to prove that the defendant was sane.[42] This defense has been attacked for a variety of reasons, but the main complaint is that the definition is ambiguous. Although the defense is raised often, it is rejected in many of the cases in which it is raised.

Intoxication   *Intoxication* may be either voluntary or involuntary. Voluntary intoxication is not a defense unless it negates the specific intent required by a statute. For example, the crime of rape requires a general intent. Intoxication, therefore, would not be a valid defense. On the other hand, assault with the intent to commit rape requires a specific intent. For that crime, intoxication may be a valid defense. By contrast, involuntary intoxication generally is a good defense. *Involuntary intoxication,* for instance, can occur if one is forced to drink an alcoholic beverage against one's will or without one's knowledge. An example of the latter would be if Jason offered Tonia a soft drink and she accepted; Jason spiked the soft drink with drugs without Tonia's knowledge.

The defense of intoxication is summarized in Exhibit 13.3, above.

Justification   *Justification* exists when a person believes an act is necessary in order to avoid harm to himself or herself or to another person. The key to this defense is that whatever the person does to avoid harm must be lesser than the harm to be avoided. For example, sometimes property has to be destroyed to prevent the spread of fire or disease. An animal control officer may destroy a rancher's sheep to prevent the spread of disease. A pharmacist may dispense a drug without a prescription in order to save a person's life.

CRIMINAL PROCEDURE

Constitutional Guarantees

Criminal procedure deals with the process in a criminal case. It is concerned with safeguarding society without unduly infringing on individual rights. The drafters of the U.S. Constitution were determined to avoid the excesses and abuses that had occurred under English rule. As a result, the Constitution contains numerous criminal procedure provisions and protections, including the guarantees of *due process* (the proper exercise of judicial authority as established by general concepts of law and morality) and *equal protection* (the assurance that any person before the court will be treated the same as every other person before the court).

At a minimum, the constitutional protections require that the defendant:

- May not be subjected to unreasonable searches and seizures;
- May not be held subject to excessive *bail* (the posting of money or property for the release of a criminal defendant while trying to ensure his or her presence in court at future hearings);
- Is entitled to a speedy trial;
- Must be informed of the charges against him or her;
- Must be tried before an impartial tribunal;
- Must be permitted to confront witnesses against him or her;
- Cannot be compelled to testify against himself or herself; *and*
- May not be subjected to cruel and unusual punishment if convicted.

Searches and Seizures

Legal disputes may arise between a suspect and the police who search the suspect's business, home, car, or person. Under the Fourth Amendment to the Constitution, people are protected from unreasonable searches and seizures. A search will be valid if any *one* of the following occurs:

- The search is properly conducted under a legal search warrant based on probable cause.
- The search is conducted without a warrant by officers acting with probable cause. In some situations, courts use a lower standard than probable cause. Common examples of the reduced standards are when an officer "pats down" a suspect because the officer is concerned that the suspect has a concealed weapon or the evidence is in a motor vehicle that could be driven away.
- The search is conducted with the permission of the owner of the property or a person with proper possession of the property, such as a tenant who rents an apartment.
- An emergency or exigent circumstance exists that requires police to enter onto the premises, such as a fire in the building.

Once police are legally on the property, they may observe and act on any criminal behavior they see. Evidence obtained through an illegal search may not be used in court in the United States; this is called *suppression of evidence.*

Sometimes a business is subjected to a search as in our Classic Case. Another example would be when the Occupational Safety and Health Administration (OSHA) wants to search a business for safety violations. Sometimes the management of a business wants to search an employee's locker, desk, or computer. The law in this area is very sophisticated and depends in part on (1) who is actually doing the search; (2) the employee's expectation of privacy in the area; and (3) the basis for the employer's suspicion. The law about search and seizure is evolving rapidly, especially in the area of government searches of computers and offices.

Stages of a Criminal Case

Exhibit 13.4 depicts the stages of criminal procedure. Note that a criminal trial is similar to a civil trial in many respects. The stages of a civil trial are discussed in Chapter 4. Many of the motions discussed in Chapter 4 can also be used in criminal trials.

The law carries a *presumption* of innocence until the defendant is proven guilty, and the burden of proof in a criminal trial is the heaviest burden in U.S. jurisprudence. The government must convince the jury of the defendant's guilt beyond a reasonable doubt, or the defendant must be acquitted.

Exhibit 13.4

The Common Stages of Criminal Procedure[a]

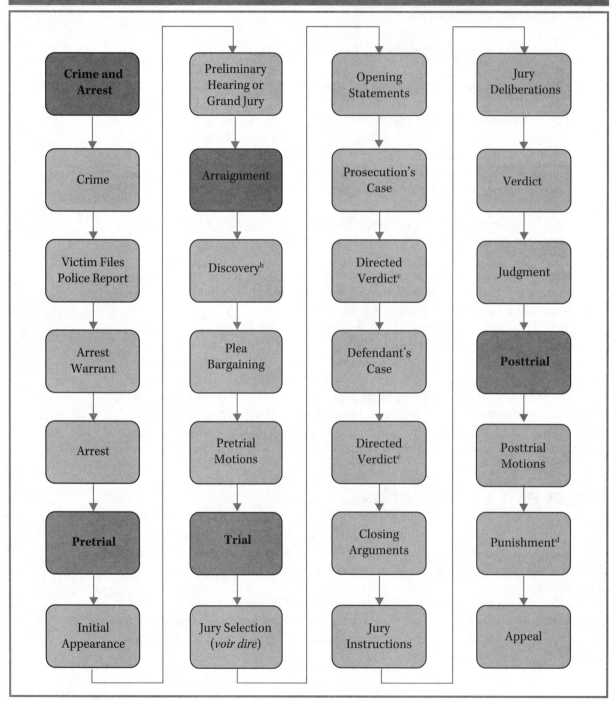

Crime and Arrest	Preliminary Hearing or Grand Jury	Opening Statements	Jury Deliberations
Crime	Arraignment	Prosecution's Case	Verdict
Victim Files Police Report	Discovery[b]	Directed Verdict[c]	Judgment
Arrest Warrant	Plea Bargaining	Defendant's Case	Posttrial
Arrest	Pretrial Motions	Directed Verdict[c]	Posttrial Motions
Pretrial	Trial	Closing Arguments	Punishment[d]
Initial Appearance	Jury Selection (*voir dire*)	Jury Instructions	Appeal

[a]The exact order may vary.
[b]Discovery is more limited in criminal cases than in civil cases.
[c]Directed verdicts are not generally granted in favor of the government.
[d]A criminal defendant may be imprisoned beginning at the time of the arrest, if the court determines that bail is not appropriate or if the defendant cannot raise the amount of bail.

Contemporary Case

In the following case, the Supreme Court of Hawaii considered whether there was adequate consent to a blood alcohol test. While this case was pending in the courts, the U.S. Supreme Court decided *Missouri v. McNeely.*[43] In that case, the U.S. Supreme Court held that there is no exigent circumstance justifying a blood alcohol test just because the human body *metabolizes* alcohol. (In other words, the level of alcohol decreases over time.)

HAWAI'I v. WON

361 P.3d 1195, 2015 Haw. LEXIS 317 (Haw. Sup. Ct. 2015)

FACTS An officer of the Honolulu Police Department observed Yong Shik Won traveling at a high speed. Won failed a standard field sobriety test. Won was arrested for operating a vehicle under the influence of an intoxicant (OVUII) and taken to the local police station. At the station, an officer read Won a form entitled "Use of Intoxicants While Operating a Vehicle Implied Consent for Testing" (Implied Consent Form). Won initialed the section of the form which told him that refusing to submit to the blood alcohol content (BAC) test is punishable by up to thirty days of imprisonment and a fine of up to $1,000. Won initialed next to "AGREED TO TAKE A BREATH TEST AND REFUSED THE BLOOD TEST" and signed the form with his name at the bottom. The results of the test showed that Won was above the legal limit for operating a vehicle.

ISSUE Was Won's election to submit to the breath test a valid consent under the circumstances?

HOLDING No, it was not consensual.

REASONING Excerpts from the opinion of Richard W. Pollack, J.:

... "An invasion of bodily integrity implicates an individual's 'most personal and deep-rooted expectations of privacy.'"... The [U.S.] Supreme Court has "never retreated ... from [its] recognition that any compelled intrusion into the human body implicates significant, constitutionally protected privacy interests."... [In precedents the U.S. Supreme Court has defined a breath test as a search.] The right to be free of warrantless searches and seizures is a fundamental guarantee of our constitution.... "[A] search without a warrant issued upon probable cause is unreasonable per se."... "[T]he warrant requirement is subject to a few specifically established and well-delineated exceptions."... One of the specific exceptions is a search conducted pursuant to consent....

This court has repeatedly recognized that an individual has a constitutional right to refuse consent to a search when consent is requested by the State.... [I]t must be shown that such consent was voluntarily given.... Voluntariness means a "free and unconstrained choice."... [C]onsent is measured ... [by] examining the totality of the circumstances.... [F]or consent to be "in fact, freely and voluntarily given," the consent "must be uncoerced."... [C]onsent may not be gained by explicit or implicit coercion, implied threat, or covert force.... "[N]o matter how subtly the coercion was applied, the resulting 'consent' would be no more than a pretext for the unjustified ... intrusion against which the fourth amendment is directed."... Our decisions demonstrate that the totality of the circumstances may indicate that an alleged waiver of a constitutional right was not voluntary even when there is a manifestation of assent by the defendant.... Verbal expression also may not be determinative of whether submission to a search is voluntary when the totality of circumstances surrounding the purported waiver is implicitly or subtly coercive....

[T]he process by which the consent to search is obtained must be meaningful and substantive; the request by the State that an individual waive the protections of the constitution must be more than a mere formality. . . . [I]f the person submits to the search under the belief that the search will occur regardless of an objection to the search or the person reasonably believed that there was no other alternative to prevent forfeiture of a right, that consent is coerced . . .

Informing the person of the right to refuse consent is a relevant factor, but it cannot decide the matter. Similarly, acquiescence or a manifestation of assent may nonetheless be insufficient to demonstrate consent when coercive elements are present. Finally, the request by the State for consent . . . must be more than perfunctory and provide the individual with a genuine and meaningful choice; that is, there must be some intimation that an objection to the search would be significant or that to withhold consent would not be futile . . .

[C]onsent to a search may be revoked or withdrawn at any time before the search has been completed. . . . In this case, two forms of consent to a bodily search are relevant to the discussion: (1) irrevocable consent allegedly deemed by statute and (2) informed and voluntary consent under the totality of circumstances.

Every person who drives on the roads of Hawai'i is deemed to have given consent to a BAC test when suspected of OVUII. . . . However, . . . police must inform the driver that his or her "deemed" consent may be withdrawn by refusing to submit to testing. . . . This court has upheld the State's OVUII "implied consent scheme" only when the driver is "afforded . . . the opportunity to make a knowing and intelligent decision whether to take an evidentiary [BAC] test." . . . [I]f a person waives the right to refuse to be searched under the belief that he or she must waive that right, then the waiver is invalid. . . . [A] person may refuse consent to submit to a BAC test, and the State must honor that refusal. . . . [C]onsent may not be predetermined by statute . . .

Where a search may not be accomplished without consent, a request for consent that subjects the person to imprisonment for refusal is calculated to overbear a defendant's will in order to impel submission. . . . [T]he Implied Consent Form that was presented to Won informed him . . . that "if you refuse to submit to a [BAC] test, you shall be subject to up to thirty-days imprisonment and/or a fine up to $1,000." . . . Thus, the threat of the criminal sanction communicated by the Implied Consent Form . . . is inherently coercive . . .

[T]he choice presented by the Implied Consent Form forces a defendant to elect between fundamental rights guaranteed by the Hawai'i Constitution. On the one hand, the person may exercise the constitutional right to refuse to be searched. . . . Alternatively, the person may "choose" to be searched in order to prevent being arrested for the refusal crime. . . . [W]ith respect to both alternatives, a person must surrender one constitutional right for preservation of another. However, the government may not condition a right guaranteed in our constitution on the waiver of an equivalent constitutional protection . . .

In exercising the constitutional right to refuse to be searched, a driver is forced to manifest to the police a willingness to commit a crime. That is, the driver must commit a crime in police presence in order to exercise the refusal allowed by statute and the right to withdraw consent provided by the constitution. The coerciveness present in such circumstances . . . is enhanced by the severity of the statutory penalty for the refusal offense. The statute criminalizing refusal to submit to a BAC test . . . authorizes imprisonment that is six times greater than that provided by the OVUII offense for a first-time offender. Specifically, the refusal offense is punishable for up to thirty days in jail, whereas a first OVUII offense carries a maximum of five days of imprisonment. . . . The threat of imprisonment is inherently coercive . . .

Won's election to submit to the BAC test was not based on voluntary consent . . .

Based on the foregoing analysis, the district court erred in not suppressing the result of Won's breath test. The judgment on appeal of the ICA [Intermediate Court of Appeals] and the district court's amended judgment of conviction are vacated, and the case is remanded to the district court for further proceedings consistent with this opinion.

Short Answer Questions

1. Three of the servers and bartenders at Devon's Bar and Grill have been swiping customers' credit cards to obtain the numbers and identifying information. They have been selling this information to others who use it for illegal purposes. What crimes, if any, are the servers and bartenders committing? Should Devon's be liable for their acts? Why?

2. Some of the employees who have entered the workplace and shot co-workers had been recently served with restraining orders. For example, in 2016 Cedric Larry Ford allegedly killed 3 people and hurt more than 12 at a Kansas factory where he worked. He was served with a restraining order 90 minutes before he started his shooting spree.[44] Should courts routinely notify law enforcement when a restraining order has been issued? Why? Should courts notify the employer even if the restraining order is not work-related? Why?

3. In 2013 16-year-old Ethan Couch killed four people and injured several others in a drunk-driving accident. At the time of the accident his blood alcohol level was three times the legal limit. Couch was apparently drunk on stolen beer. Couch pled guilty in juvenile court and was sentenced to rehab and ten years' probation. The prosecutor had recommended 20 years in prison. Couch's defense team claimed that he suffered from "affluenza." The defense is based on the concept that he was raised by wealthy parents and could not distinguish right from wrong. The American Psychiatric Association does not recognize "affluenza" as a medical diagnosis. The defense was successful and Couch is commonly called the "affluenza teen." There was evidence that his mother coddled him and did not discipline him for prior incidents, including those related to Couch's alcohol use. Should affluenza—or any other "disorder" not recognized by the American Psychiatric Association—be allowed as a defense to crimes committed by minors? Should the "disorder" reduce the punishment of minors? Why? Should any such "disorder" be a defense for adults? Why?[45]

You Decide...

1. Three children in a Tennessee Applebee's were served alcoholic root beers, which the restaurant called "Not Your Father's Root Beer." The children were ages 9, 10, and 11. One child was taken to the

hospital to be examined but all the children were expected okay. Scottie Barnett, the father, said his children ordered root beer. They received bottled drinks. He claims that when he told the server that the drinks were not root beer the employee insisted they were. "This is a 5.9 percent alcoholic drink," Barnett said. "They don't even serve root beer here at this establishment." Barnett called the police and Applebee's corporate office.

Patrick Lenow, an Applebee's spokesperson, said this was "an isolated mistake in one restaurant owned by an independent franchise operator. Strict requirements are in place to prevent this type of error and this mistake should not have happened." He also said that they immediately retrained all the team members on duty and that all team members at all restaurants owned by the same franchisee would be trained the following day. The employee that served the beverages was suspended pending an internal investigation. At this point there have been no criminal charges filed. Should there be criminal charges? Assume that criminal charges are filed in your court against Applebee's, the owner of the specific restaurant, and the server.

How would *you* decide this case? Be certain that you explain and justify your answer.

What additional information would you like to have? Why?

(See "Kids Served Alcoholic Root Beer at Applebee's," *WJHL,* March 11, 2016, http://wspa.com/2016/03/11/kids-served-alcoholic-root-beer-at-applebees/ (accessed March 13, 2016).)

2. Ingrid Lederhaas-Okun was arrested on July 2, 2013 at her home in Connecticut on charges of wire fraud and interstate transportation of stolen property. She is accused of stealing jewelry from Tiffany & Co., her former employer, and reselling the pieces for more than $1.3 million. Lederhaas-Okun was vice president of product development, which allowed her to "check out" jewelry from Tiffany's for work related purposes. Between November 2012 and February 2013, when her position was terminated, Lederhaas-Okun allegedly checked out more than 165 pieces of jewelry and did not return them. Tiffany's discovered that the jewelry was missing when it completed a company-wide inventory review.

Lederhaas-Okun claimed that she had left some of the jewelry in an envelope in her office and that some had been lost or damaged. An envelope with jewelry was not found during an office search. There were records that she resold the jewelry. There were emails between Lederhaas-Okun and a jewelry reseller on her work computer. She also signed documents with the reseller stating that the items were her own personal property. Lederhaas-Okun allegedly checked out items valued at under $10,000 because she knew that the company took a daily inventory of all checked-out items worth more than $25,000. Assume that the government files charges against Lederhaas-Okun for wire fraud and interstate transportation of stolen property in your court.

How would *you* decide this case? Be certain that you explain and justify your answer.

What additional information would you like to have? Should she be charged with federal crimes and/or state crimes? Why?

From a management perspective, does Tiffany's have any responsibility for the thefts? What checks should Tiffany's add to prevent similar thefts in the future? What inventory control techniques might be more effective?

(See Associated Press Staff, "Ex-Tiffany Exec Charged in $1.3M Jewel Theft," *NBC News Business,* July 3, 2013, http://www.nbcnews.com/business/ex-tiffany-exec-charged-1-3m-jewel-theft-6C10523876 (accessed March 18, 2016); Allie Bidwell, "Ex-Tiffany & Co. Exec Stole $1.3 Million in Jewelry," *U.S. News and World Report,* July 3, 2013, http://www.usnews.com/news/articles/2013/07/03/former-tiffany–co-executive-stole-13-million-worth-of-jewelry (accessed March 18, 2016); and Eric Spitznagel, "How a Tiffany's Employee Stole $1.3 Million in Jewelry," *Bloomberg Businessweek,* July 8, 2013, http://www.bloomberg.com/news/articles/2013-07-08/how-a-tiffanys-employee-stole-1-dot-3-million-in-jewelry (accessed March 18, 2016).)

Notes

1. The applicable portion of the statute is available on the Web site for this book.

2. Chris Matyszczyk, "Alleged Hit-and-Run Driver Arrested After Her Car Rats Her Out," CNET, December 7, 2015, http://www.cnet.com/news/woman-arrested-after-her-car-rats-her-out/ (accessed March 12, 2016), and Nicole Wakelin, "Car Rats Out Driver, Calls 911 After Alleged Hit and Run," Yahoo! Autos, BoldRide, December 7, 2015, https://www.yahoo.com/autos/car-rats-driver-calls-911-alleged-hit-run-163006123.html (accessed March 12, 2016).

3. For example, Gerald F. Uelmen, "*Simpson I* and *Simpson II*: The Jury Verdicts Can't Be Compared," *San Jose Mercury News* (California), January 26, 1997, 7C and *Rufo v. Simpson*, 2001 Cal. App. LEXIS 41 (CA 2nd Dist., Div. 4, 2001).

4. Patricia Schaefer, "Are Employees Stealing from You? Tips to Prevent Employee Theft," http://www.businessknowhow.com/manage/employee-theft.htm, © 2012 Attard Communications Inc. (accessed March 12, 2016). Although government entities investigate and prosecute crimes, it is also important for businesses to be proactive in trying to deter crimes. Employee theft can be expensive and can damage a business's reputation.

5. In 2009, the Swiss bank UBS agreed to pay the U.S. government $780 million and admitted that it schemed to help Americans hide money from the IRS. David S. Hilzenrath & Tomoeh Murakami Tse, "UBS to Name Account Holders in New Era for Swiss Banking," *The Washington Post*, August 20, 2009, http://www.washingtonpost.com/wp-dyn/content/article/2009/08/19/AR2009081901395.html (accessed March 12, 2016).

6. U.S. Constitution Article III, § 3.

7. 18 U.S.C.A. § 2381. The sections of the U.S.C.A. that follow elaborate on the crimes of treason and sedition.

8. *Granite Construction Co. v. The Superior Court of Fresno County*, 1983 Cal. App. LEXIS 2400 (Cal. App. 5th Dist., 1983).

9. In *State v. Ford Motor Co.*, Ford was indicted for manslaughter for the fiery crash of a Ford Pinto killing three Indiana girls. Ford was ultimately acquitted. Commentators have noted that the Ford case was a significant departure from prior cases against corporations. Michael B. Metzger, "Corporate Criminal Liability for Defective Products: Policies, Problems, and Prospects," *Georgetown Law Journal* 73, 1 (October, 1984), notes 15 and 16.

10. Will Oremus, "The Skimming Scam, RFID-blocking Wallets Can Work. But Do You Really Need One?," *Travel Explainer*, August 25, 2015, http://www.slate.com/articles/life/travel_explainer/2015/08/credit_cards_passports_and_rfid_fraud_are_special_blocking_wallets_necessary.html (accessed May 15, 2016) and Fahmida Y. Rashid, "How to Spot and Avoid Credit Card Skimmers," *PC Mag*, October 15, 2014, http://www.pcmag.com/article2/0,2817,2469560,00.asp (accessed March 20, 2016).

11. Mail theft is a felony in the United States.

12. Nicole Garcia, "Identity Thieves Busted: Federal Agent a Victim," KMPH Fox 26, July 31, 2012, http://kmph-kfre.com/archive/identity-thieves-busted-federal-agent-a-victim (accessed March 12, 2016).

13. FBI Announcement, Atlanta Division, "International Hacker Arraigned After Extradition, Elaborate Scheme Stole over $9.4 Million from Credit Card Processor," August 6, 2010, http://www.fbi.gov/atlanta/press-releases/2010/at080610.htm (accessed May 14, 2016).

14. Federal Deposit Insurance Corporation (FDIC), "Credit Reporting Agencies," http://www.fdic.gov/consumers/consumer/ccc/reporting.html (accessed March 12, 2016).

15. See *Regina v. Jones*, 91 Eng. Rep. 330 (1703).

16. 18 U.S.C.A. §§ 1341-1347.

17. *Ibid.*, § 1343.

18. Jack K. Levin, Computers and the Internet, X. Crimes, B. Fraud or Unauthorized Access, 2. Other Statutes, 15B Am Jur 2d Computers and the Internet, § 256 Wire Fraud, *American Jurisprudence*, Second Edition, © 2013 West Group.

19. Robert Frank & Amir Efrati, "'Evil' Madoff Gets 150 Years in Epic Fraud," *Wall Street Journal*, June 30, 2009, and "Madoff's Evil," *Wall Street Journal*, June 30, 2009. The Web site of the Madoff Recovery Initiative, http://www.madofftrustee.com/ (accessed March 12, 2016), contains interesting information about the efforts to collect assets and repay victims.

20. Clifford Krauss, "Jury Convicts Stanford of 13 Counts in $7 Billion Ponzi Fraud," *New York Times*, March 7, 2012.

21. 18 U.S.C.A. § 2314.

22. *Id.*, § 1832.

23. *Id.*, § 1341.

24. *Id.*, § 1343.

25. *Id.*, §§ 1831-1839 (1996).

26. *Id.*, § 1382.

27. 18 U.S.C.A. § 1381. One recent article focuses on the application of the EEA to the problem of Chinese espionage and encourages the government to revise the EEA to include stricter penalties for misappropriation to benefit a foreign government and to enact new comprehensive anti-hacking legislation. Jonathan Eric Lewis, "The Economic Espionage Act and the Threat of Chinese Espionage in the United States," *Chicago-Kent Journal of Intellectual Property* 8, 189 (Spring, 2009). Kevin Mandia caught the Chinese government involved in cyberattacks. See Nina Easton, "The CEO Who Caught the Chinese Spies Red-Handed," *Fortune*, July 22, 2013, 88-100.

28. When the EEA was being enacted, the FBI director, Louis Freeh, told a Senate panel that 23 countries are engaged in economic spying against U.S. businesses. Richard Behar, "Who's Reading Your E-mail?" *Fortune*, February 3, 1997, 57-70, at 64.

29. "The Enemy Within: Christian Tyler Reports on How Cold War Spy Tactics Are Being Adapted to Big Business," *Financial Times* (London), April 12, 1997, 1.

30. Richard Behar, "Who's Reading Your E-mail?," 70.

31. *Id.*, 59.

32. Jim Bundy, "How To Protect Yourself From Monday's Malware Threat," *ABC 10 News San Diego*, July 8, 2012, http://www.10news.com/news/how-to-protect-yourself-from-monday-s-malware-threat (accessed March 12, 2016) and Seth Stern, "Leftover Computer Virus Threatens Web Access, FBI Says," *Bloomberg*, July 5, 2012, http://www.bloomberg.com/news/2012-07-05/leftover-computer-virus-threatens-web-access-fbi-says.html (accessed March 12, 2016).

33. The Secret Service did much of the investigation in this case. It is responsible for combating financial fraud in addition to its responsibility to protect public officials. Brad Stone, "A Global Trail That Revealed a Cyber-Ring," *New York Times*, August 12, 2008.

34. Behar, "Who's Reading Your E-mail?," 64, *supra* Note 30.

35. See Model Penal Code (1985) § 2.07.

36. See California Penal Code § 387.

37. See 18 U.S.C. §§ 1961 *et seq*.

38. See *U.S. v. Bellomo*, 1997 U.S. Dist. Lexis 434 (S. Dist. N.Y. 1997).

39. See *Humana, Inc. v. Forsyth*, 119 S. Ct. 710, 1999 U.S. Lexis 744 (1999).

40. Federal Financial Institutions Examination Council, "Currency Transaction Reporting—Overview," https://www.ffiec.gov/bsa_aml_infobase/pages_manual/OLM_017.htm (accessed May 14, 2016).

41. The Uniform Money Services Act (2000) has been adopted by Alaska, Arkansas, Iowa, New Mexico, Puerto Rico, Texas, U.S. Virgin Islands, Vermont, and Washington. (Although technically Puerto Rico and the U.S. Virgin Islands are not states, the ULC treats them as states and for purposes of uniform laws we will also.) ULC Web site, "Legislative Fact Sheet—Money Services Act," http://www.uniformlaws.org/LegislativeFactSheet.aspx?title=Money%20Services%20Act (accessed March 12, 2016) and "Money Services Act Summary," http://www.uniformlaws.org/ActSummary.aspx?title=Money%20Services%20Act (accessed March 12, 2016).

42. Findlaw, "The Insanity Defense among the States," http://criminal.findlaw.com/criminal-procedure/the-insanity-defense-among-the-states.html (accessed March 13, 2016).

43. *Missouri v. McNeely*, 133 S. Ct. 1552, 185 L. Ed. 2d 696 (2013).

44. See John Eligon, Richard Perez-Pena and Katie Rogers, "Gunman Had Just Received Court Order; Restraining Order Might Have Set Off Kansas Man," *Dayton Daily News* (Ohio), February 27, 2016, and Christopher Haxel, Mark Berman, and Jerry Markon, "Clues Begin to Emerge in Deadly Kansas Rampage," *The Washington Post*, February 28, 2016.

45. See Jana Kasperkevic, "'Affluenza' Teen Ethan Couch's Day in Adult Court: Is This The End To His Excuse?," *The Guardian*, February 20, 2016; Lonnie Shekhtman Staff, "Why MADD Wants Ethan Couch Tried As an Adult," *The Christian Science Monitor*, January 11, 2016; and "Warrant: 'Affluenza' Teen's Mom Took $30,000 before Leaving US," *Charleston Gazette-Mail*, January 10, 2016. Postscript: When Couch was suspected of violating his probation, he and his mother left the United States. They were later apprehended in Mexico and returned to the United States.

Agency and Business Organizations

14

Agency

Learning Objectives

After completing this chapter you should be able to

- ■ Explain how agency relationships are formed and terminated
- ■ Compare agents, employees, and independent contractors
- ■ Distinguish the types of authority an agent may have
- ■ Recognize when a court may find *respondeat superior*
- ■ Describe when an injured employee is entitled to compensation from his or her employer

Classic Case

The Classic Case for this chapter is a significant Supreme Court decision confirming that it is constitutional to hold an insurance company liable for the acts of its insurance agent under *respondeat superior*. *Respondeat superior* only applies to the acts of employees, as discussed later in this chapter. The court calls Ruffin an agent because he was a licensed insurance agent. This case involved fraud, so it could have been tried under contract theories instead of tort theories. The advantages to the plaintiffs of arguing fraud under tort law is that the court can use *respondeat superior* and it can award punitive damages.

PACIFIC MUTUAL LIFE INSURANCE COMPANY v. HASLIP
499 U.S. 1, 1991 U.S. LEXIS 1306 (1991)

FACTS Lemmie L. Ruffin, Jr. was a licensed agent for two distinct companies, Pacific Mutual Life Insurance Company and Union Fidelity Life Insurance Company. Ruffin represented himself as an agent of Pacific Mutual when he provided Roosevelt City with a single proposal for both health and life insurance for its employees. Union was going to provide the health insurance policies, and Pacific Mutual was going to provide the life insurance policies. The packaging of insurance from different companies was common and Pacific Mutual knew about and approved of this practice. Roosevelt City accepted the proposal. Union was to send its bills for health premiums to Ruffin at Pacific Mutual's Birmingham office. The city clerk issued a monthly check for the premiums, which was given to Ruffin. Ruffin misappropriated most of the funds and did not pay Union for the insurance. Union sent notices that the health insurance was going to be canceled to the employees in care of Ruffin and Patrick Lupia, Pacific Mutual's agent-in-charge of its Birmingham office. Those notices were not forwarded to the employees. The employees who suffered damages filed this lawsuit against Pacific Mutual and Ruffin claiming fraud by Ruffin and seeking recovery from Pacific Mutual on the basis of *respondeat superior*.

ISSUE Does it violate Pacific Mutual's constitutional rights to hold it responsible for Ruffin's fraud based on the theory of *respondeat superior*?

HOLDING No, it does not violate Pacific Mutual's constitutional rights.

REASONING Excerpts from the opinion of Justice Blackmun:

... [Pacific Mutual, the insurer, challenges the decision to hold it responsible for Ruffin's conduct] on substantive due process grounds, arguing that it was not shown that either it or its Birmingham manager was aware that Ruffin was collecting premiums contrary to his contract; that Pacific Mutual had no notice of the actions; that it did not authorize or ratify Ruffin's conduct; that his contract with the company forbade his collecting any premium other than the initial one submitted with an application; and that Pacific Mutual was held liable and punished for unauthorized actions of its agent for acts performed on behalf of another company.... [Consequently,] the burden of the liability comes to rest on Pacific Mutual's other policyholders.

The jury found that Ruffin was acting as an employee of Pacific Mutual when he defrauded respondents.... [This finding] is amply supported by the record. Ruffin had actual authority to sell Pacific Mutual life insurance to respondents. The insurer derived economic benefit from those life insurance sales. Ruffin's [embezzlement] ... related to the life premiums as well as to the health premiums.... Pacific Mutual cannot plausibly claim that Ruffin was acting wholly as an agent of Union when he defrauded respondents.... He gave respondents a single proposal ... for both life and health insurance. He used Pacific Mutual letterhead, which he was authorized to use on Pacific Mutual business. There was ... no indication that Union was a nonaffiliated company. The trial court found that Ruffin "spoke only of Pacific Mutual and indicated that Union Fidelity was a subsidiary of Pacific Mutual." ... Pacific Mutual encouraged the packaging of life and health insurance. Ruffin worked exclusively out of a Pacific Mutual branch office. Each month he presented to the city clerk a single invoice on Pacific Mutual letterhead for both life and health premiums. Before the frauds in this case ..., Pacific Mutual had received notice that ... Ruffin was engaged in a pattern of fraud identical to those perpetrated against respondents. There were complaints to the Birmingham office about the absence of coverage purchased through Ruffin. The Birmingham manager was also advised ... [that Ruffin received subsequent premiums made payable to him] in violation of company policy.

Alabama's common-law rule is that a corporation is liable for both compensatory and punitive damages for the fraud of its employee effected within the scope of his employment. ... [This may] rationally advance the State's interest in minimizing fraud. Alabama long has applied this rule in the insurance context, for it has determined that an insurer is more likely to prevent an agent's fraud if given sufficient financial incentive to do so. ... Imposing ... damages on the corporation when its agent commits intentional fraud creates a strong incentive for vigilance by those in a position "to guard substantially against the evil to be prevented." ... Imposing liability without independent fault deters fraud more than a less stringent rule. It therefore rationally advances the State's goal. ... [I]mposing such liability is not fundamentally unfair and does not in itself violate the Due Process Clause. ...

We ... conclude that Ruffin was acting as an employee of Pacific Mutual when he defrauded respondents, and that imposing liability upon Pacific Mutual for Ruffin's fraud under the doctrine of *respondeat superior* does not ... violate Pacific Mutual's due process rights.

CREATION AND TERMINATION OF AGENCY RELATIONSHIPS

Creating the Relationship

Agency law concerns the relationships between workers and the people who hire workers. Businesses operate through their agents, and they have all levels of agents. The titles of the agents vary depending on the structure of the business, but agents include the chairman of the board of directors, the chief executive officer, the general partner, and lower level agents such as insurance agents. The tasks assigned to the agent depend on his or her position in the business. Everything a business does it does through its agents. An *agency relationship* is a consensual and representative arrangement. It is based on the concept that the parties mutually agree that (1) the agent will represent (act on behalf of) the principal and (2) the agent will be subject to the principal's direction and control. The agreement can be expressed or implied. Note that many agency relationships are based on contracts, but a contract is not a requirement for an agency relationship. The relationship is formed when the parties consent to create it.

Most agency relationships do not involve litigation because they function smoothly. To resolve the legal problems that do arise, you must look to agency law, contract law, and tort law. The court will place significant reliance on state law. You should check for any variations in your state. Much of the law of agency has been studied by the American Law Institute (ALI) and is discussed in its three *Restatements of Agency*.[1] You should note that the position of your state may vary from that in the *Restatements*.

There are few restrictions on who can form agency relationships and what can be done through agency relationships. Generally, an agent can be assigned to do almost any legal task. Some tasks are considered to be nondelegable under state law. Even when a duty is considered nondelegable, the tasks comprising the duty can still be delegated, but the *legal* responsibility for their proper completion cannot be delegated.[2] In other words, the principal will be held liable if the tasks are not properly performed.

To form a *lawful* agency relationship, the agreement must specify legal acts for the agent to perform. For example, an agreement to distribute illegal drugs such as methamphetamine could not be the basis for creating a lawful agency relationship. Since the basic agreement specifies an illegal act, no legal agency can be created.

Terminating the Relationship

Agency relationships can be terminated by (1) the agreement of the parties, for example, the agency may be established for a set period of time, such as one month; (2) the fulfillment of the purpose for which it was created, as when a realtor finds a buyer for the principal's home; (3) the revocation (termination) of the relationship by the principal, for example, the agent is fired;[3] (4) the renunciation (resignation) of the agent, in other words, the agent quits; or (5) the automatic termination of the agency by operation of law without any additional action. An agency will terminate by operation of law in the following circumstances:

- When the agent dies
- When either party becomes insane
- When the principal becomes bankrupt
- When the agent becomes bankrupt, but only if the bankruptcy affects the ability of the agent to carry out his or her duties
- When the agency cannot possibly be performed (that is, when the subject matter of the agency is destroyed)
- When an unusual and unanticipated change in circumstances occurs that destroys the purpose of the agency relationship
- When a change in law makes completion of the agency relationship illegal

The traditional rule is that the death of the principal also terminates the agency relationship immediately. Because this rule can cause undue hardship for the agent and/or the third person, many states modified their laws. In some, the death of the principal does not immediately terminate the agency relationship if immediate termination will cause a hardship. The definition of a hardship depends on the state. In some states, the termination only becomes effective when the agent has notice of the death.[4]

When either an agent or a principal terminates the agency relationship prematurely (as opposed to termination by operation of law), the party terminating the relationship has a duty to notify the other party within a reasonable period of time. This is required to ensure that the other party does not waste effort on a relationship that no longer exists. For example, if Dulce, the agent, is not aware that the agency is terminated, she will continue to make an effort to sell Ryan's—the principal's—products.

An Ounce of Prevention

When you appoint an agent, you have the power to terminate the agency, even if you do not have the right. If your agent believes the termination is wrongful, the agent can sue you for breach of express or implied contract. You may want to include provisions in your contracts for arbitrating disputes with your agents. If you include such a clause in your agency contracts, you should make sure that the provisions are fair to both sides. If a court determines that the provisions are uneven and too favorable to you, the court may refuse to enforce the arbitration provisions.

Agency at Will

If the agency agreement does not specify a set date, a set period, or a set occurrence that will terminate it, the relationship is an *agency at will.* In an at-will arrangement, either party can terminate the relationship by giving notice to the other. Neither the principal nor the agent needs cause or justification to terminate the at-will relationship. This is consistent with the theory that agency is a voluntary relationship between the parties. In many states, agency at will applies to the hiring of agents and employees. However, since most of the cases involve employees, we will use the employee/employer terminology.

The traditional concept of an employee at will is being eroded rapidly. Some courts are recognizing various theories for recovery by the discharged employee including the following:

■ Courts are holding an employer liable for a tortious discharge if the termination violates public policy. This is based on the theory that employees should not have to forfeit their jobs because they act in a manner that supports some *important* public policy. This basis is commonly used to protect whistleblowers from being discharged. Many federal and state statutes have antiretaliation provisions that prevent employers from retaliating against employees who complain to government agencies, file reports, or testify in court against them. In an early case to recognize this exception, Petermann, an employee of a union, was told to lie when he testified before a legislative committee investigating corruption inside the union. Petermann told the truth instead, and he was fired because he would not commit perjury.[5]

■ Courts are recognizing a breach of employment contract where there is an express or implied agreement that the employment (1) will not be terminated if the employee performs well or (2) will not be terminated without following specific procedures. Implied contracts often are based on procedures, policies in personnel manuals, employment interviews, and position announcements.

■ Courts are recognizing a tort of bad-faith discharge, where the employee has a right of continued employment and has developed a relationship of trust, reliance, and dependency on the employer. It is based on an implicit understanding between the employee and employer that they will deal honestly and fairly with each other. In some states, the courts may decide that employers must have "just cause" to terminate employees or that terminations made in bad faith or based on malice are prohibited.

States may not recognize any of these theories, or they may recognize some combination of them.[6] There are other public policy prohibitions on firing at-will employees. If the employee was fired on the basis of race, color, religion, national origin, gender, or some other violation of civil rights, the courts may decide that the employer cannot terminate the relationship.

The use of an employee handbook or employment manual can be beneficial to an employer in establishing a formal guide for what each party can expect of the other in the relationship. However, the handbook can also be somewhat burdensome since it is likely to impose standards for management that must be followed to protect the rights of the employees. This is especially true if the handbook or manual becomes part of the employment contract, either expressly or by implication. It is helpful to state clearly and unambiguously that employees are employees at will and that the handbook does not create an employment contract.

An Ounce of Prevention

You should maintain careful records documenting the reasons a worker is discharged, even if an agency at will is involved. A paper trail can provide important evidence if the employee sues for wrongful discharge. Workers are more likely to sue you when they have had a number of years of successful employment with promotions, awards, and/or commendations and then they are fired. Employees are likely to be surprised and shocked if they suddenly lose their position without much warning.

Independent Contractors

An *independent contractor* is hired to complete a task for someone else. The physical acts of the independent contractor are not controlled or subject to the control of the hiring party. Instead, the independent contractor relies on his or her own expertise to determine the best way to complete the job. Anyone who contracts to do physical work for another does so as either an employee or an independent contractor. Courts look at many factors in distinguishing between the two. In addition to considering the *right* to control, courts commonly consider the following factors:

- Whether the worker hires assistants
- Whether payment is by the number of hours worked or by the job completed
- Whether the services will be performed for a short period of time or a longer period of time
- Who supplies the tools and equipment to be used
- Where the work is being performed
- Whether the worker is engaged in a distinct occupation or independent business
- Whether the work is a part of the regular business of the hiring party

Independent contractors may be agents, but that is not a necessary condition for being an independent contractor. If the independent contractor does not represent the hiring party or act for the hiring party in legal or contractual matters with third parties, the independent contractor is not the hiring party's agent. In these situations, the independent contractor does not owe the hiring party any fiduciary duties. When legal questions concern fiduciary duties or contracts, the worker will simply be identified as an agent, rather than applying the cumbersome term *independent contractor agent*.

An Ounce of Prevention

If you decide that you want to hire independent contractors instead of employees, you should be careful to consistently treat the workers as independent contractors. It is not sufficient to simply label them as independent contractors or have them sign agreements that state that they are independent contractors. In addition, you need to remember that independent contractors typically can refuse to accept work. Independent contractors generally work for multiple businesses, and this may include your competitors unless there is a valid agreement to the contrary. Since the independent contractor works for others, he or she may not be available when you have a project that you want to have completed. Since he or she is independent, you will not be able to control the means he or she chooses to complete the job.

Responsibility for Independent Contractors

Principals who engage independent contractors as agents will be liable on the contract *if* the contract was authorized. Authorization will be discussed later in this chapter.

A person who hires an independent contractor is generally not responsible to third parties for the independent contractor's physical wrongdoings. However, there are a number of common exceptions to this general rule.[9] Depending on the state these exceptions include the following:

- The independent contractor is hired to engage in ultrahazardous activities.[10]
- The independent contractor is hired to commit a crime.
- The hiring party reserves the right to supervise or control the work.[11]
- The hiring party actually directs the independent contractor to do something careless or wrong.[12]
- The hiring party sees the independent contractor do something wrong and does not stop it.
- The hiring party fails to adequately supervise the independent contractor.
- The hiring party is negligent in selecting the independent contractor.[13]

In many states, the trend has been to increase the number of situations in which the hiring party can be held liable for the torts of an independent contractor. Some courts now will hold the hiring party liable for harm resulting from an independent contractor's job-related *hazardous* activities, which is a reduction from the traditional standard of *ultrahazardous* activities. The exact definitions of ultrahazardous and hazardous depend on the state. However, courts have held that the following activities were ultrahazardous: blasting boulders, drilling oil wells, transporting highly volatile chemicals, and using poisonous gases to fumigate buildings. Remember, the independent contractor is also liable for his or her own wrongdoings, regardless of whether the hiring party is liable.

DUTIES IN THE AGENCY RELATIONSHIP

Fiduciary Duties

The creation of an agency relationship creates fiduciary duties owed by the agent to the principal.[14] People other than agents can also owe fiduciary duties. *Fiduciary duties* are the duties to act with the utmost good faith, candor, confidence, and trust. They include the duty to act with the highest degree of honesty and loyalty and the duty to act in the best interests of the person to whom the duty is owed. Stockbrokers are agents for their clients.[15] As with other agents, their exact duties depend on the situation. If Raye, a broker, is buying and selling stocks selected by Carl, her client, Raye's duty is to follow his instructions in good faith.[16] The broker's fiduciary duties may extend beyond this depending on the circumstances and the types of services the broker is providing.[17] In one case, the court held that the broker, Philip Moore, had an obligation to explain short-selling to his client, Jennie Vucinich, so that she would have some idea of what she was buying.[18] The case was remanded to the trial court to determine if Moore's explanation was adequate since Vucinich was a novice investor. Ordinary business transactions, such as contracts, do not create fiduciary relationships. For example, if Kaitlyn sells Brennen her car, she does not owe him any fiduciary duties.

Other Duties of the Agent to the Principal

An agent is appointed to represent the principal. When the agent acts within his or her agency, it is the legal equivalent of the principal performing the action. The agent must protect the interests of the principal. Consequently, there are a number of duties imposed on the agent by operation of law. Some of these duties overlap. In fact, when an agent breaches one duty, most likely he or she will breach others as well. The agent's duties to the principal include:

- The obligation of faithful service, called the duty of *good faith*. To act in good faith, the agent must be conscientious in carrying out the duties of the agency and must be faithful in meeting his or her responsibilities and duties to the principal.[19] The most common violations of this duty include concealing essential facts that are relevant to the agency, obtaining secret profits, and self-dealing.
- The duty to be loyal to the principal and to protect the principal's best interests.[20] This means that an agent must not compete with the principal, work for someone who is competing with the principal, or act to further the agent's own interests without the consent of the principal. An agent may not use his or her agency position for personal benefit at the expense of the principal, such as making a secret profit.
- The duty to follow all lawful instructions as long as doing so does not subject the agent to an unreasonable risk of injury *and* the instructions are in the *course and scope* of the agency. This duty applies even if agents think the instructions are capricious or unwise. Agents must *indemnify* (repay) their principals for damages suffered because the agents failed to follow lawful instructions that were in the course and scope of their relationship.
- The duty to act as a reasonably careful agent would under the same circumstances. If the agent fails to live up to this obligation and it causes the principal a loss, the agent will be obliged to indemnify the principal.

- The duty to keep personal funds separate from the principal's funds. If the agent wrongfully uses the principal's funds to purchase something, the court can impose a constructive trust for the benefit of the principal. (A *constructive trust* is a trust imposed by a court to prevent unjust enrichment.) The court treats the situation as though the purchase was made for the benefit of the principal from the beginning.
- The duty to account for money received. This is really a combined function of recordkeeping and delivery of the funds. The funds usually must be delivered to the principal (or an authorized third party, such as a bank).
- The duty to give notice. This duty requires an agent to inform the principal about material facts that are discovered within the scope of the agent's employment. In fact, the law presumes that the principal has notice in such situations under the doctrine of imputed notice.
- The duty to perform any obligations specified in the contract. Normally, the agent's promise to act is interpreted as being only a promise to make reasonable efforts to achieve the desired result.

Duties of the Principal to the Agent

Many of the duties of the principal may be specified in the contract between the principal and the agent if there is a contract. In general, the principal has the following obligations to the agent:

- To deal with the agent fairly and in good faith,[21] including the duty not to interfere with the performance of the agency or hinder the effectiveness of the agency[22]
- To comply with the express and implied terms of any contract with the agent[23]
- To compensate the agent per the agreement
- To indemnify or reimburse the agent for expenditures and losses incurred in the performance of the duties[24]
- To maintain proper accounts so that compensation and indemnification will be correct
- To provide the agent with the means to do the job
- To continue the relationship for the time period specified in the agreement

In addition, if the worker is an employee, his or her employer has an obligation to provide the employee with a reasonably safe place to work and safe equipment to use. This obligation is based on common law and state and federal safety statutes, such as the federal Occupational Safety and Health Act (OSHA). Under OSHA, the secretary of labor may pass regulations permitting workers to refuse to work under hazardous conditions.[25] An employer also owes an employee an obligation to compensate him or her for injuries that occur on the job under state workers' compensation laws. Workers' compensation laws are discussed in Chapter 20.

Exhibit 14.2

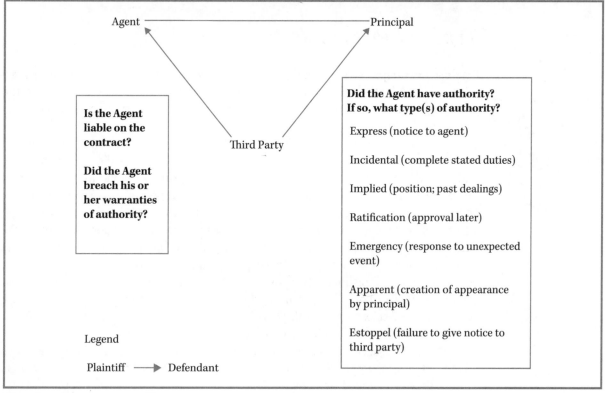

Liability to the Third Party for a Breach of Contract

Agent — Principal

Is the Agent liable on the contract?

Did the Agent breach his or her warranties of authority?

Third Party

Did the Agent have authority? If so, what type(s) of authority?

Express (notice to agent)

Incidental (complete stated duties)

Implied (position; past dealings)

Ratification (approval later)

Emergency (response to unexpected event)

Apparent (creation of appearance by principal)

Estoppel (failure to give notice to third party)

Legend

Plaintiff ——▶ Defendant

Source: Courtesy of Lynn M. Forsythe. © 2016.

LIABILITY FOR CONTRACTS

An agent may negotiate and sign contracts on behalf of the principal. This section addresses the obligations of the parties in these contracts, and the potential liability of the agent, the principal, and/or the third party when problems arise during the performance of their contracts. The distinction between employees and independent contractors is *not* significant when the agent has entered into a contract with the third party, purportedly on behalf of the principal. If the third party is the victim of a breach of that contract, who should be liable to the third party? This issue is diagrammed in Exhibit 14.2.[26]

In examining the potential liability that might arise in a contract case, one main issue is whether the principal's identity is revealed to the third party. (Another important factor is whether the principal authorized the agent to enter into the contract.

This factor will be discussed in a later section.) The principal may be classified as a disclosed, an undisclosed, or an unidentified principal. Each category affects the potential liability of the agent, the third person, and the principal. The status of the principal in this regard is determined when the agent and the third party enter the contract; the legal relationships are fixed at that time.

Types of Principals

Disclosed Principal   When an agent clearly discloses that he or she is representing a principal and identifies the principal, the principal is *disclosed*. In these situations, the principal may be bound to the contract by any of the types of authority discussed in the next section.

Normally, when an agent indicates that he or she is entering into a contract on behalf of the disclosed principal, the agent will not be liable for the contract. It is clearly understood that the third party should look to the principal alone for performance. There are exceptions. For example, if the agent fails to represent his or her capacity as an agent, the agent will be personally bound. There have even been cases where the agent was held liable because he or she failed to represent his or her capacity on the written document, even though the agent alleged that he or she orally informed the third party of his or her representative capacity. In addition, the agent will be bound if he or she intends to be bound. For example, the agent may say, "You can rely on me," or "You have my word on it." The third party will then have legal rights against both the agent and the disclosed principal. This does not mean that the third party can collect twice. The third party is limited to one recovery.

Whenever an agent of a disclosed principal enters into a contract, the agent makes all of the following implied warranties.[27] The agent does not have to state these warranties; they are implied by the situation:

- The disclosed principal exists and is competent.
- The agent is an agent for the principal.
- The agent is authorized to enter into this type of contract for the principal.

The third party can sue the agent to recover for losses that are caused by the breach of warranty of authority.

Undisclosed Principal   An *undisclosed* principal is one whose existence and identity are unknown to the third party at the time of the contract. There are many legitimate reasons why a principal might want to be undisclosed—to be able to negotiate a deal, to negotiate a better deal, or to conceal either an investment in a project or a donation to a charity. The fact that the principal prefers to remain undisclosed to the third person is not sufficient in itself to establish fraud or any other type of wrongdoing.

When the principal is completely undisclosed, the third party believes that the agent is dealing for himself or herself. The third party believes that the contract is with the agent. If there is a default on the contract, the "injured" third party can sue the agent. As far as the third party knows at the time of contracting, there are only two parties to the contract: the third party and the person with whom he or she contracted (the agent.) Consequently, the agent is liable to the third person for any breach of the contract.

If the third party later discovers the identity of the principal, the third party can sue the principal. The suit will be successful if the agent was authorized to enter into this type of contract for the principal.

The third party may in fact be the one who committed the breach. Since the third party thought he or she was liable to the agent, it is logical to allow the agent to sue the third party. The law permits this lawsuit. Under some circumstances, the undisclosed principal may also be able to sue the third party in his or her own name. Generally, the principal can file a lawsuit by himself or herself *only* if the contract is assignable. (*Assignable* means that the rights in the contract legally can be transferred from one person to another.) If the contract is assignable, the position of the third party will not be jeopardized by either an assignment or the suit by the principal rather than the agent. Since the agent can assign the contract to anyone, the principal should be able to enforce the contract rights as if those rights had been assigned to the principal. Either way, the third party will be in the same position. Remember that the third party will not have to pay both the agent and the principal: The third party will have to pay damages only once.

Unidentified Principal   An *unidentified* principal is one whose existence is known to the third party but whose identity is not known when the agent and third party interact.[28] If the principal breaches the contract he or she may be sued if the principal authorized the actions of the agent. Of course, the third party will need to discover the principal's identity. If the principal suffers damages, he or she can sue the third party. The contract need not be assignable, because the third party knew that there was another party with an interest in the contract.

The agent will be personally liable for the contract when he or she is working for an unidentified principal. The third party is probably relying on the agent's reputation and credit since the third party knows the identity of the agent but does not know the identity of the principal.

An Ounce of Prevention

When you serve as an agent, there may be situations in which you are concerned that you are exceeding your authority. Generally, you can verify your authority with your principal. You can also negate the warranties of authority (1) by telling the third party that there is no warranty or (2) by specifically stating the limitations of your actual authority to the third party. Otherwise if you exceed your authority, you may be liable to your principal and/or the third party. You also may be liable for fraud if you intentionally misrepresent your authority.

Types of Authority

The principal will not be liable for every contract entered into by the agent on his or her behalf. To determine whether the principal should be held liable, the court will examine whether the agent was authorized to enter into this type of contract. There are a number of different ways to create authority; they are commonly referred to as *types of authority*. Types of authority can overlap in a given situation, adding confusion for the businessperson.

For the third party to enforce the contract or to recover a judgment against the principal for its breach, all that needs to be shown is that one type of authority exists. In fact, if the third person can establish that *apparent* authority exists in the agent, the principal can be held liable to the third person even though the agent's conduct was *not* actually authorized by the principal. Even if the principal had expressly forbidden the conduct, the principal will be held liable if the agent possessed the apparent authority to perform the act. Remember, though, that the authority to act as an agent usually includes authority to act only for the benefit, not the detriment, of the principal.

Actual Authority   *Actual authority* is the authority that the principal actually grants to the agent: It will establish the limits of what the agent should do in the performance of his or her duties. Actual authority may be expressed by the principal to the agent or it may be implied by the principal's conduct with the agent. Most courts address the specific type or types of authority that we will discuss next.

Express Authority   *Express authority* occurs when the principal informs the agent that the agent has authority to engage in a specific act or to perform a particular task. If the agent acts within the limits of his or her express authority, generally the agent will not be liable to the principal even if the results for the principal are negative. Generally, express authority need not be in writing, and, in most cases, it is not. An agent should interpret the principal's instructions narrowly. If the agent is unclear about his or her authority, the agent should ask the principal for clarification.

Incidental Authority   Generally, the agent is given a brief explanation of his or her authority or he or she is given an objective to accomplish on behalf of the principal. This brief grant of express authority includes the power to do all acts that are incidental to the specific authority that *is* discussed. *Incidental authority* reasonably and necessarily arises to enable the agent to complete his or her assigned duties.

Implied Authority   *Implied authority* is based on the agent's position *or* on past dealings between the agent and the third party. One type of implied authority arises when an agent is given a title and a position. It is implied that the agent can enter into the same types of contracts that people with this title normally can enter. When the principal confers the title on the agent, the agent acquires the implied power that accompanies it.

Exhibit 14.3

Types of Authority for Agents

Type of Authority	Description	Example
Express	• Principal communicates with the agent using spoken and/or written words. • This occurs prior to the agent's actions. • The Statute of Frauds may require a writing.	Pablo tells Aaron to purchase a restaurant franchise on Pablo's behalf.
Implied	• Agent can acquire implied authority through a series of transactions. • Agent can also acquire implied authority by his or her position or job title.	Pauline tells Angela, her administrative assistant, not to order office supplies for the company. Several times Angela orders office supplies, and Pauline pays the bills. Pauline does not tell Angela to stop. Angela may reasonably believe that she now has the implied authority to continue to order office supplies.
	• Kendra is the VP of finance for Willow Ridge. She negotiates a loan for Willow Ridge with the firm's bank even though her express authority does not include negotiating loans. If most VPs of finance have the authority to negotiate loans with banks, Kendra would have the implied authority to do so as well.	Arthur is the Vice President of Finance for Pleasant Village Apartments. He negotiates a loan for Pleasant Village with the firm's bank even though his express authority does not include negotiating loans. If most vice presidents of finance have the authority to negotiate bank loans, Arthur also will have the implied authority to do so.
Incidental (also called incidental powers)	• Agent can carry out transactions within his or her actual or apparent authority.	Alissa is given actual authority to obtain a loan for the business. Alissa will have incidental authority to sign the loan documents and any other necessary paperwork.
Ratification	• Agent lacked authority at the time of his or her acts. • Principal approves the action *after the fact* using words or actions. • The Statute of Frauds may require a writing.	Penny tells Ann to research potential restaurant franchises that might be available and to report back to Penny with her recommendations. Instead Ann purchases a franchise on Penny's behalf. Penny approves the contract in writing.
Emergency	• Agent forms a contract in response to an emergency. • An emergency occurs that requires a quick response. • The principal cannot be located in a timely manner. • The agent's conduct was reasonable and was reasonably expected to benefit the principal.	Prudence hires Andrea to manage her gift shop. The weather service has announced that a hurricane is headed toward their community. Prudence is not available so Andrea goes to the hardware store and purchases lumber and nails to board up the store windows. She has the bill sent to Prudence.

Exhibit 14.3 Continued

Type of Authority	Description	Example
Apparent[a]	• The third party reasonably believes that an agent has authority to act in this manner because of the third party's dealings with the principal and the surrounding facts. • The third party's belief must be reasonable. • Apparent authority will exist even if the principal did not intend to create the authority.	Paul fires Adam, who had worked as his sales agent for three years. After being fired, Adam continues to call on his clients and take new orders and collect payments. (Note that the court could also use implied authority in this situation.)

Agency by estoppel[a]	• Principal will be estopped or prevented from denying the agency relationship if:
	  • principal knows that the "purported agent" is representing himself or herself as the principal's agent.
	  • principal does not speak up to prevent the third party's loss.
		Abel is not an agent for PPP, Inc. However, Abel is calling on businesses in town and representing himself as an agent for PPP. PPP becomes aware of Abel's activities, but it does not take any action to protect the public from Abel.

Source: Courtesy of Lynn M. Forsythe. © 2016.

[a] An actual agency relationship is not required for apparent authority or agency by estoppel. The person can be a purported (reputed) agent.

In the alternative, implied authority may exist because of a series of similar dealings in the past between the agent and the third party. If the principal did not object to the past transactions, it is implied that the principal authorized the earlier contracts and that this type of transaction is within the agent's power.

Ratification Authority   *Ratification authority* occurs when the agent does something that was unauthorized at the time, and the principal approves it later. Ratification requires approval by the principal after the agent forms the contract and after the principal has knowledge of the material facts. When a principal ratifies a contract, the principal must ratify the whole agreement. The principal does not need to communicate the ratification verbally to anyone.[29] Ratification may occur by an express statement or it may be implied by the principal's conduct indicating a clear intent to affirm the agent's actions. In a limited number of situations, the ratification will have to be in writing under the Statute of Frauds.

Emergency Authority   *Emergency authority* is inherent in all agency relationships. It need not be expressed. It provides the agent with authority to respond to emergencies, even though the principal and agent never discussed the type of emergency or how to respond to it. Emergency authority will be found when *all* the following circumstances exist:

■ An emergency or unexpected situation occurs that requires prompt action.
■ The principal cannot be reached in sufficient time for a response or advice.

■ The action taken by the agent is reasonable in the situation, and it is expected to benefit the principal.

Apparent Authority   *Apparent authority* occurs when the principal creates the appearance that an agency exists or that the agent has certain powers. Here, the representation of authority is made by the principal to the third party rather than to the agent.[30] The principal intentionally or carelessly causes the third party to believe that the agent had the authority. Apparent authority is not based on the conduct of the agent. An agent with apparent authority may or may not also have actual authority to perform these same acts on behalf of the principal. Before applying apparent authority, some courts require (1) that the principal's actions give rise to a reasonable belief by the third party in the agent's authority and (2) that there be detrimental reliance on the part of the third party.[31] The existence of apparent authority is a factual issue to be determined in each case, and courts faced with very similar fact situations might disagree.

Apparent authority can exist even though there is no real agent. The person acting in the agent's role may be a *purported agent* (that is, one who claims to be an agent). Sometimes this purported agent is a former agent whose position has been terminated, and sometimes the person never was an agent. When an agency relationship is terminated, a principal should take certain steps to terminate apparent authority. The principal should inform the agent that the relationship is terminated, call or send notices to people who have dealt with that agent, and sometimes advertise in newspapers and trade journals that the relationship is terminated. The principal should collect all identification tags, samples, displays, order forms, and any other materials that can be used as evidence of the agency relationship. These items are *indicia* of the agency relationship.

Apparent authority may be used to hold a principal liable on contracts entered into by the agent. It *ordinarily* will not be used to make a principal liable for physical harm caused by the agent through negligence, assault, trespass, and similar torts.

Authority by Estoppel   *Authority by estoppel* prevents a principal from denying the agent's authority. It occurs when the principal (1) *allows* the purported agent to pass himself or herself off as an agent and (2) does not take steps to prevent the purported agent's representation. Estoppel authority may occur by itself or in conjunction with other types of authority. When there is only estoppel authority and no other authority, estoppel authority will be used solely for the protection of the third party. It creates rights for the third party and liabilities for the principal; it protects the third party by providing reimbursement for the third party's damages. The courts are weighing the respective rights of two relatively innocent people—the third party and the principal. The purported agent can be sued for *fraud,* but generally that person cannot be located or has insufficient funds to pay for any losses. (*Fraud* is the intentional misrepresentation of a material fact.) The types of authority are summarized in Exhibit 14.3.

Imputing the Agent's Knowledge to the Principal

A principal may be legally responsible for information known to the agent but not actually known by the principal. This concept is called *imputing knowledge*. Because an agent has a duty to inform the principal about important facts that relate to the subject matter of the agency, it will be assumed that the agent has performed this duty. If the agent fails to perform this duty and the failure causes a loss, the principal—not the third party—should suffer the loss.

Analysis of Agent's Contracts with Third Parties

To characterize a contract situation involving any type of principal, one should answer the following questions:

- Was the person acting as an agent for the hiring party?
- Did the agent enter a contract on behalf of the hiring party or make contractual promises?
- Was the agent acting within the scope of his or her contractual authority?
- What type or types of authority were present?
- Was the hiring party a disclosed, undisclosed, or unidentified principal?
- Is the agent liable for the contractual promises?

Contract Between the Principal and the Agent

The agency relationship is consensual in nature. It does not have to be based on a contract. However, if it is a contract, both the principal and agent will give or promise to give consideration. As with other contracts, the Statute of Frauds may apply. If it does, written evidence of the contract is required for the contract to be enforceable. Even if the Statute of Frauds does not apply, it is wise to write out the contractual provisions.

Covenants Not to Compete in Employment Contracts   Some employment contracts contain *covenants* (promises) that the employee will not work for a competing firm. The contract may provide that (1) the employee will not moonlight with the competition and/or (2) the employee will not compete with the employer after this employment relationship is terminated. Some contracts contain both prohibitions.

Generally, parties are bound by their contract provisions. On the other hand, it may be a hardship on the employee to unduly restrict his or her ability to locate another job when the current position ends. It also will be detrimental to society if people are not allowed to seek the positions for which they are most highly qualified. For these reasons, courts scrutinize covenants not to compete to determine whether the covenant is legal. As a rule, courts do not favor covenants not to compete in employment contracts. The covenant will be illegal if the court concludes that it is against public policy. Some states hold that a employer cannot prevent an ordinary employee from engaging in competition once the employment is over.[32]

In many states, covenants not to compete will be legal if the employer has a legitimate business interest in the covenant and the covenant is reasonable. In these situations, the employer can sue the breaching employee or former employee for an injunction and/or contract damages.

The time and area specifications must be reasonable, and what is reasonable depends on the type of employment. Covenants containing time periods of six months to two years are generally acceptable to the courts. The covenant also must be reasonable in the area or distance specified. Courts may examine the following criteria in determining whether to enforce a covenant not to compete in an employment contract:

- Is the restraint reasonable in the amount of protection it affords the employer, or is it excessive?
- Is the restraint unreasonable because it is unduly harsh on the employee?
- If the employee works for a competitor, will that threaten irreparable injury to the employer?
- Does the employer have a legitimate interest in preventing competition by the employee? Is the employment relationship of a unique and unusual type?

An employer can prevent an employee from divulging trade secrets after the employment is terminated even without a valid covenant not to compete. Under common law, this disclosure is a violation of the employee's duty of loyalty.

LIABILITY FOR TORTS

In contract matters, there is generally a conscious desire to interact with the public and a conscious decision to enter into business arrangements with the public through the acts of the agent. In most tort situations, however, neither the employer nor the employee desires that the tort occur. But once the tort has occurred, someone has to suffer the financial burden, even if that someone is the innocent third person. The issue then becomes who should be held liable for the tort.

Respondeat Superior

Vicarious liability is legal responsibility for the wrong committed by another person, in this case the employer's liability for the wrongs committed by the employee. One important example is *respondeat superior*, where the employer has to pay for the torts committed by his or her employee in the course and scope of the employee's job. It is difficult to predict whether the court will conclude that the acts were in the course and scope of the job. This makes the application of *respondeat superior* somewhat confusing.

When the employee commits a tort that harms a third person, the employee should be responsible for the harm. However, in agency law, some circumstances exist in which the employer can also be held liable for the torts committed by the employee under the theory of *respondeat superior*. Notice that in these situations the *employer* is being held liable for the conduct of the *employee*. Since the employee is also liable for his or her tortious conduct, the liability is *joint and several*. This means that either party may be held liable individually (several liability) or that both parties may be held liable together (joint liability).

Respondeat superior has been justified on numerous grounds in court opinions, such as the Classic Case, and in legal treatises. The justifications for holding the employer liable for wrongful acts of the employee include the following:

- The employer will be more careful in choosing employees in order to avoid liability.
- The employer will be more careful in supervising employees in order to avoid liability.
- The liability for employees is a cost of conducting business.
- The employer is the person benefiting from the employee's actions.
- The employer can purchase liability insurance.
- The person with the power to control the conduct should be the person to bear financial responsibility.
- The employer can better afford the costs, especially when compared to an innocent third person who is injured by the employee's conduct.

The hiring party's *right to control* is really what distinguishes employees from independent contractors. Remember that *respondeat superior* applies only to employees. It does not apply to independent contractors because the hiring party lacks control over the conduct of independent contractors.

Respondeat superior does not make the employer an insurer for every act of the employee. The employer is only liable for those actions that are within the *course* and *scope* of the employment. Consequently, the issue in most cases based on *respondeat superior* is whether the employee was acting within the course and scope of his or her employment when the tort was committed. To resolve this question, it is important to know the employee's duties, working hours, state of mind, and work location. Courts consider a number of factors in deciding whether to impose *respondeat superior*. The factors include:

- What is the time, place, and purpose of the act
- Whether the act occurred during the normal work time and at the normal workplace

- Whether the act is of the type the employee was hired to perform
- Whether the act is one commonly done by this type of employee
- Whether the act is similar to the job or method authorized by the employer, and if so, how similar
- Whether the employee intended to serve the employer
- Whether the employer has reason to expect that the employee will do such an act
- Whether an employee's use of force against a third person should have been expected by the employer
- Whether the instrumentality used to cause the harm was provided by the employer to the employee
- Whether the act was an intentional tort or a serious crime

It is immaterial if the employer fails to exert actual control over how the worker completes the tasks as long as the employer has the *right* to use this control. *Respondeat superior* has been criticized by employers on the grounds that it is unconstitutional, but the U.S. Supreme Court has affirmed that *respondeat superior* is not fundamentally unfair or unconstitutional.[33] In most jurisdictions, there seems to be a trend toward increasing the employer's liability, even for intentional torts or serious wrongs committed by the employee, such as rape.

In many cases, certain factors may indicate that the employee is within the scope of employment and other factors may indicate the contrary. Each case is different, and no one factor controls this decision; the judge or jury weighs all the factors involved to reach a decision. Since the triers of fact exercise a lot of discretion in these cases, fact situations that seem very similar may result in markedly different decisions by different courts.

An employer can be held liable for an employee's acts even though the employer instructed the employee not to perform a specific act or commit torts. An employer is not exempt from liability when his or her employees disobey instructions. Otherwise, an employer could avoid liability by simply instructing all of his or her employees not to commit any torts during the course of employment. An employer can also be held liable under *respondeat superior* when the employee *fails* to act as directed.

Courts are less likely to hold an employer liable under *respondeat superior* for intentional wrongs such as *assault* (a threat to touch someone in an undesired manner) and *battery* (unauthorized touching without legal justification or consent) than they are for negligence on the part of the employee. Many criminal acts are also torts, and the employer may be held civilly liable under *respondeat superior* for the financial losses suffered by the victim of the employee's criminal act even if the employer is not held liable for the crime. For example, in the Classic Case of *Pacific Mutual Life Insurance Company v. Haslip,* Ruffin stole the money from the premium payments he received and the insurance company was held liable to the policyholders for his acts under *respondeat superior. Respondeat superior* is not used to impose criminal liability on the employer.

An Ounce of Prevention

Social media has moved into the mainstream. Your business should consider the use of social media outlets by your employees, both in and out of the workplace. Social media can blur the lines between your employees' personal and professional lives. A company policy can establish guidelines for use of social media outlets. The policy needs to be tailored to your individual company, its culture, and the industry. It should include what types of social media use are allowed during work hours, and employees should be informed that their social media use may be monitored. Your employees should differentiate between their personal and business identities. They should not use your trademarks without permission. Sometimes clear disclaimers on social media may be appropriate, such as "the views expressed are those of employee A and not company Z." In addition, your employees need to comply with other company policies including those dealing with discrimination, harassment, and confidential information.

Direct Liability of the Employer

Employers may be held directly responsible for some of the wrongs committed by their employees. For example, the employer is liable if the employer (1) instructed the employee to commit the wrong, (2) did not properly supervise the employee, (3) ratified or approved the employee's tort, or (3) was negligent in the selection of the employee.

Criminal law may also apply to an employer when an employee commits a crime. For example, an employer can be criminally liable based on his or her own fault. If an employer directs or encourages an employee to engage in criminal activity, the employer will probably be held personally liable for such acts under the theories of conspiracy, solicitation, or accessory to the crime. (In a *conspiracy*, the participants plan the criminal behavior together. However, in a *solicitation*, one person convinces another to engage in the criminal activity. A person is an *accessory to the crime*, when he or she assists the primary actor in the commission of the crime.) In addition, some criminal statutes create liability for the employer even though the employer does not intend to violate the statute or does not know of the illegal act or condition. For example, state liquor laws often specify that tavern or restaurant owners are liable if minors are served alcohol in their bars. In most states, the hiring party can be held directly liable and/or criminally liable whether he or she is aware of the violation.

Negligent Hiring

Careful selection of employees is important to an employer. An employer wants to know if the applicant will do a good job, work well with other members of the staff, and follow instructions. An employer can be held liable for negligent hiring if he or she is careless in the hiring process. In many states, negligent hiring also applies to the hiring of agents and independent contractors. However, since most of the cases involve employees, we will use the employee/employer terminology. *Negligent hiring* assumes that if the company had properly investigated the applicant's past, it would have learned of the prior inappropriate conduct of the applicant, and then the employer would not have hired the person. Under the theory of negligent hiring, an employer owes a duty to customers and to the public at large. In many states, the employee's acts are not required to be in the course and scope of the employment to impose liability for negligent hiring.

In negligent hiring cases, the question before the court normally will be whether the employer exercised the level of care that, under all the circumstances, a reasonably prudent employer would exercise in choosing an employee for the particular duties to be performed. The court then considers the reasonableness of the employer's efforts to check the applicant's background. The employer's duty depends on the type of position for which he or she is hiring. In 2012, Elgin Stafford's parents sued University of California, Berkeley for negligent hiring in its hiring of Dr. Robert Kevess, who worked at the school's medical center. The parents claimed that Kevess repeatedly sexually abused their son when he was a patient of Kevess. They contended that the abuse led Elgin to commit suicide. Kevess was criminally charged with sexually assaulting six male patients.[34]

Some employers are very thorough in their investigation of applicants due to the potential risks and liability. Employers should be aware that there are some restrictions on what an employer can ask. For example, as mentioned in Chapter 12, some states prohibit employers from asking applicants to divulge the usernames and passwords to their social media accounts. States generally allow employers to search the public areas of the Internet. Microsoft published a survey that indicated 70 percent of job recruiters and managers have used Internet information in their decision not to hire someone.[35] Even in the public areas of the Internet, employers may discover information about an applicant that they are not permitted to ask directly. Photos on the Internet may tell the employer the gender and race of the applicant. As we will discuss in Chapter 20, employers cannot legally discriminate on these grounds. Mug shots on the Internet will provide information about arrest records. Some states only permit employers to ask about criminal convictions.[36] It is possible with some social media for an imposter to create an account in someone else's name and post damaging false information, such as pictures depicting heavy alcohol use and drug use.

It is common to sue the employer for both negligent hiring and *respondeat superior*. In some states, if the employer admits that there will be *respondeat superior* for any employee torts, the claim for negligent hiring is dismissed.[37] Exhibit 14.4 compares the direct and the vicarious liability of the employer.

Exhibit 14.4

Employer's Liability		
Type of Liability	**Proof Necessary**[a]	**Examples**
Direct liability	• Elements of the tort	• Negligent hiring • Negligent promotion • Negligent retention • Negligence in instructing the worker • Negligence in maintaining the premises or equipment
Vicarious liability	• Worker was an employee • Worker committed a tort (includes the elements of the tort) • Tort was in the course and scope of the job	• *Respondeat Superior*

[a] The proof is what must be established in court.

Indemnification

When an employer pays a third person under *respondeat superior* for injuries caused by the employee's unauthorized acts, the employer is entitled to *indemnification* (the right to be repaid) from the employee. *Respondeat superior* is not based on the fault of the employer; it only creates legal liability for the employer. The employer should be entitled to recover from the person who caused the loss—the employee—so the law permits reimbursement. As a practical matter, the employer generally will have insurance to cover the liability he or she incurred. If the employee is still employed by the employer, the employer may be able to withhold part of the reimbursement from each paycheck until the employer is completely repaid. Continuing to employ the worker may increase the likelihood that the employer will be liable for any similar wrongs by the employee in the future under *respondeat superior* or negligent retention.

Sometimes an employee may be held liable to the third person due to the commission of a tort, but the employee may then be entitled to indemnification from the employer. Courts are influenced by what they believe to be just, considering the business and the nature of the particular relationship between the employer and the employee.[38] Under the *Restatement,* an employee is entitled to indemnification if the employee, at the direction of the employer, commits an act that constitutes a tort, but the employee believes that the act is not tortious.[39] In other words, the employee must act in good faith. Obviously, if an employee completes a task that he or she knows to be illegal or tortious, the employee is not entitled to indemnification.[40] Exhibit 14.5 illustrates the relationships among the primary parties when the employee commits a tort.

Legal Relationships Under *Respondeat Superior*

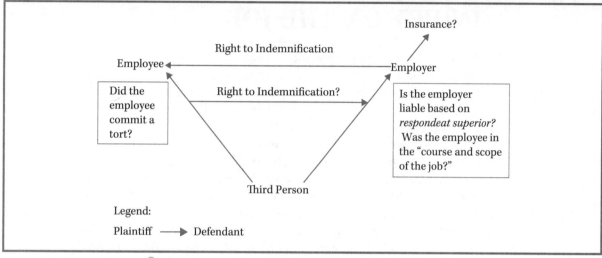

Source: Courtesy of Lynn M. Forsythe. © 2016.

Defenses Available to the Employer

Assume that an employee commits a tort and the third person is seeking damages from both the employee and employer. The employer can use three potential defenses that will shield him or her from liability:

■ The employee was not in the course and scope of employment, which means that the employer had no legal right or duty to control the employee's conduct.
■ The employee's conduct was an extreme deviation from the norm. It was not conduct that could reasonably be foreseen or expected, and therefore not something which the employer could be expected to control.
■ The employee had abandoned his or her employment and embarked on a "frolic" of his or her own. The employer should not be responsible since the employee was doing something totally unrelated to the job.

Analysis of an Employee's Torts

To characterize a tort situation, one should answer the following questions:

■ Was the person acting as an employee for the hiring party?
■ Did the employee commit a tort?

- ■ Was the employee acting within the course and scope of the job?
- ■ Is the employee entitled to indemnification from the employer?
- ■ Is the employer entitled to indemnification from the employee?

INJURY ON THE JOB

An employer has a duty to provide employees with a reasonably safe place to work and reasonably safe equipment to use at work. Both the place and equipment should be appropriate to the nature of the employment. If the workplace is not safe, the employer should warn employees about unsafe conditions that the employees may not discover even if they are reasonably careful.[41]

Under the common law, if an employee is hurt at work, the employer can use a number of defenses to avoid paying the employee. Negligence by the employee and the employee's assumption of the known risk are two such defenses. For example, the employee might have been driving the truck too fast for icy road conditions. The courts will use their law of contributory negligence (to bar recovery) or comparative negligence (to reduce recovery) for the employee. Sometimes the work itself may be inherently dangerous.[42] Some states are reluctant to apply assumption of the risk to bar or reduce recovery by injured employees; however, other states are not reluctant to do so.[43] Some states have a "firefighter's rule"[44] that has the same effect as assumption of the risk; it bars suits by firefighters, peace officers, and/or other emergency workers from recovering for on-the-job injuries.[45]

In common law, the *fellow employee doctrine* also acts to bar recovery by the employee. Traditionally, this concept was called the *fellow servant doctrine*. Under this theory, an employee cannot recover damages for work-related injuries if the damages are caused by another employee of the same employer. It acts as a complete bar to recovery.

Contemporary Case

In this Contemporary Case a group of injured plaintiffs (referred to as Hartings) and a group of insurance companies who have paid for injuries are suing Rite Rug and Jung Ho Bae for Xu's negligent driving on the way to a job site. The lower court granted summary judgment in favor of Rite Rug and Jung Ho Bae.

HARTINGS v. THE NATIONAL MUTUAL INSURANCE COMPANY
2014 Ohio App. LEXIS 1757 (3rd App. Dist., 2014)

FACTS   On October 15, 2011, Hillary Hartings was driving her vehicle with her three young cousins as passengers. Xu was driving his vehicle to a work site for Jung Ho Bae when he failed to stop at a stop sign and crashed into Hillary's vehicle. Xu's failure to stop constituted negligence and was the cause of the accident. Hillary and two cousins sustained serious injuries and the third cousin was killed. Subsequently Xu was convicted of aggravated vehicular manslaughter and deported to China. Detective Megan Baker investigated the accident scene and was unable to communicate with Xu because he could not read or speak English. Xu's Illinois driver's license was cancelled on July 10, 2009; his driving record revealed three moving violations.

Jung Ho Bae previously worked as a flooring installer for Rite Rug. Then he created a flooring business which he called Jung Ho Bae. The business operated from an office space inside the Rite Rug warehouse. Kim, his wife, worked in their office. Kim testified that Jung Ho Bae's responsibility was to locate competent drivers and installers for Rite Rug. She worked closely with the office manager of Rite Rug, who gave her the work orders and she assigned them to one of the Jung Ho Bae installers. She would give the list of completed jobs to the office manager and get paid. Kim testified that Jung Ho Bae did not train its installers. She said that Rite Rug inspects their work. She said that Jung Ho Bae has an ongoing relationship with the installers. To the best of her knowledge, the installers do not work for anyone else. Installers get paid weekly based on how many jobs they finish. Jung Ho Bae does not conduct criminal background checks or check an applicant's driving history. Kim does make sure they have a valid driver's license by examining it. She requires installers to have insurance coverage but she does not require proof or verify that they do. Kim testified that Xu signed a subcontractor agreement form before he started working for Jung Ho Bae. The agreement is in both Korean and English. Kim checked the expiration date on his driver's license. She was not aware that it was invalid and she did not ask about any accidents or moving violations. She never rode with him.

Moyer, the builder operations manager for Rite Rug, testified that the corporate office would provide a packet for the installers to fill out. When completed, the packet and a copy of the driver's license was sent to the corporate office. Moyer was not sure what they did with it. The corporate office would respond whether the applicant could work as a subcontractor. Moyer said "he is unaware whether the installers work for any other companies, but knew that in the past, some installers advertised their services for other companies."

According to Aaron Bayer, the production manager, Rite Rug requires the installers to pick up, inspect, load, and deliver the flooring material. Jung Ho Bae assigns the installers to the job sites. Rite Rug provides the installers with maps and directions. Bayer was responsible for inspecting the installers' work but he did not provide training. He admitted that Rite Rug advertises that it is a "seller and installer of floor materials." The Rite Rug website refers to the installers as Rite Rug installers.

Michael Nelson, Rite Rug's corporate warehouse manager, testified that Rite Rug meets with and trains its installers. Rite Rug does not verify whether installers are competent to drive. Installers get paid based on how many jobs they have completed. Rite Rug back-charges an installer for jobs that are not done correctly. Nelson said that he knows that Rite Rug's carpet installers are employees, however, he was unaware if the installers of hard surface flooring are Rite Rug employees.

ISSUE   Are the Hartings and the insurance companies entitled to a trial on whether Rite Rug and/or Jung Ho Bae are liable?

HOLDING Yes, they are entitled to a trial. There are genuine issues as to whether Xu was an employee of Jung Ho Bae and of Rite Rug and whether they were negligent in hiring him.

REASONING Excerpts from the opinion of Judge Rogers:

... [W]hile an employer is vicariously liable for the negligent acts of its employees committed within the scope of employment ..., an employer ... is not liable for the negligent acts of the independent contractor. [Ohio recognizes some exceptions to this rule, including that an employer may be liable for injuries that are a result of the employer's failure to "exercise reasonable care in the selection of a competent and careful independent contractor."] ...

To determine whether a party is an employee or an independent contractor, we must resolve the central question of "who had the right to control the manner or means of doing the work[?]" ... This ... requires the consideration of a number of factors, none of which are dispositive by themselves. ... Factors to be considered include "who controls the details and quality of the work; who controls the hours worked; who selects the materials, tools and personnel used; who selects the routes traveled; the length of employment; the type of business; the method of payment; and any pertinent agreements or contracts." ... Our review ... reveals that there was evidence from which a jury could reasonably infer that Xu was either an employee or an independent contractor.

On one hand, evidence was presented which tends to prove that Xu was an independent contractor. It is undisputed that the installers had to provide their own tools and vehicles. While ... Rite Rug attached a map to work orders, there was no testimony ... that the installers ... had to follow these routes. ... [T]he method of payment is also suggestive of an independent contractor since Xu was paid per job, and not at an hourly rate. While the presence of subcontractor agreements also points toward an independent contractor relationship, Xu adamantly denied signing a subcontractor agreement ...

On the other hand, evidence was presented which tends to indicate that the Baes and Rite Rug had the right to control the manner ... by which Xu performed his work. The mere fact that a contracting party reserves the right to approve the work ... does not necessarily establish an employer-employee relationship. ... Although there was testimony that Rite Rug does not train its installers, this was contradicted by Nelson's testimony that Rite Rug does, in fact, train its installers. ... [S]ometimes the Baes will "walk the job site" with new installers in order to teach them how to properly install floors. ... [A]ll the flooring materials ... are provided by Rite Rug. ... [T]he installers are directed to pick up ... flooring materials in the Rite Rug warehouse. ... [B]oth Rite Rug employees and the Baes [stated] that they retained the right to terminate installers if they did not produce satisfactory work. The fact that none of the installers were discharged is irrelevant, as long as the Baes and Rite Rug *maintained the right* to discharge. ... The ongoing nature of the Baes' and Rite Rug's relationship also points to an employer-employee relationship. ... "[A]n independent contractor is generally hired to complete a single job only and does not have a continuing, full-time relationships with a single client." Rite Rug has employed the Baes to provide them with installers for over 10 years and has even provided them with office space in its warehouse to conduct business. Rite Rug exclusively uses the Baes to install their flooring. Similarly, the Baes only work for Rite Rug. ...

[For purposes of a negligent hiring or retention claim, in Ohio it is irrelevant whether the worker is an employee or an independent contractor.] ... [I]t is undisputed that Xu was incompetent to drive and deliver Rite Rug materials, since he did not have a valid driver's license. It is also undisputed that Xu's negligence caused the Hartings' injuries. ... The Baes and Rite Rug argue that Xu's responsibility of transporting the flooring materials was incidental to his main task of installing the flooring and that since driving a car was not part of his job responsibilities, they had no duty to look into Xu's driving history. ... [T]his is contradicted by almost every employee who was deposed from Rite Rug. These employees testified that the transportation of the flooring materials is a principal responsibility of an installer. . . . [T]he matter should be submitted to a trier of fact to determine whether delivery was an integral part of Xu's job responsibilities and whether the Baes and Rite Rug exercised reasonable care in selecting Xu to deliver their goods by simply looking at his driver's license. . . .

[W]e affirm in part and reverse in part the trial court's judgment and remand this matter for further proceedings consistent with this opinion.

Judgment Affirmed in Part, Reversed in Part, and Cause Remanded.

Short Answer Questions

1. Assume that your firm is going to hire workers to "lease" to businesses and homeowners on a temporary basis. Some of the workers will do menial tasks like clean construction sites and pull weeds. Others will do clerical work such as data entry and filing. Prepare a list of questions for the job application. What other information will you collect about the applicants before you make your decision? Remember that you want to avoid liability for negligent hiring.

2. Assume you are a part-time driver for Uber. Between classes and assignments, you drive passengers in your own vehicle. One day you pick up Leila to drive her to the airport. On your way to the airport, you have an automobile accident and Leila are injured. Who is liable for her injuries? Why? What additional information would be helpful in making a decision?

3. Deric White entered an Apple Store because he was receiving strange error messages on his iPhone 5. Proper procedures were to confirm that the customer had backed up his or her information. Without confirming that White had performed a back-up procedure, the Apple staff member began working on the phone and executing a factory reset. Resetting the phone to its initial position caused White to lose 15 years of contact information and many personal photos. Should Apple be liable for the employee's actions? Why or why not?[46]

You Decide...

1. Deborah Callaway was a credit and collections manager for LA Digital Post. Callaway regularly drove her own vehicle to and from work and she was not compensated for her travel time. She often stopped at a bank on her way home to make deposits for LA Digital Post. One morning Callaway left work in her own vehicle to go to a doctor's appointment. The medical appointment was not related to her work and she did not engage in any work activity during the appointment. She had permission to go to the appointment and the time was treated as her lunch break. Callaway had an automobile accident with Raymond Maiello when she was returning to work after the appointment. Would you impose liability on LA Digital Post under the doctrine of *respondeat superior?*

How would *you* decide this case? Be certain that you explain and justify your answer.

(See *Maiello v. LA Digital Post*, 2015 Cal. App. Unpub. LEXIS 1782 (2nd App Dist., Division 7, 2015).)

2. IPC International Corporation was an independent security contractor. IPC hired Michael Juniel to provide public safety services at the Greenbriar Mall in Atlanta, GA. Juniel was responsible for "patrolling the property and deterring criminal activity." On the day of the incident Juniel arrived at work and was assigned to patrol a parking lot area. "As Juniel walked through the mall to his assigned post, he saw several masked men near a jewelry store and approached them. One of them had a gun and aimed it toward a mall patron. Juniel intervened in the confrontation, covering the patron's body with his own in an attempt to shield the patron from the gunshots. Both Juniel and the patron suffered bullet wounds in the shooting. The masked men then entered the jewelry store, shot a security guard in the store, smashed the counter, stole jewelry, and fled from the mall." Juniel sued the owner of the mall claiming that negligent management and patrol of the mall had caused his injuries. Is the owner of the mall liable or did Juniel assume the risk?

How would *you* decide this case? Be certain that you explain and justify your answer.

(See *Swope v. Greenbriar Mall Limited Partnership*, 765 S.E.2d 396, 398, 2014 Ga. App. LEXIS 712 (GA Ct. of Appeals 2014).)

Notes

1. The *Restatements* are treatises that summarize and make recommendations of what the law should be on a topic. Since the third *Restatement of Agency* was published in 2006 and is relatively new, the provisions in the second *Restatement* are still the precedents in many states. In addition, in many areas the third *Restatement* did not significantly change the rules from the second *Restatement*.

2. *Restatement (Third) of Agency* (Philadelphia: American Law Institute, 2006), § 3.04(c) explains the *Restatement's* position on duties that cannot be delegated.

3. Generally, the principal can terminate the agency at any time even though there was an agreement that the agency relationship would continue for a set time. Although the principal may have the *ability* to terminate the agency, he or she may not have the legal *right* to do so; in such a case, the agency can be terminated, but the principal may be liable for damages if this termination is a breach of contract.

4. *Restatement (Third) of Agency* (Philadelphia: American Law Institute, 2006) § 3.07(2) cited in Agency, V. Duration and Termination of Agency, C. Termination by Operation of Law, 3 Am Jur 2d Agency § 50, Termination as Dependent on Notice of Death.

5. *See Petermann v. International Brotherhood of Teamsters*, 174 Cal. App. 2d 184 (2nd Dist., Div. 2, 1959), cited in Charles J. Muhl, "The Employment-at-Will Doctrine: Three Major Exceptions," *Monthly Labor Review*, January 2001, 3.

6. *Ibid.* This article contains an exhibit of which states follow which approaches as of October 1, 2000. The table on page 4 is based on a prior article by David J. Walsh & Joshua L. Schwarz, "State Common Law Wrongful Discharge Doctrines: Update, Refinement, and Rationales," 33 *American Business Law Journal* 645 (Summer, 1965). *See also* Kevin P. Harrison, "You Can't Fire Me! State Common Law Exceptions to Employment-At-Will," 13 WAKE FOREST J. BUS. & INTELL. PROP. L. 229 (Spring, 2013).

7. The trial court decision that the drivers were employees was affirmed by the court of appeals. *Estrada v. FedEx Ground Package System, Inc.*, 154 Cal. App. 4th 1, 2007 Cal. App. LEXIS 1302 (2nd Dist. Div. 1 2007). This class action case was limited to full-time drivers who had a single work area or route (SWAs). In the words of the court, "In practice . . . the work performed by the drivers is wholly integrated into FedEx's operation. The drivers look like FedEx employees, act like FedEx employees, are paid like FedEx employees, and receive many employee benefits."

Estrada v. FedEx Ground Package System, Inc., at pp. 9 and 11. The petition for review by the California Supreme Court was denied by *Estrada v. FedEx Ground Package System Inc.,* 2007 Cal. LEXIS 13422 (Cal., Nov. 28, 2007).

8. *In re FedEx Ground Package System, Inc.,* 792 F.3d 818, 2015 U.S. App. LEXIS 11770 (7th Cir. 2015). The federal court of appeals had certified two questions to the Kansas Supreme Court. The Kansas Supreme Court responded that the drivers were employees as a matter of law. The Seventh Circuit applied this rule and remanded the case to the district court to enter a judgment for the drivers.

9. Some of these exceptions are stated in the *Restatement (Second) of Torts* (Student Edition) (St. Paul: American Law Institute, 1965), Chapter 15.

10. *Id.* Section 423 discusses highly dangerous activities; § 427A discusses abnormally dangerous activities; §§ 413 and 416 address work that creates a peculiar risk.

11. *Id.,* § 414.

12. *Id.,* § 410.

13. *Id.,* § 411.

14. There are other examples of fiduciary duties, such as those owed by a lawyer to his or her client, those owed by a corporate officer to the shareholders, and those owed by a trustee to a trust beneficiary. Principals owe their agents the duty of good faith and fair dealing. This is a narrower duty than the fiduciary duty. Thomas Earl Geu, "A Selective Overview of Agency, Good Faith and Delaware Entity Law," 10 Del. L. Rev. 17 (2008), 42-43.

15. *O'Malley v. Boris,* 742 A.2d 845, 849 (Del. Sup. Ct. 1999), cited in Note 127 of Thomas Lee Hazen, "Are Existing Stock Broker Standards Sufficient? Principles, Rules, and Fiduciary Duties," Colum. Bus. L. Rev. 710 (2010).

16. Brokers, VI. Transactions by Stock and Exchange Brokers, B. Execution of Customer's Orders, 12 Am. Jur. 2d Brokers § 181, § 181 Generally.

17. *See* Thomas Lee Hazen, "Are Existing Stock Broker Standards Sufficient? Principles, Rules, and Fiduciary Duties," Colum. Bus. L. Rev. 710 (2010). Financial reform legislation was written following the discovery of Bernard Madoff's Ponzi scheme and the Goldman Sachs investigation. During the legislative process, there was a debate about whether "to statutorily impose new fiduciary duties" on brokers. New statutory fiduciary duties were not included in the final statute. *Id.,* at 713.

18. *Vucinich v. Paine, Webber, Jackson & Curtis, Inc.,* 803 F.2d 454, 460, 1986 U.S. App. LEXIS 32494 (9th Cir. 1986).

19. "Agency; Agent; Good Faith," LawEasy, http://www.laweasy. com/q/20070606070054/agency–agent–good-faith (accessed November 20, 2012) and "Rights, Duties, and Liabilities Between Principal and Agent," USLegal, Inc., http://agency. uslegal.com/rights-duties-and-liabilities-between-principal-and-agent/ (accessed December 21, 2015).

20. *Restatement (Third) of Agency,* 2006, § 8.01 deals with the duty to act loyally. Section 8.08 deals with other duties owed by an agent.

21. *Id.,* § 8.15.

22. John Bourdeau, Romualdo P. Eclavea, Jill Gustafson, and Lucas Martin, Agency X. Rights, Duties, and Liabilities Between Principal and Agent B. Duties and Liability of Principal to Agent 1. In General, 3 Am Jur 2d Agency § 227 Contractual duties.

23. *Restatement (Third) of Agency,* 2006, § 8.13.

24. There may be a distinction between the duty to indemnify and the duty to reimburse under state law. In many states, the duty to repay the agent for necessary expenses, such as hotel bills and meals, may be a duty to reimburse. The duty to repay the agent for damages that result from the execution of the agency, such as damages paid by the agent to a third party for breach of contract by the principal, may be a duty to indemnify. The amount the agent is entitled to receive depends on the agreement and state law. Under the *Restatement (Third) of Agency* § 8.14, a principal has a duty to indemnify an agent in accordance with the contract, and unless otherwise agreed: (1) when the agent makes a payment within the scope of the agent's actual authority; (2) when the agent makes a payment that is beneficial to the principal, unless the agent acts officiously in making the payment; or (3) when the agent suffers a loss that should fairly be borne by the principal.

25. *Whirlpool Corp. v. Marshall,* 445 U.S. 1 (1980).

26. The third party should make a strategic decision about whether to sue the agent or the principal. The third party should compare the assets of the agent and the principal and any insurance they have purchased. If the agent did not have any type of authority, the third party would probably be more successful suing the agent.

27. *Restatement (Third) of Agency,* 2006, § 6.10 deals with warranties of authority.

28. The *Restatement (Second) of Agency* (Philadelphia: American Law Institute, 1958) and many courts use the label of partially disclosed principals for unidentified principals. The *Restatement (Third) of Agency,* 2006, § 1.04 (2)(c), uses unidentified principal.

29. *Restatement (Third) of Agency,* 2006, § 4.01.

30. Warren A. Seavey, *Handbook of the Law of Agency* (St. Paul: West, 1964), § 8D, p. 19.

31. *General Overseas Films, Ltd. v. Robin International, Inc.,* 542 F. Supp. 684 (S.D. N.Y. 1982), p. 688, n. 2.

32. For example, in California generally former employees can engage in any lawful business, trade, or profession. The California statute makes exceptions for covenants not to compete in other contexts, such as the termination of partnerships and limited liability companies, the sale of the goodwill of a business, or the sale of all of the shares in a

corporation. *See* California Business & Professions Code §§ 16600, 16601, 16602, and 16602.5 and *Edwards v. Arthur Andersen, LLP,* 44 Cal. 4th 937, 2008 Cal. LEXIS 9618 (CA 2008).

33. *Pacific Mutual Life Insurance Co. v. Haslip,* 111 S. Ct. 1032 (1991).

34. Alyssa Creamer, "Elgin Stafford's Parents Sue UC Berkeley, Dr. Robert Kevess," *Huffington Post,* September 5, 2012, http://www.huffingtonpost.com/2012/07/05/parents-of-elgin-stafford_n_1651324.html?utm_hp_ref=college (accessed December 6, 2015), and Henry K. Lee, "Ex-doctor Sued over Death: UC Berkeley," *San Francisco Chronicle* (California), July 1, 2012. The parents' suit was subsequently dismissed. Kevess pleaded no contest and was sentenced to five years of probation on the criminal charges for sexual misconduct with a number of other patients. Melissa Wen, "Former Tang Center Doctor Sentenced to 5 Years' Probation for Sexual Misconduct with Patients," *The Daily Californian,* December 17, 2015 (accessed April 19, 2015).

35. Survey reported in Solomon, Steiner & Peck, Ltd., "Can Your Employer Do a Background Check on You via Facebook?," http://www.ssandplaw.com/Business-Law-Articles/Can-your-Employer-do-a-Background-Check-on-you-via-Facebook.shtml (accessed December 6, 2015).

36. *See* Anita Ramasastry, "Mug Shot Mania: The Legal and Policy Issues Surrounding Private Websites' Postings of Arrest Photos," *Criminal Law,* April 24, 2012, http://verdict.justia.com/2012/04/24/mug-shot-mania (accessed December 6, 2015).

37. *See Diaz v. Carcamo,* 2011 Cal. LEXIS 6172 (CA 2011).

38. *Restatement (Second) of Agency,* 1958, § 438(2)(b).

39. *Id.,* § 439(c) and Comment on Clause (c).

40. Harold Gill Reuschlein & William A. Gregory, *Hornbook on the Law of Agency and Partnership,* 2nd ed. (St. Paul: West, 1990), § 89(B), 151-152.

41. *Restatement (Second) of Agency,* 1958, § 492.

42. Many of the professional and volunteer rescue workers from the 9/11 disaster at the World Trade Center Twin Towers are suffering from some form of respiratory problems. Workers at the site and residents of the area were exposed to pollutants that are harmful if inhaled, such as asbestos, lead, mercury, and pulverized glass. *See* Richard Perez-Pena, "Cleaning Set for Exteriors Near 9/11 Site," *New York Times,* April 6, 2002, and Margaret Ramirez, "WTC Clinic Opens; Clinton Urges $90 M More for Initiative," *Newsday, Inc.,* August 6, 2002.

43. According to the *Restatement (Second) of Agency,* 1958, § 499, absent a statute to the contrary, an employer is *not* legally liable to an employee who is injured by a risk that is inherent in the work.

44. It is also called the fireman's rule.

45. The firefighter's rule generally prevents tort recovery for firefighters and police officers who are injured by accidents of the type normally anticipated by the job. For example, the rule prevents a firefighter from suing the individual who negligently caused the fire which the firefighter was fighting. Some states do not use the firefighter's rule. For example, the South Carolina Supreme Court refused to adopt such a rule. *See* "S. Carolina High Court Rejects Firefighter's Rule," *National Law Journal,* June 3, 2002, Case, Vol. 24, No. 38.

46. This situation actually occurred in the United Kingdom. *See* Yoni Heisler, "Man Sues Apple After Retail Employee Deletes Years Worth of Photos," bgr, December 1, 2015, http://bgr.com/2015/12/01/iphone-photos-deleted-lawsuit/ (accessed December 20, 2015), and Kim Lachance Shandrow, "This Man Successfully Sued Apple for Deleting His Honeymoon Photos," Entrepreneur, December 3, 2015, http://www.entrepreneur.com/article/253529 (accessed December 20, 2015).

15

Business Organizations

Learning Objectives

After completing this chapter you should be able to

- Recognize the significance of choosing a business form
- Compare the advantages and disadvantages of the different types of business organizations
- Distinguish the types of partnerships
- Explain the concept of piercing the corporate or entity veil and recognize when a court is likely to pierce the veil
- Discuss the advantages and disadvantages of the business judgment rule

433

Classic Case

Judge Cardozo wrote the opinion in this Classic Case. His description of fiduciary duties is often quoted in other cases involving agents, partners, and joint venturers. Fiduciary duties were introduced in Chapter 14. Many people in business organizations owe fiduciary duties. Meinhard and Salmon were joint venturers, or coadventurers, as Cardozo called them.

MEINHARD v. SALMON

249 N.Y. 458, 1928 N.Y. LEXIS 830 (N.Y. Ct. of Appeals, 1928)

FACTS Louisa M. Gerry leased the premises known as the Hotel Bristol to the defendant Walter J. Salmon for a twenty-year period. Under the lease Salmon promised to reconstruct the building at a cost of $200,000. Salmon and Morton H. Meinhard, the plaintiff, agreed that Meinhard would pay half of the cost to remodel and operate the property. In return, Salmon was to pay to Meinhard 40 percent of the net profits for the first five years of the lease and 50 percent for the remaining fifteen years. The parties would share losses equally. Salmon was to have sole power to manage the building.

Near the end of the twenty years, Elbridge T. Gerry became the owner of the reversionary interest in the Hotel Bristol. He also owned a substantial amount of property in the neighborhood. Elbridge Gerry and Salmon negotiated and agreed to a twenty-year lease for the whole tract, including the Hotel Bristol. The tenant was going to be the Midpoint Realty Company, which was owned and controlled by Salmon. The lease could be renewed and possibly extended to a maximum period of eighty years. Under the lease, the existing buildings could remain unchanged for seven years, and then they were to be torn down and replaced by a new building costing $3,000,000. Salmon personally guaranteed the performance by Midpoint Realty Company.

Salmon did not tell Meinhard anything about the negotiations or the new lease. When Meinhard found out about the lease, he demanded that the lease be held in trust as an asset of the venture.

ISSUE Did Salmon breach a fiduciary duty to Meinhard?

HOLDING Yes, Salmon breached a fiduciary duty. Meinhard is entitled to an interest in the new lease.

REASONING Excerpts from the opinion of Chief Judge Cardozo:

. . . The two were coadventurers, subject to fiduciary duties akin to those of partners. . . . The heavier weight of duty rested . . . upon Salmon. He was a coadventurer with Meinhard, but he was manager as well. During the early years of the enterprise, the building . . . was operated at a loss. . . . For each [of them], the venture had its phases of fair weather and of foul. The two were in it jointly, for better or for worse. . . . Joint adventurers, like copartners, owe to one another, while the enterprise continues, the duty of the finest loyalty. Many forms of conduct permissible in a workaday world for those acting at arm's length, are forbidden to those bound by fiduciary ties. A trustee is held to something stricter than the morals of the market place. Not honesty alone, but the punctilio [fine point] of an honor the most sensitive, is then the standard of behavior. As to this there has developed a tradition that is unbending and inveterate [firmly established]. . . . Only thus has the level of conduct for fiduciaries been kept at a level higher than that trodden by the crowd. It will not consciously be lowered by any judgment of this court. . . .

[Mr. Gerry] figured . . . that the man in possession would prove a likely customer. To the eye of an observer, Salmon held the lease as owner in his own right, for himself and no one else. In fact he held it as a fiduciary, for himself and another, sharers in a common venture. . . . [I]f the lease by its terms had run in favor of a partnership, Mr. Gerry . . . would have laid before the partners . . . his plan of reconstruction. . . . [The] opportunity that was . . . an incident of the enterprise, Salmon appropriated to himself in secrecy and silence. . . . The trouble about his conduct is that he excluded his coadventurer from any chance to compete, from any chance to enjoy the opportunity for benefit that had come to him alone by virtue of his agency. This chance, if nothing more, he was under a duty to concede. The price of its denial is an extension of the trust at the option and for the benefit of the one whom he excluded.

. . . Authority is . . . abundant that one partner may not appropriate to his own use a renewal of a lease, though its term is to begin at the expiration of the partnership. . . . Certain it is . . . that there may be no abuse of special opportunities growing out of a special trust as manager or agent. . . . If conflicting inferences are possible as to abuse or opportunity, the trier of the facts must make the choice between them. There can be no revision in this court unless the choice is clearly wrong. . . . A constructive trust

is . . . the remedial device through which preference of self is made subordinate to loyalty to others. . . .

[We do not hold] that Salmon was guilty of a conscious purpose to defraud. Very likely he assumed in all good faith that with the approaching end of the venture he might ignore his coadventurer and take the extension for himself. He had given to the enterprise time and labor as well as money. He had made it a success. . . . Salmon had put himself in a position in which thought of self was to be renounced. . . . He was much more than a coadventurer. He was a managing coadventurer. . . . For him . . . , the rule of undivided loyalty is relentless and supreme. . . . [It would be a different question if there was no relationship] between the business conducted by the manager and the opportunity brought to him as an incident of management. . . . [However, here] the subject-matter of the new lease was an extension and enlargement of the subject-matter of the old one. . . . [The court ordered that a trust be established either in the lease itself or in the company . . .]

SELECTING A BUSINESS FORM

Businesses operate through the actions of their agents and employees. They select a form or type of organization to use. Some business people do this by making a conscious, informed decision. Unfortunately, others start a business without much consideration as to the form it should take. As we will see, no one form of business organization is perfect. Each has some advantages that the others lack, and each has some drawbacks the others avoid. Deciding on the proper form can be one of the most important decisions a businessperson will make. The decision to choose a type of business organization should never be made lightly or automatically. All the pros and cons for each potential alternative should be weighed carefully before a decision is made. This decision becomes more complex as new business forms are evolving and tax treatment of the various business forms are changing. People may need to consult with their accountants and attorneys as they make this decision.

Business organizations are regulated by the states; consequently the treatment will vary from state to state. Most state statutes provide a set of rules called *default rules*. These are the rules that will apply if the parties do not have an agreement to the contrary. There may also be some mandatory rules, which the parties are not allowed to modify.

Businesses that purchase franchises can operate in any form allowed by state law unless the contract with the franchisor contains restrictions. (Franchise has multiple meanings in the law. In this context, a *franchise* is the right to engage in business using a particular trademark at a particular location or in a particular territory.)

An Ounce of Prevention

Types of business organizations also vary by country. A form that may initially seem identical or similar to a U.S. form may differ in significant ways. When you are dealing with businesses formed outside the United States, you should find out what type of business it is and who might be liable if the relationship sours. In other words, are the investors personally liable for business debts? You should also find out who has authority to make decisions for the business with which you are dealing.

SOLE PROPRIETORSHIPS

The simplest business form is a *sole proprietorship,* which is owned and operated by one person. It can also simply be called a proprietorship. This one person is the boss, and there are no other owners to disagree with him or her. It is easy to form and operate a sole proprietorship. On the other hand, there is no one else to contribute expertise, knowledge, or capital to the business. The sole proprietor can hire agents and employees to assist with the enterprise. The enterprise is highly dependent on the sole proprietor, and the business will end when the sole proprietor dies or becomes incapacitated.

The sole proprietorship is easy to terminate. The owner simply pays the business debts, and then the remaining assets belong to him or her. As an alternative, the owner might sell the business to someone else. Care must be used to ensure that business liabilities are handled correctly in the sale. It is critical that the parties discuss existing liabilities and reach an agreement about who will pay them. They should also address which debts owed to the firm will be transferred to the buyer.

PARTNERSHIPS

Partnerships are formed for a variety of reasons. Many professionals form partnerships because they are not allowed to incorporate under some state laws. (In this sense, a *professional* is a member of a "learned profession," such as an accountant, a doctor, or a lawyer.) Some people create a partnership to avoid the technical steps and expense required to form a corporation. (A *corporation* is an artificial person or legal entity created by or under the authority of a state. It is owned by a group of persons known as stockholders or shareholders.) Other people form a partnership because it seems appropriate, sometimes without giving the matter serious thought.

A partnership is often defined as an association of two or more persons to carry on a business as co-owners for profit. A partnership may have a wider financial base than a proprietorship. The partnership has more expertise from which to draw. A partnership can be relatively easy to form. It can be formed by a simple, oral agreement by two or more people. On the other extreme, it can be very complex with multiple levels of partners with various rights and obligations for the parties at each level. There are a number of special types of partnerships. The simplest form is the general partnership. We will discuss the law of general partnerships before addressing the special types of partnerships.

One disadvantage to a partnership is that it is generally not perpetual, as a corporation may be. A partnership will dissolve eventually. Also, the partners face unlimited personal liability for business-related conduct, similar to a proprietor.

Most of the partnership law in the United States is based on state statutes. Some of the statutes originated from the Uniform Law Commission (ULC), formerly known as the National Conference of Commissioners on Uniform State Laws (NCCUSL). The ULC prepares uniform acts that it encourages state legislatures to adopt. The controlling law today for partnerships is found in the Uniform Partnership Act (UPA),[1] the Revised Uniform Partnership Act (RUPA),[2] or the state's own statute. As partnership law continues to evolve, there are a number of significant changes. There is a trend to view a partnership as a separate entity instead of a collection of the partners. The Revised Uniform Partnership Act (RUPA) takes the entity approach to partnerships.[3] Under the entity approach (1) a partnership is a lot more durable;[4] (2) the partnership can sue and be sued in the partnership name;[5] and (3) partnership property is owned in the partnership name. In other words, a partner has his or her partnership interest, but is not a co-owner of specific partnership property.[6]

A partnership is created by agreement of the partners. The agreement is a contract, and it may be oral unless it falls within the Statute of Frauds. No formality is required in setting up a general partnership. The partnership agreement should cover important concepts, including the partnerships' name, its duration, its purpose, how partners can withdraw from the firm, and how partners can be added to the firm. Many states do not require that a general partnership agreement be filed with any state office. Generally, the partnership agreement governs the operation of the partnership, with the state's statutes covering matters not addressed in the partnership agreement.[7] Even if the parties are very careful in drafting the agreement, situations may arise that were never considered and addressed in it. Each general partner is considered to be an agent for the partnership and for each partner, as long as the partner is acting in a business-related matter. Each general partner is personally liable, without limit, for torts or contracts if the partnership has insufficient assets to cover the debt or liability. In addition, each general partner is expected to devote service only to the partnership and not to any competing business ventures. The following rules are *imposed* on general partnerships unless the agreement contains contrary provisions:

- Each partner is entitled to an equal voice in the management of the business.
- Each partner is entitled to an equal share of profits, without regard to capital contribution.[8] (*Capital contribution* is money or assets invested by the business owners to start or encourage an enterprise.)
- Each partner is expected to share any losses suffered by the business in the same proportion as profits are shared.
- The books of the partnership are to be kept at the central office of the business. (Each partner is entitled to access the books and records of the business.)

A partner should be extremely cautious if he or she wants to loan personal property to the partnership but he or she wants to retain individual ownership. Unless the intention is made obvious, the other partners or the court may declare that the property was part of his or her capital contribution and legally belongs to the partnership.

Unless there is an agreement to the contrary, each partner is (1) a manager for the enterprise; (2) an agent for the partnership and every other partner; and (3) a principal of every other partner. As a result, all the regular rules of agency apply. Generally, any conduct by a general partner that is *apparently* authorized is binding on the partnership. Each partner is also an employee (servant) of the partnership for purposes of *respondeat superior*. This means that if the injured person can establish that the partner was in "the course and scope of employment" when the tort was committed, the partnership and each partner are jointly and severally liable for the injuries incurred. Each partner owes a fiduciary duty to the other partners and the partnership. The partners are allowed to agree on the definition of "equal voice in management." Many partnership agreements *define* the management voice of each partner. This may consist of delegating an area of responsibility to each partner. When an area has not been delegated to a specific partner, a majority vote controls. To conduct any extraordinary business, a unanimous vote is required.[9] A matter is considered extraordinary if it changes the basic nature or the basic risk of the business.

Partners are entitled to their share of the profits. A partner is *not* entitled to draw a salary from the enterprise unless the agreement contains an expressed provision for a salary. This is true even if that partner devotes extra time to running the business. Any salary provision for partners must be expressly set out in the agreement.

Being a partner may be hazardous to your financial health. Even if you are a careful, cautious person, you may face potential liability from the conduct of your partners. What rights do you have that protect you? Partners and the partnership have some protection from a creditor of one of their partners. The creditors of a debtor partner can get a charging order from a court.[10] A *charging order* is a court order permitting a creditor to receive a portion of the profits from the operation of a business. Under a charging order, the debtor/partner's *profits* are paid to the creditor until the claims are completely paid. The partnership can continue to operate. On the other hand, suppose that the partnership is in financial difficulty but that some of the partners are solvent. Generally, the creditors of the firm must first proceed against the assets of the firm.[11] This result is logical since the creditors extended credit to the firm and not the individual partners. If the assets of the firm are not sufficient to satisfy the claims, the partners are personally liable to the creditors, jointly and severally.

Taxation of Partnerships

For taxation purposes, the partnership form of business can be either an advantage or a disadvantage. Basically, the partnership is not taxed, but the individual partners are taxed on the receipts of the firm. This is commonly known as *pass-through taxation.* Federal income tax rules do not recognize the partnership as a taxable entity. The firm must file an IRS Form 1065 annually, but the form is for information purposes only. Each partner is taxed on his or her share of the firm's profits for the year, whether these profits are distributed to the partners or not. Each partner also takes his or her share of the deductions. Many states also treat the partnership as a pass-through entity.

Dissolution of Partnerships

Partners may enter and exit a partnership. Under the UPA, each entry or exit caused the partnership to dissolve. RUPA considers a partnership a much more durable entity. The entry and exit of partners does not dissolve the firm. The firm can continue.

Commonly, partnerships dissolve when (1) the partnership purpose has been completed; (2) the partnership term is over; (3) the partnership is no longer profitable; (4) it becomes unlawful for the partnership to continue the business; or (5) the partners want to dissolve the firm. When the partners are having trouble getting along, a partner can petition the court to dissolve the partnership.

The partnership can continue even if it was for a set term and that term is over or if it was for a particular project and that project is completed.[12] This can occur by an express agreement of the partners. It can also occur if the partners continue to operate the business without liquidating the firm. Assume Josh, Pamela, and Whitney have a partnership that was formed for five years. After the five years, they continue to operate it as a going concern without taking steps to dissolve it. The partnership will continue.

Change of Partners   Partners should consider the potential problems caused by the exit of a partner when they draw up the original agreement. They should address questions of (1) when a partner can voluntarily exit the firm; (2) when a partner can be expelled from the firm; (3) how the partnership interest will be valued; and (4) who will pay the exiting partner for his or her interest.

Sometimes, a new partner is brought into the business. The new partner is liable to preexisting creditors only up to the amount of his or her capital contribution. In other words, an entering partner has limited liability to preexisting creditors but faces unlimited personal liability with respect to creditors whose claims arise after his or her entry.[13]

Limited Partnerships

A *limited partnership* is a partnership in which there are two or more levels, or types, of partners. The rights and liabilities of each partner are determined by his or her status. A limited partnership must have at least one general partner and at least one limited partner. A general partner has the same liability as general partners in regular partnerships. A *limited partner* is a partner who furnishes certain funds or assets to the enterprise and whose liability is restricted to the funds provided. If the limited partner commits to provide additional funds in the future, he or she will also be liable for those funds. Although a limited partnership is an actual partnership, the limited partners are more like investors than regular partners. They have contributed cash, property, or services, and in exchange they receive an interest or share. Courts often treat the limited partners like investors in corporations or limited liability companies (LLCs). A limited partnership is more formal than a general partnership. The partners prepare and sign a written certificate that includes some of the important features of the partnership. This certificate must be filed with the state.

The law of limited partnerships is continuing to evolve. Parties who plan to establish a limited partnership need to check the statute for the state of formation. In some states (1) the limited partnership cannot use the name of a limited partner in the firm name and (2) a limited partner is not allowed to participate in the management of the enterprise without losing his or her limited liability shield.[14] Limited partners may be entitled to vote on certain decisions without being considered to be "managing."

The ULC has been revising its partnership acts.[15] Most of these changes have increased the options for partnerships and increased the protection for limited partners. The Uniform Limited Partnership Act (2001) (ULPA (2001)) made some significant changes to prior uniform acts. They include the following:

- The partnership can exist in perpetuity unless the agreement provides otherwise.
- The exit of a limited partner does not dissolve the partnership.
- Limited partners are protected from obligations of the firm based on their status. (They will not lose this protection by participating in management.)[16]
- The partnership can use the limited partner's name as the name of the partnership.

A limited partner generally does not have the right to manage even under the ULPA (2001).

Some large limited partnerships choose to be master limited partnerships (MLPs). Interests in MLPs are publicly traded either over-the-counter or in organized securities exchanges. Because they are traded, they provide some liquidity for the limited partners.

Limited Liability Partnerships

Limited liability partnerships (LLPs) are a relatively new form of business organization. LLPs are currently permitted in most states. The advantage of an LLP over a general partnership is the protection provided to all the partners. All the partners are general partners, but the partners' personal assets are protected from liability claims against the partnership. There is variation in state laws on the protection afforded partners in an LLP. Under the (ULPA (2001), the protection is from all liability for partnership obligations.[17] The exception to this is liability created by the partner himself or herself. In other words, a partner has *unlimited liability* for his or her own wrongdoings and *limited liability* for the wrongdoings of others. Generally, the statutes broadly interpret the partner's own wrongs to include the wrongs of persons under that partner's direct supervision and control.

Most states require registration of the LLP with the state. The firm must identify itself as an LLP. It is assumed that creditors will evaluate creditworthiness accordingly. The ULPA (2001) does not restrict the types of businesses that can form LLPs.[18] However, some states only allow professionals to form LLPs.[19] Other states may not permit professionals to use LLPs. Still others may permit professionals to form LLPs, but may require professional LLPs to purchase liability insurance.

Limited Liability Limited Partnerships

Limited liability limited partnerships (LLLPs) are limited partnerships with general partners who serve as managers and limited partners who serve as investors.[20] However, all the partners have limited liability and creditors are generally limited to collecting from the partnership assets.[21] This is a relatively new business form, and the type of liability does vary. Under the ULPA (2001), limited partnerships can be limited liability limited partnerships (LLLPs) simply by stating so in the agreement and the certificate that they file.[22] Some states that have adopted ULPA (2001) decided not to include the LLLP provisions.[23]

PARTNERSHIPS BY ESTOPPEL

Technically, no partnership can exist without an agreement. A third person who is dealing with someone who claims to be a partner when he or she is not, however, may be able to proceed against the alleged partnership and/or the alleged partner. Such a situation may lead to a partnership by estoppel (also called an *implied partnership* or an *ostensible partnership*). RUPA uses the new label of *purported partner.*[24] To successfully use partnership by estoppel, generally the third party must show the following:

1. Someone who is not a partner was held out to be a partner by the firm.
2. The third person justifiably or reasonably relied on the holding out.
3. The third person will be harmed if liability is not imposed.

For example, Gary Chavers operated Chavers Welding and Construction (CWC). His two sons worked in the business. CWC contracted Epsco to provide payroll and employee services its. Epsco allowed CWC to pay over time. When CWC's debt exceeded $80,000, Epsco sued to recover the debt. Gary Chavers filed bankruptcy and his debt to Epsco was discharged. Epsco then sued the sons. The sons claimed that the business was a sole proprietorship owned by Gary Chavers. The court held the sons liable based on partnership by estoppel because the Chaverses had represented to Epsco that it was a partnership and Epsco had relied on those representations.[25]

An Ounce of Prevention

A partnership by estoppel is a particular problem for young business enterprises that share space—for example, newly licensed accountants. If you do decide to share office space, you should (1) maintain your own business identities (including using your own letterheads, business cards, and plaques on office doors); (2) arrange for separate entries on the building directory; (3) maintain your own telephone lines (or if sharing a receptionist, ensure that he or she answers incoming calls with each enterprise's individual name); (4) avoid using a group name (or if using a group name, include a disclaimer of joint responsibility everywhere the name appears, for example, on business cards and telephone listings); (5) be accurate when talking about the business relationship to business associates and friends (don't say that you are "with" the other individuals or refer to the other individuals as "partners"); (6) remind the other individuals to use care; and (7) if you share work or clients with the others in the office, clearly identify the working relationship to the client.[26]

JOINT VENTURES

According to the court, the parties in the Classic Case of *Meinhard v. Salmon* had a joint venture. A *joint venture* has all the characteristics of a partnership except one. It is not set up to "carry on a business." A joint venture is established to carry out a limited number of transactions, very commonly a single deal. As soon as that deal (or those transactions) is completed, the joint venture terminates. Since the agency power in a joint venture is more limited, one member of the venture is not as likely to be held responsible for the conduct of the other members. Also, the death of a joint venturer does not automatically dissolve the joint venture. In all other respects, partnership law is applicable.

CORPORATIONS

In the United States a *corporation* is an artificial person created under the statutes of a state. Because it is considered a person, the corporation ordinarily enjoys most of the rights possessed by natural (flesh-and-blood) persons. For example, it is a citizen of the state in which it has been incorporated. Under the Fourth Amendment, it cannot be the object of unreasonable searches or seizures. Similarly, it must be afforded its rights of due process and equal protection.

Corporations are popular business forms because of their advantages over other types of business organizations. These advantages include the following:

- **Insulation from liability.** Corporate debts are the responsibility of the corporation. The shareholders' liability ordinarily is limited to the amount of their investment. Creditors of the corporation normally cannot reach the shareholders' personal assets.
- **Centralization of management functions.** Centralizing the management functions in a small group of persons with management expertise avoids some of the friction that may plague partnerships.
- **Continuity of existence.** The corporation continues to exist even after the deaths of the officers, directors, or shareholders, or the withdrawal of their shares. This potential for perpetual existence provides stability. A corporation can exist in perpetuity unless a specific length of time is stated in its articles of incorporation.
- **Free transferability of shares.** This creates opportunities for access to outside capital and permits investors to sell their interests.

These attributes influence many large and small businesses to choose the corporate form. In a given situation, another form may better suit the business's needs because there are also distinct disadvantages with the corporate form. This is a decision that requires careful thought and the advice of knowledgeable experts, such as a lawyer, accountant, and/or investment adviser. If a business does decide to incorporate, it must decide where to do so. Although there are some federal statutes, most corporate activity is controlled by state law.

The Formation Process

The Role of Promoters   The services of promoters (preincorporators) are not legally required. However, *promoters* generally begin the process of forming a corporation by taking some of the steps necessary, such as hiring a corporate attorney, leasing an office, and procuring subscribers for the stock.[27] Promoters facilitate the creation of the corporation by bringing interested parties together and by encouraging the venture until the corporation is formed. Since the promoter is working on behalf of an entity that does not yet exist, questions arise as to whether the promoter or the corporation is liable on contracts made on the corporation's behalf before its existence. The general rule is that the promoter will be liable for goods and services rendered to him or her before the corporation's formation. However, the corporation may become liable for the promoter's contracts (and possibly torts) after its formation. Generally the corporation will ratify the promoter's contracts after it is formed. *(Ratification* is accepting an act that was unauthorized when committed and becoming bound to that act upon its "acceptance.") Ratification will make the corporation liable on the contract. It does not release the promoter from liability. The possibility of double-dealing is inherent in the process of promotion. For this reason, the law treats promoters as owing fiduciary duties to the corporation. Consequently, the promoter must act in good faith, deal fairly, and make full disclosure to the corporation. In a few cases the promoter has had to pay the corporation for secret profits, embezzled funds, and other damages.

The Articles of Incorporation   The process of forming a corporation begins with filing of the *articles of incorporation*. State statutes prescribe what must be included in the articles. Once the promoters file the articles with the appropriate state official (ordinarily, the secretary of state) and pay all the required filing fees, the state issues a formal *certificate of incorporation*. In most states, corporate existence begins with the issuance of the certificate of incorporation by the secretary of state. After the state issues such a certificate, the state normally will not interfere with its grant of power to the corporation. In some jurisdictions, official corporate existence does not begin with the issuance of the certificate; it begins after the first organizational meeting following the issuance of the certificate of incorporation.

The Bylaws   *Bylaws* are the internal rules and regulations adopted by a corporation for the regulation of day-to-day matters not covered by other documents. These ordinarily are not filed in a public place. They must be consistent with the jurisdiction's corporation statute and the corporation's articles. Bylaws typically (1) list the location(s) of the corporation's offices and records; (2) describe the meetings of the shareholders and the directors; (3) set out the powers and duties of the board of directors, officers, and executive committee; (4) establish the capitalization of the corporation (that is, what types of shares may be sold and how many shares are authorized to be sold); and (5) establish the methods for conducting the corporation's business, such as execution of contracts, signatures on deeds, and notices of meetings.

An Ounce of Prevention

Corporations are taxed on their net income. In deciding whether to incorporate a business or adopt a different structure, you should consider tax issues. You should compare the corporate tax rate to the tax rates of the owners of the business. If most or all of the investors are going to work for the entity, the analysis should include wages and fringe benefits. (Common fringe benefits include deferred compensation plans, group term life insurance, health and disability insurance, and medical expense reimbursement plans.) Wages and benefits are generally deductible on your corporate tax return. In addition, many fringe benefits are not considered income on your individual tax returns as employees. Another tax consideration is whether the entity is going to retain earnings. If so, pass-through taxation may pose a hardship on some of your investors who have to claim income on their tax returns but who may not have other funds to pay the taxes due.

Taxation of Corporations

The law recognizes corporations as separate entities for federal income tax purposes. This can be a disadvantage of the corporate form. The corporation pays taxes on its income as earned. When corporate income or retained earnings is distributed to shareholders in the form of dividends, shareholders have taxable income. This structure is called double taxation. Because corporate losses are not passed on to the shareholders, shareholders do not receive the tax advantages that otherwise accompany such losses.

Regular corporations are called *C corporations* for Subchapter C of the Internal Revenue Code. There are also *S corporations* that may provide tax relief by providing pass-through taxation. For federal purposes S corporations are taxed in a manner similar to sole proprietorships or partnerships, depending on the number of owners. To elect Subchapter S status, the business must:

- Be a domestic small-business corporation. To be a domestic corporation, it must be incorporated and organized in the United States. Businesses incorporated outside the United States, certain banks, and insurance companies may not become S corporations.
- Have only one class of stock issued and outstanding. Generally, there may be different options or voting rights within that one class.
- Have one hundred or fewer shareholders. Congress has raised the number of shareholders in recent years and may continue to increase the number. In some instances, shareholders may be aggregated and treated as one shareholder; for example, a husband and wife may be treated as one shareholder.[28]
- Have no nonresident alien shareholders. If a resident alien moves outside the United States, the Subchapter S status will be terminated.
- Have only qualifying shareholders. Individuals, estates, certain tax-exempt organizations,[29] and certain trusts qualify and can be shareholders. Partnerships, corporations, LLCs, LLPs, and nonqualifying trusts are not eligible.
- Have the consent of all the shareholders.
- Not exceed the maximum allowable passive investment income.

To make a proper election, the shareholders must consent in writing on IRS Form 2553. Once the election is made, renewals are unnecessary. S status remains in effect as long as none of the triggering events occurs. An S corporation may be subject to state and local income taxes.

Disregarding Corporate Entities

The usual rule is that the shareholders in a corporation enjoy limited liability. Because the corporation is a separate entity from the shareholders, the law normally will not focus on who owns or runs the corporation. Sometimes, though, the court will *pierce the corporate veil* to serve justice. In other words, the law will ignore the "shield" that keeps the corporation and its shareholders' identities separate. For example, the corporate veil may be pierced to place liability on the shareholder when the corporate form is being used to defraud others or to achieve similar illegitimate purposes. Courts examine the facts closely to see if a particular situation justifies disregarding the corporate identity. If the corporation is a mere shell or instrumentality, or in reality is the "alter ego" of the shareholder(s), courts can use their powers of equity to impose liability on the controlling shareholder(s).

An Ounce of Prevention

One of the primary reasons for creating a corporation is to shield personal assets from liability should the business fail. To reduce the likelihood that your corporate veil will be pierced, you should (1) keep corporate affairs and transactions separate from personal transactions; (2) adequately capitalize the business initially; (3) avoid the draining off of corporate assets, especially during financial difficulties; (4) incorporate for legitimate reasons (tax savings, limitation of liability, and so on); and (5) direct the policies of the corporation toward its own interests and not the interests of the individual shareholders.

Piercing the corporate veil is also an issue in situations involving parent companies and their subsidiaries. In the parent/subsidiary situation, there are two general theories for holding the parent liable for the acts of the subsidiary: alter ego (piercing the corporate veil) and agency principles (the amount of control the parent exercises over the subsidiary). Most states are using the corporation rules regarding piercing the veil for LLCs as well. In fact, some courts call it piercing the *corporate* veil even when the entity is an LLC.

Operation of Corporations

The corporation's actions are governed by three documents—the corporation code for the state of incorporation, the articles of incorporation, and the bylaws. The management of the entity is centralized. Directors, officers, and controlling shareholders are often called "managers" for the sake of simplicity. The officers are responsible for the day-to-day operations, and the board of directors is responsible for the overall policies of a corporation. The managers ultimately answer to the shareholders, the owners. Shareholders exert only indirect control, generally through the election of directors. The sale of corporate stock is regulated by federal and state securities laws. (Securities laws are discussed in more detail in Chapter 16.)

Corporate Shareholders

Shareholders have a somewhat unique position. They own the business by virtue of purchasing shares in the corporation, but they do not manage the business. Instead, they delegate the management responsibility to the board of directors, which in turn delegates the day-to-day management duties to the officers the board appoints.

Shareholders exert indirect control over the corporation by virtue of their ownership of shares; the more they own, the more power they wield. A shareholder may own *common stock*, which allows the shareholder to receive dividends, to vote on corporate issues, and to receive property upon the corporation's liquidation. Some shareholders may own *preferred stock*, which includes priority with regard to dividends, voting, and/or liquidation rights. Preferences can involve priority with regard to *dividends* (cash, property, or other shares that the board of directors declares as payment to shareholders). Preferred shareholders may receive corporate assets before any other stockholder if the corporation is liquidated. Not all corporations issue preferred stock. If the corporation does issue preferred stock, there may be several classes, or series, that set out different priorities for each class. Under most state statutes, the articles of incorporation must spell out the preference(s) involved.

A corporation may be required to have an annual meeting of the shareholders. Sometimes, an annual meeting is not required for small, closely held corporations. However, it is important for the corporation to observe the normal formalities. Failure to observe formalities is one of the factors a court considers in piercing the corporate veil. The board of directors can also call special meetings of the shareholders. Prior to the meeting, the corporation must send written notice of the meeting to all shareholders of record. Electronic media may be used for the written notice in some states.[30]

Shareholder meetings require a quorum to take valid action. State statutes and corporate bylaws or articles usually state the percentage of the outstanding shares that must be "present" at the meeting to constitute a quorum. Delaware *permits* a corporation to conduct shareholder meetings by "remote communication" under some conditions. The board of directors can choose whether to use remote communication and how the meeting will be conducted.[31] Use of technology in shareholder meetings is likely to increase.

Shareholders generally have the right to attend and participate in shareholder meetings, to vote on matters brought before the shareholders, and to inspect corporate books and records. They may choose to exercise their rights by attending the meeting, or they may decide to grant a proxy to another person, allowing that person to act on their behalf. Shareholders do not have the right to receive dividends unless dividends are properly declared by the board of directors.

The shareholders' right to vote includes the right to vote to elect or remove directors. It also includes the right to vote on amendments or changes to the corporate bylaws.

Shareholders do not have the right to unlimited access to the corporate books and records. In general, shareholders have access to such corporate materials as stockholder lists; minutes of shareholders' meetings; minutes of board or officers' meetings; financial records, such as books of account or other periodic summaries; and business documents, including tax returns, contracts, and office correspondence or memoranda. Federal and state statutes that mandate public disclosure of information have made inspection rights somewhat less important.

Shareholders also have the right to transfer their shares to someone else (by gift or sale). This right of transferability may be restricted. If it is, any restrictions must be conspicuously placed on the stock certificate for them to be valid. The restrictions may also be included in the bylaws. Such restrictions commonly occur in close corporations.

One such restriction is a *right of first refusal.* This requires a shareholder who wishes to sell his or her shares to first offer these shares to the corporation or to the other shareholders. Rights of first refusal are generally enforceable as valid restrictions on transfer. Buy-sell agreements are also prevalent in small closely-held corporations. The agreement will state the events that will trigger it, such as the death of a shareholder. In these events, the shareholder (or his or her estate) agrees to sell the shares. The agreement will specify who must buy the shares. Either the corporation or one or more of the other shareholders will be the purchaser. It will also specify the price or the method for determining the price. The parties should strive for a fair and equitable agreement because they do not know who will be selling or purchasing the shares. In addition, a buy-sell agreement can be invalidated by a court if the court decides that it is unreasonable.

Except for situations in which courts disregard the corporate entity, shareholders normally do not become personally liable for corporate debts. However, shareholders do have certain responsibilities. Shareholders will be liable for returning an illegal dividend if the corporation is insolvent when the dividend is paid. They will also be liable if they dissolve the corporation to freeze out minority stockholders to strip them of rights or profits.

Corporate Boards of Directors

The board of directors is legally responsible for the management of the corporation although it delegates day-to-day authority to the officers. The directors are elected by the shareholders, but they act as agents of the corporation, not of the shareholders. As a result, the shareholders cannot compel the board to take any action. (Different rules may apply if the corporation is a close corporation.) The conduct of the board of directors and of corporate executives is regulated by state statutes and by federal securities laws, including the Sarbanes-Oxley Act of 2002 (SOX).[32] (SOX will be addressed in Chapter 16.)

The directors normally determine the salaries of the officers of the corporation. Possible conflicts of interest may arise when directors also serve as officers because, in effect, the directors will be helping to set their own salaries. The amount of compensation paid to officers must be reasonable. Large compensation packages may be attacked by creditors or shareholders as a waste of corporate assets. In one case, Michael Eisner recruited Michael Ovitz to serve as the new president of Disney and possibly succeed Eisner as chief executive officer (CEO). At the time, Ovitz was the head of a talent agency in Hollywood and earned over $20 million per year. The Disney board unanimously approved a five-year contract for Ovitz that provided that Disney could terminate Ovitz for good cause without liability. If Disney terminated Ovitz without good cause or if Ovitz resigned with the consent of the board, Ovitz would get his remaining salary payments, $7.5 million per year for unaccrued bonuses, an immediate vesting of his first group of stock options, and a $10 million payment for the second group of stock options. The chairman of the board's Compensation Committee participated in the negotiations. He noted that the compensation package represented an extraordinary level of compensation, but he said that Ovitz was an "exceptional corporate executive." Ovitz's term as president ended after fourteen months. Disney officials decided to treat the termination as a no-fault termination. Consequently, Ovitz's severance pay package was worth approximately $130 million. Several Disney shareholders sued claiming that the board of directors breached their duty to the shareholders in the hiring of Ovitz, the firing of Ovitz, and agreeing to pay him the severance package. The shareholders contended that the firing should have been for cause. The court found that the compensation package was reasonable under the circumstances.[33] The Dodd-Frank Wall Street Reform and Consumer Protection Act now requires public companies to hold advisory votes of shareholders on the company's pay practices for its top executives. This is commonly called the shareholders' right to a "say on pay."[34]

The state statute usually specifies the minimum number of directors a corporation must have. To avoid deadlocks, the articles or bylaws usually authorize an uneven number of directors. Generally, directors do not need to be shareholders in the corporation. Directors serve for the time specified in state statutes, the articles, or bylaws.

Generally, the board exercises its powers at board meetings. Directors traditionally had to be present to vote; they could not vote by proxy or send substitutes to deliberate for them. Some states now even allow the board to act without a meeting, if the articles or bylaws permit informal action. In fact, telephone conference calls suffice in several states. In Delaware, the directors can use all forms of teleconferencing, videoconferencing, and other communication means as long as the participants can "hear" each other.[35] In California, the directors can meet by chat room meetings or committee meetings over the Internet.[36] Given this trend toward informality, the board can hold its meetings anywhere unless the articles or bylaws declare otherwise. A quorum is required under state law. A simple majority of the directors ordinarily constitutes a quorum. Actions taken by a quorum of directors are binding on the corporation. Directors usually cannot agree in advance about how they will vote on corporate matters. Such a formal agreement is not binding because it is against public policy; directors owe fiduciary duties to the corporation and must be free to exercise their judgment in an unrestricted fashion.

Most statutes authorize the board of directors to delegate managerial authority to officers and committees of board members. Such delegations of duties ensure the smooth running of the day-to-day affairs of the corporation and promote efficiency by using the expertise of the officers and committee members.

Some corporations do not pay their directors or pay them only a token amount. An increasing number of corporations pay their directors well. Directors often are not substantial shareholders, and consequently they do not profit as owners of the firm. Directors are subject to ever-expanding duties and potential liability, so compensation seems more justifiable.

Directors make numerous decisions, collectively and individually. Increasingly, the performance of these duties exposes directors to potential personal liability. Scrutiny of directors' decisions is likely to continue to increase. Today it is legal and common for corporations to *indemnify* (pay back) their directors for liabilities accruing from their roles with the corporation. Through indemnification, directors are repaid by the corporation for the losses and expenses incurred from litigation brought against them personally for actions undertaken on behalf of the corporation. Corporations often purchase liability insurance for their directors, officers, and other employees to cover potential liability. These policies are commonly called *D and O liability insurance.*

Directors have the right to declare dividends. Directors may be personally liable for improper dividends. They also have the right to inspect corporate records. Access to corporate records is essential if directors are to properly discharge their decision-making functions.

Thirty-one states have enacted constituency statutes (also called *other constituency* statutes) that either require or permit the board of directors to consider the interests of other constituents of the corporation in their decision making. Depending on the statute, other possible constituents include the corporation's employees, customers, suppliers, and creditors. Some statutes even permit the directors to consider the economy of the state and the country.[37] Most of the state statutes are permissive and allow but do not require the directors to consider the interests of these other constituents.

Corporate Officers

While directors are responsible for the overall policies of the corporation, officers conduct the day-to-day operations of the firm and execute the policies established by the board. Officers are agents of the corporation and must live up to their fiduciary duties. Statutes often name the officers that a corporation must have. Usually, either these statutes or the corporate bylaws spell out each respective officer's authority. Typical officers include president or chief executive officer (CEO), vice president, secretary, and treasurer or chief financial officer (CFO).

The board ordinarily appoints officers, who serve at the will of the directors. The board in most jurisdictions can remove an officer with or without cause, even when the officer has a valid employment contract. But after removal *without cause*, the corporation may be liable in damages to the former officer for breach of the employment contract.

The corporation usually pays officers a fixed salary plus fringe benefits. To be lawful, compensation should be reasonable and not represent a waste of corporate assets. If waste is present, both the directors and officers may be liable to the corporation for this waste. As previously mentioned, the amount of officers' compensation has been an issue recently, particularly in corporations that are doing poorly.

Because officers are agents of the corporation, they have authority to bind the corporation to contracts. (Agency law was discussed in Chapter 14.) Officers who attempt to contract on behalf of the corporation without authority may be personally liable to the other contracting party. Even if the officer has authority, he or she may be personally liable if the officer fails to disclose the identity of the corporation. Officers who commit torts may be personally liable to the injured party; however, the corporation may also be liable for torts committed by the officer during the scope of his or her employment under the doctrine of *respondeat superior.*

Fiduciary Duties Owed to Corporations

Directors, officers, and controlling shareholders owe fiduciary duties to the corporation and sometimes to shareholders and creditors. The source of these duties is the fact that these managers occupy a position of trust and faith with regard to the corporation and other constituencies. Generally speaking, these obligations fall into three broad categories: the duty of obedience, the duty of diligence (or due care), and the duty of loyalty.

Because corporate managers act on behalf of the corporation, they are obligated to perform their duties with the amount of diligence or due care that a reasonably prudent person would exercise in the conduct of his or her own personal affairs in the same or similar circumstances. The law does not expect a manager to be perfect or all-knowing. A manager will not be liable for honest errors of judgment.

Business Judgment Rule   The law excuses the conduct if the manager made the error in good faith and without clear and gross negligence. This is the *business judgment rule.* A jury must decide whether the manager's decision satisfies the business judgment rule or is grossly negligent. A manager who is ill prepared because he or she misses corporate meetings or does not attend to corporate affairs may incur liability for breach of the duty of diligence. Similarly, failure to fire an obviously unworthy employee, failure to obtain casualty insurance, failure to heed warning signs suggesting illegal conduct (such as embezzlement), or reliance on unreasonable statements by attorneys or accountants may lead to liability. In the case of *In re Abbott Laboratories Derivative Shareholders Litigation,* the shareholders sued the directors of Abbott for negligence in ignoring six years of quality control violations noticed by the Food and Drug Administration (FDA). The board of directors had received copies of some of the FDA notices. Eventually Abbott agreed to pay a $100 million fine to the FDA and to destroy and suspend products worth $250 million because Abbott had not resolved the quality control issues. The court decided that the shareholders were entitled to a suit on the issue of whether the board was negligent. The directors were not entitled to protection by the business judgment rule.[38] A manager will incur liability only for losses caused by his or her own negligent conduct. A manager's reasonable reliance on expert reports, such as those by accountants or attorneys, is usually justified.

Conflicting Interests   Directors, officers, and controlling shareholders enjoy positions of trust with the corporation. They must act in good faith and with loyalty toward the corporation. Managers must place the interests of the corporation above their own personal interests. Sometimes corporate interests and personal interests "conflict." Usually such issues involve (1) business opportunities or (2) conflicts of interest.

The *business opportunity doctrine* (corporate opportunity doctrine) forbids directors, officers, and controlling shareholders from diverting to themselves business deals or potential deals that in fairness or in justice belong to the corporation. Personal gains at the expense of the corporation represent a breach of the managers' fiduciary duties. A business opportunity is commonly found (1) if the manager discovers the opportunity in his or her capacity as manager and (2) if it is reasonably foreseeable that the corporation will be interested in the opportunity because it relates closely to the corporation's line of business. When a manager is interested in an opportunity that might be subject to this rule, he or she should make a full and fair disclosure of all the facts and wait for a definitive statement that the corporation is not going to proceed with the opportunity. Generally the disclosure should be to the board of directors, and the decision to decline it should be made by the disinterested board members.

Another possible conflict of interest occurs when a director, officer, or controlling shareholder personally contracts with the corporation. The transaction is permitted in most states (1) if the interested manager makes a full disclosure of his or her interest to the board of directors before the board begins its deliberations; (2) if all the other relevant facts are disclosed; (3) if the final agreement is fair and reasonable to the corporation; and (4) if it is approved by the disinterested board members.

An Ounce of Prevention

Directors and officers may be shareholders even though they are not required to be. You may decide to pay them with shares or they may participate in stock options as part of their compensation package. Their stock ownership may seem positive because their fortunes will be tied to those of the corporation. This can create a conflict of interest between the directors' and officers' duties as managers and their interests as shareholders. They may be tempted to declare dividends to benefit themselves individually or to increase the price of their shares. They may also be tempted to postpone announcements or camouflage transactions on the balance sheets to sell their shares (if the news is bad) or to buy additional shares for themselves (if the news is good) before the information is released. Some of these actions may violate insider trading laws. You should consider this potential conflict of interest when you are structuring compensation packages.

LIMITED LIABILITY COMPANIES (LLC)

All fifty states and the District of Columbia now recognize limited liability companies (LLCs). Despite some disadvantages, the number of LLCs is increasing. [39] The purpose of LLCs is to provide limited liability for all investors, who are called members. Each member's liability is limited to his or her capital investment plus any additional capital contributions he or she promised to make. Most LLC statutes or the LLC articles greatly restrict the transferability of shares. LLCs may have buy-sell agreements that permit or require members to sell their membership interests to the LLC or other members under specific circumstances. Since the shares are generally not freely transferable, LLCs are not suitable when a large number of investors is anticipated. All states permit one person to form an LLC. [40] Generally, corporations, nonresident aliens, partnerships, and trusts can be members of an LLC. One unresolved issue is whether the selling of LLC interests falls under the applicable state and/or federal securities laws. Many states require LLCs to file articles of organization [41] with the state similar to the articles of incorporation filed by corporations. The statutes also require the use of "limited liability company," "limited company," "L.L.C.," or "L.C." in the name of the business. Many states limit what type of business can form an LLC. For example, professional practices and insurance businesses may not be authorized to form LLCs. [42] Some states allow professional LLCs but impose additional requirements on them. Most state statutes provide default rules for how the LLC will operate. These default rules can generally be modified by the organizers to suit their particular LLC. One of the primary disadvantages of LLCs is that they are a relatively new business form. The law is still developing. Consequently, it is difficult to predict how the law will be applied in specific situations.

Management of LLCs

Organizers decide whether the LLC should be managed by the members or managed by managers. [43] In a member-managed LLC, the members have the right to manage the enterprise and each member will have an equal say in its management. In a manager-managed LLC, the members appoint one or more managers to manage the business. These managers are generally not required to be members. The members generally elect the managers. Members can also retain the right to vote on other matters as specified in the articles of organization and the applicable state law. [44] Statutes may specify the manager's legal liability, for example, specifying that he or she owes a fiduciary duty to the minority members or he or she will be liable only for "gross negligence or willful misconduct."[45]

Taxation of LLCs

Under IRS regulations, unless the entity is actually a corporation or deemed to be a corporation, it can elect pass-through tax treatment. [46] Consequently, single-member

LLCs can be taxed as sole proprietorships. Multiple member LLCs can be taxed as limited partnerships with no general partners.[47] State income tax systems may not honor the federal tax election, resulting in a different tax treatment on the state income tax return.

Duration and Termination of LLCs

LLCs are governed by the operating agreement. Organizers will choose to create either an at-will LLC, a term LLC, or a perpetual LLC. Under the Limited Liability Company Act (2006) (last amended 2013) an LLC will exist in perpetuity.[48] Most states now allow perpetual LLCs.[49] However, some states do not and limit the duration, for example, to thirty years. An *at-will LLC* will continue as long as the members want to continue. A *term LLC* will terminate at the end of the specified time period. Of course, an LLC may fail financially prior to this time. A member has the power to withdraw from an LLC even though the withdrawal might be wrongful.[50] If an LLC is terminated, it follows a winding-up procedure similar to other types of organizations. The assets will first be used to pay off the creditors, including members who are creditors. Then the members will receive any contributions that were not returned earlier.[51]

An Ounce of Prevention

If you establish an LLC you should consider the proper duration for the entity. Even though perpetual LLCs may be permitted under state law, a perpetual LLC is not always desirable. For example, an LLC established to construct a shopping mall does not need to exist in perpetuity. Whether the LLC is at-will, for a term, or perpetual will affect your rights as members when the entity dissolves. It also influences whether a member is wrong in trying to disassociate, when or whether the exiting member will receive his or her contribution, and whether the other members can continue to operate the entity. It will also affect the LLC's ability to attract new members.

Exhibit 15.1 compares the different types of business organizations.

Exhibit 15.1

A Comparison of Different Types of Business Organizations

Attribute	Proprietorship	Partnership	Limited Partnership (LP)[a]
Creation	Proprietor opens the business, subject to state and local licensing laws and regulations.	Partners enter into an agreement, either orally or in writing; no formalities are required.	Partners enter into a partnership agreement and file a written form designating the general partners and the limited partners.
Termination	Proprietor closes the business; death, insanity, or bankruptcy of the owner also terminates the business.	Under RUPA, partnerships do not dissolve each time a partner leaves the firm. Partners can agree to continue the partnership after a partner leaves or after the partnership term is over. The terms of the agreement or a court order may dissolve the partnership. If there is a liquidation of the assets after a dissociation, the business will wind up.	Partners follow same procedure as for a partnership, except the assets will be distributed in a different priority based on the type of partner.
Taxation[b]	All business profits are taxed as the regular income of the owner; there are no federal income taxes on the business itself.	The business must file a federal tax return, but it is for information only. The income of the business is taxed as regular income to the partners.	The same tax procedure is followed as for a regular, general partnership.
Liability[c]	Proprietor has unlimited personal liability. First, business assets will be used, and then the personal assets of the owner will be used.	Partners have unlimited personal liability. First, business assets will be used, and then the personal assets of the partners. The partners are jointly and severally liable for the debts.	General partners have unlimited personal liability. First, business assets will be used, and then the personal assets of the general partners. The general partners are jointly and severally liable for the debts. Limited partners are only liable to the extent of their capital contribution. Suit can be brought against any partner to enforce his or her promise to make a contribution.[d]
Advantages	Simplicity of creation; complete ownership and control of the firm.	Informality of creation; greater potential for expertise and capital in management (because there is more than one manager).	Somewhat greater flexibility than a general partnership; increased opportunities to raise capital.
Disadvantages	Limited capital; limited expertise; limited existence (when the owner dies, the business terminates).	Limited existence; lack of flexibility; potential liability.	Some rigidity in ownership and decision making; personal liability for general partners; limited existence.

Exhibit 15.1 Continued

Attribute	Proprietorship	Partnership	Limited Partnership (LP)[a]
Capital[e]	Angels and venture capitalists generally will not invest in a sole proprietorship unless the proprietor is willing to incorporate.	Capital can be obtained by selling a partnership interest. Angels and venture capitalists generally will not invest in a partnership.	Capital can be obtained by selling a limited partnership interest. Selling of limited partnership interests may be subject to securities laws. Angels and venture capitalists generally will not invest in a partnership.

Attribute	Limited Liability Partnership (LLP)	Corporation (Inc.) (Subchapter C or Subchapter S)	Limited Liability Company (LLC)
Creation	Partners enter into a partnership agreement and the partnership files a copy or some other notice with the state.	Parties prepare and file formal legal documents known as articles of incorporation with the state of incorporation; the entity must comply with any relevant state or federal security statutes or regulations.	LLCs may be formed by one or more members. LLCs must file articles of organization with the state government.
Termination	Partners follow same procedure as for a general partnership.	Parties close the business, liquidate all business assets, surrender the corporate charter, and distribute the assets in accordance with state law; termination may also be due to the state revoking the charter.	Statute and/or agreement may limit the term of the LLC. The trend is to allow an LLC to have a perpetual existence.[f] In many states, the LLC will be at will unless it is designated a term LLC and the term is set. The LLC may dissolve when a member dies or withdraws depending on state law and the operating agreement.
Taxation[b]	The same tax procedure is followed as for a regular, general partnership.	A normal corporation (Subchapter C corporation) is treated as a separate taxable entity and pays taxes on its profits. Any dividends are also taxed to the stockholders. This is called "double taxation." A Subchapter S corporation, regulated by the IRS, is taxed as if it were a general partnership despite its corporate status. A Subchapter S corporation is treated differently only for federal tax purposes. States may also tax them as partnerships.	Most LLCs can make an election to be taxed as either a corporation or a partnership. The LLC may have different taxation for state and federal purposes.
Liability[c]	Partner is liable without limit for his or her own wrongs (malpractice) and wrongs of people he or she directly supervises; the partner's liability for the wrongs of others is limited to the partner's contribution to the firm. The partner may be personally liable for the firm's contracts.	Stockholders are *not* personally liable for debts of the corporation, so there is limited liability. Stockholders may lose their investment in the corporation if it fails.	All members are liable for association debts only to the extent of their capital contribution(s). A member can be required to pay any capital contribution he or she contractually promised to pay but is still unpaid.

Exhibit 15.1 Continued

Attribute	Limited Liability Partnership (LLP)	Corporation (Inc.) (Subchapter C or Subchapter S)	Limited Liability Company (LLC)
Advantages	Limited liability except for a partner's own wrongs and the wrongs of people he or she directly supervises.	Longevity, including the potential for perpetual existence; potentially unlimited access to capital and to expertise; freely transferrable ownership (this may intentionally be restricted in some corporations); limited personal liability for the owners.	Limited liability for all the members.
Disadvantages	Unlimited liability for partner's own wrongs; only permitted in some states. State law may restrict LLPs to professional groups, such as accountants, dentists, doctors, and lawyers or require professional LLPs to obtain liability insurance.	Double taxation of dividends (except for a Subchapter S corporation); much more federal and state regulation; formality and rigidity of the organization.	LLC statutes vary from state to state. Professionals may not be permitted to form an LLC in some states. There may be limitations on the transferability of shares.[g] Selling interests in an LLC may be subject to state and federal securities regulations. LLCs may have a limited term of existence.
Capital[e]	Capital can be obtained by selling a partnership interest. Generally, partnership interests are sold to junior associates in the profession. Angels and venture capitalists generally will not invest in an LLP.	Capital can be obtained by selling shares as long as the sale conforms to the corporation's rules and securities laws. It is easier to raise capital with corporations. Angels and venture capitalists are more comfortable investing in C corporations than most other forms. C corporations can be used for Initial Public Offerings (IPOs).[h] S corporations would have to change to C corporations for an IPO or if it seeks venture capital.	Capital can be obtained by selling memberships in the LLC as long as the sale conforms to the LLC's rules and securities laws. Angels and venture capitalists are becoming more comfortable with LLCs though some would not invest in an entity with pass-through taxation. The LLC would have to change to a corporation for an IPO.

Source: Courtesy of Lynn M. Forsythe. © 2016.

[a] This column describes limited partnerships under the Uniform Limited Partnership Act (ULPA) (2001) (Last Amended 2013), which is commonly called ULPA (2001).

[b] Any change in the business form may result in tax consequences for the business and its owners

[c] The business person will be liable on any contract he or she guarantees for the entity regardless of whether the type of entity would normally protect his or her personal assets.

[d] ULPA (2001) § 502 describes the obligation to make a contribution.

[e] Banks are willing to loan funds to any of these entities if the entity is financially sound and has good prospects for the future. Banks may require a security interest in the venture's assets and/or a loan guarantee from the venture's participants. Angels and venture capitalists only contribute advice and funds if they believe the venture can be successful.

[f] The Uniform Limited Liability Company (2006) (Last Amended 2013) takes that approach in § 108(c).

[g] This may also be an advantage.

[h] IPO offerings are influenced by the economy. For example, there were no IPOs in the United States for the last quarter of 2008 and the first quarter of 2009. These are defined as IPOs with at least one U.S. venture capital investor that trades on a U.S. stock exchange. News Release from Thomson Reuters and the National Venture Capital Association, New York, April 1, 2009, "Venture-Backed Exit Market Remains a Concern in the First Quarter; No IPO Activity for Two Consecutive Quarters; First Time on Record," available at the National Venture Capital Association Web Site at http://www.nvca.org/, under Industry Stats by Date, for April 1, 2009 (accessed September 2, 2013).

Contemporary Case

In the following case, the Wyoming Supreme Court reviewed the decision of the lower court to pierce the LLC veil. Note that in Wyoming the doctrine of piercing the veil is an equitable doctrine that is within the province of the trial court and that there is no right to a jury on the issue.

GREENHUNTER ENERGY, INC. v. WESTERN ECOSYSTEMS TECHNOLOGY, INC.

2014 WY 144, 2014 Wyo. LEXIS 165 (Wyo. Sup. Ct. 2014)

FACTS Western and GreenHunter Wind Energy, LLC (LLC) entered into a contract for Western to provide consulting services to the LLC related to the potential development of a wind turbine farm. Western performed under the contract, but the LLC did not pay Western. Western sued the LLC and obtained a judgment in the amount of $43,646.10 and $2,161.84 for attorney's fees. The LLC has no assets upon which Western can execute. Consequently Western brought this action against GreenHunter Energy, Inc., the sole member of the LLC. Western seeks to pierce the LLC's veil and hold GreenHunter Energy, Inc. liable for the LLC's contractual obligations.

During the trial Western demonstrated that GreenHunter Energy was the sole member and manager of the LLC. "The LLC consistently carried an operating capital balance which was insufficient to cover its debts, and on numerous occasions its account had a balance of zero." GreenHunter Energy decided when and how much money to advance to the LLC. GreenHunter Energy decided which of the LLC's creditors would be paid. GreenHunter Energy did not transfer any funds to allow the LLC to pay Western. The LLC did not have employees of its own. GreenHunter Energy's employees performed services

for the LLC. The LLC's chairman and general counsel held the same positions with GreenHunter Energy. Both businesses have the same business address. GreenHunter Energy's employees did all the bookkeeping and financial management for the LLC. The tax returns of the LLC were consolidated with those of GreenHunter Energy.

ISSUE Did the district court correctly pierce the LLC's veil?

HOLDING Yes, the district court's decision is affirmed.

REASONING Excerpts from the opinion of Justice Davis:

Certain legally recognized entities, such as corporations and limited liability companies, are separate and distinct from their owners. . . . The fundamental feature of these business entities is limited liability, although that protection does not extend to behavior resulting in injustice. . . . Over a decade ago, we held that even in the absence of fraud, the veil of a limited liability company can be pierced as that of a corporation can. . . . This Court observed . . . that "[c]ertainly, the various factors which would justify piercing an LLC veil would not be identical to the corporate situation for the obvious reason that many of the organizational formalities applicable to corporations do not apply to LLCs." . . . This is so because limited liability companies are intended to be much more flexible than a corporation. . . . [W]e refined the requirements for piercing the veil of a limited liability company, focusing on four factors: (1) fraud; (2) inadequate capitalization; (3) failure to observe company formalities; and (4) intermingling the business and finances of the company and the member to such an extent that there is no distinction between them. . . . [Precedents] also held that with the exception of fraud, no single factor is sufficient or required to pierce the limited liability company's veil, and that our courts must analyze all of these factors when asked to impose liability on an limited liability company's members. . . .

The first [factor] is whether there has been fraud. . . . "[A]lthough fraud in the classic sense requires an affirmative misrepresentation, this court has recognized that fraud may be perpetrated by silence as well as by affirmative representations; and when one has a duty to speak, the failure to speak may constitute fraud." . . . "[E]ven in the absence of a duty to speak, if a person does speak, he must speak the truth and make a full and fair disclosure, as half the truth may be a lie in effect." . . . Constructive fraud may be an alternative to actual fraud in certain circumstances. It "has been defined as consisting of all acts, omissions, and concealments involving breaches of a legal or equitable duty resulting in damage to another, and exists where such conduct, although not actually fraudulent, ought to be so treated when it has the same consequence and legal effects." . . .

Second, inadequate capitalization . . . may be considered. . . . Basic business practice and societal policy call for a limited liability company to be financially responsible and require that it attempt to arrange for enough capital to reasonably cover its potential liabilities at various points of its existence. . . . In determining whether a limited liability company is undercapitalized, courts must compare the amount of capital to the amount of business to be conducted and the obligations which must be satisfied. . . . Undercapitalization is a relative concept, and the weight to be given to this factor is dependent on the particular circumstances of the case. . . .

A third factor to consider is the degree to which the business and finances of the company and the member are intermingled. . . . Funds and assets should be separated and not commingled. . . . Failure

to maintain an arm's-length relationship between the member and company, as by not keeping separate bank accounts and bookkeeping records, may be weighed along with other factors. . . . Manipulation of assets and liabilities between the member and company so as to concentrate the assets in the former and the liabilities in the latter can be suggestive of improper use of the LLC as well. . . .

No single category, except fraud, alone justifies a decision to disregard the veil of limited liability; rather, there must be some combination of them, and of course an injustice or unfairness must always be proven. . . .

[The district court] considered (1) the LLC's undercapitalization and absence of assets; (2) the LLC's and Appellant's intermingling of finances and business, including commingling of funds and concentration of benefits in the member and liabilities in the LLC; (3) the lack of any separateness between the two; and (4) Appellant's course of conduct in engaging and contracting with Western in the name of the LLC for services when it knew that it could not or would not provide funds to pay Western's bills, which it found to be fraudulent and not protected by the veil of limited liability. . . .

We are satisfied that the district court applied the correct law. . . . The district court did not rely solely on undercapitalization. . . . Rather, undercapitalization was one of several factors it considered in the totality of the circumstances of this case. . . . Our review . . . confirms the accuracy of the district court's finding that during the periods when Western's invoices were submitted to the LLC, it often had no money in its operating account, and that it received periodic money transfers from Appellant, which decided how much money would be transferred to the LLC to pay specific bills it decided to pay, and when. . . . [T]he LLC was continually undercapitalized by choice, not by external forces. . . . [T]he LLC was not only owned, influenced and governed by Appellant, but the entities had ceased to be separate due to Appellant's misuse of the

LLC. . . . There is no evidence that Appellant made false statements that Western relied upon in entering into the contract with the LLC or in continuing to perform services thereunder. . . . [Although the district court used the term "fraud," we believe it applied the correct test.] It found that Appellant misused the LLC in order to improperly manipulate the situation to avoid paying for services which benefitted it, that it failed to maintain adequate separation, and that to allow it to do so would be unjust and inequitable. Thus, even though there was no fraud in the classic and technical sense, the district court's decision to pierce the LLC's veil . . . was legally correct and not clearly erroneous. . . . [W]e affirm the district court's judgment piercing the LLC's veil. . . .

Short Answer Questions

1. Portia, Tim, and Dennis have a business concept they are sure will succeed if they can establish it properly. Unfortunately, they are short of capital and cannot afford to begin the business without financial support. Marge is willing to put up the necessary capital, but she is unwilling to face the liability of a general partner. So Marge agrees to be a limited partner in the business. What must the parties do to establish a limited partnership under the RULPA? Is there anything else that they should do? If so, what?

2. You and your friends, Nathan and Shannon, are three beginning entrepreneurs. You want to start separate businesses. You are looking for ways to economize and you discover that you could save funds by sharing office space. You decide to rent a suite of offices together and share a receptionist, a reception area, and a conference room. What concerns should you have about this arrangement? What can you do to better protect yourself?

3. William Shlensky was a minority shareholder in the Chicago Cubs baseball team. During the early 1960s the Cubs did not play night games at Wrigley Field. The other major league teams played a number of night games each season. Shlensky sued based on the theory that failure to install lights at Wrigley Field and schedule night games was negligent and represented poor management. Should management's decision be upheld under the business judgment rule?[52]

You Decide...

1. Chase Walker contends that beginning on some date in 2002 he and Chuck White formed a partnership to manufacture and sell automotive scratch repair systems, finishing kits, and touch-up paints and compounds under the assumed name of Sprayless Scratch Repair (SSR). There is no evidence that Walker ever received any share of profits of the business. Walker contends that this is why he started this litigation. Stuart Keele claims he was

present when the partnership came to fruition at a dinner hosted by Walker. Keele states:

> My understanding as to the way it was going to fall out was that Chuck White was going to be the one that actually stocked and manufactured the product and that Chase [Walker] was going to handle the sales and marketing and building the business as far as distributorships and bringing people into the business and expanding the business, and Chuck's end of the business was to provide the product. . . .

A promotional video was created in which Walker appears with White's daughter. In this video, Walker states that he and White are partners in the SSR business. Walker claims that White used this tape on a loop system at trade shows. Walker also presented evidence that at a trade show in 2005, White expressed to Sam and Joanne Feil that Walker was his partner. Walker claims that in 2002 he asked White if he would be willing to split the venture into thirds, with White, Walker, and Robert Maynard each possessing one-third ownership. Mr. Maynard had a chip-fill system that would complement the SSR process. White testified that he sent a fax to Walker and Robert Maynard responding to the proposed ownership structure. Walker contributed significant amounts of money to national marketing of the SSR product and process. Walker consistently participated in national trade shows, set up such trade shows, and financed such trade show appearances. There is no evidence that Walker was paid for his services in attending. White did not refuse such contributions. It is undisputed that Walker attended these shows and paid the company's bills for the shows. Walker

footed the bill for any national marketing efforts. Apparently, White footed the bill for manufacturing the products. Walker claimed that he and White split losses "the same way we split profits"—50/50. Is Walker entitled to a trial on the issue of whether or not there was a partnership or should White's motion for summary judgment be granted?

How would *you* decide this case? Be certain that you explain and justify your answer.

(See *Walker v. White,* 2009 U.S. Dist. LEXIS 125581 (W. Dist. North Carolina, Asheville Div., 2009) and *Walker v. White,* 2010 U.S. Dist. LEXIS 20174 (W.D.N.C., 2010).)

2. Marcelo Eddy Vacaflor (Vacaflor), a Hispanic man, "enrolled in the Physician Assistant Program (P.A. Program) . . . at Pennsylvania College of Technology in Williamsport, Pennsylvania (Penn College). At the school he claims he experienced discrimination and harassment by Penn College faculty and administrators. He received failing grades on some exams and other program requirements and was dismissed from the program. Vacaflor's claims against The Pennsylvania State University (Penn State) include racial discrimination, a hostile environment, and breach of contract. Vacaflor does not claim that Penn State or Penn State employees committed any specific acts or interacted with him in any way. He wants to pierce the corporate veil between Penn State and Penn College based on "the fact that Penn College is a statutorily designated affiliate of Penn State and that Penn State's logo appears on the Penn College student manual." "Penn State is a 'State-related university and an instrumentality of the Commonwealth within the Commonwealth System of Higher Education.'" "Pennsylvania College of Technology . . . was established in 1989 by the Pennsylvania College of Technology Act" which dissolved the Williamsport Area

Community College and replaced it with Penn College. Penn College is "a nonprofit corporation organized and existing under the laws of the Commonwealth and is a wholly controlled affiliate of The Corporation For Penn State." "The Corporation For Penn State is a distinct corporate entity defined as 'a wholly controlled affiliate of the Board of Trustees of The Pennsylvania State University.'" The 1989 Act recognizes Penn College as a state-related institution, and "an affiliate corporation of The Pennsylvania State University." The Act grants Penn College "the authority to conduct educational programs consistent with the mission of The Pennsylvania State University as the Land Grant Institution of the Commonwealth of Pennsylvania." Penn College is autho-

rized to award bachelor's degrees. "The Act affords Penn College 'all the rights, powers, privileges and immunities,' and is subject to all the duties and limitations of a typical Pennsylvania non-profit corporation." Penn College has its own Board of Directors, bylaws, and funding from the Commonwealth of Pennsylvania. Penn State asked to have the claims against it dismissed. Is Vacaflor entitled to a trial against Penn State? Can the veil be pierced to reach Penn State?

How would *you* decide this case? Be certain that you explain and justify your answer.

(See *Vacaflor v. The Pennsylvania State University*, 2014 U.S. Dist. LEXIS 98541 (Middle Dist. PA 2014).)

Notes

1. Officially, this is the Uniform Partnership Act (UPA) (1914). New Hampshire is the only state that adopted UPA (1914) and is still using it. E-mail from Kaitlin Dohse, Legislative Counsel, Uniform Law Commission (ULC), October 30, 2015.
2. The ULC adopted the Revised Uniform Partnership Act. Officially, it is the Uniform Partnership Act or UPA (1997) (last amended 2013). Unofficially, it is called RUPA, even by the ULC. We will use the standard title and call it RUPA. The following states have adopted the RUPA: Alabama, Alaska, Arizona, Arkansas, California, Colorado, Connecticut, Delaware, District of Columbia, Florida, Hawaii, Idaho, Illinois, Iowa, Kansas, Kentucky, Maine, Maryland, Minnesota, Mississippi, Montana, Nebraska, Nevada, New Jersey, New Mexico, North Dakota, Ohio, Oklahoma, Oregon, South Dakota, Tennessee, Texas, U.S. Virgin Islands, Utah, Vermont, Virginia, Washington, West Virginia, and Wyoming. (The versions in South Dakota and Texas are substantially similar.) "Legislative Fact Sheet—Partnership Act (1997) (Last Amended 2013)," ULC Web site, http://uniformlaws.org/LegislativeFactSheet.aspx?title=Partnership%20Act%20%281997%29%20%28Last%20Amended%202013%29 (accessed October 28, 2015), and E-mail from Kaitlin Dohse, Legislative Counsel, Uniform Law Commission (ULC), October 30, 2015.
3. "Uniform Partnership Act (UPA) (1997) (Last Amended 2013)—Summary," http://www.uniformlaws.org/Shared/Docs/Partnership/upa%20last%20amended%202013%20

summary_Jan%202015_GH%20edits.pdf (accessed October 30, 2015).
4. *Ibid.*
5. "Uniform Partnership Act (UPA) (1997) (Last Amended 2013)—Why States Should Adopt," ULC Web site, http://www.uniformlaws.org/Shared/Docs/Partnership/upa%20last%20amended%202013%20why%20states_Jan%202015_GH%20edits.pdf (accessed October 30, 2015).
6. *Ibid.*
7. *Ibid.*
8. Revised Uniform Partnership Act § 401(a) and Comments to § 401. References to section numbers will refer to the Revised Uniform Partnership Act (1997) (last amended 2013) unless otherwise noted.
9. *Id.,* § 401(k)
10. *Id.,* § 504.
11. *Id.,* § 307(d).
12. *Id.,* § 411.
13. See Uniform Partnership Act (1997), § 306, Comment 2.
14. "Uniform Limited Partnership Act (ULPA) (2001) (Last Amended 2013)—Summary," ULC Web site, http://www.uniformlaws.org/Shared/Docs/Limited%20Partnership/ulpa%20last%20amended%202013%20summary_Jan%202015_GH%20Edits.pdf (accessed November 7, 2015) and Uniform Limited Partnership Act (2001) (last amended 2013) § 303.

15. The ULC rules for limited partnerships were codified in the Uniform Limited Partnership Act (ULPA (1916)), the Uniform Limited Partnership Act (ULPA (1976)), and the Uniform Limited Partnership Act (ULPA (2001)). ULPA (1916) is no longer followed in any state. The following states have adopted ULPA (1976): Arizona, Colorado, Connecticut, Delaware, Georgia, Indiana, Kansas, Maryland, Massachusetts, Michigan, Missouri, Nebraska, New Hampshire, New Jersey, North Carolina, Ohio, Oregon, Pennsylvania, Rhode Island, South Carolina, South Dakota, Tennessee, Texas, U.S. Virgin Islands, Vermont, Virginia, West Virginia, and Wisconsin. ULPA (2001) has been adopted by Alabama, Arkansas, California, District of Columbia, Florida, Hawaii, Idaho, Illinois, Iowa, Kentucky, Maine, Minnesota, Mississippi, Montana, Nevada, New Mexico, North Dakota, Oklahoma, Utah, and Washington. State adoption information was obtained from the following ULC web sites: "Legislative Fact Sheet—Limited Partnership Act (1916)," http://uniformlaws.org/LegislativeFact Sheet.aspx?title=Limited%20Partnership%20Act%20% 281916%29 (accessed November 7, 2015), "Legislative Fact Sheet—Limited Partnership (1976)," http://uniformlaws.org/LegislativeFactSheet.aspx?title=Limited%20Partnership%20%2 81976%29 (accessed November 7, 2015), and "Legislative Fact Sheet—Limited Partnership Act (2001) (Last Amended 2013)," http://uniformlaws.org/LegislativeFactSheet.aspx? title=Limited%20Partnership%20Act%20%282001%29 %20%28Last%20Amended%202013%29 (accessed November 7, 2015). The Uniform Limited Partnership Act (2001) (last amended 2013) is available at http://www.uniform laws.org/Shared/Docs/Limited%20Partnership/ULPA_Final_ 2014_2015aug19.pdf (accessed November 7, 2015).

16. "Uniform Limited Partnership Act (ULPA) (2001) (Last Amended 2013)—Summary," ULC Web site, http://www. uniformlaws.org/Shared/Docs/Limited%20Partnership/ ulpa%20last%20amended%202013%20summary_Jan% 202015_GH%20Edits.pdf (accessed November 7, 2015) and "Uniform Limited Partnership Act (ULPA) (2001) (Last Amended 2013)—Why States Should Adopt," ULC Web site, http://www.uniformlaws.org/Shared/ Docs/Limited%20Partnership/ulpa%20last%20amended%20 2013%20why%20states_Jan%202015_GH%20Edits.pdf (accessed November 7, 2015).

17. Uniform Limited Partnership Act (2001) (last amended 2013) § 404.

18. *Ibid.* Under § 110 (b) a limited partnership can be formed for any lawful purpose.

19. For example, California and New York follow this approach. Legal Zoom, "Limited Liability Partnerships," https:// www.legalzoom.com/knowledge/partnership/topic/lim ited-liability-partnerships (accessed November 8, 2015). New York State Department of Taxation and Finance, "Limited Liability Companies (LLCs) and Limited Liability Partnerships (LLPs)," https://www.tax.ny.gov/pit/efile/

llc_llp.htm (accessed November 8, 2015). California LLPs are limited to persons licensed to practice public accountancy, law, or architecture. In addition, engineers and land surveyors are can form LLPs until January 1, 2019. State of California Franchise Tax Board, "Limited Liability Partnership (LLP)," https://www.ftb.ca.gov/businesses/bus_struc tures/LLPartner.shtml (accessed November 8, 2015).

20. LLLPs can be formed in Alabama, Arizona, Colorado, Delaware, Florida, Georgia, Hawaii, Idaho, Illinois, Iowa, Kentucky, Maryland, Minnesota, Missouri, Montana, Nevada, North Carolina, North Dakota, Oklahoma, Pennsylvania, South Dakota, Texas, Virginia, Washington, Wyoming, and U.S. Virgin Islands. Wikipedia, "Limited Liability Limited Partnership," https://en.wikipedia.org/ wiki/Limited_liability_limited_partnership (accessed November 8, 2015). CompaniesIncorporated lists the same states, but it also lists Arkansas. CompaniesIncorporated, "Limited Liability Limited Partnership," http:// www.companiesinc.com/services/lllp.asp (accessed November 8, 2015).

21. See Uniform Limited Partnership Act (2001) (last amended 2013) § 404 (c), which states, "A debt, obligation, or other liability of a limited partnership incurred while the partnership is a limited liability limited partnership is solely the debt, obligation, or other liability of the limited liability limited partnership. A general partner is not personally liable, directly or indirectly, by way of contribution or otherwise, for a debt, obligation, or other liability of the limited liability limited partnership solely by reason of being or acting as a general partner. This subsection applies:

    (1) despite anything inconsistent in the partnership agreement that existed immediately before the vote or consent required to become a limited liability limited partnership under Section 406(b)(2); and

    (2) regardless of the dissolution of the partnership."

22. "Uniform Limited Partnership Act (ULPA) (2001) (Last Amended 2013)—Why States Should Adopt," ULC Web site. ULPA (2001) implicitly authorizes LLLPs. However, not all states which enact ULPA (2001) authorize the formation of LLLPs in their state.

23. For example, California adopted ULPA (2001) without the LLLP provisions.

24. Revised Uniform Partnership Act § 308. This section also describes the liability of a purported partner.

25. *Chavers v. Epsco, Inc.,* 98 S.W.3d 421, 2003 Ark. LEXIS 100 (Ark. Sup. Ct. 2003).

26. John W. Marshall, "Department: Case Focus: Partnership by Estoppel—Liability by Surprise," *Boston Bar Journal,* 46 B.B.J. 6, May/June 2002.

27. Subscribers enter into agreements to purchase stock from the company. Subscribers often agree to purchase stock before the actual formation of the company. There are a number of special rules that govern stock subscriptions, especially those prior to incorporation.

28. For additional information about treating family members as one shareholder, see Internal Revenue Code § 1361(c)(1) and Notice 2005-91, 2005-51 I.R.B. 1164.

29. For example, under Internal Revenue Code § 501(c)(3) corporations are not permitted to be shareholders of S corporations.

30. Del. Code Ann. § 232 (2000) provides that stockholders *may* consent to notice by "electronic transmission." New York Bus. Corp. Law § 605 (1988) and Conn. Gen. Stat. Ann. § 33-603(c)(2)(2000) authorize electronic notice of shareholder meetings. James L. Holzman & Thomas A. Mullen, "A New Technology Frontier for Delaware Corporations," *Delaware Law Review* 4, 55 (2001). Nevada permits electronic notice of shareholder meetings in NRS 75.150(2). Shawn Pearson & Shay Wells, "Special Feature: Corporate Records in the Digital Age," 22 *Nevada Lawyer* 13 (May, 2014). Wash. Rev. Code § 23B.01.410 allows electronic transmission of notices to shareholders. James L. Proctor, Jr., "Fair Notice: Providing for Electronic Document Transmissions to Shareholders in Washington State," 7 *Wash. J.L. Tech. & Arts* 59 (Summer, 2011). Proctor summarizes the different state approaches in his chart on pages 65-67.

31. Del. Code Ann. § 211. Holzman & Mullen, "A New Technology."

32. Sarbanes-Oxley Act of 2002, Pub. L. No. 107-204, 116 Stat. 745 (codified in scattered sections of 11, 15, 18, 28, and 29 U.S.C.).

33. *In re the Walt Disney Company Derivative Litigation,* 906 A.2d 27, 2006 Del. LEXIS 307 (Sup. Ct., Dela. 2006).

34. Dodd-Frank Wall Street Reform and Consumer Protection Act, Pub. L. No. 111-203, 124 Stat. 1376 (2010). There is an indication that these provisions are changing the dynamics on executive compensation. See Randall S. Thomas, Alan R. Palmiter, & James F. Cotter, "Symposium: Financial Regulatory Reform in the Wake of the Dodd-Frank Act: Article: Dodd-Frank's Say on Pay: Will It Lead to a Greater Role for Shareholders in Corporate Governance?," CORNELL L. REV. 97, 1213 (July, 2012).

35. Del. Code Ann. § 141(i). Holzman & Mullen, "A New Technology."

36. Cal. Corp. Code § 307 (a)(6) states, "Members of the board may participate in a meeting through use of conference telephone, electronic video screen communication, or electronic transmission."

37. Ohio Rev. Code § 1701.59(F) (2013) and Minn. Stat. § 302A.251(5) (2015).

38. *In re Abbott Laboratories Derivative Shareholders Litigation,* 325 F.3d 795, 2003 U.S. App. LEXIS 5998 (7th Cir. 2003).

39. "Almost 57% of all active business forms in 2011 were corporations and one-third were formed as LLCs." The author based his calculations on Internal Revenue Service data. Suren Gomtsian, "The Governance of Publicly Traded Limited Liability Companies," 40 DEL. J. CORP. L. 207 (2015), 214.

40. Carter G. Bishop, "Reverse Piercing: A Single Member LLC Paradox," *South Dakota Law Review* 54, 199, 209 (2009), citing Carter G. Bishop & Daniel S. Kleinberger, *Limited Liability Companies: Tax and Business Law,* 1.07[7], (1994, 2008-2 Supplement).

41. Depending on the state, articles of organization may be called certificates of formation or certificates of organization.

42. California specifically forbids LLCs from providing professional services, Cal. Corp. Code § 17701.04 (e). Effective January 1, 2013. Operative January 1, 2014.

43. Under the Revised Uniform Limited Liability Company Act (ULLCA (2006)) § 407(a), the LLC will be presumed to be managed by the members unless stated otherwise. ULLCA (2006) has been adopted by a number of states. The states that have adopted the ULLCA (2006) with the 2013 amendments include: Alabama, Florida, Idaho, Minnesota, North Dakota, South Dakota, Utah, Vermont, and Washington. California, District of Columbia, Iowa, Nebraska, New Jersey, and Wyoming have the 2006 version without the 2013 amendments. In 2016 the ULLCA was introduced in the state legislatures of Connecticut, Illinois, Pennsylvania, and South Carolina. "Legislative Fact Sheet—Limited Liability Company (2006) (Last Amended 2013)," ULC Web site, http://uniformlaws.org/LegislativeFactSheet .aspx?title=Limited%20Liability%20Company%20%282006 %29%20%28Last%20Amended%202013%29 (accessed May 13, 2016) and E-mail from Kaitlin Dohse, Legislative Counsel, Uniform Law Commission (ULC), November 30, 2015.

44. The ULLCA (2006) § 407 sets out the types of matters that must be put to a vote of the members and whether or not that vote must be unanimous for both LLC management structures.

45. Ark. Code Ann. § 4-32-402(1) (2015).

46. Internal Revenue Service Web site, "LLC Filing as a Corporation or Partnership," https://www.irs.gov/Businesses/ Small-Businesses-&-Self-Employed/LLC-Filing-as-a-Corpo ration-or-Partnership (accessed November 27, 2015).

47. The LLC can file an Entity Classification Election on IRS Form 8832, commonly called a "check-the-box" (CTB) election. Form 8832 is available at the IRS Web site at https://www.irs.gov/pub/irs-pdf/f8832.pdf (accessed November 27, 2015). Currently, the default for failing to file Form 8832 is that most LLCs will be taxed as pass-through entities.

48. Uniform Limited Liability Company (2006) (last amended 2013) § 108(c).

49. William Pirraglia, "What Happens When an LLC Dissolves?," Chron (*Houston Chronicle*), http://smallbusiness.-chron.com/happens-llc-dissolves-25469.html (accessed November 28, 2015).

50. Uniform Limited Liability Company (2006) (last amended 2013) § 601(a).

51. *Ibid.,* § 707.

52. *Shlensky v. Wrigley,* 237 N.E.2d 776, 1968 Ill. App. LEXIS 1107 (Ill. App., Dist. 1, Div. 3, 1968).

16

Securities Regulation

Learning Objectives

After completing this chapter you should be able to

- Recognize what the law considers a "security"
- Explain the reasons why the major securities regulation statutes were enacted
- Describe the basic steps in registering securities
- Recognize the types of offerings that are exempt from registration under the Securities Act of 1933
- Identify insider trading and short-swing profits as defined in the Securities Exchange Act of 1934
- Discuss the reasoning behind the recent securities regulations and their enactments

Classic Case

This case is one of the foundation cases that define the term *security* for purposes of the federal security laws and regulations. C. M. Joiner was basically offering his potential investors the opportunity to invest in speculative oil well drilling on land it had previously leased from the landowners. An investor could join the enterprise for as little as $5, and no investor risked more than $100.

SEC v. C.M. JOINER LEASING CORPORATION

320 U.S. 344 (1943)

FACTS The C.M. Joiner Leasing Corporation (Joiner) was engaged in a campaign to sell assignments of oil leases. Under the plan Joiner would acquire leases from landowners in exchange for a promise to drill test wells on their lands. Joiner had acquired the right to drill on thousands of acres in Texas, with a provision for the payment of one dollar ($1) per year in the event that drilling was delayed. Anthony was a driller, and he agreed to do the drilling for Joiner. Joiner expected to raise most of the funds for the project from the resale of small parcels of acreage. The sales campaign was by mail. Letters offering the opportunity to "buy in" were sent to close to 1,000 prospects scattered across the country. People who actually chose to participate were located in at least eighteen states and the District of Columbia. The parcels Joiner offered never exceeded twenty acres and usually covered 2.5 to 5 acres. The prices ranged from $5 to $15 per acre. The largest single purchase was $100, and the great majority of purchases amounted to $25 or less. Buyers were permitted to pay in installments, and some did so.

Nowhere did the sales literature mention the drilling conditions or the costs the purchaser would incur if he attempted to develop his own acreage. On the other hand, the literature assured the prospect that the Joiner Company was engaged in and would complete the drilling of a test well so located as to test the oil-producing possibilities of the offered leaseholds. The leases were offered on these terms: "You may have ten acres around one or both wells at $5 per acre cash payable by August 1st, 1941 and $5 per acre additional payable November 1st, 1941 or thirty days after both wells are completed." Other language in the advertising literature emphasized the character of the purchase as an investment and as a participation in an enterprise.

The Securities and Exchange Commission alleged that Joiner's sales campaign was the offer of securities and was in violation of the Securities Act of 1933 ('33 Act). Joiner denied that it was offering securities or that it had violated the '33 Act. The trial court found that the offers involved fraud, and the circuit court of appeals agreed. However, both courts refused injunctive relief deciding that, as the court of appeals stated, it could "find simply sales and assignments of legal and legitimate oil and gas leases, i.e., sales of interests in land." It was thought that these assignments could not be proved to be "securities" or "investment contracts."

ISSUE Was Joiner offering securities in its sales campaign?

HOLDING Yes. The leaseholds offered to the public were securities for purposes of federal law.

REASONING Excerpts from the opinion of Mr. Justice Jackson:

... Undisputed facts seem to us ... to establish ... that defendants were not, as a practical matter, offering naked leasehold rights. Had the offer mailed by defendants omitted the economic inducements of the proposed and promised exploration well, it would have been a quite different proposition. Purchasers then would have been left to their own devices for realizing upon their rights. They would have anticipated waiting an indefinite time, paying delayed drilling rental . . . until some chance exploration proved or disproved the productivity of their acres. Their alternative would have been to test their own leases at a cost of $5,000 or more per well. But defendants offered no such dismal prospect. Their proposition was to sell documents which offered the purchaser a chance, without undue delay or additional cost, of sharing in discovery values which might follow a current exploration enterprise. The drilling of this well was not an unconnected or uncontrolled phenomenon to which salesmen pointed merely to show the possibilities of the offered leases. The exploration enterprise was woven into these leaseholds, in both an economic and a legal sense; the undertaking to drill a well runs through the whole transaction as the thread on which everybody's beads were strung. An agreement to drill formed the consideration upon which Anthony was able to collect leases on 4,700 acres. It was in return for assumption of this agreement that Joiner got 3,002 of the acres, leaving Anthony about 1,700 acres for his trouble. And it was his undertaking to drill the well which enabled Joiner to finance it by the sale of acreage. By selling from 1,000 to 2,000 acres at from $5 to $15 per acre, he could fulfill his obligation to drill the well, recoup his incidental expenses and those of the selling intermediaries, and have a thousand acres left for the gamble, with no investment of his own; and if he sold more, he would have a present profit. Without the drilling of the well, no one's leases had any value, and except for that undertaking they had been obtained at no substantial cost. The well was necessary not only to fulfill the hopes of purchasers but apparently even to avoid forfeiture of their leases. . . . The terms of the offering . . . , either by itself or when read in connection with the agreement to drill as consideration for the original leases, might be taken to embody an implied agreement to complete the wells. But at any rate, the acceptance of the offer quoted made a contract in which payments were timed and contingent upon completion of the well and therefore a form of investment contract in which the purchaser was paying both for a lease and for a development project.

It is clear that an economic interest in this well-drilling undertaking was what brought into being the instruments that defendants were selling and gave to the instruments most of their value. . . . The trading in these documents had all the evils inherent in the securities transactions which it was the aim of the Securities Act to end.

It is urged that the definition of "security" which controls the scope of this Act falls short of including these transactions. . . . In the Securities Act the term "security" was defined to include by name or description many documents in which there is common trading for speculation or investment. Some, such as notes, bonds, and stocks, are pretty much standardized and the name alone carries well-settled meaning. Others are of more variable character and were necessarily designated by more descriptive terms, such as "transferable share," "investment contract," and "in general any interest or instrument commonly known as a security." We cannot read out of the statute these general descriptive designations merely because more specific ones have been used to reach some kinds of documents. Instruments may be included within any of these definitions . . . if on their face they answer to the name or description. However, the reach of the Act does not stop with the obvious and commonplace. Novel, uncommon, or irregular devices . . . are also reached if it be proved as matter of fact that they were widely offered or dealt in under terms or courses of dealing which established their character in commerce as "investment contracts," or as "any interest or instrument commonly known as a 'security.'" The proof here seems clear that these defendants' offers brought their instruments within these terms. . . . In the present case we do nothing to the words of the Act; we merely accept them. It would be necessary in any case for any kind of relief to prove that documents being sold were securities under the Act. In some cases it might be done by proving the document itself, which on its face would be a note, a bond, or a share of stock. In others proof must go outside the instrument itself as we do here. Where this proof is offered in a civil action, as here, a preponderance of the evidence will establish the case;

if it were offered in a criminal case, it would have to meet the stricter requirement of satisfying the jury beyond reasonable doubt.

We hold that the court below erred in denying an injunction under the undisputed facts of this case and its findings. The judgment is *Reversed.*

WHAT ARE SECURITIES?

The stock market crash of 1929 was caused, to some extent, by the free-wheeling, virtually unregulated practices of the nation's brokers and dealers. In the boom years leading up to the crash, companies and brokers tried to convince investors to purchase securities with inflated, untrue, or fraudulent claims. One result from the market's failure was the decision by Congress to provide some protection for investors and to put a stop to some of the more egregious practices that had led up to, and then contributed to, the financial meltdown following the market crash.

After numerous hearings, Congress recognized the scope of the fraudulent behavior that had led to the market's failure. As a result, Congress enacted two statutes, the Securities Act of 1933 and the Securities Exchange Act of 1934. The Securities Act of 1933 is normally referred to as the '33 Act or the Securities Act; the Securities and Exchange Act is normally referred to as the '34 Act or the Exchange Act. Both the '33 Act and the '34 Act have subsequently been amended, in part to address new practices that seemingly run afoul of the intent of these laws, even if these practices are not in violation of the letter of the laws. In addition, the Securities and Exchange Commission (SEC), the federal agency charged with primary responsibility for the enforcement and administration of the federal securities laws, has issued extensive rules and regulations relating to the '33 and '34 Acts and their amendments.

Essentially, the '33 and '34 Acts are *disclosure statutes*. They require companies to *disclose* information to investors about the company that is issuing the *securities*— including financial information, results of operations, management, and prospects— and the acts provide consequences for noncompliance, including failure to disclose or fraudulent disclosure of the required information.

Since the issuing of securities lies at the heart of both statutes, it is essential to know what constitutes a "security." Broadly speaking, a security is "an instrument of investment in the form of a document providing evidence of ownership."[1] This chapter's Classic Case, *SEC v. C.M. Joiner Leasing Corporation*, was the first U.S. Supreme Court case to define "'securities'" for purposes of federal security regulations. In its opinion the Court went beyond the traditional and widely accepted definition of a security, finding that a security may be found in "novel, uncommon, or irregular devices, whatever they appear to be," if those devices are shown to have been "widely offered or dealt in under terms . . . which established their character . . . as 'investment contracts,' or as 'any interest or instrument commonly known as a security.'"

The definition of a *security* has evolved and expanded over the years through case law and statutory amendments. Today *security* essentially covers anything that involves (1) an investment of money; (2) in a common enterprise; (3) whereby the investor has no managerial functions but instead expects to profit solely from the entrepreneurial or managerial efforts of others.

In other words, a security is an investment in which the investor expects to receive profits without providing any goods or services beyond his or her investment. Any profits derived from the investment will be exclusively due to the efforts of others. This is a very broad definition that follows the precedent established in the *C.M. Joiner* case. It is imperative that you keep this broad definition in mind during the discussion of the various security regulations and statutes that follow.

THE SECURITIES ACT OF 1933

The Securities Act of 1933 (the '33 Act) is also known as the "truth in securities" law.[2] The act has two main objectives:

1. To ensure that prospective investors receive detailed information about any securities being offered for sale
2. To prohibit fraud, deceit, or misrepresentation in the sale of securities

In order to meet the first objective companies must file a registration statement and a prospectus containing certain important information. At a minimum, the company must provide the following:

1. Information about the company, its properties, and its business
2. A description of the security that is to be offered
3. Information about the management of the company
4. Financial statements that are certified by independent accountants[3]

The company actually files this registration statement with the SEC; however, the information becomes available to the public shortly after it is filed. It is also important to remember that the SEC does not guarantee the truth or the accuracy of the filing, it merely acknowledges that the filing is complete and contains all the information required by law. However, there are a number of possible remedies for investors if the information contained in the statement is found to be false, fraudulent, deceptive, or misleading. Investors who are harmed because they relied on the accuracy of the statements can sue the company for damages if the statements are incomplete, inaccurate, or contain an omission. These investors are entitled to actual damages, but the damages may not exceed the purchase price of the securities. Liability can be imposed against the company that issued the security, against every person who *signed* the registration statement (this normally includes at a minimum the chief executive officer [CEO], chief financial officer [CFO], and each director of the company), and every accountant, engineer, appraiser, or any other professional expert whose statement or report appears in a document filed with the SEC and whose statement is found to be false. Liability also extends to any underwriters (firms that promote or sell the securities) involved in the sale of the securities.

The '33 Act does exempt some securities offerings from the registration requirement. Keep in mind, however, that even exempt offerings are subject to the antifraud provisions. The following are the most common types of offerings that are exempt:

1. Private offerings, which are offerings made to a limited number of persons or institutions
2. "Small offerings," which are offerings of less than $5 million in any twelve-month period
3. Purely intrastate offerings, which are made only to residents of the state in which the business is incorporated and in which it conducts a significant amount of its business
4. Securities offered for sale by municipal, state, or federal governments or government agencies

Due to the provisions found in the JOBS Act (discussed later in this chapter), firms seeking the exemption from registration are now provided three "safe harbors" for a *private offering*:

1. Under Rule 504 a firm that is otherwise not subject to the reporting requirements of the '34 Act can offer up to $1 million per year, with no limits on eligible purchasers;
2. Under Rule 505 a firm can offer up to $5 million per year to an unlimited number of accredited investors and up to 35 non-accredited investors; and
3. Under Rule 506 a firm can make offers of any size to an unlimited number of accredited investors and up to 35 non-accredited but sophisticated investors.[4] *Sophisticated investors,* according to part of the SEC's definition, have enough knowledge and experience in business matters to evaluate the risks and merits of an investment.[5] They would have access to the sort of information that is normally included in a prospectus. They must also agree not to resell or distribute the securities to the general public. There is also a more restrictive category of investors, accredited investors, to whom private offerings can be made. These accredited investors are corporations or other organizations with at least $5 million in assets and individuals with a net worth of at least $1 million.[6] Historically, the SEC prohibited the use of any general advertising for firms seeking the private offering exemption. However, on July 10, 2013 the SEC adopted a new rule, found in § 506(c), allowing firms, in some situations, to use general advertising or solicitation through mass communication outlets in connection with the sale of such securities.[7] There is no rule limiting the number of investors to whom a private offering can be made. However, if even one person does not qualify as a sophisticated investor or decides, despite any prior agreement, to resell the securities to a member or members of the general public, the exemption is lost, and the company faces potential problems for issuing securities prior to registration.

If a company offers no more than $5 million in securities in any 12-month period, it is entitled to the "small offering" exemption. This is a limited exemption, however, since the business must submit an offering statement to the SEC for review before it can take advantage of this exemption. (The offering statement contains much of the same information as a registration statement.)

A company is not required to file a registration statement with the SEC if it is involved in a purely intrastate offering. To be eligible, the firm (1) must be incorporated in the state in which it is offering to sell the securities; (2) have at least 80 percent of its revenues from business within that state; (3) have at least 80 percent of its assets within the state; (4) have at least 80 percent of the offering within the state; and (5) only offer the securities to legal residents of the state.[8] If even one offeree is not a resident of the state, the company is not eligible for the exemption. This is true even if that one offeree did not purchase any of the securities being offered.

Obviously, the rules governing the exemptions from registration under the '33 Act are complex.[9] Since one of the objectives of the act is to ensure that potential investors are given adequate and accurate information prior to their purchase of securities, it is no surprise that acquiring an exemption is difficult.

An Ounce of Prevention

When a firm is considering any offering of its securities, it should check to see if it is eligible for one of the exemptions from filing under the '33 Act. If the offering is eligible for one of the exemptions, it will save time and money and it will allow the firm to avoid the possibility of an error in the information it provides to the SEC. However, before relying on exempt status it is essential to be certain that the firm qualifies. Failure to file the necessary information when a filing is required is a serious matter. Timely consultation with legal counsel and the firm's accountants is extremely important.

THE SECURITIES AND EXCHANGE ACT OF 1934

The Securities and Exchange Act of 1934 (the '34 Act) added requirements and restrictions for companies that offer their securities publicly. It also created the Securities and Exchange Commission (SEC) as the primary watchdog and enforcement agency in the securities field. The SEC was given the authority to oversee and to regulate the securities industry. This includes the authority to register and to regulate the nation's self-regulatory organizations (SROs), such as the New York Stock Exchange (NYSE), the American Stock Exchange (AMEX), and the National Association of Securities Dealers (NASDAQ), as well as brokerage firms and transfer agencies. The '34 Act also included some additional antifraud provisions and a number of reporting requirements for public firms.[10]

When a firm "goes public," this means that the company is offering to sell a large number of securities to a large number (more than 500) of holders of the stock and that the company's stock will then be traded on a securities exchange like the NYSE or NASDAQ. Companies that have publicly traded stock (public companies) are subject to the registration and disclosure requirements of the '33 Act before they issue any new stock, and they must also comply with ongoing disclosures of information mandated by the '34 Act after the stock has been issued. The ongoing information requirements under the '34 Act include (1) quarterly reports (10-Q reports); (2) annual updates about a company's business (10-K reports); (3) reports filed within four days after significant transactions or occurrences in the business (form 8-K reports); and (4) reports with information about a company's shareholder meetings (proxy statements or DEF 14A reports).

Two of the most important provisions of the '34 Act are the rules regulating proxy solicitations and insider trading. Each of these provisions will be briefly discussed here.

Proxy Solicitations

Common stock owners have the right to vote at the annual meetings of the corporation. These annual meetings include (1) reports on the successes or setbacks from the previous year; (2) statements about the firm's plans for the future; and (3) the election of directors to the board of directors, the body that officially manages the corporation. The election results can have a significant impact on the future conduct of the business. As a result, there is keen interest in these votes, especially by the various parties trying to gain control of the right to cast these votes. Corporate management would like to control the votes of these shares to maintain control, and there may be one or more dissident groups that want to take away control by acquiring control of the votes.

Many common-stock owners are unable or unwilling to travel to the annual meeting. However, as shareholders they have the right to vote that stock or to empower someone else to vote the stock on their behalf. Allowing others to vote a person's stock is most commonly done by proxy. The current management and any dissident groups that oppose current management often actively solicit these proxies. The SEC has imposed rules and regulations on proxy solicitations to help ensure that the solicitations are done fairly and properly. Any proxy solicitation must be filed with the SEC in advance to allow the SEC to verify compliance with all disclosure rules. The solicitation must also disclose all important facts concerning the issues for which the owner's vote will be used.[11]

Insider Trading

Both the '33 Act and the '34 Act have broad antifraud provisions. One area of particular concern under the '34 Act involves insider trading. Interestingly, insider trading is not prohibited directly by the language of the '34 Act. Rather, the prohibition has evolved over time through SEC and judicial interpretations of the '34 Act's antifraud provisions and rules prohibiting the use of deceptive or manipulative practices.[12]

An *insider* is a person in possession of material information about a firm that is not generally available to the public. Information is considered material if its release is likely to have at least a small impact on the price of the firm's securities once it is released to the public.[13] It is illegal for an insider who possesses any such material inside-information to deal in the securities or to share such information with family members and friends to allow them to deal in the securities. Such conduct provides the person possessing the information with an unfair advantage over the party with whom he or she is dealing. Insider trading is a crime.

To show that a person has engaged in insider trading, the following must have occurred:

1. The person must be an *insider*, that is, must owe a fiduciary duty, including a duty of confidentiality, to the company whose securities are traded.
2. He or she must be in possession of *material* information about the company, information that has not yet been disclosed to the public.
3. He or she must trade in the securities of the company in order to achieve personal gain.

The standard for whether information is "material" is, for the most part, well settled and involves whether the relevant fact would have been viewed as significant by a reasonable investor.[14] It would be considered significant if it is likely to have at least a small impact on the price of the security when the information is released. It is usually obvious when an individual traded in the securities of a company to achieve personal gain. Consequently, most insider trading cases hinge on determining whether the person trading was an insider and if he or she owed a duty of confidentiality to the company in question.

The fact is, not everyone who has material nonpublic information is prohibited from making trades. For example, *Chiarella v. United States* [15] addressed the issue of whether "remote tippees" were insiders. A *tippee* is defined as a person who acquires material nonpublic information from a person who has a fiduciary relationship with the company to which the information pertains. The person who gives the information, the *tipper*, has breached his or her duty to the company. The tippee has violated federal security law by taking unfair advantage of any uninformed "outsiders" with whom he or she has dealt.[16]

Chiarella was a printer who worked for a firm that printed takeover bids. In one such printing job, Chiarella deduced the names of the targeted companies even though the identities of the firms had been omitted from the printing order. Based on his deduction, and without disclosing the information to anyone else, Chiarella purchased stock in the target companies prior to the announcement of the takeover bids and then sold the stock when the takeover attempts became public knowledge. As a result, he made $30,000 from his stock deals. The SEC indicted him on seventeen counts of insider trading violations under the '34 Act. The Supreme Court held that because Chiarella was a complete stranger who had dealt with the sellers only through impersonal market transactions, he did not owe a fiduciary duty of confidentiality to the company and therefore was not liable for insider trading. According to *Chiarella*, "outsiders"—those who are not in positions of trust or confidence within the companies involved—do not have a duty to abstain from trading on nonpublic material information. So, as the *Chiarella* opinion shows, a person who acquires the information by other means than by gaining the information from an insider is not a tippee and is not subject to penalties for violating Rule 10b-5 of the '34 Act. (Rule 10b-5 prohibits any act or omissions in securities transactions that result in fraud or deceit. Insider trading, for which Chiarella was charged, in covered in Rule 10b5-1.) In *United States v. O'Hagan*,[17] the U.S. Supreme Court established the misappropriation theory of insider trading, which holds that a person commits fraud in connection with a securities transaction when that person misappropriates confidential information for securities trading purposes, in breach of a duty owed to the source of the information.[18] O'Hagan was a partner in a law firm. He learned that one of the firm's clients intended to make a tender offer in an effort to gain a controlling interest in Pillsbury. Based on this information, O'Hagan purchased a number of stock options, and then sold them when the tender offer was made, netting a profit of $4.3 million.

Following the *Chiarella* and *O'Hagan* opinions, the SEC promulgated Rule 10b5-2 in 2000. This rule sets forth a nonexclusive list of circumstances that establish a "duty of trust or confidence" for purposes of the misappropriation theory. These circumstances include (1) those in which a person has agreed to maintain information confidentially; (2) when the individuals sharing the communication have a history or practice of keeping information confidential such that each should know and/or expect the other to maintain confidentiality; and (3) when a person receives confidential information from an immediate family member.[19]

The SEC also has the ability under the Insider Trading Sanctions Act of 1984[20] to penalize insider traders up to three times the amount of the profit gained or the loss avoided as a result of the unlawful purchase or sale. Such penalties are payable to the U.S. Treasury; private parties cannot seek relief based on this act. This act also increases the criminal penalties that can be levied against individual violators from $10,000 to $100,000.

In addition, the Insider Trading and Securities Fraud Enforcement Act of 1988[21] creates an express private right of action in favor of market participants who traded at the same time as those who violated the '34 Act or SEC rules by trading while in possession of material, nonpublic information and also allows private individuals who provide information that leads to the imposition of penalties to receive a bounty of up to 10 percent of any penalty.

The initial disclosure requirements and the ongoing requirements outlined above mean that publicly traded companies must file a lot of information about themselves—and this information is required to be filed electronically with the SEC and posted on the company's Web site. It is also available on the SEC's EDGAR database.[22] It is possible to find out almost anything you want to know about a publicly traded company with just a few clicks on your computer, including the salaries of a company's executives, the results of their most recent quarter or fiscal year, their future plans, detailed financial statements, and risk factors that could cause the company's business to suffer. The information in these disclosures is intended to make investing in a company's securities more transparent so investors can make informed decisions, and to give shareholders recourse if proper information is not available.

Because of the stringent and significant disclosure requirements, "going public" is not a decision to be taken lightly. Companies must plan for significant management time to be devoted to securities law compliance, must retain an independent public accountant to comply with the financial statement and audit requirements, and must hire a law firm or assemble an internal legal team to assist in navigating the disclosure requirements. The securities exchanges, such as the NYSE and NASDAQ, impose additional requirements on companies with securities listed on their exchanges—including requirements for shareholder approval of certain corporate transactions and corporate governance requirements such as independent committees of the board of directors.

Short-Swing Profits

Section 16 of the '34 Act contains a provision that requires a publicly traded company's senior management to disclose online at the SEC's Web site any purchase, sale, or other transaction made in the securities of the company they manage. This provision includes all directors of the company, the CEO and CFO, and senior officers. For most transactions, the public report must be filed within two days of the transaction and must indicate the price at which the security was purchased or sold and any other relevant details about the trade.

In addition to the reporting and disclosure requirement, § 16 also forces those officers and directors who report their trades to surrender to the corporation any profits they realize from any short-swing profits. Short-swing profits are defined as any profits realized from the purchase or sale of any security that takes place in any time period of less than six months before going public. Section 16 covers transactions resulting in profits *even when the transactions were not actually based on inside information.* In essence, this section applies strict liability to trades by insiders.

The short-swing profit rule allows the company or any holder of the company's securities to enforce the rule. Remember that under § 16, any profits are surrendered (the legal term is *disgorged*) to the company, not to any individual. To spur enforcement, § 16 provides that the company must reimburse the legal fees of any lawyers who successfully catch a short-swing profits violation. Reporting a transaction within two days can be difficult, but a firm needs to establish processes and procedures to ensure that all trades by senior officers and directors are accurately and quickly reported.

An Ounce of Prevention

Every publicly traded firm should have a formal policy addressing the issue of short-swing profits. The directors and the top executives must be made aware of the limitations imposed on them by § 16 of the '34 Act. This is especially important for a firm that has only recently gone public as its top executives and its directors may not be aware of the implications of dealing in the firm's securities over the short term, even when no inside information is involved.

THE SARBANES-OXLEY ACT

In 2001 it was revealed that the Enron Corporation, through its CEO and CFO, had repeatedly misled investors, hid corporate losses, and issued inflated and misleading financial statements to prop up the company's stock price. The ultimate bankruptcy of Enron was at the time the largest corporate bankruptcy in U.S. history and resulted in millions of dollars of losses to the company's shareholders and creditors. Unfortunately, Enron was not the only example of such conduct. In early 2002, internal auditors at WorldCom discovered similar fraudulent activity; the CEO and upper management had issued inflated and misleading financial statements for several years, again in order to maintain or increase the company's stock price.

In light of these and other scandals involving misstatement of earnings, inflation of financial statements, and similar fraudulent activity, Congress passed the Sarbanes-Oxley Act (known as SOX[23]) in 2002. Among other things, SOX requires the following:

1. Companies establish a whistleblower hotline or other reporting procedure where anonymous tips relating to a company's accounting practices can be safely reported;
2. Companies cannot take retaliatory action against employees who blow the whistle by providing information concerning alleged wrongdoing to

    (a) A federal regulatory agency,
    (b) A law enforcement agency,
    (c) A congressional committee, or
    (d) Internal investigators with the company;

3. The CEO and CFO of every publicly traded company must certify as to the accuracy of the financial statements contained in public filings with the SEC; and
4. Companies must satisfy several new and/or increased requirements relating to corporate governance and the independence of audit firms.

In addition, SOX called for the formation of a new quasi-public agency, the Public Company Accounting Oversight Board (PCAOB). The PCAOB issued new rules relating to internal controls, disclosure, and evaluation, and it requires a firm's lawyers to report to the company's board of directors if the lawyers notice any unusual activities. SOX also requires that publicly traded companies establish a code of ethics for senior management and that any waivers or violations of the code of ethics be reported to the public.

(Arthur Andersen, the accounting firm responsible for auditing Enron, was found guilty of obstruction of justice during the Enron investigation. This, in part, led to some of the provisions found in SOX relating to accounting firms and auditing procedures. The conviction was subsequently overturned by the Supreme Court, but the damage to the firm had already been done.)

An Ounce of Prevention

The number of scandals involving corporate misconduct in recent years has eroded the public trust in business. The public generally has a positive attitude toward firms that are viewed as ethical. One way to show the public that a firm is trying to act ethically is for that firm to establish some sort of whistle-blower policy. This is true even if the firm would not be required to do so under SOX. Larger firms should also consider establishing an ombudsman position within the corporate hierarchy to further encourage whistle-blowers—and others—to avail themselves of the opportunity to report wrongdoing within the firm. Improving the firm's image may justify this action.

In most companies, especially large, publicly traded companies, the financial statements are not prepared by the CEO, and they are probably not prepared by the CFO personally; yet, the CEO and the CFO must certify their accuracy. Each of these executives faces potential liability under SOX if the statements are, in fact, not accurate. This places a significant burden on them to be as careful as possible in ensuring that the financial statements are accurate and requires the CEO and the CFO, at a minimum, to be certain that the firm's internal and external accountants and auditors are highly qualified and have solid credentials and reputations. (One consequence has been for CEOs and CFOs to require the employees involved in the preparation to certify the documents' accuracy). Because of this potential liability, some people question whether it is fair or ethical to require the CEO to certify the accuracy of the statements. The answer would seem to be that a lower standard increases the likelihood of another Enron or WorldCom scandal.

Exhibit 16.1 compares these three major federal securities regulation statutes.

THE WALL STREET REFORM AND CONSUMER PROTECTION ACT[24]

On July 21, 2010, President Obama signed the Dodd-Frank Wall Street Reform and Consumer Protection Act into law. This act, the culmination of more than two years of debate, is intended to protect the United States economy against another financial

Exhibit 16.1

A Comparison of the Three Major Securities Statutes

The Securities Act of 1933 ("Truth in Securities" Law; the '33 Act)	The Securities and Exchange Act of 1934 (The '34 Act)	The Sarbanes-Oxley Act (2002) (SOX)
• Requires that investors receive significant information about securities being offered for sale to the public prior to the sale • Prohibits deceit, misrepresentation, or fraud in the sale of securities • Requires that securities be registered	• Provides broad power to the SEC to oversee all aspects of the securities industry • Identifies and prohibits certain conduct in the market • Provides disciplinary power to the SEC • Allows the SEC to require the filing of periodic reports by companies issuing publicly traded securities • Provides rules governing the information required in proxy solicitations • Prohibits fraudulent activities of any kind in securities dealings, including "insider trading" • Prohibits short swing profits for certain high-ranking officers and directors of corporations	• Reforms financial disclosures and corporate responsibility • Provides regulations dealing with corporate and/or accounting fraud • Creates the PCAOB to oversee the auditing industry • Requires that publicly traded companies establish a code of ethics and report any violations to the public • Provides protection against retaliation, including dismissal, to whistle-blowers

meltdown. It also provides a broad range of consumer protections, as well as various provisions dealing with executive compensation, corporate governance, and securities disclosure requirements. Some provisions in the statute began to have an impact on corporate reports during the 2011 reporting cycle. Many of the provisions will not take effect until later due to the need for additional rulemaking by the SEC, the Federal Reserve Board, and/or the Federal Trade Commission.[25]

Among the most important areas of reform in this statute are the following:

1. The SEC is given oversight over hedge funds and credit reporting agencies.
2. The Consumer Financial Protection Bureau was created. This is an independent agency charged with protecting consumers from deceptive financial practices and with enforcing rules on banks and mortgage companies.
3. Large companies are required to provide "funeral plans," to ensure a safe method of shutting the company down should it fail.
4. Any consumer who is turned down for a loan due to his or her credit score (FICO score) or who is charged a higher-than-expected interest rate on a loan has the right to see the score without charge. (Getting a copy of one's credit score currently costs about $15.)
5. Various state mortgage regulations will be subject to federal guidelines, including the elimination of the prepayment penalties included in many adjustable rate mortgages (ARMs).

6. The Office of Credit Ratings, charged with supervising rating agencies like Moody's and Standard and Poor's, was created.[26]

Five years after the Act was signed into law Mary Jo White, the Chair of the SEC, reported that "The Commission has taken action to address virtually all of the mandatory rulemaking provisions of the Dodd-Frank Act."[27] She reported "[t]he SEC has adopted final rules for 61 mandatory rulemaking provisions of the Dodd-Frank Act."

It may still be too soon to gauge the impact of this legislation. Many people believe that the cost of complying with the Act will have a negative impact on the financial market. The Government Accountability Office (GAO) stated in its annual report that "the full impact of the Dodd-Frank Act remains uncertain because many of its rules have yet to be implemented and insufficient time has passed to evaluate others."[28]

THE JOBS ACT OF 2012

On April 5, 2012, President Obama signed into law the Jumpstart Our Business Startups (JOBS) Act.[29] This law is designed to simplify the task of locating investors for start-up businesses. It will allow these businesses to acquire capital without meeting the registration requirements normally required under the '33 Act. Instead, start-ups will be allowed to seek "crowdfunding,"[30] a method currently used by several charities and a number of artistic groups. Once the SEC has proposed regulations to provide guidance for this innovative approach, small businesses and start-up enterprises will be able to solicit financing from individuals through offerings posted on the Internet or through brokers. There are some limitations built into the law. The businesses will only be allowed to raise up to $1 million per year through crowdfunding. In addition, investors will be limited in how much they can invest. For example, a potential investor with an annual net income or total net worth of less than $100,000 will only be allowed to invest up to $2,000 in any enterprise using crowdfunding.

The JOBS Act also provided for emerging growth companies (EGCs). A firm qualifies as an EGC if it has gross revenues of less than $1 billion in its most recent fiscal year. It retains this classification until the earliest of these four factors:

1. The end of its fiscal year when its gross revenues exceed $1 billion;
2. The end of its fiscal year that includes the 5th anniversary of its original IPO;
3. When it has issued more than $1 billion in non-convertible debt within the previous three years; or
4. The date when it qualifies as a large accelerated filer.[31]

(A large accelerated filer is a public company (1) with at least $700 million in equity at the end of its most recent quarter; (2) that has been subject to filing requirements under the '33 Act for 12 months; (3) that has previously filed at least one annual report to stockholders under the '34 Act; and (4) is therefore not able to use the small company reporting requirements for its quarterly or annual reports.[32])

While the impact will not be known for some time, this statute should greatly enhance a start-up's ability to acquire capital. This, in turn, is expected to create more opportunities for small businesses and start-ups to grow, and—it is hoped—create jobs.

THE FAST ACT OF 2015

The Fixing America's Surface Transportation (FAST) Act was signed into law December 4, 2015. While securities regulations were obviously not the primary purpose of this law, it does contain a number of amendments to the federal securities laws.

Section 71001 of the FAST Act amends the '33 Act, shortening the time period for an issuer to publicly file its registration statement from 21 days to 15 days. Section 71002 states that a firm that originally qualified as an EGC when it began the registration process but no longer qualifies as an EGC will continue to be treated as an EGC for one year, or until it issues an IPO, whichever occurs first. Section 71003 simplifies the disclosure requirements for EGCs until such time as an EGC distributes a preliminary prospectus. [33]

STATE REGULATION OF SECURITIES

Because the federal statutes preserve the states' power to regulate the offering of securities, any transactions involving securities may be subject to state law as well as federal law. Such state laws, often called "blue sky" laws, normally include three types of provisions:

1. Antifraud stipulations
2. Registration requirements for brokers and dealers
3. Registration requirements for the sale and purchase of securities

The National Securities Markets Improvement Act of 1996 (NSMIA) exempted securities that are publicly traded from regulation by state securities laws, but states still maintain rights of action for fraud with respect to these securities. State blue sky laws vary widely, and consequently any securities offering not exempted by NSMIA requires a local expert to assist in navigating the local laws.

Contemporary Case

Both Sarbanes-Oxley and Dodd-Frank have provisions intended to protect whistle-blowers, especially from retaliatory discharge. However, these protections may not be as broad as many people believe. Note how the Circuit Court addressed the issue of whether the Dodd-Frank whistle-blower provisions applied in this case.

ASADI v. G.E. ENERGY (USA) LLC

720 F.3d 620, 2013 U.S. App. LEXIS 14470 (5th Cir., 2013)

FACTS In 2006, Asadi accepted an offer from G.E. Energy to serve as its Iraq Country Executive and moved to Amman, Jordan to assume his responsibilities. In 2010, while serving in this position, Asadi was informed by Iraqi officials that G.E. Energy had recently hired a woman who was closely associated with a senior Iraqi official, hoping to curry favor with that official in negotiating a potentially lucrative joint venture agreement between G.E. Energy and the Iraq government. Asadi was concerned that this alleged conduct might violate the Foreign Corrupt Practices Act (FCPA), so he reported it to his supervisor and to the G.E. Energy ombudsperson for the region.

Soon after Asadi filed his reports, he received a "surprisingly negative" performance review. He then alleged that G.E. Energy pressured him to step down from his position as the Iraq Country Executive and take a lesser position with minimal responsibilities in the region. He refused to do so, continuing in the position for which he was hired.

Approximately a year after he initially filed his report about the possible FCPA violation he was fired from his job. He then filed suit, alleging that G.E. Energy violated the Dodd-Frank whistleblower-protection provisions by firing him after he filed an internal report of a possible securities law violation.

The district court granted G.E. Energy's motion to dismiss for failure to state a claim because he was not a whistleblower. Asadi appealed.

ISSUE Was Asadi entitled to remedies under the whistleblower-protection provisions found in Dodd-Frank?

HOLDING No. Asadi did not qualify as a whistle-blower under the Dodd-Frank Act, and therefore is not entitled to remedies under its whistleblower-protection provisions.

REASONING Excerpts from the opinion of Jennifer Walker Elrod:

... When faced with questions of statutory construction, "we must first determine whether the statutory text is plain and unambiguous" and, "[i]f it is, we must apply the statute according to its terms." ... "The plainness or ambiguity of statutory language is determined by reference to the language itself, the specific context in which that language is used, and the broader context of the statute as a whole." ... If the statutory text is unambiguous, our inquiry begins and ends with the text ...

The parties' arguments in this case implicate several additional principles of interpretation. In construing a statute, a court should give effect, if possible, to every word and every provision Congress used. ... Also, if possible, we interpret provisions of a statute in a manner that renders them compatible, not contradictory. ... With these principles in mind, we turn to the question presented in this appeal.

Congress enacted Dodd-Frank in the wake of the 2008 financial crisis. Section 922 of Dodd-Frank ... encourages individuals to provide information relating to a violation of U.S. securities laws to the Securities and Exchange Commission. ... Section

922 . . . encourages such disclosures through two related provisions that: (1) require the SEC to pay significant monetary awards to individuals who provide information to the SEC which leads to a successful enforcement action; and (2) create a private cause of action for certain individuals against employers who retaliate against them for taking specified protected actions. We must answer a relatively straightforward question relating to the latter provision in this case: whether an individual who is not a "whistleblower" under the statutory definition of that term . . . may, in some circumstances, nevertheless seek relief under the whistleblower-protection provision. For the reasons that follow, we hold that the plain language of the Dodd-Frank whistleblower-protection provision creates a private cause of action only for individuals who provide information relating to a violation of the securities laws to the SEC. Because Asadi failed to do so, his whistleblower-protection claim fails.

We start and end our analysis with the text of the relevant statute. . . . That section . . . "Securities whistleblower incentives and protection" . . . contains ten subsections. The interplay between two of these subsections—(a) and (h)—is the focus of the statutory-interpretation question presented in this case. Subsection (a) provides definitions for certain terms used throughout [including whistleblower]. . . . Specifically, "[t]he term 'whistleblower' means any individual who provides, or 2 or more individuals acting jointly who provide, information relating to a violation of the securities laws *to the Commission*, in a manner established, by rule or regulation, by the Commission." . . . This definition, standing alone, expressly and unambiguously requires that an individual provide information to the SEC to qualify as a "whistleblower." . . .

Subsection (h) . . . "Protection of whistleblowers," provides whistleblowers a private right of action against employers who take retaliatory actions against the whistleblower for taking certain protected actions. . . . Subsection (h) includes three paragraphs. Only paragraph (1) . . . is relevant to this appeal.

Paragraph (1) . . . [s]ubparagraph (A), the specific focus of this appeal, provides [that] . . . :

> No employer may discharge, demote, suspend, threaten, harass, directly or indirectly, or in any other manner discriminate against, a whistleblower in the terms and conditions of employment because of any lawful act done by the whistleblower—
>
> (i) in providing information to the Commission in accordance with this section;
> (ii) in initiating, testifying in, or assisting in any investigation or judicial or administrative action of the Commission based upon or related to such information; or
> (iii) in making disclosures that are required or protected under the Sarbanes-Oxley Act of 2002 . . . the Securities Exchange Act of 1934 . . . including section 10A(m) of such Act . . . and any other law, rule, or regulation subject to the jurisdiction of the Commission. . . .

Under Dodd-Frank's plain language and structure, there is only one category of whistleblowers: individuals who provide information relating to a securities law violation to the SEC. The three categories listed . . . represent the protected activity in a whistleblower-protection claim. They do not, however, define which individuals qualify as whistleblowers.

This construction of the whistleblower-protection provision follows directly from the plain language of [the Statute] . . . : "No employer may discharge . . . or in any other manner discriminate against, a whistleblower . . . because of any lawful act done by the whistleblower" in taking any of the three categories of protected actions. . . . This statutory language clearly answers two questions: (1) who is protected; and (2) what actions by protected individuals constitute protected activity . . .

The statutory text describing these three categories of protected activity is also unambiguous. The text ... protects whistleblowers from employer retaliation for the action that made the individual a whistleblower ... , *i.e.*, providing information relating to a securities law violation to the SEC.... The text ... protects whistleblowers from retaliation for their participation in the investigation, and possible judicial or administrative action of the SEC, that follows on the heels of the information initially provided to the SEC ...

Based on our examination of the plain language and structure of the whistleblower-protection provision, we conclude that the whistleblower-protection provision unambiguously requires individuals to provide information relating to a violation of the securities laws *to the SEC* to qualify for protection from retaliation under [the Statute] ...

We conclude that the plain language of [the Statute] limits protection under the Dodd-Frank whistleblower-protection provision to those individuals who provide "information relating to a violation of the securities laws" to the SEC.... Asadi did not provide any information to the SEC; therefore, he does not qualify as a "whistleblower." Accordingly, we AFFIRM the district court's dismissal of Asadi's Dodd-Frank whistleblower-protection claim.

Short Answer Questions

1. What information is required in a registration statement under the provisions of the '33 Act? Why do you think Congress included such requirements in a statute rather than relying on a business to "do the right thing" in registering its securities prior to a public offering?

2. What does § 16 of the '34 Act, the "short-swing profits" regulation, require of top executives and members of the board of directors of publicly traded corporations? Why do you think this regulation was put in place by the SEC? Does the SEC's definition of "short-swing profits" seem fair to you?

3. What is the purpose of the JOBS Act? Why do you think Congress provided special treatment for start-up enterprises that allow emerging growth companies (EGCs) to avoid some provisions of longstanding securities laws and regulations? What event or events led to its enactment?

You Decide...

1. Daniel F. Peterson, through his company the USA Real Estate Fund, promised investors that they could earn up to 1300 percent by investing in his firm. He claimed that there was an upcoming offering of a "secured product" backed by a number of prominent financial firms, including Merrill Lynch and BlackRock. He also claimed that the JOBS Act of 2012 would allow him to raise billions of dollars by advertising this offering to the general public, producing huge profits for early investors. Furthermore, he appealed to the patriotism of potential investors by promising that all proceeds would be invested exclusively in American businesses.

The SEC alleges that Peterson did not have a commitment from any financial firm to back the promised offering. It claims that he was using the money generated from the early investors to pay his personal expenses (rent, food, vacations, a rented Mercedes-Benz) and gifts for friends and family members.

The SEC has brought charges against him, alleging fraud. He is accused of violating both the '33 and the '34 Act.

How would *you* decide this case? Does the SEC have to establish scienter (intent) in order to get a conviction in this case? Be certain that you explain and justify your answer.

(See *Litigation Release*, "SEC Seeks to Halt Scheme Raising Investor Funds Under Guise of JOBS Act," U.S. Securities and Exchange Commission (April 25, 2013), https://www.sec.gov/litigation/litreleases/2013/lr22685.htm.)

2. Mark Cuban, an entrepreneur, owned 600,000 shares of an Internet search engine company, Mamma.com. He was contacted by the CEO of Mamma.com who told him that the firm was planning to raise capital by a PIPE offering and Cuban was asked if he was interested in participating. (A PIPE offering is a private investment in a public entity, an offering of securities at a discount from the current market price in order to generate funds. A PIPE allows a firm to generate capital quickly and with less expense than other methods of offering securities.[34]) The CEO allegedly stressed to Cuban that the information they were discussing was confidential. Cuban informed the CEO that he was not interested, that PIPE offerings were dilutive, and that he would lose money due to the offering. The CEO later e-mailed additional information about the offering to Cuban, including the name of the banker conducting the offering for the firm. Cuban then called the banker to discuss the matter. In that conversation Cuban learned that the offering would be at a discount below market price and that there would be other incentives to encourage people to invest. Within minutes of completing this phone call, Cuban sold his stock in Mamma.com. By doing so he avoided losses in excess of $750,000 when the PIPE offering was made and the price of the stock declined.

The SEC accused Cuban of violating the insider trading rules, alleging that under the misappropriation theory of insider trading he should be held liable. Cuban denied that he had any duty to refrain from selling his stock and that he was within his rights to sell the stock to a willing buyer at a mutually acceptable price.

Should Mr. Cuban be held liable under the misappropriation theory of insider trading for using this information to his benefit in selling his stock prior to the announcement of the PIPE offering by Mamma.com?

How would *you* decide this case? Be certain that you explain and justify your answer.

(See *SEC v. Cuban*, 620 F.3d 551 (5th Cir. 2010).)

Notes

1. *Merriam Webster's Collegiate Dictionary*, 11th ed. (Springfield, MA: Merriam-Webster, 2003), 1123.
2. U.S. Securities and Exchange Commission (SEC), "The Laws that Govern the Securities Industry," http://www.sec.gov/about/laws.shtml (accessed May 6, 2016).
3. *Ibid.*
4. "Noreen Weiss Adler, "A Seismic Shift In The Securities Laws: The Elimination of the Ban on the Use of General Solicitation or General Advertising in Certain Private Placements, and What It Means for Issuers, Accredited Investors, and Crowdfunding," McDonald Weiss PLLC, (October 2, 2013). http://www.jdsupra.com/legalnews/a-seismic-shift-in-the-securities-laws-11941/ (accessed May 6, 2016).
5. Kristen McNamara, "Definition of 'sophisticated investor' varies," Market Watch (April 26, 2010), http://www.marketwatch.com/story/definition-of-sophisticated-investor-varies-2010-04-26 (accessed May 6, 2016).
6. *Ibid.*

7. "Securities Exempt from Registration under the Securities Act of 1933," thisMatters.com, http://thismatter.com/money/stocks/exempt-securities.htm (accessed May 6, 2016).

8. *Ibid.*

9. The full text of the '33 Act, '34 Act, and all associated rules and regulations are consolidated and regularly updated by the University of Cincinnati College of Law and available online at http://www.law.uc.edu/CCL/xyz/sldtoc.html (accessed November 27, 2012).

10. SEC, "The Laws that Govern the Securities Industry," *supra* Note 2.

11. *Ibid.*

12. See 17 C.F.R. § 240.10b-5 (2009) and 15 U.S.C. § 78j(b).

13. "Material Inside Information," *Investopedia*, http://www.investopedia.com/terms/m/materialinsiderinformation.asp#axzz1lSVFw9o0 (accessed November 27, 2012).

14. See *Basic Incorporated v. Levinson*, 485 U.S. 224 (1988) and *TSC Industries v. Northway, Inc.*, 426 U.S. 438 (1976).

15. 445 U.S. 222 (1980).

16. *Black's Law Dictionary* (St. Paul: West Publishing Company, 1990), 1484.

17. 521 U.S. 642 (1997).

18. See *O'Hagan*, 521 U.S. at 652.

19. See 17 C.F.R. § 240.10b5-2 (2009).

20. 98 Stat. 1264, 15 U.S.C. 78a.

21. 102 Stat. 4677.

22. The EDGAR database is available at www.sec.gov.

23. 116 Stat. 745.

24. Pub. L. 111-203.

25. "The Financial Reform Act: New Corporate Governance and Executive Compensation Provisions," *JD Supra*, http://www.jdsupra.com/legalnews/the-financial-reform-act-new-corporate-46829/ (accessed November 27, 2012).

26. Dalia Fahmy, "Top 6 Changes That Financial Reform Brings to Consumers," *ABC News* (June 25, 2010), http://www.budgetclowns.com/forums/f7/top-6-changes-financial-reform-brings-consumers-206.html, (accessed November 27, 2012).

27. "Implementing the Dodd-Frank Wall Street Reform and Consumer Protection Act," U.S. Securities and Exchange Commission web site (July 16, 2015), http://www.sec.gov/spotlight/dodd-frank.shtml (accessed May 6, 2016).

28. Steve Quinlivan, "Making Sense of Dodd-Frank," Dodd-Frank.com (December 31, 2015), http://dodd-frank.com/gao-report-addresses-impact-of-dodd-frank-on-community-banks-credit-unions-and-systemically-important-institutions/ (accessed May 6, 2016).

29. Joyce M. Rosenberg, "New Law Lets Small Businesses Use Crowdfunding," *Roanoke Times*, April 15, 2012, *The Ticker*, 6.

30. Crowdfunding is a method of raising money from a "crowd," a large number of people. It is generally done online.

31. "Emerging Growth Company (EGC)," Practical Law, http://us.practicallaw.com/3-518-8137 (accessed May 6, 2016).

32. "Large Accelerated Filer," Practical Law, http://us.practical-law.com/1-382-3570 (accessed May 6, 2016).

33. Announcement, "Recently Enacted Transportation Law Includes a Number of Changes to the Federal Securities Laws," U.S. Securities and Exchange Commission, http://www.sec.gov/corpfin/announcement/cf-announcement—fast-act.html (accessed May 6, 2016).

34. "Private Investment in Public Equity—PIPE," *Investopedia*, http://www.investopedia.com/terms/p/pipe.asp#axzz1lulKPqIS (accessed November 27, 2012).

Part VI

The Regulatory Environment

17

Strategic Alliances and Antitrust Law

Learning Objectives

After completing this chapter you should be able to

- Explain the possible risks and benefits of forming a strategic alliance
- Discuss the reasons behind antitrust regulation
- Explain the coverage of the Sherman Antitrust Act
- Describe the different areas regulated by the Clayton Act and its amendments
- Recognize the scope of the Federal Trade Commission Act
- Identify unfair trade practices and their impact on competition

Classic Case

This classic case involves an unusual—and seemingly inexplicable—interpretation of interstate commerce and the scope of the Sherman Act. After reading the Court's opinion, decide whether you think the Court made a proper decision. (NOTE: The Court refers to the game as base ball, two words, as opposed to the one word, baseball, used today. We retained that usage in this case.)

FEDERAL BASEBALL CLUB OF BALTIMORE, INC. v. NATIONAL LEAGUE OF PROFESSIONAL BASEBALL CLUBS

259 U.S. 200, 42 S.Ct. 465 (S.Ct. 1922)

FACTS The Baltimore team, the plaintiff in the original case and the appellant in this proceeding, is a professional baseball club incorporated in Maryland. It was a member, with seven other teams, of the Federal League of Professional Base Ball Clubs prior to the dissolution of that League, a corporation formed under the laws of Indiana. The Federal League was formed to compete with the other two leagues, which existed prior to its formation.

The plaintiff alleged that the defendants (The National League of Professional Base Ball Clubs, the American League of Professional Base Ball Clubs [each of which was an unincorporated association of eight incorporated baseball teams], the presidents of these two leagues, the Commissioner of these leagues, as well as several persons who had wielded considerable power in the Federal League before its demise) were participants in a conspiracy to eliminate the Federal League, to the detriment of the Baltimore club. According to the allegations, the defendants conspired to monopolize the base ball business. The defendants allegedly purchased some Federal League teams and induced other teams to leave the league. Consequently, all of the teams left

the Federal League except the Baltimore team. Baltimore then had no teams to play.

At trial the Baltimore team prevailed and received an $80,000 verdict. Under the provisions of the Sherman Act, this amount was trebled, providing a judgment of $240,000. The defendants appealed, and the appellate court determined that the defendants were not subject to the Sherman Act. As a result the trial court's judgment was overturned.

ISSUE Were the Professional Base Ball Leagues involved in interstate commerce, and therefore subject to the provisions of the Sherman Act?

HOLDING No. The business of base ball is to provide exhibitions of base ball. These exhibitions are purely intrastate and therefore are not subject to federal laws. Since the Sherman Act does not apply to purely state law matters, it does not apply in this case.

REASONING Excerpts from the opinion of Mr. Justice Holmes:

. . . The decision of the Court of Appeals went to the root of the case and if correct makes it unnecessary to consider other serious difficulties in the way of the plaintiff's recovery. A summary statement of the nature of the business involved will be enough to present the point. The clubs composing the Leagues are in different cities and for the most part in different States. The end of the . . . organizations . . . described in the pleadings and evidence is that these clubs shall play against one another in public exhibitions for money, one or the other club crossing a state line in order to make the meeting possible. When as the result of these contests one club has won the pennant of its League and another club has won the pennant of the other League, there is a final competition for the world's championship between these two. Of course the scheme requires constantly repeated travelling on the part of the clubs, which is provided for, controlled and disciplined by the organizations, and this it is said means commerce among the States. But we are of opinion that the Court of Appeals was right.

The business is giving exhibitions of base ball, which are purely state affairs. It is true that, in order to attain for these exhibitions the great popularity that they have achieved, competitions must be arranged between clubs from different cities and States. But the fact that in order to give the exhibitions the Leagues must induce free persons to cross state lines and must arrange and pay for their doing so is not enough to change the character of the business. According to [precedent] . . . the transport is a mere incident, not the essential thing. That to which it is incident, the exhibition, although made for money would not be called trade or commerce in the commonly accepted use of those words. As it is put by the defendants,

personal effort, not related to production, is not a subject of commerce. That which in its consummation is not commerce does not become commerce among the States because the transportation that we have mentioned takes place. To repeat the illustrations given by the Court below, a firm of lawyers sending out a member to argue a case, or the Chautauqua lecture bureau sending out lecturers, does not engage in such commerce because the lawyer or lecturer goes to another State.

If we are right the plaintiff's business is to be described in the same way and the restrictions by contract that prevented the plaintiff from getting players to break their bargains and the other conduct charged against the defendants were not an interference with commerce among the States.

Judgment affirmed.

THE BASIS OF REGULATORY REFORM

For the first 114 years of U.S. history, business had a fairly free field in which to work. There was little federal regulation and little effective state regulation. This was, after all, the era of a *laissez faire*[1] attitude toward business. As a result, the courts and the federal government took a hands-off attitude. In such an environment, Cornelius Vanderbilt, a railroad tycoon of the 1800s, was able to boast, "What do I care about the law? Hain't I got the power?"

The tide began to turn in the late 1800s as the public tired of the irresponsible behavior of some of the so-called "robber barons." The press began to call for reforms and for protection from "big business." In response Congress enacted the Sherman Antitrust Act in 1890. This act was a good beginning to governmental regulation of business, but it was unable to curb many business excesses. One of the problems with the Sherman Act is that the act is *remedial*, only applying to situations after the conduct has occurred and caused harm. Often the harm was irreversible. In an effort to provide *preventative* protections, Congress subsequently bolstered the antitrust area with the passage of these acts:

- The Clayton Act and the Federal Trade Commission Act, both passed in 1914
- The Robinson-Patman Act, an amendment to § 2 of the Clayton Act addressing price discrimination, passed in 1936

- The Celler-Kefauver Act, which amended the merger provisions of § 7 of the Clayton Act, passed in 1950
- The Hart-Scott-Rodino Antitrust Improvements Act of 1976, which requires large companies to file a report with the Federal Trade Commission (FTC) and the Department of Justice prior to completing a merger or certain acquisitions, allowing government regulators to determine whether the proposed conduct would violate any antitrust laws
- The growth in both size and importance of international trade and its impact on the domestic market led to further amendment of the Sherman Act with the passage of the Foreign Trade Antitrust Improvement Act in 1982

We will examine the interactions and the effectiveness of the antitrust laws later in this chapter.

STRATEGIC ALLIANCES

Before addressing the antitrust laws in detail, it is important to examine the area of strategic alliances. A strategic alliance exists when two companies decide to share their resources to undertake a mutually beneficial project.[2] A strategic alliance is not the same as a joint venture or a consortium. Rather, the strategic alliance is an agreement between two firms to pool their resources to attain a result that will benefit each of the firms. Each firm maintains its autonomy and remains a separate entity. For example, a manufacturing firm may form an alliance with a research and development company to develop a more efficient distribution model. These alliances are frequently formed to improve a process, expand into new markets, or to gain a competitive advantage over competitors.

It is obvious that strategic alliances can be extremely valuable to the allying firms. Such arrangements might allow a smaller firm to gain a market niche and to successfully compete with much larger and better known firms in the industry. They also allow firms to take advantage of efficiencies or expertise that they may possess in one area by letting them team up with a similarly situated firm that has different efficiencies or expertise. The net effect of such alliances often proves to be pro-competition. Unfortunately, such alliances also run the risk of violating the antitrust laws, particularly § 1 of the Sherman Act, as will be discussed below.

An Ounce of Prevention

You can form a strategic alliance to improve your competitive position. Such alliances are normally beneficial to each of the firms involved in their formation. However, you should give careful thought and do adequate research before agreeing. If the alliance is likely to result in an increased level of competition in any line of trade or commerce, there should be no problems. But if the alliance is likely to result in decreased competition, with one or more of the firms enhancing an already strong competitive position in its industry, the Justice Department may decide that the arrangement violates § 1 of the Sherman Act. If so, criminal charges may well be filed against any or all of the participating firms.

Strategic alliances are especially important for businesses that are trying to "go global." Their use has increased dramatically in the international arena.[3]

THE SHERMAN ANTITRUST ACT

Congress passed the Sherman Antitrust Act in 1890. The intended purpose of the act was to preserve the economic ideal of a pure-competition economy. To reach this ideal, the Sherman Act prohibits combinations that restrain trade, and it prohibits attempts to monopolize any area of commerce. Violations of the act can result in fines, imprisonment, injunctive relief, and civil damages.

Section 1: Contracts, Combinations, or Conspiracies in Restraint of Trade

The Sherman Antitrust Act is a fairly short statute, but its few words cover a great number of actions. Section 1 states:

> Every contract, combination in the form of trust or otherwise, or conspiracy, in restraint of trade or commerce among the several States, or with foreign nations, is hereby declared to be illegal. Every person who shall make any contract or engage in any combination or conspiracy hereby declared to be illegal shall be deemed guilty of a felony, and, on conviction thereof, shall be punished by fine not exceeding $10,000,000 if a corporation, or, if any other person, $350,000, or by imprisonment not exceeding three years, or by both said punishments, in the discretion of the court."[4]

The original statute provided that the crime was a misdemeanor, and called for a maximum fine of $5,000, with a maximum imprisonment of one year for anyone convicted of violating the act.

Violations of § 1 require a contract, a combination, or a conspiracy. Each of these three requires two or more persons (remember that a business entity is considered a "person" for purposes of the Sherman Act) acting in concert in some manner that restrains trade or commerce among the states or with a foreign nation. Thus, § 1 requires two or more persons acting together before a violation can be found.

Courts had problems with the original language of § 1. Nearly every contract can, at least in theory, be viewed as a restraint of trade. Consequently, the prohibition against contracts "in restraint of trade" seemed too broad. If this section were to be interpreted literally, virtually all business dealings that affect interstate commerce (including foreign trade) could, theoretically, be prohibited by § 1 of the Sherman Act. Courts initially interpreted the Sherman Act very narrowly. The courts were willing to rule against combinations or conspiracies in restraint of trade, but had a more difficult time ruling that any contract was in restraint of trade. However, the courts *did* rule that some union activities were combinations or conspiracies in restraint of trade in violation of § 1 of the Sherman Act. Unfortunately these rulings tended to promote—rather than hinder—the big business of the era. These interpretations negated the impact of the act.

The Rule of Reason   Eventually, the Supreme Court found a method for evaluating conduct, particularly contracts, that allegedly restrains trade among the several states in violation of § 1 of the Sherman Act. In the case of *Standard Oil Co. of New Jersey* v. *United States,* [5] the Supreme Court introduced the "rule of reason." According to this rule, the Sherman Act does not prohibit every contract or combination in restraint of trade among the several states. Rather, the act only prohibits those contracts or combinations that *unreasonably* restrain trade among the several states. If the contract or combination is *reasonable* under the circumstances, the conduct is not in violation of the law even if it seemingly restrains trade. By applying this rule the court can determine whether a defendant accused of violating the Act conducted his or her business in a reasonable manner and adhered to the law, or acted in an unreasonable manner in violation of the law. The court determined in this particular case that the conduct by Standard Oil of New Jersey was unreasonable. However, the court in theory accepted the rule of reason defense to charges of violations of § 1.

Business lost no time in pursuing this defense to its best advantage. Given a sufficient amount of time, almost any business can develop a strong argument that its conduct was reasonable under the circumstances. The impact of this rule caused the courts to reevaluate their approach. The courts retained the rule of reason but added a new category: They declared some conduct to be so lacking in social value as to be an automatic violation of § 1. These actions, called *per se* violations, tend to directly contradict the economic model of pure competition. Since such conduct is deemed unreasonable by definition, it cannot be justified by the "rule of reason."

An Ounce of Prevention

You may have the opportunity to join some form of regional economic alliance. Such alliances are formed to encourage cooperation among the firms in the region and to enhance local economic opportunities. This form of strategic alliance can be beneficial to the area. The cooperation of the firms provides a platform for increasing the profits of all the participants. Most such businesses are likely to believe that the antitrust laws, especially the Sherman Act, are not likely to apply to their activities since the alliances are local or regional in nature. Before joining such an alliance, you should ensure that you will not be cooperating with other firms in a manner that denies "outside firms" access to the market. This could be viewed as a "combination in restraint of trade," a violation of § 1 of the Sherman Act. If the effect of the alliance does, in fact, deter outside competition in the region, all of the firms in the alliance could face criminal and civil liability under the Sherman Act.

***Per se* Violations**   As noted in the preceding section, the courts restricted the availability of the rule of reason defense for alleged Sherman Act violations by finding that the conduct in question was a *per se* violation. (A *per se* violation is inherently a violation; the act alone proves the violation.) The acts that are deemed to be *per se* violations are acts that inherently contradict pure competition. If a firm is found guilty of a *per se* violation, it is not permitted to defend its conduct; it will be found guilty by definition.

Historically the *per se* violations under the Sherman Act, § 1 were as follows:

1. Horizontal price fixing (agreements on price among competitors)
2. Vertical price fixing (agreements on price among suppliers and customers)
3. Horizontal market divisions (agreements among competitors as to who can sell in which region)
4. Group boycotts (agreements among competitors not to sell to a particular buyer or not to buy from a particular seller)

Clearly, few businesses would be careless enough to actually and overtly agree to such conduct. As a result, the courts have had to infer such agreements from the conduct of the parties. For example, in the area of price fixing, if the courts find that the parties have acted in a manner that amounts to conscious parallelism, a violation is likely to be found. Conscious parallelism, by itself, is not conclusive proof of a violation of § 1. However, it is to be weighed—and weighed heavily—by the courts in determining whether a § 1 violation is present. Generally, conscious parallelism coupled with some other fact, however slight, is sufficient to support a jury verdict of price fixing in violation of § 1. But if the conduct of the firms amounts only to price leadership, no violation is present. How can anyone distinguish conscious parallelism from price leadership? There is no easy answer to this problem; it poses a dilemma for the court every time it is raised.

Conscious parallelism occurs when several firms in an industry increase their prices at or near the same time, with no obvious reason for the increase. The courts will normally look for some circumstantial evidence that shows an implicit agreement among the firms to raise their prices and thereby increase their profits. Such evidence is considered a "plus factor" by the courts, evidence of a combination or conspiracy to restrain trade.[6] The more "plus factors" present in a given case, the more likely a violation will be found. It is also likely that there is no dominant firm in the industry.

By contrast, price leadership occurs when a dominant firm within an industry sets prices and the other firms in the industry follow the lead of the dominant firm in order to retain their relative market shares and positions. Often a price leader will use its dominant position and its efficiency to lower prices, forcing competitors to also lower prices in order to remain somewhat competitive.[7]

The Court seemed to invoke both the rule of reason and the economic theory of competition in a somewhat recent case.[8] It found that Visa's conduct was valid under the rule of reason, and that competition was enhanced by Visa's denial of membership to Sears, the applicant. Sears, Roebuck and Company applied for membership with Visa, USA, the association of credit card issuers who offer the Visa card in the United States. The association denied the application by Sears, and Sears filed suit against Visa, USA, alleging that the credit card association was combining or conspiring illegally in an effort to prevent Sears from issuing Visa cards. The court found that the harm to competition would be greater if the association admitted Sears than it would be if Sears was prevented from joining the association. According to the court, the credit card industry was better served by having Visa, MasterCard, American Express, Diners/Carte Blanche, and Discover (issued by and through Sears). Competition was keen, and the market was highly competitive. Admitting Sears to the association would reduce the number of competitors in the credit card industry and would seriously harm banks that issue Visa in head-to-head competition with Sears for the potential Visa customers in the market. According to the court, the association acted in a reasonable manner under the circumstances. Under the rule of reason, the conduct of Visa, USA was reasonable, and therefore appropriate. It did not violate § 1 of the Sherman Act.

"Quick Look" Analysis   The courts have recently added a third method for evaluating allegations that certain conduct violates § 1 of the Sherman Act. This method, the *quick look* analysis, provides a middle ground between the rule of reason and the *per se* violations. Under the quick look analysis, a defendant firm that is charged with what has historically been treated as a *per se* violation is given an opportunity to rebut the presumption that the conduct is automatically anticompetitive under the traditional *per se* standards. If the court agrees with the rebuttal evidence of the defendant firm, the court removes the conduct from the *per se* category and applies a rule of reason analysis to the case.

If the court accepts this initial argument, this quick look, it gives these firms the opportunity to show that there is a business justification for their conduct and that they should not be found in violation of the law. Exhibit 17.1 compares the three approaches to allegations of violations of § 1 of the Sherman Act.

The court began to restrict the application of the *per se* doctrine and to apply the quick look analysis to certain types of cases by 1979. In *Broadcast Music, Inc. v. CBS, Inc.*[9] the court upheld the right of an association of music copyright holders to establish a common price for the "blanket license" of their compositions. In rejecting the challenge by CBS, the court stated that, in determining whether to apply the rule of reason or the

Exhibit 17.1

Sherman Act § 1 Analyses

Type of Analysis	Violations Alleged	Treatment
Rule of reason	Contract, combination, or conspiracy in restraint of trade (excluding price fixing, market divisions, or group boycotts)	A "totality of the circumstances" test. The firm must show a reason for the conduct undertaken and the effect on competition in the industry. If the conduct is found to unreasonably restrain trade, it is illegal.
Per se violation	Price fixing Market division Group boycotts	Conduct that has a "pernicious effect" on competition or lacks any redeeming value. Practices that "always or almost always tend to restrict competition and decrease output." Evidence of a *per se* violation is, by definition, unreasonable and the firm is guilty of a violation of § 1.
Quick look analysis	To date: Some price fixing Some vertical market division	The defendant must present some evidence that the conduct is "designed to increase economic efficiency and render markets more, rather than less, competitive." If the court finds that the evidence is persuasive, the case is decided under the rule of reason.

per se rules, the court should decide "whether the practice facially appears to be one that would always or almost always tend to restrict competition and decrease output," or is "one designed to increase economic efficiency and render markets more, rather than less, competitive." This formulation provides the framework for the quick look analysis.

To date the quick look has been limited in its application to some vertical restraints and some cooperative pricing agreements. Horizontal price-fixing, horizontal market divisions, and group boycotts still are viewed as *per se* violations. The courts have evaluated some vertical market division cases and some maximum price arrangements under the quick look provisions. In addition, some tying arrangements are now being evaluated under a quick look analysis. The businesses charged with violations of § 1 of the Sherman Act are allowed the opportunity to rebut the presumption of anticompetitive effect in these cases. If they are successful, the case is decided under the rule of reason. If they are not, the conduct is found to be a *per se* violation of § 1 of the Sherman Act.

Foreign Trade Antitrust Improvement Act   Congress amended the Sherman Act in 1982 when it passed the Foreign Trade Antitrust Improvement Act (FTAIA).[10]

The FTAIA was intended to facilitate the *exporting* of domestic goods by providing an exemption to the Sherman Act for export transactions that did not injure the U.S economy, by relieving exporters from what had been a competitive disadvantage in foreign trade.[11] The act denies subject matter jurisdiction over claims by foreign plaintiffs against defendants when the *situs* of the injury is overseas and the injury arises from effects in the nondomestic market.[12]

Section 2: Monopolizing and Attempting to Monopolize

Section 2 of the Sherman Act is nearly as brief as § 1 and is equally as broad. Section 2 makes the following provision:

> Every person who shall monopolize, or attempt to monopolize, or combine or conspire with any other person or persons, to monopolize any part of the trade or commerce among the several States, or with foreign nations, shall be deemed guilty of a felony, and, on conviction thereof, shall be punished by a fine not exceeding $10,000,000 if a corporation, or, if any other person, $350,000, or by imprisonment not exceeding three years, or by both said punishments, in the discretion of the court.

As with § 1, the original statute provided that the crime was a misdemeanor, and called for a maximum fine of $5,000, with a maximum imprisonment of one year for anyone convicted of violating the act. The current penalties are the same as under § 1—a fine of up to $350,000 for an individual or up to $10 million for a corporation, and up to three years in prison.

Section 2 can be violated *either* by one person acting alone *or* by multiple parties acting in concert. In contrast, § 1 can be violated only by multiple parties acting together. (To avoid confusion, remember that it takes two people to violate § 1, while it takes only one person to violate § 2.)

Many people mistakenly believe that monopolies are prohibited by § 2. In fact, no law prohibits monopolies or possessing monopoly power. It is not illegal to gain a monopoly position through making a superior product or providing superior service, and a firm that does so would not be found in violation of § 2 of the Sherman Act. The objective of § 2 of the Sherman Act is to prohibit *monopolizing*, which involves either *seeking* to acquire monopoly power or attempting to exclude or limit competition in order to *keep* monopoly power once such power is attained. A business that is shown to have committed either of these prohibited acts is guilty of monopolizing and could be found to be in violation of § 2.

Obviously, very few pure monopolies exist in the U.S. market, and those that do exist often exist for a valid reason, such as the so-called natural monopolies. Some areas, for example, may only be served by one railroad or may only have one source of electric power. However, the provisions of § 2 do not require that a pure monopoly exists. Monopoly power may be present even if an area of commerce has several businesses in existence and seemingly competing with one another. If a firm is found to dominate an industry, it may also be found to possess monopoly power. As a rule of thumb, control of 70 percent or more of the *relevant market* is deemed to be sufficient to establish that the firm has monopoly power. However, defining the relevant market may be difficult. In determining the relevant market, the courts must determine the relevant *geographic* market (where the product in question is sold) and the relevant *product* market (what product is being sold or provided by the seller). In so doing, the courts examine the *product* produced by the defendant firm, *substitute* goods produced by other firms, and the elasticity of demand between the challenged product and the substitutes. If the courts find that the firm controls 70 percent or more of this relevant market with its product, the firm will be found to possess monopoly power under the courts' interpretation of § 2. If the firm possesses less than 70 percent of the relevant market, it lacks monopoly power under § 2 of the Sherman Act.

United States v. E. I. DuPont de Nemours and Co.[13] is a landmark case involving relevant product market. DuPont acquired the exclusive U.S. right to produce cellophane from the French patent holder of the process. By 1947, DuPont had acquired 75 percent of the cellophane market in the United States, which led the Justice Department to file charges against DuPont for violating § 2 of the Sherman Act. At trial, DuPont admitted that it controlled the market for cellophane, but denied that it controlled the relevant product market. According to DuPont, the relevant product market was for *flexible wrapping materials*, including aluminum foil, wax paper, plastic wrap, and various other materials. In this broader market, DuPont only had a 20 percent market share. The court agreed with DuPont's argument, establishing a precedent for determining the relevant product market.

When a company has a dominant position in the relevant product market there is a presumption that § 2 was, or is, violated. However, a number of defenses exist to rebut this presumption. The dominant firm may argue that (1) it is not attempting to retain its power; (2) it acquired its position legally; or (3) that its position was "thrust upon" it.

This hypothetical case shows how the "thrust upon" defense can be applied:

MicroProcessing, Inc. (MPI) is involved in nanotechnology research. (*Nanotechnology* is the engineering of functional systems at the molecular scale.[14]) The research leads to the development of a new type of computer chip that is smaller, faster, and cheaper than anything else on the market. The new chip is very popular with businesses producing computers since it is superior to other chips in every way. Soon after the chip's introduction MPI has virtually "cornered the market" for computer chips, providing more than 90 percent of the chips being installed in new computers in the United States, the relevant market. The other chip-producing firms sue MPI, alleging that MPI is guilty of monopolizing the industry in violation of § 2 of the Sherman Act.

The courts would be likely to rule in favor of MPI in this situation. MPI has done nothing to show that it is monopolizing. Its acquisition of a dominant position in the relevant market was "thrust upon" it by efficiency and innovation, not by any questionable, illegal, or unethical conduct. However, if

MPI subsequently takes steps to prevent other firms from entering the market or acts in any manner that seems to be precluding or preventing competition, it may be found guilty of monopolizing. Possessing this monopoly power is legal, but attempting to retain it is illegal!

The government has used the Sherman Act quite successfully in a number of monopolization cases, beginning with *Standard Oil Co. v. United States,* [15] decided in 1911. The Standard Oil Company was found guilty of monopolizing, using regional price-cutting to drive competition out of the market, and then asserting domination over that market segment. The court ordered Standard Oil divided into a number of smaller companies, effectively ending its ability to dominate the domestic oil market. The Justice Department was also successful in attacking American Tobacco, Alcoa, and AT&T.

Perhaps the best known recent § 2 case involved Microsoft. The case began in 1998 and was finally settled in 2002. In the Microsoft case, the judge found that Microsoft was guilty of monopolizing and was also guilty of illegal tying arrangements. He ordered that the company be divided into two separate companies, one handling the Windows operating system and the other handling Internet Explorer, Microsoft Office, and all other Microsoft holdings. These two companies were to remain separate and independent for at least ten years.

The judge also (1) prohibited Microsoft from taking any actions against computer makers who support competing technologies; (2) required that the Windows system had to be sold at the same price to all computer makers; and (3) required that Microsoft disclose certain parts of the Windows source code to software developers to ensure that newly developed software would be compatible with the Windows system.

Microsoft subsequently reached a settlement with the Justice Department and nine of the states that participated in the initial case.[16] This settlement avoided the break-up of the firm previously ordered by the court, although numerous other remedies were imposed. While some of the states that initially joined in the complaint did not participate in the settlement, Microsoft survived this action without being broken into two or more companies and has continued to thrive.

The Microsoft case provided an interesting change in the attitude of the courts to § 2 violations. In prior cases, such as Standard Oil and American Tobacco, the court ordered divestiture and broke up companies that had been formed through the acquisition of competing businesses. These firms had acquired their market dominance through mergers and takeovers, leaving one firm where there had been several competing firms. Microsoft was improperly maintaining its dominant position, but it had not acquired its position through takeovers. There was virtually no precedent under which the court should order a break-up of the company.

Remedies

When a Sherman Act violation is shown, both criminal and civil remedies are available. As originally enacted, the Sherman Act did not provide for individual civil remedies.

Instead, the law only provided for governmental prosecution of the prohibited conduct. However, §4 of the Clayton Act[17] provides for civil remedies for violations of *any* antitrust statutes, including the Sherman Act. Under this section "any person who shall be injured in his business or property by reason of anything forbidden in the antitrust laws may sue therefore . . . and shall recover threefold the damages by him sustained, and the cost of suit, including a reasonable attorney's fee."[18] In addition, as was previously mentioned, an individual who is convicted of a violation of the Sherman Act can be fined up to $350,000 and can receive up to three years in prison; a corporation that is convicted can be fined up to $10 million. Also, §4 of the Sherman Act provides that an injunction can be issued against the prohibited conduct.

Keep in mind that in a criminal case the state has the burden of proof and must establish its case beyond a reasonable doubt. In a civil suit, the plaintiff has the burden of proof, but it is a lesser burden. The plaintiff only has to show by a preponderance of the evidence that a violation occurred.

THE CLAYTON ACT

By 1914, Congress realized that the Sherman Act alone was not sufficient to solve the major anti-competitive problems of the country. The Sherman Act was remedial in nature: If a problem existed, the Sherman Act could be used to help correct the problem. Unfortunately, it is possible (if not probable) that by the time the "remedy" is sought the injured party has suffered irreparable harm or has ceased to exist as a business entity. While the Sherman Act provides deterrence, it does not prevent problems from arising.

There is an old saying that "an ounce of prevention is worth a pound of cure." Congress apparently took this adage to heart when it passed the Clayton Act. The Clayton Act was meant to be preventative in nature. It was designed to prevent problems by stopping certain conducts "in their incipiency." This intent can be shown by the language included in several of the sections of the act: certain specified conduct is prohibited "where the effect may be to substantially lessen competition or tend to create a monopoly in any line of trade or commerce." This language allows the government to challenge conduct falling within the scope of one of the act's sections when the government decides that the effect *may*—not *will*—substantially lessen competition or *may*—again, not *will*—tend to create a monopoly. This allows the government to forecast the effect of the questioned conduct and then force the challenged firm to rebut the government assumption regarding the likely effect of the conduct. Unless the firm can effectively rebut the government's assumptions, the conduct will be stopped. The intent of the law is to stop this conduct before significant harm has been caused to competing firms.

The Clayton Act has four major provisions addressing different types of conduct, each of which might reduce competition in some line of trade or commerce, or result in the acquisition of monopoly power. The Clayton Act also has a number of other provisions dealing with implementation of the various antitrust laws, including the provision for treble damages for violations of any of the antitrust laws previously mentioned. These four sections are discussed next.

Section 2: Price Discrimination

The Clayton Act, § 2, prohibits price discrimination. The original § 2 made it illegal for a *seller* to discriminate in price between different purchasers unless the price difference could be justified by a difference in costs. This provision soon placed a number of sellers in a terrible bind. Major purchasers often demanded special prices from their sellers, many of whom were not as powerful or influential as the major purchaser. If the sellers refused to give these special prices, they lost the business; if they agreed, they violated the law. This placed some sellers in an untenable position. The law shielded the buyers—who often initiated the discussion leading to the price discrimination—from liability, since the law only applied to the seller. As a result, § 2 was amended in 1936 when Congress enacted the Robinson-Patman Act. Under the Robinson-Patman Act, *buyers* were prohibited from knowingly accepting a discriminatory price. In addition, the act prohibited buyers from knowingly accepting indirect benefits such as dummy brokerage fees and promotional kickbacks. Sellers were still prohibited from granting discriminatory prices to their customers absent a cost differential justifying the price.

In interpreting and applying the provisions of the Robinson-Patman Act, the courts have developed a checklist of elements that are required in order to find that a firm is guilty of violating the law. Currently all of the following elements must be present before a violation will be found.

1. There must be discrimination in price; a different price must be charged to two or more different buyers.
2. There must be at least two consummated sales. Mere offers will not suffice; there must be at least two contracts involved.
3. There must be a difference in price quoted by the "same seller."
4. At least one of the sales must cross state lines. Since this is a federal statute, interstate commerce must be involved before the statute applies.
5. The sales must either be <u>contemporaneous</u> or they must occur within a relevant and relatively short time period.
6. The sale must relate to "commodities."
7. The goods sold must be of "like grade and quality."
8. The law only applies to goods that will be used, consumed, or resold within the United States.
9. There must be a showing of an adverse effect on competition.[19]

The mere fact that a different price is granted to different buyers in contemporaneous sales is not enough to assure a conviction for price discrimination. In fact, a number of potential defenses exist. The accused can defend against the charge by showing any of the following:

1. He or she is *meeting*, but *not* beating, the price being offered by a competitor.
2. The lower price is being offered because of obsolescence, seasonal variations, or damage to the goods being sold.
3. The difference in price is due to a difference in the cost of manufacturing or selling the goods.
4. The price differential is based on legitimate cost savings based on quantity discounts, *and* such discounts are generally available to any other customers who place orders of sufficient size. (A quantity discount that would only be available to a very limited number of large customers would not be a legitimate defense.)
5. If it charges a normal price and a reduced price, the reduced price is realistically available to any individual customer, but that the particular customer chose not to take advantage of this reduced price for whatever reason.[20]

Standard Oil Co. (of Indiana) v. FTC,[21] a landmark opinion, involved an allegation of price discrimination and a defense of meeting—but not beating—the competition's price. Standard Oil was selling gasoline to four large "jobbers" in the Detroit area at a lower price than it was selling gasoline to numerous smaller competitors in the same market. Standard showed that its lower price for the "jobbers" was only to meet—and not to beat—the price of a competitor, thus allowing Standard to retain its customers. The court accepted this defense, finding that Standard Oil was not guilty of illegal price discrimination.

The Robinson-Patman Act also changed the standards needed to show a violation. Under the original § 2, it was necessary to show that general competition had been harmed. Under the Robinson-Patman Act, a case can be prosecuted on a showing that one single competitor was injured. Courts look for two types of injuries when hearing a Robinson-Patman case: a *primary-line injury* or a *secondary-line injury*. A primary-line injury involves competition at the seller's level. The seller is providing discriminatory prices to gain a competitive advantage over one of the seller's competitors. A secondary-line injury involves competition at the buyer's level. One or more of the buyers who receive the discriminatory price are given an advantage over one or more of the buyer's competitors who did not receive the same price.

An interesting Robinson-Patman issue was raised in a case originating in Puerto Rico.[22] Caribe BMW purchased new automobiles directly from the manufacturer. Caribe's competitors in the market purchased their new BMWs from a wholly owned subsidiary of the manufacturer and were able to purchase at a lower price than that offered to Caribe. The court ruled that a manufacturer and its wholly owned subsidiary are a single entity for purposes of applying the Robinson-Patman Act, so that there was a discriminatory pricing practice in effect, entitling Caribe to remedies for violation of the act. (This ruling involves the "single seller" test, the third item listed in the checklist set out above.)

Section 3: Exclusive Dealings and Tying Arrangements

The second major prohibition under the Clayton Act is found in §3. This section actually addresses two different practices, (1) exclusive-dealing contracts and (2) tying arrangements. Both practices are prohibited when their "effect may be to substantially lessen competition or tend to create a monopoly in any line of trade or commerce." Notice again the preventative intent of the act: Actual harm need not be shown, merely the *likelihood* that harm will eventually occur.

In an exclusive-dealing contract, one party requires the other party to deal with him or her alone. For example, the seller tells the buyer that unless the buyer buys only from the seller, and not from the seller's competitors, the seller will not deal with the buyer. In most such circumstances the seller must be in a very powerful market position to make such a demand.

In a tying arrangement, one party—usually the seller—refuses to sell one product unless the buyer also takes a second product or service from the seller. For example, a manufacturer of cosmetics might refuse to sell a facial moisturizer unless the buyer agrees to also purchase the manufacturer's soap. For this sort of arrangement to be effective, usually the seller needs a highly valued, unique product to which he or she can "tie" a commonly available product. As a defense to a charge that such an arrangement tends to lessen competition or create a monopoly, the seller may attempt to show that the tied product is tied for quality-control reasons. To do so, the seller must prove that no competitors make a competing product that works adequately with the controlled product. In order to show that a firm is guilty of an illegal tying arrangement, four elements must be shown:

1. The tying arrangement must involve two separate and distinct products. (The sale of a product and a component part for the same product is not sufficient.)
2. The purchase of one product must be conditioned upon the purchase of the other product.
3. The seller must have a sufficiently strong market position to restrain competition in the market for the tying product (the product that is in high demand).
4. The arrangement must be shown to have an adverse effect on competition in the market for the tying product.[23]

Franchising is one area in which tying arrangements continue to present a problem. Franchisors insist that they must be allowed to tie the products and the materials that franchisees use to the franchise contract to assure consistent quality and to preserve the reputation of the franchise. In many cases the court will allow an exclusive dealing arrangement. For example, in *Krehl v. Baskin-Robbins Ice Cream Co.*[24] the court held that Baskin-Robbins could require its stores to sell only Baskin-Robbins ice cream. This was to prevent a store owner or franchisee from substituting less expensive ice cream while trading on the strong Baskin-Robbins brand name, to the chain's detriment.

However, many franchisees insist that these tying arrangements lead to substantially higher prices for their materials without assuring consistent quality. Instead, the franchisees argue that the tying arrangements are merely a method allowing the franchisor to gain additional profits from the franchise arrangement at the expense of the franchisees. This area has not yet been resolved and litigation will continue on this issue.[25]

The Supreme Court has ruled that a "not insubstantial" amount of commerce must be affected to have an illegal tying arrangement.[26] The Ninth Circuit went even further, ruling that there is no requirement for multiple purchasers in order to have an illegal tying arrangement,[27] so long as the effect on commerce is not insubstantial. The amount involved was approximately $100,000 per year for an indeterminate number of years, and the court ruled that such an amount was sufficiently substantial to allow the trial to proceed even though only one firm was precluded from the market due to the tying arrangement.

An Ounce of Prevention

Before purchasing a franchise, you should carefully review the disclosure documents, including any tying arrangements required by the franchisor. These arrangements may substantially reduce your profit. Some franchisees have failed because they mistakenly thought they could purchase on the open market. Most franchisees do not want to incur the expense of litigation with their franchisor even though they might be successful. The litigation will substantially strain their relationship and may affect opportunities to renew or expand.

Section 7: Antimerger Provisions

Section 7 of the Clayton Act prohibited mergers that were considered to be anticompetitive or that seemed likely to create a monopoly. This section was narrowly written and easily evaded since it considered mergers to occur only when one company purchases another company, with the two companies then becoming one. In order to avoid a violation of § 7, a firm could purchase stock in the target company or could buy the target firm's assets, but leave the targeted firm in existence.

To broaden the scope of the law, Congress amended § 7 in 1950 by passing the Celler-Kefauver Act. The amended § 7 prohibits the acquisition of stock or assets of another firm that may tend to have a negative effect on any line of commerce. As a result, firms are now potentially subject to § 7 in almost any type of merger—horizontal, vertical, or conglomerate. A *horizontal merger* is one between competing firms; a *vertical merger* is one between a firm and one of its major suppliers or customers; and a *conglomerate merger* is one between firms in noncompeting industries.

The scope of this section was then narrowed with the passage of the Hart-Scott-Rodino Antitrust Improvements Act of 1976. This Act requires certain firms and investors to file a report with both the FTC and the Department of Justice (DOJ) prior to completing a merger or, in some circumstances, purchasing securities in another firm. Basically, any investor who is trying to acquire 15 percent or more of a firm's securities or plans to purchase securities in a firm for an amount of $78.2 million[28] (for 2015) or more must file this report. The FTC and the DOJ can then investigate, determining whether either believes that the acquisition will violate any antitrust law. The firm or investor must wait at least 30 days after filing the report before proceeding. If the report raises concerns with the FTC or DOJ, that agency can either request additional information or seek an injunction to prevent the acquisition.[29]

Not all mergers are prohibited by § 7. The government must establish that if the merger is allowed, the result "may be to substantially lessen competition or tend to create a monopoly" in an industry. For example, as a challenge to a merger, the government might argue that a "concentration trend" has been established (a series of mergers within an industry that has steadily reduced the number of competitors and increased the size of the remaining firms, leading to a concentrated industry) or that one of the firms was a "potential entrant" (a firm that was likely to enter the industry from outside but instead opted to buy an existing firm, adding its economic strength to an existing firm, often in a concentrated industry). The government would argue that the industry after the proposed merger was less competitive than the industry was prior to the proposed merger. The burden then shifts to the defendants to justify the proposed merger by showing that a substantial lessening of competition is not the probable effect. For example, the merging firms might raise the failing-company doctrine, showing that without the merger one of the firms would have gone out of business. If one of the firms would have gone out of business without being saved by the merger, the same number of firms remain in the industry following the merger as would have existed without the merger. In addition, it is likely that some jobs were saved since without the merger one of the firms would have gone out of existence and its workers would have been unemployed. The firm that saved the firm may well retain a number of its employees, and it may even keep the facility open and in operation. The following example illustrates the failing-company doctrine.

> Fred's Stereo is in severe financial difficulty. Irv's Interstate Sound Store, the largest stereo dealer in the region, buys Fred's (a horizontal merger under revised § 7). Under the failing-company doctrine, if Fred's would have gone bankrupt, the merger with Irv's is probably permissible. Of course such a merger would be less likely to be challenged if the firm taking over Fred's had not been the largest competitor in the region. In such a case, the merged firms would be better able to compete with Irv's, the largest firm, and might be able to show that competition would be enhanced with the merger even if Fred's was not about to go out of business.

Section 8: Interlocking Directorates

The final substantive section of the Clayton Act is § 8, which prohibits interlocking directorates. This section was amended in 1990, and now includes officers who also serve as directors of other firms. The current language of § 8 provides that:

No person shall, at the same time, serve as a director or officer in any two corporations (other than banks, banking associations, and trust companies) that are

(A) engaged in whole or in part in commerce; and

(B) by virtue of their business and location of operation, competitors, so that the elimination of competition by agreement between them would constitute a violation of any of the antitrust laws;

if each of the corporations has capital, surplus, and undivided profits aggregating more than $31,841,000 as adjusted pursuant to paragraph (5) of this subsection."[30] [**Note:** This is the amount as of January 21, 2016.[31] The amount is adjusted annually, with the adjustment tied to the Gross National Product (GNP).]

Section 8 also has a provision for so-called "safe harbors" in some situations. Any persons serving as officers or directors for two or more competing firms will not be in violation of § 8 if:

Competitive sales of either corporation are less than $3,184,100 [**Note**: This is the amount as of January 2016.[32] Again, the amount is adjusted annually with the adjustment tied to the GNP];

Competitive sales of either corporation are less than 2 percent of its total sales; or

Competitive sales of each corporation are less that 4 percent of its total sales.

Competitive sales are defined as the gross revenues for all products and services sold by one corporation in competition with the other during its most recent fiscal year. Total sales are gross revenues for all products and services sold in the corporation's most recent fiscal year.[33]

THE FEDERAL TRADE COMMISSION ACT

The year 1914 was a very busy year for antitrust regulation. Congress passed not only the Clayton Act but also the Federal Trade Commission Act. The Federal Trade Commission Act did two important things:

1. It created the Federal Trade Commission (FTC) to enforce antitrust laws, especially the Clayton Act.

2. In § 5, it provided a broad area of prohibitions to close loopholes left by other statutes.

Section 5 of the act prohibits "unfair methods of competition" and "unfair and deceptive trade practices." This broad language permits the FTC to regulate conduct that technically might be beyond the reach of the other, more specific antitrust statutes. The area of unfair and deceptive trade practices was intentionally made broad and somewhat vague to grant the FTC leeway to proceed against any commercial practices that seem to be unfair or deceptive under the circumstances. If the statute was more specific, businesspeople would more easily find methods to circumvent it. The strength of the law has been its breadth, as well as the willingness of the FTC to attack practices that had, in some cases, been followed for many years.

To further strengthen the FTC position, a violation can be found without proof of any actual deception. A mere showing that there is a "fair possibility" that the public will be deceived is sufficient to establish that the conduct is unfair and deceptive. In addition, if a representation made by a company is ambiguous, with one honest meaning and one deceptive meaning, the FTC can choose to treat it as deceptive and as a material aspect of the transaction so that remedies are available.

An Ounce of Prevention

The marketing of your firm can be essential to success. Good marketing can enhance your firm's image, create an identity, and even develop brand loyalty. Creative advertising is a key component of the overall advertising strategy, as is evident from the attention paid to the ads that run during the Super Bowl™. However, overly creative ads that have a fair possibility of misleading or deceiving the public can result in the FTC imposing sanctions for unfair and deceptive trade practices. Before approving any advertising campaigns or commercials, you should make every effort to ensure that the ad accurately portrays your goods or services.

If the FTC opposes a business practice as unfair or deceptive, it issues a cease-and-desist order. The business must stop the challenged conduct or face a fine for disobeying the order. The fine is $16,000 per violation.[34] This may sound small, but realize that each day the order is ignored constitutes a separate violation. Thus, ignoring the order for one week costs $112,000 in fines; for a month, $480,000 in fines; and so on.

In recent years, the FTC has become particularly concerned about two business practices: deceptive advertising and "bait-and-switch" advertising. In an effort to force truth in advertising, the FTC has been carefully reviewing the commercials run by corporations and ordering corrective advertising when it decides that the advertising is misleading.

Bait-and-switch advertising involves advertising a product at an especially enticing price to get the customer into the store (the "bait") and then talking the customer into buying a more expensive model (the "switch"). The customer is informed that the advertised model is "sold out" or has some defect. An advertiser who refuses to show the advertised item to the customer or who has insufficient quantities on hand to satisfy reasonable customer demand is engaging in an unfair trade practice in violation of § 5 of the FTC Act.

UNFAIR TRADE PRACTICES

We should also mention some common law unfair trade practices, such as palming off goods and violating trade secrets. *Palming off* involves advertising, designing, or selling goods as if they were the goods of another. The person who is palming off goods is fraudulently taking advantage of the goodwill and brand loyalty of the business being imitated. This practice also frequently involves copyright, patent, or trademark infringements.

Trade secrets are special processes, formulas, and the like that are guarded and treated as confidential by the holder of the trade secret. Employees of a firm that has trade secrets must not betray their loyalty to the firm by revealing the trade secrets to others. Revealing the trade secret is a tort, and the employee can be held liable for any damages suffered by the employer. In addition, the firm or person who receives the information is guilty of appropriating the trade secret, and use of the secret can be stopped by injunction. The recipient of the information will also be liable for damages suffered by the trade secret holder. Palming off frequently involves the infringement of a copyright, a patent, or a trademark. These three areas, along with a few others, such as service marks and trade names, are protected by federal statutes, as well as under various state laws. Copyright law provides protection to artists, composers, and writers. A person who creates a book, song, work of art, or similar item has the exclusive right to the profits from the creation for his or her life plus 70 years. The owner can sue for infringement in federal court seeking injunctive relief and damages. A patent is a federally created and protected monopoly power given to inventors. If a person invents something that is new, useful, and not obvious to a person of ordinary skill in the industry, the inventor is entitled to a patent. In exchange for making the method of production public, the patent grants the inventor an exclusive right to use, make, or sell the product for 20 years (14 years for a design patent). If anyone violates this exclusive right, the patent holder can file an infringement suit. If the court upholds the patent, the infringer will be enjoined from further production and will be liable for damages to the holder of the patent.

A trademark is a mark or symbol used to identify a particular brand name or product. Copying the trademark of a competitor or using a symbol deceptively similar to that of a competitor is a violation of the Lanham Act of 1946, and the violator is subject to an injunction and the imposition of damages. (Intellectual property, including patents and copyrights, is discussed in detail in Chapter 8.)

EXEMPTIONS

Labor unions are exempt from the provisions of the Sherman Act by the Norris-LaGuardia Act, passed in 1932. They are also exempt from the Clayton Act by § 6 of the Act. The exemption applies only to "labor disputes" and normal union activities.

Farm cooperatives are also exempt from antitrust coverage so long as they are engaged in the sale of farm produce. (A number of other exemptions exist, but they have little impact on business law.)

Contemporary Case

This case required the Court to address the issues of price fixing and market division. The alleged price fixing involved conscious parallelism by the "Baby Bells" in order to prevent competition and to maintain their market positions. Note how the Court addresses the issue of conscious parallelism as proof of price fixing. The Court decided that the plaintiffs had not adequately stated a claim because they failed to show any "plus factors" that would show evidence of intent to fix prices.

BELL ATLANTIC CORPORATION v. TWOMBLY

550 U.S. 544, 127 S. Ct. 1955, 2007 U.S. LEXIS 5901 (S.Ct. 2007)

FACTS The upshot of the 1984 divestiture of the American Telephone & Telegraph Company's (AT&T) local telephone business was a system of regional service monopolies (known as "Incumbent Local Exchange Carriers" (ILECs) among other things), and a separate, competitive market for long-distance service from which the ILECs were excluded. In 1996 Congress withdrew approval of the ILECs' monopolies by enacting the Telecommunications Act of 1996, restructuring the local telephone markets and imposing a number of duties on ILECs to make market entry by other providers easier. This act also set conditions for allowing ILECs to enter the long-distance market. However, the act required ILECs to share their networks with competitors. This requirement became known as "competitive local exchange carriers" (CLECs). The ILECs opposed this requirement due to the expenses involved in making their network elements available to the CLECs at wholesale prices. In response the Federal Communication Commission revised the regulations by narrowing the range of network elements that had to be shared with CLECs.

Twombly and Marcus filed a class action lawsuit against Bell Telephone and the ILECs, alleging they had violated § 1 of the Sherman Act by conspiring to restrain trade in two ways, (1) by inflating charges for local telephone and high-speed Internet services; and (2) by refraining from competing with one another. To support their allegations, the plaintiffs pointed out that the ILECs had engaged in parallel courses of conduct to prevent competition from CLECs within their respective local telephone and/or high speed internet services markets.

The District Court found plaintiffs' allegations of parallel ILEC actions to discourage competition inadequate. The Court of Appeals reversed, holding that "plus factors are not *required* to be pleaded to permit an antitrust claim based on parallel conduct to survive dismissal." The Supreme Court granted certiorari to address the proper standard for pleading an antitrust conspiracy through allegations of parallel conduct.

ISSUE Does a complaint alleging parallel conduct that is harmful to competition sufficiently state a claim under § 1 of the Sherman Act without any factual context suggesting an agreement by the parties?

HOLDING No. The Court held that such a complaint should be dismissed absent some factual context suggesting agreement, as distinct from identical, independent action.

REASONING Excerpts from the opinion of Justice Souter:

... Because § 1 of the Sherman Act "does not prohibit [all] unreasonable restraints of trade ... but only restraints effected by a contract, combination, or conspiracy," ..."[t]he crucial question" is whether the challenged anticompetitive conduct "stem[s] from independent decision or from an agreement, tacit or express." ... While a showing of parallel "business behavior is admissible circumstantial evidence from which the fact finder may infer agreement," it falls short of "conclusively establish[ing] agreement or ... constitut[ing] a Sherman Act offense." ... Even "conscious parallelism," a common reaction of "firms in a concentrated market [that] recogniz[e] their shared economic interests and their interdependence with respect to price and output decisions" is "not in itself unlawful." ...

The inadequacy of showing parallel conduct or interdependence, without more, mirrors the ambiguity of the behavior: consistent with conspiracy, but just as much in line with a wide swath of rational and competitive business strategy unilaterally prompted by common perceptions of the market. ... An antitrust conspiracy plaintiff with evidence showing nothing beyond parallel conduct is not entitled to a directed verdict. ... [P]roof of a § 1 conspiracy must include evidence tending to exclude the possibility of independent action ... and at the

summary judgment stage a § 1 plaintiff's offer of conspiracy evidence must tend to rule out the possibility that the defendants were acting independently. ...

This case presents the antecedent question of what a plaintiff must plead in order to state a claim under § 1 of the Sherman Act. Federal Rule of Civil Procedure 8(a)(2) requires only "a short and plain statement of the claim showing that the pleader is entitled to relief," in order to "give the defendant fair notice of what the ... claim is and the grounds upon which it rests." ... While a complaint attacked by a ... motion to dismiss does not need detailed factual allegations ... a plaintiff's obligation to provide the "grounds" of his "entitle[ment] to relief" requires more than labels and conclusions. ... [A] formulaic recitation of the elements of a cause of action will not do. ... Factual allegations must be enough to raise a right to relief above the speculative level ... on the assumption that all the allegations in the complaint are true (even if doubtful in fact) ...

In applying these general standards to a § 1 claim, we hold that stating such a claim requires a complaint with enough factual matter (taken as true) to suggest that an agreement was made. It simply calls for enough fact to raise a reasonable expectation that discovery will reveal evidence of illegal agreement. And, of course, a well-pleaded complaint may proceed even if it strikes a savvy judge that actual proof of those facts is improbable, and "that a recovery is very remote and unlikely." ... In identifying facts that are suggestive enough to render a § 1 conspiracy plausible, we have the benefit of the prior rulings and considered views of leading commentators, already quoted, that lawful parallel conduct fails to bespeak unlawful agreement. It makes sense to say ... that an allegation of parallel conduct and a bare assertion of conspiracy will not suffice. Without more, parallel conduct does not suggest conspiracy, and a conclusory allegation of agreement at some unidentified point does not supply facts adequate to show illegality. Hence, when allegations of parallel conduct are set out in order to make a § 1 claim, they must be placed in a context that raises a suggestion of a preceding agreement, not merely parallel conduct that could just as well be independent action. . . .

The need at the pleading stage for allegations plausibly suggesting (not merely consistent with) agreement reflects the threshold requirement of Rule 8(a)(2) that the "plain statement" possess enough heft to "sho[w] that the pleader is entitled to relief." A statement of parallel conduct, even conduct consciously undertaken, needs some setting suggesting the agreement necessary to make out a § 1 claim; without that further circumstance pointing toward a meeting of the minds, an account of a defendant's commercial efforts stays in neutral territory. An allegation of parallel conduct is thus much like a naked assertion of conspiracy in a § 1

complaint: it gets the complaint close to stating a claim, but without some further factual enhancement it stops short of the line between possibility and plausibility of "entitle[ment] to relief." . . .

[In this case] we do not require heightened fact pleading of specifics, but only enough facts to state a claim to relief that is plausible on its face. Because the plaintiffs here have not nudged their claims across the line from conceivable to plausible, their complaint must be dismissed.

The judgment of the Court of Appeals for the Second Circuit is reversed, and the case is remanded for further proceedings consistent with this opinion.

It is so ordered.

Short Answer Questions

1. Arthur Levinson was a member of the boards of directors of both Apple and Google. Eric Schmidt was a member of the board of directors of Apple and he was CEO of Google. The FTC began an investigation of the two companies and their seeming violation of § 8 of the Clayton Act. When the investigation began, Levinson resigned from the board of Google and Schmidt resigned from the board of Apple. Both Apple and Google make Web browsers and produce software for smartphones. The two firms collaborate in some activities and compete in others. Should the FTC file charges against the two companies due to their interlocked directorates, or should the resignation of each of the men from his board position be sufficient to settle the issue? Explain and justify your answer.

2. Section 7 of the Clayton Act already addressed merger guidelines, so why do you think the Hart-Scott-Rodino Antitrust Improvement Act was passed? Should a business or an investor be required to self-report its planned activities and seek governmental approval prior to initiating a merger or an acquisition? Does this law seem to comply with the social contract theory?

3. Section 3 of the Clayton Act, as amended by the Robinson-Patman Act, prohibits price discrimination. What is necessary before the government can prove that a firm violated the current version of § 3? What will allow a firm to charge different prices to different customers despite the provisions of the amended § 3?

You Decide...

1. The National Football League (NFL) is an unincorporated association of 32 separately owned professional football teams. The 32 teams formed National Football League Properties (NFLP) to develop, license, and market the names, logos, trademarks, and related properties of the member teams. Originally, the NFLP granted nonexclusive licenses to a number of vendors to manufacture and sell team-labeled apparel. In 2000 the teams authorized the NFLP to grant an exclusive license to Reebok International, Ltd. to produce and sell trademarked headwear for all thirty-two teams. American Needle, Inc. had been licensed to manufacture and sell such headwear, but its license was not renewed. American Needle then filed suit against the NFL, alleging that the agreement between the NFLP and Reebok was a "contract in restraint of trade" that violated § 1 of the Sherman Act. According to American Needle, the thirty-two teams had combined or conspired to restrain trade by granting this exclusive license to Reebok. The NFL asserted that it is a single entity, and that an entity cannot combine or conspire, but that an entity is allowed to contract with a single vendor without violating the Sherman Act.

How would *you* decide this case? Be certain that you explain and justify your answer.

(See *American Needle, Inc. v. National Football League*, 2010 U.S. Lexis 4166 (S.Ct. 2010).)

2. Eastman Kodak is the only company that sells refurbished printheads for the large commercial printers that it produces. Eastman Kodak also sells ink for its printers, as does a competitor, Collins. Eastman Kodak began giving its customers significant "bundled discounts" on the purchase of refurbished printheads if those customers agreed to purchase their ink from Eastman Kodak. Collins filed suit, alleging that Eastman Kodak was illegally tying the sale of its ink to the purchase of the refurbished printheads, effectively precluding Collins from the ink market. Eastman Kodak argued that "bundled discounts" are legal and that its conduct did not meet the criteria to be considered an illegal tying arrangement.

How would you decide this case? What factors would be most significant in your decision? Be certain to explain and justify your answer.

(See *Collins Inkjet Corporation v. Eastman Kodak Co.*, No. 14-3306 (6th Cir. 2015).)

Notes

1. Laissez faire: An economic theory that the less the government is involved in free market capitalism, the better off business will be, and then, by extension, society as a whole. http://www.investopedia.com/terms/l/laissezfaire.asp#axzz1tovaIASI (accessed February 29, 2016).

2. "Strategic Alliance, "*Investopedia*, http://www.investopedia.com/terms/s/strategicalliance.asp#axzz1tovaIASI (accessed February 29, 2016).

3. "Definition of international strategic alliance," *Financial Times*, http://lexicon.ft.com/Term?term=international-strategic-alliance (accessed February 29, 2016).

4. 15. U.S.C. § 1.

5. 221 U.S. 1 (1911).

6. William E. Kovocic, Robert C. Marshall, Leslie M. Marx, and Halbert L. White, "Plus Factors and Agreement in Antitrust Law," Center for the Study of Auctions, Procurements, and Competition Policy, Penn State University (Feb. 14, 2011), http://capcp.psu.edu/papers/2011/plusfactors.pdf (accessed February 29, 2016).

7. "Price Leadership," *Investopedia*. http://www.investopedia.com/terms/p/price-leadership.asp (accessed February 29, 2016).

8. *SCFC ILC, Inc. v. Visa, USA, Inc.*, 36 F.3d 958 (10th Cir. 1994).

9. 441 U.S. 1 (1979).

10. 15 U.S.C. § 6(a).

11. *Carpet Group Int'l v. Oriental Rug Importers Ass'n,* 227 F.3d 62 (2000).

12. *Den Norske Stats Oljeselskap AS v. Heereman VOF,* 241 F.3d 420 (2001).

13. 351 U.S. 377 (1956).

14. Center for Responsible Nanotechnology (CRN), "What is nanotechnology?" http://crnano.org/whatis.htm (accessed February 29, 2016).

15. 221 U.S. 1 (1911).

16. "Judge OKs Microsoft's Antitrust Settlement," *Los Angeles Times,* November 2, 2002.

17. 15 U.S.C. § 15.

18. Ibid. § 15 (a).

19. List compiled from "Executive Legal Summary," a publication of Business Laws, Inc. (Chesterland, Ohio 1997).

20. *Ibid.*

21. 340 U.S. 231 (1951).

22. *Caribe BMW, Inc. v. Bayerische Werke Aktiengesellschaft,* 19 F.3d 745 (1st Cir. 1994).

23. "Tying Arrangements," The Free Dictionary by Farlex, http://legal-dictionary.thefreedictionary.com/Tying+Arrangement (accessed February 29, 2016).

24. 664 F.2d 1348 (1982).

25. See, for example, *Siegel v. Chicken Delight, Inc.,* 448 F.2d 43 (9th Cir. 1971), and *Collins v. International Dairy Queen,* Inc., 939 F. Supp. 875 (M.D. Ga. 1996).

26. *Jefferson Parish Hospital District #2 v. Hyde,* 466 U.S. 2, 104 S.Ct. 1551 (1984).

27. *Datagate, Inc. v. Hewlett-Packard Co.,* 60 F.2d (9th Cir. 1995).

28. "FTC Announces New Clayton Act Monetary Thresholds for 2016," Federal Trade Commission Web Site. (January 21, 2016), https://www.ftc.gov/news-events/press-releases/2016/01/ftc-announces-new-clayton-act-monetary-thresholds-2016 (accessed February 29, 2016).

29. "Hart-Scott-Rodino Antitrust Improvements Act of 1976," *Investopedia,* http://www.investopedia.com/terms/h/hart-scott-rodino-antitrust-improvements-act-of-1976.asp (accessed February 29, 2016).

30. 15 U.S.C. § 19, Interlocking directorates and officers, http://codes.lp.findlaw.com/uscode/15/1/19 (accessed November 29, 2012).

31. FTC Web Site, Note 28, *supra.*

32. *Ibid.*

33. "Interlocking Directorates and Officers—Section 8 of the Clayton Act," Ropes and Gray Antitrust Alert (January 31, 2011), http://www.ropesgray.com/files/Publication/833aedce-b2c5-476f-b9f4-49596124c94e/Presentation/Publication Attachment/403a9f55-7615-4526-ba9a-4e6d937a 8d7a/20110131AntitrustClaytonAct.pdf (accessed February 29, 2016).

34. Federal Trade Commission, *A Brief Overview of the Federal Trade Commission's Investigative and Law Enforcement Authority,* Federal Trade Commission Web site (July 2008), http://www.ftc.gov/ogc/brfovrvw.shtm (accessed February 29, 2016).

18

Consumer Protection

Learning Objectives

After completing this chapter you should be able to

- Discuss the importance of federal consumer protection statutes and regulations
- Explain what an APR is and how it relates to consumer credit
- Recognize the rights of consumer credit card users under Regulation Z
- Identify how a consumer can protect his or her credit reports and credit rating
- Express the importance of equal credit opportunity for consumers in the U.S. society and economy

Classic Case

In this case the Court was asked to decide the scope of the Fair Credit Billing Act, an amendment to the Truth in Lending Act (TILA). Note how the Court addressed the issue of the status of the cardholder and how that impacted the Court's decision. This opinion shows that the consumer credit protections statutes are *only* intended for consumers, not for commercial debtors.

AMERICAN EXPRESS CO. v. KOERNER

452 U.S. 233, 101 S.Ct. 2281 (1981)

FACTS In 1965, prior to the enactment of the TILA, John E. Koerner & Co., Inc., applied for a credit card account with American Express. The application was for a "company account" designed for business customers. The Koerner Company asked American Express to issue cards bearing the company's name to Louis R. Koerner, Sr., and four other officers of the corporation. Koerner was required to sign a "company account" form, agreeing that he would be jointly and severally liable with the company for all charges incurred through the use of the company card that was issued to him. American Express, before issuing the cards, investigated the company's credit rating. It did not check the credit of Koerner or the other officers.

American Express billed the Koerner Company for all charges arising from the use of the five cards issued on the company account. It sent a monthly statement showing the total due and listing individual subtotals for each of the five users. Although Koerner used his card mostly for business-related expenses, he used it occasionally for personal expenses. When he did so, he paid for these items by sending his personal check to American Express. Charges for his business-related expenses were paid by the company.

In 1975, a dispute arose between the Koerner Company and American Express concerning charges that appeared on the company account. American Express had billed the company for flight insurance for three business trips made by company employees, and for renewal fees for two of the cards that the company claimed were no longer desired. The company refused to pay the disputed amount of $55. Company officials wrote to American Express several times about this. The record does not indicate that American Express responded in any way prior to November 1976.

On September 28, 1976, Koerner attempted to use his card to purchase a plane ticket for a business trip. At that time Koerner was informed that the account was cancelled due to delinquent payments. His card was cut in two by the attendant and returned to him.

Koerner then filed suit against American Express for $25,000, alleging that American Express had cancelled his card due to the unresolved dispute over the $55 charges, in violation of the Fair Credit Billing Act. The District Court granted American Express's motion for a directed verdict, finding that the Act only applied to consumer credit. The Fifth Circuit reversed, and the Supreme Court agreed to hear the case.

ISSUE Must a creditor follow the requirements specified in the Fair Credit Billing Act for the correction of billing errors when both a corporation and an individual are liable for the debt?

HOLDING No. The section of the Act in question only applies to consumer credit. A creditor can establish its own policies for dealing with commercial credit accounts.

REASONING Excerpts from the opinion of Justice Blackmun:

. . . The threshold inquiry . . . is whether the creditor has transmitted to an obligor "a statement of the obligor's account in connection with an extension of consumer credit." If there has been no extension of "consumer credit," the section imposes no obligation upon a creditor, and the creditor is free to adopt its own procedures for responding to a customer's complaint about a billing error. We conclude that, on the undisputed facts of this case, respondent has failed to show that American Express has extended him "consumer credit" in any relevant transaction. Section 161(a), therefore, is not applicable to the dispute between these parties.

In order for there to be an extension of consumer credit, there first must be an extension of "credit." The TILA's definition of "credit" is contained in § 103(e). . . . "The term 'credit' means the right granted by a creditor to a debtor to defer payment of debt or to incur debt and defer its payment." Thus, a credit card company such as American Express extends credit to an individual or an organization when it opens or renews an account, as well as when the cardholder actually uses the credit card to make purchases.

An extension of credit is an extension of "consumer credit" if the conditions specified in the statute's definition of "consumer" are also satisfied. Section 103(h) of the TILA . . . defines "consumer" as follows:

"The adjective 'consumer,' used with reference to a credit transaction, characterizes the transaction as one in which the party to whom credit is offered or extended is a natural person, and the money, property, or services which are the subject of the transaction are primarily for personal, family, household, or agricultural purposes."

Two elements . . . must be present in every "consumer credit" transaction: the party to whom the credit is extended must be a natural person, *and* the money, property, or services received by that person must be "primarily for personal, family, household, or agricultural purposes." We . . . conclude that the Court of Appeals erred in holding respondent to be a "consumer" without deciding whether American Express had extended him credit primarily for any of the purposes specified in § 103(h). If it had considered this issue, the only permissible conclusion for it to reach would have been that the undisputed facts of this case establish that the threshold requirement of § 161(a)—an "extension of consumer credit"—has not been satisfied because none of the credit transactions relevant to the billing dispute was entered into "primarily" for consumer purposes . . .

The undisputed facts of this case reveal that the Koerner Company obtained the right "to incur debt and defer its payment" from American Express primarily for business . . . purposes. In addition, the specific transactions that were the subject of the dispute between the company and American Express also were business transactions. The facts of this case, therefore, are not encompassed within any possible interpretation of the phrase "extension of consumer credit" in § 161(a) . . .

We agree with the District Court that this evidence is sufficient to indicate that the account was opened primarily for business or commercial purposes. . . . The evidence submitted by respondent does not weaken this conclusion. In fact, it confirms it. Respondent admitted that he used the card mostly for business purposes. His answers to petitioner's interrogatories identified no more than seven nonbusiness uses of the card between 1972 and 1976 . . .

On this record, there can be no dispute that the Koerner Company's account was not covered by § 103(h)'s definition of "consumer," because it was not opened "primarily for personal, family, household, or agricultural purposes." . . .

Because Congress has restricted the operation of § 161(a) to disputes concerning extensions of consumer credit, and because the dispute between American Express and respondent did not concern an extension of consumer credit, the judgment of the Court of Appeals must be, and is, reversed.

INTRODUCTION

The states regulated consumer transactions, including consumer credit, for many years. Consumer issues were considered to be matters of local rather than national concern. Consumer transactions normally involve contracts, and contracts are governed by state law, so it was reasonable to allow the states to cover virtually all areas involving consumers. Prior to the mid-1900s, most consumer transactions did not involve the use of credit. Those transactions that did involve credit were commonly mortgage loans. Mortgages involve real estate, another area that is governed primarily at the state and local level.

However, by the mid-1900s credit transactions became more important. Some gasoline companies and department stores were issuing charge cards in the early 1900s, but their use was restricted to the issuing merchant.[1] In 1950 Diner's Club introduced credit cards, and in 1951 Diner's Club issued the first credit cards issued in the United States.[2] By 1958 American Express had introduced its "travel and entertainment" card, a competitor to Diner's Club. And in 1966 Bank of America introduced the BankAmericard, now known as Visa.[3] And it was not until standards were established for the magnetic strip on the back of the card in the 1970s that the use of credit cards became widespread.[4] Today it is estimated that about 167 million American adults have credit cards, with an average of 3.7 cards per person for those with credit cards.[5] Total credit card debt was estimated to be $884.8 billion as of January, 2015.[6]

The use of credit cards and other forms of consumer credit has become a major part of the U.S. economy. As such, consumer credit is no longer viewed as an area of local concern. It is now a national concern. Federal lawmakers and regulators increasingly focus on consumer credit issues. The financial meltdown and the turmoil in the housing market that began in December of 2007 only emphasized how important credit use—or misuse—is to the nation's economic wellbeing. The lack of uniformity among state laws, coupled with the desire to protect consumers from fraudulent practices, led to the enactment of a number of federal consumer protection statutes and regulations. Among the areas addressed in these enactments were provisions to (1) minimize the effect of erroneous information found in credit reports; (2) eliminate illegal discrimination in the extension of credit; (3) prohibit many of the harassing debt-collection practices; (4) provide guidelines for the issuing of credit cards; and (5) establish standards for consumers to challenge alleged billing errors without penalties. In this chapter we consider the most significant consumer protection laws.[7]

THE CONSUMER CREDIT PROTECTION ACT

Federal regulation of consumer credit began in 1968 with the passage of the Consumer Credit Protection Act.[8] Title I of the Consumer Credit Protection Act is more commonly known as the Truth in Lending Act (TILA). In essence, TILA is a *disclosure* statute designed to force creditors to inform consumers of the actual costs of credit using a standardized form and terminology. This information enables consumers to comparison shop, which should result in consumers making more informed decisions about credit. In order to comply with TILA, prospective creditors must provide consumers with a separate disclosure statement that satisfies the requirements of both TILA and the Consumer Financial Protection Bureau (CFPB). (The CFPB has enforced TILA since July 11, 2011. Previously the Federal Reserve Board had enforcement authority.) This statement must be provided prior to the consummation of any credit transaction. Failure to comply with these disclosure provisions subjects the creditor to various civil, criminal, and statutory penalties and/or liabilities.

An example of a TILA disclosure form is set out in Exhibit 18.1.

Federal law provides that you receive a federal Truth in Lending Disclosure Statement before consummating a consumer credit transaction. It should be studied carefully, as well as other information given to you regarding the credit transaction.[9]

If a consumer files suit against a lender for violations of TILA and/or Regulation Z (discussed below) and the lender is found to have violated either the statute or the regulation, the court can award the consumer the total of all of the following types of damages that apply:

1. Any actual damages a consumer sustained as a result of the violation
2. Statutory damages for violations of certain provisions of TILA, with a minimum amount of $100 or $200 (depending on the type of loan) and a maximum amount of $1,000 or $2,000
3. Court costs and attorney's fees
4. The sum of all fees and finance charges paid for high-cost loans[10]

Exhibit 18.1

Sample Truth in Lending Act Disclosure Form

Annual Percentage Rate	Finance Charge	Amount Financed	Total of Payments
The cost of your credit as a yearly rate.	The dollar amount the credit will cost you.	The amount of credit provided to you on your behalf.	The amount you will have paid after you have made all payments as scheduled.
A%	$B	$C	$D

An Ounce of Prevention

If you extend credit to your customers you must fully comply with TILA. You should prepare forms that include a "TILA box," providing customers with all of the required information in an approved format. Failure to satisfy the disclosure requirements of TILA can result in fines, damages, and the imposition of court costs and attorney's fees. Compliance with the standards is easy and inexpensive; noncompliance is potentially expensive, both in time and in money. Consequently, you should make every effort to comply.

TILA also limits advertising about credit. The creditor cannot advertise any deals that are not ordinarily available to everyone; any advertisements must contain all of the terms of the transaction or none of the terms can be mentioned, and if the credit calls for the consumer to make four or more payments, the agreement must include a statement that "the cost of credit is included in the price quoted for the goods and services." This required statement must be conspicuous in the advertisement.[11]

TILA also regulates transactions in which a consumer uses his or her home as collateral for a home equity or home improvement loans. (Loans for the purchase or initial construction of a home are not covered.) For these types of loans, TILA allows a three-day cooling-off period, during which the consumer may decide to rescind (cancel) the loan. The cooling-off period begins when the lender provides the consumer with the TILA disclosure information. This provision allows the consumer the opportunity to reconsider any transaction that may encumber the consumer's title to his or her home.

However, if the lender does not provide the required TILA disclosure information, or the consumer claims that the information was not provided, the cooling-off period may extend up to three years after the transaction is consummated. (This is the issue in our Contemporary Case for this chapter.)[12]

The Home Ownership and Equity Protection Act of 1994 (HOEPA)[13] amended the TILA, providing some coverage for home mortgages. It included additional disclosure requirements on certain closed-end mortgages to assist borrowers in "comparison shopping" for the best rate for the loan. It also added disclosure requirements regarding costs and other factors for consumers considering a reverse mortgage. And in 2008 Regulation Z was amended to provide protection for consumers in the mortgage market from unfair, abusive, or deceptive lending and servicing practices.[14]

There was a great deal of litigation under the original version of TILA. Some of this litigation was attributable to the disclosure requirement of the act. (The FRB apparently felt that there was significant consumer confusion due to the detailed disclosure requirements imposed on creditors.) As a result, in 1980 Congress passed the Truth in Lending Simplification and Reform Act. The Simplification and Reform Act makes it easier for creditors to comply with the disclosure requirements.

The FRB enacted Regulation Z to provide more specific guidelines for enforcement of TILA. Regulation Z covers any business that regularly offers or extends credit to its customer if the credit will be used for personal, family, or household purposes and the transaction is subject to a finance charge or, by written agreement, is payable in four or more installments. Since a consumer is defined as a person who buys products or services for personal use rather than for a commercial use, Regulation Z is only concerned with consumer credit transactions. Under the provisions of Regulation Z, the creditor must provide detailed information in a clear and conspicuous manner and in a meaningful sequence. This information must address (1) finance charges (including interest, time differential charges, service charges, points, loan fees, appraisal fees, and certain insurance premiums); (2) any other charges; (3) whether the creditor is retaining a security interest; and (4) a statement of billing rights that, when taken together, outlines the consumer's rights and the creditor's responsibilities.

Creditors must also furnish the consumer with periodic statements that disclose (1) the previous balance; (2) credits since the last statement; (3) the amount of the finance charge; (4) the annual percentage rate charged; (5) the closing date of the billing cycle; (6) the new balance; (7) the address to be used for notice of billing errors, and so on. The creditor also must promptly apply payments to the account and refund credit balances.

At one time it was common for credit card companies to issue credit cards to individuals who had not requested or applied for the card. Many people receiving such a card decided that they would keep the card and use it. Others, unfortunately, discovered—after the fact—that the card had been stolen and used, running up debts in the name of the person on the card. Such situations could harm the intended recipient's credit, and it could take a long time to resolve the matter and restore that person's credit. This issue was addressed in TILA, which prohibits the issuance of unsolicited credit cards. A credit card issuer cannot issue a credit card without an application from the person, unless the card is issued to replace an expiring card on an existing account. The person receiving the card must have submitted an oral or written request or application for the card.

FAIR CREDIT BILLING ACT

The Fair Credit Billing Act[15] (FCBA) is an amendment to TILA. It was enacted in 1975 to provide a standard method for questioning billing errors on open-end credit (credit cards) and to eliminate some of the unfair billing practices then in existence. (Open-end credit is a credit account that allows the consumer to pay a portion of the total amount due each month. Credit cards and home equity loans are examples of open-end credit.)[16] The implementation rules and regulations for the FCBA are found in Regulation Z.

Occasionally, a credit card account holder believes that his or her bill contains an error. When this happens, most such customers locate the contact information on the credit card bill and call the toll-free number to question the charge. This frequently leads to a resolution of the issue during the phone conversation with the card issuer's representative, ending the matter. But suppose that the phone call does not resolve the matter to the customer's satisfaction and that he or she still believes that the charge was posted to his or her account in error. The FCBA and Regulation Z provide for an additional, more formal step to attempt to settle the problem. In other words, the consumer still has an opportunity to have the charge removed from his or her account.

The information contained on the credit card bill in the section of "legalese" gives information about the customer's "billing rights." (It may be under a number of names, but the information must be included, and it cannot be unduly difficult for the customer to find.) The account holder should simply follow these steps to maximize his or her protections and to formally challenge the alleged billing error:

1. The customer needs to notify the card issuer in writing of the alleged error. The written notification must be sent within sixty days of the date the charge first appears on the billing statement.
2. The creditor then must notify the customer in writing that it received the information about the disputed bill.
3. The creditor then has up to ninety days after receiving the notice to
   (a) investigate the transaction giving rise to the alleged error, and then either
   (b) correct the disputed bill, or
   (c) explain in writing why the creditor believes the account is correct and supply copies of documented evidence of the consumer's indebtedness.

A creditor who complies with these provisions has no further obligations to the consumer, even if the consumer continues to make substantially the same allegations regarding the alleged error. Note, however, that until the creditor either corrects the disputed bill or notifies the consumer that the creditor believes the bill is correct (the ninety day investigatory period) the creditor may not do the following:

- Try to collect the cost of the disputed item
- Close or restrict the consumer's account during the controversy, although the creditor can apply the disputed amount to the consumer's credit limit
- Make or threaten to make an adverse credit report that the consumer is in arrears or that his or her bill is delinquent because of nonpayment of the disputed amount

A creditor who fails to comply with these provisions forfeits the amount in dispute, plus any finance charges, provided the amount does not exceed $50.

The FCBA and TILA also limit the liability of the cardholder to a maximum of $50 if the cardholder loses his or her card. If the cardholder reports the loss to the issuer before the card is used, the cardholder is not liable for any amount. Should the thief happen to use the card before the cardholder reports that it is missing, his or her maximum liability is the *lesser* of the amount charged before the lost card was reported or $50. Also, if someone steals the cardholder's credit card number, but not the card, and uses the number to make unauthorized purchases, the cardholder has no liability for any charges incurred.[17]

(Similar, but harsher, rules apply to lost debit cards. Under the Electronic Funds Transfer Act,[18] the liability of the cardholder for the unauthorized use of lost or stolen cards depend upon how promptly the cardholder gives notice of the loss of the card. If the loss is reported within two business days after the customer realizes, or should realize, that the card is missing, the maximum liability is $50. If the loss is not reported within two business days, but is reported within sixty days of the bank statement containing the first unauthorized use, the potential liability increases to a maximum of $500. If the loss is not reported within that sixty-day period, the amount that can be lost is unlimited by statute. As with credit cards, if the loss is caused by a stolen account number, the cardholder is not responsible for any transactions, provided that he or she notifies the bank within sixty days of the date of the bank statement containing the first such transaction.[19])

Individual's remedies under TILA include actual damages and statutory damages of twice the finance charges (but not less than $100 or more than $1,000). Class actions for actual damages as well as statutory damages of an amount equal to the lesser of $500,000 or 1 percent of the creditors' net worth also are possible. Awards of attorney's fees to successful litigants are available under the statute, as well. Criminal penalties for each willful and knowing failure to make the proper disclosures required by the act include fines of not more than $5,000 and one year's imprisonment. Several agencies—the CFPB and the Federal Trade Commission (FTC), for example—have responsibility for enforcement of TILA. Defenses to liability include the expiration of the one-year statute of limitations (for disclosure violations), bona fide clerical errors committed by the creditor, and the creditor's timely correction of an error.

THE FAIR CREDIT REPORTING ACT

Credit is a key element in the U.S. economy. According to the Federal Reserve, consumer debt reached $11.91 trillion as of the third quarter of 2015.[20] This amount included credit cards, mortgages, auto loans, and student loans. The availability—and the cost—of credit to consumers is an important aspect in consumer purchasing. It can affect everything from the charge card used at the local mall to acquiring a mortgage. Consumer credit providers base their decisions on providing credit, and at what interest rate, on credit reports. These credit reports are generated primarily by three major credit-reporting agencies, Equifax, Experian, and Trans-Union. These credit-reporting agencies summarize the information about individuals and sell these reports to lenders, landlords, insurers, retailers, and employers. There are also local or regional credit bureaus that may provide information on a person's credit history, especially to local or regional businesses.

Credit bureaus continually update the information they have about consumers: literally billions of pieces of information concerning private consumer transactions and millions of pieces of public record information (that is, bankruptcies, tax liens, fore-closures, court judgments, and similar activities) are reported each month.[21] Credit-reporting services facilitate a consumer's access to various types of credit and speed up credit transactions. However, the centralization of this information covering virtually the entire adult population has raised concerns about the accuracy of the information and the adequacy of the safeguards employed by these agencies to protect the privacy of individual consumers. One study from 2004 reported that as many as 80 percent of the credit reports generated contained errors, although most were minor. The study claimed that 25 percent of the reports contained major errors, errors significant enough to either prevent the applicant from getting credit or causing the applicant to receive less favorable credit terms than he or she should have received.[22]

Because of the importance of credit in the U.S. economy, and due to concerns about the impact of erroneous information in credit reports, Congress passed the Fair Credit Reporting Act[23] (FCRA) in 1970. This act is an amendment to the Consumer Credit Protection Act. The act was subsequently amended in 2001, and then supplemented in 2003 with the passage of the Fair and Accurate Credit Transactions Act, discussed later in the chapter.

Congress enacted the FCRA to require consumer-reporting agencies to adopt reasonable procedures for meeting the needs of both the consumer creditors and the businesses that are acquiring the information. Credit reports that are used in making decisions about a consumer's application for such things as credit, employment, or insurance should be reported in a manner that is fair and equitable to the consumer. They should also be handled in a manner that ensures the confidentiality, accuracy, relevancy, and proper use of such information. The FCRA applies to any entity that regularly engages in the practice of disseminating or evaluating consumer credit or other information concerning consumers for the purpose of furnishing consumer reports to third parties. Thus, the act covers credit reports generated by local credit bureaus, whose reports ordinarily set out only financial information about the consumer in question, and commercial credit-reporting agencies, whose reports may include more personal information in addition to financial information about the consumer. This "more personal information" is typically gathered through interviews with other people—for example, neighbors and colleagues might be interviewed.

The restrictions and obligations imposed on both the reporting agencies and the entity that is using the information is intended to protect consumers from harm due to inaccurate reports. They also provide some protection from potential invasions of the consumer's privacy and breaches of confidentiality that might harm the consumer. To meet these goals, the FCRA expressly obligates every consumer-reporting agency to maintain reasonable procedures designed to avoid violations of the act. Among other things, this obligation means that such agencies must report only accurate and up-to-date information, and these data can only be provided to those persons or entities eligible to receive the information.

This means that every consumer-reporting agency is required to establish reasonable procedures to verify that the users of the information use the report for only a proper purpose (e.g., to process an application for credit, employment, or insurance). Reasonable procedures include requiring prospective users to identify themselves as well as to certify the purpose for which they are seeking the information and to certify they will use the information only for the purpose certified.

In July of 2009 the FTC announced new rules and guidelines intended to promote the accuracy and integrity of information provided to credit reporting agencies. These new rules and guidelines will also allow a consumer to dispute allegedly inaccurate information directly with the providers of the information rather than the reporting agency. The intent of this "direct dispute rule" is to speed up the process of addressing alleged errors, making credit reports more accurate in a shorter time period, and lessening the negative impact on consumers whose reports contain inaccurate information.[24]

Following the enactment of these new rules and regulations, and in compliance with a congressional order, the FTC conducted a number of surveys to measure the accuracy of credit reports. In its fifth such survey, conducted in 2013, the Federal Trade Commission reported that 26 percent of consumers reported a potential error on one or more of their credit reports and had filed a dispute with at least one credit reporting agency. For at least 5 percent of the consumers the error would have resulted in paying more in credit charges for a number of purchases.[25] These results show a significant improvement from the 2004 report, although there is still room for improvement.

The reporting agency is not the only regulated party in these activities. There are also statutory obligations imposed on users of consumer reports. For example, users of investigative consumer reports must notify the consumer in writing and before requesting the information that he or she may be the subject of an investigation concerning his or her character, general reputation, personal characteristics, and mode of living. The consumer must then give written consent before the information can be requested.[26]

An Ounce of Prevention

As an employer you may want to run a credit check on applicants as one method of screening candidates. This is especially common for positions in which the employee will be handling customer funds. It is also a normal practice in many businesses to request an investigative report on candidates for managerial positions. These reports are much more intrusive, and as a result there are more safeguards built in to these requests. You should establish a policy of informing applicants in writing that you will be requesting an investigative report and of obtaining a written acknowledgment and consent from the candidate prior to requesting such a report. You may also want to consider a policy of eliminating any applicants who do not consent to the creation and use of such a report.

Whenever a user makes an adverse decision about the consumer's application that is based in whole or in part on the credit report, the user must notify the consumer of the adverse action, and the user must also supply the name and address of the reporting agency that compiled the report. Adverse decisions include the denial of credit, insurance, or employment, or charging a higher rate for the credit or insurance.

The purpose of the FCRA is to make every effort to have fair and accurate credit reporting. One way to help ensure the accuracy of these reports is to give the consumer some rights, including having provisions for challenging information contained in his or her credit report. Recall that the act prohibits the use of inaccurate and/or outdated information and that the consumer must be given notice of adverse decisions based, in whole or in part, on data contained in his or her credit report. The consumer is not entitled to see his or her file, but he or she is entitled to limited access to information in the files. The consumer is entitled to receive from the agency the nature and substance of information about the consumer in the file (except for medical information), the source of the information (except for information acquired in an investigative report), and the names of any parties who received the report. The consumer must be told of any reports furnished for employment purposes in the previous two years and for any other purpose in the preceding six months.

While the consumer is not entitled to see his or her actual file, he or she still has the right to challenge the completeness and/or the accuracy of the information contained in the agency's files. When the consumer decides to question the accuracy of any such information, he or she must inform the reporting agency. The agency must then investigate the information disputed by the consumer within a reasonable time, unless the agency has reasonable grounds to believe the consumer's claim is frivolous or irrelevant. If the agency's reinvestigation shows that the information was, in fact, not accurate, it must (a) correct the file to reflect the accurate information and (b) notify any parties who received the inaccurate information of the updated and correct information. Note that there are two distinct groups who must be notified and two markedly different time periods apply to these two groups: (1) recipients who acquired the information for *employment purposes* within the previous two years and (2) any *other recipients* within the previous six months.

If the reinvestigation results in the agency's determination that the information was accurate and up-to-date, it will not have to change its report. However, the consumer can file a statement that sets forth the nature of the dispute and his or her explanation or justification for the adverse information. Unless it has reasonable grounds to believe the statement is frivolous or irrelevant, the agency must clearly note in any subsequent consumer report containing the disputed information that the consumer disputes the information: The agency must provide either the consumer's statement or a clear and accurate summary of the statement. At the request of the consumer, the agency must send a similar notice to anyone who has received a report concerning employment within the past two years, or a report for any purpose within the previous six months. The statute expressly mandates that the agency clearly and conspicuously disclose to the consumer his or her right to make such a request.

The FCRA sets out civil remedies for violations of the act. Suits for compensatory or punitive damages are possible for willful failure to comply with the act; in cases of negligent noncompliance an injured consumer can recover only compensatory damages. In addition, for either type of violation, the injured party who successfully sues can recover court costs and attorney's fees. The act prohibits court actions brought for defamation, invasion of privacy, or negligence with respect to the reporting of information unless the suit involves false information furnished with malice or with a willful intent to injure the consumer. Any person who knowingly and willfully obtains information concerning a consumer under false pretenses faces a fine of $5,000 and/or one year's imprisonment.

The FTC functions as the principal enforcement agency for violations of the FCRA, because the law views violations of the act as unfair or deceptive trade practices. As such, the FTC can order various administrative remedies (such as cease-and-desist orders) against consumer-reporting agencies, users, or other persons. This is true even if the user or person is not subject to regulation by other federal agencies (such as the CFPB) that have enforcement authority under the act.

The Fair and Accurate Credit Transactions Act (FACTA)

As a further protection for consumers, in 2003 Congress passed the Fair and Accurate Credit Transactions Act (FACTA). This act provides new rights to consumers, including allowing each consumer (1) the right to a free credit report every 12 months from each of the three credit-reporting agencies; (2) the right to receive his or her credit score; and (3) the right to a listing of the key factors used in computing that score. The three major credit-reporting agencies are also required to provide a single point of contact so that a consumer can order all credit reports from all three companies with one communication—either a phone call to the toll-free number, a letter, or by use of the Internet Web site. The Privacy Rights Clearinghouse recommends using the mail or telephone rather than the Internet.[27]

One major reason for enactment of FACTA was concern over identity theft. Consequently, FACTA requires the truncation of account numbers for credit cards and debit cards on a customer's receipt, using only the last five digits of the account number, preceded by a series of Xs. It also prohibits the inclusion of the expiration date for the card. These measures were included as a protection against identity theft.[28]

Congress provided for the imposition of statutory damages for willful violations of FACTA; consequently, a person does not have to show any actual damages to recover. The statutory damages provision calls for a recovery from $100 to $1,000 plus attorney's fees and expenses.[29] In addition, a person who obtains a consumer's report under false pretenses or who knowingly received such a report without a proper purpose is liable to the consumer for the greater of $1,000 or the actual damages suffered by the consumer. The court may also add punitive damages at its discretion.[30]

An Ounce of Prevention

Many businesses accept credit cards as payment for goods or services rendered. If your business does so, it is imperative to ensure that you comply with FACTA. Be certain that you truncate the number on the card except for the last five digits on the bill presented to the customer for his or her signature and the receipt given to the customer. Also ensure that the form you provide to the customer does not show the expiration date of the card.

Given the concern over identity theft, you should also have portable card readers for your employees to use when customers are billed at a location other than a customer service site (e.g., restaurants). These devices allow the server to "swipe" the card at the table, in sight of the customer. The employee does not take the customer's card and then leave the customer to swipe the card.

If your business is in the restaurant industry, you might want to consider the approach of several restaurant chains. A number of these chains are now installing remote card readers on tables and asking the customers to swipe their cards themselves. With this feature the card never leaves the customer's possession, providing an even greater sense of security.

Remember that many customers are uncomfortable having their card swiped out of their line of sight. This small gesture may build customer loyalty. On the other hand, customers will be displeased if your employees steal their identity. They may believe that your business practices exposed them to identity theft.

THE EQUAL CREDIT OPPORTUNITY ACT

When Congress first passed the Equal Credit Opportunity Act[31] (ECOA) in 1974, it prohibited only discrimination based on sex or marital status in the extension of credit. Prior to this law, there was significant evidence showing that creditors denied credit to single women more often than to single men and that married, divorced, and widowed women often could not get credit in their own names. Instead, these women had to obtain credit in their husbands' names.

Congress amended the act in 1976, prohibiting discrimination in the granting of credit based on race, religion, national origin, age (provided the applicant has the capacity to contract), receipt of public assistance benefits, or the fact that the applicant has in good faith exercised any of his or her rights under the Consumer Credit Protection Act (TILA).

The FRB was originally given the responsibility of overseeing this act. (The responsibility was transferred to the CFPB under Dodd-Frank in 2011. In addition, the FTC has enforcement authority.) The FRB adopted Regulation B to provide the broad guidelines to be followed in making credit decisions. The current version of Regulation B broadly defines a credit transaction as involving every aspect of an applicant's dealings with a creditor regarding an application for credit or an existing extension of credit, including but not limited to the following:

- Information requirements
- Investigation procedures
- Standards of creditworthiness
- Terms of credit
- The furnishing of credit information, revocation, alteration, or termination of credit
- Collection procedures

The ECOA and Regulation B exempt certain transactions from coverage, such as those made pursuant to special-purpose credit programs designed to benefit an economically disadvantaged class of persons. Partial exemptions also exist for credit provided by public utilities (that is, public utilities can ask questions about an applicant's marital status) and credit for incidental consumer transactions, such as those involving physicians, hospitals, and health care.

Since creditors generally evaluate applicants' creditworthiness as a precondition of extending credit, Regulation B sets out rules that creditors must follow in making such evaluations and specifies the forms that creditors can use to ensure that they do not discriminate on any of the prohibited bases during their evaluations. In addition, ECOA requires creditors to give notice to applicants of any actions taken by the creditors concerning the applicants' requests for credit.

Creditor actions typically take three forms: approval of the application, extension of credit under different terms than those requested, or an adverse action such as a denial of the application. Regulation B imposes a notification regime[32] specifically tailored to the type of action taken. Exhibit 18.2 represents a communication that generally will satisfy these notification requirements. Creditors typically must send such a notification within 30 days of receiving a completed application.

The Consumer Financial Protection Bureau (CFPB), created under the Dodd-Frank Wall Street Reform and Consumer Protection Act of 2010, assumed oversight responsibility in July 2011. At its Web site, the bureau sets out its central mission: "The central mission of the Consumer Financial Protection Bureau (CFPB) is to make markets for consumer financial products and services work for Americans—whether they are applying for a mortgage, choosing among credit cards, or using any number of other consumer financial products."[34]

Remedies under ECOA include actual damages and/or punitive damages to a maximum of $10,000 for individual actions or a maximum of $500,000 (or 1 percent of the creditor's net worth—whichever is greater) for class actions. Equitable relief, attorneys' fees, and costs also may be granted. A two-year statute of limitations generally applies.

The usual administrative remedies are available as well. The CFBP can also ask the U.S. attorney general to institute civil actions against any creditor who has engaged in a pattern or practice of denying or discouraging credit applicants in violation of the act.

Exhibit 18.2

Form C-2, Sample Notice of Action Taken

Form C-2—Sample Notice of Action Taken and Statement of Reasons[33]

Date

Dear Applicant: Thank you for your recent application. Your request for [a loan/a credit card/an increase in your credit limit] was carefully considered, and we regret that we are unable to approve your application at this time, for the following reason(s):

Your Income: _____ is below our minimum requirement. _____ is insufficient to sustain payments on the amount of credit requested. _____ could not be verified.

Your Employment: _____ is not of sufficient length to qualify. _____ could not be verified.

Your Credit History: _____ of making payments on time was not satisfactory. _____ could not be verified.

Your Application: _____ lacks a sufficient number of credit references. _____ lacks acceptable types of credit references. _____ reveals that current obligations are excessive in relation to income.

Other: _____

The consumer reporting agency contacted that provided information that influenced our decision in whole or in part was [name, address and (toll-free) telephone number of the reporting agency]. The reporting agency played no part in our decision and is unable to supply specific reasons why we have denied credit to you. You have a right under the Fair Credit Reporting Act to know the information contained in your credit file at the consumer reporting agency. You also have a right to a free copy of your report from the reporting agency, if you request it no later than 60 days after you receive this notice. In addition, if you find that any information contained in the report you receive is inaccurate or incomplete, you have the right to dispute the matter with the reporting agency. Any questions regarding such information should be directed to [consumer reporting agency]. If you have any questions regarding this letter, you should contact us at [creditor's name, address and telephone number].

NOTICE: The federal Equal Credit Opportunity Act prohibits creditors from discriminating against credit applicants on the basis of race, color, religion, national origin, sex, marital status, age (provided the applicant has the capacity to enter into a binding contract); because all or part of the applicant's income derives from any public assistance program; or because the applicant has in good faith exercised any right under the Consumer Credit Protection Act. The federal agency that administers compliance with this law concerning this creditor is [name and address as specified by the appropriate agency listed in Appendix A].

THE FAIR DEBT COLLECTION PRACTICES ACT

In 1977 Congress passed the Fair Debt Collection Practices Act[35] (FDCPA) as Title V of the Consumer Credit Protection Act (TILA). This part of TILA regulates the activities of those who collect bills owed to others (including attorneys who regularly engage in consumer debt-collection activity, even when the activity consists of litigation).[36] The act specifically exempts from its coverage the activities of secured parties, process servers, and federal or state employees who are attempting to collect debts pursuant to the performance of their official duties. This act only covers the conduct of debt collection agents and agencies and does not apply to the original creditors who extended the credit.

The law was intended to protect consumers by eliminating abusive, deceptive, and unfair debt-collection practices. The act limits the manner in which a debt collector can communicate with the debtor. For example, the statute expressly prohibits any communications made at an unusual or inconvenient time (generally before 8:00 A.M. and after 9:00 P.M. local time) at the debtor's location without the consumer debtor's consent. The debt collector cannot communicate with the debtor at the debtor's place of employment if the debt collector knows or has reason to know that the debtor's employer prohibits the employee from receiving such communications. In most circumstances, if the debt collector knows an attorney represents the consumer with respect to the debt, the debt collector can contact only the attorney, not the debtor. A debt collector typically cannot communicate with third parties (for example, the debtor's neighbors, coworkers, or friends) concerning the collection of the debt, either.

The statute also requires the termination of further communication with the debtor if he or she notifies the debt collector in writing that he or she refuses to pay the debt and wishes all communications to stop. At that point, the debt collector can advise the consumer only of the termination of further efforts to collect the debt or of the debt collector's intention to invoke any available remedies.

Debt collectors must also refrain from unfair or unconscionable means of debt collection. For example, the debt collector is prohibited from accepting postdated checks, making collect phone calls to debtors, or adding any other amounts not expressly allowed by the underlying debt agreement or by state law.

The act requires the bill collector to send the debtor a written verification of the debt, allowing the debtor to dispute the debt if he or she believes there are grounds to do so. The debtor then has 30 days in which he or she must dispute the debt in writing; otherwise, the debt collector can assume the validity of the debt.

The FTC has primary enforcement responsibilities under the FDCPA. Civil remedies of actual damages plus additional damages, not to exceed $1,000, are possible in individual suits. In class actions, $1,000 per person may be awarded; but the total damages so awarded cannot exceed the lesser of $500,000 or 1 percent of the debt collector's net worth.

Under a separate statute, a criminal penalty of $1,000 or a sentence of one year's imprisonment, or both, may be imposed on anyone who, during the course of debt-collection efforts, uses the words *federal*, *national*, or *the United States* to convey the false impression that the communication originates from, or in any way represents, the United States or any of its agencies or instrumentalities. Successful litigants may recover costs and attorney's fees as well.

THE CONSUMER PRODUCT SAFETY ACT

The Consumer Product Safety Act of 1972[37] established the Consumer Product Safety Commission (CPSC). (This act has been amended a number of times, most recently in 2011.) The CPSC has authority over a great number of consumer products, but products expressly excluded from the commission's jurisdiction include tobacco and tobacco products, motor vehicles, pesticides covered under FIFRA (a statute discussed in Chapter 19), firearms and ammunition, food, and cosmetics.

To help protect the public from injuries from consumer products, the commission can do the following:

- Set and enforce safety standards
- Ban hazardous products
- Collect information on consumer-related injuries
- Administratively order firms to publicly report defects that could create substantial hazards
- Force firms to take corrective action (repair product, replace product, or refund payment) with regard to substantially hazardous consumer products in commerce
- Seek court orders for recalls of imminently hazardous products
- Conduct research on consumer products
- Engage in outreach educational programs for consumers, industry, and local government

Products banned by the CPSC include certain all-terrain vehicles, unstable refuse bins, lawn darts, tris (a chemical flame-retardant found in children's apparel), products containing asbestos, and paint containing lead. Products subject to CPSC standards include matchbooks, automatic garage door openers, bicycles, cribs, rattles, disposable lighters, toys with small parts, and the like. The concern over lead poisoning in children has even led the agency to regulate businesses that might seem exempt. For example, charity stores (e.g., Goodwill), used goods stores, second-hand shops, and stores selling children's books (if any of the books were printed prior to 1985) must pay for lead testing before they are allowed to sell their products. The number of items subject to testing and regulation seems to increase annually.

For example, one of the "hot" gift ideas (pun intended) for the 2015 Christmas season was the Hoverboard® (these devices are also called "smart boards" or "balance boards"). Some of these gifts were, indeed, hot—causing fires in a number of homes and at least one shopping mall. There were also reports of devices catching on fire while being ridden, although most seem to have occurred during recharging. A few airlines have banned them from being on board due to the risk of fire. The CPSC is investigating these incidents and trying to determine how much of a risk they pose.[38]

An Ounce of Prevention

Like many businesses, you might contract with manufacturers to produce your goods. You may be able to reduce your costs by relying on overseas manufacturers. However, you are still liable under the CPSC and product liability laws for the goods that are produced on your behalf. Recently, there have been numerous cases in which the goods do not comply with federal law or the businesses' own standards, for example, excessive lead in children's jewelry and toys. When this information is revealed, it harms the business's reputation and exposes it to lawsuits. Consequently, you should consider establishing an independent verification process to ensure that the manufacturer is following the standards you set in the contract. It would also be a good idea to include a clause allowing you to disaffirm the contract if the supplier violates the standards set out in the contract.

The various consumer protection statutes and their scope are summarized in Exhibit 18.3.

Exhibit 18.3

Consumer Protection Statutes

Name of Statute	*Type of Protection Provided*
Consumer Credit Protection Act (CCPA), also known as TILA (Truth in Lending Act)	• Disclosure of APR on all consumer credit • Regulations for advertising about credit • Regulation Z and credit card rules and regulations
Home Ownership and Equity Protection Act (HOEPA)	• Applies some TILA protections to home mortgages • Protects home buyers against unfair, abusive or deceptive lending and servicing practices

Exhibit 18.3 Continued

Name of Statute	Type of Protection Provided
Fair Credit Billing Act (FCBA)	• Requires creditor on open-ended credit to provide a method for consumers to challenge alleged billing errors • Establishes standards to be met in investigating the challenged charges or fees • Protects the consumer during the required investigation
Fair Credit Reporting Act (FCRA)	• Sets standards for credit reporting agencies to follow in preparing credit reports on consumers • Allows consumers to challenge information contained in a credit report • Allows consumers to add an explanation of negative, but accurate, information with the credit report, if he or she so desires • Requires the agency to send an amended report to recipients of an erroneous report within the prior six months (prior two years for employment-related reports)
Fair and Accurate Credit Transactions Act (FACTA)	• Allows each consumer one free credit report from each credit reporting agency each year • Allows each consumer to receive his or her credit score • Allows the consumer to discover the key factors used in computing the credit score • Provides numerous protections to help prevent identity theft
Equal Credit Opportunity Act (ECOA)	• Prohibits illegal discrimination on the awarding of credit • Requires a credit issuer who received an application for credit to reply with 30 days of receiving the application • If credit is denied, the reason must be given to the applicant
Fair Debt Collection Practices Act (FDCPA)	• Establishes limits on debt collection agency practices • Seeks an end to harassing and/or intimidating collection practices
Consumer Product Safety Act (CPSA)	• Creates the Consumer Product Safety Commission • Empowers the Commission to set safety standards for consumer goods, ban hazardous products, administratively order firms to publicly report known defects that could cause serious injuries • Conducts tests on consumer products • Bans hazardous products

Contemporary Case

This case is a recent interpretation of the right of a borrower to rescind a consumer credit contract. While the normal period for rescission is within three days of consummation, if the lender fails to provide proper documentation, or if the consumer creditor alleges that the documents were not provided, the rescission period extends to three years. Such was the situation in this case.

JESINOSKI v. COUNTRYWIDE HOME LOANS, INC.
135 S.Ct. 790, 190 L.Ed.2d 650 (S.Ct. 2015)

FACTS On February 23, 2007, Larry and Cheryle Jesinoski refinanced their home by taking out a $611,000 mortgage from Countrywide Home Loans. Exactly three years later, on February 23, 2010, the Jesinoskis sent a letter to Countrywide, seeking to rescind the loan. Bank of America Home Loans, which had acquired the mortgage from Countrywide, responded on March 12, 2010. Bank of America stated in its response that the attempt to rescind the loan was invalid.

The Jesinoskis then filed suit in the Federal District Court, seeking rescission of the loan and also seeking damages from the bank. Bank of America and Countrywide moved for judgment on the pleadings, which the court granted. The court found that the Jesinoskis had not properly rescinded because they had not filed suit within the three year period allowing for revocation. Their suit was filed four years and one day after the three year period had expired. The Eighth Circuit affirmed.

ISSUE Must a consumer file suit within three years in order to rescind a loan or credit agreement under the Truth in Lending Act?

HOLDING No. The statute does not require filing suit. A written notice of intent to rescind is adequate, so long as it falls within the three-year period.

REASONING Excerpts from the opinion of Justice Scalia:

. . . The Truth in Lending Act gives borrowers the right to rescind certain loans for up to three years after the transaction is consummated. The question presented is whether a borrower exercises this right by providing written notice to his lender, or whether he must also file a lawsuit before the 3-year period elapses . . .

Congress passed the Truth in Lending Act . . . , as amended, to help consumers "avoid the uninformed use of credit, and to protect the consumer against inaccurate and unfair credit billing." . . . To this end, the Act grants borrowers the right to rescind a loan "until midnight of the third business day following the consummation of the transaction or the delivery of the [disclosures required by the Act], whichever is later, by notifying the creditor, in accordance with regulations of the [Federal Reserve] Board, of his intention to do so." . . . This regime grants borrowers an unconditional right to rescind for three days, after which they may rescind only if the lender failed to satisfy the Act's disclosure requirements. But this conditional right to rescind does not last forever. Even if a lender *never* makes the required disclosures, the "right of rescission shall expire three years after the date of consummation of the transaction or upon the sale of the property, whichever comes first." . . .
The Eighth Circuit's affirmance in the present case rested upon its holding in *Keiran v. Home Capital, Inc* . . . that, unless a borrower has filed a suit for rescission within three years of the transaction's consummation, § 1635(f) extinguishes the right to rescind and bars relief.

That was error.   Section 1635(a) explains in unequivocal terms how the right to rescind is to be exercised: It provides that a borrower "shall have the right to rescind . . . *by notifying the creditor, in accordance with regulations of the Board, of his intention to do so."* . . . The language leaves no doubt that rescission is effected when the borrower notifies the creditor of his intention to rescind. It follows that, so long as the borrower notifies within three years after the transaction is consummated, his rescission is timely. The statute does not also require him to sue within three years.

Nothing in § 1635(f) changes this conclusion. Although § 1635(f) tells us *when* the right to rescind must be exercised, it says nothing about *how* that right is exercised. Our observation in . . . [a prior case] that § 1635(f) "govern[s] the life of the underlying right" is beside the point. That case concerned a borrower's attempt to rescind . . . six years after the loan's consummation. We concluded only that there was "no federal right to rescind, defensively or otherwise, after the 3-year period of § 1635(f) has run," . . . not that there was no rescission until a suit is filed.

. . . [The lenders] do not dispute that § 1635(a) requires only written notice of rescission. Indeed, they concede that written notice suffices to rescind a loan within the first three days after the transaction is consummated. They further concede that written notice suffices after that period if the parties agree that the lender failed to make the required disclosures. . . . [They] argue, however, that if the parties dispute the adequacy of the disclosures—and thus the continued availability of the right to rescind—then written notice *does not* suffice.

Section 1635(a) nowhere suggests a distinction between disputed and undisputed rescissions, much less that a lawsuit would be required for the latter. In an effort to sidestep this problem, . . . [the banks] point to a neighboring provision, § 1635(g), which they believe provides support for their interpretation of the Act. Section 1635(g) states merely that, "[i]n any action in which it is determined that a creditor has violated this section, in addition to rescission the court may award relief under section 1640 of this title for violations of this subchapter not relating to the right to rescind." . . . [They] argue that the phrase "award relief" "in addition to rescission" confirms that rescission is a

consequence of judicial action. But the fact that it can be a consequence of judicial action when § 1635(g) is triggered in no way suggests that it can *only* follow from such action. The Act contemplates various situations in which the question of a lender's compliance with the Act's disclosure requirements may arise in a lawsuit—for example, a lender's foreclosure action in which the borrower raises inadequate disclosure as an affirmative defense. Section 1635(g) makes clear that a court may not only award rescission and thereby relieve the borrower of his financial obligation to the lender, but may also grant any of the remedies available under § 1640 (including statutory damages). It has no bearing upon whether and how borrower-rescission under § 1635(a) may occur.

Finally, respondents invoke the common law. It is true that rescission traditionally required either that the rescinding party return what he received before a rescission could be effected (rescission at law), or else that a court affirmatively decree rescission (rescission in equity). . . . It is also true that the Act disclaims the common-law condition precedent to rescission at law that the borrower tender the proceeds received under the transaction. . . . But the negation of rescission-at-law's tender requirement hardly implies that the Act codifies rescission in equity. Nothing in our jurisprudence, and no tool of statutory interpretation, requires that a congressional Act must be construed as implementing its closest common-law analogue. . . . The clear import of § 1635(a) is that a borrower need only provide written notice to a lender in order to exercise his right to rescind. To the extent § 1635(b) alters the traditional process for unwinding such a unilaterally rescinded transaction, this is simply a case in which statutory law modifies common-law practice . . .

The Jesinoskis mailed respondents written notice of their intention to rescind within three years of their loan's consummation. Because this is all that a borrower must do in order to exercise his right to rescind under the Act, the court below erred in dismissing the complaint. Accordingly, we reverse the judgment of the Eighth Circuit and remand the case for further proceedings consistent with this opinion.

Short Answer Questions

1. Regulation Z, which guides implementation of TILA, has a significant number of regulations dealing with credit cards. What protections are provided to you when you use your credit cards under Regulation Z? Are you adequately protected by these regulations, or is more protection needed?

2. The Equal Credit Opportunity Act provides protections to lower-income consumers that allow them to have access to credit opportunities that might otherwise only be available to more affluent consumers. It does not ensure that everyone can obtain credit, however. What does the ECOA require of a credit provider when it receives an application for credit? What are some of the reasons that can be given when denying credit under the ECOA?

3. The Federal Trade Commission now allows a person who believes his or her credit report is inaccurate to contact the provider of the information to ask for a reinvestigation rather than contacting the credit reporting agency. This "direct dispute" provision is intended to speed up the correction of errors in a credit report and to limit the potential harm to any consumers whose reports contain inaccurate information. What benefits to you see from the "direct dispute" rules? What disadvantages to you see from these rules? Do you believe this is an improvement over the former rules? Explain your answers.

You Decide...

1. The Fair and Accurate Credit Transactions Act requires the truncation of credit card numbers on electronically printed receipts. The receipt must not display "more than the last [five] digits of the card number." The statute does not define the phrase "card number."

A Shell Oil Company credit card contains eighteen digits; fourteen of these digits are visible on the face of the card, while the remaining four digits are contained only on the magnetic strip on the rear of the card. Shell contends that the first nine numbers on the face of the card are the "account number" and that the remaining five digits are the "card number." Shell truncates the "card number" on its receipts by printing only the last four digits found on the face of the card.

Van Straaten, a holder of a Shell Oil Company credit card, insists that the proper four digits for inclusion are the four that are found only on the magnetic strip. These four digits are referred to in the industry as the "primary account number," or PAN. According to Van Straaten, Shell is printing the wrong card number on its receipts, a willful violation of FACTA. Accordingly, Van Straaten wants to file a class action against Shell Oil Company, seeking statutory damages (damages of from $100 to $1,000 per transaction).

Assume that Van Straaten filed his suit in your court. How would *you* decide this case? Be certain that you explain and justify your answer.

(See *Van Straaten v. Shell Oil Products Company, LLC*, 2012 U.S. App. LEXIS 7789 (7th Cir. 2012).)

2. Adelaide Andrews visited a doctor's office in Santa Monica, California. Since she was a new patient she was asked to complete a form that included her name, Social Security number, and other vital and pertinent personal information. A receptionist in the office copied this information shortly before her move to Las Vegas, Nevada. Once the receptionist had relocated she attempted to use Adelaide's personal information to open a number of credit accounts. Once these accounts had been opened, the imposter ran up a number of large debts that went unpaid. The credit issuers for each of these unpaid or delinquent accounts reported the situation to TRW, Inc., a credit reporting agency. TRW, in turn, included this information on Adelaide's credit report, adversely affecting her credit score and her ability to acquire credit.

Adelaide did not learn of these events until several years later when she attempted to refinance her house, only to learn that her credit report and her credit score did not support a mortgage at reasonable or favorable rates. Adelaide then filed suit against TRW, alleging that it had failed to properly verify the accuracy of her credit reports prior to disclosing their contents to any third parties.

TRW moved for summary judgment, pointing out that Adelaide had not filed suit until after the expiration of the two-year statute of limitations for initiating such an action. Adelaide argued that the two-year period for the statute of limitations should not begin until she discovered the conduct.

Assume that Adelaide filed suit in your court. How would you decide this case? Explain and justify your reasoning.

(See *TRW, Inc. v. Andrews*, 534 U.S. 19 (2001).)

Notes

1. Ben Woolsey & Emily Starbuck Gerson, "The History of Credit Cards,"*CreditCards.com*, http://www.creditcards.com/credit-card-news/credit-cards-history-1264.php (accessed February 19, 2016).
2. "History of Credit Cards," *Did You Know?*, http://didyouknow.org/creditcards/ (accessed February 19, 2016).
3. Woolsey & Gerson, "The History of Credit Cards," Note 1 *supra.*
4. "History of Credit Cards," *Did You Know?*, Note 2 *supra.*
5. Daniel P. Ray and Yasmin Ghahremani, "Credit Card Statistics, Industry facts, Debt Statistics," *CreditCards.com* (December 1, 2015), http://www.creditcards.com/credit-card-news/credit-card-industry-facts-personal-debt-statistics-1276.php (accessed May 11, 2016).
6. Tmara E. Holmes and Yasmin Ghahremani, "Credit Card Debt Statistics," CreditCards.com Web site (April 20, 2105). Found at http://www.creditcards.com/credit-card-news/credit-card-debt-statistics-1276.php (accessed May 11, 2016).
7. See, for example, Jonathan Sheldon, editor, *Fair Credit Reporting Act*, 3rd ed. (Boston: National Consumer Law Center, 1994). This and other National Consumer Law Center publications, such as Ernest L. Sarason, editor, *Truth in Lending* (1986); Gerry Azzata, editor, *Equal Credit Opportunity Act* (1988); and the annual cumulative supplements to these works provide more detailed information on consumer law, as does Gene A. Marsh, *Consumer Protection Law in a Nutshell* (St. Paul: West Group, 1999) and Howard J. Alperin & Ronald F. Chase, *Consumer Law: Sales Practices and Credit Regulation* (Minneapolis: West Publishing Co., 1986).
8. 15 U.S.C.A. § 1601 *et seq.*
9. "Truth in Lending Act, Indiana Department of Financial Institutions Web site, http://www.in.gov/dfi/2582.htm (accessed May 11, 2016).
10. Robin P. Myers, "Consumer Damages and Remedies for Truth in Lending Act and Regulation Z Violations," Federal Reserve Bank of Philadelphia Web site, http://www.philadelphiafed.org/bank-resources/publications/compliance-corner/2006/fourth-quarter/q4cc1_06.cfm (accessed February 19, 2016).
11. "Truth in Lending Act," *The Free Dictionary by Farlex*, http://legal-dictionary.thefreedictionary.com/Truth+in+Lending+Act (accessed February 19, 2016).
12. Ronald Mann, "Opinion Analysis: Shortest Opinion of the Year Explains TILA Rescission Right," SCOTUSblog Web site (January 13, 2015), http://www.scotusblog.com/2015/01/opinion-analysis-shortest-opinion-of-the-year-explains-tila-rescission-right/ (accessed May 11, 2016)

13. "Truth in Lending Act," CFPB Laws and Regulations, http://files.consumerfinance.gov/f/201503_cfpb_truth-in-lending-act.pdf (accessed February 21, 2016)

14. *Ibid.*

15. 15 U.S.C. § 1501 *et seq.*

16. "Open End Credit," *The Free Dictionary by Farlex*, http://legal-dictionary.thefreedictionary.com/Open-End+Credit (accessed February 19, 2016).

17. "Lost or Stolen Credit, ATM, and Debit Cards" Consumer Information, Federal Trade Commission Web site, http://www.consumer.ftc.gov/articles/0213-lost-or-stolen-credit-atm-and-debit-cards (accessed February 19, 2016).

18. 15 U.S.C. § 1693 *et seq.*

19. *Ibid.*

20. Erin El Issa, "2015 American Household Credit Card Debt Study," *NerdWallet.com.* http://www.nerdwallet.com/blog/credit-card-data/average-credit-card-debt-household/ (accessed February 20, 2016).

21. Sheldon, Fair Credit Reporting Act, 32, Note 7 *supra.*

22. Candace Heckman, "Study Assails Accuracy of Credit Reports," *Seattle Post-Intelligencer* (June 21, 2004).

23. 15 U.S.C. § 1681 et seq.

24. Press Release, "Agencies Issue Final Rules on Accuracy of Credit Report Information and Allowing Direct Disputes," Federal Trade Commission Web site (July 1, 2009), https://www.ftc.gov/news-events/press-releases/2009/07/agencies-issue-final-rules-accuracy-credit-report-information (accessed May 11, 2016).

25. Press Release, "FTC Testifies on Credit Reporting Accuracy Study, FCRA Enforcement, Credit Education," Federal Trade Commission Web site (May 7, 2013). Found at https://www.ftc.gov/news-events/press-releases/2013/05/ftc-testifies-credit-reporting-accuracy-study-fcra-enforcement (accessed May 11, 2016).

26. Federal Trade Commission, Bureau of Consumer Protection, "Using Consumer Reports: What Employers Need to Know," http://business.ftc.gov/documents/bus08-using-consumer-reports-what-employers-need-know (accessed February 19, 2016).

27. "Fact Sheet 6a: Facts on FACTA, The Fair and Accurate Credit Transactions Act," http://www.privacyrights.org/fs/fs6a-facta.htm (accessed May 11, 2016).

28. *Ibid.*

29. FCRA, 15 U.S.C. § 1681(n).

30. "FACTA, The Fair and Accurate Credit Transaction Act," ShredEx Web site, http://www.goshredex.com/FACTA-fair-and-accurate-credit-transactions-act.php (accessed May 11, 2016).

31. 15 U.S.C. § 1691 et seq.

32. According to the Oxford Dictionary, a regime is a "system or a planned way of doing things, especially one proposed from above." http://www.oxforddictionaries.com/definition/english/regime (accessed May 11, 2016).

33. FDIC sample form, https://www.fdic.gov/regulations/laws/rules/6500-260.html, http://www.fdic.gov/regulations/laws/rules/6500-2900.html#fdic6500appendixctopart202 (accessed May 11, 2016).

34. United States Consumer Financial Protection Bureau, "Learn about the Bureau," http://www.consumerfinance.gov/the-bureau (accessed May 11, 2016).

35. 15 U.S.C. § 1692a-1692p.

36. *Heintz v. Jenkins,* 514 U.S. 291, 299 (1995).

37. 15 U.S.C. §§ 2051-2089.

38. James Eng, "U.S. Safety Regulators Step Up Probe of Hoverboards Over Fire Risk," *NBC News* (December 10, 2105), http://www.nbcnews.com/tech/gadgets/u-s-safety-regulators-step-probe-hoverboards-over-fire-risk-n477896 (accessed February 20, 2016).

19

Environmental Protection and Sustainability

Learning Objectives

After completing this chapter you should be able to

- Explain the objectives of the National Environmental Policy Act
- Identify the common law actions and remedies available in environmental matters
- Discuss the role and the responsibility of the Environmental Protection Agency
- Describe the different types of pollution regulations
- Interpret sustainability and the impact of "going green"
- Recognize the limitations affecting international environmental regulation

Classic Case

This case involves the issue of a public nuisance. Note that it was heard several decades prior to the enactment of the National Environmental Policy Act (NEPA) and the creation of the Environmental Protection Agency (EPA). At the time this case was decided, nuisance law was virtually the only protection available to individuals when someone encroached on their living environment.

COOK v. CITY OF Du QUOIN
256 Ill. App. 452 (Ill. App. Ct. 1930)

FACTS Jackson Cook owned and operated a farm situated along Reese Creek, a natural waterway that lies on the outskirts of the City of Du Quoin. When the Cook family acquired the land and moved onto the farm, Reese Creek was suitable for watering their livestock. At some later time the City constructed a sewer system that emptied into Reese Creek. As a result of this, Cook alleged that the creek had become contaminated and polluted so that it could no longer be used by the family or their livestock. He further alleged that the creek now released noxious odors, which deprived the Cooks of the comforts and enjoyment of their home, that their health was endangered by the condition of the creek, and that he and his family had suffered damages as a result of the nuisance caused by the City. [The polluted condition of the creek was alleged to have been in existence for more than five years before this suit was filed.]

The City of Du Quoin denied the allegations and asserted that the pollution of the creek, if it existed, was due to the conduct of other towns and communities farther upstream pouring their sewage in to Reese Creek.

ISSUE Did the City of Du Quoin commit a public nuisance by discharging its sewage into Reese Creek?

HOLDING Yes. The City was guilty of creating and maintaining a continuing nuisance.

REASONING Excerpts from the opinion of Mr. Justice Newhall:

. . . The evidence shows that [Cook] moved upon the premises in question about the year 1920 and occupied the same with his family as a home; that the creek is about 40 yards from his house and three miles upstream was . . . the packing plant of the Du Quoin Packing Company; that the City of Du Quoin has about 10,000 inhabitants and some time prior to 1920 had constructed a sewer system, with a septic tank located above the packing plant and discharged the sewage through a tile sewer into a ditch leading to Reese Creek.

For some years after [Cook] moved onto his premises he used the water in the creek for watering stock, but for five years prior to the filing of the bill he had been unable to use it for that purpose; that by reason of the stream being used for a sewage outlet, the stream had become contaminated and noxious odors arose therefrom, particularly in the summertime. At times the family had to leave the home, being unable to sleep, and the odors were such as to render the members of the family sick; that the water in the stream was filled with sediment, sewage, and other deleterious elements which killed the fish in the stream and rendered the water unfit for farm uses . . .

From a review of the evidence in the record we are of the opinion that the chancellor was amply justified in reaching the conclusion that [Du Quoin] was guilty of creating and maintaining a nuisance by the pollution of the natural stream which flowed across [Cook]'s farm, and that the law and evidence justified the court in directing [Du Quoin] to abate the nuisance.

It is the right of every owner of land over which a stream of water flows, to have it flow in its natural state and with its quality unaffected. It is a part of the freehold, of which the owner cannot be disseized except by due process of law, and the pollution of a stream constitutes the taking of property, which may not be done without compensation . . .

[Du Quoin] did not attempt to offer any evidence which would refute that of [Cook], but the only offered proof on behalf of [the city], refused to be heard by the chancellor, was that other sources than that chargeable to [Du Quoin] may have been responsible for contributing to the pollution of Reese Creek, a natural watercourse. Though other wrongful acts than that of the defendant city may have been responsible for the collection of this objectionable sewage, such fact furnishes no defense to the defendant city, if it in fact contributed to the nuisance complained of and participated in the pollution of the water that caused injury . . .

Where the acts of several persons, although separate and distinct as to time and place, culminate in producing a public nuisance, which injures the person or property of another, they are jointly and severally liable . . .

The only question for review is whether the evidence supports the decree and did the court reject competent evidence . . .

The bill charges that the acts of [Du Quoin] in polluting the creek in question occasioned noxious and offensive odors which rendered [Cook's] home unfit to occupy for himself and family, dangerous to their health, as well as occasioning great physical discomfort; that [Cook] was unable to use his land for pasturage and farming purposes and that he had been unlawfully deprived of the comfort and enjoyment of said premises. The undisputed proof shows that . . . [Du Quoin] was guilty of maintaining a continuing nuisance by the polluting of said stream; that [Cook] suffered the constant annoyances and injuries charged in said bill to have been occasioned to his property and family; that during such period

the physical discomforts to himself and family constantly increased by reason of the continued unlawful acts of [Du Quoin]. No claim was made in the bill, or proofs, as to permanent damage to [Cook's] real estate and . . . the measure of damages was compensation for physical discomfort and deprivation of the comfortable enjoyment of a home, and it is clearly evident that the chancellor allowed compensation to [Cook] based upon this theory.

Where the injury is physical discomfort and results in deprivation of the comfortable enjoyment of a home, the measure of damages is not the depreciation in the rental value of the premises but compensation for such physical discomfort and deprivation of the use and comforts of home and is to be determined by the sound judgment, experience and discretion of the court or jury that may be called to determine such question in view of the facts in each particular case . . .

[Du Quoin] further contends that [Cook] would not be entitled to recover for consequential damages resulting from a public sewer where the evidence fails to show that the same was not carefully constructed or prudently operated. The mere fact that such sewer, with its septic tank and outlet, was built in the usual and customary manner, does not relieve [Du Quoin] of its legal duty to prevent injury to [Cook's] property resulting from the pollution of said natural watercourse by reason of the same being used as a means for disposal of sewage controlled by [Du Quoin]. Such sewage disposal methods adopted by [Du Quoin] were unlawful and it was the city's duty to have abated them . . .

After careful review of the record we are of the opinion that the decree of the court below is supported by the evidence and that the court did not err in its rulings, and that said decree should be affirmed.

INTRODUCTION

We all would like to have clean air, clean and safe water, and land that is free from pollution and litter. In fact, this should be an unequivocal expectation and right for all people. In addition, most of us would also like to avoid exposure to an unduly noisy environment. We favor efforts to sustain a clean, safe, and healthy environment. There is widespread agreement that our "carbon footprint" needs to be reduced in order to sustain—and even to improve—the environment. There is a growing emphasis on "going green" as a necessary step in doing so. At the same time, most people want continued access to a multitude of goods and services. Few people today, if given the choice, would want to be totally self-sufficient or to try to adapt to life without the goods, the services, or the technological devices and advances of modern life. Unfortunately, these benefits of modern life have a cost, and that cost is often paid by the environment. This cost has frequently been the result of inadequate planning or of a failure to consider the consequences of industrialization. As a result environmental protection is increasing in importance.

Environmental protection and its related laws constitute an extremely complex and controversial area. Many of the statutes and regulations are highly technical and filled with acronyms. Given the technical nature of the area, the somewhat unique terminology that is used, and the plethora of statutes and regulations covering the various areas, understanding environmental law poses a challenge to students and legal practitioners. A thorough coverage of the material is beyond the scope of this text. However, we are able to provide a broad overview of the topic and we will discuss some of the major principles and goals of this area.[1]

In the United States, environmental protection is predominantly accomplished by federal statutes and agency regulations. State laws can be used to complement the federal laws, but not to override them. Examples of state laws include: "California emissions controls" on cars that are to be sold in California, deposits on beverage cans and bottles, and restrictions on plastic bags in retail stores. And in some instances a state has taken a leading role, enacting a statute that might influence other states or the federal government to take similar action. California's Safer Consumer Products Act[2] from 2008 has led to a "Green Chemistry" Partnership between the California Department of Toxic Substances Control and the EPA that is intended to reduce the use of toxic chemicals in consumer products.[3] Many of the early environmental protection statutes were based to a significant extent on common law nuisance principles, primarily by prohibiting uses or conduct that interfered with the rights of others. While nuisance principles provided an initial framework, the sheer size and complexity of the environmental issues we face today require more than protection from "nuisances." As a result, statutes and regulations today supersede common law principles to a great extent.

COMMON LAW ACTIONS

There is an old adage that a man's home is his castle. This implies that a person is entitled to individual privacy and that his or her conduct at home should be unfettered from interference by others. Unfortunately, one person's conduct can, and often does, affect others. The common law recognized that certain conduct by one person could unreasonably interfere with the occupancy, use, and enjoyment of property owned by his or her neighbors. As a result, the common law allowed the persons whose rights were interfered with to seek remedies. One such action was a suit alleging *nuisance*. The tort of nuisance was introduced in Chapters 1 and 12. One type of nuisance occurs when a person uses his or her property in a manner that is unreasonable, unwarranted, or unlawful, and such use obstructs or injures the rights of others to use and enjoy their property, resulting in legal damages.[4]

For example, if a new factory was constructed in an area, and that factory produced smoke or soot or a stench that interfered with the rights of homeowners in the area, those homeowners could file a suit against the factory on the basis of nuisance. The court would then have to weigh the benefits the community might derive from the factory's continued operation against the loss of use and enjoyment of the homeowners: It would decide whether to shut down the factory (or at least order it to reduce or eliminate the nuisance, if possible) or to award damages to the homeowners for the decrease in their property value due to the operation of the factory. While the benefits from the factory might well be sufficient to outweigh the cost to the homeowners, other nuisances would not. Thus, a neighbor who does not maintain adequate sanitation on his or her property might be ordered to clean up the property, and a neighbor who decided to begin raising goats, pigs, or chickens—each of which brings an "exotic ambience" to the neighborhood—might be forced to stop such activities due to the negative impact the activities would have on the neighbors.

If a nuisance activity comes to a neighborhood, the neighbors may be able to seek remedies; if a person moves to a neighborhood that already has such nuisance activity, *generally* he or she cannot successfully seek remedies due to the presence of the activity. The person had at least constructive notice of the nuisance activity when he or she moved to the area; this person assumed the risk of enduring the nuisance activity.

The topic of nuisance also includes the *attractive nuisance doctrine.* This doctrine applies to any person who has "an instrumentality, agency, or condition" on his or her property, or who creates such condition on the property of others, when that condition is likely to be a source of danger to children. The person is under a duty to take such precautions as a reasonable and prudent person would take to prevent injury to children "of tender years" that he or she knows are likely to be in the area.[5] Thus, the owner of a swimming pool on his or her property needs to take reasonable steps to prevent children from entering the pool without adult supervision or parental permission. The homeowner would be liable for injuries suffered by any child "of tender years" if he or she failed to take the appropriate precautions. (A child "of tender years" generally means children aged four or younger.)

The availability of remedies for a nuisance work well locally, but they do not address the bigger problem of environmental protection for the region, the state, or the nation. A more broad-based approach is needed to protect the environment.

Another common law cause of action could be brought for *negligence* where a person or a business breached a duty of care to others in the community. A factory that did not provide adequate ventilation in its building, causing harm to its employees, could be sued for negligence. A private party might also be sued for negligence for recklessly spraying an herbicide in his or her yard, if that herbicide blew into a neighbor's yard and destroyed the neighbor's garden. Again, the available remedies for the negligence might work well locally or for a relative few, but they do not address the bigger problem of environmental protection.

In some instances, a business or an individual might even be held liable under strict liability theories for harm caused while engaged in ultrahazardous or imminently dangerous activities, such as blasting. The common law provides remedies for the individuals harmed by such activities even if the actor exercised due care and there is no showing of negligence on his or her part. And once again, such remedies may work well locally, but they will not address the larger issues.

An Ounce of Prevention

It is important for you to avoid creating a nuisance, especially as a businessperson. Failing to shovel the sidewalk after a snowstorm or blocking a street or alley when making or receiving a delivery might be viewed as a nuisance, even if such activities would not be actionable as torts. But any nuisance, whether it is simply rude or is actionable under law, may create a negative image for your business. A business's image may be hurt if it is viewed as regularly creating a nuisance: This may negatively affect your earnings. Being a "good neighbor" creates a positive image and may improve profits.

You should remember that children's views can be significantly different than those of adults. Children may be tempted to climb into cages with animals, swim in "ponds" with chemicals in the water, or climb towers holding electric lines. Most adults would avoid such activities after they assessed the risks. To avoid injury to children and the negative publicity that would result, you should install appropriate barriers and signs to discourage children from entering dangerous situations. These signs may also help deter adults who do not recognize the risks or who may be impaired.

Keep in mind that the value of preventative action goes well beyond image or perception. The essence of good environmental protection is developing proactive systems to address issues up front. That is one of the goals of NEPA and the EPA, each of which is discussed below.

THE NATIONAL ENVIRONMENTAL POLICY ACT

The National Environmental Policy Act of 1969[6] (NEPA) was intended to do the following:

- "To declare a national policy which will encourage productive and enjoyable harmony between man and his environment;
- to promote efforts which will prevent or eliminate damage to the environment and biosphere and stimulate the health and welfare of man;
- to enrich the understanding of the ecological systems and natural resources important to the nation and
- to establish a Council on Environmental Quality"[7]

This means, in essence, that it is the federal government's responsibility to ensure that the environment is used in a beneficial manner. The federal government should cooperate with state and local governments and with concerned or affected citizens or organizations to protect the environment. Policies should be enacted to avoid degradation of the environment: The policies should protect public and environmental health and safety. Policies should also be enacted that preserve a healthy environment and provide aesthetically pleasing surroundings. These high-sounding ideals provide the foundation upon which our national environmental policies and regulations have been built.

THE ENVIRONMENTAL PROTECTION AGENCY

The Environmental Protection Agency (EPA) has the primary responsibility for enforcing the various environmental protection statutes and for enacting regulations to help in such enforcement. The EPA is an administrative agency that was established by executive order in 1970. It was given the power to enforce environmental laws, adopt regulations, conduct research on pollution, and assist other governmental entities concerned with the environment. The EPA can subject suspected violators to administrative orders and civil penalties to enforce federal environmental laws. It can also refer criminal matters under the federal environmental laws to the Department of Justice (DOJ) for prosecution.

The environmental laws passed by Congress and enforced by the EPA are expected to take a "wide-angle" view of the issues. The laws and regulations should (1) consider the economic aspects of environmental law; (2) take a technological approach to environmental concerns; (3) mandate risk assessment in the implementation of these laws; and (4) use the threat of imposing liability, sometimes even strict liability, as a "hammer" to ensure compliance. Early legislation in this area was primarily concerned with the conduct of business and industry, especially the chemical industry. Increasingly, however, small businesses and state and local governments bear a large part of the costs of compliance.

ENVIRONMENTAL IMPACT STATEMENTS

At first glance, the responsibilities listed in § 101 of NEPA seem overwhelming. How can the provisions of the statute possibly be carried out? Compliance with NEPA is obviously challenging: The statute does provide a starting point in attempting to meet its objectives. Section 102 of NEPA requires virtually all federal agencies to prepare a detailed environmental impact statement (EIS) whenever the agency proposes legislation, recommends any actions, or undertakes any activities that may affect the environment. Among other things, an EIS must do the following:

- Describe the anticipated impact that the proposed action will have on the environment
- Describe any unavoidable adverse consequences of the action or activity
- Examine the possible alternative methods of achieving the desired goals
- Distinguish between long-term and short-term environmental effects
- Describe the irreversible and irretrievable commitments of resources that will occur if the proposed action is implemented[8]

The statute requires wide distribution of the EIS in draft form to other federal, state, and local agencies, as well as to the President.

Once an EIS is prepared and distributed, the public has 30 days to review the statement and to submit any comments or observations to the EPA. The EPA will then consider any comments it receives and issue an order as to whether the project should proceed. The order issued by the EPA can be challenged by filing an appeal with the U.S. Court of Appeals. (If a positive recommendation of the EPA is challenged, the EIS can be used as evidence to support the EPA's decision.)

A number of states[9] have also enacted their own state-oriented environmental policy legislation (SEPA), often called "mini-NEPAs," to allow the state to address issues that are seen as problems in the particular state. These mini-NEPA statutes operate in conjunction with the NEPA standards and often impose higher standards for the given state than the standards imposed nationally by NEPA.

POLLUTION REGULATION

Environmental regulation covers a wide range of topics, and many of the regulations are extremely technical. However, it is obvious to most people that in order to satisfy the purposes of NEPA the issue of pollution must be addressed. It is difficult to imagine a policy that does not deal with pollution and yet will "encourage productive and enjoyable harmony between man and his environment," and that will "promote efforts that will prevent or eliminate damages to the environment and biosphere"— the stated purposes of NEPA.[10]

The environmental laws address air, water, land, and noise pollution[11]. We will broadly address each of these four areas. However, it is important to remember that these statutes and regulations tend to be complex. Many of them are also extremely technical and filled with scientific terminology. The coverage here is only meant to provide a broad overview.

Air Pollution

Concerns with air pollution and the desire for clean air have been at the forefront of U.S. environmental protection efforts since the enactment of the Air Pollution Control Act of 1955.[12] This was followed by the Clean Air Act of 1963,[13] which has been expanded by numerous amendments. The original aim of the law was to control air pollution at its source, which was generally viewed as stationary and local. Thus, these first statutes were designed to provide federal assistance to the states in their own efforts to combat air pollution. It quickly became apparent that this initial effort was inadequate, and subsequent acts and amendments broadened the regulatory scope, setting new standards for mobile pollution sources (i.e., motor vehicles) and, in subsequent amendments, addressing the issues of air quality and hazardous pollutants. (A listing of the various acts addressing clean air can be found on the Web site resources for this chapter.)

Stationary Sources Stationary sources of air pollution (smokestack pollution) have long been recognized as harmful to air quality, especially in those areas near the stationary source. Factories, oil refineries, and public utilities are all major sources of air pollution. Homes, schools, and nonmanufacturing commercial sites are also sources, to a lesser extent. The Clean Air Act recognizes that state and local governments should take the initiative in regulating this area, subject to the air quality standards established by the EPA.

The EPA was directed to establish two kinds of air quality standards: (1) primary standards that are necessary to protect the public health and (2) secondary standards that are necessary to protect the public welfare—crops, livestock, buildings, and the like—from any known or anticipated adverse effects associated with the presence of air pollutants. Each type of standard should allow for an adequate margin of safety.

After these standards are established, each state must submit an implementation plan detailing how the state proposes to implement and maintain the standards. The state implementation plan must include a program that establishes any procedures necessary to monitor and control ambient air quality and include a program providing for the enforcement of emissions regulations. The EPA administrator can approve a plan once it is complete. The plan must also provide for the attainment of primary standards "as expeditiously as practicable," but in no case later than three years from the date the plan is approved. The state must also attain secondary standards within a "reasonable time" after approval.

In November 2014, President Obama announced an "historic agreement" between the U.S. and China to reduce greenhouse gas emissions. The agreement—and it should be noted that this is not a treaty, nor is it legally binding—calls for the United States to reduce its emissions, and if the U.S. does so, China will begin to reduce its emissions.[14] While this agreement does not have any enforcement provisions, it may establish a base from which multinational treaties concerning greenhouse gas emissions may emerge.

On August 3, 2015 the Clean Power Plan, a set of regulations established by the EPA, went into effect. These rules and regulations, developed after years of research and millions of comments, are intended to reduce carbon pollution from power plants.[15] One of its objectives is to reduce carbon dioxide emissions by 32 percent from the levels that existed in 2005 by no later than 2030. The EPA expects to do so by having each state develop and implement a plan for attaining the reductions.

The Paris Climate Conference of December 2015[16] involved 195 different countries and resulted in an agreement to avoid dangerous climate change by limiting the increase in global warming to less than two degrees centigrade (2°C) above pre-industrial levels. The agreement is to go into effect in 2020. Each nation submitted its own comprehensive national climate action plan for what it will do. As with the U.S.-China agreement and the Clean Power Plan, it is much too early to predict how effective any of these actions will be in reducing pollution.

Mobile Sources   Air pollution does not arise solely from smokestack sources. Motor vehicles of all types also produce pollutants that affect air quality, more so in some areas than in others. Automobiles, buses, airplanes, motorcycles, tractors, gas-powered gardening tools, and lawn mowers are mobile sources of air pollution. The EPA has sought methods for reducing harmful motor vehicle emissions since the mid-1970s. For example, the United States phased out leaded gasoline[17] and introduced catalytic converters. (A catalytic converter is the part of the auto's emission control system that converts toxic pollutants formed by fuel combustion into less toxic substances.) U.S. cities that have serious smog problems require stations to sell gas with ethanol added: The higher blend of ethanol[18] creates a higher oxygen content and cleaner combustion. Service stations in the nation's most polluting cities must sell even cleaner-burning gasoline.

Congress also established fuel mileage requirements for motor vehicles beginning in 1975 with its introduction of Corporate Average Fuel Economy, or CAFÉ, standards. Each automobile manufacturer is required to meet the CAFÉ standards for its *fleet* of vehicles, with the vehicles categorized by size and style, with the standard based on average miles per gallon based on the performance of randomly selected cars and trucks on a standardized driving model. (For 2010 cars were required to achieve an average of 27.5 mpg, and the combination of cars and light trucks must achieve an average of 23.5 mpg.[19]) In May 2009, President Barack Obama announced plans for a new fuel economy and greenhouse gas standard that would significantly change this area of the law. His plan calls for average of 37.8 mpg for cars and 28.8 mpg for trucks by

2016 and would set a national standard on greenhouse gas emissions by motor vehicles for the first time.[20] And on July 29, 2011, the EPA announced that a new CAFÉ of 54.5 miles per gallon had been agreed to by the automakers and by the state of California. This new CAFÉ would go into effect by 2025.[21]

Unfortunately, the desire to increase mileage and lessen the use of fossil fuels can occasionally lead to improper conduct. In 2015, the EPA discovered that Volkswagen had installed a "defeat device" on many of its diesel engines sold in the United States. This device was able to detect when the engine was being tested, and would then change the performance to improve test results. VW sold nearly half a million such engines in the United States. Under the "normal" operation these engines emitted nitrous oxide pollutants up to 40 times the level permitted. VW was forced to recall millions of its cars worldwide after this discovery. This situation emphasizes the importance of testing in an effort to control and limit mobile source pollution.[22]

An Ounce of Prevention

You should consider how you and your business can reduce air pollution, Adding solar panels to generate part of the energy you use; converting to electric, hybrid, or biofuel vehicles for the company's cars, vans, or trucks; and only buying products that have a high energy star rating will help to reduce the carbon footprint of your business. More recent trends include covering employee parking lots with solar panels (while providing shade for the cars) and installing electric charging stations in employee parking lots for employees who have electric or hybrid vehicles. It will also show the community that your business is "going green," which may improve your image and provide a competitive advantage over less energy-conscious firms in the industry. It may also reduce your operating costs.

Hazardous Pollutants   The 1990 amendment to the Clean Air Act addressed the issue of *hazardous pollutants*, among other things. It originally identified 188 specific pollutants that are either known to cause, or can reasonably be expected to cause, adverse effects on human health or on the environment. The list is modified as science and technology develop. These adverse effects are generally irreversible and include cancer, neurological injuries, and reproductive harm. The federal government established national emissions standards to limit the release of specified hazardous air pollutants. Ironically, these standards are not based on the health risks posed. Instead, they are "technology-based," meaning that they represent the best available control technology an industrial sector could afford. While the level of emissions allowed under the law has not been determined to be safe for the public, such emissions are limited to the greatest extent possible through the application of a standard known as MACT— the maximum achievable control technology.

An Ounce of Prevention

You should consider the type of resources you use and what consumers will do when the products wear out. For example, the first business that invented and produced blinking lights on children's athletic shoes did not consider the effect that their discards would have on the environment. They failed to consider that their technology included the use of mercury vapor switches, which obviously used mercury. Their initial response was to encourage consumers to return worn out shoes to them for recycling. Then they developed an alternate technology that did not include the use of mercury. A similar problem arises with compact fluorescent bulbs. They contain dangerous substances and should be recycled properly and not placed in landfills.

Penalties for Violations   Violators of the Clean Air Act face a number of possible penalties. The EPA can assess "administrative penalties" of up to $25,000 per day for violations of the emission standards, with fines of up to $5,000 per day for violations of other aspects of the law, such as failure to keep adequate records. In addition, the U.S. attorney general can file criminal actions, with potential fines of up to $1,000,000 for each violation and/or imprisonment of up to fifteen years in cases where one knowingly releases hazardous air pollutants into the ambient air. In setting civil penalties, the administrator or the courts may consider the size of the business, the economic impact of the penalty on the business, the violator's full compliance history and good faith efforts to comply, the duration and seriousness of the violation, and so forth. In addition to any actions taken by the EPA or the U.S. attorney general, private citizens can file suit against firms suspected of violating the Clean Air Act. Those citizens who mount successful suits may receive attorney's fees and recoup their court costs, as well as have the courts enforce the statutory provisions.

Water Pollution

Water, like air, is essential to human life. In addition, water provides a means of transportation that is of significant national interest, both commercially and in the area of national defense. As a result, the interstate or international navigable waters of the United States are subject to exclusive federal jurisdiction.

   The federal government began regulating water use in 1889 when it passed the Rivers and Harbors Act,[23] the oldest federal environmental law in U.S. history. The act makes it a misdemeanor to discharge any refuse into any navigable waters or tributaries of the United States without a permit. It also made it a misdemeanor to excavate, fill, or alter the course or condition of any port, harbor, or channel covered under the act without a permit. (Parts of the act are still enforced today.) Today, the Clean Water

Act covers navigable waters, drinking water, wetlands, and ocean dumping. It also continues to cover rivers and harbors under the original statute.

Navigable Waters   Congress passed the Federal Water Pollution Control Act[24] in 1948 in an effort to regulate and control water pollution. This act and its amendments are now called the Clean Water Act, which has three main goals:

1. To make the nation's waters safe for swimming and recreational use
2. To protect all varieties of wildlife that rely on the waters
3. To eliminate the dumping or discharge of pollutants into the waters

Municipal and industrial parties who wish to discharge any pollutants into any navigable waterways must seek a permit from the federal government before doing so. If a permit is issued, the party will be allowed to discharge some pollutants, but it must use the "best available technology" in doing so. This requirement is imposed to control the pollutants and their effects on the waterways to the greatest extent possible.

The EPA has broad regulatory powers under the Clean Water Act. It is authorized to establish water pollution standards for *point sources* of water pollution (*point sources* of water pollution are stationary sources, such as factories and plants, municipal waste treatment facilities, and public utilities) and to require any such point sources to maintain records and monitoring equipment, to keep samples of those pollutants discharged into the waterways, and to otherwise adhere to the standards established.

While the Clean Water Act allows for the discharge of some pollutants into the navigable waterways, it specifically prohibits thermal pollution. (Thermal pollution is the discharge of heated waters into waterways.) Thermal pollution decreases the oxygen level in the water, causing harm to fish and wildlife. This type of discharge is strictly regulated and monitored by the EPA.

Drinking Water   The Safe Drinking Water Act[25] of 1974 authorized the EPA to establish a set of national drinking water standards for the minimum acceptable quality of water to be used for human consumption. Public water systems must use the best available technology that is feasible, both economically and technologically, in satisfying the EPA's standards. Suppliers of public drinking water must also provide an annual statement to each of its household consumers that lists the source of the water, the level of contaminants found in the water, and possible health hazards presented by the contaminants found in the water.

The statute specifically bans the dumping of waste into wells used for drinking water. Such waste will obviously affect the water from that particular well and may reach the water tables and subsequently one or more sources of public drinking water. The EPA is also concerned about other underground pollutants that can leak or seep into the water tables and eventually contaminate public drinking waters. Leakage from landfills, runoffs that contain pesticides from agricultural lands, seepage from underground storage tanks and facilities, and other potential pollution sources can affect drinking water.

There is also a growing concern that "fracking," hydraulic fracturing of subterranean rocks in order to extract oil and natural gas, affects the water tables. After over five years of studying the issue, the EPA announced in June 2015 that there have been some instances in which drinking water was contaminated due to "fracking."[26] While the number of wells or other sites that were affected is relatively small, the concern is real. As a result, the EPA will conduct further tests and seek public comments in order to determine what rules or regulations are needed to address this issue.

The water crisis in Flint, Michigan, where unsafe levels of lead were found in the city's drinking water emphasizes how much remains to be done in order to meet the objectives of this act. Subsequent investigations by the Washington Post and USA Today show that a number of communities in the United States have lead in their water supplies that exceed the "safe" standards established by the EPA. This issue is expected to draw a great deal of attention from the EPA over the next several years.

Wetlands   Wetlands are defined by the EPA as "those areas that are inundated or saturated by surface or ground water at a frequency and duration sufficient to support, and that under normal circumstances do support, a prevalence of vegetation typically adapted for life in saturated soil conditions. Wetlands generally include swamps, marshes, bogs and similar areas."[27] The Clean Water Act forbids the filling or dredging of wetlands without a permit issued by the U.S. Army Corps of Engineers, which is authorized to adopt regulations to protect the wetlands.

Ocean Dumping   Congress passed the Marine Protection, Research, and Sanctuaries Act,[28] more commonly known as the Ocean Dumping Act, in 1972. This act regulates the dumping of *any* materials into ocean waters, and it specifically prohibits the dumping of radioactive wastes and radiological, chemical, or biological warfare agents.

In 1990 Congress passed the Oil Pollution Act,[29] a rather prompt reaction to the *Exxon Valdez* oil spill in Alaska in 1989, which was the worst oil spill/disaster in U.S. history at that time. More than ten million gallons of crude oil spilled into the Prince William Sound. The damage to the wildlife in the region was incalculable, and the cost of the cleanup exceeded $1.3 billion! In an effort to avoid such oil spills or leaks in the future, the act established new design standards for ships operating in U.S. waters. These new standards mandate that new ocean-going tankers must be of a double-hulled construction until the U.S. Coast Guard approves a superior design to protect against oil spills.[30] Existing single-hulled tankers were required to be phased out by 2010.[31] It also imposes liability on shipowners whose ships discharge oil in any manner in U.S. waters.

The Deepwater Horizon (BP) Oil Spill on April 20, 2010—the result of an explosion on a drilling platform in the Gulf of Mexico—led to a moratorium on off-shore drilling immediately following the spill. During the spill more than 200 million gallons of crude oil escaped into the gulf, causing billions of dollars in damages to the ecology and the economies of the gulf-coast states. When the moratorium was lifted, the United States put in place more stringent standards and supervision of off-shore drilling.

In April 2011, the EPA and the Army Corps of Engineers released new guidelines to clarify which waters should be protected under the Clean Water Act. One of the purposes of these guidelines is to improve the procedures for identifying wetlands and other waters that are covered by the act. A second major purpose is to extend protections to smaller waterways that feed into major streams and rivers, keeping downstream waters free of pollutants from upstream and from smaller "feeder" streams.[32]

Penalties for Violations   Violations of the Clean Water Act can result in civil and/or criminal penalties. The civil penalties run from $10,000 to $25,000 per day, depending on the type of violation. Criminal penalties, which can only be imposed for intentional violations of the act, range from a fine of $2,500 per day and possible imprisonment for up to one year to fines of up to $1 million and imprisonment for up to 15 years.

Violations of the Ocean Dumping Act can result in a civil penalty of up to $50,000, while knowingly violating the act is a criminal action carrying a fine of up to $50,000 and possible incarceration for up to one year.

Violations of the Oil Pollution Act potentially carry the most significant penalties, civil liability of $1,000 per barrel of oil spilled or $25,000 per day, and the party responsible for the oil spill is responsible for all the costs of the cleanup, to a maximum of $1 billion.[33]

Land Conservation and Pollution

The protection and preservation of land constitute the most obvious areas of federal environmental regulation. As early as the presidency of Theodore Roosevelt, concern for protecting the environment and preserving America's natural resources surfaced in the United States. The *public domain*, defined as land owned and/or controlled by the federal government, includes nearly 677 million acres. To put that in perspective, federally controlled land, national parks, and wildlife refuges in the United States occupy about as much land as does the subcontinent of India. Each state also owns and/or controls land within its borders, adding significantly to the total acreage that is government-owned. In an effort to protect and preserve the land, whether in the public domain, owned by one of the states, or owned by private entities, the federal government has enacted a number of statutes. Several of the more important ones are discussed below.

In January 2016 the Obama administration ordered a temporary halt to the granting of new coal mining leases on federal land. The administration plans to conduct a three-year review of federal policies regarding such leases. The goal is to place the policies in line with environmental concerns and to ensure that future leases properly reflect the costs the mining imposes on taxpayers and the climate. At the time the moratorium was put in place nearly 40 percent of the coal mined in the United States came from mines operating under leases on federal land.[34]

Toxic Substances   The Toxic Substances Control Act (TSCA), passed by Congress in 1976, represents the first statutory enactment that comprehensively addresses toxic chemicals and their impact on health and the environment. The act authorizes the

EPA to study chemicals, and to either ban the chemicals or limit their use, if such conduct is required to protect public health and/or the environment.

Under the terms of the act, chemicals are classified as either "existing" or "new." The emphasis of the law is to ensure that "new" chemicals are properly tested and approved by the EPA prior to their release. The manufacturer of a new chemical must provide the EPA with specific test data 90 days prior to the planned introduction of the chemical. The EPA then determines what regulations are needed in regard to the chemical. The EPA may request additional information and can ban production or distribution until it receives such data.

The act permits the EPA to require special labeling, to limit the use, to establish production quotas, or even to ban chemicals. Manufacturers of regulated chemicals are required to keep careful and detailed records of their production and distribution of the chemicals.

The EPA is expected to balance health and environmental issues on the one hand with economic considerations on the other. In effect, the agency is only to issue regulations covering any particular chemical or chemical compound when there is an *unreasonable* risk to health and/or the environment—and there is not an accepted definition of what constitutes a *reasonable* risk. This restriction, combined with the cost of testing and the regular introduction of new chemical compounds, makes the TSCA very difficult to apply. Making matters more difficult for the EPA, private citizens have the right to sue the EPA for any alleged failures to follow the TSCA or to properly apply its standards.

Insecticides, Fungicides, and Rodenticides   Sprays, chemicals, and other devices used for eradicating insects, fungi, or rodents have a valid and valuable purpose. They are also quite often toxic substances, with potentially serious consequences to unintended targets. By 1947 the use of pesticides and insecticides had become prevalent, and such use was recognized as posing a potential threat to the environment. In response to this concern, Congress passed the Federal Insecticide, Fungicide, and Rodenticide Act (FIFRA). This early version of FIFRA mandated the registration of "economic poisons [pesticides] involved in interstate commerce and the inclusion of labels, warnings, and instructions on such pesticides."

In 1970 the newly established EPA took over the enforcement of FIFRA from the Department of Agriculture. In 1972 Congress amended FIFRA when it passed the Federal Environmental Pesticide Control Act: Congress changed the focus of regulation from the accuracy of labeling to recognizing and addressing concerns for the environment. Under the amended act all persons who distribute or sell pesticides must register them with the EPA. Before the EPA will approve the registration, however, it must determine that the pesticide, when used properly, will not generally cause unreasonable adverse effects on the environment. The EPA registration of an approved pesticide can designate that the pesticide is for general use or for a restricted use, such as a use only by exterminators. The EPA can also cancel or suspend the registration of any pesticide whenever such action is necessary to prevent an imminent hazard.

Although FIFRA is basically a risk-assessment statute, the amendments to the act make it clear that in determining "unreasonable adverse effects on the environment" the EPA must take into account the benefits, as well as the costs, associated with the use of the pesticide. This means that it is possible for the EPA to register an economically beneficial pesticide even though it might pose harm to health or the environment.

Hazardous Waste Disposal   Waste disposal has the potential to cause significant harm to health and to the environment. Some waste contains toxic chemicals, but the disposal of such chemicals is not covered by the TSCA. Even the waste that does not contain any toxic chemicals can cause environmental harms, ranging from merely being an eyesore to serving as a breeding ground for various types of vermin.

The Resource Conservation and Recovery Act was passed by Congress in 1976 to address the growing concern over waste disposal in general, and toxic waste disposal in particular. The EPA was charged with monitoring this area, which includes the handling of toxic waste and solid waste. (*Solid waste* includes liquids, gases, sludges, and semisolids as well as actual solids.) The disposal of solid waste involves landfill use and regulation. The objectives of the act include the following:

- Protecting human health and the environment from the potential hazards of waste disposal
- Conserving energy and natural resources
- Reducing the amount of waste generated
- Ensuring that wastes are managed in an environmentally sound manner

In carrying out its charge, the EPA is expected to determine which types of waste are hazardous and then to develop regulations to monitor and control the disposal of these hazardous wastes. Treatment of hazardous waste is covered by Subtitle C of the act, commonly referred to as the "Cradle to Grave" system. Subtitle C imposes stringent bookkeeping and reporting requirements on generators, transporters, and operators of treatment, storage, and disposal facilities handling hazardous waste. Thus, the wastes are monitored from creation (cradle) to final disposal (grave) under (it is hoped) the watchful eye of the EPA.

The landfill of today has replaced the town dump of yesteryear. Under the provisions of the law, landfills generally are well-engineered facilities that are located, operated, and designed to protect the environment from contaminants that may be present in the solid waste stream. In addition, many new landfills are now collecting potentially harmful landfill gas emissions and converting the gas into energy.

Congress passed the Comprehensive Environmental Response, Compensation, and Liability Act (CERCLA), better known as the "Superfund," in 1980. By this statute, Congress intended to fill in the gaps in the treatment of hazardous waste by regulating hazardous waste disposal sites. CERCLA authorizes the EPA to regulate "hazardous substances," which, when released into the environment, may present substantial danger to the public health or welfare, or the environment. (Note: The act specifically excludes petroleum and natural gas from its definition of hazardous substances.) The purpose of this Superfund is to finance the cleanup of hazardous waste disposal sites when the responsible party or parties cannot be found. However, if the responsible party (referred to in the statute as a potentially responsible party, or PRP) can be found, he or she faces *strict liability*. If there are multiple PRPs, they face *joint and several liability* for the cleanup expenses. PRPs include any and all of the following:

1. The person who generated the waste disposed of at the site
2. The person who transported the waste to the site
3. The person who owned or operated the property at the time of disposal
4. The current owner or operator of the property

Any PRP who is held liable can bring a "contribution action" against any other person who is, or potentially might be, liable for his or her percentage contribution of the costs incurred.

Penalties for Violations   The TSCA is essentially a monitoring and licensing statute. Violations of the act, however, carry the potential for fines of up to $27,500 per day. It should also be kept in mind that private citizens can file suit against the EPA for its failure to carry out its duties under this act.

It is a violation of FIRFA to sell any pesticide or herbicide that is unregistered, or to sell either of them if the registration has been suspended or revoked. It is also a violation to sell a pesticide or herbicide that is mislabeled or one on which the label has been destroyed. Any commercial dealer found in violation faces a fine of up to $25,000 and incarceration for up to one year. Private users who violate these regulations face a fine of up to $1,000 and up to 30 days in jail for each offense.

Any company found in violation of the Resource Conservation and Recovery Act is subject to a civil fine of up to $25,000 per violation. Criminal penalties call for fines of up to $50,000 per day, imprisonment for up to two years, or both.

Liability for violations of CERCLA is, basically, the cost of cleaning up the site. Remember, though, that the statute imposes strict liability and that the liability is joint and several for any and all potential responsible parties, up to a maximum of $50 million. If the action creating the situation is deemed to be willful conduct or willful negligence, the $50 million cap does not apply.

Brownfields Legislation

Given the potential liability that can be imposed under CERCLA, many urban areas have been left virtually abandoned. Many developers preferred to expand outward from the city's center, developing new areas while leaving "derelict land" behind and increasing urban sprawl. In response to this problem, in 2001 Congress passed the Small Business Liability Relief and Brownfields Revitalization Act, which President Bush signed into law on January 11, 2002. This Act, an amendment to CERCLA, encourages the redevelopment of "brownfields" by reducing the potential liability under CERCLA and by providing funding for the assessment and cleanup of these areas.

Brownfields are defined as "real property, the expansion, redevelopment, or reuse of which may be complicated by the presence or potential presence of a hazardous substance, pollutant, or contaminant."[35] Cleaning and reinvesting in these properties is good for the economy and for the environment. Such use can reduce blight while reducing pressure on greenspaces and working land.[36] The act "promotes the cleanup and redevelopment of brownfields sites through policies, laws, and initiatives that explore sector-based solutions, enhance environmental quality, spur economic development, and revitalize communities."[37] The act exempts certain contributors from potential CERCLA liability and supports state and tribal response programs in cleanup efforts, expands the activities that qualify for funding of state programs, and provides Superfund liability relief for certain properties cleaned up under state programs.[38]

Under the act the EPA awards grants to communities, nonprofit organizations, workforce investment boards, and academic institutions for job training programs intended to lead to cleaning up these contaminated sites and turning them into productive assets within the community.

An Ounce of Prevention

If you are looking to expand your operations by moving to a new facility or a new community, you should consider "derelict land" for the expansion. Such sites can often be obtained at a substantially lower cost than comparable sites away from the center of the community because of the grants available for cleanup and the potential exemption from CERCLA liability. The city may even be willing to seek the initial grants and provide much of the renovation to attract your business, especially if you will provide economic development for the area.

Noise Pollution

When people think of environmental protection, they often think of protecting the air, the water, and the land. They would be likely to think of environmental protection as an effort to reduce and/or to prevent pollution of these natural resources. Not too many are likely to mention noise as an aspect of the environment, nor to think of noise as a type of pollution. This attitude is probably due to the fact that noise seems less noxious to us than filthy water or foul-smelling air. However, studies have shown that there is a direct link between noise and personal health. Noise pollution can cause problems such as stress-related illnesses, high blood pressure, and sleep deprivation. Exposure to excessive noise can lead to hearing impairment. Each of these symptoms, in turn, can lead to health problems and also to lowered productivity. Noise pollution can affect the country's economy as well as the health of its citizens.

Congress first addressed the issue of noise pollution in 1965 when it passed the federal Noise Control Act. Prior to that time, litigants seeking remedies to limit the increasingly higher decibel levels caused by post-World War II urbanization and mechanization relied on common law nuisance theories.

Congress amended the law by passing the Noise Control Act of 1972,[39] hoping to "promote an environment for all Americans free from noise that jeopardizes health or welfare."[40] The act placed responsibility for regulating this area with the EPA. The EPA defines noise pollution as "unwanted or disturbing sounds." According to the EPA, sound becomes "unwanted" when it disturbs normal activities such as sleeping or having a conversation.

These amendments also created the Office of Noise Abatement and Control (ONAC) within the EPA and charged it with overseeing noise-abatement activities and coordinating its programs with those of other federal agencies.

In 1978 Congress passed the Quiet Communities Act, an amendment to the Noise Control Act, to reinforce the significant role that state and local governments play in noise control. The amendments provide federal financial and technical assistance aimed at facilitating state and local research related to noise control and developing noise abatement plans. Similar to the remedies we have seen in other statutes, civil and criminal penalties are possible for violations of the Noise Control Act, as are citizens' suits.

The EPA determined that noise pollution was an issue that would be handled better by state and local governments than by the EPA. As a result, in 1981 the ONAC was terminated and primary responsibility for regulating noise was transferred to the states. However, the EPA still retains oversight authority: It still investigates noise and its impact on citizens, and it provides information and help to state and local agencies dealing with noise issues.[41]

WILDLIFE CONSERVATION

Congress enacted the Endangered Species Act of 1973 (ESA), the world's first attempt to protect wildlife in a comprehensive manner, in an effort to prevent the extinction of various animals and plants. Section 7 of this legislation requires every federal agency, in consultation with the secretary of the interior, to ensure that no agency action is likely to jeopardize the continued existence of an endangered or threatened species or result in the destruction or adverse modification of any critical habitat of such species. (According to scientific estimates, the world loses approximately 100 species per day.[42])

The ESA has helped bring about the stabilization or the improvement of the conditions of about three hundred threatened or endangered species, including the national symbol of the United States, the bald eagle.[43] The impact of the statute reaches beyond the borders of the United States because its prohibitions concern the international trading of wildlife. Its protection of the American habitats of migrating birds also affects transnational interests.

The national commitment to protecting species and their habitats extends beyond mere sentimentality or altruism—fully 40 percent of all ingredients in prescription medicines (including digitalis and penicillin) derive from plants, animals, and micro-organisms.[44] This means that the loss of any given species may involve the loss of the medicinal capacity to save thousands of lives.

There are different degrees of violations provided in the Endangered Species Act. The most severe punishments are for trafficking (smuggling of an endangered species) or any act of knowingly "taking," including the harming, wounding, or killing of an endangered species. The criminal penalties for such violations call for a maximum fine of up to $50,000, imprisonment for one year, or both. Civil penalties of up to $25,000 per violation may be assessed. No penalty can be imposed, however, if the accused can establish that the act was done in self-defense. No criminal penalties can be imposed for the accidental killing of an endangered species while performing farming or ranching duties.

SUSTAINABILITY

Sustainability embodies "stewardship" and "design with nature," well-established goals of the design professions. It also embodies "carrying capacity," a highly developed modeling technique used by scientists and planners.[45]

The most popular definition of sustainability can be traced to a 1987 United Nations conference. It defined sustainable developments as those that "meet present needs without compromising the ability of future generations to meet their needs."[46] Robert Gillman, editor of the *In Context* magazine, extends this goal oriented definition by stating "sustainability refers to a very old and simple concept (The Golden Rule): Do unto future generations as you would have them do unto you."[47]

Sustainability has become a hot topic on college campuses and across industrial lines as the fears of global warming and the renewed interest in environmental protection take root across society.

"Going Green"

Time magazine now runs a weekly news column addressing environmental issues. Exxon recently announced a $600 million partnership with the biotech company Synthetic Genomics Inc. to develop fuel from algae.[48] The public is being asked to change from the traditional incandescent lightbulb to compact fluorescent bulbs to save energy and money. There appears to be a movement in the United States for people and business to "go green."

What does this movement imply for the future? Increased awareness of environmental issues is likely to lead to the development of new industries and new approaches. It could mean an increase in firms seeking ISO 14000 certification. It has already resulted in an increase in CAFÉ regulations for the automobile industry. Other changes are likely, and only time will tell how this will affect business in the future.

INTERNATIONAL ASPECTS

Environmental regulation is not only on the rise in the United States, but around the world as well. While some European countries—Germany and the Netherlands, for example—have traditionally undertaken regulatory efforts that rival those of the United States, in many other countries environmental laws are practically nonexistent. The environmental contamination and degradation found in post-Communist Eastern European countries, besides providing telling examples of what results from lax environmental standards, have discouraged much-needed privatization and foreign investments.

Realizing the need for environmental oversight and modeling its efforts on U.S. legislation, the European Union has adopted the Eco-audit Management and Audit Scheme Regulation, which mandates environmental registers at each plant to catalog pollution emissions, land contamination, and the like; public disclosure of these environmental statements; and external verification of the company's environmental management system. Recently enacted environmental laws covering products now regulate product features (such as shape and recyclability), labeling, packaging, hazardous chemicals, and waste (such as waste generation, trans-boundary shipment, etc.).[49] These laws also ban certain products such as asbestos, heavy metals, and vinyl chloride.

Closer to home, the passage of the North American Free Trade Agreement (NAFTA) also shows sensitivity to environmental concerns. A subsequent environmental side agreement between the United States and Mexico attempts to address the degradation of the environment along the U.S.-Mexican border.

The EPA is working to implement the Montreal Protocol on Substances That Deplete the Ozone Layer, a treaty to which the United States is a signatory nation. As part of its efforts, the EPA will establish and enforce rules aimed at controlling the production and emission of ozone-depleting compounds and at identifying safer alternatives that reduce depletion. The Uruguay Round of the General Agreement on Tariffs and Trade (GATT) included a discussion of environmental issues. The Kyoto Protocol, an international agreement linked to the United Nations Framework Convention on Climate Change, is designed to reduce greenhouse gas emissions. The protocol sets binding targets for the reduction of these emissions for 37 industrialized nations and the European Community. The initial goal of the protocol is for industrialized countries to reduce their combined greenhouse gas emissions by at least 5.2 percent compared to 1990 levels by 2008 to 2012. The protocol became effective in 2005. To date, 184 nations have now ratified the Kyoto Protocol. The United States, the world's largest producer of greenhouse gas emissions, is not one of the ratifying nations.

Contemporary Case

In this case the EPA decided that cost should not be considered in deciding whether to enact new regulations of coal- or oil-fueled electric utility plants. Note the Court's interpretation of "appropriate and necessary" and its decision that cost must be considered in order to satisfy this standard.

MICHIGAN v. ENVIRONMENTAL PROTECTION AGENCY

135 S. Ct. 2699, 2015 U.S. Lexis 4256 (2015)

FACTS The National Emissions Standards for Hazardous Air Pollutants Program targets stationary source emissions of more than 180 specified "hazardous air pollutants." At that same time Congress established a unique procedure for determining the applicability of these standards to fossil-fuel-fired power plants (power plants). The EPA is directed to regulate emissions of hazardous air pollutants from power plants if the agency finds that the regulations are "appropriate and necessary." The EPA appears to have decided that it would regulate power plants in the same manner as it regulated other stationary sources.

Following its investigation, in 2000 the EPA concluded that regulation of coal- and oil-fired power plants was "appropriate and necessary." These findings were reaffirmed in 2012, with the EPA stating that the regulation was appropriate because power plants' emissions of mercury and other hazardous wastes posed risks to human health and to the environment and because controls were available to reduce these emissions. It found the regulations necessary because the imposition of the act's other requirements did not eliminate these risks. The EPA also found that "costs should not be considered" when deciding whether to regulate the power plants in this manner.

The EPA listed a "Regulatory Impact Analysis" with its regulation. This analysis estimated that the cost for power plants to comply with the regulations would be $9.6 billion per year, while the benefits from complying would be between $4 and $6 million per year. Certain expected ancillary results would increase the estimated benefits to $37 to $90 billion per year.

Twenty-three states challenged the EPA's regulations, asserting that it was unreasonable for the EPA to refuse to consider the cost to the power plants in formulating and implementing the regulations. The Court of Appeals upheld the Agency's decision not to consider costs, and the states appealed.

ISSUE Was it reasonable for the EPA to refuse to consider the cost of compliance with the regulations when making its findings?

HOLDING No. The statutory directive of determining whether power plant regulation was "appropriate and necessary" required at least some attention to cost.

REASONING Excerpts from the opinion of Justice Scalia:

... Federal administrative agencies are required to engage in "reasoned decisionmaking." ... "Not only must an agency's decreed result be within the scope of its lawful authority, but the process by which it reaches that result must be logical and rational." ... It follows that agency action is lawful only if it rests "on a consideration of the relevant factors." ...

EPA's decision to regulate power plants under [the statute] ... allowed the Agency to reduce power plants' emissions of hazardous air pollutants and thus to improve public health and the environment. But the decision also ultimately cost power plants, according to the Agency's own estimate, nearly $10 billion a year. EPA refused to consider whether the costs of its decision outweighed the benefits.

The Agency gave cost no thought *at all*, because it considered cost irrelevant to its initial decision to regulate.

EPA's disregard of cost rested on its interpretation of [the statute] ... which ... directs the Agency to regulate power plants if it "finds such regulation is appropriate and necessary." The Agency accepts that it *could* have interpreted this provision to mean that cost is relevant to the decision to add power plants to the program. ... But it chose to read the statute to mean that cost makes no difference to the initial decision to regulate ... ("We further interpret the term 'appropriate' to not allow for the consideration of costs") ... ("Cost does not have to be read into the definition of 'appropriate'").

[Precedent] ... directs courts to accept an agency's reasonable resolution of an ambiguity in a statute that the agency administers. ... Even under this deferential standard, however, "agencies must operate within the bounds of reasonable interpretation." ... EPA strayed far beyond those bounds when it read [the statute] ... to mean that it could ignore cost when deciding whether to regulate power plants.

The Clean Air Act treats power plants differently from other sources for purposes of the hazardous-air-pollutants program. Elsewhere ... Congress established ... criteria for EPA to apply when deciding whether to include sources in the program. It required the Agency to regulate sources whose emissions exceed specified numerical thresholds (major sources). It also required the Agency to regulate sources whose emissions fall short of these thresholds (area sources) if they "presen[t] a threat of adverse effects to human health or the environment ... warranting regulation." ... In stark contrast, Congress instructed EPA to add power plants to the program if (but only if) the Agency finds regulation "appropriate and necessary." ... One does not need to open up a dictionary in order to realize the capaciousness of this phrase. In particular, "appropriate" is "the classic broad and

all-encompassing term that naturally and traditionally includes consideration of all the relevant factors." ... Although this term leaves agencies with flexibility, an agency may not "entirely fai[l] to consider an important aspect of the problem" when deciding whether regulation is appropriate ...

Read naturally in the present context, the phrase "appropriate and necessary" requires at least some attention to cost. One would not say that it is even rational, never mind "appropriate," to impose billions of dollars in economic costs in return for a few dollars in health or environmental benefits. In addition, "cost" includes more than the expense of complying with regulations; any disadvantage could be termed a cost. EPA's interpretation precludes the Agency from considering *any* type of cost—including, for instance, harms that regulation might do to human health or the environment. The Government concedes that if the Agency were to find that emissions from power plants do damage to human health, but that the technologies needed to eliminate these emissions do even more damage to human health, it would *still* deem regulation appropriate. ... No regulation is "appropriate" if it does significantly more harm than good.

There are undoubtedly settings in which the phrase "appropriate and necessary" does not encompass cost. But this is not one of them. ... [The statute] directs EPA to determine whether "*regulation* is appropriate and necessary." ... Agencies have long treated cost as a centrally relevant factor when deciding whether to regulate. Consideration of cost reflects the understanding that reasonable regulation ordinarily requires paying attention to the advantages *and* the disadvantages of agency decisions. It also reflects the reality that "too much wasteful expenditure devoted to one problem may well mean considerably fewer resources available to deal effectively with other (perhaps more serious) problems." ... Against the backdrop of this established administrative practice, it is unreasonable to read an instruction to an administrative agency to determine whether "regulation is appropriate and necessary" as an invitation to ignore cost.

Statutory context reinforces the relevance of cost. The procedures governing power plants that we consider today appear in [the statute.] . . . In subparagraph (A), . . . Congress required EPA to study the hazards to public health posed by power plants and to determine whether regulation is appropriate and necessary. But in subparagraphs (B) and (C), Congress called for two additional studies. One of them, a study into mercury emissions from power plants and other sources, must consider "the health and environmental effects of such emissions, technologies which are available to control such emissions, *and the costs of such technologies.*" . . . This directive to EPA to study cost is a further indication of the relevance of cost to the decision to regulate . . .

EPA argues that the Clean Air Act makes cost irrelevant to the initial decision to regulate sources other than power plants. The Agency claims that it is reasonable to interpret [the statute] in a way that "harmonizes" the program's treatment of power plants with its treatment of other sources. This line of reasoning overlooks the whole point of having a separate provision about power plants: treating power plants *differently* from other stationary sources. Congress crafted narrow standards for EPA to apply when deciding whether to regulate other sources; in general, these standards concern the volume of pollution emitted by the source . . . and the threat posed by the source "to human health or the environment." . . . But Congress wrote the provision before us more expansively, directing the Agency to regulate power plants if "appropriate and necessary." . . .

Our reasoning so far establishes that it was unreasonable for EPA to read [the statute] . . . to mean that cost is irrelevant to the initial decision to regulate power plants. The Agency must consider cost—including, most importantly, cost of compliance—before deciding whether regulation is appropriate and necessary. We need not and do not hold that the law unambiguously required the Agency, when making this preliminary estimate, to conduct a formal cost-benefit analysis in which each advantage and disadvantage is assigned a monetary value. It will be up to the Agency to decide (as always, within the limits of reasonable interpretation) how to account for cost . . .

We hold that EPA interpreted [the statute] unreasonably when it deemed cost irrelevant to the decision to regulate power plants. We reverse the judgment of the Court of Appeals for the D. C. Circuit and remand the cases for further proceedings consistent with this opinion.

Short Answer Questions

1. What is the purpose of NEPA, the National Environmental Policy Act? Do you think this purpose is being satisfied? Explain why you think it is or is not being satisfied.

2. The city of Flint, Michigan is in the midst of a serious drinking water crisis. Several years ago, in the midst of a financial crisis, the state switched Flint's water supply from Lake Huron to the Flint River as a money-saving measure. The water from the Flint River is highly corrosive and apparently its use caused the city's old water lines, many of which are lead, to leach lead at levels substantially above safe levels into the water. A class action lawsuit has been filed against the Michigan Department

of Environmental Quality. The EPA has also been accused of failing to act promptly or more aggressively. How do you think a situation like this should be resolved? Who is ultimately at fault, and what should be done to prevent such events from occurring in the future?

3. The International Organization for Standards (ISO) has developed a series of environmental management standards (ISO 14000) to provide help and guidance to organizations seeking to improve their environmental efforts and images. LEED (Leadership in Energy & Environmental Design) is a "green building" certification program in the United States that recognizes and certifies buildings that are environmentally "friendly." Why might a firm decide to seek ISO 14000 certification for its operations or LEED certification for its buildings? What benefits might the firm gain? What costs would be incurred?

You Decide...

1. In 2004, eight states, the City of New York, and three private land trusts filed suit in the district court against five major electric utilities, four private companies, and the Tennessee Valley Authority (TVA). The complaint alleged that these utilities were creating a nuisance by their discharge of carbon dioxide into the atmosphere. These discharges were allegedly causing climate change, which resulted in injuries to the citizens and to the environment. They were seeking an injunction controlling or limiting these emissions (by having the court establish acceptable carbon-dioxide standards) against the utilities, under either federal or state common law nuisance principles.

The six utilities argued that the petitioners lacked standing to sue and that the complaint was "non-justiciable" since the issue raised was a "political question."

The district court dismissed the complaint on the grounds that the issue was a "political question," and not subject to court jurisdiction. On appeal, the Second Circuit reversed, finding that the issue was not a political question, that the complainants did have standing, and that they had stated a valid claim under federal common law. The Supreme Court granted *certiorari*.

How would you decide this case? Did the complaint state a valid nuisance claim under federal common law? Explain and justify your answer.

(See American Electric Power Co. v. Connecticut, 131 S. Ct. 2527, 2011 U.S. LEXIS 4565 (2011))

2. A relatively steady wind blows through the St. Lawrence Valley in Canada and Vermont. To take advantage of this steady wind, Encore Redevelopment, a Burlington, Vermont business, plans to erect wind turbines near the Vermont-Canada border. Each turbine is expected to generate enough electricity to power 900 homes.

These proposed wind turbines would be within 1,000 feet of several homes on the Canadian side of the border, although the turbines would be on U.S. soil. In Quebec, Canada, there is a law that no wind turbines can be erected with 1,640 feet of a home. There is no such statute in Vermont or in the United States. Vermont determines the distance a turbine must be placed from homes by the sound the spinning blades produce. According to Encore Redevelopment, the planned location meets the Vermont requirement. This has created a great deal of tension in the local communities on each side of the border.

The Vermont farmers support the project. They expect the turbines to provide a steady flow of income, a welcome addition to the local economy. However, the Canadian citizens oppose the project, complaining about the potential negative impact on their quality of life.

Assume that the parties agree to submit this dispute to binding arbitration.

You have been selected as the arbitrator. How would *you* decide this case? Be certain that you explain and justify your answer.

Should Encore only worry about complying with U.S. law since they will be in the United States, or should it also attempt to comply with Canadian law even though Canada has no jurisdiction here? What issues should be considered in making the final decision?

(See "Canadians Near Vermont Border Complain Wind Turbine Plan Hits Too Close to Home." *The Washington Post*, May 17, 2012, http://www.washingtonpost.com/world/the_americas/plan-for-wind-turbines-in-vermont-creates-international-furor-homeowners-in-canada-object/2012/05/17/gIQA7cuIVU_story.html (accessed May 12, 2012).)

Notes

1. John Henry Davidson & Orlando E. Delogu, *Federal Environmental Regulation*, 2 vols. (Salem, NH: Butterworth Legal Publishers, 1994); Roger W. Findley and Daniel A. Farber, *Environmental Law in a Nutshell*, 4th ed. (Minneapolis: West Publishing Co., 1996); and William H. Rodgers, Jr., *Handbook on Environmental Law*, 2nd ed. (Minneapolis: West Publishing Co., 1994) provide more detailed and comprehensive information concerning environmental law.
2. "Safer Consumer Products," California Department of Toxic Substances Control, https://www.dtsc.ca.gov/SCP/SaferConsumerProductsProgram.cfm (accessed March 1, 2016).
3. "U.S. Environmental Protection Agency and DTSC Broaden California's Push for Safer Consumer Products through Key Alliance," EPA Web site, https://www3.epa.gov/region9/mediacenter/greenchem/ (accessed March 1, 2016).
4. *Black's Law Dictionary*, 6th ed. (St. Paul: The West Group, 1990), 1065.
5. *Id.*, 130.
6. 42 U.S.C. § 4321 *et seq.*
7. Sec. 2 [42 U.S.C. § 4331].
8. Sec. 102 [42 U.S.C. § 4332].
9. At least 15 states, Puerto Rico, and the District of Columbia have enacted SEPA—or "mini-NEPA"—legislation.
10. Congressional Declaration of Intent, National Environmental Policy Act, 42 U.S.C. § 4321.
11. The EPA is also charged with materials regulation and health and safety regulations. It protects and studies the natural biosystems, monitors radiation exposure, and chemical and product safety, as well.
12. Public Law 84-159.
13. Public Law 88-206.
14. Jonathan R. Nash, "If not a historic agreement, then a historic step–Obama, China and climate change," *The Hill* (November 14, 2014). http://thehill.com/blogs/pundits-blog/energy-environment/224335-if-not-a-historic-agreement-then-a-historic-step-obama (accessed May 11, 2016).
15. "Clean Power Plan for Existing Power Plants," Environmental Protection Agency Web site, http://www.epa.gov/cleanpowerplan/clean-power-plan-existing-power-plants (accessed February 14, 2016).
16. "Paris Agreement," *Climate Action*, European Commission Web site, http://ec.europa.eu/clima/policies/international/negotiations/future/index_en.htm (accessed February 14, 2016).
17. Sharon Fabian, "Leaded Gasoline Becomes a Thing of the Past," http://edhelper.com/ReadingComprehension_54_1448.html (accessed May 11, 2016).
18. Gary Z. Whitten, *Air Quality and Ethanol In Gasoline*, "Ethanol in gasoline can favorably impact mobile source emissions in five main air quality areas." http://www.ethanolrfa.org/wp-content/uploads/2015/09/nec_whitten.pdf (accessed May 11, 2016).
19. The Energy Independence and Security Act signed into law on December 19, 2007 mandates a 40 percent increase in fuel economy by 2020.
20. Csaba Csere, "How Automakers Will Meet 2016 CAFÉ Standards," *Car and Driver* (May 2010), http://www.caranddriver.com/features/how-automakers-will-meet-2016-cafe-standards (accessed February 14, 2016).
21. Wayne Cunningham, "New CAFÉ rules nearly double fuel economy by 2025," *CNET reviews* (July 29, 2011). http://www.cnet.com/roadshow/news/new-cafe-rules-nearly-double-fuel-economy-by-2025/ (accessed May 11, 2016).
22. Russell Hotten, "Volkswagen: The scandal explained," BBC News (December 10, 2015), http://www.bbc.com/news/business-34324772 (accessed February 14, 2016).
23. 33 U.S.C. § 401 *et seq.*
24. 33 U.S.C. §§ 1251-1387.

25. 42 U.S.C. §§ 300(f)-300(j)(5).

26. Neela Banerjee, "Fracking Has Contaminated Drinking Water, EPA Now Concludes," Inside Climate News (June 5, 2015), http://insideclimatenews.org/news/05062015/fracking-has-contaminated-drinking-water-epa-now-concludes (accessed February 14, 2016).

27. EPA Regulations, 40 CFR 230.3(t).

28. 16 U.S.C. §§ 1401-1445.

29. 33 U.S.C. §§ 2701-2761.

30. Thomas D. Hopkins, "Oil Spill Reduction and Costs of Ship Design Regulation," *Contemporary Policy Issues* 10 (1992): 59. Abstract available at https://www.researchgate.net/publication/5208943_Oil_Spill_Reduction_and_Costs_of_Ship_Design_Regulation (accessed May 11, 2016).

31. *Ibid.* It was estimated in 1992 that these new standards might increase the cost of shipping oil to the United States by as much as $2 billion per year.

32. "Definitions of Waters of the United States Under The Clean Water Act," EPA Web site, https://www.epa.gov/cleanwaterrule/definition-waters-united-states-under-clean-water-act (accessed May 11, 2016).

33. "Oil Pollution Act," *The Environment, A Global Challenge*, http://library.thinkquest.org/26026/Politics/oil_pollution_act.html (accessed May 30, 2012).

34. Bobby McGill, "Obama Halts Federal Coal Leasing Citing Climate Change," *Scientific American* (January 15, 2016), http://www.scientificamerican.com/article/obama-halts-federal-coal-leasing-citing-climate-change/ (accessed February 14, 2016).

35. "Brownfield Overview and Definition," EPA Web site, https://www.epa.gov/brownfields/brownfield-overview-and-definition (accessed May 11, 2016).

36. "Brownfields and Land Revitalization," EPA Web site, http://epa.gov/brownfields/index.html (accessed February 14, 2016).

37. *Ibid.*

38. "Benefits of Brownfields Legislation—Summary of Public Law 107-118," EPA Web site, https://www.epa.gov/brownfields/benefits-brownfields-legislation-summary-public-law-107-118 (accessed May 11, 2016).

39. 49 U.S.C. §§ 4901-4918.

40. Noise Control Act of 1972, http://www.pollutionissues.com/Na-Ph/Noise-Control-Act-of-1972.html (accessed February 14, 2016).

41. "Noise Pollution," EPA Web site, https://www.epa.gov/clean-air-act-overview/title-iv-noise-pollution (accessed May 11, 2016).

42. Tim Eichenberg & Robert Irvin, "Congress Takes Aim at Endangered Species Act," *The National Law Journal*, December 13, 1995, A21.

43. *Ibid.*

44. *Id.,* A21-A22.

45. *Defining Sustainability*, http://www.arch.wsu.edu/09%20publications/sustain/defnsust.htm (accessed May 30, 2012).

46. Robert Gillman, World Commission on Environment and Development (WCED), United Nations Conference (1987).

47. *Ibid.*

48. "Exxon Makes First Big Biofuel Investment," *MSNBC.com.* http://www.msnbc.msn.com/id/31906381/ns/business-us_business/t/exxon-makes-first-big-biofuel-investment/#.T8YkhFL5OuY (accessed February 14, 2016).

49. Turner Y. Smith, Jr., "Environmental Regulation on the Rise Worldwide," *The National Law Journal* (September 1994), C15-C16.

20

Labor and Fair Employment Practices

Learning Objectives

After completing this chapter you should be able to

- Explain the development of U.S. labor law
- Recognize and discuss the areas covered by U.S. labor law
- Understand the difference between labor law and employment law
- Define bona fide occupational qualifications (BFOQs)
- Describe the difference between disparate impact and disparate treatment
- Identify conduct that may constitute sexual harassment
- Discuss other types of discrimination and the protections provided for victims of discrimination

Classic Case

The Classic Case for this chapter is a significant Supreme Court decision interpreting the Civil Rights Act of 1964. The court stated that employers' job requirements must relate to the job duties. Employers cannot impose job requirements simply because they believe that the requirements will improve the quality of their workforce.

GRIGGS v. DUKE POWER CO.

401 U.S. 424 (1971)

FACTS This suit was filed by 13 black employees who worked at Duke Power Company's Dan River Steam Station. [The authors will use "black." People also use the term African American. The Court uses the label "Negroes," which was the socially correct term at the time.] Prior to the Civil Rights Act of 1964, Duke Power openly discriminated on the basis of race. The plant was organized into five operating departments. Blacks were employed only in the Labor Department. In 1965 when the company abandoned its policy of limiting blacks to the Labor Department, it made high school graduation a requirement for transfer from the Labor Department to any other department. The company added a requirement for new employees hired on or after July 2, 1965, the date on which the Civil Rights Act became effective. To qualify for positions in all departments except the Labor Department applicants had to have a high school education and to achieve satisfactory scores on two professionally prepared aptitude tests. Neither test was created or intended to measure the ability to learn to perform a particular job or category of jobs. The test standards were more stringent than the high school requirement, since they would screen out approximately half of all high school graduates. The 1960 North Carolina census data shows that 34 percent of white males had completed high school, and only 12 percent of black males had done so.

The Equal Employment Opportunity Commission (EEOC) found that use of a battery of standardized tests, including these particular tests, resulted in 58 percent of whites passing the tests, as compared to only 6 percent of blacks. There was no showing of a racial purpose or offensive intent in the adoption of the high school diploma requirement or general intelligence tests. These standards have been applied fairly to whites and blacks alike.

ISSUE Does the Civil Rights Act of 1964 prohibit an employer from requiring a high school education or the passing of standardized general intelligence tests as a condition of employment in or transfer to jobs when (1) neither standard is shown to be significantly related to successful job performance; (2) both requirements operate to disqualify black applicants at a substantially higher rate than white applicants; and (3) the jobs in the past had been filled only by white employees as part of a longstanding practice of giving preference to whites?

HOLDING Yes, the Civil Rights Act prohibits the use of these requirements.

REASONING Excerpts from the opinion of Chief Justice Burger writing for a unanimous court:

. . . The objective of Congress in the enactment of Title VII is plain from the language of the statute. It was to achieve equality of employment opportunities and remove barriers that have operated . . . to favor an identifiable group of white employees over other employees. . . . [P]ractices, procedures, or tests neutral on their face, and even neutral in terms of intent, cannot be maintained if they operate to "freeze" the status quo of prior discriminatory employment practices. . . . Congress did not intend by Title VII . . . to guarantee a job to every person regardless of qualifications. . . . What is required . . .

is the removal of artificial, arbitrary, and unnecessary barriers to employment when the barriers operate invidiously to discriminate on the basis of racial or other impermissible classification.

... The Act proscribes not only overt discrimination but also practices that are fair in form, but discriminatory in operation.... If an employment practice which operates to exclude Negroes cannot be shown to be related to job performance, the practice is prohibited.... [N]either the high school completion requirement nor the general intelligence test is shown to bear a ... demonstrable relationship to successful performance of the jobs for which it was used. Both were adopted ... without meaningful study of their relationship to job-performance ability.... [T]he requirements were instituted on the Company's judgment that they ... would improve the overall quality of the work force. The evidence ... shows that employees who have not completed high school or taken the tests have continued to perform satisfactorily

and make progress. ... Congress directed the thrust of the Act to the *consequences* of employment practices, not simply the motivation. ... Congress has placed on the employer the burden of showing that any given requirement must have a manifest relationship to the employment in question.

... Nothing in the Act precludes the use of testing or measuring procedures. ... What Congress has forbidden is giving these devices and mechanisms controlling force unless they are ... a reasonable measure of job performance. Congress has not commanded that the less qualified be preferred over the better qualified simply because of minority origins. Far from disparaging job qualifications as such, Congress has made such qualifications the controlling factor, so that race, religion, nationality, and sex become irrelevant. ...

The judgment of the Court of Appeals is, as to that portion of the judgment appealed from, reversed.

INTRODUCTION

Labor law and fair employment law provide the framework under which workers are regulated and protected. Labor law deals with the relationship between management and the workers. It tends to view the workers as a group, and provides for group protection. It defines unfair labor practices and unfair management practices. Fair employment practices law deals with employer rights and responsibilities that help to guarantee the equitable treatment of all the employees. Fair employment practices view the workers as individuals and provides for the protection of each worker within the employment setting. There are both federal and state protections. Each of these areas is in a state of change that requires the businessperson to check the laws regularly for new rules. Many federal and state laws require that employers provide written notice to employees. Employers often comply with this requirement by posting appropriate signs in the workplace and/or including the information in employee manuals. However, the fact that an employee is given written notice does not mean that the employer can act with impunity. Consider the following situation:

Dawnmarie Souza was employed by American Medical Response (AMR) as an emergency medical technician. AMR had a policy that said that employees could not depict the company in any way on social media sites. It also had a policy that prohibited "employees from making 'disparaging' or 'discriminatory' 'comments when discussing the company or the employee's superiors' and 'co-workers.'"[1] Despite these policies, Souza criticized her boss on Facebook. She also mocked her supervisor and said, "love how the company allows a 17 to become a supervisor" (17 is the company's lingo for a psychiatric patient). Souza's comments were followed by supportive comments from her coworkers. Souza made the postings on her own time using her own computer. AMR fired Souza for violating the company's policies, and Souza filed a complaint with the National Labor Relations Board (NLRB).

The NLRB sided with Souza, deciding that her comments were protected. Employees are entitled to talk about their employment and they are entitled to do so face-to-face and/or on-line. The NLRB also took issue with the company policy that prohibited employees from making negative comments about the company, superiors, and co-workers.[2] The case between the NLRB and AMR was ultimately settled, and the employer agreed to change some of its policies.[3] (When disputes are settled without litigation they do not provide precedents, so other employees facing similar policies may not be as fortunate as Souza was in her dispute.)

LABOR LAWS

Federal Labor Laws

Unions are commonplace in the United States today. But this was not always so. The rise of unionism in the United States was marked by violence and bloody battles. The courts were hostile to unions. In the 1800s and early 1900s, both state and federal courts viewed workers' concerted activities (such as strikes and picketing) as common law criminal conspiracies, tortious interference with contract, and/or antitrust violations. The Sherman Act was initially used against unions since union activities were viewed as "combinations in restraint of trade." Exhibit 20.1 provides an overview of the most significant federal labor laws.

The Norris-LaGuardia Act (1932) Congress passed the Norris-LaGuardia Act to protect certain activities from negative federal court decisions, for example peaceful *strikes* (organized refusals to work), *boycotts* (concerted refusals to deal with firms so as to disrupt their business), and *picketing* (demonstrations near a business to publicize a labor dispute and to encourage the public to refuse to do business with the employer). The act allowed employees to organize and to engage in collective bargaining free from court or employer intervention, as long as the concerted activity did not involve *wildcat strikes* (unauthorized withholdings of services or labor during the term of a contract),

Exhibit 20.1

Significant Labor Statutes

Name of Statute	Behavior Allowed or Prohibited
Norris-LaGuardia Act (Labor Disputes Act) [1932]	Protects certain activities from federal court action; activities protected include peaceful refusals to work, boycotts, and picketing. It also promotes collective bargaining.
Wagner Act (National Labor Relations Act) [1935]	Allows employees to organize and to engage in collective bargaining; specifies employer unfair labor practices; establishes the National Labor Relations Board (NLRB).
Taft-Hartley Act (Labor Management Relations Act) [1947]	Prohibits unfair labor practices by unions; separates the NLRB's functions; empowers courts to grant various civil and criminal remedies; creates the Federal Mediation and Conciliation Service.
Landrum-Griffin Act (Labor Management Reporting and Disclosure Act) [1959]	Requires extensive reporting of unions' financial affairs; allows civil and criminal sanctions for union officers' financial wrong-doings; mandates democratic procedures in the conduct of union elections and meetings.

violence, sabotage, trespass, and similar activities. The underlying policy was aimed at keeping the courts out of labor disputes. Employees and employers could advance their respective goals using the economic tools available to them. Consequently unions resorted to strikes, picketing, and boycotts; and the employers discharged employees.

The Wagner Act (1935)   The Wagner Act, also called the National Labor Relations Act, began a positive approach to labor organizations. Congress approved the right of employees to organize themselves and "to form, join, or assist labor organizations, to bargain collectively through representatives of their own choosing, and to engage in concerted activities for the purpose of collective bargaining or other mutual aid or protection." The right to refrain from engaging in concerted activities is protected as well. The act lists employer *unfair labor practices* such as (1) coercion of or retaliation against employees who exercise their rights; (2) domination of unions by employers; (3) discrimination in employment (hiring and firing, for instance) designed to discourage union activities; and (4) refusals by employers to bargain collectively and in good faith with employee unions. It sets out the process for conducting secret elections for employees to choose their representative in the collective bargaining process.[4] The Wagner Act also established a new administrative agency, the National Labor

Relations Board (NLRB), to oversee such elections and to investigate and remedy unfair labor practices.

The Taft-Hartley Act (1947)   After the Wagner Act was passed, unions grew in size and influence. As a result, the balance of power shifted toward unions. Consequently, Congress passed the Taft-Hartley Act, also called the Labor Management Relations Act (LMRA), in an attempt to adjust the balance of power and to curb union excesses. It prohibited certain unfair labor practices by unions, including (1) engaging in *secondary boycotts* (boycotts at an employer's customers or suppliers in an attempt to influence the employer); (2) forcing an employer to discriminate against employees on the basis of their union affiliation or lack of union affiliation; (3) refusing to bargain in good faith; (4) requiring an employer to pay for services not actually performed by an employee (*featherbedding*); and (5) *recognitional picketing* (picketing in which a union attempts to force recognition of a different union from the one that has been certified). It also allowed employees to refrain from joining a union and participating in its collective activities.

The Taft-Hartley Act decreased the NLRB's authority by separating the NLRB's functions. The Office of General Counsel became responsible for prosecuting the unfair labor practices cases. The decision-making (or *adjudicatory*) function remained with the five-person NLRB. This reconfiguration significantly changed the nature of the NLRB, which previously had served as both prosecutor and decision maker. The Taft-Hartley Act also (1) empowered courts of appeals to set aside NLRB decisions concerning unfair labor practices where it was appropriate; (2) authorized district courts to issue injunctions requested by the NLRB to stop unfair labor practices; (3) created fines and imprisonment for anyone resisting NLRB orders; and (4) provided for civil remedies for private parties damaged by secondary boycotts or various union activities. NLRB orders now become law only when imposed by a federal circuit court of appeals. This limits the NLRB's enforcement powers. If the court affirms the NLRB order, the court issues an injunction. In the meantime, the allegedly unfair labor practices may continue and may stifle the opponent's interests.

Other sections (1) protect the employer's right of free speech (by refusing to characterize as unfair labor practices an employer's expressions of its opinions about unions when the expressions contain no threats of reprisal); (2) preserve the employees' rights to engage in peaceful informational picketing; and (3) prohibit *closed shop agreements* that obligate the employer to hire and retain only union members. When United Food and Commercial Workers (UFCW) attempted to unionize a Smithfield Foods meatpacking plant, both the plant manager and the company president told the employees that they did not favor the union. They also repeatedly told the employees about the history of the plant. The facility had been owned by three other companies in the past: Each time after the UFCW unionized the workers, the plant closed. The Smithfield manager and president said in their statements that they were not sure that the union caused the closures, they could not predict the future, and that they wanted the plant to be a success. The court affirmed the NLRB's decision that the company was not threatening the employees with plant closure.[5]

While closed shop agreements are prohibited, *union shop* clauses that require an employee to join a union after being hired are legal. The Taft-Hartley Act also created a Federal Mediation and Conciliation Service for settling disputes between labor and management. It requires a cooling-off period in certain situations before strikes can occur. States can prohibit certain union techniques designed to consolidate the unions' power under the states' right-to-work laws. Right-to-work laws are discussed later in this chapter.

The Landrum-Griffin Act (1959)   By the 1950s, Congress had discovered substantial corruption among union leaders. Union members had been harmed by officers' plundering of union treasuries and by officers' often oppressive treatment of the rank-and-file members. Congress responded with the Landrum-Griffin Act, also called the Labor Management Reporting and Disclosure Act (LMRDA). This act (1) requires extensive reporting of financial affairs; (2) allows civil and criminal sanctions for financial wrongs by union officers; and (3) mandates democratic procedures in the conduct of union affairs by providing a "bill of rights" for union members. The Landrum-Griffin Act amended portions of the Taft-Hartley Act to outlaw *hot cargo clauses* (clauses that required the employer to cease doing business with nonunion companies).

Covered Workers   These federal statutes apply to most employers and employees. The acts exempt employees covered under the Railway Labor Act; agricultural workers; domestic workers; independent contractors; most supervisors; and federal, state, and local government employees.[6] Federal, state, and local government employees may be permitted to engage in collective bargaining under various executive orders and statutes.

State Labor Laws

The supremacy clause of the Constitution empowers Congress to pass laws that will preempt the states' ability to regulate labor law. The Supreme Court has held that federal preemption powers are broad in this area. Because of the NLRB's expertise and a desire for uniform results, federal laws ordinarily will supersede state laws governing the same or similar activities.

Matters that only marginally affect the federal statutory scheme or matters that are of deep local concern may constitute legitimate state interests that state legislatures and courts may control. The law in this area is unsettled. Generally, state courts can adjudicate lawsuits involving damages from criminal or tortious activity, retaliatory discharges, and those causes of action covering employees excluded from the federal statutes. States may enforce any right-to-work statutes that they have enacted.[7] A *right to work law* is a statute that prohibits requiring union membership as a condition for employment. In other words, a state can prohibit "agency shop" agreements between unions and management.

Exhibit 20.2

Federal Employment Statutes

Name of Statute	Type of Protection	Covered Employers and Employees[a]
Social Security Act [1935]	Provides federal benefits to retired workers, disabled workers, and the workers' spouses and minor children.	Most employers and people who are self-employed. Some state and local governments do not participate in Social Security and have created their own retirement system. Some churches and religious organizations are exempt.[b]
Federal Unemployment Tax Act [1954]	Provides (through a coordinated federal and state effort) economic security for temporarily unemployed workers.	Employers who paid wages of $1,500 or more to employees in any calendar quarter during the current or prior calendar year; also employers who had one or more full- or part-time employees for at least some part of a day in any 20 or more different weeks in the current or prior calendar year.[c]
Equal Pay Act [1963]	Prohibits discrimination in wages on the basis of sex.	Executive, administrative, and professional employees; outside sales people; and all employees who are covered by the federal minimum wage laws.
Title VII of the Civil Rights Act [1964]	Prohibits discrimination in the terms, conditions, and privileges of employment on the basis of color, race, religion, sex, or national origin.	Employers in interstate commerce with 15 or more full- or part-time employees for each working day in each of 20 or more weeks in the current calendar year or the prior calendar year; includes federal, state, and local governments; also applies to national or international labor organizations and employment agencies.
Age Discrimination in Employment Act [1967]	Protects certain workers (in general those aged 40-70) from discrimination in employment based on age.	All private employers with 20 or more full- or part-time employees for each working day in each of 20 or more weeks in the current calendar year or the prior calendar year; includes state and local governments, employment agencies, and labor organizations.[d]
Occupational Safety and Health Act [1970]	Mandates safe and healthful workplace conditions.	Most employers that are involved in interstate commerce and employ at least one employee. Atomic energy workers are not covered.
Pregnancy Discrimination Act [1978]	Protects workers from pregnancy-related discrimination based on pregnancy or pregnancy-related symptoms. Amends Title VII.	Employers in interstate commerce with 15 or more full- or part-time employees for each working day in each of 20 or more weeks in the current calendar year or the prior calendar year; includes federal, state, and local governments; also applies to national or international labor organizations and employment agencies.

Exhibit 20.2 Continued

Name of Statute	Type of Protection	Covered Employers and Employees[a]
Consolidated Omnibus Budget Reconciliation Act (COBRA) [1985]	Allows employees or qualified beneficiaries to extend their coverage under the employer's group health insurance for a period of time; the employee or beneficiary has to pay the entire premium for the coverage.	Employers with 20 or more employees on a typical business day during the last quarter; does not apply to churches or government entities.
Immigration Reform and Control Act [1986]	Prohibits immigration-related discrimination based on national origin or citizenship status.	Employers with four or more employees.
Title I of the Americans with Disabilities Act [1990]	Protects disabled workers from employment discrimination. Disabilities are defined as physical or mental impairments that sub-stantially limit one or more major life activity.	Employers with 15 or more full- or part-time employees for each working day in each of 20 or more weeks in the current calendar year or the prior calendar year; also applies to labor organizations and employment agencies; exempts religious entities.
Civil Rights Act [1991]	Amends earlier civil rights statutes to broaden the scope of protections afforded under anti-discrimination law; prohibits "race norming" of employment tests.	Employers in interstate commerce with 15 or more full- or part-time employees for each working day in each of 20 or more weeks in the current calendar year or the prior calendar year; includes federal, state, and local governments; also applies to national or international labor organizations and employment agencies.
Family and Medical Leave Act [1993]	Mandates that eligible employees receive up to 12 weeks of leave during any 12-month period for certain family- or medical-related events.	Public employers of any size and private employers with 50 or more employees for each working day in each of 20 or more weeks in the current calendar year or the prior calendar year.
Lilly Ledbetter Fair Pay Act [2009]	Specifies that the statute of limitations to file a suit based on pay discrimination begins to run with each discriminatory pay check. Amends Title VII, the Age Discrimination in Employment Act, and the Americans with Disabilities Act.	Victims of pay discrimination who do not learn of the discrimination until sometime after it began.

Source: Courtesy of Lynn M. Forsythe. © 2016.

[a] The federal government's control of employment is generally based on the Commerce Clause and is limited to enterprises involved in interstate commerce.

[b] This only describes new employment. For example, in the past self-employed workers, federal government workers, members of the military, and workers for nonprofit organizations were not covered. Past employees of this type may or may not receive benefits due to complicated rules.

[c] IRS 2015 Instructions for Form 940, http://www.irs.gov/pub/irs-pdf/i940.pdf (accessed May 12, 2016). The dollar limit is different for household employees. IRS Publication 15 (2016), *Employer's Tax Guide*, pp. 2 and 38, https://www.irs.gov/pub/irs-pdf/p15.pdf (accessed May 12, 2016) and IRS Publication 51 Agricultural Employer's Tax Guide (2016), https://www.irs.gov/pub/irs-pdf/p51.pdf (accessed May 12, 2016).

[d] "Federal Laws Prohibiting Job Discrimination, Questions and Answers," http://www.eeoc.gov/facts/qanda.html (accessed May 12, 2016).

FAIR EMPLOYMENT PRACTICES LAWS

Federal and state governments have enacted statutes to ensure equal employment opportunity for persons historically disadvantaged in the workplace. Exhibit 20.2 provides an overview of the most significant federal employment laws.

The Civil Rights Act of 1964

One of the most important of these laws is the Civil Rights Act of 1964. Title VII of this act prohibits discrimination in employment on the basis of color, race, religion, sex, or national origin. Under Title VII, an employer cannot lawfully make decisions to hire, discharge, compensate, or establish the terms, conditions, or privileges of employment for any employee based on these protected categories. In addition, an employer cannot segregate, limit, or classify employees or applicants for employment in discriminatory ways. Title VII generally covers (1) employers in interstate commerce that have on their weekly payrolls at least fifteen full- or part-time employees[8] for at least twenty weeks per year; (2) any national or international labor organizations that consist of at least fifteen members or that operate a hiring hall; and (3) employment agencies that regularly obtain employees for employers or work opportunities for potential employees. In addition none of these three groups can discriminate against any individual who has opposed unlawful employment practices.

Title VII authorized the creation of the Equal Employment Opportunity Commission (EEOC), a bipartisan, five-member panel appointed by the president to enforce the various equal employment opportunities statutes. The EEOC is currently the enforcement agency for a number of statutes including (1) Title VII; (2) the Pregnancy Discrimination Act; (3) the Equal Pay Act; (4) the Age Discrimination in Employment Act; (5) the Americans with Disabilities Act; and (6) the Civil Rights Act (1991). The EEOC also can bring lawsuits relating to broad patterns of discrimination. Its jurisdiction may be triggered by complaints by individuals, charges filed by the EEOC, or charges filed by a state fair employment or human rights commission.

Recently, some employers have begun asking applicants and employees to divulge the usernames and passwords to their social media accounts. One concern about this practice is that the employer will discover information that the employer is not allowed to ask directly, including the race and religion of the applicant or employee. There seems to be a trend by state legislatures to prohibit this practice.[9]

Disparate Treatment   Employers may be liable for the *disparate treatment* of their employees. Such cases may involve an employer who only considers women for clerical positions, only considers men for positions on an assembly line, or only considers white males for managerial positions. An employer that allows whites or males to break rules without penalty but punishes blacks, Hispanics, Asians, or women who break the same rules is also likely to be found guilty of disparate treatment. The reverse is also true.[10]

Disparate Impact   Selection criteria that seem outwardly neutral may actually preclude members of one or more protected classes from jobs. This was the issue in the Classic Case for this chapter. For example, statistically fewer blacks than whites may graduate from high school. Any job requirement that prevents a disproportionate number of blacks or other minorities from securing employment or promotion has a *disparate impact* (that is, an unequal effect) on minorities and may be illegal. The EEOC and the courts look at statistical evidence to determine if there is a disparate impact. One statistic that is used is the 4/5 rule set out by the EEOC.[11] Under the 4/5 rule, if the selection rate for a protected class is less than 4/5 (or 80 percent) of the selection rate for the group with the highest selection rate, this constitutes statistical evidence that there is a disparate impact. For a simple example, if 90 percent of the white applicants are accepted (and they are the group with the highest selection rate) and only 30 percent of the Asian applicants are accepted, then the 4/5 rule is violated. Asian applicants would have to be accepted at a rate of 72 percent or more under the rule (4/5 of the 90 percent acceptance rate for white applicants). The 4/5 rule is some evidence but it is not conclusive. A test that violates the 4/5 rule can still be shown to be non-discriminatory by other proof, such as a showing that the sample size was not typical in this instance.[12] One the other hand, a test may be shown to create a disparate impact by other means even if it does not violate the 4/5 rule. For example, the Supreme Court has recognized that a statistical disparity of more than two standard deviations from the mean creates an inference of discrimination.[13]

Once the plaintiff has made his or her initial case, the employer has the burden of proving either that (1) the employment practice does not cause a disparate impact or (2) that the requirement is legitimately related to the position (a *bona fide* occupational qualification, or BFOQ). As one might expect, there is a significant amount of litigation over whether a requirement is a BFOQ. The plaintiff may respond to a claim that a requirement is a BFOQ by showing that the requirement is a pretext for unlawful discrimination. (A *pretext* is a false or weak motive used to hide the real or strong motive.)

An Ounce of Prevention

You should strive to provide equal opportunities to applicants of all colors, genders, races, religions, and national origins. It is required by the law and also may help you attract customers or clients from diverse backgrounds. You should include a statement in advertisements and position announcements that you are an equal employment opportunity (EEO) enterprise. During the interview process, you should strive to hide any personal biases that you may have. For example, you should not say anything negative about a woman's ability to do the job. You should also be careful about your nonverbal communication. In other words, conceal negative feelings when you interview an older applicant or a disabled applicant. Negative statements or nonverbal communication may cause an applicant to initiate a lawsuit.

Affirmative Action Plans   The term *reverse discrimination* refers to claims by whites that they have been subjected to adverse employment decisions because of their race. Affirmative action plans and resulting allegations of reverse discrimination are very controversial. There are two sets of interests that clash. There are those of the minority candidate who in the past may have been disadvantaged because of race. There are also those of the white candidate who did not participate in this discrimination but who now loses opportunities because the employer is seeking to bring about equal opportunity for minority workers. Some employers and universities continue to try to develop affirmative action plans that will survive judicial review. The EEOC also attempts to provide guidance on how to develop a lawful affirmative action plan that complies with Title VII.

Religious Discrimination   Title VII also prohibits religious discrimination. Sincere religious beliefs (or the lack thereof) are protected under Title VII. Under Title VII, the employer must make a "reasonable accommodation" to the employee's religious beliefs unless doing so would pose an "undue hardship" on the conduct of the business. Problem areas include scheduling an employee to work on his or her Sabbath and restrictions on beards, length of hair, and clothing that are mandated by an employee's religion. Kimberly Cloutier wore an eyebrow ring as a symbol of her affiliation with the Church of Body Modification. She was employed by Costco Wholesale Corp., which had a policy prohibiting employees from wearing visible facial or tongue jewelry except for earrings. Cloutier asked for an accommodation for her religion. Costco informed her that she could cover the jewelry with an adhesive bandage or insert a clear plastic retainer in its place. She refused to do so. She argued that the only reasonable accommodation was to allow her to wear her piercings. The court decided that Costco had no duty to accommodate Cloutier because Costco could not do so without undue hardship. Costco had a legitimate interest in requiring its employees to be reasonably professional in their appearance.[14] Notice the approach the Supreme Court took to accommodations in the Contemporary Case in this chapter.

Bona Fide Occupational Qualifications (BFOQs)   Religion, sex, or national origin can be a BFOQ. Race, however, cannot. Private educational institutions may make religion a BFOQ. Loyola University of Chicago, a Jesuit university, refused to consider Jerrold Pime for a full-time tenure track position in its philosophy department because he was Jewish. The court upheld the university's decision to hold the full-time tenure track positions for Jesuits.[15] A movie director can cast only women in women's roles for authenticity. A restaurant can hire only women to be restroom attendants in the women's restroom. However, the fact that an employer or his or her customers *prefer* men or women in a particular occupation does not make gender a BFOQ. Problem areas for some employers include (1) their stereotypes about employees' ability to perform a job; (2) height/weight requirements that are not job-related (women usually are smaller than men); and (3) so-called sex-plus cases. In sex-plus cases, the employer adds a selection criterion for women that is not added for men (such as when women with preschool-aged children are not hired, but men who have such children are).

Sexual Harassment   Title VII attempts to protect employees from sexual harassment in the workplace by imposing liability on the harassing party and, possibly, on the employer. There are two types of sexual harassment recognized under Title VII: Quid pro quo, in which a supervisor requests sexual favors in exchange for employment benefits or opportunities; and hostile workplace sexual harassment, which involves misconduct that creates an intimidating, hostile, or offensive workplace for the victim.[16] Workplace sexual harassment is actionable under Title VII when women are harassed by men, men are harassed by women, and when the offender and the victim are the same sex.[17] Employers may have to pay large recoveries if they fail to take corrective actions to end sexual harassment once they know, or should have known, that it had occurred.

An Ounce of Prevention

You should work to minimize sexual harassment. Sexual harassment can be costly.[18] It distracts the victim and his or her coworkers from their jobs. Any litigation and court judgment can also be disruptive and expensive. You should make it clear to your employees that sexual harassment will not be tolerated. You should also establish, publicize, and vigorously enforce anti-sexual harassment policies. An important part of the policy should include designating who will take the reports of employees. Managers charged with this responsibility should promptly and thoroughly investigate reports. Many companies are held liable because they fail to investigate allegations of sexual harassment. On the other hand, the company may avoid liability if it has an effective policy and the employee fails to use it.[19] Some companies release the names of employees who report sexual harassment. This is labeled retaliatory disclosure. You should avoid publicizing this information because managers and other employees may harass the person who reported the alleged harassment.

Courts use different standards based on who is engaging in the harassing behavior. If the harassing employee is the victim's co-worker, the employer generally is liable only if the employer was negligent in controlling the work conditions. When the harasser is the victim's supervisor, different rules apply. If the supervisor's harassment results in a tangible employment action, the employer is strictly liable. (*Tangible employment action* is "a significant change in employment status, such as hiring, firing, failing to promote, reassignment with significantly different responsibilities, or a decision causing a significant change in benefits."[20]) If no tangible employment action is taken, the employer may escape liability by establishing that (1) the employer exercised reasonable care to prevent and correct any harassing behavior and (2) that the plaintiff unreasonably failed to take advantage of the preventive or corrective opportunities that the employer provided.[21]

Computer use can be the basis for sexual harassment. Typical examples involve employees' uploading, downloading, or displaying inappropriate content (for example, pornographic material on a firm's electronic bulletin board) or employees' using e-mail to make unwelcome sexual overtures to other employees. Employers should include clear statements in their anti-harassment policy that the policy applies to the firm's e-mail system. Companies will want to monitor social media and any bulletin boards to identify and remove any inappropriate content.

An Ounce of Prevention

You can be liable for your employees' use of technology, including sexual harassment, defamation, copyright violations, and the disclosure of trade secrets or other proprietary information on-line. This potential liability is a powerful incentive and rationale for establishing a policy for monitoring employees' usage of the Internet, e-mail, and social media. Once a policy is established and communication to employees, you should also inform employees that monitoring is being instituted at the company. You should confine monitoring to work-related email and target specific problems rather than totally banning all personal e-mail and Internet usage.[22] A few states have enacted laws pertaining to the monitoring of e-mail, so you should check the coverage of these statutes.

National Origin Discrimination   Title VII's ban on national origin discrimination also prevents harassment in the form of ethnic slurs. Repeated jokes and other derogatory statements directed at an employee's ethnic origins may constitute national origin discrimination. If an employer fails to hire a worker on the basis of the applicant's language difficulties or accents, the employer must prove that the criteria are job related. Some employers have established English-only rules, requiring that employees speak English at the work place. The courts are still developing the precedents for valid "English only" rules.

Narrow BFOQs may exist in national origin cases. It may be legal to refuse to hire noncitizens: The prohibition in Title VII does not include citizenship[23] unless the discrimination in favor of citizens has the purpose or effect of discrimination on the basis of national origin. The protected categories under Title VII do not specifically include being an alien.[24] Other anti-discrimination laws may protect legal residents, however. It is not a violation of Title VII for an employer to refuse to hire persons who are unable to obtain security clearances because they are not U.S. citizens or have relatives in countries that have hostile relationships with the United States.

The Pregnancy Discrimination Act of 1978

The Pregnancy Discrimination Act (PDA) requires an employer to treat pregnancy in the same fashion as he or she would treat any other temporary disability. Failure to do so constitutes actionable sex discrimination.[25] Sex discrimination is also called gender discrimination. The Supreme Court interpreted the PDA and the Civil Rights Act in *International Union v. Johnson Controls, Inc.*[26] Johnson Controls' battery-manufacturing process used lead. Occupational exposure to lead involves health risks, including the risk of harm to a fetus carried by a female employee. Johnson Controls decided to bar all women, except those whose infertility could be medically documented, from jobs involving actual or potential lead exposure exceeding the OSHA standard. The union filed a suit on behalf of the employees, claiming that the policy constituted sex discrimination in violation of Title VII. According to the Supreme Court, by excluding women with childbearing capacity from these jobs, Johnson Controls's policy created a classification that was based on gender and explicitly discriminated against women on the basis of their sex. When Johnson Controls used the words "capable of bearing children," it explicitly classified on the basis of potential for pregnancy. Johnson Controls's alleged concerns about the welfare of fetuses was not sufficient to establish a BFOQ of female sterility. The Court concluded that decisions about the welfare of future children must be left to the parents who conceive, bear, support, and raise them rather than to the employers who hire those parents.

The Immigration Reform and Control Act of 1986

The Immigration Reform and Control Act (IRCA) is principally aimed at stemming the flow of illegal aliens into the United States. However, it also bans discrimination based on national origin or citizenship. An employer cannot refuse to hire applicants because they appear to be aliens or noncitizens. IRCA is narrower in scope than Title VII because it only covers hiring, recruitment of workers for a fee, and discharges. Title VII preempts this act whenever Title VII covers the conduct in question.

The Equal Pay Act of 1963

The Equal Pay Act prohibits discrimination in wages on the basis of sex. This means that men and women performing work in the same establishment under similar working conditions must receive the same rate of pay *if* the work requires equal skill, effort, and responsibility. Different wages may be paid if the employer bases the pay differential on seniority, merit, piecework, or any factor other than sex (for example, participation in training programs). Unequal pay continues to be a problem. In January 2016, President Obama announced a plan to require companies with at least 100 employees to report their wage data by gender, race, and ethnicity to the federal government. The proposed plan would be effective September 30, 2017 if it is approved by the Equal Employment Opportunity Commission.[27] States such as California also are taking additional steps to prevent unequal pay.[28]

The Age Discrimination in Employment Act of 1967

The Age Discrimination in Employment Act (ADEA), in general, protects workers aged forty or older from adverse employment decisions based on age. BFOQs based on safety, such as requiring police officers or airplane pilots to retire at age sixty, may be upheld. An employer claiming an age related BFOQ based on public safety must convince the court that the challenged practice is effective in protecting the public and that there is no acceptable alternative. Courts have reached various results in interpreting the public safety standard. For example, in one case the court held that the employer could not be successful in court until it established and enforced minimum fitness standards for all its employees.[29]

The Lilly Ledbetter Fair Pay Act of 2009

The Lilly Ledbetter Fair Pay Act was a response to the Supreme Court's decision in *Ledbetter v. Goodyear Tire & Rubber Co.*[30] The Supreme Court ruled against Ledbetter because she failed to file her complaint within 180 days of the *first* act of discrimination when Goodyear started paying her less than male employees performing the same jobs.[31] Claimants may not be aware of the discrimination within 180 days. Even when the claimant is aware that his or her pay is less, the claimant may believe that the disparity is not based on illegal discrimination. The act amends Title VII of the Civil Rights Act, the Age Discrimination in Employment Act, and the Americans with Disabilities Act by specifying that the statute of limitations begins when a discriminatory compensation decision is adopted, when the individual becomes subject to a discriminatory compensation decision, or when the individual's compensation is affected by a discriminatory compensation decision.[32]

The Civil Rights Act of 1991

Congress passed the Civil Rights Act of 1991 to strengthen the rights of plaintiffs alleging employment discrimination.[33] The act's amendments to § 1981 of the Civil Rights Act of 1866 specify that this statute covers all forms of racial discrimination in employment (including racial harassment). The act mandates the impartial use of tests and consequently prohibits "race norming" of employment tests. This means employers are unable to modify scores, use different cutoff scores, or otherwise adjust the results of employment-related tests on the basis of color, race, religion, sex, or national origin. This is so even if employers want to take these actions to ensure the inclusion of minorities in the applicant pool.

The Americans with Disabilities Act of 1990

The Americans with Disabilities Act (ADA) seeks to correct employment discrimination against individuals with disabilities and to guarantee such individuals equal access to public services. Title I prohibits employment discrimination. The ADA requires an employer to provide "reasonable accommodations to the known physical or mental limitations" of a person with a disability unless such accommodations "would impose an undue hardship on the operation of the business."[34] It is not possible to create a comprehensive list of disabilities. Disabilities can include physical problems such as cancer, diabetes, epilepsy, heart disease, HIV, speech impediments, and tuberculosis. Mental disabilities can include emotional illness, depression, mental illness, mental retardation, and specific learning disabilities such as dyslexia. Homosexuality and bisexuality are not considered disabilities under the ADA.[35] In addition to having a disability, the employee or applicant must show that the impairment substantially limits one or more major life activity.[36] In some cases, this is easy to prove. For example, a blind person cannot see, and seeing is a major life activity.

Significant changes were made by the ADA Amendments Act (ADAAA) in 2008.[37] The amendments do the following:

- Require that the disability definition be construed in favor of broad coverage of individuals under the ADA
- State that "the question of whether an individual's impairment is a disability under the ADA should not demand extensive analysis"
- Broaden the definition of disability by stating that "[a]n impairment that substantially limits one major life activity need not limit other major life activities in order to be construed as a disability"
- State that an impairment that is episodic or in remission qualifies as a disability if it would substantially limit a major life activity when it is in an active state
- Direct the EEOC to redefine the term *substantially limits* as used in the ADA
- Expand the EEOC definitions of *major life activity* in the ADA. The nonexclusive list of major life activities now includes all the activities identified in the EEOC regulations. It adds eating, sleeping, standing, lifting, bending, reading, concentrating, thinking, and communicating. The definition adds the operation of "major bodily functions" including "functions of the immune system, normal cell growth, digestive, bowel, bladder, neurological, brain, respiratory, circulatory, endocrine, and reproductive functions."[38]
- Make clear that the courts should not take into consideration mitigating measures in determining whether an individual is impaired[39]

Reasonable accommodation by employers includes such actions as making existing facilities accessible to and usable by persons with disabilities, restructuring jobs, and providing part-time or modified work schedules. However, the act does not require the employer to implement any job accommodation if the employer can demonstrate that the accommodation would impose an "undue hardship" on the operation of the business. *Undue hardship* is an action requiring "significant difficulty or expense" with reference to the following factors: (1) the nature and cost of the accommodation; (2) the size, type, and financial resources of the specific facility where the accommodation would have to be made; (3) the size, type, and financial resources of the covered employer; and (4) the covered employer's type of operation, including the composition, structure, and functions of its workforce and the geographic separateness and administrative or fiscal relationship between the specific facility and the covered employer. Congress rejected attempts to put a cap on the level of difficulty or expense that would constitute an "undue hardship."

The ADA expressly protects employees or applicants who are participating in or who have completed drug rehabilitation programs and no longer are using illegal drugs. Employers do not violate the ADA if they impose sanctions against employees who currently are using illegal drugs, and employers may hold such employees (and/or employees who are alcoholics) to the same performance and conduct standards to which it holds other employees, even if the unsatisfactory performance or behavior is related to the employees' drug use or alcoholism.

The Family and Medical Leave Act of 1993

The Family and Medical Leave Act (FMLA) provides generally that "an eligible employee[40] shall be entitled to a total of 12 work weeks of leave during any 12 month period"[41] for the following family-related events: (1) the birth of a child; (2) the placement of a child with the employee for adoption or foster care; (3) the care of a seriously ill spouse, child, or parent; and (4) a serious health condition of the employee that makes him or her unable to perform any of the essential functions of his or her job.[42] In 2015 the Department of Labor enacted a rule that spouses in legal same-sex marriages are entitled to leave under the FMLA.[43] The FMLA does not require the employer to pay for any leave taken under the act. However, eligible employees can use any accrued vacation or personal leave for FMLA purposes. The act obligates employers to reinstate an employee who has used FMLA leave to the employee's former position or to one that involves "substantially equivalent skill, effort, responsibility, and authority."[44] The FMLA allows an employer to refuse to reinstate "key employees" if an employer can show that substantial and grievous economic injury would occur if the key employees were restored to their original positions.

The regulations explain that a *serious health condition* is (1) one that requires either an overnight stay in a hospital; (2) a period of incapacity requiring an absence from work of more than three days and that involves continuing treatment by a health-care provider; or (3) continuing treatment for a chronic or long-term health condition that, if left untreated, likely will result in a period of incapacity for more than three days. Prenatal care and care administered for a long-term or chronic condition that is incurable and for which condition the person is not receiving active treatment by a health-care provider are included.

The Occupational Safety and Health Act of 1970

The purpose of the Occupational Safety and Health Act (OSHA) is to assure a safe and healthful workplace for employees. The act accomplishes this (1) by authorizing enforcement of the standards developed under the act by the Occupational Safety and Health Administration (also called OSHA); (2) by assisting and encouraging the states' efforts to ensure safe and healthful working conditions; and (3) by providing for research, information, education, and training in the field of occupational safety and health, through the National Institute for Occupational Safety and Health (NIOSH). The act requires each employer to furnish a safe and healthful workplace, one that is free from "recognized hazards" that may cause or are likely to cause death or serious physical harm to employees. The act covers most employers and employees, including agricultural employees, nonprofit organizations, and professionals (such as accountants, brokers, doctors, and lawyers). In fact, the act reaches almost any employer that employs at least one employee and whose business in any way affects interstate commerce.

OSHA allows inspectors to enter the workplace to inspect for compliance with regulations. Inspections are generally unannounced. OSHA regulations require the inspector to obtain a warrant if the employer refuses to admit the inspector. The standards for obtaining a warrant are low so the warrant requirement does not significantly hinder OSHA's functions. Employees may request an inspection by writing to the secretary of labor if they believe there is a violation. When an employee has initiated the complaint, he or she can request that his or her identity be withheld. The act protects employees from discrimination or discharge based on the employee's filing a complaint, testifying about violations, or exercising any rights guaranteed by the act.

An Ounce of Prevention

Your best strategy is to avoid OSHA violations; however, this is not always possible. You should make reasonable efforts to be aware of both the standards and the work conditions. Employers can defend themselves by showing they did not know and could not know about the condition or hazard even with the exercise of "reasonable diligence." If you wish to contest any penalties, you can use the appeals procedures. You can also request temporary exemptions from OSHA standards by proving that you cannot comply within the required time because of the unavailability of materials, equipment, or personnel. You may be granted a permanent exemption if your method of protecting employees is as effective as that required by the standard.

OSHA prohibits employees from stopping work or walking off the job because of "potential unsafe conditions at the workplace" unless the employee would subject "himself [or herself] to serious injury or death arising from a hazardous condition at the workplace."[45] The Supreme Court held that the secretary of labor has the authority to promulgate a regulation allowing workers to refuse to perform in hazardous situations.[46]

International and State Application of U.S. Employment Laws

Americans employed abroad by U.S.-owned or U.S.-controlled firms can use the protection of Title VII, the ADA, and the ADEA, unless compliance with these U.S. laws will constitute a violation of the host country's laws. The Supreme Court held that state employees cannot sue their employers for damages under the ADA because Congress had exceeded its power under the Fourteenth Amendment when it applied the ADA to state workers.[47]

EMPLOYEE BENEFITS AND PROTECTIONS

There are a number of standard benefits and protections which employers provide to attract applicants. Some of the more important of these are discussed in this section.

Group Health Insurance through Employers

One common and popular employee benefit is group health insurance. The premiums are generally significantly less than the cost of purchasing health insurance as an individual. When employees lose their jobs, have their hours reduced, or voluntarily sever their employment, they generally lose their health insurance. The Consolidated Omnibus Budget Reconciliation Act of 1985 (COBRA) allows employees or their qualified beneficiaries to continue their health insurance with the group, so long as the employee or qualified beneficiary pays for the insurance.[48] A number of "qualifying events" will trigger COBRA, including death, termination (other than for misconduct), reduction of hours, retirement, Medicare entitlement, or employer's bankruptcy.[49] For a qualified beneficiary, a divorce or legal separation from the employee spouse or the cessation of a child's dependency is a qualifying event.

Health Care Reform

President Obama signed the Patient Protection and Affordable Care Act (PPACA) and the Health Care and Education Reconciliation Act (HCERA).[50] These acts are important to businesses and their employees because they encourage more businesses to offer health insurance to their workers. Small businesses will receive tax credits to make health care more affordable.[51] In 2012, a majority of the U.S. Supreme Court upheld many parts of PPACA that were being challenged.[52] There will continue to be legal and political challenges to these acts. A change in the composition of the legislative and/or executive branches may result in reversal of the acts or parts of the acts. In addition, opponents to the acts may limit budget allocations, impeding implementation.[53]

Social Security and Medicare

The federal Social Security Act, first enacted in 1935, created retirement benefits for workers. Since then, Social Security benefits have been extended to the worker's spouse and minor children (1939) and severely disabled workers (1956). The 1939 amendments added coverage for families of retired workers and workers who had died.[54] The Social Security Administration is working on processing instructions for handling claims based on same-sex marriages.[55] The current debate about Social Security focuses on fears that the system will become bankrupt and on proposed plans to prevent its bankruptcy.

In general, Social Security benefits are computed on the worker's earning records. This is true for all four basic types of payments—retirement, disability, dependents, and survivors. Generally, a *fully insured* worker is one who has worked at least forty quarters (ten years). To use 2016 as an example, such workers will earn one-quarter of coverage for each $1,260 in covered earnings, including wages, farm wages, or income from self-employment, up to a maximum of four quarters per year.[56] A fully insured worker is entitled to retirement benefits. A worker or his or her family may be eligible for other benefits with less than forty quarters.

Computing the actual benefit amount involves complicated formulas based on the worker's age; date of retirement, disability, or death; and yearly earnings history (including the amount of salary). The amount of the benefit is dependent on the type of payment—retirement, disability, dependent, or survivor—and who is receiving it. Cost-of-living escalators tied to the *consumer price index* (the measurement of how the price of a group of consumer goods changes between two time periods) may raise benefits.

The Federal Insurance Contribution Act (FICA) taxes are paid by both employees and employers on wages earned by workers. FICA taxes fund Social Security and Medicare. In 2016, the combined tax rate paid was 7.65 percent (6.2 percent Social Security tax and 1.45 percent Medicare tax). Social Security tax is not assessed on that portion of the annual wages that exceed $118,500.[57] The Medicare tax is assessed on all wages. Employers and employees each pay the 7.65 percent.

Unemployment Compensation

Unemployment compensation is a coordinated federal and state effort to provide economic security for temporarily unemployed workers. Generally, unemployment compensation only covers employees. The funds used for payments come from taxes, or contributions, paid predominantly by employers. In a few states, employees also pay these taxes. Under the Federal Unemployment Tax Act (FUTA), employers must report and pay the federal tax on their employees' wages. Wages include anything paid as compensation for employment and may consist of salaries, fees, bonuses, and commissions. In 2016, the maximum amount of wages subject to FUTA was $7,000 per employee and the FUTA rate was 6 percent on each employee's wages up to the $7,000.[58] The federal government allows a credit for participating in a state unemployment program.

States generally use "experience rating" or "merit rating" systems where the rate employers pay reflects each individual employer's experience with unemployment. Under such systems, employers pay higher rates if their workers suffer more involuntary unemployment. Since the goal of unemployment compensation is the prevention of unemployment, such systems provide incentives to employers to keep their workforces intact.

State provisions regarding the criteria for eligibility and the amount of benefits vary greatly. However, generally a worker will not be eligible if he or she:

- Is discharged for good cause
- Quits voluntarily without cause
- Is unemployed due to a strike in which he or she actively participates
- Refuses to remain available to work and/or refuses to accept a similar substitute position

Workers' Compensation

Under workers' compensation statutes, payments are made to injured workers for injuries suffered on the job. Generally, only employees are covered by workers' compensation. Injured workers receive compensation for their injuries in the form of medical care and disability benefits. Disability benefits are often based on a fixed schedule of compensation for listed injuries. This enables workers to easily determine how much they are entitled to receive. This procedure allows for the quick settlement of claims and discourages costly litigation. The employer usually (1) self-insures; (2) buys insurance; or (3) pays money into a state fund at a "merit" or "experience" rate based on the employer's actual history.

Workers' compensation laws impose *strict liability* on the employer for injuries to employees during the scope of their employment. Workers' compensation statutes are not based on the fault of the employer. The worker only needs to show that his or her injury was caused in the course and scope of the job. In some states the employee can elect to sue under the common law *or* to collect under workers' compensation. Under common law, three defenses tend to prevent recovery by the employee: The defenses are contributory negligence, assumption of the risk, and the fellow employee rule.[59] Workers' compensation statutes arose in part as a response to these defenses. If the workers' compensation statute does not apply, generally the employee will be permitted to sue based on common law theories.

The classes of employees covered by such acts depend on the particular statute involved. Agricultural workers, household workers, or casual laborers are not covered in some states. Workers' compensation statutes presumably do not cover corporate directors, officers, or stockholders. Yet under the *dual capacity doctrine,* these people can receive compensation if they are performing the ordinary duties of the business when they are injured. For example, Brett, a general manager of a tree-pruning service, will be able to recover if he is injured while pruning trees. Typically, the covered employee is eligible for workers' compensation for just about any employment-related injury or disease. Usually even a negligent employee can recover for injuries suffered while he or she was acting as an employee.

Workers' compensation statutes vary in the following respects:

- Some are the exclusive remedy of employees; others permit employees to sue on other theories.
- Some cover only major industrial occupations.
- Some exclude small shops with few employees.
- Some exclude injuries caused intentionally by the employer or other workers.

Because of the variations, it is important to examine the applicable state statute.

Contemporary Case

The Supreme Court agreed to hear this Contemporary Case to resolve the issue of whether a job applicant has to inform the employer that she would need a religious accommodation for her headscarf. The employer's dress policy prohibited caps which on its face is a neutral policy.

EQUAL EMPLOYMENT OPPORTUNITY COMMISSION v. ABERCROMBIE & FITCH STORES, INC.

135 S. Ct. 2028, 2015 U.S. LEXIS 3718 (2015)

FACTS Abercrombie & Fitch Stores, Inc. owns and operates several lines of clothing stores. Abercrombie imposes a Look Policy that governs its employees' dress to project the desired image. The Look Policy prohibits "caps" but does not define what a "cap" is. Samantha Elauf applied for a position in an Abercrombie store. She is a practicing Muslim and wears a headscarf which is consistent with her understanding of her religion's requirements. Her scarfs were purchased at regular clothing stores. Elauf was interviewed by Heather Cooke, the store's assistant manager. Cooke determined that Elauf was qualified to be hired, however, Cooke was concerned that the headscarf would conflict with the Look Policy. Cooke attempted to get clarification from the store manager as to whether the headscarf would be a "cap." When this was not successful, Cooke asked Randall Johnson, the district manager. Cooke told Johnson that she thought Elauf wore her headscarf because of her religion. Johnson told Cooke that all headwear, religious or otherwise, would violate the Look Policy and he told Cooke not to hire Elauf. (These facts are from the Supreme Court opinion, however, Abercrombie denied that Cooke told Johnson that the headscarf was probably being worn for religious reasons.)

ISSUE Under Title VII, does an applicant have to inform an employer that her headscarf is being worn for religious reasons? Is there a separate legal claim for failure to accommodate a religious practice?

HOLDING No. An applicant does not have to inform the employer that her scarf is worn for religious reasons. It is sufficient that the employer refuses to hire her because the employer wants to avoid making an accommodation. No. There is no separate claim for failure to accommodate. It is a failure to accommodate under either disparate impact or disparate treatment.

REASONING Excerpts from the opinion of Justice Scalia:

. . . Title VII of the Civil Rights Act of 1964 . . . prohibits two categories of employment practices. It is unlawful for an employer:

> (1) to fail or refuse to hire or to discharge any individual, or otherwise to discriminate against any individual with respect to his compensation, terms, conditions, or privileges of employment, because of such individual's race, color, religion, sex, or national origin [disparate treatment]; or

> (2) to limit, segregate, or classify his employees or applicants for employment in any way which would deprive or tend to deprive any individual of employment opportunities or otherwise adversely affect his status as an employee, because of such individual's race, color, religion, sex, or national origin [disparate impact].

. . .

These two proscriptions . . . are the only causes of action under Title VII. The word "religion" . . . [includes] "all aspects of religious observance and practice, as well as belief, unless an employer demonstrates that he is unable to reasonably accommodate . . . " a "religious

observance or practice without undue hardship on the conduct of the employer's business." . . .

Abercrombie's primary argument is that an applicant cannot show disparate treatment without first showing that an employer has "actual knowledge" of the applicant's need for an accommodation. We disagree. Instead, an applicant need only show that his need for an accommodation was a motivating factor in the employer's decision. . . .

The disparate-treatment provision forbids employers to: (1) "fail . . . to hire" an applicant (2) "because of" (3) "such individual's . . . religion" (which includes his religious practice). Here . . . Abercrombie (1) failed to hire Elauf. The parties concede that (if Elauf sincerely believes that her religion so requires) Elauf's wearing of a headscarf is (3) a "religious practice." All that remains is whether she was not hired (2) "because of" her religious practice. . . . [Title VII prohibits] even making a protected characteristic a "motivating factor" in an employment decision. . . .

It is significant that . . . [Title VII] does not impose a knowledge requirement. . . . Instead, the intentional discrimination provision prohibits certain *motives*, regardless of the state of the actor's knowledge. Motive and knowledge are separate concepts. An employer who has actual knowledge of the need for an accommodation does not violate Title VII by refusing to hire an applicant if avoiding that accommodation is not his *motive*. Conversely, an employer who acts with the motive of avoiding accommodation may violate Title VII even if he has no more than an unsubstantiated suspicion that accommodation would be needed.

. . . [T]he rule for disparate-treatment claims based on a failure to accommodate a religious practice is straightforward: An employer may not make an applicant's religious practice, confirmed or otherwise, a factor in employment decisions. For example, suppose that an employer thinks (though he does not know for certain) that a job applicant may be an orthodox Jew who will observe the Sabbath, and thus be unable to work on Saturdays. If the applicant actually requires an accommodation of that religious practice, and the employer's desire to avoid the prospective accommodation is a motivating factor in his decision, the employer violates Title VII. . . .

[R]eligious practice is one of the protected characteristics that cannot be accorded disparate treatment and must be accommodated. . . . Title VII does not demand mere neutrality with regard to religious practices . . . Rather, it gives them favored treatment, affirmatively obligating employers not "to fail or refuse to hire or discharge any individual . . . because of such individual's" "religious observance and practice." An employer is . . . entitled to have . . . a no-headwear policy as an ordinary matter. . . . Title VII requires otherwise-neutral policies to give way to the need for an accommodation. . . .

The Tenth Circuit misinterpreted Title VII's requirements in granting summary judgment. We reverse its judgment and remand the case for further consideration consistent with this opinion.

Short Answer Questions

1. Reyco hires computer technicians to provide web support for Reyco's software. The techs work from home on computers and cell phones provided by Reyco. Reyco's policy states that the company computers, cell phones, and e-mail accounts can only be used for official company business. You represent a labor union, which seeks to become the bargaining representative for the computer technicians. What challenges would you have? How would this be similar to unionizing workers who work together in the same office? How would it be different?

2. Nagheen is Muslim. Her religious practices require her to cover her hair and most of her face with a traditional veil when she is in public. Rob, her direct supervisor, is uncomfortable seeing Nagheen in the veil and believes that customers will also be uncomfortable. He transfers Nagheen from the front reception desk to a phone bank where she will primarily deal with customers by phone. Nagheen complains to you since you are the human resources manager. Are Rob's actions illegal? Why or why not? Is there a better way for Rob to handle the situation? If so, what is it?

3. Arbitration Answers (AA) provides arbitration services in the Detroit metropolitan area. AA set up an application portal on its Web site to hire new arbitrators. Tanya has applied for one of the positions. You are the human resources manager responsible for the initial screening of applicants. You want to consider applicants' choices of username and to review information that the applicants have posted on social networking sites, such as Facebook and YouTube, in your initial screening. Would this review be legal? Is it fair to applicants like Tanya? How should AA handle the information that you locate?

You Decide...

1. Steve Sarkisian was the head football coach at University of Southern California (USC) when he was fired in December 2015. Sarkisian claims his anxiety, depression, and alcohol use spiked after his team was upset by the University of Washington, where he used to coach. Sarkisian appears to have a history of problems with alcohol. There are numerous reports about his alcohol use when he was at Washington. For example, one former player said Sarkisian smelled of alcohol at some morning meetings.

At USC there were a number of reports of Sarkisian appearing to be intoxicated at work. One news reporter claimed that there were over 12 alcohol-related incidents at USC.[60] In one highly publicized example, Sarkisian appeared to be drunk at a booster event in August 2015, where he slurred his speech and made inappropriate comments. After the booster incident, USC required Sarkisian to sign a letter agreeing to apologize and undergo counseling. The doctors prescribed medication for stress. At a news conference a few days after the booster incident, Sarkisian said he did not think he had a problem with alcohol.

Sarkisian filed a lawsuit against USC. According to the suit, Sarkisian finally realized that he had a problem and needed serious help, and the school fired him. The lawsuit claims the school discriminated against him based on his alcoholism and that the school had an obligation to accommodate his disability. It also claims breach of contract. USC claims that it is not liable for breach of contract because Sarkisian was fired for cause. The school also claims that Sarkisian denied he had a problem with alcoholism, did not ask for time to get help, and resisted the school's efforts to obtain help for him.

In December, when Sarkisian acknowledged that he was not okay and needed to get help, Athletic Director Pat Haden put him on indefinite leave. The next day, Sarkisian went to an inpatient treatment facility. That day Haden sent Sarkisian an email firing him for not performing according to USC standards.

Assume that Sarkisian's American's with Disabilities (ADA) claim has been filed in your court. How would *you* decide this case? Be certain that you explain and justify your answer.

(See Guardian Sport, "Former USC Coach Steve Sarkisian Checks into Rehab, Reports Say; Coach Reportedly Appeared Intoxicated at Work Friends of Sarkisian Express Concern," *The Guardian*, October 13, 2015; Nathan Fenno, "Steve Sarkisian Sues USC, Alleging Discrimination and Breach of Contract," *Los Angeles Times*, December 7, 2015, http://www.latimes.com/sports/usc/la-sp-usc-sarkisian-lawsuit-20151208-story.html (accessed December 28, 2015), and Scott Wolf, "USC Fires Football Coach Steve Sarkisian," *Whittier Daily News* (California), December 9, 2015.)

2. Pennsylvania Supreme Court Justice J. Michael Eakin was suspended with pay and benefits by Pennsylvania's Court of Judicial Discipline. Eakin opened a private Yahoo.com account in the fictitious name of "John Smith." Using the account Eakin shared e-mails including some that joked "about slapping a female employee's backside" and "about a woman beaten black and blue by her husband."[61] The private e-mail address contained information "degrading to women, gays and racial minorities."[62] Two of the e-mails included sexually suggestive comments about Eakin's female secretary and his female office manager. Many of the e-mails were sent to other government employees and some were sent from his work computer. Eakin contends that he did not intend for the e-mails to become public. Eakin responded, "Perhaps my demeanor is one of the boys. . . . But what I sent was to people who were also one of the boys. It was in the locker room."[63] He argues that the e-mails have "nothing to do with (his) performance on the job."[64] Pennsylvania's Court of Judicial Discipline said it "is deeply and profoundly troubled by even a remote possibility that the patently discriminatory and offensive views and attitudes expressed" "may have impacted Justice Eakin's judicial work."[65] According to Pennsylvania's judicial canons judges must avoid "both impropriety and the appearance of impropriety in their professional and personal lives [while always showing] independence, fairness, impartiality, integrity and competence."[66] It is interesting to note that a year earlier the Judicial Conduct Board examined the e-mails

available at the time and concluded that they did not violate any rules for judicial conduct.

Assume that the issue of Eakin's discipline has been filed in your court. How would *you* decide this case? Be certain that you explain and justify your answer.

(See Steve Esack, "Kane Lets Public Judge Eakin Emails," *Morning Call* (Allentown, Pennsylvania), A1, October 23, 2015, "In Our Words, Court Right to Judge Eakin's 'Private' Emails," *LNP* (Lancaster, PA), A 16, December 29, 2015, and "Pennsylvania SC Judge Eakin Suspended over Lewd Emails," *Legal Monitor Worldwide*, December 26, 2015.)[67]

Notes

1. Quotes from Steven Greenhouse, "Labor Board Says Rights Apply on Net," *New York Times*, November 9, 2010, B1.
2. *Ibid.*
3. Bloomberg News, "Company Settles Case in Firing Tied to Facebook," *New York Times*, February 8, 2011, B7.
4. The proposed Employee Free Choice Act would make secret ballots unnecessary if a majority of the employees sign authorization cards. This proposal is currently stalled in Congress. In addition, the National Labor Relations Board may have the administrative power to change from a secret election to a card-check system of selecting a union. A recent article has suggested that although it has the power, it should not exercise it. Halima Woodhead, "Can Card-Check Be Unilaterally Imposed by the NLRB?" 1 *American University Labor & Employment Law Forum* 85 (Winter, 2011).
5. *United Food and Commercial Workers Union Local 204 v. National Labor Relations Board*, 506 F.3d 1078, 2007 U.S. App. LEXIS 25759 (D.C. Cir. 2007).
6. Courts and the NLRB have wrestled with the question of who is a supervisor.
7. 29 U.S.C.A. § 164(b), cited in George Blum, John Bourdeau, Keith A. Braswell, Paul M. Coltoff, Romualdo P. Eclavea, John A. Gebauer, John Glenn, Lucas Martin, Lonnie E. Griffith, Jr., Amy G. Gore, Eleanor L. Grossman, Jill Gustafson, Glenda K. Harnad, Janice Holben, Alan J. Jacobs, Sonja Larsen, Anne E. Melley, Kristina E. Music Biro, Karl Oakes, Karen L. Schultz, Jeffrey J. Shampo, Thomas Smith, Barbara J. Van Arsdale, Labor and Labor Relations I. Overview of Laws Governing Labor-Management Relations G. State Laws; Federal Pre-emption 3. Particular Statutory Allowances of State Jurisdic-

tion, 48 Am Jur 2d Labor and Labor Relations § 527 State Right-to-work Statutes
8. *Walters v. Metropolitan Educational Enterprises, Inc.*, 519 U.S. 202 (1997).
9. For an annotated list of state statutes dealing with access to usernames and passwords, see the National Conference of State Legislatures Web site, "Access to Social Media Usernames and Passwords," updated October 29, 2015, http://www.ncsl.org/research/telecommunications-and-information-technology/employer-access-to-social-media-passwords-2013.aspx#2014 (accessed December 29, 2015). In 2015 legislation was introduced or considered in at least 23 states. *Ibid.* In 2012 federal legislation was proposed but it was not passed. Sarah Perez, "House Shoots Down Legislation That Would Have Stopped Employers from Demanding Your Facebook Password," Techcrunch, March 28, 2012, http://techcrunch.com/2012/03/28/house-shoots-down-bill-that-would-have-stopped-employers-from-demanding-your-facebook-password/ (accessed December 29, 2015) and Correy Stephenson, "New Federal Bill Would Protect Employee Social Media Use," *Lawyers Weekly USA*, Dolan Media Newswires, August 2, 2012.
10. *McDonald v. Santa Fe Trail Transportation Co.*, 427 U.S. 273 (1976), held that whites can sue for racial discrimination when they receive disparate treatment. In this case, the employer had accused two whites and one black of misappropriating a shipment of antifreeze. The company fired both white employees but retained the black worker. The Supreme Court concluded that Title VII prohibits all forms of racial discrimination, including *reverse discrimination* of this type.

11. EEOC Uniform Guidelines of Employee Selection Procedures, 29 C.F.R. 1607.4(D). The Supreme Court has said that great deference should be given to the guidelines issued by the EEOC. *See Griggs v. Duke Power Co.,* 401 U.S. 424, 433-434, as cited in Michael J. Songer, "Going Back to Class? The Reemergence of Class in Critical Race Theory Symposium," Note: "Decline of Title VII Disparate Impact: The Role of the 1991 Civil Rights Act and the Ideologies of Federal Judges," 11 Mich. J. Race & L. 247, 251 (2005). For an explanation of the 4/5 rule, *see* Tracy Bateman Farrell et al., 46 Am Jur. 2d Job Discrimination, § 313 Four-fifths or 80% rule (2015).

12. *Ibid.*

13. *Hazelwood School District v. United States,* 433 U.S. 299, 311 (1977), as cited in Songer, 251.

14. *Cloutier v. Costco Wholesale Corp.,* 390 F.3d 126, 2004 U.S. App. LEXIS 24763 (1st Cir. 2004). The U.S. Supreme Court denied certiorari in *Cloutier v. Costco Wholesale Corp.,* 125 S. Ct. 2940, 162 L. Ed. 2d 873, 2005 U.S. LEXIS 4923 (2005). The appeals court did seem a little skeptical of when Cloutier joined the religion and her interpretation of its tenets. Cloutier interpreted the religion as requiring that the piercings be visible at all times.

15. *Pime v. Loyola University of Chicago,* 585 F. Supp. 435, 1984 U.S. Dist. LEXIS 17154 (N.D. Ill, E. Div. 1984), judgment affirmed, 803 F.2d 351 (7th Cir. 1986).

16. In fiscal year 2014, 6862 claims of sexual harassment were made to the EEOC. EEOC Web site, "Charges Alleging Sexual Harassment, FY 2010-FY 2014," http://www.eeoc.gov/eeoc/statistics/enforcement/sexual_harassment_new.cfm (accessed December 29, 2015).

17. *Oncale v. Sundowner Offshore Services, Inc.,* 523 U.S. 75 (1998).

18. To illustrate the need for an effective policy, in 1998 Mitsubishi Motor Manufacturing Company agreed to a $34 million settlement for sexual harassment. Courts will frequently ask employees whether they were aware of the sexual harassment policy and the extent to which they used it to resolve their claims.

19. *Pennsylvania State Police v. Suders,* 542 U.S. 129, 2004 U.S. LEXIS 4176 (2004).

20. *Burlington Industries, Inc. v. Ellerth,* 524 U.S. 742, 761, cited in *Vance v. Ball State University,* 133 S. Ct. 2434, 186 L. Ed. 2d 565 (2013).

21. These are affirmative defenses that the employer can use. This summary is from *Vance v. Ball State University,* 133 S. Ct. 2434, 186 L. Ed. 2d 565 (2013).

22. *Espinoza v. Farah Mfg. Co., Inc.,* 414 U.S. 86 (1973).

23. Legal aliens generally have the right to work under the Fourteenth Amendment's Equal Protection Clause. They may be excluded from certain jobs if it is necessary for the public welfare. George Blum, John Bourdeau, James Buchwalter, Paul M. Coltoff, Russell J. Davis, John A. Gebauer, John Glenn, Amy G. Gore, Lonnie E. Griffith, Jr., Eleanor L. Grossman, Jill Gustafson, Glenda K. Harnad, Janice Holben, Alan J. Jacobs, John Kimpflen, Sonja Larsen, Jack K. Levin, Lucas Martin, Anne E. Melley, Mary Babb Morris, Kristina E. Music Biro, Karl Oakes, Karen L. Schultz, Thomas Smith, Jeffrey J. Shampo, Eric C. Surette, and Barbara J. Van Arsdale, Aliens and Citizens, VII. Rights, Privileges, and Duties of Aliens Living in United States, A. Constitutional and Statutory Rights, 7. Right to Engage in Trade, Business, Occupation, or Profession, 3B Am Jur 2d Aliens and Citizens § 1859 Basic Rule of Right to Work.

24. In this regard, some employers provide a computer terminal that employees can use for a limited duration for personal e-mails—during their breaks, for example—as long as the usage is lawful and nondisruptive of ordinary business operations.

25. In 2014, 3400 claims of pregnancy discrimination were made to the EEOC. EEOC Web site, "Pregnancy Discrimination Charges FY 2010-FY 2014," http://www.eeoc.gov/eeoc/statistics/enforcement/pregnancy_new.cfm (accessed December 29, 2015).

26. 499 U.S. 187 (1991).

27. Jim Puzzanghera and Shan Li, "Obama Moves to Close Gender Wage Gap," *Los Angeles Times,* C1, January 30, 2016.

28. *Ibid.*

29. *E.E.O.C. v. Com. of Pa,* 829 F.2d 392 (3rd Cir. 1987), cited in Tracy Bateman Farrell, George Blum, John Bourdeau, Paul M. Coltoff, Romualdo P. Eclavea, Lonnie E. Griffith, Jr., Jill Gustafson, Glenda K. Harnad, Janice Holben, Alan J. Jacobs, John Kimpflen, Sonja Larsen, Jack K. Levin, Lucas Martin, Anne E. Melley, Tom Muskus, Karl Oakes, Jeffrey J. Shampo, Eric C. Surette, Barbara J. Van Arsdale, Mary Ellen West, Job Discrimination, V. Exceptions to Prohibitions Against Discriminatory Conduct, B. Bona Fide Occupational Qualification (BFOQ), 2. Particular Characteristics as BFOQs, b. Age, 45A Am Jur 2d Job Discrimination § 266 Safety-related BFOQs.

30. 127 S. Ct. 2162 (2007).

31. A five-justice opinion spoke for the majority. Justice Ruth Bader Ginsburg wrote and spoke for the four dissenting justices. She read her dissent aloud from the bench to express "more than ordinary disagreement." Justice Ruth Bader Ginsburg, The 20th Annual Leo and Berry Eizenstat Memorial Lecture: The Role of Dissenting Opinions (October 21, 2007), http://www.supremecourtus.gov/publicinfo/speeches/sp_10-21-07.html, cited in Lani Guinier, "Symposium: The Most Disparaged Branch: The Role of Congress in the Twenty-First Century: Panel IV: Beyond Legislatures: Social Movements, Social Change, and the Possibilities of Demoprudence: Courting the People: Demoprudence and the Law/Politics Divide," 89 B.U. L. Rev. 539 (2009).

32. U.S. Equal Employment Opportunity Commission Web site, "Notice Concerning the Lilly Ledbetter Fair Pay Act of 2009," http://www.eeoc.gov/laws/statutes/epa_ledbetter.cfm (accessed December 29, 2015).

33. The act has been criticized as providing vague standards for disparate impact. *See* Songer, where the author compares disparate impact decisions prior to and following the 1991 act.

34. ADA Title I, § 102 (5)(A) available from the U.S. Equal Employment Opportunity Commission Web site, "Titles I and V of the Americans with Disabilities Act of 1990 (ADA)," http://www1.eeoc.gov/laws/statutes/ada.cfm (accessed December 30, 2015).

35. Kathy E. Hinck, C. Angela Van Etten, & John F. Wagner, Am. Jur. 2d Americans with Disabilities Act Analysis and Implications § 7, Conditions Covered.

36. Ibid., § 10, Activities Covered.

37. The amendments redefined disability and created new rules for interpreting the term because Congress thought that the standard established by the Supreme Court in *Toyota Motor Manufacturing, Kentucky, Inc. v. Williams* was too high. Kathy E. Hinck et.al., § 2 ADA and Implementing Regulatory Provisions, Am. Jur. 2d Americans with Disabilities Act Analysis and Implications § 2. The EEOC issued its ADAAA regulations in March 2011.

38. 42 U.S.C. § 12102(2)(B) (2012).

39. See Philip A. Kilgore & John T. Merrell, "Redefining 'Disabled': The ADA Amendments Act of 2008," *South Carolina Lawyer* 21, 24 (July 2009) and its summary of the 2008 Amendments.

40. Employees eligible to take leave under the FMLA must have worked for the employer for at least 12 months and for at least 1,250 hours in the 12 months immediately preceding any leave taken under the act. Employees who work at job facilities that employ fewer than 50 persons are ineligible for FMLA leave unless the employer has 50 or more employees working within a 75-mile radius of the work site.

41. FMLA § 102 (a)(1).

42. FMLA § 102.

43. United States Department of Labor Web site, "Family and Medical Leave Act, Final Rule to Revise the Definition of 'Spouse' Under the FMLA," http://www.dol.gov/whd/fmla/spouse/ (accessed December 30, 2015). Under the rule, the Department of Labor moved from a place of residence test to a place of celebration test. In other words, the place where the marriage was entered into governs whether it is a legal marriage. *Ibid.*

44. 29 CFR 825.215 (a), "Equivalent Position," available at Legal Information Institute, https://www.law.cornell.edu/cfr/text/29/825.215 (accessed December 30, 2015).

45. *Whirlpool Corp. v. Marshall,* 445 U.S. 1, 3 (1980), footnote 3 citing the text of 29 CFR § 1977.12 (1979).

46. *Ibid.*

47. *Board of Trustees of the University of Alabama v. Garrett,* 531 U.S. 356 (2001).

48. If an employee has health insurance that is partly paid for by the employee and partly paid for by the employer, the ex-employee or beneficiary will have to pay the full premium under the COBRA extension.

49. Tracy Bateman Farrell, Sonja Larsen, Lucas Martin, and Karl Oakes, Employment Relationship, V. Employee Benefits, D. Required Continuation of Employee Health Benefit Plans, 8. Notice Requirements, a. In General, 27 Am Jur 2d Employment Relationship § 146 Group Health Plan Notice Requirements and § 149 Employer's Notice Requirements.

50. There are numerous articles about the constitutionality of the Affordable Health Care Act. For example, *see* Mark A. Hall, "The Factual Bases for Constitutional Challenges to the Constitutionality of Federal Health Insurance Reform," 38 N. Ky. L. Rev. 457 (2011).

51. If a business qualifies as a small business under the Internal Revenue Service rules, it may be eligible for a refundable tax credit of 50 percent of the health insurance premium it paid. In addition, the amount not taken as a credit can be taken as a deduction on the business's tax return. Internal Revenue Service Web site, "Small Business Health Care Tax Credit and the SHOP Marketplace," https://www.irs.gov/Affordable-Care-Act/Employers/Small-Business-Health-Care-Tax-Credit-and-the-SHOP-Marketplace (accessed December 31, 2015).

52. *National Federation of Independent Business v. Sebelius,* 2012 U.S. LEXIS 4876 (2012).

53. For a discussion of the history of health care reform and some of the obstacles facing the Affordable Health Care Act, *see* David Pratt, "Health Care Reform: Will It Succeed?," 21 Alb. L.J. Sci. & Tech. 493 (2011).

54. Social Security Web site, "Legislative History, 1939 Amendments," http://www.socialsecurity.gov/history/1939amends.html (accessed December 31, 2015).

55. "On June 26, 2015, the Supreme Court issued a decision in *Obergefell v. Hodges,* holding that same-sex couples have a constitutional right to marry in all states." The Social Security Administration will update its Web site when more information becomes available. Social Security Web site, "Same-Sex Couples," https://ssa.gov/people/same-sexcouples/ (accessed December 30, 2015).

56. "[T]he amount of earnings needed for a quarter of coverage changes automatically each year with changes in the national average wage index." Social Security Web site, "Quarter of Coverage," http://www.ssa.gov/oact/COLA/QC.html (accessed December 31, 2015).

57. The rates and the cut-off point can change annually. Social Security Web site, "OASDI and SSI Program Rates & Limits, 2016," https://www.ssa.gov/policy/docs/quickfacts/prog_highlights/index.html (accessed December 31, 2015).

58. IRS Publication 926, Household Employer's Tax Guide, dated December 23, 2015, https://www.irs.gov/pub/irs-pdf/p926.pdf (accessed December 31, 2015).

59. The fellow employee rule (also known as the fellow servant rule) bars recovery from the employer when the employee was injured by the acts of a fellow employee.

60. Scott Wolf, "USC Fires Football Coach Steve Sarkisian," *Whittier Daily News* (California), December 9, 2015.

61. "In Our Words, Court Right to Judge Eakin's 'Private' Emails; The Issue," *LNP* (Lancaster, PA), A 16, December 29, 2015.

62. *Ibid.*

63. *Ibid.*

64. *Ibid.*

65. *Ibid.*

66. Steve Esack, "Kane Lets Public Judge Eakin Emails," *Morning Call* (Allentown, Pennsylvania), A1, October 23, 2015.

67. Postscript: On March 15, 2016, Justice Eakin resigned. Eakin's resignation may be motivated by an attempt to keep his retirement benefits. Angela Couloumbis, Craig R. McCoy, and Mark Fazlollah, "Amid Porn Email Furor, Eakin Resigns from High Court," *The Philadelphia Inquirer,* March 16, 2016, A1 and Mark Fazlollah and Craig R. McCoy, "In Porngate, Prosecutors Urge That Most Serious Charge against Eakin Be Dropped," *The Philadelphia Inquirer,* March 18, 2016, A1.

Glossary

Acceptance: a communication to the offeror that the offeree agrees with the proposed terms. A manifestation of assent by the offeree.

Accessory to the crime: a person who assists the primary actor in the commission of the crime. One who contributes to or assists in the commission of a crime.

Accord and satisfaction: the settlement of a disputed claim in which the parties agree to a settlement (accord) and then perform the agreed terms (satisfaction).

Acts of God: acts caused exclusively by forces of nature.

Actual authority: the authority that the principal actually grants to the agent and that establishes the limits of what the agent should do in the performance of his or her duties.

Actual notice: notice expressly and actually given to the party directly, e.g., the defendant in a civil suit is personally served by an officer of the court or is mailed service by registered mail.

Actus reus: wrongful act; the prohibited action required for a crime.

Administrative law: law relating to government agencies: includes the creation and operation of administrative agencies and the powers granted to them; also includes the rules that agencies make the relationship between agencies and the other branches of government.

Administrative regulations: rules promulgated by government agencies when they are performing their quasi-legislative functions.

Advisory opinions: opinions rendered by a court at the request of the government or of an interested party that indicate how the court would rule on a matter should litigation develop.

Affirm: approval by an appeals court of a lower court's decision.

Agency law: the law dealing with a consensual representative relationship between a party being represented (the principal) and the person he or she has designated as his or her representative (the agent).

Agent: the person appointed and authorized by another to act as his or her representative.

Alien: a person or corporation that is a citizen of another country.

Alternative dispute resolution: methods of resolving disputes other than traditional litigation.

Answer: document filed by the defendant in a civil suit that denies some or all of the allegations made by the plaintiff in the complaint.

Apparent authority: authority that a third person reasonably believes an agent possesses, as when the principal creates the appearance that an agency exists or that the agent has certain powers. Apparent authority may be used to hold a principal liable on contracts entered into by the agent. It ordinarily will not be used to make a principal liable for physical harm caused by the agent through negligence, assault, trespass, and similar torts.

Appellate court: court that has the power to review the decisions of lower courts.

Arbitration: the process of submitting a dispute to a person or group of persons called arbitrators for a decision.

Arson: the intentional or willful burning of property by fire or explosion.

Assault: a threat to touch someone in an unauthorized, undesired, and/or offensive manner; a threat to inflict harm on another person, coupled with the apparent present ability to do so, that puts the threatened person in reasonable fear or apprehension of the touching.

Assumption of the risk: the plaintiff takes or assumes the risk of damage, injury, or loss; in tort law assumption of the risk is a defense to a negligence action if the plaintiff voluntarily assumed a known risk.

Attachment: the legal process of seizing another's property in accordance with a writ or judicial order.

Attractive nuisance doctrine: this doctrine applies to any person who has an instrumentality, agency, or condition on his or her property, or who creates such condition on the property of others, that is likely to lure children onto the property and to be a danger to them.

Authority by estoppel: authority that arises when the principal (1) is aware that the purported agent is passing himself or herself off as an agent and (2) does not take steps to protect the third party.

Bail: the posting of money or property for the release of a criminal defendant while trying to ensure his or her presence in the court at future hearings.

Battery: the unauthorized and offensive touching of another person without either legal justification or that person's consent.

Beyond a reasonable doubt: the standard used in criminal cases to determine if the defendant is guilty. The trier of fact must be convinced that there is no real possibility that the defendant is innocent.

Bilateral treaties: treaties that involve two nations.

Bill of attainder: a "legislative trial" in which a person is judged a felon or worse by the legislature and not by a court of law.

Bona fide occupational qualification (BFOQ): a valid defense to a claim of employment discrimination; used when gender, national origin or religion are a legitimate job qualification and are essential and reasonably necessary to the operation of the business. Race cannot be a BFOQ. An employer can use a BFOQ as a defense to a claim of employment discrimination.

Boycotts: concerted refusals to deal with firms in order to disrupt their business.

Burglary: the breaking and entering of a building with the intent to commit a felony inside the structure.

Bylaws: the internal rules and regulations adopted by a corporation for the regulation of its day-to-day matters. Bylaws supplement the articles of incorporation and state law.

Capital contribution: money or assets invested by the business owners to start or encourage an enterprise.

Case: claims brought before the court in regular proceedings to protect or enforce rights or to prevent or punish wrongs; also called a *controversy*.

Caveat emptor: let the buyer beware.

Cease and desist order: an order delivered by an administrative agency or a court to an individual or an organization to discontinue the practice described or face sanctions.

Certification mark: mark on a product used to identify the place of origin, materials used, method of manufacture, quality, or some other characteristic.

Certiorari: to be more fully informed. When the Supreme Court decides to grant *certiorari*, it issues a writ of *certiorari*, which orders the lower court to certify a record of the proceedings and send it to the Supreme Court.

Charging order: a court order permitting a creditor to receive a portion of the profits from the operation of a business.

Choice of laws: the rules used to select which jurisdiction's substantive laws should be applied to a particular incident; that is, what laws should govern the subject before the court.

Civil law: private law where one person sues another person.

Class action lawsuit: a lawsuit involving a group of plaintiffs or defendants who are in substantially the same situation.

Common stock: stock that allows the shareholder to receive dividends, to vote on corporate issues, and to receive property when the corporation is liquidated. Shareholders of common stock are not entitled to any preferences in receiving dividends or receiving assets when the corporation is liquidated.

Comparative negligence: the decider of fact weighs the relative negligence of the plaintiff(s) and defendant(s) in a negligence suit; damages are apportioned based on the parties' fault.

Complaint: the plaintiff's first pleading in a civil suit. It informs the defendant that he or she is being sued.

Concurrent condition: a condition that requires the parties to exchange their performance obligations at the same time. A mutually dependent condition.

Concurrent jurisdiction: more than one court has the right to exercise jurisdiction over a dispute.

Condition precedent: a condition that must be satisfied before the promisor's duty to perform becomes legally binding.

Condition subsequent: a condition to which the parties agree that will discharge an existing obligation to perform.

Conglomerate merger: merger between firms in two industries that do not compete with each other.

Consideration: the exchange of value that is required for a contract. The assumption of a duty that did not previously exist *or* the surrender of a right that did previously exist, bargained for and given in exchange for the other party's assumption of a duty or surrender of a right.

Conspiracy: when participants plan criminal behavior together.

Constitution: the fundamental law of a nation.

Constitutional law: law relating to the government and its activities under the Constitution.

Constructive discharge: a situation in which an employer makes an employee's working conditions so intolerable that the employee is forced to resign.

Consumer price index: the measurement of how the price of a group of consumer goods changes between two time periods.

Contingency fee: a fee to be paid to an attorney based on some contingency or event. The most common provisions are that the fee is due only if the case is settled or won in court.

Contract law: the law governing contracts; law that interprets and applies the rights and duties that arise from legally enforceable agreements.

Contributory negligence: a plaintiff in a negligence suit is barred from recovering if he or she was also negligent in causing the accident.

Conversion: when a person intentionally exercises exclusive control over the personal property of another without the permission of the owner or the person who is legally entitled to possession.

Copyright: a property right in an original work of authorship, including artistic, film, literary, musical, and photographic works, that are fixed in a tangible medium of expression.

Copyright law: body of law that protects an original work of authorship fixed in any "tangible medium of expression" from which the work can be perceived, reproduced, or otherwise communicated.

Corporation: an artificial person or legal entity created by or under the authority of a state. It is owned by a group of persons known as stockholders or shareholders.

Court of Common Pleas: title used in some states for trial courts of general jurisdiction.

Courts of general jurisdiction: courts having unlimited or almost unlimited trial jurisdiction in civil and criminal cases.

Covenants: promises.

Criminal forfeiture: when the government confiscates property as a punishment for certain specified criminal activities.

Criminal law: the body of law dealing with public wrongs called crimes.

Criminal procedure: the rules that govern how crimes are investigated, prosecuted, tried, and punished.

Cyberlaw: law dealing with computers and the Internet.

Damages: money claimed by a person, such as a plaintiff, or ordered to be paid by a court. It is to compensate for a loss or injury suffered by a person.

De novo: from the beginning.

Decider of fact: the entity in a trial that decides what happened. It is the jury, if there is one; the judge is the decider of fact if there is no jury.

Defamation: an actor makes an untrue statement concerning a victim that exposes the victim to public ridicule or injures the victim's reputation. The statement must be published, which means that it must be heard or read by someone other than the victim.

Default judgment: a judgment entered against a party who fails to appear in court to defend himself or herself in civil action brought by another party.

Defendant: the one who responds to the lawsuit; the party being sued in a civil action; the person accused of the crime in a criminal action.

Demeanor evidence: the witnesses or the parties' behavior, speech, mannerism, and dress.

Deposition: the formal process of orally asking a potential witness questions under oath outside the courtroom; a witness's sworn testimony taken outside of court and then reduced to writing by a court reporter.

Deterrent: something that impedes or prevents. It can be something that discourages certain behavior.

Dictum: language included in the opinion of a judge that is not necessary to the opinion of the court.

Discovery: a general term that applies to a group of specific methods used to find information, to preserve information, and to narrow the issues to be decided during the trial.

Disenfranchised groups: groups restricted from enjoying certain constitutional or statutory rights due to systemic prejudice or bigotry.

Disparagement: defamation of a business product. This is also called product disparagement or trade libel.

Disparate impact: unequal effect on persons based on innate characteristics such as race, religion, color, national origin, gender, or disability; based on the rule, policy, or procedure that may seem neutral on its face but that has a discriminatory effect; discriminatory effect may be unintentional.

Disparate treatment: unequal treatment of persons due to bias or bigotry; overt treatment or categorization of people because of innate characteristics such as race, religion, color, national origin, gender, or disability.

Diversity of citizenship: when the plaintiff is a citizen of one state and the defendant is a citizen of another; it also exists when one party is a foreign country and the other is a citizen of a state. It is a basis of jurisdiction in federal courts when the trial does not involve a federal question.

Dividends: cash, property, or shares of stock that the board of directors declares as payment to shareholders.

Domicile: the place where a person is physically present and he or she considers as home; when the person leaves he or she intends to return to this place.

Due process: the proper exercise of judicial authority as established by general concepts of law and morality.

Duress: when one party enters into a contract due to a wrongful threat or coercion.

Egoists: people who make their decisions on the basis of self-interest, choosing the course of conduct that will provide the greatest benefit to themselves. Egoists believe that other people should also make decisions based on their own self-interest.

Egotists: people who are self-centered; they often refer to themselves excessively.

Electronically stored information (ESI):   electronic records.

Embezzlement: the fraudulent taking of money or other property that was lawfully entrusted to the person.

Emergency authority: the agent's authority to respond to emergencies, even though the principal and agent never discussed the type of emergency or how to respond to it.

Eminent domain: the power of the government to take private property for public use. The government pays the owner for the property.

Enabling statute: statute that creates a government agency and/or specifies the power and authority of the agency.

Equal protection: a constitutional principle requiring that similarly situated people be treated similarly under the law.

Equity: a body of rules applied to legal controversies when there is no adequate remedy at law. Monetary damages would not be fair compensation.

Ethics: a guiding philosophy; the principles of conduct governing an individual or a group.

Ex post facto law: a law passed after an occurrence or act, which retroactively changes the legal consequences of the act.

Exclusive jurisdiction: a court's power to hear a certain type of case to the exclusion of other courts.

Execute: to perform a contract obligation or to sign a legal document.

Express authority: when the principal informs the agent that the agent has authority to engage in a specific act or to perform a particular task.

Fact-finding: a process where an arbitrator investigates a dispute and issues findings of fact and a non-binding report.

False imprisonment: the unlawful detention of one person by another against the victim's will and without just cause.

Featherbedding: the practice of requiring an employer to pay for services not actually performed by an employee.

Federal district courts: general trial courts in the federal court system.

Federal questions: questions that pertain to the federal Constitution, statutes of the United States, regulations of federal administrative agencies, and treaties signed by the United States.

Felonies: major offenses punishable by confinement from one year to life in a state or federal prison, a large fine, or both.

Fiduciary duties: the duties to act with the utmost good faith, candor, confidence, and trust. These duties are imposed on a number of people including agents, executors, and trustees.

First impression: when an issue is presented to the court for an initial decision; the issue presents a novel question of law and is not governed by any precedent.

Force majeure clause: contract clause that excuses performance due to *acts of God* (an act caused exclusively by forces of nature) or due to acts of a foreign enemy that interfere with and/or prevent performance of the contract.

Foreign corporation: a corporation that was formed and had its articles of incorporation approved in another state or country.

Foreseeability: the knowledge or notice that a certain act is likely to cause a certain result.

Forgery: the making or altering of a negotiable instrument or credit card invoice in order to create or to shift legal liability for the instrument.

Forum: the court that is or will be conducting the trial.

Franchise: the right to engage in business using a specific trademark at a particular location or in a particular territory. The franchisor is the owner of the trademark. The franchisor gives the franchisee the permission to use the trademark.

Fraud: the intentional misstatement of a material fact made with the intention of inducing another party to enter a contract or to part with something of value.

Fundamental rights: rights expressly or impliedly guaranteed in the Constitution.

Gag order: order by a judge to be silent and not discuss a pending case.

Garnishment: procedure to obtain possession of the defendant's property when it is in the custody of another person. This procedure is often used to gain possession of some portion of the defendant's wages or salary.

Good faith: a state of mind where a person is honest in his or her belief or purpose or faithful in fulfilling his or her duty or obligation.

Goods: items that are tangible personal property, meaning the items are moveable; the items are not land or anything permanently attached to land.

Habeas corpus: the name given to a variety of writs issued to bring a party before a court or judge. It is often used to test the legality of imprisoning the party.

Hackers: outsiders who gain unauthorized access to computers or computer networks.

Homicide: the killing of one human being by another.

Horizontal merger: merger between competing firms.

Hostile environment harassment: workplace misconduct that creates an intimidating, hostile, or offensive working environment. The hostile environment may be due to harassment based on the sex, race, religion, national origin, age, or disability of the harassed individual.

Hot cargo clauses: contract clauses that require the employer to cease doing business with nonunion companies.

Implied authority: authority based on the agent's position or title or on past dealings between the agent and the third party.

In personam jurisdiction: the court's authority over the defendant; also called *personal jurisdiction.*

In rem jurisdiction: the court's authority over property, such as land, or status of something, such as a partnership, that is located within the control of the court.

Incidental authority: a grant of express authority includes the power to do all acts that are incidental to the specific authority that is expressed. Incidental authority reasonably and necessarily arises to enable the agent to complete his or her assigned duties.

Indemnification: the right to be repaid.

Indemnify: repay.

Identity theft: the taking of personal information, such as the name, address, and/or Social Security number, name of another, and then using this information to access the victim's accounts or credit.

Independent contractor: a person who is hired to complete a task for someone else. The independent contractor relies on his or her own expertise to determine the best way to complete the job. He or she is not subject to the control of the person who hires him or her.

Indictment: a written accusation submitted by a grand jury against a person charged with a crime.

Infraction: the violation of a rule or a local ordinance.

Injunction: a court order that directs a person to do or not do something.

Insanity plea: criminal defense where the accused claims that, as a result of a mental disease or defect, the accused either did not know what he or she was doing was wrong or he or she could not prevent himself or herself from doing what he or she knew to be wrong.

Insider: a person in possession of material information about a firm that is not generally available to the public.

Intentional torts: wrongs in which the actors behaved in a willful or intentional manner; the actors either wanted the act to occur or knew that the act would probably occur.

Interrogatories: a method of discovery in which one party sends written questions to the other party in the lawsuit, the recipient answers under oath and returns the answers.

Interstate: between two or more states.

Intrastate: begun, carried on, and completed wholly within the boundaries of a single state.

Invasion of privacy: an intrusion into a person's personal activity or exploiting their personality in an unjustified manner. Invasion of privacy is recognized as a tort.

Invidious discrimination: discrimination stemming from bigotry or prejudice.

Judicial question: a question that is proper for a court to decide.

Judicial restraint: a judicial policy of refusing to hear and decide certain types of cases.

Judicial review: the power of the courts to review and uphold or overturn the decisions of other departments or branches of government.

Justification: a lawful and sufficient reason for a person's actions; if the person proves a sufficient reason in court it may be a defense for some crimes and torts.

Laissez faire economy: an economy where the government does not interfere in commercial and economic affairs.

Larceny: the wrongful taking and carrying away of the personal property of another without the owner's consent and with the intent to permanently deprive the owner of the property. Larceny is a crime.

Legislative apportionment: the ratio of legislative representatives to constituents.

Libel: a written, printed, or other permanent communication of an untrue statement that causes a person to suffer a loss of reputation.

Libel per quod: a statement that is not libelous on its face, the libel must be proven by the context.

Libel per se: a statement that is libelous on its face without having to consider the context in which the remark appeared.

Limited liability company (LLC): a business form in which the owners are called members; members are not generally liable for the debts and obligation of the entity.

Limited liability limited partnerships (LLLPs):   limited partnerships with general partners and limited partners; both types of partners have limited liability and creditors are generally limited to collecting from the partnership assets.

Limited liability partnership (LLP): a partnership in which the partnership is liable for debts and obligations; individual partners are liable for their own torts and the torts of the people they supervise.

Limited partnerships (LPs):   partnerships with general partners who serve as managers and limited partners who serve as investors. Limited partners generally have limited liability. They can lose their investment in the partnership but their personal assets are not at risk.

Long-arm statutes: statutes that permit the state to exercise *in personam* jurisdiction over defendants over whom the state would not ordinarily have jurisdiction.

Majority rule: the rule adopted by most states.

Malice aforethought: deliberate purpose or design.

Manslaughter: the unlawful killing of one human being by another; the killing is unlawful, but there is no malice.

Mediation: the use of an impartial third party, a mediator, who attempts to help the parties find a mutually acceptable resolution to their dispute.

Mens rea: criminal intent; guilty mind; the state of mind required for a crime.

Merchant: a person who regularly deals in goods of the kind involved in the contract; a person possessing knowledge or skill particular to transactions involving such goods; a person who employs another person possessing such knowledge or skill as an agent, broker, or intermediary.

Minitrial: a type of alternative dispute resolution where the parties' attorneys present an abbreviated form of their best case.

Minority rule: the rule adopted by a smaller number of states.

Misappropriation of trade secrets: the unlawful acquisition and use of the trade secrets of a business enterprise.

Misdemeanors: minor criminal offenses that are punishable by confinement of up to one year in a city or county jail, a small fine, or both.

Moot: a subject for argument; unsettled; undecided; a point not settled by judicial decisions.

Moot cases: court cases that cannot have any practical effect on the controversy; a question is moot when it presents no actual controversy or when the issues have ceased to exist.

Morals: principles of right and wrong behavior as sanctioned by or operative on one's conscience.

Motion: request to a judge to take certain action. A motion is usually in writing.

Motion for a change of venue: a request to the judge asking him or her to move the case to another court; for example, to another county within the state.

Motion for a new trial: a request to the trial judge asking him or her to grant a new trial because of errors in the first trial.

Motion for a summary judgment: a request to the judge asking him or her to declare that side the "winner" because there are no material issues of fact.

Multilateral treaties: treaties that involve more than two nations.

Murder: the willful, unlawful killing of a human being by another with malice aforethought.

Mutual assent: when the parties agree to be bound by exactly the same terms.

Nationalization: when the government takes private property from the owner and makes it government property.

Negligence: the failure to do something a reasonable and prudent person would do, or doing something that a reasonable and prudent person would not do.

Negligence per se: inherent negligence; negligence without a need for further proof because a person violated a statute, ordinance, or regulation that specified how he or she should behave.

Negotiation: the discussion and resolution of a matter by the parties involved.

Nondepository providers: providers of services such as check cashing and currency exchange. These providers do not hold funds such as savings accounts.

Nuisance: a condition that interferes with the use of property. A private nuisance is the unreasonable interference with the interest of a person in the use or enjoyment of his or her land. A private nuisance is a tort. A public nuisance is an action that causes inconvenience or damage to the public at large. Public nuisance can lead to a civil suit or a criminal prosecution.

Objective standard: standard based on what a reasonable person would think.

Offer: a communication of an intent to make a contract by the offeror.

Offeree: the person to whom an offer is made.

Offeror: the person who initiates the formation of a contract; the person who makes the offer.

Ordinances: laws passed by municipal governments.

Partnership: an association of two or more persons to carry on a business as co-owners for profit.

Patent: a monopoly (exclusive right) granted to an inventor by the federal government upon application and demonstration that the invention is new, useful, and non-obvious.

Per se violation: something that is inherently a violation; the act alone proves the violation.

Peremptory challenge: technique to remove a prospective juror. With peremptory challenges, the attorney does not need to discuss his or her reasons for wanting to remove the juror.

Perfect tender: performance that completely fulfills the promisor's commitments.

Personal property: all property with the exception of real property. Personal property includes property that is tangible or intangible.

Petit jurors: ordinary jurors on the panel for the trial of a civil or criminal court case.

Picketing: demonstrations near a business to publicize a dispute and to encourage the public to refuse to do business with the business.

Plaintiff: the one who files a civil lawsuit.

Pleadings: formal statements filed in court specifying the claims of the parties.

Plenary: exclusive.

Point sources of water pollution: stationary sources of water pollution, such as factories and plants, municipal waste treatment facilities, and public utilities.

Political questions: questions that the court refuses to decide, due to their purely political character or because determination of the question would encroach on powers of the other branches.

Preferred stock: stock that includes priority rights with regard to dividends, voting, and/or liquidation.

Preponderance of the evidence: evidence showing that one's argument is more likely than not; the evidence that is more convincing or has greater weight. This is the standard used in most civil cases.

Preventive law: law designed to prevent harm or wrongdoing before it occurs. It is also called preventative law.

Prima facie case: a case that is obvious on its face; it may be rebutted by evidence to the contrary.

Principal: a person who appoints an agent to act for him or her.

Private law: the body of law that deals with the property and relationships of private persons.

Privatization: the process of changing from government ownership of business and other property to private individual ownership.

Privilege: an exception to a legal duty; in tort law, a defense to an intentional tort where the defendant claims that his or her conduct was authorized or sanctioned by the law; a rule of evidence that permits a witness to refuse to provide certain information in a legal proceeding, such as the attorney-client privilege.

Pro persona: when a person represents himself or herself in court. This is also called appearing *pro se.*

Pro se: appearing in one's own behalf in court.

Proactive: to identify potential problem areas and actively participate in avoiding or resolving them.

Probable cause: a reasonable ground to suspect that a person is committing or has committed a crime, or that a place contains specific evidence of a crime. This is the standard that the judge or magistrate uses to determine whether to issue an arrest or search warrant.

Procedural law: the law specifying the methods used to enforce legal rights or obtain compensation for the violation of these rights.

Promoters: those who generally begin the process of forming a corporation by taking some of the positive steps necessary, such as hiring a corporate attorney, leasing an office, and procuring subscribers for the stock. Promoters are also called incorporators.

Property law: law that deals with the ownership and transfer of assets.

Prothonotary: the title used in some states to designate the chief clerk of courts.

Public domain: land owned and/or controlled by the government. In copyright and patent law, artistic works and patents that are not protected by law; they can be used by members of the public without being liable for infringement.

Public figure: a person who has a degree of prominence in society.

Public law: law that deals with the relations between private individuals and the government. It also deals with the structure and operation of the government itself.

Public official: a person who is elected or appointed to perform government functions.

Quasi-contract: obligation created by the court in the absence of an agreement; it is created by a court where there is an unjust enrichment.

Quasi in rem jurisdiction: authority obtained through property under the control of the court.

Quid pro quo: something for something. In contract law, the exchange of value (consideration) supporting the contract.

Quid pro quo sexual harassment: sexual advances or requests for sexual favors in exchange for employment benefits made to employees by coworkers and/or supervisors' employees.

Racketeer Influenced and Corrupt Organizations Act (RICO): federal statute that makes it a crime to obtain or maintain an interest in, use income from, or conduct or participate in the affairs of an enterprise through a pattern of racketeering activity.

Ratification authority: when the agent does something that was unauthorized at the time and the principal approves it after the fact. For ratification to be valid, the principal must have knowledge of all the material facts. After the principal ratifies the act he or she is liable for it.

Reactive: waiting to see what develops and then reacting to those developments.

Real property: land and whatever is permanently attached to the land, such as a house.

Recognitional picketing: picketing in which a union attempts to force recognition of a different union from the certified bargaining representative.

Reformation: a court-ordered correction of a written contract in order to make the writing reflect the true intentions and agreement of the parties.

Rejection: the offeree informs the offeror that he or she will not accept the offer to form a contract.

Remand: the appeals court returns the case to the lower court for correction because the lower court made a mistake of law.

Remedial law: designed to deal with problems that have already arisen; a law that provides a way to enforce rights or compensate for injuries; a statute passed to correct or modify a prior law.

Remedies at law: money; in contracts a monetary assessment of the harm suffered by the nonbreaching party, it only includes the harm that should have been reasonably anticipated by the breaching party if he or she did not perform.

Remedies in equity: generally remedies where the court orders that some action be done; in contracts it is specially tailored remedies for those situations in which money won't make nonbreaching party "whole."

Renunciation of agency: termination of the agency relationship by the resignation of the agent.

Replevin: a legal action to recover possession of goods that have been taken unlawfully.

Res judicata: a rule of civil law that prevents a person from being sued more than once by the same party for the same civil wrong. This is also called *res adjudicata.*

Rescission: an equitable remedy relieving the parties from their obligations under the contract on grounds such as mutual mistake, fraud, and impossibility. Rescission returns the parties to their original position prior to entering the contract.

Respondeat superior: the doctrine that requires the superior (employer) to answer or pay for the torts of employees that occur in the course and scope of employment.

Restatements: treatises published by the American Law Institute that summarize the law on a subject; restatements are not actually part of the law. Restatements can become part of precedent when they are cited by a judge in a court opinion.

Restitution: the return or restoration of something to its rightful owner or its rightful status; compensation for the loss caused to the plaintiff to make him or her whole. Restitution is available in contract cases and tort cases. It is also sometimes ordered by a judge in criminal cases as a condition for probation.

Reverse: an appeals court's overturning of a decision by a lower court that made an error of law.

Revocation of agency: termination of the agency relationship by the principal discharging the agent.

Revocation of an offer: the offeror informs the offeree that he or she no longer wants to form the contract; the offeror terminates the offer.

Right against double jeopardy: a rule of criminal law that states that a person cannot be tried in court more than once by the same government for the same criminal offense.

Right of privacy: an individual's right of autonomy; the right of a person and his or her property to be free from public scrutiny; the right to be left alone.

Right to work law: a statute that prohibits requiring union membership as a condition for employment.

Robbery: a form of aggravated theft; larceny plus the threat to use force or violence.

Sale: the passing of title from a seller to a buyer for consideration.

Scienter: guilty knowledge; an intent to deceive, manipulate, or defraud. Scienter is an element of fraud.

Secondary boycotts: boycotts directed at a business's customers or suppliers in an attempt to influence the business. Boycotts often take place in labor disputes.

Security: any instrument relating to finances, including a note, stock, bond, put, call, or option; any investment from which a person expects to receive benefits solely from the efforts of others rather than his or her direct participation; collateral to guarantee the fulfillment of an obligation.

Sedition: an agreement, communication, or some other activity intended to incite treason or some lesser commotion against the public authority.

Service mark: the use of a word, symbol, or phrase to identify the provider of that service.

Service of process: the delivery of a legal notice to inform the person served of the nature of the legal dispute.

Severance pay: wages paid upon the termination of a person's job.

Slander: defamation that occurs when the statement is oral.

Slander per quod: an oral statement that injuries a person's reputation. A victim of slander per quod must show that, in context, the statement was defamatory and that it harmed him or her.

Slander per se: oral defamation that occurs when a person says that another person is seriously immoral, seriously criminal, has a social disease, or is unfit as a businessperson or professional. In these cases, there is no need to prove actual damages.

Sole proprietorship: a business form in which the business is owned and operated by one person.

Solicitation: when one person convinces another to engage in criminal activity.

Solid waste: waste that includes solids, liquids, gases, sludges, and semisolids.

Specific performance: an equitable remedy in which the court requires performance of a contract in the specific form in which it was made, or according to the precise terms agreed upon.

Standing: when the party has a sufficient interest in the outcome of a controversy to assert his or her rights.

Stare decisis: the legal question has been decided; there are precedents on this issue.

Status quo ante: parties' respective positions prior to the contract. The situation that existed before something being discussed occurred.

Statute of limitations: a statutory time limit within which a cause of action must be initiated or rights can be enforced.

Statutes: the laws created by federal or state legislative bodies.

Strikes: organized refusals to work.

Subject matter jurisdiction: the power of a court to hear certain kinds of legal questions.

Subjective standard: standard based on what this person actually thought.

Subpoena: an order to compel a person to testify in a judicial proceeding.

Subpoena duces tecum: an order to appear with records or evidence at a judicial proceeding.

Substantial performance: in contract law, substantial performance occurs when performance does not exactly satisfy the terms of the contract, but the party has (1) made a good faith effort to perform the contract and (2) performed at a level that is good enough to satisfy a reasonable and prudent person.

Substantive law: that part of law that creates and defines legal rights.

Summons: a writ beginning a legal action and notifying the person named that the person must appear in court to answer a complaint.

Tender: an unconditional offer of money or performance to fulfill a legal obligation.

Trademark: a graphic symbol, logo, phrase, or word used by a business to distinguish its products from the products of others.

Trade dress: a specific design, including color, shape, or sound, used to identify a business, its goods, or its services. It can include the packaging and product displays for goods.

Trade secret: a device, formula, process, or other business information that is kept secret and used by a business. It provides the owner with a competitive advantage.

Treason: the crime of betraying one's country.

Treaties: formal agreements between two or more nations. Treaties are often categorized by the number of nations involved.

Trespass: an unlawful interference with one's property or right; for example, when a person intentionally goes onto the real property of another without permission.

Trial de novo: a new trial on the entire case, including questions of fact and issues of law.

Tort law: the body of law dealing with civil wrongs for which the victim is entitled to remedies.

Undue influence: a person takes advantage of a victim's weakened condition or takes advantage of a fiduciary relationship to persuade the victim to make a contract he or she would not otherwise have made. Undue influence can also be used to persuade a victim to make gifts or provisions in wills.

Universal treaties: treaties, such as the Geneva Convention, that are recognized by almost all nations.

Venue: the proper geographical area or district where a suit can be brought.

Verdict: the stated opinion of the jury.

Vertical merger: a merger between a firm and one of its suppliers or customers.

Vicarious liability: legal responsibility for the wrong committed by another person. Respondeat superior is an example of vicarious liability.

Voir dire: examination of potential jurors to determine their competence to serve on the jury.

White-collar crimes: generally crimes committed in a commercial context by professionals and managers.

Wildcat strikes: unauthorized withholdings of services or labor during the term of a contract.

Writ: a writing issued by a court in the form of a letter ordering some designated activity.

Wrongful death: unlawful death. It does not necessarily have to involve criminal activity.

Table of Cases

Principal cases are indicated by italics.

Index